FOUR DAYS
IN NOVEMBER

FOUR DAYS
—— IN ——
NOVEMBER

THE ORIGINAL COVERAGE OF
THE JOHN F. KENNEDY ASSASSINATION
BY THE STAFF OF

The New York Times

INTRODUCTION BY Tom Wicker

EDITED BY Robert B. Semple Jr.

St. Martin's Press
New York

www.stmartins.com

Library of Congress Cataloging-in-Publication Data

Four days in November : the original coverage of the John F. Kennedy assassination / by the staff of the New York times ; edited by Robert B. Semple Jr. ; introduction by Tom Wicker.—1st ed.
    p. cm.
  Includes index (p. 603)
  ISBN 0-312-32161-9
  1. Kennedy, John F. (John Fitzgerald), 1917–1963—Assassination. I. Title: 4 days in November. II. Semple, Robert B. III. New York times.

E842.9.F63   2003
973.922'092—dc21   2003046871

10   9   8   7   6   5   4   3   2

CONTENTS

PREFACE

By Robert B. Semple Jr.

When Mike Levitas, then the director of book development for *The Times,* asked me to edit and organize this book, I welcomed the project as a chance to recapture a fateful moment in American history and to relive, as well, an extraordinary moment in the history of the paper. My own role in *The Times*'s coverage was modest, to say the least. I had been hired by James (Scotty) Reston, the Washington bureau chief, two months before the assassination to be an assistant editor on the bureau's news desk.

Like most people of a certain age, I can remember exactly where I was when the news from Dallas came across the radio—in a car wash in Northwest Washington, getting ready to head north for a weekend with friends in New Haven. I immediately returned to the *Times* bureau, then located above a Drug Fair at 17th and K Streets, and spent the next four days doing pretty much what Alvin Shuster, the deputy news editor, told me to do—run copy, edit copy, shovel copy through the wire room (those were the days of teletype) to the anxious editors in New York. What I had was a ringside seat for four of the most tumultuous days in the life of the nation and the history of American journalism—the four days encompassing President Kennedy's assassination in Dallas, the murder of Lee Harvey Oswald and Kennedy's burial in Arlington National Cemetery.

In retrospect, *The Times* was unusually well equipped to cover this story, with enormous resources in New York, in offices throughout the country and the world, and especially in Washington, the epicenter of most of the

journalistic action. Over the years, Scotty Reston had assembled an exceptional pool of journalists—Max Frankel covering the State Department,
Tom Wicker at the White House, Tony Lewis at the Supreme Court, Jack
Raymond at the Pentagon, Ned Kenworthy on Capitol Hill, to name only
a few stars in a luminous constellation. To this day I marvel at what these
people were able to do under the most demanding professional and emotional pressures.

That things went as smoothly as they did was in part a tribute to Al
Shuster, an even-tempered editor (I cannot recall him raising his voice once
during the four days) who was thrust into a leadership role by the temporary absence of his two superiors. Reston, who was lunching in Winston-
Salem with the governor of North Carolina when the shots were fired,
returned late in the day to write his column for the next day's paper and
to begin organizing the coverage for the next three days. Shuster's immediate boss, Fendall Yerxa, had been conferring with editors in New York
and was dispatched to Dallas to set up a minibureau.

The main nerve center, of course, remained the newsroom in New York;
Washington just happened to be my perch. And at the center of the New
York action was the national desk, presided over by Harrison Salisbury, a
veteran editor and a Pulitzer Prize winner for his reporting from the Soviet
Union. Summoned from lunch when news of the shooting flashed across
the wires, Salisbury ordered a half-dozen reporters to Dallas to assist Tom
Wicker, the paper's White House correspondent and the only *Times* reporter on the scene. He assembled a "universal" copy desk consisting of
the top editors from the national, foreign and metropolitan desks to process
the enormous flow of copy that would be arriving during the course of the
afternoon, meanwhile coordinating his efforts with the metropolitan editor,
A. M. Rosenthal, his deputy, Arthur Gelb, and the foreign editor, Manny
Freedman. Rosenthal and Gelb sent dozens of reporters all over the city
to gather reaction while deploying others to assemble biographical material
on Kennedy and Johnson (there was no formal obituary). Freedman, meanwhile, organized coverage abroad.

The first day's paper was a remarkable achievement on all levels, mechanical as well as literary—250 columns of news or about 200,000 words,
twice the size of an ordinary novel (not all of it devoted to the assassination—there was other news to cover). The next three days' papers were

equally exhaustive. Harry Reasoner, then an anchorman for CBS News, was later moved to write: "I want to extend my thanks and commendation for the Saturday, Sunday, Monday and Tuesday issues of *The Times*. I don't recall in my lifetime ever seeing the profession of journalism carried on at a higher level. All the facts—the exhaustive, accurate news of events, the careful study of implications in allied areas, the authoritative special comments, the wise counsel on the editorial page—were so shining and splendid that you would think *The Times* had been planning its coverage for years. In a way, of course, I suppose it had."

No less remarkable is how well the coverage has held up over the years. There were, of course, glitches and miscalculations, especially on the first day. For instance, the Saturday paper carried an overheated political assessment suggesting that the Democratic party's presidential aspirations had been irreparably damaged. (As things turned out, Johnson swamped Barry Goldwater in 1964. The Sunday paper carried a more measured and ultimately more accurate political analysis.) And while the Sunday, Monday and Tuesday papers were virtually glitch-free, Turner Catledge, the managing editor, would later say that his greatest regret was the headline on the third day, "President's Assassin Shot to Death," which effectively convicted Oswald even though he had not been—and never would be—tried for the crime.

On the whole, though, these editions have stood the test of time—all the more remarkable given the emotions of the moment and the insatiable demand from editors in New York for details about subjects that, until the assassination, nobody had much thought about. I remember to this day, with some amusement, an exasperated and exhausted Pentagon correspondent, Jack Raymond, trying to answer a fusillade of questions about the riderless horse, Blackjack, which followed the caisson bearing Kennedy's coffin on Monday. Why riderless? Why were the stirrups and boots reversed? Why this horse, and not some other? And what did Genghis Khan have to do with it?

Even more impressive than the accuracy of the reporting was its professional detachment. The tone throughout was measured, the urge to canonize resisted. Except for some overwrought prose in the first day's lead editorial (perhaps forgivable under the circumstances), this was true even on the editorial page, which had been largely admiring of Kennedy. Indeed, practically nowhere in these pages is more claimed for the Kennedy presidency than history has ultimately awarded it. Similarly, the reporting on the grieving Kennedy family was for the most part respectful without descending to mournful excess. And the early portraits of Lyndon Johnson and his staff, and of his legislative aspirations, were accurately drawn and extraordinarily prescient.

A word about the organization of this book. Though *The Times*'s editors in New York did a heroic job of organizing each day's news coverage by subject matter (foreign reaction in one place, for example, local reaction in another, biographical material in still another), a literal page-by-page reproduction of the news in each day's paper would confuse and overwhelm the reader. We therefore superimposed another layer of order on the process by grouping the stories thematically. These themes are identified in a brief editor's comment before each day's paper.

Readers will also note that, following standard practice in morning newspapers like *The Times,* the dateline on stories reflects the actual date an event took place and the story was written, while the newspaper itself is dated the following day.

There was inevitable duplication, especially on the first day; some of that duplication has been eliminated. Of three reaction stories from Moscow on the first day, for instance, one survives here. Various quotes popped up in more than one story: That got fixed, too. From time to time, words were dropped from sentences, obscuring their meaning. We have supplied substitute words, noting them in brackets. Many of these glitches were first spotted by *The Times*'s Mary Ellen LaManna, who heroically transcribed four days of coverage onto computer disks for later editing, and whose suggestions were invaluable.

To make matters still easier for the reader, the many one-and-two-paragraph reaction stories (known in the newsroom vernacular as "shirttails") from foreign capitals have been modestly culled. Two very similar stories about the assassinations of previous presidents have been combined. Most but not all of the eulogies from the pulpits of New York, Washington and the nation are preserved. All in all, more than 90 percent of the coverage from the four days' papers is here, just as it was originally printed, along with many of the photographs. It makes compelling reading 40 years later. Journalism, it is often said, is the first rough draft of history. This rough draft made history of its own.

FOUR DAYS
IN NOVEMBER

INTRODUCTION

By Tom Wicker

Forty years after the death of John F. Kennedy, the world is obviously a different place. Since Nov. 22, 1963, numerous developments—most recently, those of Sept. 11, 2001—have shaken the nation and the world until both would have been all but unrecognizable from the perspective of the Kennedy years.

The young president's more extreme admirers lamented in 1963 that even the greatness of the nation, the future that had seemed so glowing, might suffer decline with the loss of the Kennedy touch. Some political analysts calculated that the Democratic party would not for years recover from the loss of so attractive a leader. Many were deeply affected personally. "We may laugh again," said Daniel P. Moynihan, then an assistant secretary of labor, "but we'll never be young again."

In the shock of the assassination—the first of a president since Leon Czolgosz had shot William McKinley more than a half century earlier—no one could be sure how the cold war would be affected by a new man at the head of American policy. What about Kennedy's civil rights bill, deadlocked and stymied in Congress? Could his space program, including the promise to put a man on the moon, be continued? Might the war in Vietnam be won—or should it be abandoned?

Four decades after the shooting in Dallas, it's surprising how little the assassination—at the time a veritable thunderclap among events—affected these specific questions, much less the inexorable tide of history. Kennedy's absence from the government and the political scene, of course, immediately changed the presidential succession—but politics already was changing, not necessarily for the better, and would have changed even if Kennedy had lived.

In the long perspective of time, sad to say for those who believe in the primacy of the individual, John Kennedy's death mattered less to the future than the mushroom development of television.

When Lee Harvey Oswald fired from a window of the Texas School Book Depository, television was only just beginning to be what it is today and has been for most of the four decades since—something like the national nervous system. If it doesn't twitch, if an event is not televised live or in endless recaps, the nation scarcely notices; and even if something does happen off camera—say, the shootings at Columbine High School— television quickly arrives with its glaring lights and its talking heads competing for airtime, so that people everywhere realize something shocking has happened. A century ago, weeks would have passed before many Americans got the news, and some never would have.

As late as John Kennedy's day, television still occupied itself primarily with entertainment—*Leave It to Beaver, Sergeant Bilko, I Love Lucy.* Though JFK recognized its news potential, he won the presidency in the closest election of modern times not so much with canned commercials or crafted speeches as because of his televised debates with Richard Nixon— maybe only the first of the four. It was not burdened with substance but sharply contrasted the candidates.

I well remember, too, how resentful were those of us in the "print media," not just of that fancy-pants appellation, but to find that Kennedy had decided to allow TV cameras*—those cranelike, three-legged intruders into *our* business—a privileged place in the news conferences he opened, for the first time, to live coverage. That decision relegated newspapermen who had covered Roosevelt and Truman and Eisenhower to the back rows of the State Department auditorium, but it was in those televised news

---

*Many of them operated by the same cynical and profane technicians who only a year or so earlier had manned film cameras for "the reels"—the newsreels once prominent in movie theaters but put abruptly out of business by television news.

conferences that Americans most often saw their president, as the cameras graphically transmitted the Kennedy wit and charm to the nation, contributing immeasurably to his continuing legend.

Even the evening news programs had been held, until 1963, to 15 hurried minutes, five nights a week. When the major networks (then NBC and CBS) reluctantly offered 30-minute newscasts (with Huntley-Brinkley and Walter Cronkite as anchormen), John F. Kennedy—again recognizing an important new medium—appeared to inaugurate each half-hour program. That was only a few months before the fatal trip to Dallas; he was dead in that city shortly after noon on Nov. 22, an hour that marked not only the death of a president but the birth of the television phenomenon that now dominates the national attention and very nearly the national life, not least its political competitions.

For all of the three days following Kennedy's assassination, the networks devoted their entire airtime to coverage of the shooting and its consequences (would they do that today for *anything*?), Cronkite staying tirelessly before the camera all those 72 hours. In a dire time of fear and uncertainty (Did the Communists do it? What might be coming next? Who's this cowboy that's president now?), television unquestionably held the nation together, as a wise friend might support a bereaved family at the funeral of a brother. Not coincidentally, therefore, the cameras were right at hand for Jack Ruby's revenge shooting of the defiant Oswald— and they have been rather relentlessly "on the spot" ever since.

No more presidential debates were held until 1976, when a single misstatement by President Ford tilted the outcome, and perhaps the election, to Jimmy Carter. Even before then, however, political campaigning had become virtually *all* television, as it remains today, from the state level up, and even in some cities and Congressional districts. Ronald Reagan made himself a national political figure in 1964 with a single speech (now remembered as "the speech") on behalf of Barry Goldwater, aired on a patched-together statewide television network in North Carolina and delivered without graphics or gimmickry while Reagan sat in an easy chair.

In 1988, for another example (among many), Senator Bob Dole of Kansas had come from 18 points behind in a Gallup poll, to *lead* Vice President George Bush 32 to 27 in a CBS News report on the eve of the New Hampshire Republican primary. Bush turned his deficit into a nine-point victory, the most important of his presidential campaign, mostly with a single TV commercial that suggested a two-faced Dole, if elected, would raise taxes. Later, in that year's general election, Bush helped himself overcome a *16-point deficit* nationwide with the famous Willie Horton attack ad. As much as any single factor, that commercial contributed to Bush's victory over the complacent and miscast Michael Dukakis.

That's the way it's done today, and probably would be if John F. Kennedy had never gone to Dallas in 1963. If your candidate is behind in Indiana, or among Roman Catholics, or in the ethnic wards somewhere, don't bother to send in your candidate; get a new ad on TV right away and aim it specifically at the target. If you're running for president, hit the major media markets, and hit 'em again, even if it means jetting from Oregon to Florida between 2 P.M. and the six o'clock news. And those astronomical sums for modern political campaign costs? Most of that money goes not for bumper stickers, billboards, full-page ads, "street money" or even to set up personal appearances by flesh-and-blood candidates—but for airtime and professionally crafted commercials,

If JFK had been alive to run for Congress or any other office after 1968, the end of his presumed second term and of his presidential eligibility, or if his political career had been timed 20 or 30 years later, he'd have had to make it as today's candidates have to—on television, with commercials, his good looks still an obvious asset, but his spontaneity and sense of humor caught and conveyed, if at all, by script and videotape.

Kennedy did have individual and lasting impact on modern politics. The man who landed on the moon during Nixon's Administration actually was sent into space by JFK, who turned Dwight Eisenhower's embryonic space program into a budgetary giant and a scientific success. No one blanches anymore at the mere thought of a Roman Catholic in the White House. Looks and personality count more than ever in election campaigns, and even wit may now be an asset. Lyndon Johnson knew what he was doing, or not doing, when he refused to hold his presidential news conferences in the State Department auditorium, where they surely would have been contrasted with JFK's star turns in that venue.

All of those Kennedy legacies seem insignificant, however, compared to the television colossus that now towers over the political landscape. He had played a vital part in creating that monster—promoting 30 minutes of evening news, angling his news conferences toward the living-room screen rather than the morning headline, involuntarily providing those three televised days of national mourning—but in the end the monster, like Frankenstein's, probably would have turned on him, too.

Who can say, nearly a half century later, that JFK would have been able to exploit television as Bush did in 1988? Might not he, too, have succumbed to its appetites, as Bush later did to Bill Clinton's easy command of "the tube"?

In 1963, everybody knew, of course, that the war in Vietnam—though not yet a consuming national preoccupation—was bound to be affected by the president's death. Indeed, some of the war's darker events, like the death of Ngo Dinh Diem in a United States–backed coup d'état, might have been orchestrated by Kennedy himself and therefore could have been a cause of revenge murder.

That was a fringe view; more widely held was the notion that the Pentagon no longer would have to fight the war with "one hand tied behind its back" by a president too soft to use the full range of American power— often meaning the bomb. Therefore, Kennedy's "no-win policy" could quickly be turned to victory after his removal from power. Even in 1963, however, a vociferous minority (later termed "nervous Nellies" by Lyndon Johnson) never had fully understood or believed in the war. These few, in sharp contrast to those who talked knowingly about that hand tied behind the back, hoped that with the arch–cold warrior Kennedy—as they saw him—out of the way, a diplomatic end to the war could be achieved; perhaps it could even be abandoned outright.

Indeed, for most of the year 1964, before Johnson was himself elected in November, he loudly promised that American boys would not be sent to do what Asian boys ought to do for themselves. Even after Johnson won his landslide over Barry Goldwater (voters obviously did not want a *third* president in less than a year) and sent more troops, then more, and even more, to Indochina, as well as great flights of United States bombers over Hanoi and Haiphong, he at least kept a tight leash on target selection, fearing that an errant bombload could bring Communist China into the war. Nor did he or President Nixon later order use of the bomb. So the Nellies seemed to have been at least half prescient.

In fact, however, the war raged on for nearly a decade after LBJ expanded it. A half million American troops were at one time deployed; two more countries, Cambodia and Laos, were engaged; 50,000 American and untold numbers of Asian lives were lost, most of them violently. So Kennedy's murder actually may have made a difference in Vietnam—though not the one so often predicted. The most compelling evidence is that before Nov. 22, 1963, John F. Kennedy's was the strongest voice for moderation within his Administration—telling the Joint Chiefs, for example, that using United States troops in Laos was "a last step" and turning from support for pro-Western elements to acceptance of Laotian neutralism, "an independent country not dominated by either side."*

It's possible, therefore—though by no means a certainty—that after Kennedy had won re-election in 1964 (probably over Goldwater), the war would have been prosecuted with less belligerence and determination. Johnson, with his paranoid fears of the "right wing" and of being the first president to lose a war, saw no alternative to a tough war policy; neither did his successor, Nixon, until he was forced finally to settle with North Vietnam on terms that he and his Machiavellian security adviser, Henry Kissinger, could have had years earlier. That would have meant far less American and Asian bloodshed and might have precluded some of the domestic political crises that recurred from 1969 to 1974.

Four decades after the war became Johnson's, then Nixon's, dividing the nation more profoundly than at any time since the Civil War, the hand-behind-the-back theory nevertheless persists. So, too, for most of that time did the so-called Vietnam syndrome—until the first President Bush proclaimed it dispelled by the successful Gulf War. That supposed "syndrome," articulated in various ways, sometimes by events, sometimes in speeches and documents, held in broad general effect that if the United States should again get into a war abroad, it should be as a last resort, with indisputable national-security causes, clear objectives and wide public support.†

Both the theory and the syndrome could be, and often are, attributed to Kennedy. But the war in Vietnam did not become truly unwinnable, nor

---

American Tragedy by David Kaiser (Cambridge: Harvard University Press, 2000), pp. 39–40.
†Stated in detail by Secretary of Defense Caspar Weinberger in 1984. Eliot A. Cohen, *Supreme Command* (New York: Free Press, 2000), p. 187.

much of a domestic problem, while he was commander in chief. And though he *was* a moderating influence on the Pentagon in the war's early stages, no evidence exists—quite the opposite—that the war ever could have been won, then or later, by unleashing the Pentagon to go at it with both hands, whatever that might have meant (and if it *did* mean using the bomb on Asians a second time in two decades, the consequences would have been incalculable).

As for the "Vietnam syndrome," to the extent that it ever really existed, it's a plausible interpretation that it was for some years a useful public restraint on presidents and generals—a commonsense warning that when contemplating the use of its power, the United States should more nearly know what it's doing, and can do, than three Administrations ever knew in Vietnam. That's a lesson that John Kennedy, with his hard-earned distrust of experts, following the Bay of Pigs fiasco in 1961, might indeed have learned. But he died too soon to realize it, and it had little effect on the policies of his immediate successors.

The civil rights revolution, only slightly less than television, also has remade the country since 1963—including the transformation of the Democratic "solid South" into the Republican "nearly solid South." That revolution, too, was mightily helped along by John F. Kennedy, before and especially after his death, when blacks began to see him as a hero and an inspiration, a view they had not always taken of the live president. Sentimental regard for a recently murdered leader also may have swayed some Congressional votes in favor of his long-stymied 1963 civil rights bill. That sweeping measure was only reluctantly submitted and given little chance before it was pushed through Congress by Johnson, the legislative wizard, in 1964.

Kennedy's support for the mob-resisted admission of James Meredith to the University of Mississippi, his confrontation at "the schoolhouse door" with Governor George Wallace of Alabama,* above all, the young president's insistence in his Boston accent on something no earlier president had had the courage or the vision to say: that blacks' struggle for

---

*Actually that of Kennedy's deputy attorney general, Nicholas Katzenbach, at the University of Alabama.

civil rights constituted a "moral issue" for the rest of the nation—all these actions were vital to the civil rights movement.

Equally important, however, were LBJ's "we shall overcome" speech to Congress, his Howard University commencement address in 1964, his appointments of blacks to high office—Thurgood Marshall, notably, to the Supreme Court—much of his Great Society legislation, and his major achievements in securing passage not only of Kennedy's civil rights bill but also of his own Voting Rights Act of 1965.

Yet, it seems probable that the civil rights revolution would have happened about as it did, even if these presidents had not acted as they did. More nearly indispensable than any political effort were the bravery and sheer persistence of the black Americans who led, often at risk of their lives, their people into the streets, as well as the courage of those who followed—in the face of Bull Connor's police dogs, against flailing billy clubs on the Edmund Pettus Bridge, along the bleak highway from Selma to Montgomery.

The long-delayed rise of black Americans to full citizenship, to voting and officeholding rights, to legal and social equality (though still too often ignored), was a development whose time had come, whose triumph owed as much to the relentless pressures of its foot soldiers as to visionary leaders of either race, even a murdered but not martyred president—whose death, unlike that of Martin Luther King Jr., five years later, was neither on behalf nor because of the black struggle.

Immediately after the shots rang out in Dealey Plaza, conspiracy theorists began their endless plaints of betrayal, venality and cover-up. I was riding that day toward the "triple underpass" in one of the motorcade press buses—not yet knowing for sure what had happened, or if anything serious had—when I saw a police motorcycle with an empty sidecar laboring up the railroad embankment. Beside the disaster that later took shape in my notes, that motorcycle seemed so insignificant that I did not include it in my long account for *The New York Times* of the presidential assassination. Later, when I mentioned the motorbike—as merely an oddity of a confused day—in a summary for our house organ, *Times Talk*, I was promptly accused as a conspirator who had "covered up" an important sighting that allegedly supported the presence of a "second gunman" on the embankment.

The flood stream of conspiracy theories—Castro did it, or the Mafia, or the South Vietnamese; perhaps the Pentagon in cahoots with the CIA; maybe the prime beneficiary, Vice President Johnson (it happened in Texas, didn't it?)—ironically was speeded along by the Warren Commission report. Johnson had hardly succeeded Kennedy in the White House when he appointed the commission to investigate and report on what had happened in Dallas on Nov. 22. In doing so, he pulled off a near miracle by persuading Senator Richard Russell of Georgia, a relentless critic of Chief Justice Earl Warren, to serve on a group to be chaired by Warren.

The Warren Commission soon reported in September 1964 that Lee Harvey Oswald was the lone assassin. A disappointed young former marine, who had tried life in the Soviet Union and found it wanting, Oswald had brought a Russian bride back to a seemingly aimless and certainly unsuccessful career in the United States. The commission concluded that he had acted out of rather mixed and indeterminate motives: frustration, envy and lust for fame and recognition.

That was not good enough for many Americans, who wanted a more serious cause—political, military or international—and a more plausible perpetrator for the murder of their president. Many found gaps in the commission's chain of reasoning: It seemed unlikely, for instance, that Oswald could have fired all the shots so accurately in so short a time; and some flatly disbelieved the commission's theory of a "single bullet" supposedly wounding Kennedy first and then Gov. John Connally of Texas (who was in the presidential limousine). These and other disputed points in the report itself, as well as numerous new "facts" turned up by zealous critics, quickly served to undermine the credibility of the Warren Commission—which had been appointed to discover, once and for all, what actually had happened on Nov. 22, 1963.

The tide of conspiracy notions reached high water in 1991, when Oliver Stone's film *JFK* reflected the discredited theories of a discredited New Orleans prosecutor, whose unsupported fantasies had been debunked long before the movie was released. *JFK* undoubtedly lent brief, hollow credence to the widespread belief in conspiracy, but the film's sheer implausibility, its high-pitched assertion of rumor and half- (even quarter-) truth, also may have launched an undercurrent against the rush of conspiracy hysteria.

That rush had been set off by Americans' inability to believe that a cat *could* look at a king, that a pathetic loser like Oswald, with no definable motive and using a cheap mail-order rifle, could destroy—despite the Secret Service, the atom bomb and the MX missile—a sort of young American emperor, whose office, even to those who disliked or distrusted the man, was a symbol of the most powerful nation in history.

Not altogether unpredictable, but unlikely, in 1963 was the remarkable later political emergence of Robert Kennedy from the imposing shadow of JFK.

When in 1961 the president-elect had chosen his younger brother—a former disciple of Senator Joseph R. McCarthy of Wisconsin, the notorious Red-hunter—to head the Justice Department, the youthful appointee was widely derided for inexperience, and the president-elect's own suspected ties to McCarthy* (deplored by many Democrats, including their reigning queen, Eleanor Roosevelt) were exhumed and re-examined. Robert Kennedy nevertheless proved himself in short order an able attorney general (one of the few officials in Washington willing to stand up to J. Edgar Hoover, the menacing but iconic director of the Federal Bureau of Investigation), a scourge of organized crime and a valuable adviser to the president even in foreign affairs—notably the Cuban missile crisis. He also gained a reputation as an "enforcer," a partisan "ruthless" in pursuit of his own and his brother's interests.

After the assassination, the attorney general stayed on in the new Administration, but bitter rivalry soon developed between him and President Johnson—believed by many Democrats, perhaps including Robert Kennedy, to have somehow "usurped" the presidency from its rightful occupant. Bobby, as he was known to millions, ultimately resigned his office, ran in 1966 against Senator Kenneth Keating, Republican of New York, defeated him, became a major, if still junior, figure in the United States Senate (junior even to his younger brother, Edward, a senator from Massa-

---

*John F. Kennedy had been the only senator who did not vote when the Senate condemned McCarthy in 1957. That he was in hospital at the time was regarded by some as an excuse to skip the vote.

chusetts since 1963) and a political leader widely expected to be a presidential candidate in 1968.

He seemed a different man from the raw young attorney general of 1961. The assassination apparently had wrought profound changes in him, in addition to deep personal grief. He began to exhibit an extraordinary identification—far beyond that of his murdered brother—with the deprived, the disadvantaged, the dispossessed, and these new and unsuspected attitudes of "soul" brought him a passionate following, particularly among minorities and those most stricken by what they saw as the unfinished mission of John F. Kennedy. Even a number of usually independent reporters developed similar personal devotion to "Bobby."

No documentary evidence exists that his transformation, as some called it (natural development, others thought), came about *because* his brother was killed. But it seemed plausible—and obvious to Bobby's aficionados—to believe that like Saul struck off his horse on the road to Damascus, Robert Kennedy had seen a great light and now held it up before his followers. But as with many charismatic leaders, the aura of passion that quickly surrounded him aroused the suspicion and animosity of those who did not share it—among them Lyndon Johnson and those old Democrats whose loyalty was devoted to him.

Was this new Robert Kennedy the genuine article or a political construct? Didn't his reluctance to take on Johnson and the Democratic party's leadership reflect conventional political considerations? Could he have achieved such a place of eminence if JFK had not been murdered, if his brother's followers had not been desperately in search of a new leader? Was he really a self-anointed heir rather than a presidential possibility in his own right?

On the other hand, had John Kennedy lived and served a second term, with his brother as a feared and respected attorney general—or maybe moved up to be secretary of state, as Washington rumor had predicted— might not Bobby have built up his own program and position and acceded to the White House more or less expectably? (With the application of judicious political muscle by JFK, of course—natural and only to be expected in a close-knit family, or from a president to a loyal and valued associate.) And anyway, who besides a second Kennedy could more surely defeat a resurgent but still despised-by-Democrats Richard Nixon?

After some clearly political hesitation, Robert Kennedy did enter the 1968 race for the Democratic presidential nomination—but only after it was virtually "locked up" by Vice President Hubert Humphrey. Despite popular mythology, "Bobby" and his fervent supporters probably could not have won it. That will never be known for sure, because on the night of his triumph over Eugene McCarthy in the important California primary, Robert Kennedy, like his brother John before him, was shot and killed by an improbable assassin.

He left behind him a three-month campaign that—just as his death left his presidential capacities forever uncertain—did not truly answer the question whether "Bobby" had somehow been called to a greatness beyond politics after—or because of—Nov. 22, 1963. His was a shrewd, tough, professionally conceived and operated political campaign by an exciting candidate who won hotly contested primaries in Indiana, Nebraska and California, and lost only one, in Oregon.

It also was a rare and sometimes "soulful" campaign, exceptionally marked by Kennedy's grieving and eloquent words to an Indiana rally on the night of Martin Luther King Jr.'s murder, and by an enormous later turnout of cheering blacks lining the mean streets of Oakland—leaping for a look at the candidate, reaching out to touch the cars of the passing motorcade. No other politician in recent memory would have been so personally moved or so intellectually prepared to make the extemporaneous Indianapolis speech, nor could any have inspired by his mere presence the passionate adulation of Bobby's reception in Oakland.

Much pseudo-psychological speculation following John F. Kennedy's assassination in 1963 postulated that Oswald's deed had been dangerously contagious. All kinds of loners, losers, envious wanna-bes, mental cases and what Ronald Reagan later called "Looney Tunes," it was often suggested and sometimes believed, would see a splendid way out of their real or imagined predicaments by the killing of a president or some other luminary. How better to enter history and win the glory so far unfairly denied? So they would take up an unregistered and unregulated firearm, as easily obtained as Oswald's rifle had been, and blow away some public figure, perhaps even a president, who might unwittingly have stumbled against the fragile threads that bound disturbed psyches to sanity.

That, of course, is a theory, not necessarily a condition. Still, it's hard to blink the horrendous record that followed after—maybe *from*—Dallas in 1963.

Jack Ruby, who took Oswald out before he even could be tried (thus first setting off the flood of conspiracy notions), did not quite fit the theory or the predicted profile of the demented killer venting personal frustration. Nor had he had much time to work himself up over Kennedy's death, and he might even have been, in the public eye, a hired assassin, trying to cover up a Mafia hit on the president (Ruby's Dallas nightclub apparently had Mafia connections). No convincing evidence, however, has ever shown Ruby to be anything but what he claimed to be—an outraged Kennedy admirer, acting on vigilante impulse.

The shooting death of Malcolm X in Harlem in 1965 might more nearly have fit the theory of a demented killer acting for no good reason—except that subsequent revelations made it reasonably clear that Malcolm was a victim of internal conflicts and rivalries among Black Muslims. And though it's still doubted, even by Martin Luther King Jr.'s surviving family, the shooting death of the great black leader in Memphis in 1968 appears to have been a paid hit—financed by vengeful whites, never certainly identified. The trigger almost certainly was pulled by the ineffable James Earl Ray, who was captured after an international hunt, first confessed, served hard time in prison, recanted without much plausibility and died without ever having fit the Looney Tunes idea.

Sirhan Sirhan, who murdered Robert Kennedy in a Los Angeles hotel kitchen later in 1968, may well have been the kind of brooding, frustrated time bomb waiting to explode that pseudo-psychology had long predicted. Moreover, as the prominent younger brother of a dead president, one who at the time of his death appeared possibly to be a future president himself, Kennedy was just the kind of prominent target the madness-awakened theory had predicted. So no one criticized Edward Kennedy when later in 1968 he refused the pleas of some Democrats that he replace Robert as a presidential candidate; for it was widely believed that Edward, the lone surviving brother, would be a likely, if not certain, target for someone else seeking a strange kind of moment in the sun.

Arthur Bremer, who stalked, then shot but did not kill George Wallace in the parking lot of a Maryland mall in 1972, fits almost exactly the predicted profile of a disturbed man trying to kill someone in the public eye—not for a personal reason, or even on sudden impulse, but to satisfy some deep urge for miscalculated glory. Those members of the murderous Charles Manson gang who tried but failed to shoot President Gerald Ford in Sacramento in 1975 seemed more nearly "kill crazy," as they already had shown themselves to be in the gruesome Hollywood murders.

Not, however, until John Hinckley almost succeeded in assassinating Ronald Reagan in 1981, outside a hotel in Washington, did a potential killer and his postulated victim so nearly fit the old speculative notion. Hinckley harbored a secret love, an obsession decidedly unrequited, for the actress Jodie Foster. This passion was thwarted at every turn, as later investigation showed; therefore, Hinckley thought to impress Miss Foster with some headline deed—which the attempted murder of a president certainly was. Reagan barely survived, through the quick work of aides and the Secret Service, but his gallantry and humor under fire ("Honey, I forgot to duck") undoubtedly added to the great affection the American people already were showing for him.

From 1963 to 1981, of course, is a long time; it might well be too much to suggest that the murder of John Kennedy by one tortured loser set in motion, nearly 20 years later, in the mind of a differently frustrated misfit, a plan to kill another president. Still, the record of those years is shocking, probably unmatched in any civilized nation, and some still believe that the long bloody parade began in front of the Texas School Book Depository in 1963, with one lunacy leading inexorably to another.

All these killings and efforts to kill—save possibly the murder of Malcolm X—were connected in a more important way. Theodore Roosevelt, who succeeded McKinley, thought Leon Czolgosz, the assassin, had deliberately aimed at the "heart of the American Republic" and that his act constituted "an assault upon representative government and civilized order."* While none of the assailants from 1963 to 1981 had the conscious intent to bring down a government (in contrast, as Roosevelt knew, Czolgosz had anar-

---

*These actually are the words of Edmund Morris, Roosevelt's biographer, ostensibly describing TR's thoughts as he traveled to succeed William McKinley in 1901. Morris, *Theodore Rex* (New York: Modern Library, 2001), p. 4.

chist beliefs), singly and in the totality of their actions, men like Oswald and Hinckley have contributed heavily to what is today a palpable lack of trust and confidence in government. I'm not referring to such widely believed notions as that government—any government, state or federal—is a scheme to fleece the "common man" for the benefit of the rich, or the popular chestnut that all politicians have their hands in the till. There's enough truth in those charges to explain if not to vindicate them.

No, I mean the contemporary fantasy that Washington is dominated by a shadowy, octopuslike conspiracy to deliver the free citizens of the United States to the evil hands of some (never defined) international despotism, or the equally absurd belief that an elected government is an enemy determined to disarm American citizens by taking away their legitimately held guns. I don't, of course, argue that these idiocies were produced by that long line of attempted and successful assassinations, but I do contend that the repeated assaults on presidents and political leaders, drumming home the fear that no one is safe, that no threat can be dismissed, have had the insidious side effects of making conspiracy seem plausible, high officials suspect and "self-defense" necessary.

Why should Americans, in such an era, give up their "constitutional right" to own firearms? Much less the weapons themselves? If both the Kennedys could be murdered, together with Martin Luther King, on the one hand, and if Ronald Reagan and George Wallace barely survived, on the other, it's easier to believe that no one's life is safe, that nothing is to be trusted.

This vague sense of threat was exacerbated in the same years by a number of unhappy circumstances that undermined Americans' confidence in their government and/or their nation:

¶The cold war realization that the oceans no longer protected "God's country"; Soviet missiles could reach the heartland, and American housewives stocked bottled water in suburban basements during the Cuban missile crisis.

¶A "bitch of a war on the other side of the world"* that could not be adequately explained or defended, that dragged on endlessly, consuming

---

*As Lyndon Johnson, after his retirement, described the war in Vietnam to Doris Kearns Goodwin.

thousands of young lives, while those who fostered it were "unresponsive" to the protests of millions.

¶The Watergate scandal, in which a president repeatedly lied to the people, seemed to be undermining the Constitution and became the first forced to resign to avoid impeachment.

¶The loss of the kind of industrial pre-eminence on which Americans had prided themselves since World War II, with Japanese and German automobiles prominent on United States streets and the nation's trade deficit soaring to astronomical heights.

This list of major factors could be augmented with a number of others—particularly the popularity of hyped-up movies and other fictions that presented presidents as evil schemers of one kind or another, the Pentagon as a secret haven of malignant intent, and the C.I.A. as a nest of vipers dedicated to deception of the people and power for themselves. The film *JFK* suggested that virtually the entire Federal Government had joined in a conspiracy to get rid of the president and cover up the deed. Some of this chorus of innuendo, mistrust and betrayal in the "pop culture" is bound to have had chilling effect on the public's view of government propriety.

When in 1993 the F.B.I., for instance, overreacted—as it probably did—at Waco, Texas, against an armed band of cultists, demands quickly followed—not just that those responsible be punished but also that the supposedly overweening power of Government itself be checked by an aroused citizenry. And on the anniversary of the Waco fire and shoot-out, the Murrah Federal Building in Oklahoma City was blown up, with great loss of innocent life, apparently as a demonstration that some citizens *were* aroused against Government intentions—indeed were willing to risk prison or execution for their overwrought convictions. We do not yet know how many they are, but we may find out.

Government power in a democracy must always be regarded with skepticism; the governor or the president who promises never to raise taxes is perfectly capable of doing it anyway. But that kind of mendacity is not the same as plotting a coup or a murder, or planning to destroy free institutions; in America, it's paranoid, not patriotic, to hoard bombs and bullets against the day when Government itself tries to deliver the nation and its freedoms to foreign or international control.

· · ·

In looking back to the Kennedy years, and over the decades since, it's finally necessary to examine the man himself—the life that was lived, and lost on Nov. 22, 1963. Books have been written about JFK, his thousand days in office, his personality, his war record, his family—so many books and articles that little could be added at this late date.

Nor is it likely that anything can alter the general perception, born of revelations after his death, that he was a playboy president, unfaithful to his wife and thereby deceiving the public about his "character." Recently, too, disinterested review of his medical records has shown that he suffered far more from various physical problems than he acknowledged, or was generally known to his associates. Those records disclose, too, that Kennedy took a variety of medications, some of which now are considered dubious—leading to one critical characterization of him as a "pill-popping president."

No one has shown, however, and medical records can't, that "pills" adversely affected his presidential performance—any more than associates' allegations that Richard Nixon had a "drinking problem" demonstrate that he took important actions under the influence of alcohol, or that Nancy Reagan's belief in horoscopes dictated Ronald Reagan's official actions. In defense of all these presidents, at least on those points, it ought to be understood that presidents are human—would we want them *not* to be?— and that "character" is composed of many elements, not to be summed up by a few episodes or personal traits. Should Dwight Eisenhower be judged entirely on the fact that he did not support the Supreme Court's 1954 school desegregation ruling?

We reporters in the Kennedy years heard lots of innuendo and bandied about much locker-room talk about the president's sex life. Sometimes Kennedy's face appeared puffy—from cortisone treatments, we were told. We could see, on occasion, that he was in pain from the back problems we knew he endured, and that he bore such trials with fortitude and grace. Once, it was reported—from what source I don't recall—that he was wearing a sort of corset under his shirt. Dr. Janet Travell, the White House physician, was a specialist in back pains.

Beyond those indications, I believe most reporters had no evidence solid enough to be reported by careful journalists or made public by reputable publishers and broadcasters of the president's medical problems or of his sexual liaisons. At least I didn't; if others in the White House press did have such evidence, they failed to confide it to me. These many years later, however, I don't consider this excuse good enough. We should have obtained such evidence—given the hints and indications we *did* have—for it was our duty to report to the American people on the president's health and on what many would have regarded as his immorality.

Why didn't we have that evidence? After long and unhappy consideration of my own and others' failure, I believe we didn't work hard enough, didn't *try* hard enough to get behind the surface to reality. In the early 1960s, in what still was basically the Washington of the 1950s, still under the spell of Eisenhower the father figure, White House reporters—including me—were not skeptical enough, challenging enough, diligent enough, *dedicated* enough to the watchdog function of the press, its best reason for First Amendment protection. We didn't work hard enough to find out the facts, and that meant we didn't do our duty as reporters.

Many critics—of the press as well as of John Kennedy—believe that reporters in his time "covered up" for him; Richard Nixon certainly thought so. It's a plausible belief; perhaps not in every reporter's case can it be denied, but I believe the greater fault was a complacent belief among reporters like me that we were being told what we needed to know and that what we were being told was the truth. "Handout journalism" still was the custom of the day, until dislodged by the lies of Vietnam and Watergate—dislodged, at that, only among those willing to learn the lesson.

My acquaintance with John F. Kennedy was brief and distant—a year or two as *The Times*'s White House correspondent while he was president, some rather formal interviews, a quick, mistaken intrusion into his presidential cabin on Air Force One. On a weekend trip to Cape Cod—one of many—I had been assigned as part of "the pool" on the president's plane for his return flight to Washington.* I misjudged the time of departure and arrived a few minutes late at the airport—astonished but relieved to find

---

*A pool represents the rest of the press. If members, in their privileged location, see or hear or are told anything newsworthy, they are obliged to report it to colleagues.

that the president of the United States had ordered Air Force One held for me, or more probably for *The New York Times*.

I stumbled up the front stairway and rushed back toward the pool seats, necessarily passing through the presidential cabin, where JFK was at work. I'd like to report that we exchanged jovial remarks. But he only glared, as if he wanted no further interruption, and even as the great plane was beginning its takeoff, I rushed on back to the pool seats.

I cherish even that as a rare personal moment with President Kennedy. And *my* strongest impression of him has nothing to do with sex or health— it's of a man able to draw about him in Washington a large group of talented people and remain always not just their titular "boss" but, more important, their leader by natural force. Among the political figures I have known, few have had that naturally dominant quality to the extent that Kennedy did. Lyndon Johnson, for instance, admired and even envied it in his predecessor—though it came as a surprise to him, after having observed Kennedy's easygoing Senate years.

JFK also exhibited an unusual capacity to inspire, not necessarily by brilliance or eloquence (though at his news conferences, with no writers to shape his words, he was highly articulate), but again by natural force. After the lethargies of the Eisenhower years, John Kennedy seemed to challenge people in all walks to "do better"—one of his favorite phrases— as in his inaugural address he had urged Americans to ask "what you can do for your country." In 1961 and thereafter, there was an avalanche of response—in the Peace Corps, elsewhere in the federal service, in voluntary and private enterprises—almost as if Americans were glad to resume their natural energies. Even of difficult goals, those not to be finished in 1,000 days "nor even perhaps in our lifetime on this planet," he urged, "let us begin."

A president who could lead and inspire: We never cease to need them, but we have had, and no doubt will have, too few.

So even aside from Kennedy's concrete achievements in the Cuban missile crisis, in civil rights and in disarmament, though his time in office lasted only a few years and his conduct seems in retrospect to have been less than pristine, no ordinary president rode in that last motorcade, on that sunlit day, through those cheering crowds in Dallas, to the shattering moment in front of the School Book Depository. For all I know or care, John Kennedy may have played such tricks before high heaven as make the angels weep, but for a while he lifted his people and, as he had promised, got his country moving again.

Therefore, neither Republicans nor Democrats, liberals nor conservatives, nor any of the rest of us should ask for whom the bell tolled on Nov. 22, 1963.

DAY ONE

November 22, 1963

"All the News That's Fit to Print"

The New York Times.

LATE CITY EDITION

VOL. CXIII...No. 38,654.   NEW YORK, SATURDAY, NOVEMBER 23, 1963.   TEN CENTS

KENNEDY IS KILLED BY SNIPER AS HE RIDES IN CAR IN DALLAS; JOHNSON SWORN IN ON PLANE

TEXAN ASKS UNITY

Congressional Chiefs of Both Parties Promise Aid

By FELIX BELAIR Jr.
Special to The New York Times

WASHINGTON, Nov. 22 — Lyndon B. Johnson returned to a stunned capital shortly after 6 P.M. today to assume the duties of the Presidency.

The new President asked for and received from Congressional leaders of both parties their "united support in the face of the tragedy which has befallen our country." He said it was "most essential that ever before that this country be unified."

Partisan differences disappeared in the chorus of assurances with which the Congressional leaders responded.

But Mr. Johnson was described by those who talked with him as "stunned and shaken" by the assassination of President Kennedy.

Discusses U.S. Security

But he moved quickly from problems of national security and foreign policy to funeral arrangements for Mr. Kennedy.

Across the street from the West Wing of the White House, the President conferred with officials in his old Vice-Presidential offices in the Executive Office Building.

Senator George A. Smathers, Democrat of Florida, a personal friend of the dead President, was one of those who described Mr. Johnson as shaken.

"Everyone is," he added. "But the President is the more so because he was right there when the tragedy occurred."

While flying to Washington aboard the Presidential plane, Mr. Johnson arranged for a meeting with Cabinet members to ask that they remain at their posts. He made the same request of staff members in the executive offices.

Meets With Hariman

"Calm and confident" was the way Senator J. W. Fulbright described the President's manner during a discussion of foreign-policy matters with Under Secretary of State W. Averell Harriman. The Arkansas Senator said the President had been working on "what looked like a statement"—presumably an assurance of continuity of the nation's foreign policy.

The new President's first conference was aboard the helicopter that flew him the 15 miles from Andrews Air Force Base

Continued on Page 11, Column 6

"This is a sad time for all people. We have suffered a loss that cannot be weighed. For me it is a deep personal tragedy. I know the world shares the sorrow that Mrs. Kennedy and her family bear. I will do my best. That is all I can do. I ask for your help —and God's."—President Lyndon Baines Johnson.

PRESIDENT'S BODY WILL LIE IN STATE

Funeral Mass to Be Monday in Capital After Homage Is Paid by Public

By JACK RAYMOND
Special to The New York Times

WASHINGTON, Nov. 22 — The body of John F. Kennedy President Kennedy's assassination will lie in state in the rotunda of the Capitol Sunday and then will be borne to St. Matthew's Roman Catholic Cathedral for a pontifical requiem mass at noon Monday.

The President's body was returned to Washington today in the same Air Force jet that carried him to Texas. The assassinated President's widow, with Mrs. Kennedy, the new President, Lyndon B. Johnson, and Mrs. Johnson aboard, arrived at Andrews Air Force Base at 5:58 P.M.

It was announced later that Mr. Kennedy's body would lie in the White House tomorrow from 10 A.M. to 6 P.M., during which time Government and diplomatic officials will pay their respects.

The coffin will be taken from the White House to the Capitol Monday morning, where it will lie in state.

Continued on Page 6, Column 2

LEFTIST ACCUSED

Figure in a Pro-Castro Group Is Charged— Policeman Slain

By GLADWIN HILL
Special to The New York Times

DALLAS, Tex., Nov. 22 — The Dallas police and Federal officers leveled a charge of murder late tonight in the assassination of President Kennedy.

The accused is Lee Harvey Oswald, a 24-year-old former marine, who went to live in the Soviet Union in 1959 and returned to Texas last year.

Capt. Will Fritz, head of the Dallas police homicide bureau, identified Oswald as an adherent of the left-wing Fair Play for Cuba Committee.

Oswald was arrested about two hours after the shooting, in a movie theatre three miles away, shortly after he allegedly shot and killed a policeman on a street nearby.

He was arraigned tonight on a charge of murdering the police officer. The charge related to the Kennedy killing was made later.

Appears in Line-Up

After the arraignment, the suspect, a slight, dark-haired man, was taken downstairs to appear in a line-up, presumably before witnesses of the Kennedy assassination.

While being escorted, handcuffed, through a police building corridor, he shouted: "I haven't shot anybody."

Captain Fritz and Oswald was employed—the exact jot was unknown—at the Texas School Book Depository, a warehouse from which the assassin's bullets came. The captain said some witnesses had placed Oswald in the building at the time of the assassination.

The sequence of events leading to his arrest was as follows:

As a citywide manhunt began during the hour following the assassination, an unidentified man notified police headquarters, over a police-car radio, that the car's officer had been

Continued on Page 6, Column 1

PARTIES' OUTLOOK FOR '64 CONFUSED

Republican Prospects Rise —Johnson Faces Possible Fight Against Liberals

By WARREN WEAVER Jr.
Special to The New York Times

WASHINGTON, Nov. 22 — The body of John F. Kennedy President Kennedy's assassination cast a new into turmoil today.

It removed at a single blow the man who would have been renominated for a second term in the White House by acclamation nine months from now.

It elevated into the Presidency and the leadership of the Democratic party an older, more conservative man still emerging from his Southern heritage.

It increased immeasurably the leaders of the Republican party prospects of electing a President next November.

The shock of the President's death stilled the official voices of politics in the capital. But so profound was the potential effect on the government, and leadership that primaries consideration could not be silenced.

There has been fast and strong probabilities on that

Continued on Page 6, Column 6

John Fitzgerald Kennedy 1917-1963

Why America Weeps

Kennedy Victim of Violent Streak He Sought to Curb in the Nation

By JAMES RESTON

WASHINGTON, Nov. 22 — America wept tonight, not alone for its dead young President, but for itself. The grief was general, for somehow the worst in the nation had produced the best in her. The dominant note of all the reactions was sorrow for itself, it seemed, beyond the immediate tragedy itself, some strain of madness and violence, had destroyed the highest symbol of law and order.

Speaker "John McCormack, now 71 and, by the peculiarities of our politics, next in line in succession after the Vice President, expressed this sense of national dismay and self-criticism:

"My God! My God! What are we coming to?"

The irony of the President's death is that his whole Administration was devoted almost entirely to various attempts to curb this very streak of violence in the American character.

When the historians get around to assessing his three years in office, it is very likely that they will be impressed with his efforts to restrain those who wanted to be more violent in the cold war over-seas and those who wanted to be

Continued on Page 5, Column 6

The City Goes Dark

By ROBERT C. DOTY

The center of New York, the restless night city, was darkness and went in near silence after the murder of President Kennedy last night.

In and around Times Square the normal, frantic Friday night noise slowed as near to a halt as it ever comes. Mournful, illuminate and movie theatres dimmed their lights and dance halls closed their doors and darkened their marquees.

As dusk came, automatic devices turned on the huge, gaudy display signs that normally start up the night. Then, one by one, the lights blinked out, turning the great carnival strip into what was almost a mourning.

There were exceptions, of course. Restaurants, by decision of their trade associations, remained lighted and open as a

Continued on Page 3, Column 1

Gov. Connally Shot; Mrs. Kennedy Safe

President Is Struck Down by a Rifle Shot From Building on Motorcade Route— Johnson, Riding Behind, Is Unhurt

By TOM WICKER
Special to The New York Times

DALLAS, Nov. 22—President John Fitzgerald Kennedy was shot and killed by an assassin today.

He died of a wound in the brain caused by a rifle bullet that was fired at him as he was riding through downtown Dallas in a motorcade.

Vice President Lyndon Baines Johnson, who was riding in the third car behind Mr. Kennedy's, was sworn in as the 36th President of the United States 99 minutes after Mr. Kennedy's death.

Mr. Johnson is 55 years old; Mr. Kennedy was 46.

Shortly after the assassination, Lee H. Oswald, a one-time defector to the Soviet Union, active in the Fair Play for Cuba Committee, was arrested by the Dallas police. Tonight he was accused of the killing.

Suspect Captured After Scuffle

Oswald, 24 years old, was also accused of slaying a policeman who had approached him in the street. Oswald was subdued after a scuffle with a second policeman in a nearby theater.

The shooting took place at 12:30 P.M., Central standard time (1:30 P.M., New York time). Mr. Kennedy was pronounced dead at 1 P.M. and Mr. Johnson was sworn in at 2:39 P.M.

Mr. Johnson, who was uninjured in the shooting, took his oath in the Presidential jet plane as it stood on the runway at Love Field. The body of the President was aboard. Immediately after the oath-taking, the plane took off for Washington.

Standing beside the new President as Mr. Johnson took the oath of office was Mrs. John F. Kennedy. Her stocking was saturated with her husband's blood.

Gov. John B. Connally Jr. of Texas, who was riding in the same car with Mr. Kennedy, was severely wounded in the chest, ribs and arm. His condition was serious, but not critical.

The killer fired the rifle from a building just off the motorcade route. Mr. Kennedy,

Continued on Page 7, Column 4

NEWS INDEX

THE NEW PRESIDENT: Lyndon B. Johnson takes oath before Judge Sarah T. Hughes in plane at Dallas. Mrs. Kennedy and Representative Jack Brooks are at right. To left are Mrs. Johnson and Representative Albert Thomas.

WHEN THE BULLETS STRUCK: Mrs. Kennedy moving to the aid of the President after he was hit by a sniper yesterday in Dallas. A guard mounts rear bumper. Gov. John B. Connally Jr. of Texas, also in the car, was wounded.

RAY O'NEILL, *The Times*'s national news editor and Harrison Salisbury's deputy, usually came to work during the noonday lull. On this Friday, Nov. 22, he had just settled in at his desk on West 43d Street when a copy editor named Bill Lamble handed him a bulletin from The Associated Press, datelined Dallas and timed at 1:39 P.M. E.S.T. "PRESIDENT KENNEDY WAS SHOT TODAY JUST AS HIS MOTORCADE LEFT DOWNTOWN DALLAS." Thus began four of the most tumultuous days in the history of the nation and of *The Times*. The major events of that first day unfolded in just over two hours—the assassination, which in fact occurred at 12:30 P.M. Dallas time; Lee Harvey Oswald's arrest shortly thereafter; and Lyndon Johnson's swearing-in at 2:39. Washington and the world were thrown into confusion. Politics, diplomacy, the financial markets—all were subject to instant recalculation. For a moment the nation itself seemed to tremble. It was a huge, sprawling story—and *The Times* had seven hours to pull it together before the presses started for the first edition, stretching its considerable resources to limits they had rarely if ever seen. A team of reporters and editors was sent winging to Dallas from New York and Washington, while the entire metropolitan staff was requisitioned to gather reaction and write background and biographical pieces. The first section of the paper was cleared of all advertising, and the deadline was moved up to accommodate a longer press run and still get the paper delivered on time. Tom Wicker's lead story from Dallas began to move at 5 o'clock and was edited and cleared by 7:30. The last page of the first edition was locked up at 8:24 P.M.; the presses rolled at 8:40. The assassination story covered the first 16 pages in the final edition of Nov. 23 and included 47 pictures.

That edition is rearranged here as follows: The first section, essentially, is the story as it unfolded in Dallas—the shooting itself, the scene at the hospital, Oswald's arrest, Johnson's swearing-in, and so on. The second section focuses on the Kennedy family, the third section on local, national and world reaction, the fourth on Kennedy's career and accomplishments. The fifth section includes analytical pieces and editorial comment.

Despite the confusion and time pressures, there were some extraordinary individual achievements—among them Wicker's 4,000-word lead piece, written in short bursts, then dictated from the Dallas airport. (Mr. Wicker would later jot down his memories of that frantic day for *Times Talk,* the paper's house organ. That piece is included in the appendix.) James (Scotty) Reston, the Washington bureau chief, produced an Olympian news analysis that captured in 1,200 or so words his sense of the Kennedy presidency. The biographical pieces, covering most of four pages of the paper, remain to this day a serviceable summary of Kennedy's personal and professional life. The reader will also find some excellent local reporting from New York, including two reaction pieces by Robert Doty and George Barrett that provide a portrait of a shaken city so rich in detail, so endowed with immediacy that it almost seems as if they could have been written yesterday—not 40 years ago. The normal Friday night press run was increased by 50 percent, to 864,000 copies. It was, not surprisingly, a sellout.

KENNEDY IS KILLED BY SNIPER AS HE RIDES IN CAR IN DALLAS; JOHNSON SWORN IN ON PLANE

Gov. Connally Shot; Mrs. Kennedy Safe

President Is Struck Down by a Rifle Shot From Building on
Motorcade Route—Johnson, Riding Behind, Is Unhurt

By TOM WICKER
Special to The New York Times

DALLAS, Nov. 22—President John Fitzgerald Kennedy was shot and killed by an assassin today. He died of a wound in the brain caused by a rifle bullet that was fired at him as he was riding through downtown Dallas in a motorcade. Vice President Lyndon Baines Johnson, who was riding in the third car behind Mr. Kennedy's, was sworn in as the 36th President of the United States 99 minutes after Mr. Kennedy's death. Mr. Johnson is 55 years old; Mr. Kennedy was 46.

Shortly after the assassination, Lee H. Oswald, described as a onetime defector to the Soviet Union, active in the Fair Play for Cuba Committee, was arrested by the Dallas police. Tonight he was accused of the killing. Oswald, 24 years old, was also accused of slaying a policeman who had approached him in the street. Oswald was subdued after a scuffle with a second policeman in a nearby theater.

The shooting took place at 12:30 P.M., Central standard time (1:30 P.M., New York time). Mr. Kennedy was pronounced dead at 1 P.M. and Mr. Johnson was sworn in at 2:39 P.M. Mr. Johnson, who was uninjured in the shooting, took his oath in the presidential jet plane as it stood on the runway at Love Field. The body of the president was aboard. Immediately after the oath-taking, the plane took off for Washington. Standing beside the new president as Mr. Johnson took the oath of office was Mrs. John F. Kennedy. Her stocking was saturated with her husband's blood. Gov. John B. Connally Jr. of Texas, who was riding in the same car with Mrs. Kennedy, was severely wounded in the chest, ribs and arm. His condition was serious, but not critical.

The killer fired the rifle from a building just off the motorcade route. Mr. Kennedy, Governor Connally and Mr. Johnson had just received an enthusiastic welcome from a large crowd in downtown Dallas. Mr. Kennedy apparently was hit by the first of what witnesses believed were three shots. He was driven at high speed to Dallas's Parkland Hospital. There, in an emergency operating room, with only physicians and nurses in attendance, he died without regaining consciousness. Mrs. Kennedy, Mrs. Connally and a Secret Service agent were in the car with Mr. Kennedy and Governor Connally. Two Secret Service agents flanked the car. Other than Mr. Connally, none of this group was injured in the shooting. Mrs. Kennedy cried, "Oh no!" immediately after her husband was struck.

Mrs. Kennedy was in the hospital near her husband when he died, but not in the operating room. When the body was taken from the hospital in a bronze coffin about 2 P.M., Mrs. Kennedy walked beside it. Her face was sorrowful. She looked steadily at the floor. She still wore the raspberry-colored suit in which she had greeted welcoming crowds in Fort Worth and Dallas. But she had taken off the matching pillbox hat she wore earlier in the day, and her dark hair was windblown and tangled. Her hand rested lightly on her husband's coffin as it was taken to a waiting hearse.

Mrs. Kennedy climbed in beside the coffin. Then the ambulance drove to Love Field, and Mr. Kennedy's body was placed aboard the presidential jet. Mrs. Kennedy then attended the swearing-in ceremony for Mr. Johnson. As Mr. Kennedy's body left Parkland Hospital, a few stunned persons stood outside. Nurses and doctors, whispering among themselves, looked from the window. A larger crowd that had gathered earlier, before it was known that the president was dead, had been dispersed by Secret Service men and policemen.

Two priests administered last rites to Mr. Kennedy, a Roman Catholic.

They were the Very Rev. Oscar Huber, the pastor of Holy Trinity Church in Dallas, and the Rev. James Thompson.

Mr. Johnson was sworn in as president by Federal Judge Sarah T. Hughes of the Northern District of Texas. She was appointed to the judgeship by Mr. Kennedy in October, 1961. The ceremony, delayed about five minutes for Mrs. Kennedy's arrival, took place in the private presidential cabin in the rear of the plane. About 25 to 30 persons—members of the late president's staff, members of Congress who had been accompanying the president on a two-day tour of Texas cities and a few reporters— crowded into the little room. No accurate listing of those present could be obtained. Mrs. Kennedy stood at the left of Mr. Johnson, her eyes and face showing the signs of weeping that had apparently shaken her since she left the hospital not long before. Mrs. Johnson, wearing a beige dress, stood at her husband's right.

As Judge Hughes read the brief oath of office, her eyes, too, were red from weeping. Mr. Johnson's hands rested on a black, leather-bound Bible as Judge Hughes read and he repeated: "I do solemnly swear that I will perform the duties of the President of the United States to the best of my ability and defend, protect and preserve the Constitution of the United States."

Those 34 words made Lyndon Baines Johnson, onetime farmboy and schoolteacher of Johnson City, the president. Mr. Johnson made no statement. He embraced Mrs. Kennedy and she held his hand for a long moment. He also embraced Mrs. Johnson and Mrs. Evelyn Lincoln, Mr. Kennedy's private secretary. "O.K.," Mr. Johnson said. "Let's get this plane back to Washington."

At 2:46 P.M., seven minutes after he had become president, 106 minutes after Mr. Kennedy had become the fourth American president to succumb to an assassin's wounds, the white and red jet took off for Washington. In the cabin when Mr. Johnson took the oath was Cecil Stoughton, an armed forces photographer assigned to the White House.

Mr. Kennedy's staff members appeared stunned and bewildered. Lawrence F. O'Brien, the Congressional liaison officer, and P. Kenneth O'Donnell, the appointment secretary, both long associates of Mr. Kennedy, showed evidences of weeping. None had anything to say. Other staff members believed to be in the cabin for the swearing-in included David F. Powers, the White House receptionist, Miss Pamela Turnure, Mrs. Kennedy's press secretary, and Malcolm Kilduff, the assistant White House press secretary.

Mr. Kilduff announced the president's death, with choked voice and red-rimmed eyes, at about 1:36 P.M. "President John F. Kennedy died at approximately 1 o'clock Central standard time today here in Dallas," Mr. Kilduff said at the hospital. "He died of a gunshot wound in the brain. I have no other details regarding the assassination of the president." Mr. Kilduff also announced that Governor Connally had been hit by a bullet or bullets and that Mr. Johnson, who had not yet been sworn in, was safe in the protective custody of the Secret Service at an unannounced place, presumably the airplane at Love Field. Mr. Kilduff indicated that the president had been shot once. Later medical reports raised the possibility that there had been two wounds. But the death was caused, as far as could be learned, by a massive wound in the brain.

Later in the afternoon, Dr. Malcolm Perry, an attending surgeon, and Dr. Kemp Clark, chief of neurosurgery at Parkland Hospital, gave more details. Mr. Kennedy was hit by a bullet in the throat, just below the Adam's apple, they said. This wound had the appearance of a bullet's entry. Mr. Kennedy also had a massive, gaping wound in the back and one on the right side of the head. However, the doctors said it was impossible to determine immediately whether the wounds had been caused by one bullet or two. Dr. Perry, the first physician to treat the president, said a number of resuscitative measures had been attempted, including oxygen, anesthesia, an endotracheal tube, a tracheotomy, blood and fluids. An electrocardiogram monitor was attached to measure Mr. Kennedy's heartbeats. Dr. Clark was summoned and arrived in a minute or two. By then, Dr. Perry said, Mr. Kennedy was "critically ill and moribund," or near death. Dr. Clark said that on his first sight of the president, he had concluded immediately that Mr. Kennedy could not live. "It was apparent that the president had sustained a lethal wound," he said. "A missile had gone in and out of the back of his head causing external lacerations and loss of brain tissue." Shortly after he arrived, Dr. Clark said, "the president lost his heart action by the electrocardiogram." A closed-chest cardiograph massage was attempted, as were other emergency resuscitation measures.

Dr. Clark said these had produced "palpable pulses" for a short time, but all were "to no avail." The president was on the emergency table at the hospital for about 40 minutes, the doctors said. At the end, perhaps eight physicians were in Operating Room No. 1, where Mr. Kennedy remained until his death. Dr. Clark said it was difficult to determine the exact moment of death, but the doctors said officially that it occurred at 1 P.M.

Later, there were unofficial reports that Mr. Kennedy had been killed instantly. The source of these reports, Dr. Tom Shires, chief surgeon at the hospital and professor of surgery at the University of Texas Southwest Medical School, issued this statement tonight: "Medically, it was apparent the president was not alive when he was brought in. There was no spontaneous respiration. He had dilated, fixed pupils. It was obvious he had a lethal head wound. Technically, however, by using vigorous resuscitation, intravenous tubes and all the usual supportive measures, we were able to raise a semblance of a heartbeat." Dr. Shires said he was "positive it was impossible" that President Kennedy could have spoken after being shot. "I am absolutely sure he never knew what hit him," Dr. Shires said. Dr. Shires was not present when Mr. Kennedy was being treated at Parkland Hospital. He issued his statement, however, after lengthy conferences with the doctors who had attended the president.

Mr. Johnson remained in the hospital about 30 minutes after Mr. Kennedy died.

The details of what happened when shots first rang out, as the president's car moved along at about 25 miles an hour, were sketchy. Secret Service agents, who might have given more details, were unavailable to the press at first, and then returned to Washington with President Johnson.

Mr. Kennedy had opened his day in Fort Worth, first with a speech in a parking lot and then at a Chamber of Commerce breakfast. The breakfast appearance was a particular triumph for Mrs. Kennedy, who entered late and was given an ovation. Then the presidential party, including Governor and Mrs. Connally, flew on to Dallas, an eight-minute flight. Mr. Johnson, as is customary, flew in a separate plane. The president and the vice president do not travel together, out of fear of a double tragedy. At Love Field, Mr. and Mrs. Kennedy lingered for 10 minutes, shaking hands with an enthusiastic group lining the fence. The group called itself "Grassroots Democrats." Mr. Kennedy then entered his open Lincoln convertible at the head of the motorcade. He sat in the rear seat on the right-hand side. Mrs. Kennedy, who appeared to be enjoying one of the first political outings she had ever made with her husband, sat at his left. In the "jump" seat, directly ahead of Mr. Kennedy, sat Governor Connally, with Mrs. Connally at his left in another "jump" seat. A Secret Service agent was driving and the two others ran alongside.

Behind the president's limousine was an open sedan carrying a number of Secret Service agents. Behind them, in an open convertible, rode Mr. and Mrs. Johnson and Texas's senior senator, Ralph W. Yarborough, a Democrat. The motorcade proceeded uneventfully along a 10-mile route through downtown Dallas, aiming for the Merchandise Mart. Mr. Kennedy was to address a group of the city's leading citizens at a luncheon in his honor.

In downtown Dallas, crowds were thick, enthusiastic and cheering. The turnout was somewhat unusual for this center of conservatism, where only a month ago Adlai E. Stevenson was attacked by a rightist crowd. It was also in Dallas, during the 1960 campaign, that Senator Lyndon B. Johnson and his wife were nearly mobbed in the lobby of the Baker Hotel.

As the motorcade neared its end and the president's car moved out of the thick crowds onto Stemmons Freeway near the Merchandise Mart, Mrs. Connally recalled later, "we were all very pleased with the reception in downtown Dallas." Behind the three leading cars were a string of others carrying Texas and Dallas dignitaries, two buses of reporters, several open cars carrying photographers and other reporters, and a bus for White House staff members.

As Mrs. Connally recalled later, the president's car was almost ready to go underneath a "triple underpass" beneath three streets—Elm, Commerce and Main—when the first shot was fired. That shot apparently struck Mr. Kennedy. Governor Connally turned in his seat at the sound and appeared immediately to be hit in the chest. Mrs. Mary Norman of Dallas was standing at the curb and at that moment was aiming her camera at the president. She saw him slump forward, then slide down in the seat. "My God," Mrs. Norman screamed, as she recalled it later, "he's shot!" Mrs. Connally said that Mrs. Kennedy had reached and "grabbed" her husband. Mrs. Connally put her arms around the governor. Mrs. Connally said that she and Mrs. Kennedy had then ducked low in the car as it sped off. Mrs. Connally's recollections were reported by Julian Read, an aide to the governor. Most reporters in the press buses were too far back to see the shootings, but they observed some quick scurrying by motor policemen accompanying the motorcade. It was noted that the president's car had picked up speed and raced away, but reporters were not aware that anything serious had occurred until they reached the Merchandise Mart two or three minutes later.

Rumors of the shooting already were spreading through the luncheon crowd of hundreds, which was having the first course. No White House officials or Secret Service agents were present, but the reporters were taken quickly to Parkland Hospital on the strength of the rumors. There they encountered Senator Yarborough, white, shaken and horrified. The shots, he said, seemed to have come from the right and the rear of the car in which he was riding, the third in the motorcade. Another eyewitness, Mel Crouch, a Dallas television reporter, reported that as the shots rang out he saw a rifle extended and then withdrawn from a window on the "fifth or sixth floor" of the Texas School Book Depository. This is a leased state building on Elm Street, to the right of the motorcade route. Senator Yarborough said there had been a slight pause between the first two shots and a longer pause between the second and third. A Secret Service man riding in the senator's car, the senator said, immediately ordered Mr. and Mrs. Johnson to get down below the level of the doors. They did so, and Senator Yarborough also got down. The leading cars of the motorcade then pulled away at high speed toward Parkland Hospital, which was not far away, by the fast highway. "We knew by the speed that something was terribly wrong," Senator Yarborough reported. When he put his head up, he said, he saw a Secret Service man in the car ahead beating his fists against the trunk deck of the car in which he was riding, apparently in frustration and anguish.

Only White House staff members spoke with Mrs. Kennedy. A Dallas medical student, David Edwards, saw her in Parkland Hospital while she was waiting for news of her husband. He gave this description: "The look in her eyes was like an animal that had been trapped, like a little rabbit— brave, but fear was in the eyes." Dr. Clark was reported to have informed Mrs. Kennedy of her husband's death.

No witnesses reported seeing or hearing any of the Secret Service agents or policemen fire back. One agent was seen to brandish a machine gun as the cars sped away. Mr. Crouch observed a policeman falling to the ground and pulling a weapon. But the events had occurred so quickly that there was apparently nothing for the men to shoot at. Mr. Crouch said he saw two women, standing at a curb to watch the motorcade pass, fall to the ground when the shots rang out. He also saw a man snatch up his little girl and run along the road. Policemen, he said, immediately chased this man under the impression he had been involved in the shooting, but Mr. Crouch said he had been a fleeing spectator.

Mr. Kennedy's limousine—license No. GG300 under District of Columbia registry—pulled up at the emergency entrance of Parkland Hospital. Senator Yarborough said the president had been carried inside on a stretcher. By the time reporters arrived at the hospital, the police were guarding the presidential car closely. They would allow no one to approach it. A bucket of water stood by the car, suggesting that the back seat had been scrubbed out. Robert Clark of the American Broadcasting Company, who had been riding near the front of the motorcade, said Mr. Kennedy was motionless when he was carried inside. There was a great amount of blood on Mr. Kennedy's suit and shirtfront and the front of his body, Mr. Clark said. Mrs. Kennedy was leaning over her husband when the car stopped, Mr. Clark said, and walked beside the wheeled stretcher into the hospital. Mr. Connally sat with his hands holding his stomach, his head bent over. He, too, was moved into the hospital in a stretcher, with Mrs. Connally at his side.

Robert MacNeil of the National Broadcasting Company, who also was in the reporters' pool car, jumped out at the scene of the shooting. He said the police had taken two eyewitnesses into custody—an 8-year-old Negro boy and a white man—for informational purposes. Many of these reports could not be verified immediately. An unidentified Dallas man, interviewed on television here, said he had been waving at the president when the shots were fired. His belief was that Mr. Kennedy had been struck twice—once, as Mrs. Norman recalled, when he slumped in his seat; again when he slid down in it. "It seemed to just knock him down," the man said.

Governor Connally's condition was reported as "satisfactory" tonight after four hours in surgery at Parkland Hospital. Dr. Robert R. Shaw, a thoracic surgeon, operated on the governor to repair damage to his left chest. Later, Dr. Shaw said Governor Connally had been hit in the back just below the shoulder blade, and that the bullet had gone completely through the governor's chest, taking out part of the fifth rib. After leaving the body, he said, the bullet struck the governor's right wrist, causing a compound fracture. It then lodged in the left thigh. The thigh wound, Dr. Shaw said, was trivial. He said the compound fracture would heal. Dr. Shaw said it would be unwise for Governor Connally to be moved in the next 10 to 14 days. Mrs. Connally was remaining at his side tonight.

Mrs. Kennedy's presence near her husband's bedside at his death resulted from somewhat unusual circumstances. She had rarely accompanied him on his trips about the country and had almost never made political trips with him. The tour on which Mr. Kennedy was engaged yesterday and today was only quasi-political; the only open political activity was to have been a speech tonight to a fund-raising dinner at the state capitol in Austin. In visiting Texas, Mr. Kennedy was seeking to improve his political fortunes in a pivotal state that he barely won in 1960. He was also hoping to patch a bitter internal dispute among Texas's Democrats.

At 8:45 A.M., when Mr. Kennedy left the Texas Hotel in Fort Worth, where he spent his last night, to address the parking lot crowd across the street, Mrs. Kennedy was not with him. There appeared to be some disappointment. "Mrs. Kennedy is organizing herself," the president said good-naturedly. "It takes longer, but, of course, she looks better than we do when she does it." Later, Mrs. Kennedy appeared late at the Chamber of Commerce breakfast in Fort Worth. Again, Mr. Kennedy took note of her presence. "Two years ago," he said, "I introduced myself in Paris by saying that I was the man who had accompanied Mrs. Kennedy to Paris. I am getting somewhat that same sensation as I travel around Texas. Nobody wonders what Lyndon and I wear."

The speech Mr. Kennedy never delivered at the Merchandise Mart luncheon contained a passage commenting on a recent preoccupation of his, and a subject of much interest in this city, where right-wing conservatism is the rule rather than the exception. Voices are being heard in the land, he said, "voices preaching doctrines wholly unrelated to reality, wholly unsuited to the sixties, doctrines which apparently assume that words will suffice without weapons, that vituperation is as good as victory and that peace is a sign of weakness." The speech went on: "At a time when the national debt is steadily being reduced in terms of its burden on our economy, they see that debt as the greatest threat to our security. At a time when we are steadily reducing the number of Federal employees serving every thousand citizens, they fear those supposed hordes of civil servants far more than the actual hordes of opposing armies. We cannot expect that everyone, to use the phrase of a decade ago, will 'talk sense to the American people.' But we can hope that fewer people will listen to nonsense. And the notion that this nation is headed for defeat through deficit, or that strength is but a matter of slogans, is nothing but just plain nonsense."

Texan Asks Unity

Congressional Chiefs of Both Parties Give Promise of Aid

By FELIX BELAIR Jr.

Special to The New York Times

WASHINGTON, Nov. 22—Lyndon B. Johnson returned to a stunned capital shortly after 6 P.M. today to assume the duties of the presidency. The new president asked for and received from Congressional leaders of both parties their "united support in the face of the tragedy which has befallen our country." He said it was "more essential than ever before that this country be united." Partisan differences disappeared in the chorus of assurances with which the Congressional leaders responded. Mr. Johnson was described by those who talked with him as "stunned and shaken" by the assassination of President Kennedy. But he moved quickly from problems of national security and foreign policy to funeral arrangements for Mr. Kennedy. Across the street from the West Wing of the White House, the president conferred with officials in his old vice-presidential offices in the Executive Office Building. Senator George A. Smathers, Democrat of Florida, a personal friend of the dead president, was one of those who described Mr. Johnson as shaken. "Everyone is," he added. "But the president is the more so because he was right there when the tragedy occurred."

While flying to Washington aboard the presidential plane, Mr. Johnson arranged for a meeting with Cabinet members to ask that they remain at their posts. He made the same request of staff members in the executive office. "Calm and contained" was the way Senator J. W. Fulbright described the president's manner during a discussion of foreign-policy matters with Under Secretary of State W. Averell Harriman. The Arkansas senator said the president had been working on "what looked like a statement"—presumably an assurance of continuity of the nation's foreign policy.

The new president's first conference was aboard the helicopter that flew him the 15 miles from Andrews Air Force Base to the south lawn of the White House. He was briefed during the flight by Secretary of Defense Robert S. McNamara and the White House assistant for national security affairs, McGeorge Bundy. Under Secretary of State George W. Ball also took part.

During the afternoon two Johnson aides moved into the White House. They were Walter Jenkins, his administrative assistant as vice president, and George Reedy, his press secretary. Bill D. Moyers, top aide to Mr. Johnson during the 1960 campaign, went out to the Johnson home this evening to spend the night. Mr. Moyers, who is 29 years old, is now deputy director of the Peace Corps. Before leaving his old offices in the Executive Office Building for his Spring Valley residence, President Johnson discussed with J. Edgar Hoover, director of the Federal Bureau of Investigation, the progress of the investigation into the assassination. He talked by telephone with the physician of Gov. John B. Connally of Texas, who was wounded while sitting across from President Kennedy, and was relieved to learn that the governor's condition was satisfactory. He arranged to meet with Secretary of State Dean Rusk at 9 A.M. tomorrow and with former President Eisenhower at 11:30 A.M. tomorrow. He had already talked by telephone with General Eisenhower as well as with former Presidents Herbert Hoover and Harry S. Truman. One of the first acts of the president tomorrow will be to issue a proclamation fixing Monday, the day of Mr. Kennedy's funeral, as a day of national prayer and mourning.

The presidential jet landed at Andrews Air Force Base in nearby Maryland after the flight from Dallas. Both President Johnson and his wife, Lady Bird, remained aboard the jet aircraft until the coffin bearing the body of the slain president had been removed from a forward compartment to an enclosed ramp and then to a waiting Navy ambulance. A large delegation of Administration officials was on hand as the plane taxied to a stop. President Johnson solemnly shook hands with a few persons and then walked toward a large Congressional delegation. The president was somberly attired in a black three-button suit and stood hatless in a breeze as he spoke a terse message to the country. Mrs. Johnson was at his side. A thin silver stripe across his black four-in-hand necktie was the only deviation in his somber appearance.

It was 6:23 P.M. when the Army helicopter with the President and Mrs. Johnson aboard skirted the illuminated Washington Monument and descended to the White House lawn. Two more helicopters came roaring in moments later. The first carried the presidential assistants, Lawrence O'Brien, Kenneth O'Donnell and Malcolm Kilduff, who was acting press secretary on the trip to Dallas. Other staff members and Secret Service agents were aboard the second craft. Several staff members wept. It had been the same at Andrews Air Force Base. Several among the diplomatic corps made no attempt to hide their grief as the new president passed among them. President Johnson seemed to move with confidence into his new responsibilities.

Compared with former President Harry S. Truman's lack of preparation for the White House, it was as though Lyndon B. Johnson had been tutored every step of the way by President Kennedy himself. It was at the insistence of the late president that Mr. Johnson attended all Cabinet meetings as a matter of a vice president's right. It was President Kennedy's idea that his second in command should participate actively in the administration of the Executive Branch as well as in the formulation of policy. As vice president, he was named chairman of the National Aeronautics and Space Council and made responsible for setting up the president's Committee on Equal Employment Opportunity. Mr. Johnson had viewed the vice presidency in a more traditional sense—that of presiding over the Senate and furthering the Administration's legislative program while increasing his knowledge of Federal affairs at the highest level. It was also President Kennedy's idea that his vice president should become better known abroad as well as at home. Thus Mr. Johnson became the president's special emissary. He went around the world on a goodwill tour in

1961 on an itinerary that included battle-scarred South Vietnam. Later he visited the Middle East on a fact-finding mission for the president. More recently he visited the Scandinavian countries on a tour that ended with a whirlwind visit to the capitals of the European Economic Community. Returning from the tour he acknowledged being tired. But he was off again the next day to make a speech in West Virginia.

Mr. Truman had been excluded so completely as vice president from affairs of the presidency and his official family that he remarked a few years after assuming the highest office that he was the worst prepared man for the responsibilities since Andrew Johnson succeeded Abraham Lincoln. In this sense Mr. Johnson may be the best prepared vice presidential successor in American history. He has had access, as a member of the National Security Council, to the nation's most closely held military and diplomatic secrets.

Leftist Accused

Figure in a Pro-Castro Group Is Charged—Policeman Slain

By GLADWIN HILL

Special to The New York Times

DALLAS, Tex., Nov. 22—The Dallas police and Federal officers issued a charge of murder late tonight in the assassination of President Kennedy. The accused is Lee Harvey Oswald, a 24-year-old former marine, who went to live in the Soviet Union in 1959 and returned to Texas last year. Capt. Will Fritz, head of the Dallas police homicide bureau, identified Oswald as an adherent of the left-wing Fair Play for Cuba Committee. Oswald was arrested about two hours after the shooting, in a movie theater three miles away, shortly after he allegedly shot and killed a policeman on a street nearby. He was arraigned tonight on a charge of murdering the police officer. The charge related to the Kennedy killing was made later.

After the arraignment, the suspect, a slight, dark-haired man, was taken downstairs to appear in a line-up, presumably before witnesses of the Kennedy assassination. While being escorted, handcuffed, through a police building corridor, he shouted: "I haven't shot anybody."

Captain Fritz said Oswald was employed—the exact job was unknown—at the Texas School Book Depository, a warehouse from which the assassin's bullets came. The captain said some witnesses had placed Oswald in the building at the time of the assassination. Dallas County District Attorney Henry Wade said there were "a few loose ends" in the case to be wrapped up, and he expected that the case would not go to the grand jury next week. Oswald faces a death sentence if convicted. The sequence of events leading to his arrest was as follows:

As a citywide manhunt began during the hour following the assassination, an unidentified man notified police headquarters, over a police-car radio, that the car's officer had been shot and killed. The car was in the 400 block of East Jefferson Boulevard in the Oak Cliff section, on the edge of the downtown area. The car's driver, Patrolman Tippit, had not made any call that he was going to question anyone. Eight other officers converged on the spot. They found Patrolman Tippit lying on the sidewalk, dead from two .38-caliber bullet wounds. They began a search of nearby buildings for the killer. Then another call came to police headquarters from Julie Postal, cashier of the Texas Theatre at 231 West Jefferson Boulevard, six blocks from the scene of the policeman's slaying. She said an usher had told her that a man who had just entered the theater was acting peculiarly. The investigating police officers were dispatched to the theater. They began checking patrons, starting at the front of the house. One of the officers, Sgt. Jerry Hill, said that when they came to Oswald, sitting in the rear four seats in from the aisle, the suspect jumped up and exclaimed: "This is it!" The Dallas Police Department appeared to be the nerve center of the overall investigation of the president's death, although the various lines this might be taking were not defined. The justice of the peace before whom Oswald was arraigned, David Johnston, said the assassination was a matter of state jurisdiction so far.

Little was known here about Oswald, except reports published locally in 1959 when he went to the Soviet Union after his discharge from the Marine Corps. He was said to have tried to renounce his United States citizenship by turning in his passport to the United States Embassy in Moscow. The Embassy, it was reported then, advised him to hold on to it until he had some assurance of Soviet citizenship. He was reported to have worked in factories in the Soviet and to have married a Russian girl. At the time of his quasi-defection, his mother and his brother, a milkman in nearby Fort Worth, sent messages vainly trying to dissuade him.

Shortly after he was escorted from his arraignment last night, a tall, slender woman with a little girl about 2 years old and a baby in her arms left the homicide bureau. An officer said they were the suspect's wife and daughter.

A housekeeper at Oswald's rooming house said the young man entered his room shortly after the shooting of the president, got a coat, and went back out. The housekeeper, Mrs. Earlene Roberts, said: "He came in in a hurry in his shirt sleeves and I said, 'Oh, you're in a hurry,' and he didn't say anything. He went on in his room and got a coat and put it on. He went out to the bus stop and that's the last I saw of him." Mrs. Roberts said Oswald rushed into the rooming house, at 1026 North Beckley Road in suburban Oak Cliff. This was shortly after Mrs. Roberts had learned, in a telephone call from a friend, that the president had been shot. She said she had not connected Oswald's appearance with the shooting. She described Oswald, who had lived in the house since the end of October, as quiet.

Justice of the Peace Johnston said he was one of four from outlying communities, assembled for the Kennedy visit, who had been recruited to assist law enforcement officers with the inquiry. Judge Johnston said Judge Theron Ward had been assigned to the president's death and Judge Joe B. Brown Jr. to the death of the policeman. Judge Johnston and Judge Lloyd Russell were assisting in such matters as the issuance of search warrants and handling the arraignment. The arraignment involved no plea. Oswald was held without bail for grand jury action and was advised of his rights to counsel.

Captain Fritz emerged from the homicide bureau after the arraignment and said: "We've charged this man with the killing of the officer." Asked whether Oswald had been linked with the assassination, the officer replied: "He doesn't admit it—we have some more work to do on that case." The revolver carried by Oswald in the theater was not suspected of having figured in President Kennedy's death. Police ballistics experts were still studying, with apparently no conclusive findings, the rifle found in the book warehouse. Captain Fritz said it was of obscure foreign origin, possibly Italian, of about 1940 vintage, and of an unusual, undetermined caliber. He displayed a bullet he said fitted the gun. It was about .30 caliber and about two and one-half inches long, with a narrow tapered nose. Sergeant Hill said Oswald had a .38-caliber revolver under his shirt, and that in a scuffle that ensued, it was fired once, harmlessly. The time was 2:15 P.M. yesterday.

Oswald was subdued, handcuffed, rushed to downtown police headquarters and put in a fifth-floor cell. At 6:35 P.M. he was taken down to the third-floor homicide bureau. He wore black slacks, black loafer shoes, a white undershirt and an olive plaid sport shirt, unbuttoned. His left eye was slightly blackened, and there was a contusion on his right cheekbone.

Career of Suspect Has Been Bizarre

U.S. Loan Enabled Oswald to Return From Soviet

By PETER KIHSS

It was a $435.71 United States Government loan that enabled Lee Harvey Oswald to return to this country 18 months ago after living two and a half years in the Soviet Union. The 24-year-old Texan who was charged last night with the murder of President Kennedy has had a bizarre career. An ex-marine, he applied for Soviet citizenship in Moscow in 1959, only to appeal later to a United States senator for help in getting back home on the ground that the Soviets were holding him and his Russian wife against his will. Last July, he tried to infiltrate the Cuban Student Directorate, seeking to overthrow Cuban Premier Fidel Castro, according to Cuban exiles in New Orleans and Miami. Turned down, he appeared later as asserted chairman of a New Orleans chapter of the Fair Play for Cuba Committee, propagandizing in favor of the Castro regime. Currently he has been holding a passport obtained on his contention that he was a photographer and wanted to go abroad during October, November and December

of this year to visit the Soviet Union, Britain, France, Germany, the Netherlands. Finland, Italy and Poland.

In Buffalo yesterday, a man who said he served in the same Marine
Corps unit at El Toro, Calif., in 1954–55, said that Oswald was a "lonely,
introverted aloof boy" during that time. The Buffalo man, Allen D. Graf,
of 31 West Utica Street, said Oswald "always said he hated the outfit,"
and was bitter about the "tough time his mother had during the depression.
We all thought it was the usual gripes of a guy in service," Mr. Graf said,
according to The Associated Press. Mr. Graf said Oswald stayed by himself
much of the time, and was "somewhat of a problem boy then."

It is also as "an introvert" that Oswald is remembered by Mrs. Howard
Green, wife of a Texas State representative from Fort Worth. Mrs. Green
said yesterday in Austin that she had taught him in the sixth grade at
Ridgelea Elementary School in Fort Worth. He was a loner who sought
escape in books, but did not apply himself in school and wound up with
below-average grades, Mrs. Green said according to United Press International.

Recently Oswald has described himself as a "Marxist." The Dallas police said he had been working in the Texas School Book Depository Building, from which, it is believed, the rifle bullet that killed President Kennedy
was fired. Newsmen called him arrogant when they saw him yesterday in
the custody of the Dallas police. A sharp-featured man with dark, intent
eyes, he raised his handcuffed hands in a clenched fist. As pieced together
from various quarters, including reports of The Associated Press and
United Press International from various points, Oswald's career has gone
like this:

He was born in New Orleans, Oct. 18, 1939, after his father had died.
He lived two years in New York. He attended two Fort Worth elementary
schools and then enrolled in a high school in September, 1956. But he
withdrew from high school only 23 days after starting classes, and joined
the Marines. He served three years in the Marines, including service in
Japan, and was discharged Sept. 11, 1959, as a radar operator. The discharge was granted on a plea of hardship. When he was discharged, he
visited a sister-in-law, Mrs. Robert L. Oswald, in Fort Worth. She recalled
later that "he said he wanted to travel a lot and talked about going to

Cuba." Instead, he turned up in Moscow as a tourist on Oct. 13, 1959. His occupation was then listed as shipping export agent, his permanent address as 3124 West Fifth Street, Fort Worth. On Oct. 31, 1959, the former marine, then 20 years old, walked into the United States Embassy and slapped his passport down on a desk. He said he had applied for Soviet citizenship. The embassy suggested that he refrain from signing any papers until he was sure the Soviet Union would accept him.

His brother, Robert L. Oswald, a Fort Worth milk route carrier, cabled him a plea to change his mind, and also telegraphed Secretary of State Christian A. Herter asking for help in making contact with the would-be defector. "Lee, through any means possible, contact me," Robert's cable read. "Mistake. Keep your nose clean." But on Nov. 2, 1959, Lee Oswald swore out an affidavit: "I affirm that my allegiance is to the Soviet Socialist Republic." His passport was accepted by embassy officials and sent to the Justice Department in Washington.

Aline Mosby, a United Press International correspondent who interviewed him in Moscow then, wrote from Paris last night that she had "judged him as a person very determined but unsure of himself, naive and emotionally unbalanced." "I'm a Marxist," she quoted him as saying. "I became interested about the age of 15. An old lady handed me a pamphlet about saving the Rosenbergs. I still remember that pamphlet about the Rosenbergs. I don't know why. Then we moved to North Dakota and I discovered one book in the library, *Das Kapital*. It was what I'd been looking for. It was like a very religious man opening the Bible for the first time. I started to study Marxist economic theories. I could see the impoverishment of the masses before my eyes in my own mother. I thought the worker's life could be better. I found some Marxist books on dusty shelves in the New Orleans library and continued to indoctrinate myself for five years." He said he had been waiting to get out of the Marine Corps "like waiting to get out of prison." Dispatches at the time had also quoted him as saying he considered the occupation of Japan "imperialistic."

Oswald was said to have told embassy officials he planned to inform the Soviets about everything he learned while he had been a radar operator during his three-year enlistment in the Marines. On Nov. 11, 1959, he said Soviet officials had refused to grant him citizenship, but had told him he could live in the Soviet Union as an alien resident. In the Soviet Union he was understood to have worked in a factory at Minsk, where he ostensibly became disillusioned with life under Communist rule. He married a Minsk hospital employee, Marina Nikolaevna, now about 22 years old. The United States Embassy in Moscow said yesterday that a daughter was born to the couple last year.

In Washington, Senator John G. Tower, Republican of Texas, made public yesterday a letter he had received from Oswald from Minsk in January, 1962: With misspellings, it read:

"Dear Senator Tower,

"My name is Lee Harvey Oswald, 22, of Ft. Worth up till Oct. 1959, when I came to the Soviet Union for a residenual stay. I took a residenual document for a non-Soviet person living for a time in the U.S.S.R. The American Embassy in Moscow is familiar with my case.

"Since July 20th, 1960, I have unsuccessfully applied for a Soviet exit visa to leave this country, the Soviets refuse to permit me and my Soviet wife, (who applied at the U.S. Embassy Moscow, July 8, 1960 for immigration status to the U.S.A.) to leave the Soviet Union. I am a citizen of the United States of America (Passport Number 1733242, 1959) and I beseech you, Senator Tower, to rise the question of holding by the Soviet Union of a citizen of the U.S., against his will and expressed desires.

"Yours very truly,

"Lee H. Oswald."

Senator Tower passed on this word by a letter Jan. 26, 1982, to Frederick G. Dutton, assistant secretary of state for congressional relations. The senator said he did not know Oswald or any of the facts, or what action, if any, this Government should take. A memorandum by one of the senator's aides, Miss Linda Lovelady, said the State Department reported on Feb. 1, 1962, that Oswald "now wishes to return to U.S. with his Soviet wife, who is pregnant." The memorandum said his mother was living in Vernon, Tex., and "unable to pay for his return—State Department will probably finance this on a loan basis." The State Department decided Oswald had not expatriated himself, and still held United States citizenship. As it does for United States citizens stranded abroad, it provided for a loan—listed at $435.71—to pay for the transportation of Oswald, his wife and newborn child. Government records indicate he left Moscow at the end of May, 1962. It is not clear whether he ever repaid the loan.

The Soviet authorities had granted exit permits for him and his family, not always the easiest problem for foreigners with Russian wives. In Miami, José Antonio Lanuza, spokesman for the Cuban Student Directorate, said yesterday that Oswald had approached that anti-Castro group's New Orleans delegate, Carlos Bringuier, last July. Mr. Lanuza said Oswald asserted he wanted to help Cubans in a fight against Communism, and offered a $10 contribution and his aid in military training for an invasion. "I was suspicious of him from the start," said Mr. Bringuier, 29, who has lived in New Orleans since February, 1961, and who operates a retail clothing store. "But frankly I thought he might be an agent from the F.B.I. or the C.I.A. trying to find out what we might be up to." Mr. Bringuier said in New Orleans that Oswald had given him a blue paperback, *Guidebook for Marines,* with his name penciled on the first page, "Pvt. Lee H. Oswald." According to Mr. Lanuza, Oswald showed up with some pickets on Canal Street, New Orleans, some days later. Their signs read: "Hands Off Cuba," "Viva Castro!" and "Let's Send Medicine and Food to Cuba Instead of Cuban Raiders." Mr. Bringuier and some other anti-Castro Cubans grabbed his literature away, and Mr. Bringuier and Oswald and some others were arrested. The New Orleans police reported that Oswald was fined $10 in City Court last August for disturbing the peace.

On Aug. 21, Oswald took part in a panel discussion on radio station WDSU in New Orleans. He had identified himself as secretary of the New Orleans Chapter of the Fair Play for Cuba Committee—although last night that national organization's director, Vincent Theodore Lee, said there was no such chapter and denied knowing Oswald. In the discussion, Oswald said he was a Marxist but denied he was a Communist, and said there was "a very great difference." He noted that many diverse parties were "based on Marxism." Oswald said his three-year residence in the Soviet Union "gives me excellent qualifications to repudiate charges that Cuba and the Fair Play for Cuba Committee's Communist controlled." He said the committee had been investigated and "the total result was zero. The principles of the Fair Play for Cuba," he went on, "consist of restoration of diplomatic trade and tourist relations with Cuba. We are striving to get the United States to adopt measures which would be more friendly toward the Cuban people and the new Cuban regime in this country. . . . Our aims and our ideals are very clear, and in the best keeping with American traditions of democracy."

A participant asked if Oswald agreed with a Castro statement describing President Kennedy as a ruffian and a thief. "I would not agree with that particular wording," Oswald said. The panel program "so discredited" Oswald, Mr. Lanuza asserted in Miami, that "the Fair Play for Cuba Committee transferred him to Dallas." Mr. Lee denied last night that there were any Fair Play chapters in Texas.

Recently he and his wife have been living in Irving, a suburb of Dallas. The Dallas police said they now have two children. He wife does not speak English. His mother, Mrs. Marguerite Oswald, lives in Fort Worth. When told yesterday her son had been arrested, she said: "I am heartbroken about this. He is really a good boy."

Oswald, When a Marine, Was Not a Crack Shot

As marines go, Lee Harvey Oswald was not highly regarded as a rifleman. When he first entered the Marine Corps in 1956, he qualified as a sharpshooter with a score of 212 out of a possible 250. On his second proficiency test two years later, he fell back to marksman category with a score of 191. The Marine rifle ratings are: marksman, 190 to 209; sharpshooter, 210 to 219, and expert, 220 to 250.

Eyewitnesses Describe Scene of Assassination

Sounds of Shooting Brought Cars to Halt—Motorcade Sped Kennedy to Hospital

Following is a description of the assassination of President Kennedy yesterday, written by Jack Bell of The Associated Press, who witnessed the shooting from the fourth car behind the president:

DALLAS, Nov. 22 (AP)—There was a loud bang as though a giant firecracker had exploded in the caverns between the tall buildings we were just leaving behind us. In quick succession there were two other loud reports. The ominous sound of these dismissed from the minds of us riding in the reporters' "pool" car the fleeting idea that some Texan was adding a bit of noise to the cheering welcome Dallas had given John F. Kennedy.

The reports sounded like rifle shots. The man in front of me screamed, "My God, they're shooting at the president!" Our driver braked the car sharply and we swung the doors open to leap out. Suddenly the procession, which had halted, shot forward again.

In the flash of that instant, a little tableau was enacted in front of a colonnade toward which the velvety green grass swelled upward to a small park near the top of an underpass for which we had been headed. A man was pushing a woman dressed in bright orange to the ground and seemed to be falling protectively over her. A photographer, scrambling on all fours toward the crest of the rise, held a camera trained in their direction. As my eye swept the buildings to the right, where the shots—if they really were shots; and it seemed unbelievable—might have come, I saw no significant sign of activity.

Four cars ahead, in the president's Continental limousine, a man in the front seat rose for a moment. He seemed to have a telephone in hand as he waved to a police cruiser ahead to go on. The presidential car leaped ahead and those following it attained breakneck speed as the caravan roared through the underpass and on to a broad freeway, police sirens whining shrilly. These sirens had been silenced by presidential order throughout Mr. Kennedy's Texas trip. Up to the highway we thundered, careening around a turn into the Parkland Hospital and screeching to a stop at the emergency entrance. As we piled out of our car, I saw Mrs. Kennedy, weeping, trying to hold her husband's head up. Mrs. John Connally was helping hold up the governor of Texas.

Mr. Connally's suit front was splattered with blood, his head rolling backward. By the time I had covered the distance to the presidential car, Secret Service men were helping Mrs. Kennedy away. Hospital attendants were aiding Mr. and Mrs. Connally. For an instant I stopped and stared into the back seat. There, face down, stretched out at full length, lay the president, motionless. His natty business suit seemed hardly rumpled. But there was blood on the floor.

"Is he dead?" I asked a Secret Service man. "I don't know," he said, "but I don't think so." I ran for a telephone. A few minutes later I was back for more information.

The president and Mr. Connally had been moved into an emergency operating room. Vice President Johnson, Mrs. Johnson and Mrs. Kennedy had been escorted into the hospital.

The shiny White House automobile, a manufacturer's dream, stood untouched. It had been flown 1,500 miles from Washington only to become the death vehicle of the president, to whom it was designed to give maximum protection. On the front seat floor lay the soft felt hat the president often carried but seldom wore. Beside it in mute comradeship was the wide-brimmed, light-colored Texas-style hat that Mr. Connally wore. In the wide area between the seats, now cleared of its jump seats, three twisted and torn roses lay in a pool of blood on the floor. Beside them was a tattered bouquet of asters. It all seemed so unreal. This was the conveyance for what had been in the nature of triumph for Mr. Kennedy and the first lady, who had been smiling, shaking hands and filled with happiness at a day of meeting the folks in the streets, the airports and the hotels. Ironically, if their reception in Texas had not been so warm, precautions might have been taken to raise the shatter-proof side glasses, even though the top of the convertible was down. Such protection might have saved the president. But Dallas, where the president's policies had raised a storm of conservative protests, had been warm in its welcome to the handsome, bronzed president and his pretty, chic wife.

The presidential party appeared to be chatting gaily among themselves after they had left the crowds of downtown Dallas behind and their caravan had swung into a quiet area where admirers had not chosen to stand. But there the assassin took his stand. His three well-aimed shots plunged America and the world into grief.

10 Feet From President

TORONTO, Nov. 22 (Canadian Press)—A man from suburban Willowdale who was only 10 feet away when President Kennedy was assassinated today said he first thought the gunfire was the sound of firecrackers. Norman Similas, 34 years old, told *The Star* in a telephone conversation that he had been in Dallas on business. He was taking pictures of the motorcade when he saw the president slump to the floor, he said.

Here is his story: "I was in Dallas on a convention and I decided to snap a picture of the president as the motorcade rolled by. The crowds had thinned out just past an overpass near the Trade Mart, so I had a good position when the motorcade came by at about 8 miles an hour. Then I suddenly heard a sharp crack. The first thing that came to my mind was that someone was setting off firecrackers. I turned away from the president's car and looked back to where the noise seemed to come from. Then somebody—I don't know who it was—yelled: 'The president's been shot.' I swung back to look at the car. A Secret Service man ran up with his gun drawn. A policeman beside me drew his revolver and his eyes searched the crowd. Then another shot rang out and a third almost immediately on top of it. I was still staring at the car. The Secret Service man opened the car door and I saw the president slumped down to the floor and falling toward the pavement. Jackie Kennedy was sitting on the left side of the car and Governor Connally on the president's right. I could see a hole in the president's left temple and his head and hair were bathed in blood. The agent looked in and gasped: 'Oh, my God, he's dead.' "

Boy Described Shooting

Special to The New York Times

CHICAGO, Nov. 22—The *Chicago Tribune* published today an eyewitness report by a 14-year-old boy who was standing 10 feet away and looking directly at President Kennedy at the time of the assassination. The boy, Alan Smith, a Boy Scout and a ninth-grade pupil at the Stockyard Junior High School, gave the following description:

"It made me weak. I felt like sitting down. It was horrible. I was standing on the curb watching the parade along Main Street. We were permitted to skip school, if we had a note from our parents, to watch it. The crowds were cheering, but all at once they changed to screaming. The car was about 10 feet from me when a bullet hit the president in his forehead. The bullets came from a window right over my head in the building in front of which my friends and I were standing. Mr. Kennedy had a big wide smile. But when he was hit, his face turned blank. There was no smile, no frown—nothing. He fell down over Jackie's knees and didn't say anything. She stood up screaming, 'God, oh God, no.' There was blood all over her and everything. She tried to raise him up but he fell back over her."

Ambush Building Chosen With Care

Looms Over Kennedy Route—6th Floor Little Used

Special to The New York Times

DALLAS, Nov. 22—The building in which President Kennedy's assassin hid today could hardly have been more suited to the use made of it. The Texas School Book Depository is a seven-story brick building that looms above the route Mr. Kennedy's motorcade took through Dallas. It is at the corner of Houston and Elm Streets, but set back and above the street on which Mr. Kennedy's car was traveling. The killer fired a high-powered rifle from the southeast corner window of the sixth floor. Jack C. Cason, president of the depository, said someone could have hidden on that floor for several days without being discovered. The floor is used solely for storage. In many areas it was stacked eight feet high with books. Reserve stocks of books are more readily available in the basement and on the second and fourth floors. Only when additional copies are needed did employees of the building have occasion to go to the sixth floor. These circumstances indicated that the killer was well aware of the layout of the building and the uses of the various floors. No elevator goes to the sixth floor from the front entrances. The killer would have had to get off the elevator on the fourth floor, walk to the back of the building and take the stairs or one of two freight elevators to reach the sixth floor.

Mr. Cason said he did not know Lee H. Oswald, arrested as a suspect in the president's assassination. Oswald had told the police he was an employee of the book depository. Late tonight the depository's personnel manager had not been located to comment.

The book depository is a building said to be about a half-century old. Its first floor apparently has been remodeled and is surrounded with grill-work. Above the first floor, however, the building's exterior has not been touched. The sixth floor windows are surmounted by arches. But the window from which the killer is believed to have fired has a square of brick-work about it. Immediately above the sixth floor there is a cornice. The seventh floor then has windows differing from the rest of the building. Atop the book depository building is a large neon sign. About 90 persons are employed in the building but most of them were out watching the president's motorcade pass when the fatal shots were fired.

Agents Checked Kennedy's Route

Dallas Police Also Helped in Security Precautions

By JOHN HERBERS

Special to The New York Times

DALLAS, Nov. 22—The Secret Service made elaborate and painstaking security preparations for President Kennedy's visit here. Agents made a minute check of the parade route he was to follow, the food he was to eat, the flowers that were to decorate the platform and potential trouble-makers. Secret Service men who were all around the president when he was shot, looking into the crowds and the buildings, were ready for any eventuality. In addition, 350 uniformed officers of the Dallas police provided additional security for the president.

It was impossible, however, for agents to make sure that every room, every window and every alleyway and rooftop along the six-mile route from the airport to the Trade Mart did not contain a sniper. Secret Service agents had been in Dallas for several days making security preparations.

At first, agents were reluctant to approve the Trade Mart for the scheduled luncheon. It is a huge modern building for showing merchandise and holding meetings. They said a number of balconies overlooking the speaking stand might pose a problem, but after further study they approved the site.

The Dallas police provided agents with a list of known agitators who might cause trouble. The agents studied their pictures and habits. Buildings along the route were checked. Detailed security was arranged for the 14 entrances to the Trade Mart. Agents secured a guest list and planned to check the tickets of everyone attending. Agents poked through 5,000 yellow roses that were arranged in the Trade Mart to make sure they contained no explosive or weapons. It was decided that the president and his party would receive the same kind of steak at the luncheon as everyone else. The president's steak was to be selected at random in the belief that nobody would attempt to poison the entire lot. Employees of the Trade Mart and those persons in the official greeting party at the airport were thoroughly looked over by agents. Before the president arrived, agents gave the airport a thorough check. Balconies, windows and other vantage points were covered. The Dallas police said the preparations were as thorough as could have been made.

Kennedy Car Built for Security

CINCINNATI, Nov. 22 (UPI)—The automobile in which President Kennedy was fatally shot today was custom built here in 1961 to rigid Secret Service specifications. Delivered to the White House in June, 1961, the car, called the Presidential Continental, had more specially designed features than any car ever before used for Government duties. The metallic navy blue vehicle is owned by the Ford Motor Company and was leased to the White House. Hess & Eisenhardt, which outfitted the auto, said today it had a protective "bubble top" but declined to specify whether the cover was bulletproof. The vehicle was equipped with radiotelephones to keep the president and his guards in communication with staff members along any parade route.

Texas Governor a Self-Made Man

Connally, a Johnson Friend, Was Born on Small Farm

Gov. John B. Connally Jr., a husky six-footer, is a self-made man who has prospered in business and politics. A conservative Democrat, he won his party's nomination for governor in June, 1962, by a close margin in a run-off primary against Don Yarborough, his liberal opponent. He then fought off a strong Republican threat to defeat Jack Cox, a former Democrat.

Mr. Connally is a highly controversial figure in a state known for its political fights. He is at odds not only with Don Yarborough, who is expected to oppose him again for the nomination, but also with another, unrelated Yarborough, Senator Ralph W. Yarborough.

The governor has been closely associated with Lyndon Johnson. He served as executive director of the Johnson-for-President organization in 1960. His appointment as President Kennedy's first secretary of the navy was attributed to Mr. Johnson's sponsorship. When Mr. Connally resigned as secretary of the navy in December, 1961, to seek the governorship, the president praised him and paid tribute to the state of readiness of the Navy and the Marine Corps, both of which were under his direction. But he differed with the president on civil rights and other issues. His campaign for governor was described, even by his opponents, as the best-organized, best-financed and most effective in Texas history.

Mr. Connally, one of seven children, was born on a small farm near Floresville, Tex., on Feb. 27, 1917. He attended public schools in Floresville and San Antonio. He worked as a batch-weigher for a highway construction gang to pay his way through law school at the University of Texas. It was at the university that he first proved his ability as a politician. He was elected president of the student body, of his law class and of various organizations as well as winning the Inter-Society Oratorical Contest. On Dec. 21, 1940, he married Idanell Brill, a classmate who was Cactus Beauty, Relay Queen and University Sweetheart. She has proved a considerable campaign asset. They have three children, John B., 3d, Sharon and Mark. Soon after Mr. Connally was licensed to practice law in 1938, he went to Washington to become an assistant in the office of Mr. Johnson, then a United States representative.

During World War II, he entered the Navy as an ensign and emerged as a lieutenant commander. He served aboard the carriers *Essex* and *Bennington* and in Algiers, and was awarded the Legion of Merit and the Bronze Star. After the war, he managed a radio station in Austin, practiced law and then served briefly on Mr. Johnson's Senatorial staff. In 1952, he moved his law practice to Fort Worth and became attorney for the oil interests of the late Sid W. Richardson. He became executor for the estate of Mr. Richardson, a multi-millionaire. Mr. Connally, who is wealthy even by Texas standards, says that his greatest personal interests are Hereford and horse breeding and a coastal Bermuda grass pasture program on his Floresville ranch.

PRIEST DESCRIBES HOW HE ADMINISTERED LAST RITES AFTER THE PRESIDENT'S DEATH

Absolution Given at the Hospital

Mrs. Kennedy Takes Part in 15-Minute Ceremony but Appears to Be in Shock

By RONALD SULLIVAN

The priest who administered the last rites of the Roman Catholic Church to President Kennedy said last night that when he arrived at the hospital the president was dead. The priest, the Very Rev. Oscar L. Huber, said he had to draw back a sheet that was covering the president's face so that he could anoint his forehead with oil. Father Huber said the president's body was on a portable treatment table in an emergency room on the first floor of Parkland Hospital in Dallas. In the room, he said, were the president's wife, a few aides and a number of Secret Service agents. Father Huber, who is 70 years old, was accompanied by another priest, the Rev. James Thompson, who drove their car to the hospital.

Because the president was dead, Father Huber said, a "short form" of conditional absolution was administered. Then the last sacrament of the Church, Extreme Unction, or The Anointing of the Sick, was administered. Father Huber answered questions in a telephone interview from Dallas. He said that everyone in the president's room stood during the ceremony. He said a few, but he was not certain, might have blessed themselves with the Sign of the Cross. The ceremony took about 15 minutes, Father Huber said. Afterward, he added, he and Father Thompson left the room and remained in a hospital corridor for a half an hour.

Father Huber was the first to report that the president was dead. He and the other priests at Holy Trinity Church in Dallas were in the rectory when they heard that the president had been shot. Almost immediately, since the hospital was in his parish, Father Huber, the pastor, went upstairs for his small black prayer books. Father Thompson, a curate, met Father Huber coming downstairs and they both got into Father Thompson's car. The drive to the hospital normally would take just a few minutes. But the shooting had drawn swarms of cars and pedestrians. Traffic was jammed. Father Huber said they felt shocked as their car inched through the crowds, and Father Thompson kept repeating: "It just couldn't happen. It just couldn't happen." The two priests were met by members of a police emergency squad when they arrived at the hospital. They were quickly ushered inside the room where the president had been taken.

Father Huber said he thought he had arrived at nearly 1 P.M. (2 P.M. New York time). But he said that because of his shock, he was not certain. Father Huber administered conditional absolution. This is given when a priest has no way of knowing the mind of the recipient and whether the soul has left the body. In doing this, he said in Latin: "I absolve you from all censures and sins in the Name of the Father, and of the Son, and the Holy Spirit. Amen." Father Huber then said: "If you are living, may the Lord by this Holy Anointing forgive whatever you have sinned. Amen." As Father Huber spoke these words, he anointed the president on the forehead, making a small Sign of the Cross with his thumb, which had been dipped in the oils. Father Huber then gave the Apostolic Blessing: "I by the faculty given to me by the Apostolic See grant to you a plenary indulgence and remission of all sins and I bless you. In the Name of the Father, and of the Son, and of the Holy Spirit.

Amen." With that, Father Huber replaced the sheet over the president's face. He went on in English with the Prayers for the Dying and for the Departed Soul:

"May the most clement Virgin Mary, Mother of God, the most loving consoler of the afflicted, commend to her Son the soul of this servant, John, so that through her maternal intercession he may not fear the terror of death, but in her company may he joyfully enter the desired heavenly home. Amen.

"Into Thy hands I commend my spirit O Lord Jesus Christ. Receive my spirit. Holy Mary pray for me. O Mary Mother of Grace, Mother of Mercy, do thou protect me from the enemy and receive me at the hour of death. St. Joseph pray for me. St. Joseph in the company with the Blessed Virgin, thy spouse, open to me the bosom of divine mercy. Jesus, Mary and Joseph I give my heart and my soul. Jesus, Mary and Joseph assist me in my last agony. Jesus, Mary and Joseph may I sleep and rest in peace in Your holy company.

"Let us pray.

"To Thee O Lord we commend the soul of Thy servant, John, that being dead to the world he may live unto Thee and whatever sins he has committed through the frailty of his mortal nature do Thou in Thy most merciful goodness forgive and wash away through Christ our Lord. Amen.

"Grant O Lord that while we here lament the departure of your servant, we may ever remember that we are most certainly to follow him. Give us grace to prepare for that last hour by a good life, that we may not be surprised by a sudden death but be ever watching, for when Thou shalt call that soul we may enter eternal glory, through Christ our Lord. Amen.

"Eternal rest grant him O Lord and let perpetual Light shine upon him."

After this Mrs. Kennedy took a place beside Father Huber near the president's body. Father Huber led a recitation of the Lord's Prayer and Hail Marys. Mrs. Kennedy, with a clear and audible voice, responded as did others in the room who knew the endings of the prayers. Before leaving the room, Father Huber consoled the president's wife. He said she appeared to be in a state of shock, even though she was erect, clear-eyed and coherent. Mrs. Kennedy followed Father Huber out of the room. In the corridor, she thanked the priest for his expressions of sympathy and for praying for her husband.

6 Cabinet Members Turn Back
After Getting News Over Pacific

By HENRY RAYMONT

Special to The New York Times

WASHINGTON, Nov. 22—A plane carrying six members of the Cabinet turned back over the Pacific today at the news of President Kennedy's death. The officials were bound for Japan for political and economic talks. Secretary of State Dean Rusk was first to receive word of the assassination, an hour after a special Air Force jet carrying the party had left Hickam Air Force Base in Honolulu for Tokyo. The news was radioed to the pilot of the aircraft, who notified Mr. Rusk. The secretary of state is fourth in line of succession to the presidency after the vice president, the speaker of the House, and the president pro tempore of the Senate. Mr. Rusk, after consulting with the other Cabinet officers, ordered the pilot to turn around and fly to Washington, where the party is expected at 1 A.M. tomorrow. The officials, most of whom had had close personal bonds with the late president, were reported to have been stunned at the news.

The other Cabinet members were Douglas Dillon, secretary of the treasury; Stewart L. Udall, secretary of the interior; Orville L. Freeman, secretary of agriculture; W. Willard Wirtz, secretary of labor and Luther H. Hodges, secretary of commerce. They were accompanied by their wives. Also on the aircraft were Pierre Salinger, the White House press secretary, and Robert Manning, assistant secretary of state for public affairs. Richard I. Phillips, press officer of the State Department, said that Acting Secretary George Ball had had a brief radio conversation with Mr. Rusk after the secretary had decided to turn back. The talks in Japan, which had become an annual event for the review of diplomatic and trade relations, were canceled.

The slaying came as a shock to the diplomatic corps here. West German Ambassador Heinrich Knappstein said that "the people of Germany and Berlin, who recall so vividly President Kennedy's recent visit, mourn together with the free world the tragic loss of a very good friend and most able statesman." British Ambassador Sir David Ormsby Gore, a close personal friend of the Kennedys, called the assassination a "horrible, wicked and senseless act. Jack Kennedy was the best and the most loyal friend one could ever hope to have and I feel a sense of loss beyond description," he said. Hervé Alphand, the French ambassador, said President Kennedy "died as a soldier and we shall never forget his example or his memory."

Networks Drop Regular Shows

News and Solemn Music Heard on Radio and TV

By VAL ADAMS

National television and radio networks and independent stations here canceled all entertainment programs and commercial announcements yesterday soon after the first bulletin that President Kennedy had been wounded. Throughout last night networks and stations confined themselves to news of the assassination and related developments. Between news reports, many radio stations played religious music. The Columbia Broadcasting System announced that its television and radio networks would carry no commercial announcements and no entertainment programs until after the funeral. Dr. Frank Stanton, president of C.B.S., made the announcement. The American Broadcasting Company and the National Broadcasting Company announced that entertainment programs and commercials would be suspended indefinitely. They indicated the suspension would continue until after the funeral. The National Broadcasting Company said its radio network had dropped regular shows for several days when President Roosevelt died. Many independent stations indicated they would forgo normal programs for the weekend, at least. Some also said they would omit commercials.

Less than two hours after the president died, a video-taped message by him was transmitted from the United States to Japan by the communications satellite Relay. His message, part of the first trans-Pacific telecast from the United States to Japan, had been taped at the White House on Wednesday. The program was sent from a National Aeronautics and Space Administration ground station in the Mojave Desert near Goldstone, Calif. Last night N.B.C. sent a 15-minute news program on President Kennedy's death to Japan via Relay.

It was reported from London that the British Broadcasting Corporation and the Independent Television Authority, which operates commercial television there, had suspended their regular programs.

Some of the network reporters and commentators who reported the tragedy seemed as stunned as their audiences. Initially, they had great difficulty in trying to speak. But they settled down to long hours of reporting. The American Broadcasting Company's television section pressed into service its former news chief, James C. Hagerty, now vice president of corporate affairs for American Broadcasting–Paramount Theaters, Inc. He had been White House news secretary in the Eisenhower Administration. Mr. Hagerty described some of the protective measures used by the Secret Service. He said the bubble on the open car that had been used by Dwight D. Eisenhower had not been bulletproof, although he did not know about the one used by President Kennedy.

Deaths in Office Show a 20-Year Coincidence

WASHINGTON, Nov. 22 (AP)—President Kennedy's death continues the coincidence that presidents elected at 20-year intervals in zero-numbered years die in office. The presidents and the years they were elected are:

1840	William Henry Harrison.
1860	Abraham Lincoln.
1880	James A. Garfield.
1900	Willlam McKinley.
1920	Warren G. Harding.
1940	Franklin D. Roosevelt.
1960	John F. Kennedy.

Roosevelt did not die in the third term to which he was elected in 1940 but in his fourth term. Three of the previous presidents on the list were assassinated—Lincoln, Garfield and McKinley.

KENNEDY FOURTH PRESIDENT KILLED BY AN ASSASSIN; ATTACKS ON TWO OTHERS FAILED

Truman Escaped Assailants in '50

Lincoln the First to Be Shot While in Office—Fanatic Slew McKinley in 1901

John F. Kennedy is the fourth president to be killed by an assassin. Two other presidents were attacked, but the attempts failed. In addition, attempts were made on a former president and two on presidents-elect. Abraham Lincoln, William McKinley and James A. Garfield were killed in office. The abortive attempts were on Andrew Jackson and Harry S. Truman. The two presidents-elect were Lincoln and Franklin D. Roosevelt. The former president who escaped an assassin's bullet was Theodore Roosevelt. He was wounded in the chest.

The first president assassinated was Lincoln, who was shot on Good Friday, April 14, 1865, at a theater performance he had not wished to attend. He had gone to Ford's Theater out of a sense of obligation to a public that had expected to see General Grant, who was unable to attend. Lincoln was killed by a bullet that entered the back of his head. The thin, but strong, president lingered unconscious until 7:22 A.M. the next day, when he died. The plot to kill him was formulated by a 26-year-old actor, John Wilkes Booth, a passionate defender of the Confederate cause. He shot Lincoln through a hole that had been bored through the door of the president's box. As he fired his Derringer, Booth said in a low voice the Latin phrase *"Sic semper tyrannis"* ("Thus always to tyrants"). Booth leaped by an Army officer who tried to stop him and jumped to the stage. His foot caught in a flag, breaking his left leg in two places. Despite this he left through the stage wings. He was later cornered in a Virginia barn and shot. Three associates in the crime were hanged and another was imprisoned. A plot to kill Lincoln had been foiled in February, 1861. The assassination was supposed to have taken place in the railway station at Baltimore, where the inaugural train carrying Lincoln from Springfield, Ill., to Washington was scheduled to stop. The conspirators were seized.

James A. Garfield, the second president to be murdered in office, was fatally shot in a Washington railroad station as he traveled to make a speech at Williamstown, Mass. Garfield lingered between life and death for weeks before he died of blood poisoning. He was shot by a disappointed office-seeker, Charles Jules Guiteau, who fired twice from a .44-caliber revolver. He was later hanged. The bullets struck the 20th president in the arm and in the back near the spine. He fell, momentarily unconscious, and bystanders carried him to a nearby building. He was later removed to the White House. Guiteau was seized before he could fire a third shot.

The third assassinated president, William McKinley, was shot twice at point-blank range on Sept. 6, 1901, as he stood in a receiving line at the Pan American Exposition in Buffalo. Eight days later, at the home of a friend, he died. His assailant, a fanatic named Leon F. Czolgosz, was grabbed, beaten and handcuffed. President McKinley's guards had failed to notice Czolgosz as he stood in line with a handkerchief around his hand. The handkerchief contained a .32-caliber revolver. Czolgosz was later electrocuted.

The unsuccessful attempt on the life of Andrew Jackson took place on Jan. 30, 1835, when the two pistols of Richard Lawrence both misfired. Lawrence, a Washington house painter, was found to be insane and died in a mental hospital 16 years after the attempt.

The attack against President Truman occurred on Nov. 1, 1950, when two Puerto Rican nationalists attempted to fight their way into Blair House, where the Trumans were living. The two—Oscar Collazo and Griselio Torresola—were shot by policemen before they could reach the steps. Torresola died with a bullet in his head and Collazo, seriously wounded, survived and was sentenced to death. Mr. Truman subsequently commuted his sentence to life imprisonment. The two men, who had participated the day before in a rally for Puerto Rican independence, approached Blair House together and opened fire. They were armed with 66 rounds of ammunition and two guns. In the blazing gunfight, Leslie Coffelt, a policeman, was killed. Two other policemen were wounded.

Franklin D. Roosevelt was attacked only a few weeks before his inauguration. He landed in Miami on the afternoon of Feb. 15, 1933, after a cruise on a yacht owned by Vincent Astor. The assassin was Giuseppe Zangara, a 32-year-old bricklayer, who said later that he had planned to kill President Hoover but had changed his plan because Mr. Roosevelt happened to be in the city. He fired five shots at the president as he sat in his car. One bullet hit Mayor Anton Cermak of Chicago, who had just spoken to Mr. Roosevelt. Mr. Cermak died of his wound on March 6. Zangara, believed by many to be insane, was later electrocuted in Florida State Prison.

The former president who escaped death, Theodore Roosevelt, was on a stumping tour as the candidate of the Progressive, or Bull Moose, party in 1912. On the evening of Oct. 13, in Milwaukee, John Schrank, a New York bartender of German ancestry, fired one shot at him as he entered his car outside the Gilpatrick Hotel. Roosevelt was struck in the chest and a rib was fractured. His life was probably spared because the bullet passed first through the manuscript of a speech and then through his spectacle case in his breast pocket. The president went on to make his scheduled address and spoke for 50 minutes before going to a hospital to have his wound dressed. Seventeen days later, he resumed his unsuccessful campaign. Schrank was tried, but was found to be insane. He died in a mental hospital in 1943.

Among other historic assassinations of recent times were those of Gandhi in 1948, Trotsky in 1940, and Archduke Francis Ferdinand of Austria-Hungary and his wife, the Duchess of Hohenberg, in 1914, which touched off World War I. Other major assassinations have included Huey P. Long in 1935, King Alexander of Yugoslavia in 1934, Francisco "Pancho" Villa in 1923 and Count Folke Bernadotte in 1948.

PRESIDENT'S BODY WILL LIE IN STATE

Funeral Mass to Be Monday in Capital After Homage Is Paid by the Public

By JACK RAYMOND

Special to The New York Times

WASHINGTON, Nov. 22—The body of John F. Kennedy will lie in state in the rotunda of the Capitol Sunday and then will be borne to St. Matthew's Roman Catholic Cathedral for a pontifical requiem mass at noon Monday. The president's body was returned to Washington today in the same Air Force jet that carried him to Texas. The airliner, with Mrs. Kennedy, the new president, Lyndon B. Johnson, and Mrs. Johnson aboard, arrived at Andrews Air Force Base at about 5:58 P.M. It was announced later that Mr. Kennedy's body would lie in the White House tomorrow from 10 A.M. to 6 P.M., during which time Government and diplomatic officials will pay their respects. The coffin will be taken from the White House to the Capitol Rotunda Sunday morning, where it will be placed under honor guard in ceremonies to be attended by the president's family, United States officials and foreign representatives. The public will be allowed to file past all day tomorrow until 9 P.M. The body was taken to the White House on a catafalque similar to the one used for a martyred predecessor, Abraham Lincoln. Lighted candles burned on both sides of the dark mahogany coffin. Two Roman Catholic priests were in attendance, kneeling in constant prayer beside the bier. A military guard of honor stood watch.

Richard Cardinal Cushing, archbishop of Boston, a longtime friend of the Kennedy family, will officiate at the mass. Former Presidents Harry S.

Truman and Dwight D. Eisenhower were expected to appear but former President Herbert Hoover, who is 89 years old, will be unable to come to Washington. The president was expected to be buried at the Kennedy family plot in Holyhood Cemetery, near Brookline, Mass. He is a native of Boston.

The presidential plane was met by an honor cordon of airmen in dress uniform, with rifles and bayonets, and by high-ranking officials. The coffin containing the president's body was placed in a Navy ambulance and taken to the naval hospital at Bethesda, Md. Mrs. Kennedy and the president's brother, Attorney General Robert F. Kennedy, rode in the ambulance after making their way to it through the crowd. Cabinet and Congressional officials had stayed apart from the crowd near the ambulance, waiting to greet the new president formally when he alighted moments later from the plane. By the time the ambulance arrived at Bethesda shortly after 7 P.M., a crowd of several hundred people had gathered at the front entrance. They stood back in silence.

An honor guard of 200 sailors that had waited marched to the front entrance. Mrs. Kennedy, tearless but looking dazed, and Attorney General Kennedy conferred with the commanding officer of the hospital, Admiral C. B. Golloway. They were joined by Secretary of Defense Robert S. McNamara. Later a White House chauffeur appeared at the hospital with two suitcases for Mrs. Kennedy. She spent the night in the special 17th-floor suite for high officials.

Four Roman Catholic priests arrived to offer their services and the Roman Catholic chaplain at the hospital, Comdr. Robert B. Brengartner, consoled Mrs. Kennedy. Others who joined her were the president's aides and close friends, Lawrence F. O'Brien, P. Kenneth O'Donnell and David F. Powers, and Pamala Turnure, her secretary. Charles Bartlett, a newspaper columnist and close friend of the Kennedys, also arrived at the hospital. A spokesman for Mrs. Kennedy, asked whether she was under doctors' care, replied: "I wouldn't say she is under the care of a doctor in the usual sense, but obviously there are a lot of doctors here."

At Andrews Air Force Base tension had prevailed as the great blue and white jet, known as Air Force 1, and with the words "United States of America" on its fuselage, ended its journey from Dallas. Slowly the plane turned at the end of the runway, its landing lights piercing the darkness in the unusually warm November evening. Heading directly for the terminal building where the Cabinet and other officials waited, it came to a halt with its rear door slightly open. A yellow lift ramp was rolled to it, with four Navy men, two officers and two sailors, aboard.

Some difficulty developed in moving the heavy bronze coffin. Finally, with help from aides of the president, they succeeded in turning the coffin so it could be placed on the lift and lowered to the ground. There was more hauling as military men and civilians sought to lend a hand, as though by this act they could help the president. At last they managed to get the coffin into the ambulance. Then Mrs. Kennedy and the attorney general came down on the lift. A Navy officer reached up and caught Mrs. Kennedy under the arms to help her to the ground.

Kennedy's Wife Kept Composure

Accompanied His Body to Bethesda Naval Hospital

By MARJORIE HUNTER

Special to The New York Times

WASHINGTON, Nov. 22—Mrs. John F. Kennedy returned tonight to a city she had left 31 hours earlier as the wife of the president of the United States. Clutching the hand of her brother-in-law, Attorney General Robert F. Kennedy, she watched the coffin bearing the body of her husband as it was lowered to the ground by a yellow lift drawn up beside the presidential jet and loaded onto an ambulance. She then climbed into the ambulance beside the coffin for the ride to Bethesda Naval Hospital. She wore the pink wool suit she had been wearing, hours earlier, when her husband collapsed by her side, the victim of an assassin's bullet, on the streets of Dallas. Mrs. Kennedy spent the night on the 17th floor of the Naval Hospital. She is expected to go to the White House tomorrow morning.

There was no indication where her two children, Caroline and John Jr., slept. They were taken from the White House about 5:30 P.M., but aides would not say where they went or who had accompanied them. The children had been left in the care of their nurse, Mrs. Maude Shaw, when the Kennedys left yesterday morning for a two-day swing through Texas.

The Texas trip, plainly a political one, was to have been the first of many such trips in which Mrs. Kennedy planned to campaign with her husband for 1964. It was the first political appearance she had made with him in the United States, outside of Washington, since the early presidential primaries in the spring of 1960. While generally shunning politics, Mrs. Kennedy proved to be a sparkling addition to the presidential party on several trips abroad. She was such a hit in Paris in the summer of 1961 that President Kennedy referred to himself as "the man who accompanied Jacqueline Kennedy to Paris." On another occasion, President Kennedy jokingly said that Mrs. Kennedy and Caroline "are the only things keeping the Democratic party going." Certainly, not since the days of Mrs. Franklin D. Roosevelt had the publicity spotlight been focused so steadily on a president's wife. She was one of the youngest and prettiest women ever to occupy the White House.

No humanitarian crusader, as Mrs. Roosevelt was, Mrs. Kennedy set the pace in fashions and the arts. She became the most talked-about and copied woman in the nation. It was a role that she once told close friends that she would liked to have avoided. Just before moving into the White House in 1961, she confided: "I feel as though I had just turned into a piece of public property. It's really frightening to lose your anonymity at 31."

Some months later, she expressed misgivings about the official life that was closing around her and her family. She was not sure, she told friends, that she was up to the rigors of her husband's New Frontier, but she kept trying. She insisted on spending part of the mornings and the afternoons with her children. She devoted several hours each day to her favorite project—refurnishing the White House with antiques of the early 1800's.

Long interested in the arts, and an amateur artist herself, Mrs. Kennedy made the White House one of the most glittering social gathering spots in the nation. Artists and writers, musicians and actors mingled with politicians at the White House dinners and other socials. There were command performances by many of the most famous names of the age—for example the cellist, Pablo Casals, and the violinist, Isaac Stern. White House performers ranged from ballet stars to readers of Elizabethan poetry.

Kennedys Gather at Hyannis Port

Senator and Sister Join President's Parents

By JOHN H. FENTON

Special to The New York Times

HYANNIS PORT, Mass., Nov. 22—Senator Edward M. Kennedy, and his sister, Mrs. Eunice Shriver, flew from Washington today to join their sorrowing parents, Mr. and Mrs. Joseph P. Kennedy, at the family compound here where President Kennedy had spent many summers. The town was shocked by the news of the president's assassination. A cordon of grim state and local policemen stood guard at the gate of the compound to assure the family complete seclusion. Newsmen and photographers, who were at the Hyannis Airport in Barnstable when the senator and his sister arrived shortly before 5 P.M., apologized for having to be on hand. The senator said, "I understand, gentlemen," and entered a car to be driven here.

The president's mother, Mrs. Rose Kennedy, was playing golf at the Hyannis Port Golf Club when she learned of the tragedy. Her chauffeur was reported to have told her the news after hearing it on a Secret Service radio in the car. Mrs. Kennedy left immediately to join her husband, who is convalescing here from a stroke suffered a year ago. Attorney General Robert F. Kennedy was expected later.

In Boston, the Most Rev. Richard Cardinal Cushing, a close friend of the president and his family, spent more than an hour in his private chapel praying. Later, he issued a statement expressing his deep grief. He then left for Hyannis Port to join the Kennedy family. The cardinal married the president and his wife, Jacqueline, and baptized their two children, Caroline and John Jr. He also presided at a Mass for a third Kennedy child, Patrick Bouvier Kennedy, who died shortly after birth last summer.

Much of the area where the Kennedy summer home is situated is quiet at this time of year. Many homes, motels and other summer resorts have been boarded up for the winter. Radio stations throughout the area immediately canceled regular programs to broadcast a continuing report of developments.

State Representative Paul D. Reed, a Republican, recalled that on the first day he had attended Choate School, a private secondary school in Connecticut, the student body was called into the chapel to pray for a classmate, John F. Kennedy, who was ill with pneumonia. "I prayed again today," Mr. Reed said, "but this time it was too late."

Gov. Endicott Peabody, a long-time friend of the president, turned back during a flight to Tennessee where he was to attend a Civil War memorial ceremony. Later, the Massachusetts Legislature, which ended its 1963 session last Saturday, was summoned to a special session to memorialize the president.

News Withheld From 2 Children

They Leave the White House Without Seeing Mother

By EILEEN SHANAHAN

Special to The New York Times

WASHINGTON, Nov. 22—President Kennedy's children, Caroline and John Jr., went to bed tonight without having been told of their father's death. Mrs. Kennedy apparently wished to tell them herself and they were shielded from the news throughout this afternoon and evening. The children, after following their regular schedules until late afternoon, under the custody of their nurse, Maude Shaw, were taken from the White House to an unknown destination shortly before Mrs. Kennedy arrived back in Washington with the body of the president. It was thought that Caroline and John Jr. had probably been taken to the home of their uncle, Attorney General Robert F. Kennedy, in nearby McLean, Va. White House assistants would not say, however, where the children were.

Mrs. Kennedy, who at first had been expected to join the children before their bedtime and tell them that their father was dead, decided instead to spend the night at the Bethesda Naval Hospital, just outside Washington.

The president's body was taken there before being returned to the White House.

Caroline, whose sixth birthday is next Wednesday, went to school as usual this morning in the private schoolroom on the third floor of the White House. She returned to the family living quarters on the second floor about 1:15 P.M., before the assassination of the president. John spent the day in the family living quarters. The only break in their routine before they left the White House around 5:30 P.M. was a brief visit from their uncle, Senator Edward M. Kennedy, and their aunt, Mrs. Eunice Shriver, the president's sister. They saw the children before leaving Washington for Hyannis Port, Mass., to be with President Kennedy's father and mother, Mr. and Mrs. Joseph P. Kennedy. White House staff assistants assumed that Mrs. Shaw, Senator Kennedy and Mrs. Shriver had all agreed that the children should not be told of their father's death until Mrs. Kennedy returned to Washington.

The assassination was the second tragedy to befall the family in four months. Patrick Bouvier Kennedy, the president's third child, born prematurely Aug. 7, died in Boston two days later of a lung ailment. For the president's parents, this was the third of their nine children to die. The president's oldest brother, Joseph P., Jr., was killed in the explosion of a Navy plane over the English Channel in World War II. A sister, Kathleen, also perished in an airplane crash. She was the widow of the marquess of Hartington.

The president's brother, Senator Kennedy, was presiding over the Senate when he received word that the president had been shot in Dallas. He left the Senate chamber immediately and went to the White House. The attorney general was lunching at his home in nearby McLean, Va., when the assassination occurred. He apparently remained there through the afternoon. Mrs. Shriver and her husband, the Peace Corps director, were reportedly in the White House at the time of the shooting. Mr. Shriver remained in Washington to help make the funeral arrangements. The Kennedy family had been planning a traditional gathering for Thanksgiving next week at the home of the president's father on Cape Cod, Mass. Mrs. Kennedy and Caroline and John, with most of the children's cousins, were scheduled to attend.

ROBERT KENNEDY MAY KEEP CABINET POST AS ATTORNEY GENERAL UNDER JOHNSON

Capital Expects Offer to Be Made

Associates Believe Younger Man Will Accept—Note Closeness to Brother

By ANTHONY LEWIS

Special to The New York Times

WASHINGTON, Nov. 22—The expectation here tonight was that President Johnson would ask Attorney General Robert F. Kennedy to remain in the Cabinet. If asked, Mr. Kennedy will accept. That was the view of his close friends and associates, though they did not minimize the difficulty of his position.

John F. Kennedy was more than a brother to Robert. He was hero, closest friend, sharer of the spirit. In his brother's Administration, Robert Kennedy played an extraordinary role as intimate adviser beyond his Cabinet duties. Now, if he stays on as attorney general, he will be subordinate to a stranger—one, moreover, symbolizing different forces in the country and in the Democratic party. Inevitably, Robert Kennedy will inherit some of his brother's following. Not that he has the same image in the country—he is a much more controversial figure. But some of the Kennedy mantle will surely pass to him. In the long run, therefore, it will be a great test for both President Johnson and Robert Kennedy to work together instead of following independent paths.

Friends thought tonight that both would try to meet that test, in the interest of the country and of the party. Moreover, they both have strong immediate interests pushing them toward cooperation. Mr. Johnson assumes the presidency toward the end of a term and a bare half-year before the Democratic National Convention. His interest in at least the short run must be to hold the Government and the party together, not in making drastic changes. The attorney general has jobs undone—and that he wants to get done. Foremost among them is the passage of civil rights legislation.

Despite President Johnson's Southern background, no experienced observer here tonight doubted that he would push for the passage of that civil rights legislation. No less than total cooperation between him and Mr. Kennedy will be needed to get it past a reluctant Congress.

As vice president, Mr. Johnson spoke around the country in behalf of Negro rights. As the Senate majority leader in 1957 and 1960 he steered to pass the only two civil rights acts to go on the books since Reconstruction days after the Civil War.

The attorney general received word of the shooting of his brother while he was having lunch with the United States attorney for the Southern District of New York, Robert M. Morgenthau. They were at Mr. Kennedy's home in suburban McLean, Va.

Justice Byron R. White of the Supreme Court, an old friend and the attorney general's deputy before going on the bench, came out from town to be with him. The director of the Central Intelligence Agency, John A. McCone, came over from the nearby C.I.A. headquarters.

Mr. Kennedy's wife, Ethel, got the children home from school. The attorney general walked with them on the back lawn and under the tall, bare trees. At 5 o'clock Mr. Kennedy drove to the Pentagon building. He talked with Robert S. McNamara, the secretary of defense, for 20 minutes, and then the two men flew by helicopter to Andrews Air Force Base to meet the plane carrying the body of the fallen president.

Kennedy Family Asks Flowers Be Omitted

WASHINGTON, Nov. 22 (AP)—The Kennedy family asked tonight that no floral tributes be sent for the services for the late president. The Kennedy family has expressed the desire that no flowers be sent to the White House or to the funeral. They asked that anyone wishing to do so donate an equivalent amount to charity.

Sister Sees Dallas Telecast

JEFFERSON, Wis., Nov. 22 (UPI)—President Kennedy's younger sister, Rose, learned of his assassination today while watching a television broadcast from Dallas, Tex., where he was shot. "She knows he is dead," said a spokesman at St. Colleta's, a school for the retarded, where she has lived for the last 20 years. "She was watching on television."

THE CITY GOES DARK AND CANCELS ACTIVITIES AS THE PRESIDENT IS MOURNED

By ROBERT C. DOTY

The center of New York, the restless night city, wore darkness and went in near silence after the murder of President Kennedy last night. In and around Times Square, the normal, frenetic Friday night pulse slowed as near to a halt as it ever comes. Most legitimate and movie theaters, night clubs and dance halls closed their doors and darkened their marquees. As dusk came, automatic devices turned on the huge, gaudy signs that normally blot out the night in the Times Square area. Then, one by one, the lights blinked out, turning the great carnival strip into what was almost a mourning band on the city's sleeve.

The Harvard-Yale and Princeton-Dartmouth football games and scores of other contests at colleges and schools were canceled for Saturday. Dinner dances, cocktail parties, banquets and other social events were called off throughout the metropolitan area. All the city's major hotels canceled entertainment in their public rooms.

There were exceptions, of course. In outlying Manhattan neighborhoods and in the other boroughs, the visible evidence of shock and sorrow was less spectacular. Movie theaters and shops remained lighted and open, but crowds were sparse and subdued. Restaurants, by decision of their trade associations, operated as usual for public convenience and necessity. Bars were open, often with customers three deep, talking in hushed tones, eyes glued to television sets that repeated the news over and over again. Twelve all-night movie houses on 42d Street between the Avenue of the Americas and Eighth Avenue darkened their main display signs but were open for business. One of them expressed the street's attitude with a picture called *Carry On, Regardless.*

In the same area, in a penny arcade, rifle shots snapped against moving targets and none of half a dozen marksmen seemed to think it was an odd way to pass the time. Two record stores blared music into the otherwise subdued street.

Elsewhere in the city's five boroughs, stores and most theaters remained open as usual, but in many centers crowds were well below normal for Friday night. Most neighborhood movie theaters remained open, but they had nearly empty houses. In Greenwich Village most of the major night spots that offer entertainment were closed and the majority of off-Broadway legitimate houses also canceled performances. In Brooklyn, only the young seemed to be out in normal force and spirits. In the King's Highway area, the police and store-keepers found activity off by at least 60 per cent. There was a similar relative hush at Flatbush and Church Avenues, where a taxi driver commented, "It looks like a different town." Most Brooklyn movie houses were open, but the Albemarle Theater on Flatbush Avenue turned away would-be patrons with a sign: "Out of respect for the late President John F. Kennedy this theater will be closed for the rest of the day." Along Jamaica Avenue in Queens, the three big department stores that dominate most busy Friday nights—Macy's, May's and Gertz—had closed their doors. Many smaller stores also closed, and those that remained open had little or no business.

The early evening pattern was less distinct in Harlem, where night life normally gets under way at a later hour. Crowds appeared nearly normal and the only notable closing reported was that of the Apollo Theater, a vaudeville house on 125th Street. Harlem bar conversation centered nervously and with some hostility on the new president, Lyndon B. Johnson, and speculation that the drive for integration and a major civil rights bill would be slowed or halted with a Texan in the White House. "Let's see what your cracker president is going to do for you now," a Harlem bartender said to his customers.

At the Chinese Public School, supported by Chinatown residents, Kenneth Chan, the principal, called 700 students together for a special memorial service at nightfall. Earlier in the day, hundreds of public and private events—school and university classes, receptions, formal dinners, dances—were halted in mid-course or canceled. All city, state and Federal courts closed as soon as word of the assassination spread.

George Szell, conducting the New York Philharmonic at Philharmonic Hall, ended the concert abruptly after completing Beethoven's "Leonore" Overture No. 3. Among scores of social events abruptly canceled was the Annual Freedom Award Dinner of the Order of Lafayette at which former President Dwight D. Eisenhower and Gen. Lucius D. Clay were to have received awards.

FIRST, "IS IT TRUE?" THEN ANGER AND ANGUISH AMONG NEW YORKERS AND VISITORS

News of Tragedy Spreads Quickly

Men Say "My God!" and Cry, Shoppers Stop to Pray and Many Businesses Close

By GEORGE BARRETT

The cry rang across the city, echoing again and again: "Is it true?" Another cry quickly took its place as the news of the death of President Kennedy swept with stunning impact: "My God!" Women wept, and men wept. A refusal to believe the report of the assassination was the immediate reaction, but swiftly came horror, then anguish, and then, among many, both city residents and visitors, deep anger. The news spread quickly, and the shocked hundreds of thousands reached for so many telephones that the system blacked out and operators had to refuse calls. Shoppers in department stores clustered instinctively, and in at least one store they stopped buying and prayed together, some of them silently, some aloud.

In all parts of the five boroughs motorists pulled up their cars and sat hunched up over their dashboard radios. At red traffic lights the cry cascaded from car to car, from pedestrian to motorist: "Is it true?" In some

hospitals physicians and nurses went on emergency rounds to give seda-
tives to patients who were agitated by the news. Uptown, midtown, downtown, work in offices came to an abrupt halt as employees hovered over
transistor radios. Some people went home at once, and many managements
shut up shop for the day.

The grief, shock and incredulity were a terrible mirror of April 12, 1945,
when the news of President Franklin D. Roosevelt's death toward the end
of World War II hit the city and the world. But there was another dominant
emotion yesterday—anger. Bitterness and even savagery were expressed.
A question repeated time and again was: "Where was his protection?"

It was a truck driver, Griff Clarke of Huntington Beach, L.I., who caught
the sentiment that so many shared with this outburst: "This is a disgrace
to the country!" It was Michael Baruth of Yonkers who reflected the feeling of horror with the query: "What kind of madmen would do a thing
like that?"

All flags on municipal buildings were ordered to half-staff by Mayor
Wagner, and throughout the city businesses, theaters and apartment houses
lowered their flags without waiting for instructions. Typical of the business
community's reaction to Mr. Kennedy's death was the order that went out
from the Fifth Avenue Association to all member stores. They were asked
to fly flags at half-staff and to turn off all Christmas lighting, including
the annual spectaculars in Fifth Avenue windows, until further notice. Saks
Fifth Avenue and Best & Company changed Fifth Avenue windows late
in the afternoon to pay homage to Mr. Kennedy. At Saks a photograph of
President Kennedy was placed on a chair and flanked by urns of red roses.
At Best's the window contained an American flag with a black crepe on
its staff and a watercolor of Mr. Kennedy. Crowds gathered in front of the
displays, and tears were openly shed.

At hundreds of places all flags were taken down—the flags of members
of the United Nations, the city flag, the state flag, house and club flags—to
express full homage with the United States flag alone. Texas was the target
of wrath for scores of persons, who used phrases like "damned Texans"
and other profanities.

A number of persons said that they did not take subways or buses on
short trips after the news, but decided to walk just to be alone with their

thoughts. One common scene was the tight grasp of one man's hand on another's arm as they discussed the assassination.

In the Bronx, at the corner of Fordham Road and Grand Concourse, a predominantly Jewish and Irish area where the president had been popular, immediate reaction was as much anger as shock. Max Schechter, a newsstand dealer, said: "Our president traveled to practically every country in the world and was safe. In his own country he had to be assassinated. It's a disgrace." Mrs. Anne Nightingale, a department store saleswoman who lives at 966 East 181st Street, declared: "He didn't deserve it. I would do anything to bring him back."

The grief and the acts of mourning knew no special group, no particular section of the city and no political convictions. The sorrow and the shock were unfolded in the human vignette, the collection of individuals who stared as though in a trance from their subway seats, their stools at luncheon counters, their chairs near television sets.

At the intersection of Court and Centre Streets, one motorist stopped his car in the middle of traffic and walked over to a sidewalk luncheonette. He asked the counterman: "Is it true?" The counterman didn't look up. "Yes, he's dead," he said. The motorist returned to his car, slipped under the wheel and sat, motionless and staring. Horns blared, then went soundless as word of the president's death filtered from driver to driver. Strangers talked to each other in the subway, mostly in soft voices or whispers. Again the awful question, "Is it true?" One man, eyes watering as he heard the answer, spoke as though to himself: "Another Lincoln; he's another Lincoln."

For some hours there was an almost eerie quality as numbers of men and women seemed totally unable to grasp the reality. They ate their lunches automatically; they typed letters without really seeing the unwinding sentences; they reached for the telephone to call home, to talk to someone they know. Those who had no one familiar at hand walked up to strangers and talked about President Kennedy.

The bells of St. Patrick's Cathedral tolled solemnly, and thousands of Roman Catholics went to churches to pray for the nation's first Catholic president. Msgr. Timothy Flynn of the New York Archdiocese spoke for Catholics and non-Catholics alike when he described the reaction at the archdiocese: "Stupefied horror."

Four servicemen sat in the recruiting booth in Times Square dazed at the news of the loss of their commander in chief. Recruiting was halted for the day. The Astor Bar was grim and silent. One bartender said: "Everybody feels dead, real dead. Everybody feels like crying."

The death of the president was tied in by many Harlem mourners with the fight for civil rights. Miss Dorothy Cooper of 85 West 119th Street said she was convinced that the assassination "would put quite a damper on the civil-rights fight." "I think it's going to be terrible, as far as civil rights are concerned," Mrs. Anna Thomas of 226 Edgecombe Avenue said. However, an attorney, Ivan Michael, said he felt the drive for civil rights would now have greater impetus. "I think we are going to witness a more vigilant drive toward the individual liberty of man," Mr. Michael declared.

Many in the suburbs heard the news quickly because television programs were interrupted. Fred Tracz, a postman in Greenwich, Conn., encountered many housewives who wept as they told him the news. "They talked about it just as if they lost their son or daughter," he said. Like hundreds of motorists, James Falabella of Pleasantville, N.Y., had to pull his car to the side of the road and try to absorb the tragedy. "I couldn't drive for a half-hour after I heard the news on my car radio," he said. Mrs. John Andrews, a housewife in Greenwich, said: "We all have our ideas about this and that in politics. But when the president dies, we are all one family." "This is an indictment of the American people," Robert L. Tooker, a lawyer in Riverhead, commented. "We have allowed certain factions to work up such furor throughout the South with fanatic criticism of the office of president that a demented person can feel confident that such atrocious action is justifiable." A farmer in a clothing store said: "I feel sick to my stomach. Maybe in Europe or Asia, but not in the United States in 1963." Mrs. Edith Bouvier Beale of Apaquoque Road, East Hampton, an aunt of Mrs. Kennedy, said, "My heart is broken." Misthopoulos Georges, a Greek-born barber who came to the United States 10 years ago, sat in his shop, hunched over, and wept. "I feel he was a very good boy," he said. "I cry."

For many of the grief-stricken there was special bitterness that such brutality was still possible in the United States. A counter girl commented that the president had traveled over so much of the world and "yet here, in our own country, a savage kills him." At the intersection of Flatbush Avenue and Sixth Avenue, in the Park Slope area of Brooklyn, pedestrians and office workers out for lunch groped to describe their emotions, and often just shook their heads and refused to speak. "Oh, my God, oh, my God, oh, my God," were the only words that Mrs. Louis Greenberg could say. She did not buy the lamp that she and her husband had decided to get yesterday. In Trenton grief spread through the corridors of the New Jersey State House, and at 3 P.M. Gov. Richard J. Hughes ordered all state offices closed for the day. Dr. Edward Brailove, a dentist, weeping said: "Wasn't it horrible? I can't work. I've sent two patients home and I've closed my office."

Churches Fill Up on News of Death

By PAUL L. MONTGOMERY

Many New Yorkers filed solemnly to their houses of worship yesterday to pay homage to the dead president. In the hour when no one here knew whether President Kennedy was alive, they went to pray for his life. When the news of his death came, they prayed for his soul. At Roman Catholic and Protestant churches and Jewish synagogues alike weeping men and women went to seek comfort in their grief.

During the afternoon more than 20,000 people passed in and out of St. Patrick's Cathedral to pay their respects. At 5 P.M. Bishop John Maguire, vicar general of the archdiocese, presided at a memorial service. A catafalque covered with an American flag rested before the altar. Bishop Maguire sprinkled holy water on the catafalque as 15 priests joined with the crowd of 7,000 in repeating prayers. The scene was repeated over the city in Catholic churches. In the churches and synagogues of other faiths memorial and remembrance services were held. The nation's religious leaders, numbed by the president's death, paid tribute to him and prayed for guidance in the time ahead.

By 2 P.M. St. Patrick's Cathedral was filling up. Six priests of the cathedral knelt in a row before the white altar and prayed for the president. Girls in bright scarves and businessmen with attaché cases knelt at the altar rail, their heads bowed. In the aisles the votive candles flickered as Auxiliary Bishop Joseph Flannelly, administrator of the cathedral, intoned the prayers. Many of the congregation anxiously fingered their rosaries. At 2:30 Bishop Flannelly broke off the prayer and turned to face the growing crowd.

"We have just been informed that President Kennedy is dead," he said softly. And then, softer still, "May God have mercy on his soul." For a moment, there was not a whisper in the huge cathedral. Then a muffled wail, subtle as smoke, crept over the crowd. Women bowed down sobbing and men cradled their heads in their arms. Bishop Flannelly began the ancient litany for the dead:

"O God the creator and redeemer of all the faithful, hear our supplication, and through Thy infinite mercy graciously grant to the soul of Thy servant departed the remission of all his sins."

Five minutes later, the great bells of the cathedral began to toll solemnly. The crowd passing on Fifth Avenue looked up and knew. "Oh my God," a woman said. "He's dead." Two blocks up Fifth Avenue, at St. Thomas Protestant Episcopal Church, the carillon took up the toll. A sidewalk Santa Claus slowed his vigorous bell ringing to keep time.

Inside St. Patrick's, the prayers continued. Many who seemed never to have been there before stopped for a moment in the back and bowed their heads. Women used improvised ways to cover their heads—paper napkins, envelopes and pocketbooks. The altars at the sides were bright with the candles lit for the president. Services at the cathedral continued through the evening. A solemn pontifical mass for the president will be sung at 10 A.M. today.

Elsewhere in the city, people began filing into churches and synagogues soon after the announcement that the president had been shot. In the Cathedral Church of St. John the Divine a prayer service was held in front of the great choir. In old Trinity Church, at Broadway and Wall Street, the Rev. Thorley Bridgeman led a memorial prayer service. At many of the services, the sincerity of the worshipers' grief overrode the impromptu nature of the gatherings. Bishop Maguire led the congregation at St. Patrick's in singing the national anthem, something that is rarely done in a Catholic church. At St. Thomas Church the carillon played "My Country, 'Tis of Thee."

Jewish men, women and children went to their houses of worship to pray and intone the Kaddish, the traditional prayer for the dead, in homage to the president. At the same time, the Synagogue Council of America, the representative body of the Orthodox, Conservative and Reform branches of Judaism, called on spiritual leaders to lead their congregations in special prayers at the beginning of the Sabbath last night and through today. The churches of the city planned memorial services for the late president. At the Cathedral of St. John the Divine there will be a service at 4 P.M. tomorrow. There will also be a service at the time of the president's funeral. Three other Episcopal churches in the city also announced services— St. Bartholomew's at Park Avenue and 51st Street, St. George's at 207 East 16th Street and the Church of the Resurrection at 115 East 74th Street—for tomorrow morning. The one at St. George's will be at 10:30, the others at 11. Christ Church Methodist, Park Avenue and 60th Street, will also have a service tomorrow at 11 A.M. The Rev. Dr. Adam Clayton Powell Jr. will lead the memorial service at 3 P.M. tomorrow at the Abyssinian Baptist Church, 132 West 138th Street. Archbishop Iakovos of the Greek Orthodox Church of North and South America instructed the 400 churches in this country to hold services for the president Sunday morning. The archbishop will preside at a memorial observance at Holy Trinity Cathedral, 319 East 74th Street, tomorrow at 10 A.M.

The Protestant Council of the City of New York urged all church and synagogue members to offer prayers for "President Johnson, our nation and the entire free world in this most tragic crisis." Harold E. Stassen, president of the American Baptist Convention, requested the churches of the denomination to join in mourning for "the tragic loss of our president." The Rev. Oliver R. Harms, president of the Lutheran Church–Missouri Synod, said that tomorrow would be observed as "a day of penitence and prayer" in the 6,000 churches of the denomination. The Rev. Theodore M. Hesburgh, president of the University of Notre Dame in South Bend, Ind., pledged in messages to the Kennedy family that 100 masses would be offered at Notre Dame for the late president.

Kennedy Quoted Psalm in Talk He Never Gave

The speech that President Kennedy was to have delivered in Dallas yesterday ended with these words: ". . . and the righteousness of our cause must always underlie our strength. For as was written long ago: 'Except the Lord keep the city, the watchman waketh but in vain.' "

The quotation, ironic in the light of events, is from Psalm 124 in the Bible. The complete verse reads:

> *Except the Lord build the house,*
> *They labor in vain that build it:*
> *Except the Lord keep the city,*
> *The watchman waketh but in vain.*

People Across U.S. Voice Grief and Revulsion

Many Weep as Bells Toll and Flags Are Lowered at Word of the President's Death

CHICAGO

Special to The New York Times

CHICAGO, Nov. 22—The president's assassination left people here in a state of stunned outrage. Women wept in the streets. Flags throughout the city dropped to half-staff as though a single hand had pulled the halyards.

"I wanted to do something. But there was nothing to do but pray for him and his family," Mrs. T. S. Rivera, a housewife, said. In a crowded bar–lunch room at State and Kinzie Streets, laborers from a nearby construction project gasped as the announcement of the death came over a radio. A husky Negro workman knocked a glass of whiskey from the bar, said "for God's sake" and rushed out the door. Women at a table burst into tears. All was silent except for the radio announcer's voice. "I thought we were living in a civilized country," a man finally said.

In a luxurious restaurant on Michigan Avenue, the crowd melted away, customers leaving large sums of money on the tables rather than waiting for the waitresses to present a bill. Down the avenue, in front of a television store where sound was piped to the street from sets behind the show window, women in a crowd of spectators wiped away tears. Farther along, Tom Busekrus, a student who had a transistor radio held to his ear, could hardly speak. "There is nothing I can say, it's thoughtless," he said at last. Mrs. Elizabeth Carter, a housewife, said: "They must be crazy—they'd have to be crazy." A meatcutter said, "It's a pathetic thing." William A. Lee, president of the Chicago Federation of Labor, said: "It is the most terrible moment in our history."

Mayor Richard J. Daley, who was close to Mr. Kennedy, burst into tears when he learned the news during a luncheon with several associates. Many city and private business offices, as well as the Federal courts, closed for the day.

The bells of Holy Name Cathedral tolled as 700 school children and hundreds of adults filed into the sanctuary for a special recitation of the rosary for the repose of the soul of the president. Religious leaders of all faiths asked for prayers for the president's family.

Edwin C. Berry, executive director of the Chicago Urban League, said the president's civil rights program was the most forward looking ever advanced by a president, and his death was a setback for those who believed in equality for all.

The commercial center almost came to a standstill. Shoppers moved toward television departments. In some stores the soft music played over loudspeakers stopped and radio bulletins were cut in. Prices plunged on the Board of Trade, which stayed open beyond its customary closing hour of 1:15 P.M. Wheat closed 1 to 4¼ cents a bushel lower, soybeans 2½ to 4¾ lower, corn ¾ to 1¼ lower, oats 1 to 1½ lower, and rye ½ to 3¼ lower.

The Illinois Bell Telephone Company had a surge of traffic immediately after the announcement of the shooting. "We haven't seen anything like this since the death of President Roosevelt and the end of World War II," a company official said. A Negro civil rights demonstration, scheduled at City Hall to protest segregation, evaporated. A National Association for the Advancement of Colored People membership meeting was turned into a memorial service. Dark clouds covered the city during an unseasonable warm rain.

LOS ANGELES

Special to The New York Times

LOS ANGELES, Nov. 22—Grief and revulsion was the reaction here to Mr. Kennedy's assassination. From mayor to bootblack, from executive to laborer, the general response mixed a sense of deep loss with a welling up of indignation. Even those who admitted little personal involvement appeared shocked. "It would appear we're going back to the days of the jungle," said one young real estate dealer. "I didn't agree with the man, but this sort of thing can't be condoned." A group of executives, strongly opposed to Mr. Kennedy's policies, expressed shock and disgust. Most of the women and many of the men in an elevator wept as the news of the death was confirmed.

Downtown banks, stores and streets were alive with people carrying transistor radios and wearing dazed expressions for at least an hour after the news. "I have the kind of feeling that I had the morning of Pearl Harbor," said Melvyn Rivkind, a public relations man. "This is a legacy of the hate that has arisen. Frankly, I feel pretty sick." Mayor Sam Yorty called the assassination "an awful black mark" on the nation's history and added: "Maybe the American people will stop and think about the hate groups who encourage this type of thing." A salesman in a hotel bar said it more pungently: "It's those flag-waving screwballs, they're only about 10 per cent of the people, but it's people like them that cause this kind of thing. I'm a conservative and I didn't agree with him. But, my God, he was our president."

"I feel like I've lost a real friend," a shoeshine man said. At various levels, from a hotel chef up to a city councilman and clergymen, Negroes seemed to be in general agreement. The Rev. Maurice E. Dawkins, pastor of the Peoples' Independent Church, called President Kennedy "the new Lincoln" and said he died "for the freedom of all people of all races and creeds." A Negro assemblyman in the California legislature, Mervin Dymelly, expressed the fear "that this uncivilized act" might set the Negroes' civil-rights cause "back to the Civil War days."

Flags were at half-staff minutes after the president's death was verified. Many families felt a sense of personal bereavement. One mother, crying despite her daughter's efforts to comfort her, said: "Why do people have to be cavemen? Why can't people progress at all?"

PHILADELPHIA

PHILADELPHIA, Nov. 22—News of President Kennedy's assassination stunned the people of Philadelphia this afternoon. Mayor James H. J. Tate called the murder "a sin against humanity" and likened Mr. Kennedy to Abraham Lincoln. At the Academy of Music, Eugene Ormandy abruptly halted the regular Friday afternoon concert of the Philadelphia Orchestra. The Pennsylvania Supreme Court, the United States District Court and the county courts all adjourned until Monday. Mr. Tate, his eyes red and his face flushed, recalled that President Kennedy visited Philadelphia three weeks ago in support of Mr. Tate's successful candidacy. The mayor said: "He told me how he looked forward to coming here for the Army-Navy game next week and to the Democratic National Convention in Atlantic City next year. He told me he looked forward to bathing in the surf and spending some time on the beach in Atlantic City.

"President Kennedy was the world's leading spokesman of goodwill and tolerance for all men and all nations. I pray that Vice President Johnson will be able to lead us in the path that was laid out by President Kennedy."

SENATE, STUNNED AND CONFUSED BY WORD OF THE SHOOTING, ADJOURNS UNTIL MONDAY

Brother in Chair as News Arrives

Edward Kennedy Leaves the Dais Quickly—Party Leaders Voice Grief

By CABELL PHILLIPS

Special to The New York Times

WASHINGTON, Nov. 22—The Senate was stunned into somber confusion today with news that President Kennedy had been shot. Majority Leader Mike Mansfield was too overcome to offer a motion for adjournment. The task fell to Minority Leader Everett McKinley Dirksen. Nowhere does the official record show the reason for the sudden cessation of the day's activities. In the confusion, the shooting was not mentioned.

By ironic coincidence, the president's brother, Senator Edward M. Kennedy of Massachusetts, was occupying the presiding officer's chair when a Senate aide whispered the news in his ear. He gathered his papers and quickly left the dais.

About 50 visitors were scattered about the galleries. They apparently had no intimation of the tragedy until Senate Chaplain Frederick Brown Harris invoked God's assistance "as the president of the Republic goes down like a giant cedar." Suddenly, they stirred in consternation. The word spread quickly, however, after the first bulletins arrived over the news wires. Expressions of shock, sympathy and anger against the assassination poured forth as the news spread over Capitol Hill. The familiar roles of partisan and ideological difference dissolved in a common wave of grief and dismay.

Senator Mansfield, in a statement issued later in the afternoon, said: "I will miss him as a friend, the nation will miss him as a President and the world will miss him as a leader." Senator Dirksen told reporters: "Only someone suffering from aberrations of personality and motivated [by] insane passion would be guilty of the assassination of the great leader of the greatest country on earth." The House of Representatives was not in session today and many of its members were out of the city.

First word of the attack on the president was taken to the Senate floor by Richard Riedel, press liaison officer. He spotted the bulletins on the Associated Press news ticker in the senators' lobby at 1:42 o'clock. He darted onto the floor where a handful of members were in desultory debate over a bill on Federal library services. Senator Winston Prouty, Republican of Vermont, was speaking. Neither the Republican nor Democratic leader was present. The leader's seat was occupied by Senator Wayne Morse, Democrat of Oregon, manager of the library bill. Mr. Riedel gave his message to the first senator he encountered, Spessard Holland, Democrat of Florida. "The president has just been shot," he whispered. He went next to Senator Morse and repeated the message. Then he spotted Senator Kennedy on the dais and went to him. "Senator," he said, "your brother has just been shot." Mr. Riedel said that Senator Kennedy gasped: "No!," quickly left his seat and went into the lobby. There he put through a telephone call to the White House and another to Attorney General Robert F. Kennedy, his brother. He then departed hastily for his office in the Old Senate Office Building. Senator Holland quietly replaced Senator Kennedy in the presiding officer's chair.

Meanwhile, Senator Morse had interrupted debate to ask for a quorum call. This most familiar of delaying tactics, he said later, was used to gain time until he could get the two Senate leaders on the floor. Senators Mansfield and Dirksen had already been apprised of the news in their offices by a call from a reporter in the press gallery. They hurried to the floor. Mr. Mansfield withdrew the quorum call and announced that the Senate would be in recess "pending further developments."

As a dozen or more senators gathered in knots to discuss the news, the two leaders withdrew to the majority leader's office. Mr. Mansfield talked briefly by telephone with a presidential assistant, Ralph Dungan. It was not certain at that time whether the president had succumbed. The two leaders returned to the Senate and the session was reconvened at 2:10. About 50 senators, anxiety marking their faces, had assembled. In a voice that occasionally quavered with emotion, Mr. Mansfield rose to address the chair. "Mr. President," he said, "after discussing the tragic situation which now confronts the nation and the free world, the distinguished minority leader and I feel that it is only appropriate and proper, in view of the tragic circumstances which have arisen, and the extreme danger which confronts a good, decent and a kindly man, that it would not be inappropriate for the chaplain of the Senate to deliver a prayer at this time of hope that he and the governor of Texas [John B. Connally Jr.] will recover. On the completion of that prayer, we shall move to adjourn until 12 o'clock noon Monday next."

The chaplain asked the Senate to stand for a moment of silent prayer. Then, with deep gravity, he said: "Our Father, Thou knoweth that this sudden almost unbelievable news has stunned our minds and hearts. We gaze at a vacant place against the sky, as the president of the Republic goes down like a giant cedar, green with boughs. We pray that in Thy will his life may still be spared. In this hour we cry out in words that were uttered in another hour of deep loss and bereavement: 'God lives and the Government at Washington still stands.' Hold us, we pray, and the people of America, calm and steady and full of faith for the Republic this tragic hour of our history. God save the state and empower her for whatever awaits the great world role she has been called upon to fill in this time of destiny. Amen."

The Senate Republican conference formally adopted a resolution describing President Kennedy as a "friend" and a "distinguished chief executive." The resolution was approved at a midafternoon meeting in the office of Senator Dirksen of Illinois, after news of the president's death had been received. It expressed "profound regret and sorrow over his untimely and tragic passing" on behalf of the Senate's 33 Republicans. As a former Senate colleague, it said, the president "maintained with the Respublican members a cordial and understanding relationship which endeared him as a friend and a fellow public servant." The resolution will be sent to the Kennedy family.

OTHER CONGRESSIONAL COMMENT

WASHINGTON, Nov. 22 (UPI)—"My God . . . My God . . . what are we coming to," were the only words that John McCormack, speaker of the House of Representatives, could utter when told that President Kennedy had been shot down in Dallas. Mr. McCormack's dazed response was echoed throughout the tragic afternoon by other senators and representatives who had served with the slain chief executive before he entered the White House. Senator Margaret Chase Smith, Republican of Maine, burst into tears when she was told the news while eating lunch. Senator Richard B. Russell, Democrat of Georgia, leader of the Senate's Southern bloc, spoke of "this dastardly crime." He said: "The assassin's bullet has stricken a brilliant and dedicated statesman at the very height of his powers." The House Republican leader, Charles A. Halleck of Indiana, branded the assassination "an unspeakable crime against all the people of this country. The world should know," he eulogized, "that in this hour of national tragedy, Americans stand together as one—shocked and grieved at this unbelievable news." The Senate Democratic whip, Hubert H. Humphrey of Minnesota, who contested the presidential primaries with Mr. Kennedy in 1960, said: "America has lost a great president. The world has lost a great leader. I have lost a good friend. What an incredible tragedy." Representative Adam Clayton Powell, Democrat of New York, said every Federal and state effort should be made to punish the guilty. He also said that "all Americans who have any sanity, any character, any religious beliefs, irrespective of color, political creed or religion, should now rally around Lyndon Johnson to try to lift America back to the level of prestige that has now been destroyed."

Throng Gathers at White House

Capital Church Bells Toll—Embassy Flags Lowered

By NAN ROBERTSON

Special to The New York Times

WASHINGTON, Nov. 22—The sound of Washington today was the sound of church bells endlessly tolling and transistor radios conveying the unbelievable horror that the president of the United States was dead from an assassin's bullet. A thousand people gathered along Pennsylvania Avenue opposite the White House as dusk settled, drawn irresistibly to stand and wait—for what they did not quite know. A car with a poster on the roof rolled around and around the square. "The wrath of God is upon us," it said. "Jesus Christ saves from all sin."

On Massachusetts Avenue's embassy row, flags of every hue and nation hung at half-staff in the muggy, breathless atmosphere. In a Washington supermarket, men and women wept unashamedly as the news blared from the radio. Check-out clerks fled their stations in tears. Strangers stopped one another on the streets. "My God, my God!" they said. "Did you hear?"

In a Washington office, a man ranted against the assassin. "Look what the Birchers have done!" he cried. Neither he nor fellow workers who listened to him knew then that a prime suspect had been picked up in Dallas—a left-winger. The first word of the shooting, coming during the lunch hour, nearly emptied restaurants.

Robert Auburn of Pasadena, a travelogue producer, was at a restaurant with his wife when he heard a waitress say: "Assassinated!" "I knew it was somebody important," he said. "Ordinary people get killed. Important people are assassinated. The last thought in my mind was that our president was the one." A woman tourist, impelled like so many others to wait near the White House, said: "It seems unpardonable in a country that is so blessed with all the good things. I wouldn't have thought the man would have any enemies that felt that wickedly."

Those who refused to believe it was true—and there were many dis-believers in Lafayette Square facing the White House—finally accepted it when the flag above the Executive Mansion was lowered to half-staff at 2:45 P.M. David S. Urey, a law student, watched the flag flutter down the staff. "I certainly wasn't pro-Kennedy," he said. "As a matter of fact, I was supporting Goldwater. But the thought that comes to me is that this is the second president we've lost now on the civil-rights issue—Lincoln and Kennedy. I don't know how anyone could have strong enough senti-ment on another issue to assassinate him."

A strapping man standing nearby did not bother to wipe away the tears that streamed down his cheeks. Haltingly, he said: "I was driving to pick up my little girl at school. I heard it over my radio. I don't know why I came here. I had a feeling." A retired civil servant heard the "unbelievable news that he was dead" on her radio at home. "I felt as if I couldn't stay at home alone and endure it," she said, so she walked more than a mile to join the throng at the White House.

Before policemen asked the crowd to leave the fence in front of the Executive Mansion and step behind ropes across the street, a young girl thrust a bunch of chrysanthemums through the bars. It hung there, flowers for the dead, until White House policemen took it away.

On street corners all over the city, people huddled close around anyone who carried a transistor radio. Others walked or stood gazing at newspaper extras with large headlines reading, "JFK Is Slain!" or "President Is Killed by Sniper in Texas!" Worshipers knelt or sat with bowed heads and brimming eyes in St. John's Episcopal Church, known as the "Church of the presidents," a block from the White House. Every president from Madison to Eisenhower attended services there occasionally. In the gold-topped spire above, the bell tolled through the long afternoon. A 20-year-old busboy was standing in front of the White House clutching four-color postcards of Mr. Kennedy. "When I heard the news, I was so shocked I just went out and bought these for my own personal use," he said.

"This is a black day," said Philip Warren, an employee of the National Association of Counties. "This doesn't make sense at all. I thought this country was beyond that." A bearded student from George Washington University felt "as if the end of the world had come along and you're not prepared for it." When he first heard the news, he said, "I went for a drive to calm myself down; when that didn't work, I finally came to the White House." Few of those clustered in the area could give a reason for their presence. No one could understand why the president had been assassinated. "It must have been a maniac," one said. "What will happen to us now?"

Racial Hostility Ignored by South

Many Who Fought Policies of Kennedy Voice Grief

By CLAUDE SITTON

Special to The New York Times

BIRMINGHAM, Ala., Nov. 22—Many of this city's residents expressed grief today over the assassination of President Kennedy. Among them were whites who had bitterly opposed Federal policies in a series of racial crises here. T. Eugene Connor, the former police commissioner, known as "Bull," said Mr. Kennedy's slaying "was one of the most terrible things that have happened in my lifetime. I regret it very much. My sympathy goes out to his wife and his whole family." David Vann, a lawyer who has attempted to steer Birmingham toward moderation on racial issues, said the city had lost a friend.

"While many disagreed with him, in depth of concern he was one of the city's closest friends," Mr. Vann said. "Emotion often prevented our seeing this, but Birmingham has a big share in the world's tragic loss." He continued: "I cannot help but feel that this tragedy is in many ways symbolic of . . . professionally promoted hate into what is always its natural and ultimate consequences. The Scriptures say that 'he who hates his brother kills him.' Often we fail to realize that in every community, there are some emotionally disturbed people who need but little encouragement to carry out the faultlessly unintended consequences of the type of deliberate, organized heckling that met the president yesterday in Texas, which met Adlai Stevenson on his last visit to Texas and which we have seen in this city and other cities around the country. I can only hope that the nation's sorrow will be a sobering sorrow."

Frances Green, a student at Phillips High School, said, "I think it was the most horrible thing that has happened since I've been living. Anyone that would do something like that would have to be insane. The president was a great person, despite the racial trouble. A girl came through the halls at school screaming about it when it happened," she said. "When my teacher found out about it, she laid her head down and cried."

Some in Birmingham, while expressing sorrow, saw in the president's assassination further evidence of the "Communist plot" they hold responsible for racial troubles here. Among them was former Mayor Arthur J. Hanes. "I, like all Americans, am grieved and shocked over the tragic, cowardly and dastardly assassination of the highest elected official of our beloved country," Mr. Hanes, a caustic critic of the late president, said. "In the untimely death of President Kennedy is apparently another episode in the long and sordid history of Communistic–left wing policy—of control by revolution and assassination," he declared, adding: "How much longer will this great and proud nation permit the deadly Cuban-Communist cancer to eat away at the unity and vitality of this nation?"

Not even death could remove the bitterness felt by some whites. A youth who identified himself as Rusty Wesson of Birmingham telephoned radio station WQXI in Atlanta tonight and voiced these sentiments over its "Open Mike" show before the announcer cut him off: "I feel sure, and I'm sure that the majority of the people of Alabama feel, that Mr. Kennedy got exactly what he deserved. I'm sorry for his family. But I want to say that any man, any white man, who did what he did for niggers should be shot."

McCORMACK, NEXT IN LINE OF SUCCESSION TO THE PRESIDENCY, IS GIVEN SECURITY GUARD

Speaker Shaken by News of Death

He and Other House Officials Meet Plane as Coffin Is Taken to Washington

By JOHN D. MORRIS

Special to The New York Times

WASHINGTON, Nov. 22—House Speaker John W. McCormack became first in line of succession to the presidency today and was immediately made acutely aware of it. Within minutes after President Kennedy's death had been announced a Secret Service detail arrived at the Capitol to begin an around-the-clock guard of the Massachusetts Democrat. Secret Service agents were also assigned to the Washington Hotel, where Mr. and Mrs. McCormack maintain a suite. The guard is required under a 1962 law designed to insure the safety of the person next in line to the presidency. Such protection had been available to Mr. McCormack on request, but the speaker valued his privacy to a greater extent than he feared for his safety. When he became speaker in 1961, he was understood to have turned down suggestions that he ask for a guard.

Mr. McCormack's official role in the Government is not changed by Mr. Kennedy's death. However, it seemed likely that President Johnson would bring him into continuously close consultation and keep him fully informed of the Administration's affairs in view of his position as first in line of succession. After Mr. McCormack, those next in the line of succession are the president pro tempore of the Senate, Senator Carl Hayden, Democrat of Arizona, and the secretary of state, Dean Rusk. The speaker, who will be 72 years old on Dec. 21, was visibly shaken on receiving word of the shooting of Mr. Kennedy. He was having lunch in the House restaurant with Dr. Martin Sweig, an aide, and Edward Fitzgerald, administrative assistant to the clerk of the House. Two news correspondents went to the table and told the three men President Kennedy had been shot.

"My God! My God! What are we coming to?" Mr. McCormack exclaimed.

He finished his lunch and went to his office just off the House floor. He was joined by Representatives Carl Albert, the House Democratic leader, and Carl Vinson, Democrat of Georgia. A short vigil there was ended by a call from the White House. Theodore C. Sorensen, special counsel to the president, was on the telephone. He reported that President Kennedy was dead. "I was stunned," the speaker told reporters later. "I just simply said, 'My God, it's tragic.' "

A three-man Washington police detail of plainclothes men regularly assigned to the Capitol went immediately to the speaker's office at the request of the Secret Service to provide an interim guard. Within minutes, a Secret Service detail commanded by Inspector Burrill A. Peterson arrived and went to the corridor and anteroom of the speaker's private office.

Speaker McCormack's first official act on being informed of Mr. Kennedy's death was to order flags on Capitol Hill lowered to half-staff. Then he prepared a public statement, called reporters into his office and read it to them.

He sat at his desk, looking pale and tense. Representative Albert, in a nearby chair, was red-faced, and his eyes were bloodshot. Representative Vinson sat staring at the floor, an unlighted cigar in his mouth. "This is a tragic event," Mr. McCormack began. "I feel very inadequate in expressing my thoughts. The nation has sustained a staggering loss . . ." He choked momentarily. ". . . the significance of which," he continued, "is stupendous. Our country and the entire world will never forget President Kennedy. His leadership was superb in meeting the challenges of this period of world history. The warmth of his personality will never be forgotten." Again the speaker paused, fighting back tears. "The relationship that existed between the president and myself throughout the years has been close and most friendly," he went on. "In his tragic passing I have lost a dear and personal friend. The nation has lost a great leader. I mourn for his family, for the nation, for Mrs. McCormack and myself."

The group in the speaker's office was joined a few minutes later by Representative Hale Boggs of Louisiana, the House majority whip, or assistant Democratic leader. The four House leaders, Representatives McCormack, Albert, Boggs and Vinson, went to Andrews Air Force Base in the speaker's limousine. There they joined other Congressional and Administration leaders who met the plane bearing Mr. Kennedy's body. Speaker McCormack and other Congressional leaders of both parties then went to the White House for a conference with President Johnson. The white-haired Mr. McCormack, tall, erect and vigorous, will continue his duties as presiding officer of the House and principal leader of its Democratic majority. He declined to discuss his new status as first in line of presidential succession.

The late Speaker Sam Rayburn of Texas was first in line of succession to the presidency from July 18, 1947, when the present succession law was enacted, until Jan. 20, 1949, when Harry S. Truman was inaugurated for a full term as president. With Mr. Truman's inauguration, the late Alben W. Barkley became vice president, and Mr. Rayburn reverted to second in the line of succession. Mr. Rayburn performed no executive duties during the 1947–49 period when there was no vice president. However, President Truman consulted with him almost daily, in person or by telephone. He was kept fully informed of Administration affairs.

Right-Wing Senator Receives Threats

Special to The New York Times

WASHINGTON, Nov. 22—Threatening telephone calls to the office of Senator John G. Tower, Republican of Texas, caused the senator to move his family to the home of friends in Maryland tonight as a safety precaution. The senator is regarded as a right-wing conservative. He had been highly critical of President Kennedy. Representative Bruce Alger of Dallas, also a Republican, is also reported to have received a number of anonymous calls and telegrams. An aide said tonight that Senator Tower was in St. Louis for a Republican conference. When advised of the threats, he directed that his wife and three daughters be conducted to the home of a friend. The aide said that about a dozen anonymous and threatening telephone calls had been received at the senator's office this afternoon, as well as a number of telegrams. The telegrams came from as far away as California. "The senator recognized these as coming from crackpots," the aide said, "but he was unwilling to take any chances with the safety of his wife and children. He arranged for them to stay with friends until he returns to Washington."

Lasky, Critic of Kennedy, Says Book Sale Is Halted

Victor Lasky, author of *JFK: The Man and the Myth,* a best-selling book sharply critical of President Kennedy, said last night that "the publisher has stopped the presses." Mr. Lasky said he had canceled 12 lecture engagements and three scheduled television appearances. "I've canceled out of everything," he said. "As far as I'm concerned Kennedy is no longer subject to criticism on my part."

About the assassination, he said: "I have been a critic of the president, but when I heard the sad news, I turned to my wife and asked her to join me in praying for God's mercy for our president."

A spokesman for the publisher, the Macmillan Company, said that all distribution and promotion of the book had been halted.

Captain of Japanese Ship That Sank PT-109 Mourns

FUKUSHIMA, Japan, Saturday, Nov. 23 (UPI)—The captain of the Japanese destroyer that rammed and sank PT-109, commanded by Lieut. (jg.) John F. Kennedy in World War II, expressed shock and sorrow today on learning of the president's death. "I think his death is a great loss to Japan," said Kohei Hanami, 54-year-old former captain of the Japanese destroyer *Amagiri.* Mr. Hanami, now mayor of Shiyokawa, a town in northern Japan, said he was sorry that he had now lost the opportunity to meet Mr. Kennedy personally.

FINANCIAL AND COMMODITIES MARKETS SHAKEN; FEDERAL RESERVE ACTS TO AVERT PANIC

Exchanges Close as Traders React

Stocks Plunge in a Sudden Rush of Sales, but Prices Are Mixed Elsewhere

By JOHN M. LEE

President Kennedy's assassination had an immediate and crushing impact on the nation's financial and commodities markets yesterday. Securities and commodities markets closed soon after 2 P.M. when news of the shooting was circulated. The New York Stock Exchange experienced some of its heaviest trading in history, as prices broke sharply in the worst drop since the market plunge of May 28, 1962. Other markets conducted mostly by telephone came to a standstill, but prices were generally mixed. The Federal Reserve System moved quickly to prevent panic when the markets reopen and issued an extraordinary statement declaring there was agreement "that there is no need for special action in the financial markets." The statement was issued at 5:20 P.M. by the Federal Reserve Bank of New York.

The expression of confidence by Alfred Hayes, president of the New York bank, was taken as an avowal that the Federal Reserve and European central banks would work in concert to thwart any speculation against the dollar in foreign exchange markets in this country.

Word of the shooting spread during the lunch hours, and heavier-than-usual crowds filled the narrow streets of the financial district. The air was described by one observer as "one of stupefaction." Bells tolled from historic Trinity Church at the head of Wall Street. Normal operations in factories, offices and stores throughout the nation were disrupted as news of the president's death passed through corridors by word of mouth and into offices by transistor radios. Several large corporations, such as the Standard Oil Company (New Jersey), closed offices throughout the nation and sent employees home. The business community was stunned. Roger M. Blough, chairman of the United States Steel Corporation; Frederic G. Donner, chairman of the General Motors Corporation, and W. P. Gullander, president of the National Association of Manufacturers, were among the executives issuing statements of shock and grief.

Most businessmen were in no mood to discuss the impact on the economy. Some, however, feared that confidence would be affected and that a delicately poised stock market, which has shown little tendency to rise on favorable business news, could be in for a further decline. General Lucius Clay, former supreme allied commander and now a partner in the investment banking firm of Lehman Brothers, said, when asked for comment, "I rather think there would be an immediate depressing effect on the market. However," he added, "I think firm underlying factors will carry it through this critical period." The market collapse yesterday erased about $11 billion in paper values from the stocks listed on the Big Board.

Robert P. Baruch, chairman of the executive committee of the securities firm of H. Hentz & Co., said "hasty liquidation of sound investments is ill advised at this time. It is our conviction that when sober judgment prevails, confidence in the economy will assert itself," he added. A quick sampling of national business sentiment by The Associated Press concluded that business would go into a lull because of the assassination but that there would not be any real slump.

An anonymous executive of a large metals producer was quoted as having said, "Business will certainly stop, look and listen, and they will surely postpone expansion plans. It's quite a shock to confidence." William Butler, a vice president of the Chase Manhattan Bank, said, "There might be some leveling, but I don't see it leading to a recession." Many businessmen believe the economy is in a strong position now to sustain a shock. Corporate profits this year are expected to beat the 1962 record by a substantial margin, capital spending is advancing and consumer attitudes are regarded as favorable.

However, some corporate executives have emphasized that a tax cut was needed to stimulate the economy and prevent it from stagnating at a high level. Stock market activity has been disquieting to some observers. Prices have failed to rise appreciably in recent weeks despite a wave of favorable business developments, including higher dividends. Instead, the market has reacted adversely to an imbroglio over soybean oil. In addition, some businessmen observed that although there had been differences with President Kennedy over certain issues, they at least knew where he stood. President Johnson represented to them something of an unknown.

The Government issued a statement from the Treasury Department apparently designed to strengthen confidence. Noting that all markets except those for foreign exchange had closed upon word of the tragedy, the Treasury said: "The foreign exchange markets absorbed the initial shock without change, and the close cooperation of central banks and financial officials assures the maintenance of orderly conditions." The Securities and Exchange Commission, which regulates the market, met late yesterday to discuss a reopening of the stock markets. The S.E.C. had no other statement concerning the resumption of trading, but it was expected that an additional statement would be made, perhaps over the weekend or at least before the scheduled reopening at 10 A.M. Monday.

The Dow-Jones industrial average, which had been rising before the news flashed on the exchange floor at 1:41 P.M., was off 21.16 points when the Board of Governors closed the exchange at 2:07 P.M. The market usually closes at 3:30 P.M. It was the worst drop since the market break of May 28, 1962, when the closing average was off 34.95. The New York and the American Stock Exchanges said last night they planned to open as usual on Monday unless the president's funeral was held then. The exchanges plan to close the day of the funeral.

Yesterday was the first time that the market had closed during a session since Aug. 4, 1933, when the floor was pervaded by gas fumes. Keith Funston, president of the exchange, said a flood of orders to the floor had necessitated yesterday's early close. The exchange announced that all market orders of any type that remained unexecuted when trading was stopped had expired.

Other exchanges quickly followed the Big Board in closing. They were the American Stock Exchange, the Cotton and Wool Exchanges, the Midwest Stock Exchange, the Pacific Stock Exchange and the Cocoa, Coffee and Sugar Exchanges. The S.E.C. asked all broker-dealers to cease over-the-counter trading. In a statement following the suspension of trading on the New York Stock Exchange, the exchange's Board of Governors said: "It was the opinion of the board that the market would reflect more realistic values after the public had an opportunity to apprise the effect of this great national and international tragedy." Volume on the New York exchange was extremely heavy for the five-and-a-half-hour session, climbing to 6.63 million shares from the 5.67 million shares traded the preceding day.

The big department stores here that usually remain open until 9 o'clock Friday nights closed at 5:45, and many others locked their doors before normal closing time. Most stores said that they were planning to open today, but would close on the day of the president's funeral. Advertising was canceled by many companies. More than 100 pages of retail store advertising were dropped from the Sunday main section of *The New York Times* alone.

WORLD LEADERS VOICE SYMPATHY AND SHOCK AS THEIR COUNTRIES MOURN PRESIDENT

Elizabeth Sends Her Condolences

Americans in London Weep at Embassy—Erhard and de Gaulle Sorrowful

Special to The New York Times

LONDON, Nov. 22—Queen Elizabeth and Sir Alec Douglas-Home, the prime minister, led the British tonight in mourning for President Kennedy. The queen, staying with friends in the country, sent an immediate message of sympathy to Mrs. Kennedy. A statement from Sir Alec's office spoke of "shock and horror" at the news of the assassination. The royal court will go into mourning for a week. The queen sent "heartfelt and sincere sympathy" to Mrs. Kennedy. In a message to President Johnson, she said she had been "shocked and horrified" by the news.

Sir Alec heard the news at Arundel, home of the duke of Norfolk, in Sussex. He rushed back to London. In a nationally televised tribute, Sir Alec said Mr. Kennedy had left "an indelible mark" on the entire world. "There are times in life when the mind and heart stand still," Sir Alec said, "and one such is now. He was young and brave and a great statesman. The loss is a deep and sad one because he was the most loyal and faithful of allies."

The word that the president had been shot spread swiftly through Britain. When he died, millions were watching the British Broadcasting Corporation's evening news telecast. The announcer interrupted his broadcast to answer the telephone. Then he told viewers: "We regret to announce that President Kennedy is dead." Americans in London began to receive calls from their British friends. The United States Embassy switchboard was overwhelmed with calls from people who wanted to know if it was true. The news spread through the streets in central London. Some, not believing, walked in the clear, cold night to the embassy. Within an hour the crowd grew to 200. American visitors at the Savoy Hotel gathered around a teleprinter in the lobby. Some were in tears. Alexander Orr, a timekeeper at Gamage, a London department store, said: "I'm very sorry. He has done a lot for the world. He's a countryman of mine—Irish. It's a funny country, America. There are so many different races. We're more level-headed here."

The De Profundis was said in Westminster Cathedral for the repose of the soul of President Kennedy, and the tenor bell of Westminster Abbey will be rung every minute between 11 A.M. and noon tomorrow. Dr. Arthur Michael Ramsey, the archbishop of Canterbury, described President Kennedy as a "statesman of Christian ideals whose service to his fellows was inspired by his faith in God." Harold Wilson, leader of the Labor party, got the news while addressing a public meeting in Flintshire, Wales. "I am sure I am speaking for everyone in this country when I express our deep horror at this evil act," Mr. Wilson said. He added: "I pay tribute to one who has been a good friend of this country, a great world statesman and a great fighter for peace. His great struggle for racial equality in the United States is something that will in memory long outlive his life."

Sir Winston Churchill issued a statement saying, "This monstrous act has taken from us a great statesman and a wise and valiant man." The loss to the world is "incalculable," the 88-year-old former prime minister said. He added, "Those who come after Mr. Kennedy must strive the more to achieve the ideals of world peace and human happiness to which his presidency was dedicated."

De Gaulle Salutes Memory

Special to The New York Times

PARIS, Nov. 22—President de Gaulle paid a soldier's tribute to President Kennedy tonight, saying he had died "as a soldier, under fire, doing his duty in the service of his country. In the name of the French people, a friend always to the American people, I salute this great example and this great memory," General de Gaulle added. General de Gaulle also addressed a telegram to President Johnson. He wrote: "Be assured more than ever,

Mr. President, of the friendship, faithful and confident, of France for the United States of America."

Chancellor Tells of Sorrow

Special to The New York Times

BONN, Nov. 22—On his return to Bonn from Paris, Chancellor Erhard drove to a television studio, where he expressed sorrow. "We all have lost John F. Kennedy," he said. "In this hour, words cannot express the pain and sorrow we feel." Dr. Erhard and former Chancellor Konrad Adenauer sent telegrams of sympathy to Mrs. Kennedy and to President Johnson.

"A Flame Went Out"

Special to The New York Times

BERLIN, Nov. 22—Mayor Willy Brandt expressed West Berlin's sadness when he said, "A flame went out for all those who had hoped for a just peace and a better life." Mr. Brandt, who was known to have friendly personal relations with the president, intends to travel to Washington for the funeral. Many West Berliners lighted candles in their windows in a demonstration of mourning that has been a custom in the city since the death of Mayor Ernst Reuter in 1953. Theaters broke off their performances. "We are too moved to go on," said Albrecht Schönhals, a 75-year-old actor, in closing the performance at the Forum Theater. The audience quietly filed out.

Austria Sends Sympathy

Special to The New York Times

VIENNA, Nov. 22—President Adolf Schärf, in a message to Mrs. Kennedy, said: "I convey to you and your children and the American people my heartfelt condolences." To President Johnson, Mr. Schärf wrote: "I am profoundly distressed by the tragic death of President Kennedy. I express my sincerest sympathies in my own name and that of the Austrian people, who feel very close to the people of the United States in this hour."

Dutch See Disaster

Special to The New York Times

THE HAGUE, Nov. 22—President Kennedy's assassination was termed "disastrous" by Premier Victor Marijnen. "His death will undoubtedly have serious consequences for world politics," he added. "The murder fills me with the deepest indignation," the premier said.

Spaak: "I Cannot Speak"

BRUSSELS, Nov. 22 (Reuters)—Foreign Minister Paul-Henri Spaak of Belgium said today in a sobbing voice: "What can I say about this hideous news, except that I am stunned, and that a terrible, frightening thing has happened. I cannot speak tonight."

Segni Notes "Grave Loss"

ROME, Nov. 22—Italy was stunned with disbelief. President Antonio Segni said the death of the president was a "very grave loss for all humanity."

Franco Tells of Grief

Special to The New York Times

MADRID, Nov. 22—Spaniards learned of President Kennedy's death through a special bulletin on the state radio. Generalissimo Francisco Franco and his ministers were holding a routine Cabinet meeting here when they were informed. Shortly afterward, an official spokesman expressed Spain's deep mourning. In a message to President Johnson, General Franco said all Spain condemned the assassination of President Kennedy. In his condolences to Mrs. Kennedy, General Franco said that her husband's death "fills all Spanish hearts with grief."

Portugal to Mourn 3 Days

Dispatch of The Times, *London*

LISBON, Nov. 22—Portugal will mourn President Kennedy for three days. Both Premier Antonio de Oliveira Salazar and President Américo Deus Rodrigues Tomás have sent telegrams of condolences to President Johnson.

Norwegian Laments Loss

Special to The New York Times

OSLO, Norway, Nov. 22—Premier Einar Gerhardsen said Norwegians had "had a peculiar feeling of security" and had believed in President Kennedy's "will to create peace and justice in the world." The premier addressed the nation by radio and television soon after hearing of the president's death.

Denmark: "An Evil Deed"

Special to The New York Times

COPENHAGEN, Denmark, Nov. 22—Premier Jens Otto Krag, addressing the Danish people on television and radio, said: "What we have heard is inconceivable. It is an evil deed, another dark spot on the history of our time."

Swedes Weep at News

Special to The New York Times

STOCKHOLM, Nov. 22—King Gustav VI Adolf and his subjects expressed shock and sorrow. The king sent a message to Mrs. Kennedy and the United States Embassy was flooded with calls from Swedes, many of whom wept as they told of their distress and sorrow. Premier Tage Erlander eulogized Mr. Kennedy as a great American statesman who gave his life in a battle for ideals.

Kekkonen Sends Condolences

Special to The New York Times

HELSINKI, Finland, Nov. 22—President Urho K. Kekkonen sent a telegram of condolence to Mrs. Kennedy and expressed the shock of the Finnish people. Serious music replaced the regular programs on the Finnish radio.

Swiss Call Death Tragic

Special to The New York Times

GENEVA, Nov. 22—President Willy Spühler said tonight that the Swiss government had learned "with consternation" of President Kennedy's "particularly tragic" death. Mr. Spühler, in a message to President Johnson, expressed "the profound sympathy of the Swiss government and people."

Greece Shares in Sorrow

Special to The New York Times

ATHENS, Nov. 22—The news information minister of Greece, George Athanasiades-Novas, reported the president's death to the nation. He said: "I feel, as all Greeks do, pain and indignation for this abominable act. The Greek people share in the American people's mourning."

Turk Assails Crime

Dispatch of The Times, *London*

ANKARA, Turkey, Nov. 22—President Cemal Gürsel described President Kennedy on the Turkish radio tonight as "a pioneer in the great struggles of humanity, a determined fighter for world peace, and a firm friend of the Turkish nation. Every Turkish family feels a personal grief at this horrible crime," he said.

Canada: "Tragedy for All"

Special to The New York Times

OTTAWA, Nov. 22—Coupled with the initial shock and grief produced by the first news of President Kennedy's assassination was a sense of anxiety for the future throughout Canada today. Not since President Franklin D. Roosevelt died in the closing days of World War II has any event had so great an impact on this nation. Prime Minister Lester B. Pearson and members of the opposition parties joined in expressions of grief. Mr. Pearson announced the news to Parliament. He said: "This is a tragedy not only for the president's family and for his people; it is a tragedy for all of us. No people outside the United States will share more deeply in this tragedy than the people of Canada."

Impact Great in Latin America

Special to The New York Times

LIMA, Peru, Nov. 22—When President Kennedy was elected three years ago, Latin America greeted his victory as the promise of a brighter future. This afternoon the news of Mr. Kennedy's death hit with an impact seemingly greater than the assassination of a Latin president would have caused. At first there was the emotional reaction of millions of simple, hopeful people. To them President Kennedy was the symbol of United States interest in their fate and of the peace they wished so deeply for themselves and the world. Then, later, came the fear that Mr. Kennedy's death might mean the ending or slowing down of United States programs in Latin America typified by the Alliance for Progress. But the overwhelming impact was one of shock, grief, incredulity and personal loss.

Peru's president, Fernando Belaúnde Terry, a young and aggressive liberal who shared many of Mr. Kennedy's ideas, heard of the assassination as he was lunching with his Cabinet at the presidential palace. An aide reported that President Belaúnde, visibly shaken, asked his ministers to rise with him in tribute to Mr. Kennedy's memory. Then he telephoned Ambassador J. Wesley Jones to say that he was "deeply shocked."

President Kennedy's personal popularity was so great in Latin America that it seemed to overcome the real and imagined grievances of this continent against the United States. In San José, Costa Rica, eight months ago, crowds engulfed him so deeply that the Secret Service men feared for his safety. People embraced him, patted his back, shook his hand—and even kissed it.

Sirens Sound in Buenos Aires

Special to The New York Times

BUENOS AIRES, Nov. 22—Sirens on the buildings of the newspapers *La Nación* and *La Prensa* were sounded today when the news of President Kennedy's death became known. The sirens are used only on occasions of extraordinary events.

Betancourt Weeps

CARACAS, Venezuela, Nov. 22 (AP)—President Rómulo Betancourt was speechless when he was told the news. He sent condolences to Washington, then tried to read the message to newsmen. But he broke into tears and was unable to go on.

3 Days of Mourning for Brazil

Special to The New York Times

RIO DE JANEIRO, Nov. 22—President João Goulart declared three days of official mourning in Brazil and canceled all of his official engagements.

Chilean Leader Deeply Moved

Special to The New York Times

SANTIAGO, Chile, Nov. 22—Deeply moved, President Jorge Alessandri Rodriguez expressed his sorrow to Ambassador Charles W. Cole. The Government declared national mourning and the radio stations replaced all programs with funeral music.

López Mateos Mourns

Special to The New York Times

MEXICO CITY, Nov. 22—President Adolfo López Mateos expressed "sorrow and consternation" and expressed hope that the death of "such an illustrious personage would not affect world peace."

Colombian Sees Setback

Special to The New York Times

BOGOTA, Colombia, Nov. 22—President Guillermo Léon Valencia of Colombia said to the nation in a broadcast this evening: "The news of the assassination of President John F. Kennedy constitutes a disastrous setback for the entire world, especially for the free world and above all for the American continent."

Soviet People and Leaders Grieve for Kennedy

Radio Plays Funeral Music—Gromyko Expresses "Greatest Sympathy"

By HENRY TANNER

Special to The New York Times

MOSCOW, Saturday, Nov. 23—The Moscow radio interrupted a concert of classical music at 10:55 o'clock last night to report the death of President Kennedy. Then it played funeral music until it signed off at midnight.

Tass, the official Soviet press agency, in its first announcement, reported it was thought that "extreme right-wing elements" were the assassins. [A pro-Castro leftist was arrested in Dallas in connection with the assassination.] The press agency later distributed a short biography of Mr. Kennedy that called him an "outstanding American statesman."

There was consternation and genuine grief on the faces of the Muscovites who heard the news. An elderly woman in humble clothes who tends the elevators in a building where foreigners live had been listening to the radio. "He was so young!" she said. "Those wretches! In his own country! Wasn't he protected?"

Ambassador Foy D. Kohler was stricken. "It's terrible, terrible!" he said. In their apartments at the Kremlin and in suburban Lenin Hills, Soviet Government and Communist party officials were informed immediately, a Soviet source reported. Foreign Minister Andrei A. Gromyko telephoned Ambassador Kohler at midnight. He wanted to "express his shock and greatest sympathy to the American people," he told the ambassador. Mr. Gromyko said that official condolences would be conveyed later at the "highest level."

Today's issue of *Pravda,* the official Communist party newspaper, carried a two-column front-page picture of President Kennedy along with a column and a half of text. Under the headline "Murder of the President of the U.S.A., John Kennedy," *Pravda* printed a biography of Mr. Kennedy. It noted that in a speech at American University June 10, the president declared that all countries "have a deep mutual interest in just and genuine peace and in stopping the arms race."

A 15-year-old Russian boy ran a mile through darkened Moscow streets to tell an American schoolmate that President Kennedy had been killed. The boy was upset. His words were the same as those of Ambassador Kohler. "It's terrible, terrible!" he said.

Western diplomats were aghast. "This is a terrible tragedy for his family, his country, my country and the world," the British ambassador, Sir Humphrey Trevelyan, said. Western diplomats immediately expressed the conviction that Mr. Kennedy's death would have a profound effect on Soviet–United States relations and on East-West relations in general. A high-ranking Western diplomat said President Kennedy had "commanded the respect of Soviet leaders and of Premier Khrushchev personally to a greater degree than any other Western statesman in recent years." Mr. Khrushchev, the diplomat added, was deeply impressed by the young president's "determination and courage" when he met him in Vienna in 1961. He said the Soviet leader's impression of the American president had been confirmed through a series of crises from Berlin to Cuba in which Mr. Kennedy showed that he was "ready to resist even at the greatest risk."

While the Russian leaders thus respected Mr. Kennedy as a bold opponent in the cold war, they also recognized him as a "reasonable and unemotional man" with whom they could negotiate and "do business," the diplomat said. Even in recent days—as tension rose over the Soviet arrest of Prof. Frederick C. Barghoorn and the Berlin autobahn incidents—President Kennedy's speech of June 10, in which he called for strong efforts for peace, was often quoted in the Soviet press. The passage that was singled out was his call for a reappraisal of American views of the Soviet Union. The passage was often quoted out of context, in connection with the 30th anniversary of the establishment of diplomatic relations between the United States and the Soviet Union.

Premier Rushes to Moscow

MOSCOW, Saturday, Nov. 23 (UPI)—Premier Khrushchev was rushing back to Moscow by train from the Ukraine after receiving reports of President Kennedy's assassination, informed sources said today. The premier was said to have ordered Foreign Minister Gromyko to stand by to go to the United States to attend Mr. Kennedy's funeral.

Ulbricht Expresses Grief

Special to The New York Times

BERLIN, Nov. 22—Walter Ulbricht, Communist chief of East Germany, sent a message of condolence today to President Johnson. He said his government's "horror of the terrorists is as deep as our sympathy with the American people, who have lost one of their most outstanding statesmen."

Yugoslav's Voice Quavers

BELGRADE, Yugoslavia, Nov. 22 (Reuters)—The voice of the leading commentator of Yugoslavia quavered tonight as he broadcast the news of President Kennedy's death.

Hungarians "Shocked"

Special to The New York Times

BUDAPEST, Hungary, Nov. 22—The Budapest radio interrupted a music program tonight to announce the death of President Kennedy. It said the news had "profoundly shocked" the people of Hungary. "What will become of us all?" cried one Hungarian woman in tears.

Kennedy Impact Felt in Moscow

It Remembers Him for Gain in Exchange of Ideas

By THEODORE SHABAD

Special to The New York Times

MOSCOW, Nov. 22—When John F. Kennedy was elected president of the United States in 1960, Soviet leaders viewed him as a man who might carry on the philosophy of Franklin D. Roosevelt in seeking an accommodation with Moscow. Although Soviet hopes fell short of realization as the new president grappled with the realities of the persistent cold war, his death will undoubtedly produce genuine regret among the Kremlin's policymakers. Mr. Kennedy will be remembered as the man who achieved an improvement of communications between the United States and the Soviet Union. A relatively freer flow of information and ideas has been regarded as essential by Washington to prevent any miscalculation by Moscow that might lead to a nuclear war. Perhaps the most concrete expression of the improved communications was the hot line established between United States and Soviet command centers for use in an emergency that both sides hoped would never come. However, there were other equally significant advances, such as the personal exchanges of messages between President Kennedy and Premier Khrushchev in times of crisis and the publication of texts of several Kennedy statements in the Soviet press. It was not until after his election that Mr. Kennedy evoked hope in Moscow for a change in American-Soviet relations.

Before the Democratic nominating convention, Soviet sympathies were with Adlai E. Stevenson, who was described in the press here as being "for a policy of realism and not adventurism." The limited press comment in Moscow during the election campaign was directed mainly against the Republicans. It was in a message of congratulations after the election that Premier Khrushchev first pinned the F.D.R. label on the new president. The Soviet premier expressed the hope that "relations between our countries will return to the state in which they were during Franklin Roosevelt's time." However, Mr. Kennedy's first State of the Union message made it clear to the Kremlin that the new president was determined to keep up American defenses while exploring avenues of understanding with the Soviet Union.

Premier Khrushchev and President Kennedy met in Vienna in June, 1961. At the meeting Mr. Kennedy sought to caution Mr. Khrushchev against misjudging the United States' will to act whenever its vital interests were threatened. A high point in President Kennedy's efforts to put his views before the Soviet people came in November, 1961, when *Izvestia,* the Soviet Government newspaper, published an interview that the president had given to *Izvestia*'s editor Aleksei I. Adzhubei, who is Premier Khrushchev's son-in-law. It was the first time that such an East-West dialogue, in which Mr. Adzhubei represented the Soviet view, had been published in the Soviet Union.

The solution of the Cuban missile crisis a year ago was attributed in part to the effectiveness of the direct communications between President Kennedy and Premier Khrushchev. The latest improvement of United States–Soviet relations is usually credited here to the "Moscow spirit" that followed the signing in August of the treaty for a limited nuclear test ban. But a significant role was undoubtedly played by President Kennedy's speech of last June appealing to Americans to reappraise their attitude toward the Soviet Union and the cold war. That speech was published by *Izvestia* and evoked a warm response. "Have you read Kennedy's speech?" one Russian was overheard to have said. "It's all about peace."

The latest evidence of Moscow's respect for President Kennedy was shown in the recent incident involving the arrest in the Soviet Union of Prof. Frederick C. Barghoorn of Yale University. President Kennedy said Professor Barghoorn had not been on an intelligence mission. The Soviet authorities released the professor and made it clear that they had done so as a result of the president's intervention.

Setback to Unity of Europe Feared

Allied Diplomats See Peril of Weakened U.S. Backing

By DREW MIDDLETON

Special to The New York Times

PARIS, Nov. 22—The United States' leadership of the Atlantic community, desperately needed in a time of change, has been dealt a grievous blow by the assassination of President Kennedy. Diplomats here and in other capitals of Western Europe emphasized tonight that the conflict between the president's view on the organization of the Atlantic community and those of General de Gaulle and his followers was nearing a climax. The president's death, they said, has left General de Gaulle as the senior Western leader. Within three months Chancellor Konrad Adenauer of West Germany and Prime Minister Harold Macmillan of Britain have retired and Mr. Kennedy has been killed. General de Gaulle, himself a target for at least four known assassination attempts, survives able to continue preaching his policies of European independence to a Continent temporarily bereft of United States leadership and uncertain about the new masters of the great powers.

The immediate need, diplomats agreed, is for an early and authoritative reassertion by President Johnson of continued United States interest in two cardinal policies laid down by Mr. Kennedy. These were specified as: The American belief that integration of conventional and nuclear forces provides a better defense for Europe than the national military organizations advocated by General de Gaulle. The conviction that, whatever difficulties arise in dealing with the Soviet Union, discussions should continue over the future of Germany, Berlin and Central Europe generally. Implicit in this assessment, the sources declared, is the fear that the new Administration may veer away from internationalism toward the political philosophy of "fortress America."

President Kennedy's assassination came at a moment when many European governments were hoping for a firm reassertion of United States policy toward Europe. Diplomats conceded regretfully that they had been critical of the late president for not making his policies better known. One Scandinavian minister remarked that avowals of European dependence on the United States, such as that made today by Chancellor Ludwig Erhard of West Germany, while welcome, were no substitute for equally firm assertions of American interdependence with Europe. The first duty of the new Administration toward Europe, most sources believed, would be a statement that the United States, in this troubled time, has no intention of discarding its responsibilities overseas.

Reports from The Hague, Brussels, Bonn and Copenhagen indicated a deep-seated fear that the United States was planning a sizable withdrawal of military forces from Europe. This fear has been strengthened by former President Dwight D. Eisenhower's suggestion that five American divisions could be recalled and by Secretary of Defense Robert S. McNamara's statement discounting the strength of the Soviet army in Eastern Europe. In these circumstances, General de Gaulle's warnings that the United States would not forever protect Europe have gained credibility in Western Europe. This mood inevitably will gain new importance in Western Europe in the aftermath of President Kennedy's death. But even before that, a Belgian source said, Europeans had begun to question the long-term intentions of the United States. Europe, a West German source said, is now at a halfway house between independence and interdependence. The path it takes, he said, will be indicated by the force and clarity with which the new Administration reasserts United States policy toward this questioning Continent.

U.N. Mourns Loss; Session Adjourns

Assembly Delegates Pray and Ponder the Future

By SAM POPE BREWER

Special to The New York Times

UNITED NATIONS, N.Y., Nov. 22—News of President Kennedy's death brought official mourning here. But more than that, it produced a profound sense of shock among delegates and officials. The most general reaction was: What will this mean to the state of balance in world affairs and the recent progress toward understanding?

Official mourning was declared when the General Assembly met at 3 P.M. only long enough to stand for a minute of silent prayer and brief expressions of sorrow by the president, Dr. Carlos Sosa Rodriguez, and the secretary general, U Thant. All other meetings were canceled. The 111 national flags that fly in front of headquarters were taken down and the United Nations flag lowered to half-staff.

As delegates gathered in the Assembly's plenary hall, they crowded past to offer condolences to Adlai E. Stevenson as chief United States delegate. Nikolai T. Fedorenko, chief Soviet delegate, took pains to shake hands with each of the United States delegation. He had been at a luncheon with Mr. Stevenson when the news of the shooting was received.

Long after the Assembly adjourned, the delegates' lounge and the corridors were filled with little groups of delegates discussing the assassination and what it would mean. A typical comment came from Abdul-Monem Rafa'i, chief delegate of Jordan. He said: "He died when he was needed most, both nationally and internationally." A South American delegate said: "It is hard to believe in assassination in cold blood like that in this country. What purpose can it serve?" Carlos M. Lechuga Hevia, Cuban chief delegate, said that "in spite of the existing antagonism between the United States Government and the Cuban revolution, we have heard with deep sorrow the news of the tragic death. All civilized men," he added, "will always be saddened by events such as this. Our delegation to the organization of the United Nations wishes to express that this is the sentiment of the people and Government of Cuba."

First news of the shooting of President Kennedy burst on the delegates as they were leaving earlier meetings and gathering for pre-luncheon drinks and conversation in the delegates' lounge. Within minutes, the huge room emptied as delegates hurried out to get further information. The word came first from a Secretariat member who ran into the room to tell a group of newspapermen what had just come over the radio. The clatter of conversation was suddenly hushed as the news spread from group to group. Members of the United States delegation bolted out of the headquarters and across First Avenue to the United States Mission building.

Mr. Stevenson was attending a luncheon in a private dining room here given by Luis Bossay of Chile for chief delegates. An aide who gave him the news said Mr. Stevenson was too shocked to make any comment as he excused himself and hurried back to his office to keep in touch with developments. Mr. Stevenson's formal statement later said: "The tragedy of this day is beyond instant comprehension. All of us who knew him will bear the grief of his death to the day of ours. And all men everywhere who love peace and justice and freedom will bow their heads. At such a moment we can only turn to prayer—prayer to comfort our grief, to sustain Mrs. Kennedy and his family, to strengthen President Johnson and to guide us in time to come. May God help us."

Capitals of Asia Express Sorrow

Sleeping Cities Awaken to News of Assassination

Special to The New York Times

TOKYO, Saturday, Nov. 23—News of President Kennedy's death reached here shortly before 4 A.M. today when most of the nation was sleeping. It was announced on radio and television soon afterward and repeated news bulletins quickly relayed the information throughout a shocked nation.

The foreign minister, Masayoshi Ohira, voiced the Japanese Government's sympathy and cooperation. Premier Hayato Ikeda and Emperor Hirohito sent messages of condolence to the White House. Foreign Minister Ohira said that a leading Japanese official, possibly Premier Ikeda, would go to the United States for the funeral of Mr. Kennedy. Many Japanese were up early today to view the first live transmission of a television program across the Pacific from the United States to Japan by way of the Relay satellite. A taped greeting from President Kennedy to the Japanese people was to have been the high point in the 20-minute program.

Shinzo Koike, minister of postal services, who was in the television receiving station for the broadcast, announced before the program that President Kennedy had been assassinated. He expressed shock and extended the condolences of the Japanese people. A brief greeting from the president was deleted from the Relay transmission. Radio and television stations immediately picked up the news. Morning newspapers, most of which had published their final editions, distributed extras speedily, with the news in large black headlines. Initial radio announcements termed the assassination of Mr. Kennedy the "saddest possible news" to the world and of such major importance that an assessment of its impact was impossible.

Mr. Kennedy was highly popular with the Japanese, who admired his youthful energy and his generally liberal political views. There were high hopes that the president, who was known to be eager to visit Japan, would come here early next year. All political elements except the extreme left had made clear that they would afford him a warm welcome. Foreign Minister Ohira met with Ministry officials to assess the impact of the president's death on Japanese foreign policies.

Tributes Cite Loss to U.S. and World

Following are comments on the assassination of President Kennedy and tributes to his leadership expressed yesterday by a wide array of political, religious, cultural, diplomatic and labor leaders:

U THANT, United Nations secretary general—"As secretary general of the United Nations I would like to express profound sorrow at this most tragic event and to be associated in the condolences to Mrs. Kennedy, to the members of the bereaved family and to the Government and people of the United States."

HERBERT HOOVER—"I am shocked and grieved to learn of President Kennedy's assassination. He loved America and has given his life for his country. I join our bereaved nation in heartfelt sympathy to Mrs. Kennedy and their two children."

HERBERT H. LEHMAN—"This is the greatest catastrophe that our nation has suffered since the assassination of President Lincoln."

MAYOR WAGNER—"President Kennedy has joined the company of the martyrs. The enormity of the loss the world has today suffered is incalculable. The world mourns; the nation mourns; the city mourns. My grief and that of all New Yorkers I know is personal and irreparable. He was my friend. He was also a friend of man, a friend of peace, a champion and sword of justice. Hate has reaped its harvest. Now we must not leave undone any of the great works he was doing, and doing so valorously, so eagerly, so brilliantly."

RICHARD M. NIXON—"The assassination of the president is a terrible tragedy for the nation. Mrs. Nixon and I have sent a personal message expressing our deepest sympathy to the members of the family in this hour of sorrow."

SENATOR BARRY M. GOLDWATER—"It is both shocking and dreadful that a thing like this could happen in a free country. The president's death is a profound loss to the nation and the free world. He and I were personal friends. It is also a great loss to me. Mrs. Goldwater and I offer our heartfelt sympathies to Mrs. Kennedy and the president's family."

SENATOR EVERETT McKINLEY DIRKSEN—"There are some things that are simply incredible, and leave one absolutely speechless. This is one of them. I knew John Fitzgerald Kennedy as a representative, as a senator and as the president, for 14 years or more. And my last visit with him was on Tuesday morning of this week. I say it's an incredible thing. And my heart goes out to the family and I'm a little bewildered by this turn of events as I know the nation and the whole wide world will be."

GEN. DOUGLAS MacARTHUR—"I realize the utter futility of words at such a time, but the world of civilization shares the poignancy of this monumental tragedy. As a former comrade in arms, his death kills something within me."

CHIEF JUSTICE EARL WARREN—"A great and good president has suffered martyrdom as a result of the hatred and bitterness that has been injected into the life of our nation by bigots, but his memory will always be an inspiration of good will everywhere. The entire world is poorer because of his passing. May God protect our nation in this hour of crisis."

GEORGE MEANY, president of the American Federation of Labor–Congress of Industrial Organizations—"No words can express our shock and grief. The president was a great man and history is certain to regard him as one of our greatest presidents. He was a warm friend of all the working people of America."

GOV. WILLIAM W. SCRANTON of Pennsylvania—"This hideous crime, with all its tragedy, leaves the heart and soul of America lifeless and in sorrow. Pennsylvanians join all Americans in prayer for our president, his wife and his family, and for our nation. All the world stands still, stunned to silence by this evil deed."

ALF M. LANDON—"I cannot say anything else in this national tragedy, except that the sympathy of the entire country goes out to the president's loved ones."

JAMES FARMER, national director of the Congress of Racial Equality—"We believe that this assassination was the result of the president's efforts to bring about a more democratic America and we hope that this nation will rededicate itself to those ideals of his."

GEORGE ROMNEY, governor of Michigan—"It is imperative that the assassin or assassins who had any influence behind them or associated with them be identified. Upon behalf of all Michigan citizens, I extend our heartfelt grief and sympathy to the president's family. Let us unite behind our new president and give him our loyal support. Our grief should renew our dedication to serve our country."

ENDICOTT PEABODY, governor of Massachusetts—"I am deeply grieved by the shocking, untimely and unbelievable death of our beloved President Kennedy at the hands of an assassin. He will live forever in the hearts and memories of people in our Massachusetts—his home state—our nation and throughout the world as a humanitarian and as a leader who gave his life for his principles and beliefs."

PAUL ZUBER, a civil rights leader—"This is just more horrible proof of the breakdown of law and order in this country."

ORVAL E. FAUBUS, governor of Arkansas—"This is a tragedy of the greatest magnitude. It is shocking beyond belief and seems incomprehensible. The president was a great American—the chosen leader of his people."

DR. ANGUS C. HULL, executive director of the Baptist City Societies of Greater New York—"Every American will be deeply shocked that this could happen to a president who so ably expressed the concern of all of us that we might be a united people across all differences of race, culture and religious faith."

GEORGE C. WALLACE, governor of Alabama—"We may disagree with people in public office because of philosophy and attitudes, but this attack upon the chief executive is an attack upon the American system and I'm sure that whoever did it had the universal malice for all people of this country."

ROSS BARNETT, governor of Mississippi—"I am profoundly shocked and deeply distressed at the cowardly act."

ROY WILKINS, executive secretary, National Association for the Advancement of Colored People—"The assassination of President Kennedy is a grim tragedy reminding us anew of the depth of hatred that some Americans are capable of harboring. The president's consistent commitment to and espousal of basic human rights for all earned the undying enmity of frantic and loathsome bigots. We have no doubt that the assassin was motivated by a hatred of the president's ideals."

WILLIAM SCHUMAN, president of the Lincoln Center for the Performing Arts—"Even while we mourn President Kennedy's loss, as Americans and as artists, we pledge ourselves anew to the realization of his vision."

ROBERT S. McNAMARA, secretary of defense—"As the leader of our nation and the free world, President Kennedy demonstrated a courage and strength of spirit that insured his place in history. By those of us privileged to work with him he will be cherished for his human warmth and the humor that never failed him."

RICHARD CARDINAL CUSHING of Boston—"My heart is broken with grief over his martyrdom for the cause of the free world. John F.

Kennedy, known to me for a lifetime, loved by me as a devoted friend, has laid down his life for all men. Greater love than this no man has."

ROBERT H. W. WELCH JR., founder of the John Birch Society, in a message to Mrs. Kennedy—"On behalf of the council of John Birch Society and our members and myself, I wish to express our deep sorrow at so untimely a loss to our nation of its youngest elected president and to convey more particularly to you and to all members of President Kennedy's family our sincere and heartfelt sympathy in your overwhelming personal loss."

JOHN N. DEMPSEY, governor of Connecticut—"I know that I speak for every citizen of Connecticut in expressing outrage at the senseless act of the assassin, grief in our great loss and the deepest sympathy for the president's family. Let us all pray to Almighty God to give [President Johnson] the strength he will need to carry on the causes to which President Kennedy gave his life."

ZENON ROSSIDES, ambassador from Cyprus—"President Kennedy's dedication to the cause of peace, justice and freedom engaged the conscience of mankind and made of him a symbol of its trust and hope for survival and human progress amid the growing dangers of self-annihilation in a nuclear age."

DR. T. F. TSIANG, ambassador from Nationalist China—"The death of President Kennedy is a great loss both to the United States and to her many friends in the world, among whom I count my own country, China. He combined practical statesmanship with idealism. His valiant fight for human freedom will, I have no doubt, be continued by freedom-loving peoples everywhere."

HORACE W. B. DONEGAN, bishop of the Protestant Episcopal Diocese of New York—"I speak for all the clergy and laity of the Diocese when I say that we are numbed with shock at the assassination of the president. He is now joined with Lincoln and McKinley in the ranks of the martyred leaders of our people. God grant him rest and give our citizens calmness and courage in the days that are immediately before us."

SAMUEL EDWARD PEEL, Liberian ambassador—"I know my own president and the people of Liberia, who had such great esteem, affection and respect for him, will be deeply grieved to hear of this tragic death."

BRITISH AMBASSADOR SIR DAVID ORMSBY GORE—"This horrible, wicked and senseless act has deprived not only the American people but the world of a great and wonderful man. Jack Kennedy was the best and most loyal friend one could ever hope to have and I feel a sense of loss beyond description."

THE REV. DR. ROSWELL P. BARNES, executive secretary of the New York Office of the World Council of Churches—"The assassination of the president is a shocking tragedy. We express our profound sympathy to his family and to all who shared his life and responsibilities in intimate comradeship. His assassination is an unmitigated shame to a nation that prides itself on its high civilization."

LABEL A. KATZ, president of B'nai B'rith—"President Kennedy's boundless devotion to the causes of world peace, civil rights for all, and social and economic advancement not only for the United States but for the whole world has earned for him a place among the greatest of our presidents."

BISHOP LLOYD C. WICKS, bishop of the Methodist Church of the New York area—"Ours is the loss of a great countryman. His life had been given in valiant defense of the nation's better self."

Huey Long's Slaying in '35 Recalled by Son, a Senator

NEW ORLEANS, Nov. 22 (AP)—Senator Russell B. Long, Democrat of Louisiana, speaking as "one who saw his father die of an assassin's bullet," said today that President Kennedy "did not die in vain. None of us is blessed with the wisdom to understand why the Almighty wanted it this way," he said in a statement, "but we should live in faith that John F. Kennedy did not die in vain."

Mr. Long's father, Huey Long, was shot to death in a corridor of the Louisiana Capitol in September, 1935. Mr. Long said today: "Americans should realize that it is Almighty God who in his infinite wisdom determines the outcome of such events rather than the unworthy person who appears to be the immediate cause."

KENNEDY BOYHOOD AND YOUTH WERE OFTEN A TALE OF SHARP RIVALRY OF 2 BROTHERS

Joseph Jr. Ruled John With Fists

Future President Offered Few Signs Then of His Interest in Politics

John Fitzgerald Kennedy grew up under the shadow of his brother Joseph. It laid a mark on his character. In later life, some persons were to see in the rivalry of the two Kennedy boys at least one reason for the success of the surviving brother. But during the years of growing up it did not seem exactly that way to John. Joseph was not only two years older than John. He was also taller, heavier, stronger. In the absence of the boys' father, young Joseph took on some of his authority. In the big family it was Joseph Jr. who laid down the law. He had a quick temper and he tended to enforce his rulings with his fists.

All through childhood and early adolescence Joseph Jr. and John fought. The outcome was inevitable—John was smaller, slimmer and less developed than his brother. But still the boys fought. Their younger brother, Robert, remembered years later how he and his sisters had cowered in an upstairs room while the two boys fought below. The rivalry was not confined to the physical. Joseph Jr. was an able, aggressive, outgoing youngster.

John Kennedy gave few signs in his youth that he might some day head for the presidency. He was born on May 29, 1917, in Brookline, a Boston suburb. His first years were spent in Brookline at 83 Beals Street, a comfortable white frame house in a pleasant upper middle-class neighborhood. In Brookline, John started his education at the Dexter School, a private school rather than a parochial institution. By 1926 Joseph Kennedy's business interests were concentrated in New York and he decided to uproot his family from the Boston milieu. John went to fourth, fifth and sixth grades in the Riverdale Country Day School. Years later he was dimly remembered by his teachers as a likable youngster, moderately studious, polite and hot-tempered. The family then moved to nearby Bronxville where Joseph Kennedy had purchased an 11-bedroom red brick house. Only one year of John's education was spent in a Catholic institution. This was Canterbury, a preparatory school at New Milford, Conn., where John went for a year at the age of 13. The next fall he shifted to Choate at Wallingford, Conn. Choate was a rather exclusive boys' school with a strong Protestant Episcopal orientation. His brother, Joseph Jr., had gone to the school two years ahead of John and was a leader.

There was nothing brilliant about John Kennedy's record at Choate. To his teachers he gave no outward sign of special ability. His grades were average. At Choate John made friends with Lemoyne Billings, a boy from Baltimore. This was one of the earliest of his school friendships that were to endure and grow as his political career began to gather headway. John Kennedy was graduated from Choate in 1935, when he was 18. He was tall, thin, wiry, good-looking and energetic. John had decided to break with family tradition and go to Princeton rather than Harvard, where his father had studied, and where Joseph Jr. was already cutting out an important career. However, John had a recurrence of jaundice in December and left Princeton. In the autumn of 1936 he entered Harvard.

His first two years at Harvard were undistinguished. He got slightly better than a C average as a freshman and about the same as a sophomore. John went out for freshman football but was too light to make the team. He suffered a back injury that was to plague him seriously later on. But football gave him another of his lifetime friends. This was Torbert H. Macdonald. The turning point in John's college career probably was a trip to Europe that he made in the summer of 1937 with Billings. John had an audience with the pope and met Cardinal Pacelli, who was to become Pope Pius XII. "He is quite a fellow," John wrote his parents. John also admired the Fascist system in Italy "as everyone seemed to like it," but took a balanced view of the civil war in Spain.

Toward the close of 1937 his father was named ambassador to the Court of St. James's by President Roosevelt. Ambassador Kennedy was in the thick of the controversy over United States policy. He took the side of the supporters of Prime Minister Neville Chamberlain, backed the Munich agreement and, in general, expressed views regarded by his critics as those of isolationism and appeasement. John Kennedy's interest in foreign affairs was further stimulated when he obtained permission from Harvard to spend the second semester of his junior year in Europe.

John's final year at Harvard was by far the best of his educational career. For the first time he demonstrated intellectual drive and vigor. He was determined to be graduated with honors and took extra work in political science toward this end. His grades improved to a B average. But his principal achievement of the year was the writing of a thesis, "Appeasement at Munich." In it, his basic point was: Most of the critics have been firing at the wrong target. The Munich Pact itself should not be the object of criticism but rather the underlying factors such as the state of British opinion and the condition of Britain's armaments which made "surrender" inevitable. "To blame one man, such as Baldwin, for the unpreparedness of British armaments is illogical and unfair, given the condition of democratic government." In June, 1940, John Kennedy was graduated cum laude in political science. His thesis had won a magna cum laude.

Coconut Shell in the White House Recalled Rescue in World War II

On John F. Kennedy's desk in the White House a scarred and battered coconut shell held a place of honor. On its rough bark was scratched this message: "Native knows posit he can pilot 11 alive need small boat kennedy." This crude memento was a souvenir of as close a brush with death as John Kennedy—or any other man—was likely to experience and live to talk about. It also marked the climax of his brief but daring and courageous military career.

Mr. Kennedy was graduated from Harvard in June, 1940, just after the so-called "phony war" had ended in Europe. With World War II more and more dominating the world's headlines and the thoughts of men, Mr. Kennedy found it impossible to settle down to civilian existence. He had talked of entering Yale Law School in the fall of 1940. But he changed his mind at the last moment and enrolled at the Stanford University business school for graduate work. He was restless, however, and left school to make a long tour of South America. By the time he got back he had but one interest—to get into the armed forces.

He undertook a rigorous course of conditioning and exercises and managed to pass a Navy physical in September, 1941. He was assigned at first to a desk in Naval intelligence in Washington, preparing a news digest for the Navy chief of staff. This was not to his liking. He invoked his father's influence and managed to get transferred to the torpedo boat training station at Melville, R.I., where a number of his friends, including his Harvard roommate, Torbert H. Macdonald, were already stationed. In March, Lieutenant (j.g.) Kennedy had command of PT-109, a boat that was part of a PT squadron based at Rendova, south of New Georgia. Not long after midnight Aug. 2, 1943, PT-109 was on patrol in Blackett Strait in the Solomon Islands, about forty miles from the Rendova base. The 26-year-old Lieutenant Kennedy was in charge, leading three other PT boats. His first officer, George Ross, a Princeton graduate, was at the wheel. Suddenly out of the murk the Japanese destroyer, *Amagiri,* bore down on them at 30 knots. It rammed the boat squarely, cutting it in two, and steamed on without loss of speed.

Two members of the PT crew were killed outright. Lieutenant Kennedy was hurled onto the deck, falling on his back. But he was not killed. Nor was his craft sunk. The after half of the PT remained afloat although the sea was covered with burning gasoline. Although his back had been injured by his fall, Lieutenant Kennedy and several of his crew members managed to aid two men who were badly hurt—Patrick H. McMahon, the engineer who was severely burned, and Harris, a fellow Bostonian who had hurt his leg. The men hoped for an early rescue but no help came. Apparently the other PT boats had assumed all men were lost.

The next night the hull capsized and Lieutenant Kennedy led his party to a small island. Most of the way he swam, breast-stroke, pulling the injured Mr. McMahon by life preserver straps that he clasped in his teeth. Lieutenant Kennedy left his exhausted mates on the atoll and swam on further to Ferguson Passage through which PT boats frequently operated. He carried with him a heavy ship's lantern for signaling. All night long he swam and drifted in the Ferguson Passage, hoping a PT boat would come along. Sometimes he dozed in the water. No PT boats appeared. In early morning he swam back to the reef where his comrades waited and sank exhausted and sick on the sand. The next night Mr. Ross swam to Ferguson Passage but had no more luck. The next day Lieutenant Kennedy moved his men to another island closer to Ferguson Passage. All were hungry and thirsty. Some were ill. On the fourth day Mr. Kennedy and Mr. Ross swam to Cross Island, even closer to Ferguson Passage. Here they made a great find—a keg of water and a box of biscuits and hard candy left behind by the Japanese. They also found a native dugout canoe. Mr. Kennedy left Mr. Ross on Cross and paddled back to his crew with food and water. On the fifth day he returned to Cross, but on the way a storm swamped the canoe. But, in imminent peril of drowning, he was sighted by a group of Solomon Islanders in a large canoe. They took him to Cross and Mr. Ross. Here they led the Americans to a larger canoe concealed on the island. Mr. Kennedy took a coconut, scratched on it the message: "Native knows posit he can pilot 11 alive need small boat kennedy." He told the natives again and again "Rendova, Rendova." They paddled away. That night he and Mr. Ross again went out to Ferguson Passage. Again their canoe was capsized and they nearly drowned. They made it back to Cross and sank on the beach in exhausted slumber. But on that morning—the sixth since the disaster—Mr. Kennedy and Mr. Ross were awakened by four natives, one of whom spoke excellent English and said: "I have a letter for you, sir." More than seventeen years later, after Lieutenant Kennedy had become President Kennedy, the man who received the message and summoned help was identified as A. R. Evans, an Australian serving in his country's Naval Reserve. Mr. Evans was now an accountant at Sydney. Within a matter of hours the PT survivors had all been rounded up and were back at their base, the worse for wear and tear, but happily alive.

The commander of the destroyer *Amagiri* Kohei Hanami, now a farmer in Japan, sent Mr. Kennedy congratulations on his election. Mr. Kennedy sent him a bronze medal commemorating the ceremony. Lieutenant Kennedy's conduct won him the Purple Heart and the Navy and Marine Corps

Medal with a citation from Adm. William F. Halsey that paid tribute to "his courage, endurance and excellent leadership in keeping with the highest traditions of the United States Naval Service." But his career with the PT boats quickly ended. He contracted malaria. His weight dropped to 125 pounds. He was suffering some pain from the aggravation of his old back injury. In December, 1943, he was sent back to the United States. Mr. Kennedy still hoped for more active duty and thought he might be sent to the Mediterranean. But he was not well and late in the spring of 1944 he entered Chelsea Naval Hospital, near Boston.

Almost a year to the day after his adventure in the South Pacific the Kennedy family was gathered at Hyannis Port when two priests appeared and asked to see Joseph P. Kennedy Sr. Joseph Jr. had been reported missing in action. Beginning in September, 1943, Joseph had flown combat duty with a Liberator bomber squadron attached to the British Coastal Command. By July, 1944, after a second tour of duty, Joseph had orders to go home when he learned about and volunteered for an experimental mission called "Project Anvil." The plan was to load a Liberator with 22,000 pounds of TNT, take it into the air with a pilot and co-pilot and then fix its flight controls on a course for the German V-2 rocket bases. The pilot and co-pilot would then parachute to safety.

On Aug. 12, 1944, Joseph Jr. and Lieut. Wilford J. Willy of Fort Worth took off in the robot plane with two control planes accompanying them. About 6:20 P.M., as the plane [neared the] coast, it blew up. The two pilots were instantly killed.

The death of Joseph Jr. at the age of 29 was but the first of a series of tragedies to strike the Kennedys. Less than four weeks later, on Sept. 10, 1944, the British War Office announced the death in action in France of Lord Hartington. He was the husband of Kathleen, oldest of the Kennedy girls and the only member of the family to marry outside the Roman Catholic Church. Kathleen and Lord Hartington were married at the Chelsea Registry Office, London, in early May, 1944. She herself became the second member of the Kennedy family to die when, in May, 1948, she was killed in the crash of a small private plane in France.

John Kennedy remained in the hospital near Boston for a disc operation on his back. Finally, thin and in far from robust health, he appeared before a Navy board and was mustered out of service. His military career was at an end. His civilian life opened ahead of him.

Death of Brother in War Thrust Kennedy Into Career of Politics

"Just as I went into politics because Joe died, if anything happened to me tomorrow, my brother Bobby would run for my seat in the Senate. And if Bobby died Teddy would take over for him." So John F. Kennedy once described his decision to enter politics.

Early in 1945, John Kennedy was working for The International News Service as a special correspondent. He covered some important events, including the Potsdam Conference and the founding conference of the United Nations in San Francisco. But he did not appear to have made up his mind about his career. By this time, however, he was seriously considering entering politics. For this decision his father, Joseph P. Kennedy Sr., has taken full credit. He told an interviewer in 1957: "I got Jack into politics. I was the one. I told him Joe was dead and that it was therefore his responsibility to run for Congress. He didn't want to do it. He felt he didn't have the ability and he still feels that way. But I told him he had to do it."

That was not the way President Kennedy remembered it. He said he had been attracted strongly to journalism, but finally concluded that "it was too passive. We all liked politics," he said, "but Joe seemed a natural to run for office. Obviously, you can't have a whole mess of Kennedys asking for votes. So when Joe was denied his chance, I wanted to run and was glad I could."

By a quirk of political fortune, James Michael Curley, long a dominant figure in Boston politics, was vacating the Congressional seat in the Eleventh District in 1946. Mr. Curley, a political enemy of both of John Kennedy's grandfathers—Patrick J. Kennedy and John F. Fitzgerald—was about to become mayor of Boston. Thus, it was in the old Eleventh District that John Kennedy first tried his political fortunes. The district included

East Boston, where John Kennedy's father was born. It included the North End, where his mother, Rose, and her father, John F. Fitzgerald, had been born. It included Cambridge, where the Kennedys had gone to Harvard. It was a great district for a young Kennedy to run in—except for one thing. John Kennedy had no roots there, or hardly any roots in Boston. He had been born and spent a few childhood years in Brookline. He had gone to college at Harvard. He had summered at Hyannis Port on Cape Cod. But he was not a genuine Bostonian. He had kept a Boston address—the Bellevue Hotel, next door to the State House, where his grandfather maintained rooms.

Regardless of any handicaps, John Kennedy got into the race with all he had. He was still yellow from the Atabrine he had taken to combat malaria picked up in war service in the South Pacific. He was only 28 years old and looked about 21. He was scrawny and he was shy about meeting people. But he had determination. He had the Kennedy name and the Kennedy money. He also had a rapidly growing group of fervent supporters, built around his family and his friends of prep school, college and Navy days.

Mr. Kennedy started campaigning early in the year for the June primary. If he was inept about treating the boys in the East Boston saloons he proved to be one of the most energetic campaigners the Eleventh District had ever seen. And his organization began to grow, turning his headquarters at 122 Bowdoin Street into a bustling political center. Mr. Kennedy ran largely on his war record. Reprints of articles about his exploits in the South Pacific were widely circulated.

On Election Day, Mr. Kennedy swamped his opponents. His political career was now fairly launched and he won the final election without difficulty in November. In January, 1947, he presented himself at the House of Representatives. He was 29 years old but so boyish in appearance that he was often mistaken for a college student. He had a shy smile, a great shock of hair and a thin but wiry frame. Mr. Kennedy served three terms in the House. His record was not spectacular but his votes usually were on the liberal side. He demonstrated flashes of independence, such as in his refusal to kowtow to Representative John W. McCormack, long-time leader of the Massachusetts Democratic delegation. He also fought the American Legion for its opposition to housing projects, declaring that the Legion "hasn't had a constructive thought since 1918."

Meantime, Mr. Kennedy was beginning to focus his eye on wider horizons. He had considered running for the Senate in 1948 against Leverett Saltonstall, but, after weighing the prospects, decided against it. His chance came in 1952 when Gov. Paul A. Dever decided not to run for the Senate against Henry Cabot Lodge. Senator Lodge was a redoubtable candidate. Once more the Kennedy family turned out in force to campaign. John Kennedy's brother, Robert, 27, was his campaign director. His sisters, Jean, Eunice and Patricia, went from door to door, poured tea and presided over coffee hours. His mother also took a leading part.

During the later part of the campaign an old back injury bothered Mr. Kennedy and he was forced to make appearances on crutches. But there was always a Kennedy to substitute for another Kennedy. The year 1952 was the year of the Eisenhower landslide. But Mr. Kennedy felt confident of victory. His confidence was well founded. He defeated Mr. Lodge by 1,211,984 votes to 1,141,217—a margin of 70,000—while the Republican presidential ticket won in Massachusetts by 208,800 votes. It was 36 years since John Kennedy's grandfather, Mr. Fitzgerald, had been defeated by Henry Cabot Lodge's grandfather of the same name, in the United States Senatorial election.

Mr. Kennedy's first years in the Senate were marked by three major events—one personal, one political and one physical. The personal event was his marriage. In 1951 he first met Jacqueline Lee Bouvier, then 21 and a student at George Washington University. She was the daughter of Mr. and Mrs. John V. Bouvier 3d, who were divorced. She was brought up in New York and Washington, attended Vassar College and the Sorbonne in Paris and was a Roman Catholic. Miss Bouvier was a striking young woman with soft, abundant hair, modulated voice and an independent, inquisitive mind. Although Mr. Kennedy was instantly attracted to the dark, slender girl, it was months before he saw much of her. They met just on the eve of his Senate campaign. Not until he returned to Washington in 1953 as a senator did the courtship begin in earnest. They were married on Sept. 12, 1953, at St. Mary's Roman Catholic Church in Newport. The Most Reverend Richard J. Cushing, then archbishop of the Archdiocese of Boston and later a cardinal, performed the ceremony.

Meanwhile, Mr. Kennedy's back was giving him new difficulty. The trouble grew worse. On Oct. 21, 1954, he entered Manhattan's Hospital for Special Surgery and underwent a double fusion of spinal discs in a long, difficult operation. The operation was not altogether successful. He was in the hospital until late December. After a brief vacation, he had another operation in mid-February, 1955. The most frequent rumor was that he suffered from Addison's disease, a serious malfunctioning of the adrenal glands. He had experienced some malfunctioning of the adrenals because of his wartime malaria. But after his critical back operations his health soon built back to the typically vigorous Kennedy level.

Against the background of these personal events a major political crisis occurred. This was once again on the subject of McCarthyism, a word given to the activities of Senator Joseph R. McCarthy of Wisconsin, a crusader against communism. Senator Kennedy had, in effect, evaded the McCarthy issue in his campaign of 1952. But now as the Wisconsin senator's activities impinged more and more on the national scene and sentiment rose in the Senate for curbing Mr. McCarthy's activities, the question of Mr. Kennedy's position came to the fore. As the issue was drawn tighter Senator Kennedy continued to steer a cautious course in correspondence with his constituents and in public speeches.

Senator Kennedy did vote against Mr. McCarthy on certain issues. He voted for confirmation of James B. Conant as ambassador to West Germany and Charles E. Bohlen as ambassador to the Soviet Union, two appointments opposed by Mr. McCarthy. But the direct issue of Senate censure of Mr. McCarthy was building up rapidly. Mr. Kennedy decided to vote for censure—but on the narrow technical ground that Mr. McCarthy had jeopardized the dignity and honor of the Senate. Senator Kennedy prepared a speech outlining his views. But he never delivered it and he was not in the Senate when the censure issue arose. When the vote on the censure was taken on Dec. 2, 1954, and Mr. McCarthy's power was checked by a 67-to-22 vote of the Senate, Mr. Kennedy was "absent by leave of the Senate because of illness." He was still recuperating from back surgery.

This was not the end of the matter, however. The question of Mr. Kennedy's attitude toward Mr. McCarthy and McCarthyism was to persist through his broadening political career. As late as 1959, the satirists of the Washington Press Club sang at a Gridiron dinner:

> *"Where [were you,] John,*
> *Where were you, John,*
> *When the Senate censored Joe?"*

Visitors to Family Were Advised to Be Ready for Football Game

The characteristics of the Kennedy clan probably were best summarized in a semi-humorous set of "Rules for Visiting the Kennedys," which were drafted by a close friend, Dave Hackett. Here is what Mr. Hackett advised:

"Prepare yourself by reading *The Congressional Record, U.S. News and World Report, Time, Newsweek, Fortune, The Nation, The Democratic Digest, The Ensign* and the manual *How to Play Sneaky Tennis*. Memorize Page 2 of *Jokes Guaranteed to Lay Them in the Aisles*. Anticipate that each Kennedy will ask you what you think of another Kennedy's (a) dress, (b) hairdo, (c) backhand, (d) latest achievement. You will find that 'Terrific!' is a satisfactory answer. They won't listen to much detail.

"It's touch football but it's murder. The only way I know of to get out of playing is not to come at all or to come with a broken leg. If you don't have a broken leg, and if you come, you will play; that is, you will if you don't want to take your supper in the kitchen, or if you don't want to talk to anyone for the rest of the week-end.

"Make a lot of noise and make out that you never had a better time in your life. Things will go smoother if you do. Don't overdo this, though. Don't make out that you're having altogether too much fun. If you do, you'll be accused of not taking the game seriously enough.

"Look glum if your team doesn't score a touchdown and become gleeful when your team does. Don't sacrifice your teammates (it's a team game). And for goodness' sake don't harp on any error of the enemy, because the enemy will be made up of Kennedys, too, and the Kennedys don't like that sort of thing."

BOOK ON "COURAGE" AND '56 CONVENTION ROLE PUT KENNEDY ON ROAD TO WHITE HOUSE

Volume Written During '55 Illness

Drive for Vice-Presidency a Year Later Failed but Brought Wide Publicity

The precise moment when John Fitzgerald Kennedy determined to run for the presidency of the United States may never be determined. Some historians feel that a campaign for the presidency was implicit in John Kennedy's decision late in 1945 to embark upon a political career. They point out that he took over, in effect, the projected ambitions of his late brother, Joseph P. Kennedy Jr., whose intention to try for the presidency had been explicit as early as his college days at Harvard. To some, the Kennedy ambition for the presidency stemmed from a frustrated drive originally possessed by Joseph P. Kennedy Sr., and transmitted by him first to his son Joe and then to his son Jack. Whatever the influence of these psychological factors may have been upon John Kennedy, it seems certain that his decision to make a bid for the highest American political honors stemmed from his own year of deep crisis, 1954 to 1955.

He spent most of that period in and out of hospital beds. He underwent surgery several times at grave risk of his life to correct his chronic and painful back injury. During almost the whole period he was away from Washington, he was out of the mainstream of political life, isolated from ordinary affairs and in a position to think deeply about himself and about questions of human and political philosophy. John Kennedy did not spend his months of illness and recuperation in idleness. He turned his mind and his interest to a task that intimately linked his personal and political interests. This was the writing of the book that he published in 1956 under the title *Profiles in Courage*.

Before he picked up the political mantle of his brother Joe, John Kennedy had been headed for a career as a writer. He had dabbled in journalism and had written many articles for periodicals. And on the eve of World War II he had turned his college political science thesis into a widely read book called *Why England Slept.* This was an analysis of the Baldwin-Chamberlain era that led England down the Munich staircase into World War II.

Then, just as the surgeons fused the injured discs of his spine, so he fused his literary and political aspirations and produced a study of notable examples of political courage in America. John Quincy Adams, Daniel Webster, Edmund Ross, George W. Norris, Sam Houston, Thomas Hart Benton, Robert A. Taft—these were some of the men whose lives Mr. Kennedy incorporated in his study. Many vehicles have launched public men onto the stage of national politics. But seldom has the instrument been a best-selling collection of historical biographies. But such was the case with John Kennedy.

Profiles in Courage lifted him into a special category—a category of statesmanship and scholarship beyond the reach of most men in politics. It served a more subtle purpose as well. For in the process of writing about the great and brave men of American politics Mr. Kennedy acquired a stature and fiber of political philosophy that he had not had before. His book won a Pulitzer Prize in biography in 1957. And this honor helped lift him, in public-opinion polls, into a leading position among presidential possibilities. There was one discordant note connected with the book. Rumors circulated that it had been ghost-written by his close friend and intimate political aide, Theodore C. Sorensen. Warnings by Senator Kennedy that he would sue for libel and slander finally halted the circulation of the rumors.

He returned to Washington on May 23, 1955, not completely recuperated from his operations. It was early 1956 before he moved into the clear as a national figure. In view of his age and the general political situation—the renomination of Adlai E. Stevenson as the Democratic presidential nominee was virtually certain—Senator Kennedy set his sights for the vice-presidential nomination. Actually, this was merely a gambit toward a possible presidential nomination four years hence. He wanted the advertising and political experience of a bid for a vice-presidential nomination. He would have liked the nomination but a brisk fight for it was almost as useful to his purposes. In the end, after numerous ups and downs and a few moments of coming close, Senator Kennedy did not make it. He took the spotlight at the Democratic convention, placing Mr. Stevenson in nomination.

Mr. Stevenson then threw the race for the vice-presidency open. There was a scramble between Senators Kennedy and Estes Kefauver of Tennessee. On the second ballot, Mr. Kennedy led 618 to 551½. But on the third ballot Mr. Kefauver swamped Mr. Kennedy. Four years of intensive political activity and organization lay ahead of Senator Kennedy before his presidential ambitions could be achieved.

Mr. Kennedy turned full time attention to presidential politics. He stumped 26 states for Mr. Stevenson in 1956. Then, in 1957, he began to build a national legislative record. He criticized the level of ambassadorial appointments of the Eisenhower Administration. He backed aid for Poland and for India. He called for the independence of Algeria. He published incisive critiques of United States foreign policy in the quarterly *Foreign Affairs*. He warned of a missile gap. In domestic policy he steered a difficult course. He compromised on features of civil rights legislation, drawing criticism from the left. He backed better budgeting and fiscal housekeeping. He fought for moderate labor reform. And he tucked away an indispensable demonstration of his live political appeal. In 1958 he ran for a second term for the United States Senate. It was a rough, tough campaign in which Mr. Kennedy first had to clear away some minor roadblocks put in his path by dissident Democrats in Massachusetts.

The biggest winning margin ever to be piled up by a candidate in Massachusetts had been achieved by Leverett Saltonstall in 1944. He won his Senate race that year with a majority of 561,668 votes. Mr. Kennedy's enthusiasts hoped that he might make as good a showing. He did—and a good deal better. His margin was 874,608, the biggest in history and the biggest margin any Senatorial candidate in the United States won by in 1958. From that time forward presidential politics seemed almost completely to preoccupy Senator Kennedy. He was constantly on the go, appearing in every part of the country. Behind him he had a small but well organized and seasoned political staff. It was built around the Kennedy family. John was running for the presidency. But it was still a clan operation.

Always there were some Kennedys traveling with him on the plane. His brother Robert was campaign manager. His principal aides were the old team—the group of close friends and associates he had gathered over the years, dating back to preparatory school days, plus a few acquired in his Washington years. The key members of his organization were Lawrence F. O'Brien, experienced in Boston political battles; P. Kenneth O'Donnell, a Harvard football star and Boston political pro; Mr. Sorensen, who had become virtually a Kennedy alter ego in the years of his Senate service; Timothy J. Reardon Jr., who had roomed with Joseph Kennedy Jr., at Harvard; Torbert H. Macdonald, by now a United States representative from Massachusetts; Francis X. Morrissey, another Boston pro, and others of this type.

A suite of offices was rented in the Esso Building in Washington, just under the brow of Capitol Hill—and the Kennedy campaign was moving fast. The first task was to obtain the nomination. Senator Kennedy chose to go after that by competing in the primaries. This pitted him in two major contests with Senator Hubert H. Humphrey of Minnesota—first in Wisconsin in February and then in West Virginia in April. Senators Kennedy and Humphrey campaigned in Wisconsin for a month, running up and down the state through bitter cold and winter snowstorms. Mr. Kennedy won the state but Mr. Humphrey put up a good showing—good enough so that the coalescing opposition to Mr. Kennedy within the Democratic party could raise questions about his vote-getting ability in the Middle West. Senator Kennedy had picked the Wisconsin primary boldly. He wanted to demonstrate two things—his ability to run well in the agricultural Middle West and his ability to overcome the "Catholic issue."

Although Mr. Kennedy had been in political life for nearly fifteen years, the issue of his religion loomed larger than ever when he entered openly upon his presidential course. For overhanging the prospects of a Roman Catholic candidate was the long memory of the religious turmoil raised by the candidacy of Alfred E. Smith, a Catholic Democrat, who ran a disastrous race against Herbert Hoover in 1928. Senator Kennedy was determined to meet the religious issue head-on. Indeed, he seemed to seek opportunities to emphasize his belief in the traditional separation of church and state and of the right of a Catholic to political equality with a non-Catholic.

With the indecisiveness of the Wisconsin primary leaving these questions somewhat unsettled, Senators Kennedy and Humphrey were rematched in the West Virginia primary. Here for the first time Mr. Kennedy fought the religious issue out from one end of the state to another. And here he encountered voters who were hard-bitten in their opposition to any candidate of the Catholic faith. There were many predictions that Mr. Kennedy might be defeated because of anti-Catholic prejudice among the voters or that he might just squeak through. But to the surprise of his own staff he won a big victory—a commanding success that drove Mr. Humphrey out of the presidential competition and was hailed by the Kennedy supporters as conclusive evidence that the omen of the Al Smith defeat in 1928 no longer overhung his campaign chances. From that time on the Kennedy bandwagon picked up overwhelming momentum.

By the time the Democratic National Convention opened in Los Angeles in July, experienced political observers were certain that Mr. Kennedy had put together a winning combination even though Senator Lyndon B. Johnson of Texas was still openly in the field against him and Mr. Stevenson still hoped for a third nomination. But the hopes of Mr. Johnson and Mr. Stevenson were dependent upon holding the line with sufficient favorite-son candidates to prevent the Kennedy nomination on the first ballot. It was a hopeless task.

The big Democratic states had begun to line up behind Senator Kennedy. Gov. David L. Lawrence of Pennsylvania, Mayor Richard J. Daley of Chicago and most of the New York State delegation swung in behind Mr. Kennedy. He won easily on the first ballot. Senator Kennedy moved swiftly to heal the breaches in the party. He asked and got Mr. Johnson's acceptance as his running mate. Mr. Stevenson introduced Mr. Kennedy for the acceptance speech. The stage was set for the final drive for the presidency.

From the moment that Vice President Richard M. Nixon was made the Republican candidate, it was apparent that he and Mr. Kennedy would wage vigorous campaigns. Each proposed to utilize all of the technological devices of the new age to present themselves to the electorate. Each scheduled heavy programs of television time. Each utilized the jet airplane to carry out dazzling schedules, which whisked him from one end of the country to another. For the first time, with the admission of Hawaii and Alaska into the Union, the candidates had 50 rather than 48 states to campaign in. The major innovation of the campaign, however, was not the jet airplane. It was the national television debate of the presidential candidates.

During the West Virginia presidential primary Mr. Kennedy and Mr. Humphrey met in a television debate and as early as the Wisconsin primary the Kennedy strategists had discussed the possibility of national television debates if the senator won the nomination. However, the initiative for the presidential campaign debates came from the national television networks, which had long been interested in trying such a procedure. After considerable consultation by the broadcasters and representatives of each candidate, a series of four debates was agreed upon. The first of the four debates, conducted on Sept. 26 in Chicago, proved, in retrospect, to be by far the most important. Indeed, when the election was over many observers felt that this encounter had been the turning point of the campaign. It was not so much a clash of issues at the first debates as a contrast of personalities.

Kennedy partisans credited this debate with clearing away two major issues that had been raised against their candidate. The first was the issue of youth, inexperience and immaturity, which the Republicans had planned to make a cornerstone of their campaign. But after the first and subsequent debates, the Republicans conceded, the issue lost most of its bite because Senator Kennedy presented himself to the national audience as an assured, mature figure with a wealth of specific information about government and policy at his finger tips. The second handicap removed by the television debates was the fact that Mr. Kennedy was less widely known than Mr. Nixon. The vice president had been on the national stage continuously for eight years. Mr. Kennedy had been campaigning vigorously for four, but there was no doubt that he still lagged behind in the public awareness. After the debates, this disadvantage was eliminated.

There was a third factor of major consequence involved in the initial television appearance. In this debate, Mr. Nixon appeared thin, tired, nervous. He looked below par physically. In contrast, Mr. Kennedy was ebullient and self-confident and radiated health and energy. The religious issue refused to be put down in the campaign. Mr. Kennedy was compelled to return to it again and again. However, the climax of these efforts occurred early in the campaign when he appeared before a group of Protestant ministers in Houston, Tex. The group was notably hostile to him and apparently convinced that a Catholic could not act with independence and freedom in the White House. Mr. Kennedy confronted his accusers in a dramatic hour-long session, which was televised nationally and rerun again and again in areas in which religious prejudices were known to be high. The high point of his presentation was a declaration that he would resign the office of the presidency if he ever thought that his religious beliefs would not permit him to make a decision in the national interest.

Mr. Kennedy relied upon virtually ceaseless physical activity. He campaigned all day long by airplane in long trips from one coast to another. Then he set up late night campaign meetings and tours that sometimes seemed to turn night into day—as in the case of a notable foray into Connecticut, which began at 12:30 A.M. and went on until nearly 4 A.M. the following day. By Nov. 8, Election Day, each candidate had traveled more thousands of miles than any of his predecessors in American political history. Each had spoken more times and to more millions of people than any candidate before. Mr. Kennedy wound up his campaign on home territory. He spent the Monday before election in a whirlwind tour of New England, culminating in a rally in his old Boston territory. He was up early in the morning to vote in Boston and then went to his home in Hyannis Port, Mass., to wait for results.

In Hyannis Port the whole Kennedy family was gathered—Mr. Kennedy's wife, awaiting the birth of their second child (the youngster, John F. Kennedy Jr., was born Nov. 25), his parents, his brother Robert and all the rest of the brothers, sisters, in-laws and children. As they waited for the returns to come in, the family, in the old tradition, played touch football on the lawn and demonstrated that not all the Kennedy energy had been exhausted in the election campaign. That is, all played football, except for the senator's wife, Jacqueline. She went for a long walk, alone, along the sandy beach. Twenty-four hours later, on the morning of Nov. 9, Mr. Nixon conceded the election to Mr. Kennedy—after one of the closest votes in recent national history.

Irish Wards of Boston Forged Kennedy's Political Weapons

President's Grandfathers Laid the Base for Family's Arrival on U.S. Scene— Joseph's Fortune Abetted Move

Not since the days of the Roosevelts has so numerous, so vigorous and so political a family as the Kennedys appeared on the national political horizon. In energy, animal spirits and physical exuberance the Kennedys displayed closer affinity to Theodore Roosevelt and his dictum of "the strenuous life" than the more commonly evoked images of the Franklin D. Roosevelt family. And, in numbers, the Kennedy family set a record, unmatched in modern White House annals. The family is a product of and has long been a principal component of one of America's greatest political forging grounds—the Irish wards of old Boston.

The head is Joseph P. Kennedy, father of the thirty-fifth president. The matriarch is his wife, Rose, beautiful, gracious and energetic in her seventh decade. The relationship of the Kennedy children, the Kennedy in-laws, the Kennedy grandchildren, the Kennedy connections to one another have little counterpart in contemporary American society. It is marked by loyalty, affection and cohesiveness so intense that an observer once remarked: "When an outsider threatens to thwart the ambitions of any one of them, the whole family forms a close-packed ring, horns lowered, like a herd of bison beset by wolves."

What is the origin of the Kennedy clan? In the present generation it has been formed by the union of two Boston Irish political families, the Kennedys and the Fitzgeralds. Before that union, there had been a minimum of love and a maximum of hard-bitten antagonism between the two families. The Kennedys were products of County Wexford. One day in 1947 John F. Kennedy, then a 30-year-old Massachusetts congressman, made a sentimental pilgrimage back to County Kilkenny. He repeated the visit this year. He went to Lismore Castle on the River Blackstone and then drove across the green countryside to the market town of New Ross on the Barrow River, where the Kennedy ancestral home had been. It was still standing—a thatch cottage with dirt floor and white-washed wall. It was from this place that Patrick Kennedy set out to venture in America soon after 1845, at the height of the dreadful potato famine.

Like thousands of other emigrants, Patrick paid his $20 for steerage passage on a Cunard ship and landed on Noddle's Island in East Boston, across a narrow arm of land from Boston Harbor. By 1850 Patrick Kennedy was working as a cooper. He married and had four children. The last of them, named Patrick J., was born in January 1862. A little later the original Patrick died. Patrick J. Kennedy began his working life as a dock roustabout and longshoreman. He was 5 feet 10 inches tall, had a sandy complexion, bright blue eyes and a handsome flowing moustache. He was quiet-spoken, industrious, ambitious. Soon Patrick J. had founded a saloon across from the East Boston shipyard. He prospered. He added a retail liquor business, then more saloons. Eventually he had a coal company, a wholesale liquor company and a bank, the Columbia Trust Company. He had moved up a long way from the roustabout days on the docks. But more important, perhaps, than any of these activities, he had gone into politics, deeply, skillfully and intensively.

By the 1880's he was a man of influence. Five times he ran for state representative—and always won. He tried for the State Senate and won. He was fire commissioner, street commissioner, election commissioner. Whatever he went after, he got. He became a member of the famous "Board of Strategy"—the inner circle of Boston Irish ward leaders who met daily in Room 8 of the Old Quincy House on Brattle Street near Scollay Square. The "Board" decided all of Boston's political business in informal caucus.

Side by side with Patrick J. Kennedy's growth in political influence, wealth and community standing another political figure was making his way forward. He was John F. Fitzgerald—known as "Honey Fitz," "Little Nap" or "The Little General." John F. Fitzgerald, third oldest in a family of nine, grew up in an eight-family tenement in Lower Hanover Street. By the time he was 16 he had lost both his parents. Soon he had a job as clerk in the Custom House under Leverett Saltonstall, grandfather of the present-day governor and senator from Massachusetts. Honey Fitz was 5 feet 2 inches tall. He was as outgoing as Patrick J. Kennedy was retiring. Mr. Fitzgerald bounced around Boston like a rubber ball. He wore a boutonnière in his coat. He was merry, ebullient, garrulous. His eyes sparkled, his sandy hair was parted down the middle and when he sang his campaign song, "Sweet Adeline," he rolled his eyes toward heaven. Honey Fitz was elected councilman, alderman and state legislator. He ran successfully twice for the United States House of Representatives and later was Boston's mayor.

Patrick J. and Honey Fitz were fellow workers in Boston politics but not much more. Patrick J. found Honey Fitz insufferable. The feeling seems to have been mutual. It was the next generation, however, that produced the merging of these two vigorous strains of Boston political stock. In 1914, Joseph P. Kennedy, Patrick J.'s eldest son, married Rose Fitzgerald, daughter of Honey Fitz. Joseph P. Kennedy began almost immediately to make money prodigiously. And his wife had babies at a fast rate—five in six years, nine in all. Seven of the children survived.

Few men in their lifetime have amassed as much wealth as Joseph P. Kennedy. His fortune by 1960 was estimated from $200,000,000 to $400,000,000. He was rated as one of the world's most wealthy men. He displayed financial shrewdness from the start. He persuaded his political father and father-in-law to get him a job as state bank examiner at $1,500 a year. He worked a few months, long enough to learn the banking situation from the inside. The next move was to become, at 25, the president of the family-owned bank, the Columbia Trust, and to put his inside knowledge to work. World War I found him associated with the late Charles M. Schwab, the self-made millionaire head of Bethlehem Steel. At war's end Mr. Kennedy plunged into Wall Street.

He started out in the amusement industry, piling up millions in various film and theater operations. He ran stock pools. He branched out into liquor and, with the repeal of Prohibition, got a firm grip on the import to the United States of scotch whiskies. He spread out into real estate. As his fortune grew, Mr. Kennedy turned the drive and perfectionism of his character toward his clan-like family, inculcating it with a fierce kind of intrafamily competitiveness and combativeness against the outside world. The slogan of the Kennedy family was, "Second Best is a Loser." To encourage independence in his family, Mr. Kennedy settled on each of the children a $1,000,000 trust fund. As Mr. Kennedy put it, he wanted each child to be able to look at him—if he wished—and tell him to go to hell, that he would follow his own way.

First of the Kennedy children was Joseph P. Jr., born in 1915. He died in a crash of his plane over Europe in World War II. John F. Kennedy was born on May 29, 1917. Four girls followed. They were: Rosemary, born in 1919; Kathleen, born in 1920, who married the marquess of Hartington in 1944, was widowed the same year and died in a plane crash in 1948; Eunice, born in 1921, wife of Sargent Shriver, a business man who became head of the Peace Corps; Patricia, born in 1924, wife of Peter Lawford, British actor. Robert F., manager of his brother's presidential campaign, was born in 1926. He now is head of a household that numbers eight children. Finally, came Jean, born in 1928, who is the wife of Stephen Smith, executive of Kennedy real estate interests in New York, and Edward (Teddy), born in 1932.

There has been endless speculation about the source of the political drives that have possessed the Kennedy family. On the surface the drive seems to have skipped from the generation of Grandfather Kennedy and Grandfather Fitzgerald to the generation of Joseph and John and Robert. But other observers are not so certain of this. Once Joseph P. Kennedy had begun to accumulate his millions, he moved more and more into the political sphere, although he never ran for elective office. He was an early backer of Franklin D. Roosevelt. He worked energetically in the campaign of 1932, and was in the thick of the early New Deal. He was named to several important offices in that period. The most important was the chairmanship of the Securities and Exchange Commission. He was its first head. His next Federal post was the chairmanship of the United States Maritime Commission. He backed President Roosevelt for a second term in 1936. Then, he was named ambassador to the Court of St. James's. About this time, and closely connected with the rising threat of World War II in Europe, Mr. Kennedy's views and those of President Roosevelt began to diverge. At the same time Washington political observers noted signs that they believed indicated that Mr. Kennedy was nourishing major political ambitions himself. However, the speculations about Mr. Kennedy's political ambitions were never to be tested. With the war already on in Europe, Mr. Roosevelt decided to run for a third term, thus ending any hopes Mr. Kennedy might have had of running himself.

KENNEDY CONCENTRATED ON DOMESTIC ISSUES AFTER SHOWDOWN OVER CUBA IN '62

Major Programs Met Frustration

Plans for Civil Rights, a Tax Cut and Health Insurance Balked by Congress

The Administration of John F. Kennedy was marked by a breathless series of major events—the abortive Bay of Pigs invasion, the Berlin Wall, riots at the University of Mississippi and other places in the battle for civil rights, and the Cuban showdown. But from the moment Premier Khrushchev announced the dismantling of the missile bases and withdrawal of the missiles from Cuba in October, 1962, a period of comparative relaxation in cold war tensions began, a tranquil time internationally that was only mildly disturbed by incidents such as the recent arrest and release of Prof. Frederick C. Barghoorn. For 13 months the nation has been living without fear of imminent war. In this period the president was able to turn his main attention to domestic issues such as civil rights and the lagging economy, issues he had made part of his program from the beginning.

Mr. Kennedy's inaugural address was only 1,355 words long—one of the shorter introductory messages of recent American presidents. "Now the trumpet summons us again," he declared, "not as a call to bear arms, though arms we need—not as a call to battle, though embattled we are—but a call to bear the burden of a long twilight struggle year in and year out, 'rejoicing in hope, patient in tribulation'—a struggle against the common enemies of man: tyranny, poverty, disease and war itself."

And in what probably became his most celebrated passage, he implored: "And so, my fellow Americans: ask not what America will do for you—ask what you can do for your country."

Polls showed that his popularity declined somewhat as a result of Administration support for militant civil rights leaders. President Kennedy himself said he expected a close race in 1964. Yet his Administration received a heartening vote of confidence in the Congressional elections of 1962. Normally, the Congressional forces of the party in power are cut sharply in the mid-term elections. But in 1962 the Democrats broke the jinx, adding four Senate seats. They lost four seats in the House but this was only a fraction of the usual off-year loss. And among the new Democrats in the House were many liberals.

The president's handling of the Cuban crisis was a major factor in the upset victory. Republicans groaned: "We were Cubanized." But not all the news was good. A jarring disappointment was the defeat of Democratic candidates for governor in four big states: New York, Pennsylvania, Ohio and Michigan. Nelson Rockefeller easily won re-election in New York; Representative William W. Scranton was elected governor in Pennsylvania; George Romney won in Michigan and James A. Rhodes won in Ohio. This lineup contained three prospects for the Republican presidential nomination: Governors Rockefeller, Scranton and Romney. So far only Governor Rockefeller has declared his candidacy.

The president's popularity, according to the Gallup poll, reached a crest in 1961, following the attempt to invade Cuba, when his approval rating was 83 per cent, and sank to 57 per cent in October of this year. Two weeks ago the poll indicated a slight rise: 59 per cent approved of the job Mr. Kennedy was doing as president. The November poll showed that the president enjoyed his greatest popularity among Roman Catholics, Negroes and Jews and with younger adults. There was strong anti-Kennedy sentiment in the South.

The president's legislative program was having an exceptionally difficult time in Congress, and the lack of results on major items reduced his popular support. He had begun the year with a sweeping and ambitious program. But at his last White House news conference, a week ago, he publicly accepted what had become a foregone conclusion: the legislative achievements of this session of Congress would be among the most meager ever.

Congress, bogged down on routine appropriation matters, had not yet taken up the civil rights bill. Other items on the president's program that were still languishing were education, mental health and health insurance for the aged under Social Security. The Administration's tax bill, promising lower taxes as a stimulus to economic recovery, passed the House Sept. 25 but stalled in the Senate Finance Committee. There was little hope that controversial issues such as civil rights and taxes would come to a final test before next summer, on the eve of the national conventions, and their impact on the presidential campaign was expected to be heavy.

The president was especially exasperated at the slashing of his foreign aid bill. At his news conference, the president described the Senate's treatment of the bill as "the worst attack on foreign aid . . . since the beginning of the Marshall Plan." On Nov. 15, the Senate passed a $3.7 billion aid bill, an amount $800 million less than the president had requested. The House was even more hostile, and cut the president's program by $1 billion. There seemed little possibility that a money bill for much more than $3 billion would emerge from conference.

Critics assailed the president, saying that more vigorous leadership was necessary to persuade Congress that the cuts would be catastrophic. President Kennedy had promised to reinvigorate the domestic economy, to "get the country moving again." Today the nation is at a peak of affluence. Yet unemployment remains above 5.5 per cent. The president worried over regions that lagged behind the rest of the nation. In April he appointed an Appalachian Regional Commission, which is now drawing up a massive program of Federal aid for a ten-state swath of chronic poverty running from the Pocono Mountains of Pennsylvania to northern Alabama.

His relations with the business community had improved considerably since the spring of 1962, when he raised hackles by forcing the steel companies to hold the price line. At that time he made a withering attack on United States Steel and other leading corporations, which had increased steel prices $6 a ton. The president called the price rise "a wholly unjustifiable and irresponsible defiance of the public interest." Privately, he called the industry leaders "sons of bitches." Big Steel backed down. Last spring, when business was good and profits at record levels, steel announced modest price increases on selected items. This time the industry drew White House praise for "restraint." What was to be his last attempt to woo business was Monday in a speech to the Florida Chamber of Commerce in Tampa. He sought support for the tax-cut by assuring business leaders he was not anti-business. He reminded businessmen that corporate profits were at an "all-time high," and denied that Democrats sought to "soak the rich."

The civil rights front became grimmer suddenly in the late months of 1962. In October, a Negro named James Meredith, grandson of a slave and a nine-year veteran of the Air Force, sought to register at the University of Mississippi. The university town of Oxford was torn by rioting. A mob, harangued by former Maj. Gen. Edwin A. Walker, who had flown from Dallas, attacked United States marshals who were guarding Mr. Meredith. Gov. Ross Barnett pleaded with the president by telephone: "Get Meredith off the campus . . . I can't protect him." "Listen, Governor," the president shouted, "we're not moving anybody anywhere until order is restored. . . . You are not discharging your responsibility, Governor. . . . There is no sense in talking any more until you do your duty. . . . There are lives in jeopardy. . . . I'm not in a position to do anything, to make any deals, to discuss anything until law and order is restored and the lives of the people are protected. Good-by." President Kennedy slammed down the phone. He ordered Federal troops into Oxford. Governor Barnett was charged with contempt. But the White House feared that the arrest of Governor Barnett might trigger violence throughout the South. So the governor was considered to have purged himself of contempt by allowing Mr. Meredith on the campus.

The victory for integration at Oxford cost one life, that of a reporter. Disorders in Birmingham followed. Birmingham had been plagued by bombings, all with racial overtones, since World War II. On Sunday morning, Sept. 15, 1963, a dynamite explosion shook the 16th Street Baptist Church in Birmingham's downtown Negro section. When the smoke cleared, rescuers found the bodies of four girls beneath a pile of debris. Their teacher had just dismissed them after a lesson on "The Love That Forgives." President Kennedy called the affair a consequence of the "public disparagement of law and order." He appeared to mean Alabama's governor, George C. Wallace, a segregationist who had tried to block integration at the University of Alabama in Tuscaloosa.

The president named a two-man committee, Kenneth C. Royall, former secretary of the Army, and Earl. H. Blaik, a former West Point football coach, to try to reconcile the white and Negro communities of Birmingham. The president had promised a broad civil rights program. But he was forced to appeal for a softening of a bill drafted by a bipartisan group of Northern liberals in the House. He felt the bill ranged so widely as to risk defeat. This action irritated civil rights groups. But the watered-down bill, as drafted by the House Judiciary Committee in late October, was still considered the broadest civil rights program ever recommended to Congress.

DEATH CAME AS KENNEDY SOUGHT TO SHAPE A NEW FOREIGN POLICY GEARED TO CHANGES IN THE WORLD OUTLOOK

The death of President Kennedy came at a time when his Administration was seeking to shape a new foreign policy to cope with far-reaching changes in the world outlook. The Soviet Union, still recoiling from the rebuff suffered in its thwarted effort to install nuclear missiles in Cuba in the fall of 1961, seemed receptive to a new accommodation with the United States. In July of this year, the United States and Britain successfully negotiated with the Soviet Union a treaty that banned nuclear testing in space, the atmosphere and under water. Amid worldwide talk of a breakthrough in East-West relations, President Kennedy in a broadcast report to the nation spoke of the great opportunities and at the same time warned against over optimism.

"This treaty is not the millennium," he said. "It will not resolve all conflicts, or cause the Communists to forgo their ambitions, or eliminate the dangers of war. It will not reduce our need for arms or allies or programs of assistance to others. But it is an important step—a step toward peace—a step toward reason—a step away from war." The treaty culminated five years of negotiations on a test ban treaty. It did not bar testing underground because of continued Soviet opposition to on-site inspection. As the president had warned, the signing of the nuclear test ban treaty also did not end serious and dangerous disputes with the Russians. Only three months later, the Western world was shocked by Soviet action in halting the movement of a United States convoy on the autobahn to West Berlin.

Moscow represented the interference as a quarrel over control technicalities and subsequently once again granted unhampered rights of passage to allied convoys. However, the incident raised serious doubts about Soviet intentions. The doubts were reinforced this month when a United States scholar, Prof. Frederick C. Barghoorn of Yale University, was arrested in Moscow on espionage charges. He was released after President Kennedy had denounced the arrest as "unwarranted and unjustified" and a wave of indignation had swept the United States.

The doubts of many Americans about the feasibility of arriving at an accommodation with the Russians had been reflected in the debate and Senate hearings that preceded the Senate ratification of the test ban treaty. There were fears that the treaty might jeopardize American security by giving the Russians some military advantage. There were misgivings that the United States might be agreeing to stop testing at a time when the Russians had research data not yet revealed to the West. There was suspicion that the Russians might somehow be able to cheat and get away with it. However, the Senate decided to go along with the president on a calculated gamble for an enduring peace that would avert the horror of nuclear war. Last Sept. 24, the Senate approved the treaty by a vote of 80 to 19.

The president took heed of warnings from military leaders and such critics as Senator Barry Goldwater, Republican of Arizona, who opposed ratification, that a euphoria might settle over the United States public attitudes toward the Communist challenge. In a speech at the University of Maine on Oct. 19, the president sought to dispel any idea "that the cold war is over, that all outstanding [issues] between the Soviets and ourselves can be quickly and satisfactorily settled." Mr. Kennedy declared that the nation had been "strengthened by both the increased power of our defenses and our increased efforts for peace." The president concluded: "In the months and years ahead we intend to build both kinds of strength, during times of détente as well as tension, during periods of conflict as well as cooperation, until the world we pass on to our children is truly safe for diversity and freedom, and the rule of law covers all."

The Kennedy Administration sought to reassure the nation of strength. In a speech before the Economic Club of New York the secretary of defense, Robert S. McNamara, said that the United States possessed a "strategic nuclear deterrent far superior to that of the Soviet Union" as well as tactical conventional arms at least the equal of that deployed by Moscow. Mr. McNamara said that the United States possessed 500 operational long-range ballistic missiles and planned by 1966 to have 1,700 operational.

In moving cautiously toward a possible détente with the Russians, the Kennedy Administration was encouraged by the troubles within the Communist bloc. The quietly simmering ideological dispute between the Soviet and Chinese Communist parties burst into the open in an aggravated form last spring. A de facto split now exists, in the opinion of Government analysts.

A host of factors brought on the Sino-Soviet quarrel. Competition for leadership of the international Communist movement, disagreements over economic policy, and differences over the means of achieving world Communism. Premier Khrushchev favored a strategy of "peaceful coexistence" that put the emphasis on ideological, economic, propaganda and diplomatic competition with the West. The Chinese Communist leader, Mao Tze-tung, advocated more violent tactics of revolutionary and subversive penetration of the non-Communist world. Mr. Khrushchev agreed with Peking's goals, but balked at the risks of nuclear war with the United States that the Chinese Communist strategy entailed. This was made clear in a public exchange of acrimonious letters between the two parties. While Mr. Khrushchev attempted to protect his position within the Communist world from Peking's attacks, he indicated a desire to relax tensions with the West.

The Kennedy Administration saw opportunities in the breakup of the formerly monolithic Soviet bloc and also in the economic difficulties that plagued the Russians and compelled them to turn to the West for help in feeding the millions behind the Iron Curtain. On Oct. 9, Mr. Kennedy approved the sale of $250 million worth of wheat to the Soviet Union. Apparently suffering from the effects of a disastrous failure in their crops, the Russians on Sept. 16 had concluded a deal with Canada to buy $500 million worth of wheat. Moscow then turned to the United States for more. The president described his action as "not inconsistent with many smaller transactions over a long period of time," and emphasized that it did not constitute a new Soviet-American trade policy. He added: "But it does represent one more hopeful sign that a more peaceful world is both possible and beneficial to us all."

Conservative critics accused the president of bailing Mr. Khrushchev out of his economic difficulties. (At the time of the president's death, the wheat deal was bogged down in bargaining over shipping rates and credits between Soviet officials and private American firms.)

In his speech at the University of Maine, the president retorted: "It is in our national self-interest to sell surplus wheat in storage to feed Russians and Eastern Europeans who are willing to divert large portions of their limited foreign exchange reserves away from the implements of war." In the same way, he hailed as an achievement of his Administration the conclusion of an agreement last spring with the Soviet Government for the establishment of a "hot line" communications link between Moscow and Washington for exchanges of messages if war threatened.

While the Administration saw glimmers of hope for a détente with the Russians, it struggled to cope with crises in other areas. In Latin America it was alarmed about the tendency of military juntas in such countries as Honduras and the Dominican Republic to take over through military coups. In Cuba the Russians were cutting back on their military forces, but the Administration still viewed Cuba as a dangerous focal point for Communist subversion of Latin America. Within the Western Alliance, serious cracks had developed. President Charles de Gaulle of France struck a blow at what had been described as the Grand Design of President Kennedy. General de Gaulle vetoed the entry of Britain into the European Common Market. Mr. Kennedy had hoped that Britain would be able to join the European organization as a first step toward the creation of a "United Europe" which would be both an economic and political union. The president had looked forward to the subsequent forging of a "concrete Atlantic partnership" between such a Europe and the United States.

General de Gaulle also rejected the Washington concept of a centrally controlled nuclear deterrent. He insisted on the creation of an independent French nuclear deterrent as part of his vision of organizing Western Europe under French leadership. France declined, as did Communist China, to sign the nuclear test ban treaty, which had been widely acclaimed elsewhere in the world.

The Kennedy Administration also found no solution for dealing with Communist China, a problem that officials conceded privately might be the principal foreign policy headache of the next decade. In Southeast Asia, Communist pressure, with the encouragement of Peking, was sustained in South Vietnam and in Laos. Despite a United States investment of about $2.5 billion in aid to the Government there and the presence of 16,500 American troops, the Communist-led Vietcong guerrillas sustained their offensive. The situation in the country, which President Kennedy regarded as possibly the key to control of other non-Communist sections of Southeast Asia, was complicated by a political crisis.

Earlier this month, the Government of President Ngo Dinh Diem was swept out by a military coup led by generals friendly to the United States. President Diem and his brother, Ngo Dinh Nhu, regarded as the real power in the Government, were assassinated. The Diem Government had incurred the wrath of the generals and the displeasure of the United States by a political repression of Buddhist elements in the country. Buddhist priests had committed suicide on the streets to dramatize what they insisted was the persecution of their movement by the Roman Catholic Diem family. They transformed themselves into human torches.

President Diem resisted the appeals of the Kennedy Administration to adopt a more lenient attitude toward the Buddhists. The position of the Administration was that the measures against the Buddhists had made the Diem Government so unpopular that a victory against the Communists would be unlikely unless there were political reforms. The disappearance of the Diem regime left many questions about the future of South Vietnam unanswered. There was no certainty that the new regime would be able to unite the country and prosecute the war against the Vietcong effectively. Communist control of South Vietnam would almost surely mean collapse of the shaky coalition regime in Laos and endanger pro-Western Thailand and the neutralist regimes in Cambodia and Burma.

In the first two years of the Kennedy Administration, the Cuban crisis of October, 1962, provided the president with his sternest test. Grave questions of foreign policy had confronted the young president from the moment he entered the White House. These included strife in the Congo, the Soviet challenge to the United Nations, the creeping Communist advance in Laos and the deadlock over a nuclear test ban. But the Cuban problem, which Mr. Kennedy had inherited, involved him in probably his worst setback just three months after his inauguration. A year and a half later it brought him to a bold and successful confrontation with the Soviet Union. The setback of April, 1961, was the failure of an invasion of Cuba by exiles seeking to overturn the regime of Premier Fidel Castro.

American prestige—and that of President Kennedy personally—was at stake, because the invading forces had been assembled and trained by the

Central Intelligence Agency. In the protracted post-mortem of the abortive landing, the president was criticized for having vetoed the use of American air cover for the invaders. The president accepted responsibility and made plain that he had learned a lesson.

Although he did not say so himself, defenders of the fledgling Administration pointed out that Cuban-American relations had begun to deteriorate before Mr. Kennedy was elected or even nominated; and that just before his inauguration, the Eisenhower regime had severed relations with Havana and closed down all diplomatic and consular agencies in retaliation for Premier Castro's increasingly violent anti-Americanism. Moreover, the involvement of the C.I.A. in the situation and the basic planning of the assault on the Playa Giron, a beach on Cuba's south coast fronting the Bay of Pigs, had begun under President Eisenhower. But none of this was generally known during the first two months of the incoming Administration. It was not until April 8—12 days before the debacle—that the White House, smarting under Premier Castro's words and actions against United States interests, issued a sweeping indictment of the rulers of Cuba. It charged that the premier—whose ouster of Fulgencio Batista in 1959 had been widely hailed in this country—had betrayed the hopes of the revolution that he had led and was binding the country closer and closer to Communism. For a long time, Premier Castro had denied that he was a Communist. On Dec. 2, 1960, however, he had proclaimed in a five-hour speech that he was a "Marxist-Leninist" and would be "till the day I die."

The successful defense against the invaders, and the capture of about 1,500 of them, was a great triumph for Premier Castro. But in the next round of the critical relations between his country and the United States, the bearded Cuban did not fare so well. For in October, 1962, the issue was not Premier Castro versus the United States but the United States versus the Soviet Union over the question of Soviet offensive missiles in Cuba. In its resolution, Dr. Castro was reduced to a figure of relatively little consequence. President Kennedy set the terms. Premier Khrushchev chose to meet them. The missiles were dismantled, loaded and shipped back to the Soviet Union. Premier Castro kept insisting that he would never allow on-site inspection, to verify that the missiles and between 30 and 40 Ilyushin-28 bombers had been removed. But although he had been essential to the build-up of a tense drama of the cold war, Dr. Castro was barely on stage for its conclusion. He had been shrewdly and deliberately by-passed by President Kennedy, and in the solution of the crisis his prestige suffered a serious if not fatal blow.

Mr. Kennedy's command decision on Cuba, when reconnaissance flights confirmed beyond doubt that Soviet missiles had been assembled and placed at launching sites on the island, was to blockade the island. He announced this on Monday, Oct. 22, in a speech to a nation that had sensed that a showdown was coming but that had been kept in almost unbearable doubt over the weekend. Rumors were widespread that what was imminent was a full-scale invasion by American battle forces. But when the president faced the microphones and television cameras and his countrymen tuned in their sets, he announced not assault or bombardment but "quarantine"—his word for a naval blockade.

And in perhaps the gravest lines of his speech, he said: "It shall be the policy of this nation to regard any nuclear missile launched from Cuba against any nation in the Western Hemisphere as an attack by the Soviet Union on the United States requiring a full retaliatory response upon the Soviet Union."

It was not until five weeks later that the Pentagon gave details indicating the deadly preparation that had been undertaken with a view to imple-menting the president's words. The Department of Defense disclosed that Air Force missile crews—the men who tend, aim and would fire the 6,300-mile-range Atlases and Titans—had been put on a "maximum" alert during the crisis. And the ICBM readiness was part of an air, sea and ground mobilization that brought to combat posture more than 300,000 men, in-cluding Army and Marine invasion forces. The Naval blockade was lifted on Nov. 20. Announcing this, the president said the Soviet Union had gone a "long way toward reducing the dangers which faced this hemisphere." The last Soviet step, after the dismantling and shipment of 42 missiles, was a promise to withdraw the IL-28 bombers. This message followed ten days of negotiation on the issue of the planes.

In the earlier and more acute phase of the crisis, the president and Mr. Khrushchev had exchanged ten letters—five each way—in seven days. It was the last letter from the Soviet leader that said work on the Cuban bases had stopped and that the missiles had been crated and returned to where they had originated. In return, the premier said he placed faith in the president's assurance that there would be no attack on Cuba, no invasion. This in effect ended the crisis. In an apparent effort to soothe the vanity of Premier Castro, Mr. Khrushchev sent his chief trouble-shooter, Anastas I. Mikoyan, a Soviet first deputy premier, to Havana. The visit lasted 24 days. Mr. Mikoyan then flew to New York and Washington, where negotiations on the final stages of the question continued at the United Nations and in Washington.

The Cuban crisis cost the life of one American flier in action. He was Maj. Rudolf Anderson Jr., whose U-2 was apparently shot down during a reconnaissance flight.

When Mr. Kennedy became president on Jan. 20, 1961, conditions had seemed favorable for progress in the field of international affairs. The president sought to introduce a new momentum and a new atmosphere in the conduct of foreign policy. On his side, Premier Khrushchev seemed eager for a meeting with his opposite number. First, however, Mr. Kennedy wanted to familiarize himself with the many facets of the global conflicts. He proposed, in effect, a recess; possibly with discussions with the Soviet Union at the end of the summer or by early autumn of his first year in office. The lull, he thought, would give him time to get his Administration under way, to prepare for negotiations of substance with the Soviet leader, and to reconnoiter the ground of the immediate past so that he might avoid the pitfalls uncovered by President Eisenhower's talks with Mr. Khrushchev in 1955 and 1959.

President Kennedy's first official act in the sphere of United States–Soviet relations was to reply to the congratulations he received from Premier Khrushchev. "We are ready and anxious," he told the Soviet premier, "to cooperate with all who are prepared to join in genuine dedication to the assurance of a peaceful and more fruitful life for all mankind."

With that as the keynote, there quickly followed a meeting in Moscow between Premier Khrushchev and United States Ambassador Llewelyn E. Thompson Jr. Then came the announcement at Mr. Kennedy's first news conference, four days after he took office, that the Soviet Union had released Capt. John A. McKone and Capt. Freeman B. Olmstead, survivors of an American RB-47 reconnaissance plane that had been shot down by the Russians on July 1, 1960. Two months later Igor Y. Melekh, a Soviet diplomat who had been held as a spy, was freed to advance "the national and foreign policy interests of the United States." On both sides it appeared that new approaches were under way to break rigid, long-deadlocked positions.

United States policy toward the rising nations of Asia and Africa also was modified. Neutralists were wooed instead of reviled, and anti-colonialism was sharpened. But the old problems did not disappear. Communist forces continued to advance in Laos and President Kennedy had to choose between the massive military intervention asked by some of his military advisers and the warnings against such action by the nation's allies, particularly France and Britain.

The president expanded the United States air and naval forces in Southeast Asia, but at the same time he resolved to try to end the Laotian crisis by negotiation and diplomacy. Amid charges and countercharges of aggression and intervention by the two great centers of power, agreement was finally reached among the major factions that Laos would be provisionally governed by a coalition representing the established government of Boun Oum; the neutralist Prince Souvanna Phouma, and the Communist-directed Pathet Lao forces. It was an uneasy truce at best.

JOHNSON, KNOWN AS AN ADEPT LEADER, SERVED KENNEDY AS ADVISER AND POLITICAL AIDE

Texan Was Active as Vice President

He Worked Way Through College and Once Taught Debating in High School

President Lyndon Baines Johnson has long been known as a master tactician, a political leader whose specialty is getting things done. Determined, persuasive, with an intuitive sense of legislative bodies and the individuals in them, he knows the ways of the cloakrooms and corridors on Capitol Hill. Intense, sometimes even mesmeric, he is adept in the personal approach and skilled in the art of give and take.

A Democratic senator once said of him: "The secret is, Lyndon gives and takes. If you go along with him, he gives you a little here and there—a dam, or support for a bill you're specially interested in. Lyndon never forgets."

Former Vice President Richard M. Nixon once described him as "one of the ablest political craftsmen of our time." It is perhaps a measure of his talents that in 1957, as majority leader of the Senate, he piloted through the Senate the first civil rights bill in more than 80 years. Three years later, he overcame a Southern filibuster and had another such measure passed. Meanwhile, he had promoted a change in Senate rules that made it easier to cut off debate.

The new president is 55 years old and the embodiment of a lanky Texan. He weighs 200 pounds and is 6 feet 3 inches tall. He leans to affability, to back-slapping and shoulder-hugging, but on occasion he can be irascible. He is an indefatigable worker. When Senate majority leader, he worked an 18-hour day. He suffered a severe heart attack in the summer of 1955, but within a day or two he was surrounded in his hospital room with telephones and mimeograph machines. His working day still has been running to 16 hours or more.

He has been accustomed to awakening at 7 A.M. to the buzzing of his wrist watch alarm—he is fond of all kinds of gadgets—and between shaving and breakfast turning through the *Congressional Record* and several daily newspapers. He usually breakfasted heartily and arrived at his office about 9. His office day rarely has ended before 6:30 P.M., and evening engagements followed. The new president's Texan background is sometimes reflected in his dress. Although he usually appears in conservative attire, he is given to 10-gallon hats and vivid shirts. An ebullient kind of vanity is a Johnson characteristic. His initials, LBJ, adorn his possessions— from cuff links to his cattle ranch near Johnson City, Tex.

In conversation, his speech is homespun. Discussing the plight of a political leader in difficulty, he is likely to phrase the circumstances: "The point of the knife is right at his belly." Or, in another connection: "My daddy used to tell me that the time to kill a snake is when you've got your hoe in your hands."

Although well-to-do—as is his wife—the president is not wealthy by Texas standards. He was not born to wealth, and while working his way through college had to leave for a time because of money needs.

As vice president, Mr. Johnson was one of the most active and influential men to hold the office in modern times. As an adviser to President Kennedy's Cabinet, as a presidential envoy abroad, as a political lieutenant at home, he developed a relationship with President Kennedy that became close and cordial after an uncertain beginning. Probably half a dozen members of the Cabinet and the White House staff were more influential than Mr. Johnson in the Kennedy Administration, and probably several other men were personally and politically closer to the president. Nevertheless, as vice president Mr. Johnson had easy and frequent access to the president. He saw him several times a week when the two were in Washington, and there were frequent telephone contacts. Through these contacts, and through his collateral duties in the National Security Council, the National Aeronautics and Space Council, the Advisory Committee to the Peace Corps and the President's Committee on Equal Employment Opportunity, Mr. Johnson kept in close touch with what was going on in the Administration. He was said to have had a haunting memory of how President Truman moved into the White House, after the death of Franklin D. Roosevelt, and learned only then that the United States possessed an atomic bomb. For that reason, Mr. Johnson took a particular interest in the National Security Council. By law, he was required to sit on the council. By choice, he regarded his seat as an opportunity to keep in touch with the most vital decisions.

He rarely talked about his office as vice president. When he did, he laid great stress upon his constitutional duties as the presiding officer of the Senate. He rarely mentioned his work in the space program or race problems in industry. This was generally interpreted as evidence that the vice president wanted to avoid seeming to compete with the president for headlines and political power, and to avoid offending sensitive senators with any suggestion that he was trying to "run the Senate." As presiding officer of the Senate, where he had been Democratic leader during much of his 12-year tenure, he rarely sat through the speeches and debates. At most sessions he would begin the day's proceedings, then turn over the gavel to a junior member of the Democratic majority. Once in a great while, especially in his early days as vice president, he would lapse into old ways as majority leader. Growing impatient at some parliamentary interruption, he would ask: "Can't we get this vote out of the way?"

Usually, however, he avoided dabbling in the business of the Senate. Most of his time was spent in the duties given him by the president. Early in the Kennedy Administration, Mr. Johnson was given large responsibility for the space program, as chairman of the National Aeronautics and Space Council, and for race relations in industry, as chairman of the Committee on Equal Employment Opportunity. The Space Council oversees the operations of the National Aeronautics and Space Administration, but the vice president's hand upon the administration was a light one. Rather than acting as a policy-maker, he co-ordinated policies and arbitrated disputes. He did, however, urge that the administrator of the agency be a layman, rather than a scientist, and a layman, James E. Webb, got the job. A former aide of Mr. Johnson's in the Senate, O. B. Lloyd, became a public relations man for the agency. Otherwise, the vice president's influence was scarcely visible.

As chairman of the Committee on Equal Employment Opportunity, he lunched privately with board chairmen and senior executives of the large corporations, talking with businessmen about race relations. He spoke softly but he carried a big stick—power over Government contracts. Under his persuasion, nearly 50 major companies were brought to agreement on rejecting racial barriers in personnel practices. As a political lieutenant of the president, Mr. Johnson was a frequent speaker at political dinners. His talks, as a rule, pressed for Administration policies and defended the president from his critics. On his last appearance in New York City, on Oct. 16, Mr. Johnson was on a typical political mission. As the guest of the Liberal party, he spent a major part of his day shaking hands with voters in the garment district, where the Liberal vote is strong. Then, at a dinner for 2,000 Liberals in the Americana Hotel, Mr. Johnson called upon the party to strengthen its alliance with the Kennedy Administration. He defended the nuclear test ban treaty, argued for a tax cut and demanded "equal rights for all American citizens." A few days later, Mr. Johnson was off to Europe in another of his roles—as the president's personal envoy to foreign chiefs of state. It was only on Nov. 10 that he returned from this last mission, a visit to Belgium, the Netherlands and Luxembourg.

His part in foreign affairs began before the Kennedy Administration was three months old. On April 3, 1961, Mr. Johnson represented Mr. Kennedy at a celebration in Dakar, marking the first anniversary of the new Republic of Senegal. Senegalese crowds found the vice president's mastery of the warm handshake and the friendly smile both a novelty and a pleasant experience. There were risks at home for a Texas politician, for dozens of newspaper photographs showed the vice president with Africans. But Mr. Johnson ignored the political hazards.

In August that year, the vice president took one of his more celebrated trips abroad. The Communists had just built the Berlin Wall, and Mr. Kennedy dispatched Mr. Johnson for a weekend visit to Berlin as a symbol of American determination to resist Communist pressure. Reporting later on his visit, Mr. Johnson said: "No person can see what we saw without deeply feeling the great responsibilities that America has to the people of West Berlin, and to humanity. They look to us for encouragement, for hope, and for leadership—and together we are going to march shoulder to shoulder to the end that freedom is preserved in the world."

Among his trips this year was a visit to Scandinavia in September. His tour of Sweden, Norway, Denmark, Finland and Iceland, countries that had never before received an American official of his rank, was intended to reassure them of United States interest in their welfare. Mr. Johnson also represented the United States at the Jamaican independence celebration in 1962, and in the same year made a swing through the Middle East and the Mediterranean area. He also represented the United States at the funeral, in Stockholm, for Dag Hammarskjold, former secretary general of the United Nations.

In Washington, Mr. Johnson occupied a six-room suite in the Executive Building, next door to the White House. No vice president, including Richard M. Nixon, had ever occupied quarters physically so close to the president. Mr. Johnson also occupied the vice president's ceremonial chamber in the Capitol, and the sumptuous suite usually assigned to the majority leader. Senator Mike Mansfield of Montana, who succeeded him as Democratic leader, preferred smaller quarters. In addition, Mr. Johnson maintained an office in the Senate Office Building. It was the same suite he had occupied in his days as a senator from Texas.

In this multiple role, Mr. Johnson was considered by many political observers to be more active and influential than Vice President Nixon had been during the Administration of President Eisenhower. It was said that one had to look back to former Vice President John Nance Garner, in the days before he broke with President Roosevelt, to find a vice president who was on such close terms with the president. This relationship was one that began in keen rivalry. In the days before the Democratic National Convention of 1960, Mr. Johnson eagerly sought the presidential nomination, and spurned any talk of a vice presidential nomination.

At the convention, he fought hard against Mr. Kennedy's forces. At that time he was asked what he thought of becoming vice president; his answer was a short, unprintable word. Four days later he accepted the nomination for the vice presidency. It is not recorded whether Mr. Johnson changed his view of the vice president's job after he assumed it. His own record in the post, however, indicates that he found in it more of an opportunity and more of a challenge than he had expected.

Lyndon Johnson was born in a farmhouse in Stonewall, Tex., on Aug. 27, 1908. He comes from a political family. His grandfather and father, both named Sam Johnson, served in the Texas Legislature. According to an old story, his grandfather, on the day the boy was born, declared: "He'll be a United States senator some day." The president's father was a colleague in the Texas Legislature of Sam Rayburn, later to become the long-time speaker of the House of Representatives. Mr. Rayburn was for years one of Lyndon Johnson's best friends and his mentor in Washington. At the age of nine, when most boys his age were hunting squirrels in the valley of the Pedernales River, Lyndon Johnson was shining shoes in the single barber shop of Johnson City. He finished high school at 15 and went to work on a road-building gang. He worked his way to California doing odd jobs as an elevator operator, a car washer and a handyman in a cafe. Returning home, he went back to his road-building job. But by this time, as he said later, "it became increasingly apparent to me that there was something to this idea of higher education."

He hitchhiked to San Marcos, Tex., and entered Southwest State Teachers College. He got a part-time job as janitor at the college, sold hosiery door-to-door and worked as secretary to the college president. Nevertheless, money ran short and he had to drop out of college for almost a year. During this time he taught school in a small South Texas town. When he was 22, just three and one-half years after he had arrived at the college,

Lyndon Johnson received his Bachelor of Science degree. For two years he taught public speaking and debating in a Houston high school. In 1931 he entered politics as secretary to Representative Richard M. Kleberg of Texas. It was in this period that he met his wife-to-be, Claudia Alta (nicknamed Lady Bird by a Negro nurse) Taylor, daughter of a wealthy Marshall, Tex., rancher. He married her after a whirlwind six-week courtship and took her back to Washington.

In the capital, Lyndon Johnson came to the attention of President Roosevelt, who, in 1935, appointed him Texas state administrator of the National Youth Administration. He served two years, then resigned to run for the Congressional seat made vacant by the death of James P. Buchanan of Brenham. He defeated nine other candidates to win the race. In 1938 he was elected to a full term.

With the outbreak of World War II, Lyndon Johnson, as a member of the Naval Reserve, became the first member of Congress to enter active duty. He won the Silver Star for gallantry in action on a flight over enemy positions in New Guinea. After a year in service—he held the rank of lieutenant commander—he returned to the House when President Roosevelt ordered all members of Congress in the armed forces to return to their offices. After five successive terms in the House, Mr. Johnson was elected to the Senate in 1948, defeating the conservative Texas governor, Coke Stevenson, by 87 votes. In 1954, he was re-elected to the Senate by an overwhelming majority. Shortly after his arrival in the Senate, he became, with the backing of the powerful Southern leader Richard B. Russell of Georgia, the Democratic whip, or assistant leader.

In 1952 the Democratic leader, Senator Ernest McFarland of Arizona, was defeated for re-election, and Mr. Johnson took over the post. Then 44 years old, he was the youngest Senate leader in history. Mr. Johnson's name was entered as the Texas favorite-son candidate for the presidential nomination at the Democratic National Convention in 1956. In 1960, although Mr. Johnson was Mr. Kennedy's strongest opponent for the Democratic presidential nomination, he lost to the Massachusetts senator on the convention's first ballot, 806 votes to 409. After teaming up with Mr. Kennedy on the Democratic ticket, he campaigned vigorously and was an important factor in the narrow victory over the Republican slate, Mr. Nixon and Henry Cabot Lodge. At a recent press conference, Mr. Kennedy denied emphatically rumors that Mr. Johnson might not be on the Democratic ticket in 1964.

It has been Mrs. Johnson who has looked after the family's financial interests in all the years since they were married, on Nov. 17, 1934. Mrs. Johnson's father was a businessman and landowner as well as rancher; her mother, who died when she was 5 years old, also left her a substantial inheritance. Mrs. Johnson invested some of her money in an Austin radio station, which she bought at a comparatively modest price in 1942. From that base, she has built up a group of radio and television stations which are considered to be prosperous properties.

When not in Washington, Mr. and Mrs. Johnson live at their Texas ranch. They have two daughters, Lynda Bird and Lucy Baines Johnson. Mr. Johnson is a member of the Christian Church. His wife and daughters, however, are Episcopalians, and he usually attends the National Cathedral or All Saints Episcopal Church with them in Washington.

New First Lady Has Many Roles

She Is a Leading Hostess and a Businesswoman

Special to The New York Times

WASHINGTON, Nov. 22—Mrs. Lyndon B. Johnson is the most politically minded woman to enter the White House as first lady since Mrs. Franklin D. Roosevelt. As one of Washington's most active hostesses, Mrs. Johnson carried out her role as the wife of the vice president with a zest that few of her predecessors had shown. She toured the slums of Athens. She stood in a Peace Corps chow line in Puerto Rico. She visited depressed area projects in West Virginia. She guided an illiterate camel driver from Pakistan around Washington and treated him like a visiting monarch.

Her own view of being the wife of a public official was summed up a few months ago when she said: "For 25 or 26 years I've been on the other end asking people, mostly voters, to do things for Lyndon and the party. Now, I feel I have an obligation to them."

As frankly political as her husband, she stumped the country in 1960 seeking votes for the Democratic team of Kennedy and Johnson. "I like to go campaigning with Lyndon whenever I can," she said recently. "I find it interesting and exhilarating. I think people can assess a man a little in relation to what kind of a wife and family he has." To prepare for the 1960 campaign, she took speaking lessons to overcome her fear of audiences. It was a fear so deep-seated that when she was offered the valedictorian medal on graduating from the University of Texas in 1933, she turned it down because she would have had to make a speech of acceptance. Though shy in those days, she quickly displayed a flair for business. She ran a $67,000 family inheritance into a fortune in companies, lands and investments worth more than $1 million—without the help of her husband. She meets a weekly payroll for her radio-television station KTBC in Austin, Tex., keeps the family's tax records, and handles stacks of mail, both personal and official. She also manages two homes—the stone and frame house on the 400-acre LBJ ranch near Johnson City, Tex., and the 12-room Washington mansion, The Elms, which once was the home of Mrs. Perle Mesta. She hunts deer, takes motion pictures, studies Spanish, rolls bandages with the Senate Red Cross Wives and maintains a back-breaking schedule of social events and benefit performances. Though busier than most Washington wives, she has attempted to make their home "off limits" to problems that might upset her husband. President Johnson had a heart attack in the mid-1950's. That is seldom mentioned around the Johnson home.

Claudia Alta Taylor—Lady Bird even in her husband's official biography—was born 50 years ago in Karnack, Tex. She will be 51 years old on Dec. 22. She acquired her nickname as a baby, when the family cook declared that she was as "purty as a ladybird." It stuck, despite repeated efforts to cast it off. The name became even more of a permanent fixture after her marriage to Lyndon B. Johnson in 1934, for the initials fitted perfectly into what is now a Johnson trademark: L.B.J. The ranch bears those initials. So do the two Johnson daughters, Lynda Bird, 19, a student at the University of Texas, and Lucy Baines, 16, who lives with her parents and attends school in Washington.

Lynda Bird's engagement was recently announced to Ensign Bernard Rosenbach of Comfort, Tex., but no wedding date has been set. Mrs. Johnson has tried to avoid having her daughters think "they are important" because their father is a public figure. In fact, Mrs. Johnson once said, the two girls claimed they were "deprivileged children" because they so seldom saw their father.

Johnson's Choice in '60 a Surprise

Texan Was Picked Despite Attacks on Kennedy

By RUSSELL BAKER

Special to The New York Times

WASHINGTON, Nov. 22—When President Franklin D. Roosevelt died in Georgia 18 years ago, Lyndon B. Johnson was a rising but uncelebrated representative from Texas. That afternoon, with the shock still reverberating through Washington, a newspaperman found him in a gloomy Capitol corridor with tears in his eyes. "There are plenty of us left here to try to block and run interference," he said, "but the man who carried the ball is gone—gone."

Of Mr. Roosevelt, who had taught him politics, he said: "He was just like a daddy to me always." The episode illuminates the emotionalism and irony of this complicated politician who entered public life a New Deal liberal, found his ambition for the presidency blocked by men who thought him too conservative and accepted the anonymity of the vice-presidency against the counsel of his friends and advisers.

In most respects, he was the political antithesis of John F. Kennedy. In the 1950's, when they were both in the Senate, the contrasts were striking. Where Mr. Kennedy was cool, immaculate, intellectual and seldom seen, Lyndon Johnson was flamboyant, rumpled, emotional and constantly moving, both on and off stage. As Mr. Kennedy developed his presidential campaign, he turned his back on the Senate and took to the stump. His strategy was based on the assumption—sound, as it proved—that nominations are won out in the states in the battle for popular backing and delegates.

The Johnson strategy was tied to the Senate floor. With his Southern accent, the animosity of the labor-liberal group, and his lack of a well-known public image, he sought to establish himself as a Westerner and as the Democrat who "got things done," the leader who made a record for the party while other candidates talked. It proved hopeless. Indeed, it must have always seemed so to Mr. Johnson, for though he made a few trips into the country in a futile search for non-Southern delegates, he insisted vehemently until the Democratic convention met in Los Angeles that he was not a candidate for the nomination.

Although Mr. Johnson arrived at the convention with the Kennedy nomination a virtual certainty, he nevertheless attacked with a ferocity that startled his admirers and seemed likely to create a permanent chasm between himself and Mr. Kennedy. In a televised confrontation with Mr. Kennedy, he tried to laugh off the Kennedy candidacy as the presumption of a young upstart and broadly suggested that Mr. Kennedy's father had been soft on Nazism in World War II. Mr. Kennedy turned his cheek, destroyed the attack with a few characteristic lines of understated wit, and went down to the arena to accept the nomination.

The history of the vice-presidential nomination that followed is still garbled. It came as a shock to Mr. Johnson's family, his advisers, his staff, his Senate colleagues, everyone who had assumed that he had alienated himself permanently from the Kennedys.

When Mr. Kennedy first proposed it, the Johnson camp seemed to receive the offer as an insult. The late Sam Rayburn, then speaker of the House, and Mr. Johnson's closest friend and confidant, advised against accepting. His family was opposed. Most of his staff and most political veterans of the scene assumed that the man who ran the Senate would scarcely surrender his position of power for the anonymity of the vice-presidency. The next day when his decision was announced, the secretaries in his convention headquarters wept. There are many theories about his reasons for stepping into what most observers at Los Angeles considered oblivion. One is that he reasoned that his position as Senate leader would inevitably dwindle under a Democratic president. Another holds that he yielded to party loyalty under Mr. Kennedy's arguments that without him the Democrats could not hold the South and, therefore, could not win. In any case, the personal relationship that developed between the two during the campaign and after was closer than any other between president and vice president in modern times.

Mr. Johnson, often uncomfortable and obviously at loose ends in the vice-presidential power vacuum, applied himself with characteristic vigor to the labor of the secondary position. Shortly after taking office and having an intimate interior view of the presidency, he told an interviewer: "The president carries heavier burdens than I ever envisioned. You feel little goose pimples coming up on your back because it's such a frightening, terrifying responsibility."

Now, finally, after so much history, it is Lyndon Johnson who has to carry that ball that passed from Franklin Roosevelt to Harry Truman and from Dwight Eisenhower to John Kennedy.

Constitution Vague on President's Successor

Lyndon B. Johnson inherited the immense powers of the presidency because of 83 words in the 173-year-old United States Constitution. Article II, Section 1, Clause 5, provides for presidential succession as follows: "In case of the removal of the President from office, or of his death, resignation, or inability to discharge the powers and duties of the said office, the same shall devolve on the Vice President, and the Congress may by law provide for the case of removal, death, resignation or inability, both of the President and Vice President, declaring what officer shall then act as President, and such officer shall act accordingly, until the disability be removed, or a President shall be elected."

Contrary to popular notion, the Constitution does not specifically state that the vice president shall become president in the event of the president's death. It says that the "powers and duties" of the office "shall devolve on the Vice President." But while constitutional lawyers have debated the issue, the succession of the vice president to the presidency has been established by what scholars call "constitutional custom."

John Tyler established the precedent when William Henry Harrison died in 1841. The principle laid down by him, of assuming the title as well as the powers and duties of the president, was followed by six other vice presidents. Mr. Johnson is the seventh. If President Johnson should die, the speaker of the House of Representatives, John W. McCormack of Massachusetts, would succeed him, under a law adopted by Congress in 1947. Next in line is the president pro tem of the Senate, Senator Carl Hayden, Democrat of Arizona. Senator Hayden is now entitled to the vice president's $35,000-a-year salary. The title of vice president is vacant. Next on the list is the secretary of state, Dean Rusk, and other members of the president's Cabinet. Prior to the change in the law in 1947, the secretary of state was next in line after the vice president. The law was changed to place elected officials, who theoretically are more responsive to the will of the people, ahead of appointive officials, like the secretary of state.

Following Dean Rusk, these officials, in this order, would be in line to succeed Mr. Johnson: Secretary of the Treasury Douglas Dillon, Defense Secretary Robert S. McNamara, Attorney General Robert F. Kennedy, Postmaster General John A. Gronouski, Interior Secretary Stewart L. Udall, Agriculture Secretary Orville L. Freeman, Commerce Secretary Luther H. Hodges, Labor Secretary W. Willard Wirtz, and Secretary of Health, Education and Welfare Anthony J. Celebrezze.

Arts Encouraged by the Kennedys

Frost's Poem at Inaugural Showed Family's Intent

By MILTON ESTEROW

From the moment of the inauguration ceremony when the late Robert Frost read a poem, President Kennedy made clear his interest in the arts. With Mrs. Kennedy, he established an image of artistic patronage. Not since Thomas Jefferson had there been such an interest in culture in the White House. For the first time in history, the White House had a special consultant on the arts, August Heckscher. By executive order, Mr. Kennedy created the country's first President's Advisory Council on the Arts.

The flow of guests from the arts to the White House was significant. The guests included Metropolitan Opera stars, a troupe of Shakespearean actors and the cellist Pablo Casals, all of whom performed in the East Room at state dinners. The list of private guests included Gian Carlo Menotti, Leonard Bernstein, Igor Stravinsky, George Balanchine, Elia Kazan and Ralph Richardson.

Mr. Heckscher said yesterday, "He cared about the life of the mind; he cared for excellence in all fields. And so he was led to care for the arts, which he felt to be bound up with the well-being and the vitality of the nation. The precedents he set, the initiative he made in bringing the arts and government into a better relationship, will be remembered as part of the brightness of his tragically curtailed Administration."

The president and his wife attended the opening performances of both the Opera Society and the National Symphony Orchestra. Mr. Kennedy took a public stand in favor of the National Cultural Center to be built in Washington. He also went out of his way to commend various groups for their artistic achievements. He wrote to Jack Landau, who staged a command performance of Shakespearean scenes at the White House in 1961, congratulating him on "a very exciting performance" and expressing his and Mrs. Kennedy's pride in "our American theater."

With the nation in a period of attention to its cultural life, Mr. Kennedy appointed Mr. Heckscher to his post in March, 1962. Mr. Heckscher acted as liaison between the White House and governmental and private agencies. He surveyed the relationship between the Government and the arts in general. Mr. Heckscher resigned last June. He had served more than twice as long as the six months to which he had agreed. He stayed on at the president's request until a successor could be named. Mr. Kennedy had been expected to appoint Richard N. Goodwin, a former White House aide, next month. At the same time, Mr. Kennedy was expected to announce the names of 35 to 40 private citizens as members of the Advisory Council on the Arts.

Mr. Kennedy created the council last June because he had been persuaded that there was no hope of gaining Congressional legislation to achieve his goals in the field. Mr. Kennedy had a skill in the arts himself, beyond his appreciation of others' achievements. He established that he had a gift for writing when *Profiles in Courage* appeared in 1956. The book won the Pulitzer Prize in biography in 1957.

Mr. Kennedy, a senator at the time, produced the book while recuperating in 1955 from an operation on his back. The Library of Congress sent him cartons of books and Theodore Sorensen, an aide, checked facts to help the convalescent senator. The book was a series of biographical essays about men who had shown courage in defying public opinion and voting according to their consciences. Friends say that the Pulitzer Prize remained to Mr. Kennedy the most precious award he ever received. He gave the $500 award to the United Negro College Fund.

The surprise many reviewers expressed at the literary quality of the book indicated that the public had forgotten Mr. Kennedy's earlier book. At Harvard he won an honors degree in political science with a theme on Munich. He turned this into a book that came out in July, 1940. He chose the title *Why England Slept* to follow the title of Prime Minister Churchill's book, *While England Slept.* It sold 40,000 copies in the United States and as many more in Britain. In 1960, another Kennedy book, *The Strategy of Peace,* appeared. In this he argued for, among other things, unification of all American defense forces.

WHY AMERICA WEEPS

Kennedy Victim of Violent Streak
He Sought to Curb in the Nation

By JAMES RESTON
Special to The New York Times

WASHINGTON, Nov. 22—America wept tonight, not alone for its dead young president, but for itself. The grief was general, for somehow the worst in the nation had prevailed over the best. The indictment extended beyond the assassin, for something in the nation itself, some strain of madness and violence, had destroyed the highest symbol of law and order.

Speaker John McCormack, now 71 and, by the peculiarities of our politics, next in line of succession after the vice president, expressed this sense of national dismay and self-criticism: "My God! My God! What are we coming to?"

The irony of the president's death is that his short Administration was devoted almost entirely to various attempts to curb this very streak of violence in the American character. When the historians get around to assessing his three years in office, it is very likely that they will be impressed with just this: his efforts to restrain those who wanted to be more violent in the cold war overseas and those who wanted to be more violent in the racial war at home.

He was in Texas today trying to pacify the violent politics of that state. He was in Florida last week trying to pacify the businessmen and appealing to them to believe that he was not "anti-business." And from the beginning to the end of his Administration, he was trying to damp down the violence of the extremists on the Right. It was his fate, however, to reach the White

House in a period of violent change, when all nations and institutions found themselves uprooted from the past. His central theme was the necessity of adjusting to change and this brought him into conflict with those who opposed change.

Thus, while his personal instinct was to avoid violent conflict, to compromise and mediate and pacify, his programs for taxation, for racial equality, for medical care, for Cuba, all raised sharp divisions with the country. And even where his policies of adjustment had their greatest success—in relations with the Soviet Union—he was bitterly condemned. The president somehow always seemed to be suspended between two worlds—between his ideal conception of what a president should be, what the office called for, and a kind of despairing realization of the practical limits upon his power. He came into office convinced of the truth of Theodore Roosevelt's view of the president's duties—"the president is bound to be as big a man as he can."

And his Inaugural—"now the trumpet summons us again"—stirred an echo of Wilson in 1913 when the latter said: "We have made up our minds to square every process of our national life with the standards we so proudly set up at the beginning and have always carried at our hearts." This is what the president set out to do. And from his reading, from his intellectual approach to the office, it seemed, if not easy, at least possible. But the young man who came to office with an assurance vicariously imparted from reading Richard Neustadt's *Presidential Power* soon discovered the two truths which all dwellers on that lonely eminence have quickly learned. The first was that the powers of the president are not only limited but hard to bring to bear. The second was that the decisions—as he himself so often said—"are not easy."

Since he was never one to hide his feelings, he often betrayed the mood brought on by contemplating the magnitude of the job and its disappointments. He grew fond of quoting Lord Morley's dictum—"Politics is one long second-best, where the choice often lies between two blunders." Did he have a premonition of tragedy—that he who had set out to temper the contrary violences of our national life would be their victim?

Last June, when the civil rights riots were at their height and passions were flaring, he spoke to a group of representatives of national organizations. He tolled off the problems that beset him on every side and then, to the astonishment of everyone there, suddenly concluded his talk by pulling from his pocket a scrap of paper and reading the famous speech of Blanche of Spain in Shakespeare's *King John*:

> *The sun's o'ercast with blood: Fair day, adieu!*
> *Which is the side that I must go withal?*
> *I am with both; each army hath a hand.*
> *And in their rage, I having hold of both,*
> *They whirl asunder and dismember me.*

There is, however, consolation in the fact that while he was not given time to finish anything or even to realize his own potentialities, he has not left the nation in a state of crisis or danger, either in its domestic or foreign affairs. A reasonable balance of power has been established on continents. The state of truce in Korea, the Taiwan Strait, Vietnam and Berlin is, if anything, more tolerable than when he came to office. Europe and Latin America were increasingly dubious of his leadership at the end, but their capacity to indulge in independent courses of action outside the alliance was largely due to the fact that he had managed to reach a somewhat better adjustment of relations with the Soviet Union.

Thus, President Johnson is not confronted immediately by having to take any urgent new decisions. The passage of power from one man to another is more difficult in other countries, and Britain, Germany, Italy, India and several other allies are so preoccupied by that task at the moment that drastic new policy initiatives overseas are scarcely possible in the foreseeable future. At home, his tasks lie in the Congress, where he is widely regarded as the most skillful man of his generation. This city is in a state of shock tonight and everywhere, including Capitol Hill, men are of a mind to compose their differences and do what they can to help the new president.

Accordingly, the assumption that there will be no major agreements on taxes or civil rights this year will probably have to be revived. It is, of course, too early to tell. But it is typical and perhaps significant that the new president's first act was to greet the Congressional leaders of both parties when he arrived in Washington and to meet with them at once in the White House.

Today's events were so tragic and so brutal that even this city, which lives on the brutal diet of politics, could not bear to think much about the political consequences of the assassination. Yet it is clear that the entire outlook has changed for both parties, and the unexpected death of President Kennedy has forced Washington to meditate a little more on the wild element of chance in our national life. This was quietly in the back of many minds tonight, mainly because President Johnson has sustained a severe heart attack, and the constitutional line of succession places directly back of him, first Speaker McCormack, and then the president pro tempore of the Senate, 86-year-old Senator Carl Hayden of Arizona. Again a note of self-criticism and conscience has touched the capital. Despite the severe illnesses of President Eisenhower just a few years ago, nothing was done by the Congress to deal with the problem of presidential disability.

For an all too brief hour today, it was not clear again what would have happened if the young president, instead of being mortally wounded, had lingered for a long time between life and death, strong enough to survive but too weak to govern. These, however, were fleeting thoughts, important but irritating for the moment. The center of the mind was on the dead president, on his wife, who has now lost both a son and a husband within a few months, and on his family which, despite all its triumphs, has sustained so many personal tragedies since the last war. He was, even to his political enemies, a wonderfully attractive human being, and it is significant that, unlike many presidents in the past, the people who liked and respected him best were those who knew him the best. He was a rationalist and an intellectual, who proved in the 1960 campaign and in last year's crisis over Cuba that he was at his best when the going was tough. No doubt he would have been re-elected, as most one-term presidents are, and the subtle dualism of his character would have had a longer chance to realize his dream.

But he is gone now at 46, younger than when most presidents have started on the great adventure. In his book *Profiles in Courage,* all his heroes faced the hard choice either of giving in to public opinion or of defying it and becoming martyrs. He had hoped to avoid this bitter dilemma, but he ended as a martyr anyway, and the nation is sad tonight, both about him and about itself.

There is one final tragedy about today: Kennedy had a sense of history, but he also had an administrative technique that made the gathering of history extremely difficult. He hated organized meetings of the Cabinet or the National Security Council, and therefore he chose to decide policy after private meetings, usually with a single person. The result of this is that the true history of his Administration really cannot be written now that he is gone. He had a joke about this. When he was asked what he was going to do when he retired, he always replied that he had a problem. It was, he said, that he would have to race two other members of his staff, McGeorge Bundy and Arthur Schlesinger Jr., to the press. Unfortunately, however, he was the only man in the White House who really knew what went on there during his Administration, and now he is gone.

Foreign Policy Role

As Kennedy Grew in the Presidency Effective Diplomacy Was His Forte

By MAX FRANKEL

The death of President Kennedy was evaluated in the gravest terms yesterday by foreign diplomatic circles. Mr. Kennedy, by the testimony of all who watched him, had learned in three years to become an effective diplomat. He managed to assemble and hold together a knowledgeable team of foreign affairs specialists. He developed an awareness of the nuclear power at his command and persistently sought a working relationship with his principal adversary, Premier Khrushchev. Even those who have disagreed at times with Mr. Kennedy's policy came to value his grasp of international issues and his simultaneous firmness toward and prudence in dealing with the Soviet Union.

Mr. Kennedy acquired most of his knowledge and skill in office, and it is doubtful that his successor, though widely traveled and reasonably well-briefed, can quickly display comparable talent. President Kennedy learned from the early mistakes at the Bay of Pigs in Cuba and in complex diplomacy with Europe, and he was soon praised as a man determined to become a forceful leader of the noncommunist world. President Johnson will have to work to match that reputation, which in itself is an indispensable tool of American diplomacy.

Premier Khrushchev had come to have a measure of respect for and understanding of Mr. Kennedy. He valued the American leader's lack of belligerence even as he came to appreciate his agility and toughness in a crisis—as in the Cuban missile affair a year ago. Soviet propaganda always pulled its punches when it came to Mr. Kennedy's person. Though the first and only Khrushchev-Kennedy meeting in Vienna in 1961 did not go well for the American side, the two men learned each other's habits later on, and depended even in the worst of times on their private channels of communication, on which they realized the peace of the world would hang.

When Mr. Kennedy demanded the release of Prof. Frederick C. Barghoorn last week, Mr. Khrushchev readily yielded, with a bow to the personal interest of the president. Among the Western allies, although diplomacy will remain turbulent, Mr. Kennedy's personality, his grasp of economic issues and his devotion to unity were widely appreciated. Repeatedly, where diplomats failed, it was the president himself—by letter to Rome or Bonn or, more often, by telephone call to Paris or London—who kept negotiations on the rails and who restored a confidence bruised by events. The fear of another wave of American isolationism began to spread through Western Europe in recent years. Everywhere, however, there was confidence that as long as John F. Kennedy held office, the United States would remain true to its commitments and forceful in its leadership.

In other nations, especially the smaller nations that themselves are held together often by a single personality, the loss will be even more manifest. Dozens of those leaders have been to Washington in the Kennedy years, and they have gone away impressed by the president's interest in their problems and dedication to their independence. None of the more important foreign-policy projects of the Kennedy Administration has come anywhere near completion. The test ban treaty with the Soviet Union, by the president's own definition, was a first step toward relaxing East-West tensions. The Alliance for Progress, a 10-year project of social reform and economic development in Latin America, was noticeably in trouble. The grand design of partnership between North America and Western Europe was wracked by dissension, by new nationalism in Europe and by the complexities of economic relations. But the broad themes of policy behind these projects were beginning to be felt around the world. Mr. Kennedy, it was recognized, stood for toughness against the Russians, but only to achieve more lasting settlements and never at the risk of destroying essential confidence between Moscow and Washington.

In a world increasingly preoccupied by nationalist struggles, it was also becoming plain that Mr. Kennedy stood for the gradual erosion of national sovereignty, for the institutional as well as philosophic unity of the Western world. His central theme in relations with all countries was that the United States wished nothing more than the right of every people to be independent. Leaders in the newer countries—in Ghana and Guinea and Indonesia—came to understand and value that concept.

The president also found that the range of new policies that any Administration can introduce is severely limited by history, by economic forces beyond a nation's control and by the swirl of events. He had hoped, for instance, to move much further toward cooperation with the Russians, and even, one day, to take a new look at policy on Communist China. These limitations are certain to be felt by President Johnson. The chances are that, like Presidents Truman, Eisenhower and Kennedy, the new leader will preserve, and in any case will usually find himself forced to preserve, the essential lines of international policy.

Mr. Kennedy had a temperament that kept his passions out of world affairs most of the time. He had personal charm, wit and grace that often made the difference in relations with other leaders. His traits of personality and intelligence were thought to be solely responsible for keeping together the varied personalities of his foreign-policy staff—men like Secretary of State Dean Rusk; Secretary of Defense Robert S. McNamara; the president's special assistant, McGeorge Bundy; Under Secretaries of State George W. Ball and his deputy, Averell Harriman, and Adlai E. Stevenson, representative at the United Nations. Behind them served other admirers of Mr. Kennedy, men from the universities and foundations and law offices who answered the call of the New Frontier and allowed the Kennedy charm and intelligence to hold them in Washington and in embassies around the world much longer than they wished to serve.

Foreign Affairs

—At the End of a Sudden Day

By C. L. SULZBERGER

PARIS—The two foreign statesmen with whom President Kennedy had most trouble and in whom he was at the same time perhaps most interested were President de Gaulle and Premier Khrushchev. It was scarcely accidental that on his first journey abroad, in 1961, he chose to meet the Frenchman whose role as an ally so perplexed him and the Russian who, although the U.S.A.'s principal adversary, ultimately began to show signs of working toward an accommodation.

During that trip, Mr. Kennedy told me: "I think it is tremendously important for a man with my responsibility to know something about the people I have to deal with. That helps me make up my mind when the moment for decision comes. You have to know the men themselves in order to be able to evaluate their words." His initial impression of de Gaulle was somewhat confusing because, while confessing admiration for the general's courteous and grandiose manner, he noted that "his anti-American feeling and suspicions go way back and are very deep-rooted." The president always retained the essence of this first impact. He could not escape fascination for de Gaulle's personality but he also could not establish the kind of forthright human contact he sought.

De Gaulle, on his part, expressed himself somewhat diffidently about Kennedy and seemed to be holding a true evaluation in abeyance until history itself had had a chance to judge. This is de Gaulle's habit; he has not yet made up his mind just how to measure the importance of Khrushchev, a man who has been in power far longer. What de Gaulle was really trying to gauge was whether Kennedy would prove to be a strong leader because, as the general contends: "In our age nations need greater direction by their governments. Whatever his intentions, President Kennedy will find himself increasingly pushed toward strong administration and the American economy will find itself increasingly pushed toward *dirigisme*. This is a necessity of our times. There is no escape."

Kennedy left Paris for Vienna and his Khrushchev confrontation. He came away coldly disillusioned and determined to face the worst. But Khrushchev himself, as he later confided, was impressed. "When I talked with him in Vienna I found him a worthy partner," he said. Trying to analyze his opponent, Khrushchev told me: "The advantages Eisenhower had over Kennedy were that he was an older man, hero of World War II, a man who commanded great respect in the U.S.A., and therefore if he said the U.S.A. should not go to war, no one would dare accuse him of being afraid.

"President Kennedy is in a different position. Politically he has a much broader outlook. He himself conducted the talks without depending on Rusk the way Eisenhower always depended on Dulles. Kennedy formulates his own ideas. That is his superiority to Eisenhower. I had a feeling he could understand things better. Kennedy is not a lawyer" [an apparent reference to Dulles]; "he is a president. Kennedy is perhaps too young and he lacks authority and prestige. But he doesn't want to fight; only an idiot wants war."

It is interesting that both de Gaulle and Khrushchev seemed to have more affection for Eisenhower but a hint of more respect for Kennedy. Certainly the late president proved to each, troublesome ally and dangerous rival, that he did not lack resolution. The Cuban crisis confirmed de Gaulle's belief that these times require decisive leadership and Khrushchev's belief that Kennedy was "a worthy partner"—even if "partner" was scarcely the word.

Once, in a philosophical colloquy, de Gaulle observed to me, in discussing contemporary leaders: "People speak of giants when it is all over. Sophocles said that one must wait until the evening to see how splendid the day has been." Well, it is not evening now but night, and the judgment of history, imposed with premature brutality, sets in at the end of a sudden day.

John Fitzgerald Kennedy

The incredible, devastating news that engulfed all America and the world yesterday afternoon is still difficult of comprehension. Hours after the event it remains almost inconceivable that John Fitzgerald Kennedy, president of the United States, whose every word and action typified life and youth and strength, now lies dead of an assassin's bullet.

All of us—from the country's highest leaders to the humblest citizen— all of us are still in a state of shock from this stunning blow, that even now seems unreal in its grotesque horror. And hundreds of millions of people beyond our borders—throughout the hemisphere and across the seas—mourn, too, the loss of a president who gave worldwide reality to the American ideals of peace and freedom.

One's first thought turns in human sympathy to the president's family, to his wife, who was by his side when he was struck down, to his little children, to his parents, to his brothers and sisters. The acutely personal loss they have suffered is intensified by the unusual closeness of their relationships within this tight-knit family.

The personal loss is deep and crushing; the loss to the nation and the world is historic and overpowering. John F. Kennedy was a man of intellect as well as action. He represented the vitality and the energy, the intelligence and the enthusiasm, the courage and the hope of these United States in the middle of this 20th century. On that day less than three years ago when he took the oath of his great office, he said: "Let the word go forth from this time and place, to friend and foe alike, that the torch has been passed to a new generation of Americans—born in this century, tempered by war, disciplined by a hard and bitter peace, proud of our ancient heritage—and unwilling to witness or permit the slow undoing of those human rights to which this nation has always been committed, and to which we are committed today at home and around the world."

John F. Kennedy died in and for this belief, the belief in those human rights to which this nation has always been committed, and to which in his day it recommitted itself—rights which we hope to see exercised around the world, but which we are determined to see exercised within our borders. No madman's bullet can stop this inexorable march of human rights; no murder, however tragic, can make it falter. In death as in life, the words and spirit of this our most newly martyred president will lead the nation ever closer toward fulfillment of the ideals of domestic brotherhood and international peace by which his Administration has been guided from the start.

Among the last words John F. Kennedy wrote were these: "In a world full of frustrations and irritations, America's leadership must be guided by the lights of learning and reason." The light of reason was momentarily extinguished with the crack of a rifle shot in Dallas yesterday. But that light is, in reality, inextinguishable; and, with God's help, it will show the way to our country and our country's leaders as we mourn for John F. Kennedy in the darkening days ahead.

President Johnson

Mourning a lost leader, let us close ranks behind his successor and demonstrate before the world that we are a united and a dedicated people. The burden of responsibility that now falls upon the shoulders of Lyndon Johnson is heavy. He must rally the country from the profound shock into which it has been plunged. He must establish as swiftly as possible a confident relationship between the coordinate branches of the Government. He must convince the country that this bitter tragedy will not divert us from our proclaimed purposes or check our forward movement. He must demonstrate to our friends and allies overseas that our goals remain unchanged and that our strength is undiminished. To these tasks Lyndon Johnson brings experience and qualities of character that should stand him in good stead. He is thoroughly at home in the Congress, which must now share with him the responsibility of steadying the country through the crisis which confronts it. He is well known in all parts of the country, but no one can really know his qualities as leader until he has had a chance to demonstrate them in an assignment more difficult than any other on earth. He is a man of moderate views, with a talent for bringing concord out of disagreement.

A man of the South, he has aligned himself unmistakably with President Kennedy's civil rights program. In another equally important field of action he has played an increasingly constructive role in the expression of this nation's foreign policy. Particularly in recent years he has traveled much abroad, looked closely into problems with which he will have to deal, made contacts which will be of value to him and been accepted as a trustworthy representative of the American people and an authoritative spokesman of their ideals. These are assets he will bring to the presidency in this sad hour. On his side he can count upon the great fund of goodwill which will flow to him spontaneously. He can be sure that every move he makes to steady the country and to lead it forward will meet with a ready response. He can be confident that in a time of crisis the traditional resourcefulness and determination of the American people will help to sustain him. The challenges are great; the country will support greatness in its new president.

The Task in Congress

"We have made a beginning—but we have only begun. Now the time has come to make the most of our gains—to translate the renewal of our national strength into the achievement of our national purpose." That was the charge John F. Kennedy gave to the 88th Congress in his State of the Union Message last January. It remains his legacy that must be fulfilled, its urgency made more acute by eleven months of Congressional inaction.

Lyndon Johnson has dedicated himself to the same ends of equal opportunity, full employment, better education and human progress that animated President Kennedy in domestic affairs. Only last week Mr. Kennedy declared that putting the jobless back to work was the paramount task confronting the nation. For six years one out of every 18 workers has been idle. The civil rights program is moving with painful slowness in the House and faces even slower progress when it gets to the Senate. The tax cut bill is in trouble, and tax reform has been quietly buried. Dozens of other vital measures are stalled. Ethical standards for Congress need shoring up to restore full faith in government.

As Senate majority leader in the Eisenhower Administration, the new president—and the late Speaker Sam Rayburn—established a record for effectiveness in conducting legislative affairs that has rarely been surpassed on Capitol Hill. The respect he won from members of both parties then will be much needed now. Even more needed will be a clear expression of resolve to achieve passage of programs that have the scope and vision imperative to achieve the "new era of human progress" Mr. Johnson has set as his goal.

Which Way the World?

In international affairs President Kennedy was a crusader for peace with honor, justice and liberty. The assassin's bullet that struck him down struck also at his work, and a paralysis of program will exist until President Johnson can announce his program and the means and methods of putting it into effect.

The policies of the United States are so rooted in our principles that they can be justly described as fixed. They varied little under Presidents Roosevelt, Truman and Eisenhower, and President Johnson can be counted upon to continue them. But each president gave them his own interpretation and put his own personal stamp on them. That makes the transfer of the world's most august and powerful office to new hands of the utmost importance to all men, especially in this revolutionary age when the whole world is in a state of transition and disarray.

The test ban treaty is Mr. Kennedy's monument on the course toward peace and disarmament. It is a beacon in a still stormy sea; our alliances are in bad repair in many areas, the foreign aid program is being hacked to bits in Congress, the nature of Soviet intentions remains murky and the policies of Communist China are a hazard to Moscow as well as to the West. President Johnson's travels and conversations with world leaders have given him an awareness of the magnitude of the problems and a warm understanding of the importance of a strong Atlantic alliance. Destiny has entrusted him with decisions that will determine the fate of this nation and the free world and perhaps of all mankind.

"This Old but Youthful Union"

The Republic goes on. That is the history of the United States even in times of tragedy when a president dies in office and the nation is choked with grief. Out of violence and revolution the Founding Fathers created a Republic that is the freest and greatest in the world today. This Government of democratically elected leaders has survived grim moments of civil war and world wars; of presidential transfers of power caused by sudden death as well as normal succession. The assassination of Abraham Lincoln came at a far gloomier period in the nation's affairs.

Four presidents have been slain in office and Franklin D. Roosevelt had the narrowest of escapes. It is a shocking indictment of our civilization that presidents must live in such peril. Yet the strength of our Government of law, not men, insures that no assassin's act can overturn the institutions of the United States. Few men who have been entrusted with the role of chief executive understood the depth of our historical past better than President Kennedy. He who risked his life often as a naval commander in wartime knew the perils of the presidency in peacetime. Yet he always recognized the long view for the country that lay behind his Administration and would extend beyond it—this is part of his heritage and our appreciation.

He defined the United States and its continuity in his third State of the Union Message at the beginning of this year: "Today, having witnessed in recent months a heightened respect for our national purpose and power— having seen the courageous calm of a united people in a perilous hour— and having observed a steady improvement in the opportunities and well-being of our citizens—I can report that the State of this old but youthful Union, in the 175th year of its life, is good."

The life of the old but youthful Union continues because of men like John F. Kennedy—and also because of the laws governing our Republic.

Remembered From Robert Frost

Be wary of the simplifying snow
And cautious of the reassuring night.
They seem, he said, to smooth the path you go—
To veil the harsh realities of light.
He did not mean to hint that easy words
Give easy answers—that brooks and pasture springs
Or provident woodchucks and mid-April birds
Bespeak a comfortable peace in common things.
But eyes for orchids at a meadow's rim
Can readier pause at riddles of design—
In a moth's chill tryst with white on white, or the stark
Loneliness of an old man's winter dark;
And minds that quiet to a thrush's hymn
May stronger bear death's quick demanding whine.

ROBERT PRICE

DAY TWO

November 23, 1963

"All the News That's Fit to Print"

The New York Times.

NEWS SUMMARY AND INDEX, PAGE 25

LATE CITY EDITION
U.S. Weather Bureau Report (Page 56) Forecast:
Cloudy, windy, colder today; clearing tonight. Sunny, milder tomorrow.
Temp. Range: 52—34; yesterday: 41—32

SECTION ONE

VOL. CXIII. No. 38,655.

NEW YORK, SUNDAY, NOVEMBER 24, 1963.

THIRTY CENTS

KENNEDY'S BODY LIES IN WHITE HOUSE; JOHNSON AT HELM WITH WIDE BACKING; POLICE SAY PRISONER IS THE ASSASSIN

CABINET CONVENES

Johnson Sees Truman and Eisenhower on First Day in Office

By JAMES RESTON
Special to The New York Times

WASHINGTON, Nov. 23—President Johnson took over the machinery of government today and won broad leaders of the nation and the non-Communist world.

It was a bleak and melancholy day, with the rain falling slowly out of gray skies and the body of the assassinated 35th President of the United States lying in the East Room of the White House.

Like a family tracing the imperatives of both life and death, citizens of the Union came quietly to the Executive Mansion to look at the coffin of John Fitzgerald Kennedy and to express their best wishes to his successor.

Will Address Congress

The President announced that he would address a joint session of Congress at 12:30 P.M. Wednesday. White House sources indicated that the speech would be telecast to the nation.

President Kennedy's funeral will take place on Monday. The address to Congress was delayed to allow Mr. Johnson to spend Tuesday conferring with the many foreign leaders who will be in Washington for the funeral.

Later it was announced that the President, would meet at 3 P.M. tomorrow on the war in South Vietnam with Henry Cabot Lodge, Ambassador to Saigon; Secretary of Defense Robert S. McNamara, Secretary of State Dean Rusk and McGeorge Bundy, special Presidential assistant on security affairs. The President, apparently wishes to know about their discussions in Hawaii last week on the Vietnamese situation since the overthrow of the Diem regime.

Meeting Opens With Prayer

President Johnson held his first Cabinet meeting this afternoon. He opened it with a minute of silent prayer for President Kennedy and then asked all members of the Cabinet to continue to serve as before. Attorney General Robert F. Kennedy was present.

Earlier, President Johnson had received former Presidents Harry S. Truman and Dwight D. Eisenhower, attended church and conferred with Secretary Rusk, Secretary McNamara and other officials.

Unity and continuity were the themes of President Johnson's first full day in office. He was clearly concerned today to make plain to all nations that the authority of state had passed smoothly and quickly into his hands and that he intended to proceed on the same

Continued on Page 1, Column 1

Aldous Huxley Dies Of Cancer on Coast

Special to The New York Times

LOS ANGELES, Nov. 23—Aldous Leonard Huxley, the novelist - philosopher - historian whose satirical "Brave New World" set a model for writers of his generation, died here yesterday at the home of friends. He and his wife had been living there since their home was destroyed by fire last year.

The mustard-80-year-old scholar and writer—and poet, essayist, playwright and botanical probor into the human command-place and the esoteric—died of cancer.

Mr. Huxley, in his own right the youngest of a nest of distinguished literary intellectuals, was a grandson of Thomas Henry Huxley, throw Arnold and a brother-of

Continued on Page 37, Column 1

JOHNSON ORDERS DAY OF MOURNING

He Proclaims Tomorrow as Time for Entire Nation

By E. W. KENWORTHY
Special to The New York Times

WASHINGTON, Nov. 23—Lyndon B. Johnson, the new President of the United States, issued a proclamation today designating a national day of mourning for his slain predecessor.

In one of his first official actions, Mr. Johnson called on all Americans to go to their churches on Monday and pay "the homage of love and reverence" to the memory of John P. Kennedy.

He also ordered all Federal offices in the country to close on that day, the day of Mr. Kennedy's funeral.

The proclamation was issued in midafternoon shortly after the new President and his wife, Lady Bird, returned from a special prayer service.

It marked the apogee of the anguish who shared "our grief" to join in mourning the untimely death of a "great and good man."

The White House
By the President of the United States

A Proclamation

To the People of the United States:

John Fitzgerald Kennedy, 35th President of the United States, has been taken from us by an act which outrages decent men everywhere.

He upheld the faith of our Fathers, which is freedom for all men. He broadened the frontiers of that faith, and backed it with the energy and the courage which are the marty of his Nation that he led.

A man of wisdom, strength and peace, he molded and moved the power of our Nation in the service of a world of growing liberty and order. All who love freedom will mourn his death.

As he did not shrink from his responsibilities, but welcomed them, so he would not have us shrink from carrying on his work beyond this hour of national tragedy.

He said to himself: "The energy, the faith, the devotion which we bring to this endeavor will light our country and all who serve it—and the glow from that fire can truly light the world."

Now, therefore, I, Lyndon B. Johnson, President of the United States of America, do appoint Monday next, Nov. 25, the day of the funeral service of President Kennedy, to be a day of national mourning throughout the United States. I earnestly recommend the people to assemble on that day in their respective places of divine worship, there to bow down in submission to the will of Almighty God, and to pay their homage of love and reverence to the memory of a great and good man. I invite the people of the world who share our grief to join us in this day of mourning and rededication.

IN WITNESS WHEREOF, I have hereunto set my hand and caused the Seal of the United States of America to be affixed.

DONE at the City of Washington this twenty-third day of November in the year of our Lord nineteen hundred and sixty-three, and of the Independence of the United States of America the one hundred and eighty-eighth.
LYNDON B. JOHNSON.

63 Elderly Patients Are Killed As Fire Razes Ohio Rest Home

By United Press International

NORWALK, Ohio, Nov. 23—Sixty-three elderly men and women died in a fire that destroyed a rural rest home today. It was the worst fire tragedy in this country since 26 persons perished in 1958 when a Chicago school burned.

State Fire Marshal Fred Ron, after an inspection with Gov. James A. Rhodes, confirmed that the three employes on duty at the Golden Age Nursing Home and 21 elderly residents, many of them invalids, had escaped.

The one-story building near Fitchville, 15 miles south of here, burned rapidly as firemen whipped through it.

The tragedy was the most disastrous rest home fire in the United States this week. On Monday, 25 elderly persons.

IN REPOSE: The flag-draped coffin of President Kennedy in East Room of the White House. A priest kneels in prayer at left. The guard of honor represents the armed services.

CAPITAL WEIGHING POLITICAL EFFECT

Party Chiefs Expect Johnson to Push Kennedy Program and Be Nominee in '64

By WARREN WEAVER Jr.
Special to The New York Times

WASHINGTON, Nov. 23—A shaken capital began to piece together today a new pattern of national politics to replace the one shattered by an assassin's bullet 24 hours before.

There were no certainties. There were only degrees of speculation, as the indications talked in the aftermath of President Kennedy's death and the accession of President Johnson.

As party leaders looked forward after a day of turmoil and tragedy, they reached one major conclusion. The new President seems almost certain to be his party's standard-bearer when the Democratic convention meets in Atlantic City nine months from tomorrow.

Legislative Doubt

On the legislative side, Congressional sources expected that the President would adopt and push the Kennedy program.

Although Mr. Johnson was silent on politics, as he may for some time, no one among his associates questioned that the former Vice President would expect the nomination and fight for it, if necessary.

One of the major advantages that President Johnson will enjoy in this bid potential opposition is almost hopelessly divided.

When the political harmony of Washington's present attentiveness has faded, the President can expect to face two major groups of detractors within his own party: those liberals who find him too conservative and those Southerners who feel he has deserted their cause.

Both of these groups may feel next August that they might prefer one of their own as a nominee. But the possibility of their agreeing on a candidate is slim.

Then is also on Mr. Johnson's side the fact that he owns the party leadership across the entire

Continued on Page 6, Column 4

Evidence Against Oswald Described as Conclusive

By GLADWIN HILL
Special to The New York Times

DALLAS, Nov. 23—Police officials said today they had amassed evidence enough to convict Lee Harvey Oswald of the assassination of President Kennedy.

"We're convinced beyond any doubt that he killed the President," said Capt. Will Fritz, chief of the Dallas Police Homicide Bureau, after questioning Oswald and others. "I think the case is clinched."

While the 21-year-old warehouse worker continued to deny the killing under prolonged questioning, the Dallas County District Attorney, Henry Wade, said this afternoon: "I think we have enough evidence to convict him now but we are still trying to get more evidence in the case for days."

Oswald was arrested yesterday afternoon after the President had been killed by a sniper's rifle bullet. He was charged with murder. District Attorney Wade said he planned to present the case to the grand jury next Wednesday or the following Monday. He thought the case might come to trial in mid-January.

Police Chief Jesse Curry announced tonight that the Federal Bureau of Investigation had identified as Oswald's handwrit-

Continued on Page 2, Column 1

KHRUSHCHEV PAYS SPECIAL RESPECTS

Calls to Kohler and Sends Messages—Mikoyan Will Attend Capital Rites

The texts of the messages of condolence, Page 12.

By HENRY TANNER
Special to The New York Times

MOSCOW, Nov. 23—Premier Khrushchev, in a series of unusual actions, emphasized today the Soviet Union's deep concern over the death of President Kennedy.

Mr. Khrushchev called this morning at the residence of the United States Ambassador, Foy D. Kohler, to pay his tribute and to sign the condolence book. Anastas A. Grontckhn, the Foreign Minister, who accompanied the Premier, said that in his eyes as he took leave of the Ambassador.

Anastas I. Mikoyan, a First Deputy Premier and one of Mr. Khrushchev's closest associates will go to Washington for the funeral.

It was not known whether the fight of the decisions by President de Gaulle and Dr. Alec Douglas-Home to go to Washington, Mr. Khrushchev contemplated attending himself

In death, Mr. Kennedy was praised and mourned in Moscow

Continued on Page 8, Column 1

RITES TOMORROW

Burial in Arlington— Many World Leaders to Attend Funeral

By JACK RAYMOND
Special to The New York Times

WASHINGTON, Nov. 23—The body of John Fitzgerald Kennedy lay in repose today, a closed, flag-draped coffin in the East Room of the White House.

Two priests, kneeling in air prayer, and a military guard honor kept constant watch.

Tall candles at each corner shed her flickered under dimly lighted giant chandelier. At the root of the coffin the was a mahogany crucifix; the head a spray of carnations and lilies.

Mrs. Kennedy, who for two drsn and other members of family were the first to view the room.

Visits by Ex-Presidents

Throughout the day many others, including former Presidents Dwight D. Eisenhower and Harry S. Truman, Government officials and representatives of foreign nations, paid their private respects to Kennedy, who was assassinated yesterday in Dallas.

Tomorrow, the coffin will taken to the great Rotunda the Capitol to lie in state as to permit public viewing. It be closed at 9 P.M.

On Monday, proclaimed President Johnson as a nationwide day of mourning, a funeral to be held in St. Matthew's Roman Catholic Cathedral here.

Mourning on the Two

The news from the wires crn ken caused the muscle or modification of some nor mal activities. A listing of such changes as are prese

Among those who have said they will attend the state funeral are President de Gaulle of France; Prince Philip, husband of Queen Elizabeth II of Britain, and Prime Minister Alec Douglas-Home; King Baudouin of the Belgians; Fr Deputy Premier Anastas Mikoyan of the Soviet Union; Ludwig Erhard, Chancellor of West Germany, and President Eamon de Valera of Ireland.

Military Cortege Set

The White House announced that a horse-drawn caisson with ceremonial troops would take the casket from the Capitol and from there to the church on Monday in a traditional military procession.

The plans were similar to those for the funeral procession that escorted President Roosevelt along a similar route in 1945. A corps of drummers will beat muffled cadence for the procession.

Mr. Kennedy will be buried Arlington National Cemetery accordance with the wishes of the family. So will the com since the deceased President be buried near the famed shrine

Continued on Page 5, Column 4

Sections of Today's Paper

This main news section consists today of one part only. Out of respect for the memory of President Kennedy, advertisers have curtailed their notices.

Section		Section	
2 Drama, Screen, Music, TV		"Employment Advertising	
3 Real Estate		Resorts and Travel	
4 News, Gardens, Home			
5 Sports			
6 Financial and Business			
7 Review of the Week			
8 The Week in Review			

Index to Subjects

IF THERE WAS anything approaching a calm, "normal" day in *The Times*'s four-day, assassination-to-funeral coverage of John F. Kennedy's death, it was Saturday, Nov. 23. Though still riveted to millions of television sets, the nation had begun to regroup, however slowly. For one thing, the failure of any other potential assassin to emerge provided comfort—though by no means firm proof—that Kennedy had not, as many feared, been the victim of an organized conspiracy. Meanwhile, the machinery of democratic government began to whir, with power flowing in an orderly manner from the Kennedy team to the new president. Most reassuring of all, quarrels among nations were temporarily suspended as world leaders made plans to come to Washington for the funeral.

The stories from the Sunday paper of Nov. 24 are grouped accordingly. The first section focuses, appropriately, on the slain president. His body lies in state, elaborate preparations are under way for his funeral, the world (Fidel Castro being a conspicuous exception) continues to mourn. The second section focuses on Lyndon Johnson and his first full day in office, the third on the continuing police investigation in Dallas, the fourth on appraisals and editorial comment on Kennedy, Johnson and the tasks ahead.

Some of these stories are all the more striking with the passage of time. The funeral arrangements, for example, were impossibly elaborate (they certainly seemed so for the reporters trying to get them down on paper). That the armed forces, the local police, the White House and the grief-stricken Kennedy family orchestrated all this in the brief time available to them still seems incredible.

The press was lucky in one respect: because Lyndon Johnson had been such a towering presence as Senate majority leader, more was known about him than would have been the case with most vice presidents. Even so, the second-day analysis of the new president was uncannily on the mark—especially Anthony Lewis's detailed, intimate 1,800-word portrait of LBJ's character and style, a tour de force of deadline reporting.

There are two additional points of interest in Day Two that readers might easily overlook. One, it's worth noting the speed and certainty with which the Dallas police concluded that Oswald had acted alone and decided (it's almost an aside in the Gladwin Hill story) that there had been no "organizational" conspiracy. This was obviously a bit hasty. Nevertheless, despite a robust trade in conspiracy theories that endures even to this day, no subsequent investigation, including the Warren Commission's, has ever shaken that verdict.

Second, though they constitute formidable blocks of text, Mr. Kennedy's two speeches are worth reading, both for style and substance. (One was delivered Friday morning, hours before the assassination, in Fort Worth. The other, of course, was never delivered.) Stylistically, both are written in the rhythmic cadences and balanced sentences that Kennedy's speech-writers had perfected as long ago as the Inaugural Address. Substantively, they were prototypical cold war speeches, delivered in an unabashedly patriotic part of the country that also happened to manufacture large quantities of advanced weaponry. Like every American president in the bipolar world, Kennedy saw the United States as the world's strongest and surest defender against tyranny in all its forms. His rhetoric reflected not only a sure sense of his audience but also his deepest beliefs.

KENNEDY'S BODY LIES IN WHITE HOUSE; JOHNSON AT HELM WITH WIDE BACKING; POLICE SAY PRISONER IS THE ASSASSIN

Rites Tomorrow

Burial in Arlington—Many World Leaders to Attend Funeral

By JACK RAYMOND

Special to The New York Times

WASHINGTON, Nov. 23—The body of John Fitzgerald Kennedy lay in repose today in a closed, flag-draped coffin in the East Room of the White House. Two priests, kneeling in silent prayer, and a military guard of honor kept constant watch. Tall candles at each corner of the bier flickered under the dimly lighted giant chandeliers. At the foot of the coffin there was a mahogany crucifix; at the head a spray of carnations and lilies. Mrs. Kennedy, her two children and other members of the family were the first to visit the room.

Throughout the day many others, including former Presidents Dwight D. Eisenhower and Harry S. Truman, Government officials and representatives of foreign nations, paid their private respects to Mr. Kennedy, who was assassinated yesterday in Dallas.

Tomorrow, the coffin will be taken to the great Rotunda of the Capitol to lie in state and to permit public viewing. It will be closed.

On Monday, proclaimed by President Johnson as a national day of mourning, a funeral will be held in St. Matthew's Roman Catholic Cathedral here. Among those who have said they will attend the state funeral are President de Gaulle of France; Prince Philip, husband of Queen Elizabeth II of Britain, and Prime Minister Sir Alec Douglas-Home; King Baudouin of the Belgians; First Deputy Premier Anastas I. Mikoyan of the Soviet Union; Ludwig Erhard, chancellor of West Germany, and President Eamon de Valera of Ireland.

The White House announced that a horse-drawn caisson, with ceremonial troops representing each service, would bear Mr. Kennedy's body to the Capitol and from there to the church on Monday in a traditional military procession. The plans were similar to those for the funeral parade that escorted Franklin D. Roosevelt along a similar route in 1945. A corps of drummers will beat muffled cadence for the procession.

Mr. Kennedy will be buried at Arlington National Cemetery in accordance with the wishes of the family. He will thus become the second president to be buried near the famed shrine of the Tomb of the Unknowns. William Howard Taft, 27th president, lies buried near a towering iron gate at the cemetery entrance.

Today the White House, which had gleamed in unseasonable springlike sunshine almost every day for weeks, was gray under leaden skies and a constant downpour. Small crowds braved the rain to watch the procession of limousines that ceaselessly brought visitors to the columned North Portico.

The body of Mr. Kennedy, which had been flown to Washington from Dallas yesterday, was carried into the White House at 4:28 A.M. after being prepared by undertakers at the Naval Hospital at Bethesda, Md.

Mrs. Kennedy, who had been in constant attendance of the body since her husband was slain, still wore the raspberry colored suit she had on in Dallas as she walked into the White House. Beside her was the president's brother, Attorney General Robert F. Kennedy, his arm protectively around her.

At 10:30 A.M. in the East Room, where the Kennedys and their companions had once danced gaily at parties, a private mass was said by the Rev. John J. Cavanaugh, former president of the University of Notre Dame and longtime friend of the Kennedy family. About 75 close friends attended the mass with Mrs. Kennedy and her two children, Caroline and John Jr. A spokesman for Mrs. Kennedy said the children had been told of the assassination last night.

After the private mass and viewing by the family, the ritual procession of Government leaders and dignitaries began.

Earlier, the press had been permitted to see the room. The coffin, with the American flag draped over it, the field of stars at the head, rested on a catafalque, or platform, similar to the one that bore the coffin of Abraham Lincoln. The catafalque was draped in black. The two priests, who attended in shifts with other clergymen of their faith, knelt in silent prayer, one with eyes staring unseeing, the other with eyes closed. At each corner of the coffin stood a uniformed enlisted man, one from each armed service.

A Navy lieutenant in full dress stood at rigid attention, his ceremonial sword sheathed. On the wall behind the coffin were portraits of George and Martha Washington. The marble mantels of two huge fireplaces were draped in black. The tops of the crystal chandeliers also were draped in black, with the tiny candle-like bulbs emitting only a faint glow.

The Government leaders, who walked on a black rubber carpet next to the bier, were led by John W. McCormack, the 71-year-old speaker of the House, who is next in the line of succession after President Johnson. Secretary of State Dean Rusk and Mrs. Rusk were driven to the west wing entrance and walked silently through the press offices to the main part of the White House, where they joined the others. Chief Justice of the United States Earl Warren and Mrs. Warren arrived at the columned North Portico entrance a few minutes later.

Soon the pace of arrivals quickened. As each visitor reached the portico steps, a 10-man mixed service honor guard snapped to attention. Maj. Gen. Chester V. Clifton, the White House military aide, greeted each arrival. Inside the White House, Sargent Shriver, director of the Peace Corps, and brother-in-law of the late president, received them.

Angier Biddle Duke, State Department chief of protocol, helped in receiving the visitors and identified the foreign diplomatic representatives.

The Chief Justice and Mrs. Warren stayed only briefly. When they emerged, Mrs. Warren wiped tears from her eyes and then cried openly as they waited for the car.

President Truman arrived at 2:45 P.M. after a flight from Independence, Mo. He passed by the coffin and then went upstairs to visit Mrs. Kennedy for 15 minutes.

Other early arrivals included Defense Secretary Robert S. McNamara, who had consulted with President Johnson during the morning; Gen. Maxwell D. Taylor, chairman of the Joint Chiefs of Staff; Deputy Defense Secretary Roswell L. Gilpatric and Ambassador Carl Rowan. Mr. Rowan, back from Finland for consultations, had conferred with Mr. Kennedy early this week. In the continuing procession of mourners, Governor and Mrs. Rockefeller, accompanied by Senator and Mrs. Jacob K. Javits, arrived shortly before 3 P.M. Gov. Ross R. Barnett of Mississippi and Gov. George C. Wallace of Alabama also called. Mr. Kennedy had clashed bitterly with both men over civil rights.

Pierre Salinger, the White House press secretary, said that the formal procession to the Capitol Rotunda tomorrow would begin at 1 P.M. A police motorcycle escort will lead the procession, followed by an armed services escort with muffled drums and a company of Navy personnel. This will be in special recognition of Mr. Kennedy's service in the Navy during World War II. A special honor guard, made up of the members of the Joint Chiefs of Staff, will march in front of a detail of flag bearers. Clergymen of various faiths will then walk in advance of the caisson bearing the coffin. The caisson will be drawn by white horses, flanked by twenty servicemen, ten on each side. Then a single serviceman will walk with the folded presidential flag in his arms. Behind him will come the limousines bearing the members of the immediate family, President and Mrs. Johnson, and a rear guard of police.

The metropolitan police said the Rotunda would remain open to the public until 9 P.M. tomorrow. It will be open to the public again Monday between 9 and 10 A.M. The same cortege, in the same order, will also escort the coffin from the Capitol to the funeral service, Mr. Salinger said.

He reported that, although the Kennedy family had requested wellwishers not to send flowers but to contribute money to a charity, a number of bouquets had arrived and had been accepted by White House guards. He added, however, that "we are still asking people not to send flowers."

The Military District of Washington said the procession from the White House would follow a route similar to one used for inaugural parades. The procession will leave the White House grounds at 1 P.M. and proceed down Pennsylvania Avenue to 16th Street, turning there to follow Pennsylvania Avenue again until it reaches Constitution Avenue. Then it will proceed along Delaware Avenue until it reaches the Capitol Plaza, site of the president's inauguration less than three years ago.

On Monday, it was announced, the cortege will leave at 11 A.M. and follow a similar route back to the White House. On the White House grounds, the procession will re-form to include additional Government leaders.

Mrs. Kennedy may walk eight blocks from the White House in the final stage of the funeral procession to St. Matthew's Cathedral. The route will be west on Pennsylvania Avenue to 17th Street, then north on 17th Street to Rhode Island Avenue where the church is located.

Johnson Orders Day of Mourning

He Proclaims Tomorrow as Time for Entire Nation to Honor Kennedy

By E. W. KENWORTHY

Special to The New York Times

WASHINGTON, Nov. 23—Lyndon B. Johnson, the new president of the United States, issued a proclamation today designating a national day of mourning for his slain predecessor. In one of his first official actions, Mr. Johnson called on all Americans to go to their churches on Monday and pay the "homage of love and reverence" to the memory of John F. Kennedy. He also ordered all Federal offices in the country to close on that day, the day of Mr. Kennedy's funeral. The proclamation was issued in midafternoon shortly after the new president and his wife, Lady Bird, returned from a special prayer service. It invited the people of the world who shared "our grief" to join in mourning the untimely death of a "great and good man."

Mr. Johnson's day was one of brisk activity. At 8:40 this morning the tall Texan left home, flanked by motorcycle outriders and followed by a Secret Service car, and sped to the White House. He had been elevated to the presidency only 19 hours before when an assassin's bullet struck down Mr. Kennedy in Dallas. Through 9:15 tonight, when Mr. Johnson went home, his day was filled with intelligence briefings; conferences with top officials on foreign and defense policies; a meeting with the Cabinet; talks with former Presidents Dwight D. Eisenhower and Harry S. Truman; a session with legislative leaders of both parties; a visit with Mr. Kennedy's widow, and an interlude of prayer in St. John's Episcopal Church across Lafayette Square from the White House.

The old Johnsonian habits—an affable carelessness about time, for instance—had vanished. He kept to his schedule with precision. One official who is close to the new president said he was moving with the "natural grace of the gentleman he is, but also with a sense of responsibility." Others said they detected at once a new strain of dignity, especially in Mr. Johnson's awareness of the worldwide impact of his accession.

Thus it was Mr. Johnson who insisted during meetings with high officials that he wished them all to remain at their jobs, while the officials themselves replied that this would work only for a time. Sooner or later, they told their new chief, he must consider himself free to shape a "Johnson Administration" responsive to his own ideas, habits and personality.

All day long, when Mr. Johnson showed himself publicly at the White House or in the corridors of the Executive Office Building, his demeanor was a mixture of sorrow and constraint. If he was already a burdened man, he carried his burden this first day without evidences of tension. Once or twice he managed a faint smile.

Aside from an early morning security briefing and an afternoon meeting with the Cabinet, President Johnson, with a sense of the fitness of things, carried on all business in his suite on the second floor of the Executive Office Building, a rococo stone pile across West Executive Avenue from the White House.

On 52d Street, at the edge of the wooded Spring Valley section of northwest Washington, a gray dawn revealed the great change that had overtaken the family of Lyndon Baines Johnson. His home there is a luxurious, French provincial–style house of white-washed brick sitting among small pines and large magnolias at the crest of a hill. Its former owner, Perle Mesta, a renowned party-giver, called the house "Les Ormes." It was typical of Mr. Johnson that he had "Les Ormes" on the stone gate posts translated into plain Texan, "The Elms."

Outside the gilded, wrought-iron gates of the house a crowd of reporters, television technicians, local police, White House guards and Secret Service men, 50 or 60 in all, was gathering by 7 A.M. As President Johnson's car came through the gates at 8:40, a light rain was beginning to fall. He was accompanied by Bill D. Moyers, now second in command at the Peace Corps. Mr. Moyers, a former Baptist clergyman, is a close personal friend who played a large role in Mr. Johnson's unsuccessful campaign for the nomination in 1960. He had spent the night at The Elms.

The president reached the White House at 8:55 and went into the side entrance on West Executive Avenue. There he first conferred briefly with the dead president's brother, Attorney General Robert F. Kennedy. At 9:05, John A. McCone, director of the Central Intelligence Agency, and McGeorge Bundy, special White House assistant for national security affairs, arrived. President Johnson joined them shortly in the "situation room," where they gave him an intelligence briefing. The "situation room," near Mr. Bundy's office, may best be described as the "nerve center" or "operational headquarters" for the president.

At 9:20, Secretary of State Dean Rusk arrived at West Executive Avenue. Mr. Rusk entered the Executive Office Building and took the elevator to the second floor. Eight minutes later President Johnson walked briskly out of the White House, across the street and down the alley to the office building. He was accompanied by Mr. Moyers and Representative Homer Thornberry of Texas, an old friend.

Mr. Johnson's suite is elegant but not lavish. The inner office is about 15 feet by 30, deep-carpeted and furnished with a desk, a small, rectangular mahogany table, green leather chairs and a sofa. A fairly small marble fireplace is surmounted by a massive square mirror with a gilt frame.

No other officials were present at the talks between the president and Mr. Rusk. Mr. Johnson sat at the head of the table in a straight chair; Mr. Rusk sat in a lower chair beside him. The substance of their conversation was not disclosed, but presumably Mr. Rusk gave the president his views on foreign policy problems in Vietnam, Berlin and the Western alliance.

Mr. Rusk remained about 40 minutes, leaving at 10:12. As he strode out of the building, looking neither right nor left, a reporter asked: "Can you tell us anything about your conference?"

"No, not at all," Mr. Rusk said.

On his way out of the president's office, Mr. Rusk had passed Secretary

of Defense Robert S. McNamara going in. Mr. McNamara also was clos-
eted alone with the president.

When a small group of reporters and photographers was admitted toward the close of Mr. McNamara's 50-minute conference, they saw the
two men with their heads close together. On the table were four or five
typewritten pages. The only word overheard was "billions"—spoken by
Mr. McNamara.

Meanwhile, at 10:20, the president's wife arrived, accompanied by Elizabeth Carpenter, her press secretary. They went into the anteroom of the
president's office. At 10:36 Mr. Bundy, looking strained and preoccupied,
arrived, spent seven minutes and left. Between 10:45 and 11:00 Congressional leaders arrived singly or in pairs. They went into a side room to
await the conclusion of the president's conference with Mr. McNamara.
Present were the Senate majority leader, Mike Mansfield; the speaker of
the House, John W. McCormack; the Senate majority whip, Hubert H.
Humphrey; the House majority leader, Representative Carl Albert; the
House Democratic whip, Representative Hale Boggs; Republican Senators
George D. Aiken of Vermont and Bourke B. Hickenlooper of Iowa; the
House minority leader, Charles A. Halleck, and the House minority whip,
Leslie S. Arends.

There was an air of cluttered incongruity about the scene in the old
building. High Government officials were often in line with workmen moving boxes of documents in and out. At one point the elevator, overcrowded
with reporters and photographers, refused to budge, and the newsmen had
to scramble up the winding staircase.

President Johnson talked only briefly with the Congressional leaders.
One senator said he had asked them in chiefly because he wished them to
accompany him to the White House.

About 11 A.M., the president and Mrs. Johnson, followed by the leaders,
made their way across the street to the White House. It was now raining
hard, and Senator Mansfield, who was without hat or raincoat, got
drenched. The president and Mrs. Johnson spent about 20 minutes with
Mrs. Kennedy in the upstairs living quarters of the mansion.

Then, at about 11:20, former President Eisenhower arrived at the north
portico of the White House, where an honor guard was drawn up on the

lawn. He was followed by Earl Warren, chief justice of the United States. The president and General Eisenhower spent about half an hour in the East Room, where Mr. Kennedy's body lay in repose. General Eisenhower did not see Mrs. Kennedy.

The president and his wife and General Eisenhower then drove across the street to the Executive Office Building. With Mrs. Johnson between them, the two men walked down the narrow corridor in the dazzling white light of photographers' lamps. Mrs. Johnson was dressed in black with a black lace net hat. As they talked, messengers were hauling papers and books and the treasured ships' models from Mr. Kennedy's office in the White House.

Then Mr. Johnson and his wife left for the prayer service at St. John's Church, known as the "Church of the Presidents." Presidents have worshipped there for a century and a half. The rector, the Rev. John C. Harper, said that Mr. Johnson had requested the service.

Afterward Mrs. Johnson drove off alone, apparently returning home. The president went back to his office, where he lunched with General Eisenhower. The two men discussed various trouble spots around the world. The president arranged for Mr. Bundy to give General Eisenhower a briefing.

He conferred by telephone during the morning with J. Edgar Hoover, director of the Federal Bureau of Investigation, on the agency's investigation of the assassination.

The Cabinet meeting began at 2:30 and lasted half an hour. The president told the assembled members that he needed their help. The response for the group was made by Mr. Rusk and Adlai E. Stevenson, chief delegate to the United Nations. They pledged the Cabinet's support and assured the president that all were prepared to serve him in their present capacities as long as he wanted them to. In addition to Mr. Stevenson and the statutory members of the Cabinet, the following were present: Dr. Jerome B. Wiesner, the president's science adviser; Dr. Walter W. Heller, chairman of the Council of Economic Advisers; Kermit Gordon, director of the budget; Timothy Reardon, special assistant to Mr. Kennedy; George E. Reedy, press secretary to President Johnson, and Mr. Salinger and Mr. Moyers. Later, Secretary of Agriculture Orville L. Freeman, Supreme

Court Justice Arthur J. Goldberg, who was formerly secretary of labor, and R. Sargent Shriver, director of the Peace Corps, all paid brief calls on the president.

A few minutes later the president again walked across the street to the Executive Office Building for a talk with former President Truman. When newsmen were admitted, the president was smiling. At one point Mr. Truman grasped Mr. Johnson's hands across the table and patted them approvingly, as if to say that he knew what the president felt and what he faced, and he was with him.

One of Mr. Johnson's final visitors was Secretary of Labor W. Willard Wirtz, who spent an hour and 45 minutes with the president. Upon leaving, Mr. Wirtz was asked whether the report by an arbitration board on the railroad labor crisis would be issued on Tuesday as scheduled. He replied that he thought the report would be out on time.

The White House

By the President of the United States of America

A Proclamation

To the People of the United States:

John Fitzgerald Kennedy, 35th President of the United States, has been taken from us by an act which outrages decent men everywhere.

He upheld the faith of our Fathers, which is freedom for all men. He broadened the frontiers of that faith, and backed it with the energy and the courage which are the mark of the Nation that he led.

A man of wisdom, strength and peace, he molded and moved the power of our Nation in the service of a world of growing liberty and order. All who love freedom will mourn his death.

As he did not shrink from his responsibilities, but welcomed them, so he would not have us shrink from carrying on his work beyond this hour of national tragedy.

He said it himself: "The energy, the faith, the devotion which we bring to this endeavor will light our country and all who serve it—and the glow from that fire can truly light the world."

Now, therefore, I, Lyndon B. Johnson, President of the United States of America, do appoint Monday next, Nov. 25, the day of the funeral service of President Kennedy, to be a day of national mourning throughout the United States. I earnestly recommend the people to assemble on that day in their respective places of divine worship, there to bow down in submission to the will of Almighty God, and to pay their homage of love and reverence to the memory of a great and good man. I invite the people of the world who share our grief to join us in this day of mourning and rededication.

IN WITNESS WHEREOF, I have hereunto set my hand and caused the Seal of the United States of America to be affixed.

DONE at the City of Washington this twenty-third day of November in the year of our Lord nineteen hundred and sixty-three, and of the Independence of the United States of America the one hundred and eighty-eighth.

LYNDON B. JOHNSON.

Kennedy Will Lie in a Quiet Cemetery That He Knew Well

Special to The New York Times

WASHINGTON, Nov. 23—A caisson drawn by white horses will bear the body of President Kennedy on Monday to the quiet, wooded cemetery he visited just 12 days ago. Arlington National Cemetery, on the Virginia side of the Potomac River, was a spot Mr. Kennedy knew well. He drove there Nov. 11, along the winding driveways bordered by trees whose leaves had turned golden, to lay a Veterans Day wreath on the Tomb of the Unknowns. It is there, near the tomb, that his body will be laid to rest.

Mr. Kennedy was alternately somber and smiling on that last visit to the cemetery. He stood quietly, staring straight ahead at the tomb, while a bugler played taps. He had planned to leave then, and not stay for the ceremony of music and speaking inside the nearby amphitheater. He changed his mind. Taking his son, John Jr., by the hand, he went to the amphitheater. The boy stayed in the audience with a Secret Service agent. The president walked to the stage. He made no speech.

A man with a sense of history, Mr. Kennedy had visited Arlington often. He had spoken at Veterans Day ceremonies there in 1961. He went there last May to lead Memorial Day rites at the Tomb of the Unknowns. On that day in May the president stopped briefly by the grave of James Forrestal, the first secretary of defense.

More than 150,000 persons—members of the military or veterans or members of their families—are buried at Arlington. The cemetery, 100 years old next year, covers 419.4 acres that once belonged to Gen. Robert E. Lee. When General Lee left Arlington on April 22, 1861, to take command of the Virginia troops, Federal soldiers took possession of the Lee mansion and converted it into a headquarters. The rolling acres became an army camp. Later, a hospital was set up there. In 1864, by order of the secretary of war, the land became a military cemetery. The first person buried there was a Confederate soldier who had died in the hospital.

Children Learn Father Is Dead; Mother Returns to White House

Caroline and John Jr. Receive the News—Mrs. Kennedy Stays Most of the Night at Bethesda Naval Hospital

By NAN ROBERTSON

Special to The New York Times

WASHINGTON, Nov. 23—President Kennedy's two children were told last night that their father was dead. It was not known who had told them or what words had been used. Almost certainly it was not their mother.

Mrs. Kennedy stayed close to her husband from the moment he was shot by an assassin until his body was returned to the White House before dawn today. His body now lies in the East Room. Mrs. Kennedy spent most of the night at Bethesda Naval Hospital, where the slain president was first taken from nearby Andrews Air Force Base. She rode in the ambulance with the body and remained at the hospital from 7 o'clock last night until 4 A.M. today.

Her children were taken late yesterday afternoon from the White House to the home of Mrs. Hugh D. Auchincloss, their maternal grandmother, in Georgetown, an exclusive section of Washington. There they had dinner. Then the children, Caroline and John Jr., were taken back to the White House. They went to their private quarters upstairs about 7:30 P.M. with their nurse, Maude Shaw, who has been with the Kennedys since Caroline was 11 days old. John Jr., nicknamed "John John" by his father, will be 3 years old Monday, the day of his father's funeral. Caroline's sixth birthday will be Wednesday.

This morning the grief-stricken mother took both children to a private mass in the East Room. The closed bronze coffin reflected the flickering candles set about it. The Roman Catholic mass, believed to be the first ever celebrated in the White House, was said by the Rev. John J. Cavanaugh, former president of the University of Notre Dame, who is a close friend of the family. About 75 friends and relatives attended the mass.

Princess Stanislas Radziwill flew in from France today to be with Mrs. Kennedy, her sister. The president's mother, Mrs. Joseph P. Kennedy, will arrive from Hyannis Port tomorrow. Her husband, who suffered a stroke nearly three years ago, will remain in Hyannis Port.

There were reports yesterday that Caroline and John had been carefully protected from the news of their father's death and would not be told until their mother returned to the White House. Mrs. Kennedy went directly from the airport to Bethesda, however. By the time she arrived at the White House at 4:25 this morning, the children had long been asleep. Mr. Kennedy's press secretary, Pierre Salinger, said that by that time John Jr. and Caroline already knew their father was dead.

"They were told last night," he said at a briefing today. "I don't know who told them. I can't say whether any relatives are staying with the children." He did say, however, that Mrs. Edward M. Kennedy, the Peter Lawfords, the Stephen Smiths, Sargent Shriver and Attorney General and Mrs. Robert F. Kennedy "are all here."

At 11 o'clock this morning, President and Mrs. Johnson visited Mrs. Kennedy in her second-floor living quarters. They stayed 20 minutes.

Last night at the Bethesda Naval Hospital, Dr. John W. Walsh kept vigil with Mrs. Kennedy. Dr. Walsh, her obstetrician and a good friend, also saw her through the birth and death of her infant son, Patrick Bouvier Kennedy, last August. The baby lived 39 hours 12 minutes before his heart failed from the stress of a lung ailment.

Also by Mrs. Kennedy's side was her brother-in-law, the attorney general. At Andrews Air Force Base, he rushed up the ramp as the presidential plane arrived from Dallas last night and folded her in his arms.

She wept and asked him: "Would you come with us?"

On her arrival at Andrews, Mrs. Kennedy's wish to accompany the coffin by ambulance to the hospital caused a major miscue. The authorities at the hospital had expected the president's body to arrive by helicopter. Two helicopters arrived shortly before 7 P.M., bearing the honor guard of all services that had been posted at Andrews. They took position on the hospital's helicopter pad. Instead, Mrs. Kennedy, the attorney general and the flag-draped coffin arrived at the main hospital building in a gray Navy ambulance, its window curtains closed. A crowd of about 3,000 persons surged about the vehicle. Mrs. Kennedy and her brother-in-law walked up the steps into the hospital.

Later, when the coffin was carried into the White House, Mrs. Kennedy walked slowly behind it, still wearing the blood-spattered pink suit she had worn in Dallas. The attorney general kept step with her, his arm protectively about her.

Father Informed of Death of Son

Senator Breaks the News as Medical Aides Stand By

By JOHN H. FENTON

Special to The New York Times

HYANNIS PORT, Mass., Nov. 23—President Kennedy's ailing father, Joseph P. Kennedy, was told today of his son's death. There was no immediate report of how the 75-year-old former ambassador to Britain took the news. He has been an invalid for nearly two years as a result of a stroke. Senator Edward M. Kennedy, the president's youngest brother, broke the news. His mother, Mrs. Rose Kennedy, and a sister, Mrs. Eunice Shriver, were present. Dr. Russell S. Boles Jr., a Boston neurologist, was standing by at the Kennedy summer home, as were four nurses. Senator Kennedy and Mrs. Shriver, the wife of Sargent Shriver, director of the Peace Corps, temporarily delayed returning to Washington. They flew here late yesterday to join their parents.

The president's mother, dressed in black, attended two masses early today at St. Francis Xavier Roman Catholic Church, where the Kennedy family had worshiped summers and at other times when they were in residence on Cape Cod. She was accompanied by Miss Helen Gargan, a niece. A special requiem mass at 7 A.M. replaced the usual daily low mass at that hour. The Right Rev. Leonard J. Daley, the Kennedys' summer pastor, was the celebrant. The mass was celebrated at an altar donated by the Kennedys in memory of an elder son, Joseph Jr., who was killed as a Navy flier in World War II.

The president was well liked, particularly by those who remembered him as a gangling youngster who summered here. A later generation recalled the president's trips into town with his children, Caroline and John Jr., on candy buying trips for youngsters from the neighborhood.

Tomorrow in Boston, Richard Cardinal Cushing, archbishop of Boston, will celebrate a requiem mass at 9:15 A.M. at the Catholic Television Center and deliver a eulogy. The mass will be nationally televised.

2,500 CROWD INTO SAINT PATRICK'S CATHEDRAL FOR A PONTIFICAL REQUIEM MASS

Mourners Weep at Sound of Taps

250 Clergymen Take Part in Service—Catafalque Is Draped by Flag

By PAUL L. MONTGOMERY

Twenty-five hundred persons attended a mass at St. Patrick's Cathedral yesterday for President Kennedy.

This was their prayer:

"O God, whose nature is ever to give mercy and forbearance, we humbly entreat Thee for the soul of Thy servant John, who at Thy bidding has departed from this world."

The congregation at the pontifical requiem mass for the president was somber as the 250 seminarians, priests and prelates filed down the main aisle to begin the service. At the end, when the slow, single notes of Taps sounded from the choir loft and the soft answering echo hung in the vaulting, they wept.

There were some empty places in the 2,300-seat cathedral when the clergy filed in at 10 o'clock. Twenty minutes later, as the antiphonal choirs finished chanting the Dies Irae (Day of Wrath), all the seats were filled and the aisles were crowded.

The long line of clergy made a stir as they walked to their places around the altar. The seminarians and priests wore black cassocks and white surplices. The celebrant of the mass and his assistants were dressed in embroidered black vestments and the prelates wore purple—the color of penitence and mourning.

The day was gloomy and overcast. Only a little light showed through the stained-glass windows to illuminate the upper reaches of the cathedral. The muffled sounds of traffic came through the opened doors at the sides and on Fifth Avenue.

The Dies Irae, a description of the Last Judgment and a prayer to Jesus for mercy that is a part of the requiem mass, was last heard in the cathedral in June. Then too it referred to "Thy servant John"—Pope John XXIII.

The congregation displayed little outward emotion as the choirs from the archdiocesan seminary in Yonkers chanted and sang through the ordinary of the mass—a symbolic reenactment of the Crucifixion and sacrifice of Jesus. The red lights on television cameras winked and the white, gull-wing cornets of the Sisters of Charity of St. Vincent de Paul fluttered. The sisters operate the Kennedy Child Study Center in East 67th Street, which is endowed by the Kennedy family.

Several hundred people received communion after filing past a flag-covered catafalque representing the coffin, that was placed at the head of the main aisle. The end of the mass was taken up with prayers in English, including the Lord's Prayer and one for the dead:

"Eternal rest grant unto him, O Lord, and let the perpetual light shine upon him. May his soul and the souls of all the faithful departed, through the mercy of God, rest in peace."

The catafalque was illuminated by six tall candles. One guttered and went out.

The celebrant of the mass, Auxiliary Bishop John J. Maguire, vicar general of the archdiocese, circled the catafalque and pronounced absolution by sprinkling it with holy water. Then he repeated the absolution with a censer, distributing incense above the catafalque. When the celebrant returned to the altar, the mass ended. Then Dr. Charles J. Courboin, sitting at the organ at the back of the edifice, played Taps and the stillness was shattered. The clergy and the congregation, many of them brushing away tears, sang the National Anthem and the memorial service was over. As they left, it began to rain.

Among the guests in the front of the congregation were representatives of the armed forces, a Protestant Episcopal priest and Metropolitan Leonty of the Russian Orthodox Church outside Russia.

There will be a requiem mass for the president at St. Patrick's today at 10 A.M. Ordinarily, such observances are forbidden on Sundays and other major holidays. However, Pope Paul VI, through the apostolic delegate in Washington, has granted permission to Catholic churches in the nation to offer a requiem mass for the president today. A spokesman for the archdiocese of New York said that, to his knowledge, this was the first time that such dispensation had been granted to pay homage to a layman.

Tomorrow there will be two pontifical requiem masses at the cathedral—at noon and 5:30 P.M. The noon observance is being offered at the request of the United States delegation to the United Nations, which has sent notification of it to all foreign delegations and diplomats here. The masses are called pontifical because they are celebrated by bishops—considered representatives of the pope. The requiem mass differs from the ordinary mass in that several exclamations of joy are left out and some special sections—including the Dies Irae—are added.

Jews Here Recite Mourning Prayer

1,100 in Temple Say Kaddish in Tribute to Kennedy

By McCANDLISH PHILLIPS

Eleven hundred Jews stood in the temple of Congregation B'Nai Jeshurun yesterday and recited a Mourner's Kaddish, one of the most sacred of Jewish prayers—in tribute to John Fitzgerald Kennedy, who was a Roman Catholic. A Kaddish is usually recited only for deceased Jews. The prayer mentions neither death nor the dead, but affirms faith in God and in the justice of His ways. Some read the Kaddish, most knew it.

"Magnified and sanctified be the name of God throughout the world which He hath created according to His will," an English translation begins. It continues: "May we behold His Kingdom established on earth speedily and in our day, so that God may rule over us all. Amen. May He who maketh peace in the high places make peace for Israel and for all mankind say ye. Amen."

About 350 more people than might normally have attended the service came for the memorial portion in the final hour of the three-hour-and-20-minute service. By 9:15 A.M. only a dozen men in black hats and white prayer shawls and three women had pushed through the heavy wooden doors of the temple at 257 West 88th Street, just west of Broadway. Cantor

Robert Segal led the scattered congregation in chanting the introductory hymns and psalms. These were the temple regulars, the especially faithful ones.

The Torah service followed with the opening of the Ark and the withdrawal of the Torah scroll with its red cloth covering and silver breastplate. In this second hour, with 90 persons present, the cantor's rich, sure baritone and the congregation's strong choral response filled the temple with hymns and Psalms in Hebrew.

By 11, when the memorial service was about to begin, hundreds had been led down the five aisles on the main floor to seats in the blue-cushioned pews. Others began to take places in the three-sided balcony. Jewish men, women and children attended special memorial services at their houses of worship throughout the city yesterday.

At the temple of B'nai Jeshurun, Rabbi Joel Geffen of the Jewish Theological Seminary of America took the marble pulpit at the center of a 40-foot-wide platform. He was robed and capped in black with a knee-length shawl. He likened the late president to the ancient Jewish patriarch Jacob, who dreamed at Beth-el that he saw a ladder reaching to Heaven and the Lord standing above it. Dr. Geffen said that Mr. Kennedy, too, had had dreams—dreams of a world at peace and of equality of rights for all mankind. He quoted the slain man's prophetic vision of a world "where the weak are safe and the strong are just." As guest preacher for Rabbi William Berkowitz, the congregation's spiritual leader, Dr. Geffen had been prepared to speak on "The Status of Jews and Jewry in the World." Instead, he had stayed awake most of the night to study his personal file of statements and speeches by Mr. Kennedy. He entered the pulpit with no text but with a fistful of clippings and a paperbound copy of Mr. Kennedy's book *Profiles in Courage,* and weaved excerpts from these into an eloquent sermon-eulogy.

A young man kept a handkerchief to his nose for most of the next half-hour and two women near him with reddened eyes dabbed at their tears with tissues. In the balcony, a heavy man with a full and wiry black beard sat with his great hands folded, a picture of meditation and deep composure. A boy of 10 leaned forward in the front row and grasped the railing with his hands. Most of the mourners were solemn but not tearful until near the end, when the words of the 23d Psalm stirred many to weeping.

In a tribute to Mr. Kennedy, Charles H. Silver, president of the congregation and former president of the Board of Education, said: "This is our untimely day of atonement." He said there would be time later to assess "our code of tolerance toward the terrorist and hate-maker in our midst."

After the Mourner's Kaddish, Dr. Geffen returned to the pulpit. "May the soul of our beloved president, John Fitzgerald Kennedy, be bound up in the bonds of eternal life. May his soul dwell with all the righteous and blessed of the peoples of the world."

At Temple Emanu-El at 65th Street and Fifth Avenue, the regular sermon by Rabbi Julius Mark was canceled. Instead, Dr. Mark, as well as Dr. Nathan Perilman, rabbi of the congregation, and Rabbi Ronald B. Sobel, assistant spiritual leader, delivered separate sermons in tribute to Mr. Kennedy.

On the temple's walls outside, a notice read:

"In Memoriam. John F. Kennedy, President of the United States. We are shocked and grief-stricken."

Nixon Voices Grief Before TV Audience

Former Vice President Richard M. Nixon appeared briefly on television yesterday to express his sorrow over the death of President Kennedy. "President Kennedy yesterday wrote the last and greatest chapter of his *Profiles in Courage,*" Mr. Nixon said. "Today, millions of people throughout the world are trying to find words adequate to express their grief and sympathy to his family," Mr. Nixon continued. "The greatest tribute we can pay to his memory is in our everyday lives to do everything we can to reduce the forces of hatred which drive men to do such terrible deeds."

Mr. Nixon, dressed in a dark gray suit and wearing a dark gray tie, stood in the doorway of the apartment house at 810 Fifth Avenue, at 62d Street, where he lives. Live cameras of the three television networks, film units and radio broadcasters were ranged in a semicircle on the sidewalk. Mr. Nixon, who lost the presidential election of 1960 to Mr. Kennedy, spoke solemnly and prefaced his remarks about Mr. Kennedy by saying: "In view of the nature of this statement I would appreciate it if we did not go into any other questions at this time."

The former vice president and Mrs. Nixon will fly to Washington to-morrow to attend the funeral service for Mr. Kennedy.

Negro Women's Group Postpones Its Cotillion

The National Council of Negro Women has postponed Friday's International Cotillion, a debutante presentation involving about 100 young women from the United States, Europe, Asia and Africa. The event has been rescheduled for Jan. 3 in the Imperial Ballroom of the Americana Hotel.

The young women were expected to arrive here last night and early today. All but two, one from St. Louis and another from Monroe, La., were notified of the change before they had left home, a spokesman for the ball said.

A rehearsal for the cotillion was to be held today as planned, but only young women from this area were expected. The cotillion committee and the National Council of Negro Women will have a memorial service for President Kennedy Friday at 8 P.M. at the Americana.

KHRUSHCHEV AND THE SOVIET PEOPLE, IN UNUSUAL ACTION, PAY SPECIAL RESPECTS

Calls on Kohler and Sends Messages— Mikoyan Will Attend Capital Rites

By HENRY TANNER

Special to The New York Times

MOSCOW, Nov. 23—Premier Khrushchev, in a series of unusual actions, emphasized today the Soviet Union's deep concern over the death of President Kennedy. Mr. Khrushchev called this morning at the residence of the United States ambassador, Foy D. Kohler, to pay his tribute and to sign the condolence book. Andrei A. Gromyko, the foreign minister, who accompanied the premier, had tears in his eyes as he took leave of the ambassador.

Anastas I. Mikoyan, a first deputy premier and one of Mr. Khrushchev's closest associates, will go to Washington for the funeral. Premier and Mrs. Khrushchev sent personal messages of condolence to Mrs. Kennedy, and President Leonid I. Brezhnev and the premier sent official messages to President Johnson. The texts were made public by Tass, the Soviet press agency.

In death Mr. Kennedy was praised and mourned in Moscow as no Western statesman before him had been. For the first time the Moscow television station broadcast a live newscast from Washington via Telstar, the United States communications satellite. The program showed the scene as marines carried Mr. Kennedy's coffin into the White House and as family and friends gathered. There could be no doubt about the depth of the feeling that the death had evoked among plain Soviet citizens. There was not an American in the city who did not receive calls from Soviet friends and even distant acquaintances.

At the *New York Times* bureau, Soviet employees clipped the president's portrait from a discarded magazine, put black type around it and pinned it to the wall. They placed a large bunch of white flowers beneath it.

The father of a schoolboy sent a telegram to the American parent of one of his son's classmates. "With deep sincere grief, anger and condolence, I heard about the premature death of your president," it said. It was signed, "Soviet citizen and your friend."

The figure of the youthful president in death appeared to have captured the imaginations of Soviet citizens to a far greater extent than anyone here had realized. Many of the condolences expressed not only grief over his death but also concern over the future and fear of the unknown.

"What will U.S.-Soviet relations be in the future?" several Muscovites asked. "Will the hope of peace be diminished?"

Some of their questions were implied also in a report in *Izvestia*, the Government newspaper. In the first public assessment of President Johnson, the newspaper's New York correspondent quoted American observers as having said that it was "improbable" that there would be "basic changes" in American foreign policy.

To the Soviet public the new president is largely an unknown. Premier Khrushchev met him formally during a visit to Washington in 1959.

Mr. Khrushchev, who had hurried to Moscow from Kiev, arrived at Spaso House, Ambassador Kohler's colonnaded residence, at 12:30 P.M. with Mr. Gromyko and Mikhail N. Smirnovsky, head of the American desk of the Foreign Ministry. Mr. Kohler, still obviously stunned, took his guest by the arm and led him to a small table where the condolences book lay next to a framed photograph of the president inscribed to the ambassador "With high esteem and warm personal regards." The frame bore a black mourning band.

A marine stood stiffly to one side of the table. An American flag with black crepe stood on the other. Not a word passed between the Soviet leader and the ambassador. The only sound was the whirring of television cameras crowding in as Mr. Khrushchev slowly, almost ponderously, put on his glasses and then stepped forward to sign at the top of a page. Mr. Gromyko and Mr. Smirnovsky signed next. Then, still silent, the group stepped back and posed for pictures. Mr. Kohler then led Mr. Khrushchev and his aides to another part of the residence, where they stayed for 20 minutes. A spokesman said later that the premier had presented his condolences to the ambassador and that the rest of the conversation was a reminiscence of the Vienna conference of 1961—the only personal meeting between Mr. Kennedy and Mr. Khrushchev.

Moscow's show of grief and compassion, according to longtime residents, surpassed even those at the death of Franklin D. Roosevelt, another president who had captured the Soviet people's imagination.

"There was no television then and few radios," an elderly Muscovite said. "Roosevelt was old and sick, and he died a natural death. It was wartime and we were used to hearing of death.

"There was no indignation then. Now there is. Here was a man who tried to do good, and they would not let him live."

All Soviet news media gave extensive coverage to the assassination. Residents said they recalled nothing even remotely comparable. All morning newspapers had revised their front pages to announce the death. Soviet newspapers do not normally carry foreign news on their front pages. *Izvestia* gave a large and prominent space on its front page to the Soviet leaders' messages of condolence, and a major part of an inside page to reports from Washington, Dallas and New York. The Moscow radio broadcast extensive news programs all through the day. The state television suspended its schedule at 6 P.M. for a special program entitled, *In Memoriam of President John F. Kennedy.* In addition to the Telstar newscast, it included films of Mr. Kennedy's inauguration and his appearance last June 10 at American University, where he made a speech regarded here as a milestone in better East-West relations. The passages from the speech that Moscow viewers heard included one saying: "As Americans, we fight Communism . . . but we can still hail the Russian people."

Mr. Khrushchev, in his message to Mr. Johnson, described Mr. Kennedy as a "person of broad outlook who realistically assessed the situation and tried to find ways for negotiated settlements on the international problems which now divide the world.

"The Soviet Government and the Soviet people share the deep grief of the American people over this great loss," he said. He added that President Kennedy had made "a tangible contribution" to the search for peace.

In his message to Mrs. Kennedy, the premier said: "It was with deep personal grief that I learn about the tragic death of your husband. All people who knew him greatly respected him, and I shall always keep the memory of my meetings with him."

British to Sound Johnson on Ties

Home to Accompany Philip on Trip to U.S. Today

By SYDNEY GRUSON

Special to The New York Times

LONDON, Nov. 23—Sir Alec Douglas-Home will fly to Washington tomorrow to attend the memorial service for President Kennedy and, presumably, to have a first meeting with President Johnson. Sir Alec, Britain's new prime minister, will accompany Prince Philip, the Duke of Edinburgh.

Buckingham Palace announced today that Queen Elizabeth's husband would represent the monarch at the service. Harold Wilson, leader of the Labor party, will travel with Prince Philip and the prime minister.

Sir Alec's decision to go to Washington is meant as a mark of the esteem and affection in which the murdered president was held here. But it is also a reflection of the concern aroused by the replacement of the Western world's leader by a man virtually unknown to the British Government and people.

Sir Alec was Britain's foreign secretary until five weeks ago. As foreign secretary he was Prime Minister Macmillan's chief lieutenant in forging British-American policy toward the worldwide problems in which the two countries are immersed.

In contrast with the new president, Mr. Kennedy had a circle of close British friends. His sister Kathleen was married to the heir of the duke of Devonshire. She and her husband were killed soon after they married. Through this marriage Mr. Kennedy was related to Sir David Ormsby Gore, British ambassador in Washington, who is a kinsman of former Prime Minister Harold Macmillan. Another of Mr. Kennedy's sisters, Patricia, is married to the English-born actor Peter Lawford.

The feeling of deep personal loss and grief over President Kennedy's death were still evident throughout Britain today. The prime minister attended a memorial service at the Roman Catholic Westminster Cathedral. He will attend a Church of England memorial service in Westminster Abbey tomorrow. Similar services were held in churches of all denominations and synagogues throughout the country. A week's court mourning has been ordered and the House of Commons will sit only long enough Monday for tributes to be paid the late president before it rises for the day.

Pope and Council Join Us in Mourning

Spellman Officiates at Mass for Kennedy in Rome

By MILTON BRACKER

Special to The New York Times

ROME, Nov. 23—President Kennedy was mourned today by the pope in his private chapel, by Cardinal Spellman at a requiem mass in the Church of Santa Susanna, by the churchmen here for the Ecumenical Council, and by American and Italian residents of Rome alike.

All day crowds lingered in the driveway of the United States Embassy on the Via Veneto. Gifts of flowers were displayed in the entrance, while men and women lined up to sign the two visitors' books. A United States marine presided over one, a sailor over the other.

Members of the diplomatic corps were received in the embassy. Ambassador G. Frederick Reinhardt and his wife later sat in the front row at the American Catholic church while Cardinal Spellman celebrated the requiem mass.

Besides saying mass in his Vatican chapel for the repose of the president's soul, Pope Paul sent telegrams of condolence to Mrs. Kennedy, to Attorney General Robert F. Kennedy, to the late president's parents, and to his successor, President Johnson.

To Mrs. Kennedy—whom the previous pope, John XXIII, had greeted at the Vatican with widespread arms and the one word, "Jacqueline!"— Pope Paul said in his message:

"We hasten to send you, beloved daughter, the assurance of our heartfelt sympathy on your deep sorrow and of our fervent prayers for the repose of the soul of your husband.

"Upon you and your children, we bestow in pledge of sustaining and consoling divine grace, our affectionate apostolic blessing."

Sending condolences to President Johnson, the pontiff referred to "President John Fitzgerald Kennedy, whom we have known personally and whose intrepid character and high qualities we admired."

Pope Paul received President Kennedy in private audience on July 2.

At Saint Peter's Basilica this morning, a requiem mass had been arranged for cardinals and other prelates who had died this year. When the churchmen had gathered, they were told by Eugene Cardinal Tisserant, dean of the College of Cardinals, that the mass also was being said for the repose of the soul of the president.

Independently, the American bishops here for the Council—presently about 180 out of a total of 237—issued a statement declaring that the president's death "deprives mankind of a compassionate champion of peace and brotherhood, his country of a loyal husband and father, his parents of a dutiful and devoted son."

The Church of Santa Susanna, on the Via XX Settembre, was packed for the 5 P.M. mass celebrated by Cardinal Spellman. Cardinal Spellman was assisted by two seminarians from the North American College, William Varvaro and John Strynkowski, both of Brooklyn. Both youths are deacons, and both are to be ordained next month.

Regime in Vietnam Expresses Sorrow

Special to The New York Times

SAIGON, South Vietnam, Nov. 23—The new military junta sent cables today to Mrs. John F. Kennedy, President Johnson and Secretary of State Dean Rusk and expressed its sorrow publicly.

Gen. Paul D. Harkins, the United States military commander, said: "The bold decision to come to the aid of the Republic of Vietnam in its fight against the Communist Vietcong was one of the highlights of President Kennedy's tragically abbreviated but illustrious term as our chief of state."

Some Vietnamese military officers were worried over the effect of the president's death on American commitments here. A Vietnamese colonel, about to lead his troops into the field, stopped a reporter and asked whether this might mean the United States would pull out of Vietnam.

Castro Mourns "Hostile" Leader

Deplores Slaying but Says Kennedy Courted War

MIAMI, Nov. 23 (AP)—Premier Fidel Castro, voicing disapproval of President Kennedy's assassination, told Cuba tonight that the late president had carried the world "to the brink of nuclear war." In a radio and television address the premier said that despite Mr. Kennedy's "hostile policies toward us," the news of his assassination was "grave and bad."

"People feel repugnance to such a slaying because we should not consider this method a correct form of battle," he added. "We Cubans must react as conscientious revolutionaries and not confuse systems with the individual. We fight against systems, not the man."

The Administrations of President Kennedy and his predecessor, Dwight D. Eisenhower, Dr. Castro said, "were characterized by hostile and implacable policies toward us." He went on: "Cuba was a victim of attacks of all kinds that cost blood. Hundreds of our compatriots lost their lives defending against Yankee imperialism." Dr. Castro recalled the unsuccessful Bay of Pigs invasion of 1961 and the naval quarantine of Cuba in 1962, and he declared that nuclear warfare could have resulted.

Ireland Mourns "Death in Family"

Recalls Kennedy's Hope to Return There in Spring

Special to The New York Times

DUBLIN, Nov. 23—Ireland is in mourning today for President Kennedy. A radio commentator summed up the nation's feelings when he said, "It's as if there was a death in every family in Ireland." All public functions, sporting events, dances and other entertainment have been canceled.

One of the most moving tributes to the late president was paid by President Eamon de Valera. In a voice charged with emotion the 81-year-old president told a nationwide radio audience:

"During his recent visit we came to regard the president as one of ourselves, though always aware that he was the head of the greatest nation in the world today.

"We were proud of him as being of our race and we were convinced that through his fearless leadership the United States would continue increasing its stature among the nations of the world and its power of maintaining world peace."

At the request of Mrs. Kennedy, a contingent of the Irish Army will take part in the funeral ceremonies for her husband, it was announced tonight. A contingent from the officer cadet unit will leave Dublin tomorrow on the plane that will take President de Valera to the United States. The group will be accompanied by Gen. Sean McEoin, chief of staff of the Irish Army.

The mayor of Limerick, Mrs. Frances Condell, compared the loss of President Kennedy to that of Pope John XXIII. She said, "The president, like Pope John, walks with God today."

Archbishop William Conway, primate of the Roman Catholic Church in Ireland, said in a message from Rome: "President Kennedy's high ideals, his hope for peace and social justice will long remain an inspiration to the world."

In no part of Ireland is there such grief as in the little County Wexford towns of New Ross and nearby Dunganstown, where Mr. Kennedy's forefathers were born. Andrew Minihan, chairman of the New Ross urban council, who received President Kennedy last June, said the assassination "has shocked the entire town." Mr. Minihan recalled that the president, during his visit to New Ross, had thrilled the people by his reading of the Gerald Griffin poem "On the River Shannon," the text of which had been given to him the previous night by Mrs. de Valera.

The reading ended with the lines:

> *"To see old Shannon's face again;*
> *Oh the bliss entrancing."*

The president then turned to the great gathering of Wexford people and promised: "I am going to come back to see old Shannon's face again. This is not the land of my birth, but it is the land for which I have the greatest affection and I certainly hope to be back in the springtime."

CABINET CONVENES

Johnson Sees Truman and Eisenhower on First Day in Office

By JAMES RESTON
Special to The New York Times

WASHINGTON, Nov. 23—President Johnson took over the machinery of government today amid pledges of support from the other leaders of the nation and the non-Communist world. It was a bleak and melancholy day, with the rain falling slowly out of gray skies and the body of the assassinated 35th president of the United States lying in the East Room of the White House. Like a family facing the imperatives of both life and death, citizens of the Union came quietly to the Executive Mansion to look at the coffin of John Fitzgerald Kennedy and to express their best wishes to his successor.

The president announced that he would address a joint session of Congress at 12:30 P.M. Wednesday. White House sources indicated that the speech would be telecast to the nation. President Kennedy's funeral will take place on Monday. The address to Congress was delayed to allow Mr. Johnson to spend Tuesday conferring with the many foreign leaders who will be in Washington for the funeral.

Later it was announced that the president would meet at 3 P.M. tomorrow on the war in South Vietnam with Henry Cabot Lodge, ambassador to Saigon; Secretary of Defense Robert S. McNamara; Secretary of State Dean Rusk and McGeorge Bundy, special presidential assistant on security affairs. Pierre Salinger, White House press secretary, said the president would talk to Mr. Rusk, Mr. Lodge and Mr. McNamara about their discussion in Hawaii last week on the Vietnamese situation since the over-throw of the Diem regime.

President Johnson held his first Cabinet meeting this afternoon. He opened it with a minute of silent prayer for President Kennedy and then asked all members of the Cabinet to continue to serve as before. Attorney General Robert F. Kennedy was present. Earlier, President Johnson had received former Presidents Harry S. Truman and Dwight D. Eisenhower, attended church and conferred with Secretary Rusk, Secretary McNamara and other officials.

Unity and continuity were the themes of President Johnson's first full day in office. He was clearly concerned today to make plain to all nations that the authority of state had passed smoothly and quickly into his hands and that he intended to proceed on the same course and with the same associates for the time being. At the same time, he emphasized again today a nonpolitical approach to the leaders of the Republican party.

As boxes of President Kennedy's official papers were being moved into the old State Department Building from the White House, President Johnson and General Eisenhower, who developed a close working relationship when Mr. Johnson was majority leader of the Senate, chatted together and then called in photographers to record the meeting. Although President Johnson spent more time today with Secretary Rusk, Secretary McNamara and John A. McCone, director of the Central Intelligence Agency, than with anyone else, it was stated officially that these meetings did not involve any new developments in foreign or defense policy. President Johnson has been representing the former Administration abroad, most recently in the Low Countries and Scandinavia, but he has not been deeply involved in all foreign policy questions, mainly because President Kennedy tended to have few meetings of the Cabinet or the National Security Council.

Therefore, today's meetings were only the first of a series of briefings by Cabinet members. The preliminary estimates of next year's budget have already gone in. President Kennedy was familiar with the broad outlines of these estimates and with the details of many. But President Johnson will now have to review all of these and settle some controversial questions that have both financial and political implications. One of these, for ex-

ample, concerns the question of a major slum clearance and low-cost housing program. This is deeply involved in the racial controversy in the North
and the new president's decision on this is expected to give some indication
of his approach to the problem. President Kennedy had been under considerable pressure to hold down Government expenditures next year as part
of an arrangement to get Republican and Southern Democratic support for
a tax cut. Now President Johnson must decide how he wishes to negotiate
this to get the tax cut he has supported in the past.

In the foreign field, the decision of President de Gaulle, Chancellor
Ludwig Erhard, and Anastas I. Mikoyan, a first deputy premier of the
Soviet Union, to attend the Kennedy state funeral raised the immediate
question of whether to invite them to stay over for discussion. President
Johnson decided to hold at least brief talks with them. President de Gaulle
has been at odds with the United States on the defense of the Atlantic
Community, the future of the North Atlantic Treaty, and the whole issue
of avoiding the spread of nuclear weapons. This had led to some division
among President Kennedy's advisers before his death. Some favored making a new effort to compromise these differences with President de Gaulle.
Others felt that this would be a mistake. Yet the indications tonight were
that President Johnson would at least want to have an exchange of views
with these and other leaders, even if no new negotiations were started. A
Johnson-Mikoyan meeting took on added interest in the light of Premier
Khrushchev's statement about the assassination of President Kennedy. Mr.
Khrushchev has risked opposition within his own government to try to
reach an accommodation with Washington, and it was assumed here that
he would wish to be reassured through Mr. Mikoyan that President Johnson
intended to carry on the Kennedy policy.

The new president is likely to find, however, as President Kennedy did
before him, that reassuring one major nation has a way of making another
unhappy. For example, just before the assassination of President Kennedy,
the new chancellor of West Germany had arranged his first state visit here.
One of the purposes of this was to discover just how far Washington cared
to go in reaching agreements with Moscow. The Eisenhower Administration, for example, insisted that Soviet agreement to the reunification of
Germany should be a precondition of any Washington-Moscow accom-

modations. The Kennedy Administration, while always insisting on German reunification as a goal, has nevertheless sought limited accommodations with the Soviet Union. Here again President Johnson will no doubt be asked for his approach to this question, at a time when Mr. Mikoyan is seeking assurances that Mr. Johnson will carry on the Kennedy approach to Moscow. Both the White House staff and the State Department were studying today how all these probable demands on the president's time could be met in the next week.

Johnson's Attitudes on Major Issues

Following are recent statements by President Johnson on major issues:

COMMUNISM

"Khrushchev is committed to the proposition that only under a dictatorship can the world find prosperity and economic abundance. His whole life is wrapped around the concept that free enterprise must fall."—San Augustine, Tex., Aug. 29, 1959.

"Mr. Khrushchev does not understand that Americans of whatever their political creed—Republican or Democratic—will stand united against him in his effort to divide the country and weaken the hopes of freedom. We also stand united in our determination to preserve our freedoms and to promote peace in the world."—Washington, June 2, 1960.

"We are united in America, regardless of party and regardless of religion, in our concern and understanding for the German people in their present ordeal. The endangered frontier of freedom now runs through divided but dauntless Berlin. The Communist dictatorship has the power temporarily to seal a border; but no tyranny can survive beyond the shadow of its own evil strength."—Berlin, August 19, 1961.

"If the Communists have chosen to lay aside pretense of morality by resort to their many forms of aggression, we must not do the same. The highest morality between nations is the integrity of mutual agreements. Where we have asked nations to stand with us for freedom—where men are willing to stand for their own freedom—we must honor our pledge to stand with them."—New York, May 4, 1961.

"Khrushchev has boasted that the Soviet Union will destroy us in economic competition. And the Soviets have been working for years on the uncommitted peoples of the earth. It would be foolish to pretend that their work has not been effective."—Washington, April 16, 1959.

COMMUNIST CHINA

"The Communists exiled and assassinated Leon Trotsky. But they did not exile this idea. And one of the greatest single blows that ever has been dealt against the free world was the Communist conquest of 650 million Chinese, who are gaining at the rate of 13 million people a year."—Washington, May 10, 1961.

"America stands firm with her Chinese [Nationalist] allies and we shall continue to do so until freedom is secured."—Taipei, Taiwan, May 15, 1961.

CUBA

"We shall not be content until the last of Soviet forces are withdrawn from Cuban soil. The members of the Organization of American States also are mutually determined that the Cuban people shall have an opportunity to choose their own government freely and without oppression."—Fort McNair, Wash., March 20, 1963.

"It has been said truthfully that wherever we look in this world today we see the advancing peril of Communism. In some faraway lands, it is a creeping peril. But in this hemisphere—in this homeland of the ancient faith and ancient security of the Monroe Doctrine—it is a peril that is galloping across the waters of the Caribbean. For—incredible, unbelievable, unthinkable as it may seem—there is tonight a Soviet beachhead only 90 miles from our Gulf Coast. A bad neighbor, a very bad neighbor, holds power in Havana."—New Orleans, Oct. 15, 1960.

"Cuba is a showcase of Communist failure that is costing the Soviet Union more than $1 million a day to prevent complete and final collapse. This Administration's policy is to get rid of Communism and Castro."—Milwaukee, May 4, 1963.

"The purpose of the United States remains unchanged toward this hemisphere; we intend that the Americas shall be free of Communism."—Chicago, Nov. 14, 1962.

LATIN AMERICA

"Either we launch now a positive and dynamic program to redeem democracy or we will leave the field clear for a massive Communist penetration into Latin America. What can we do?

"One of the first steps we must take is to reaffirm that we are on the side of progress in Latin America. We must support, morally and financially, the struggle of our Latin friends against political, economic and social injustice—not only to improve their standard of living but to foster the democratic way of life in every country.

"We must revitalize our diplomatic corps with ambassadors who know and understand our neighbors and their language and who have qualifications other than contributing to campaign chests.

"We must offer to the people of Latin America the very best technical know-how which will help them to develop their skills and to make and sell their own products.

"We should establish in the Panama Canal Zone an Inter-American Center for the training of government administrators. There is a widespread need in Latin America for skilled and well-trained government administrators; this center would help to meet that need."—New Orleans, Oct. 15, 1960.

NUCLEAR TESTING

"If a treaty is to be effective and to command the confidence of all participating nations it must provide an efficient, reliable, prompt system of verification and controls not subject to crippling vetoes. There is no point to a treaty for a treaty's sake. For our part we want a sound, effective and workable treaty. A sound treaty could contribute importantly to a reduction of international tension, and to progress on the critical problem of disarmament."—Geneva, April 6, 1961.

"We are not going to accept the verdict of those who would equate the morality of breaking the atomic test truce with the morality of purely defensive measures [now] that the truce is broken. We are not going to stand abashed before those who are willing to excuse the deadly sins of Communist tyrannies because of sins—many times atoned—that were committed in the last century."—Las Vegas, Oct. 2, 1961.

DISARMAMENT

"We now face the prospect of destroying ourselves not as the result of an armaments race but merely by indulging in the race. I am calling for an open curtain for full discussion of the immediate, urgent problems facing our people. We should insist on the right to state our case on disarmament in detail to the Soviet people. And when the Soviet people know, they will insist that the arms race, the nuclear explosions, the intercontinental missiles all be banished. They will insist upon systems that safeguard us against world suicide."—New York, June 9, 1957.

"A disarmament proposal, to hold real promise, must at the minimum have one feature: reliable means to ensure compliance by all. It takes actions and demonstrated integrity on both sides to create and sustain confidence. And confidence in a genuine disarmament agreement is vital, not only to the signers of the agreement, but also to the millions of people all over the world who are weary of tensions and armaments."—Washington, Jan. 7, 1958.

FOREIGN AID

"No nation can long enjoy great affluence when all the other nations are impoverished."—San Marcos, Tex., May 28, 1961.

"We will vigorously pursue the drive against ignorance, poverty and disease not only at home but throughout the world."—New York, May 4, 1961.

"India's experience in dealing with these basic problems [hunger, illiteracy and disease] is of great value to the United States, which wishes to use its resources for aiding the peoples of the underdeveloped countries."
—New Delhi, May 19, 1961.

NATO

"Our nations together gave birth to the concept of alliances made not for the protection of governments but for the protection of common people.

"Such an alliance, for such a purpose, could only have been the product of nations governed by representatives and responsible parliaments serving responsible constituents.

"But our great alliance is not the final accomplishment of which we are capable. The bonds of our alliance in NATO are strong.

"Together we shall maintain that strength. Standing on that strength, all of us can, and must, move together to build together new strength for freedom.

"The challenge before us is to add new dimensions to the purposes of our alliances. We can go beyond allaying fears to fulfilling dreams.

"Beyond mutual military purposes, we can do much more to implement concepts of economic progress and social gain.

"Where we have sought to protect the integrity of the individual against aggression by force, we can now turn our alliances to the work of raising the standards by which the individual lives in integrity as a free man."
—Paris, Nov. 21, 1960.

DEFENSE

"We cannot be done with our dangers, or even our duties, by next weekend, or even next year. We are in for a long pull and it is our duty to begin pulling."—New York, May 5, 1961.

"We have not threatened in a put-up or shut-up fashion and we have not sought to upset the peace. We hope that reason and negotiation will prevail."—Los Angeles, June 25, 1961.

"We seek peace but we shun appeasement because we know it is appeasement on the installation plan and the signal for ultimate war. Our power is a pledge of peace, not an incitement to conflict."—Nashville, Sept. 25, 1961.

"We must not libel the roads that lead to peace or glamorize the roads that lead to war. We learned at a tragic price the folly of heeding orators who insisted that our national strategy must be permanent isolation. We would pay a higher price for heeding orators who insist our national strategy be instant intervention."—Annapolis, Md., June 5, 1963.

CIVIL RIGHTS

"The Negro today asks justice. We do not answer him, we do not answer those who lie beneath this soil when we reply to the Negro by asking, 'Patience.'

"It is empty to plead that the solution to the dilemmas of the present rests on the hands of the clock. The solution is in our hands. Our nation found its soul in honor on these fields of Gettysburg 100 years ago. We must not lose that soul in dishonor now on the fields of hate.

"We as a nation have failed ourselves by not trusting the law and by not using the law to gain sooner the ends of justice which law alone serves."—Gettysburg, Pa., May 30, 1963.

"It is difficult to raise a man's status by legislation, but if you give him the right to vote he can help himself."—New York, Jan. 22, 1960.

TAXES

"If we are not to default the integrity of our free enterprise system, we must concentrate vigorous effort on its future rather than hold to easy concepts of the past.

"We must not surrender to inflation.

"We must not surrender to poverty.

"We must not surrender to educational blight or medical mediocrity or social depression in any field of our society.

"We must not abandon regions or cities or classes or ages to despair.

"We must not allow ourselves to forfeit the goals of equal standards of freedom, opportunity and equality for want of boldness.

"We certainly must not abdicate progress to the rule of tension and strife.

"In a world reborn—facing the new youth of a new age and a new dimension of space—we must certainly not default the leadership of vigor to the totalitarians.

"Fiscal solvency concerns us all. It is a first concern, for no course is honest without the courage of financial prudence. But we cannot afford to bankrupt the national conscience to serve the ends of political bookkeeping."—Washington, Jan. 7, 1959.

SPACE

"We cannot wishfully and unrealistically assume that no nation will extend its objectives of world domination by means of space weapons. To reach for the moon is a risk, but it is a risk we must take. Keep in mind that failure to go into space is even riskier."—Dallas, April 23, 1963.

"We are going to the moon because it is a logical step in the exploration of the universe, and we know that the steps we have already taken have paid off a valuable return on our investment and paid off handsomely."—New Orleans, April 19, 1962.

"The whole field of space needs one head—one man to be accountable, one man with the powers to accomplish. If the Executive Department cannot or will not meet this responsibility, then the Congress must act. America cannot sit out 1960 and wait to start up, again, somewhere down the road."—Washington, Dec. 17, 1959.

"We ought to spend the money, the time and the effort to surpass the Russian effort. I don't think we have the proper sense of urgency."—Washington, Oct. 11, 1959.

JOHNSON WEIGHS MAKE-UP OF STAFF BUT ASKS KENNEDY AIDES AND CABINET TO STAY

Changes Likely in a Few Weeks

New President Is Expected to Put Some of Own Men in Key White House Posts

By CABELL PHILLIPS

Special to The New York Times

WASHINGTON, Nov. 23—President Johnson has asked the Kennedy Cabinet and White House staff to remain in their jobs. Early next week, however, if established custom is followed, their formal resignations will be placed on his desk, to be accepted or rejected at the president's pleasure. And within the next few weeks there almost certainly will be some new faces on the scene, at least among the more intimate staff positions. Later, undoubtedly, there will be changes in the Cabinet.

This will not represent a "house cleaning." There has been an unusual rapport between Mr. Johnson as vice president and most Kennedy aides. Rather, it will be a demonstration of the inescapable need of a president to surround himself with aides of his own choice and with whom he shares a deep confidence. In the most recent and nearly comparable example, when Harry S. Truman moved into the presidency after Franklin D. Roosevelt's death in 1945, there was an almost complete turnover in less than 90 days. But the personal relationships underlying that transition differed considerably from those existing now.

A president has his personal 1,500-man bureaucracy, officially called the Executive Office of the President. It is a collection of specialized agencies such as the Bureau of the Budget, Council of Economic Advisers and National Security Council. They extend his managerial grasp on the reins of Government. Central to this, and more intimately involved in helping a president carry out his day-to-day duties, is the White House staff. This group of personal aides and deputies has no responsibilities other than those assigned by the president.

This staff structure varies from president to president. Dwight D. Eisenhower, for example, modeled his after a quasi-military command staff, with Sherman Adams as a chief of state. The Kennedy staff was less rigidly organized. Over-all, however, precedence has gone to Theodore C. Sorensen, a brilliant young Nebraska lawyer who served Mr. Kennedy in the Senate for many years. His title is special counsel to the president. This was also the title of Clark M. Clifford when he was the top aide to President Truman.

The Kennedy staff collectively has often been referred to jokingly as "the Irish Mafia" because of the number of Boston Irish friends of the president's who served on it. Altogether, there are 17 special assistants, a press secretary and a deputy press secretary on this roster, plus a handful of lesser functionaries. Among the more familiar names in the group are Pierre Salinger, the press secretary; Lawrence F. O'Brien, Congressional liaison; P. Kenneth O'Donnell, appointments and political liaison; McGeorge Bundy, national security affairs, and Arthur Schlesinger Jr., Ralph A. Dungan and Timothy J. Reardon Jr., among others, whose assignments were more flexible.

Such a group bears a peculiarly close and confidential relationship to a president. Mr. Truman inherited a competent corps of assistants from President Roosevelt. But in less than a week, he installed his own man, Charles Ross, as press secretary, replacing Steve Early. Mr. Ross, a boyhood friend of the new president, was a Washington correspondent for the *St. Louis Post-Dispatch*. He had covered Mr. Truman as senator and vice president. In the next few weeks thereafter, President Truman replaced practically every top White House assistant with persons who had formerly worked for him in the Senate and with friends from the political world. It would be surprising if President Johnson did not, for the same reasons, make some early staff changes himself.

The Cabinet bears a different relationship to a president. He is no less dependent upon it than upon his staff for the success of his Administration, but he has less freedom in choosing it and less control over its members' performance. Mr. Truman faced a particularly awkward problem in this respect. He scarcely knew some members of the Roosevelt Cabinet, and was regarded with light disdain by others. As Jonathan

Daniels wrote in his Truman biography, *Man of Independence:* "Mr. Truman was to find the same sort of Cabinet contentions which began with Jefferson and Hamilton at the table of George Washington. He was to discover that some who accepted places as his subordinates did so with no lapse of their sense of superiority. No other President in history ever had at his table two men who so deeply felt that somehow they had been cheated out of his chair." (The last sentence of the quoted passage referred to Secretary of State James F. Byrnes and Secretary of Commerce Henry A. Wallace, both of whom had hoped for the vice-presidential nomination in 1944.)

Although Mr. Truman regarded himself as little more than a "caretaker" president when he was sworn in in April, 1945, he had replaced six of the Roosevelt Cabinet by the end of July, and three of the remaining four by September, 1946. Whatever reasons President Johnson finds for making changes in the Cabinet and White House staff, they will not, it seems, be the same ones that motivated President Truman.

As Mr. Truman wrote in his memoirs: "The President, by necessity, builds his staff (and Cabinet), and the Vice President remains an outsider, no matter how friendly the two may be."

In the 83 days between the inauguration and death of Mr. Roosevelt Vice President Truman saw the president four times.

20 Johnson Aides Form Cadre for an Enlarged Personal Staff

Group, Nearly All Texans, Is Expected to Be Doubled or Trebled— Some Hold Space and Defense Posts

By BEN A. FRANKLIN

Special to The New York Times

WASHINGTON, Nov. 23—President Johnson's personal staff was a closely knit cadre of about 20 persons during his three vice-presidential years. It will be doubled or trebled in the ensuing transition at the White House. The change is expected to be distinct and revealing. Mr. Johnson, like President Kennedy, has had the good fortune to attract able and devoted staff aides who have the knack of anticipating the moves and reflecting the moods of their chief. Among the closest and brightest of Mr. Johnson's intimates is a 29-year-old Baptist clergyman, Bill D. Moyers, who was summoned to the White House last night and today. Mr. Moyers was a newsman in Texas when Mr. Johnson made him his executive assistant in his 1960 campaign for the Democratic presidential nomination. He has never had a congregation. After the 1960 campaign, Mr. Moyers joined the Peace Corps, becoming an assistant public affairs officer in 1961 and then being appointed to the $20,000-a-year post of deputy director under President Kennedy's brother-in-law, Sargent Shriver.

The best-known Johnson staff member around Washington is George E. Reedy, the bushy-haired press assistant, who is the only non-Texan in the Johnson entourage. A 46-year-old Chicagoan, Mr. Reedy left the Capitol staff of the United Press in 1951 to join Mr. Johnson, then a senator. Mr. Reedy is regarded as the likely successor to Pierre Salinger as White House press secretary. They are considered equally colorful spokesmen.

Walter Jenkins, who has worked for Mr. Johnson since 1939, has the greatest seniority on the staff. An important and trusted adviser on political matters, Mr. Jenkins, now in his 40's, has had the title of administrative assistant to Mr. Johnson both as senator and as vice president.

Mrs. Elizabeth Carpenter, a former correspondent here for Texas newspapers, joined the Johnson staff in 1960 as Mrs. Johnson's press secretary. Her role, however, has not been limited to social affairs. She is considered likely to continue to be Mrs. Johnson's press secretary.

O. B. Lloyd Jr., 49, another former Texas newspaperman, served until 1961 on the Johnson staff. He is now public affairs director of the National Aeronautics and Space Administration and a close associate there of another Johnson protégé, James E. Webb, the NASA administrator.

Mr. Johnson's influence in the space and defense programs has been formidable. In the Senate he was chairman of the Aeronautical and Space Sciences Committee and a member of the Armed Services Committee. As vice president he headed the National Aeronautics and Space Council. Thus he has been close to a number of leading space and defense officials.

Among them is Kenneth E. Belieu, now assistant secretary of the navy. He was close to Mr. Johnson in the Senate as a staff assistant on the Armed Services Committee and later as staff director of the Committee on Aeronautical and Space Sciences. Another such specialist is Edward C. Welsh, executive secretary of the National Aeronautics and Space Council. Mr. Welsh was formerly an assistant to Senator Stuart Symington, Democrat of Missouri, and is an economist of some international repute. An associate of Mr. Belieu in various Senate committee assignments was Max Lehrer, an expert on space policy and defense budget matters. Mr. Lehrer is now an official of the Radio Corporation of America.

Assigned by the State Department to brief the vice president on Foreign Affairs, Samuel R. Gammon, a career Foreign Service officer with a doctorate from the University of Texas, is expected to continue in some special foreign policy post. Another official in this category is Carl T. Rowan, a Negro, a former newspaperman who has been a deputy assistant secretary of state and is now ambassador to Finland. Mr. Rowan reportedly received word from Mr. Johnson today to "come see me this afternoon." He had accompanied the vice president on many of his foreign travels. There was also some speculation that Dean Acheson, former secretary of state and a strong supporter of President Johnson, might be called upon for at least an informal role in foreign policy.

It is considered likely that Mr. Johnson will invite Gerald W. Siegel to return to Government service. Mr. Siegel, a lawyer, resigned as head of the Senate Democratic Policy Committee to become a vice president and general counsel of *The Washington Post*. Another veteran of Mr. Johnson's Capitol staff is Arthur C. Perry, a former aide to the late Senator Tom Connally, Democrat of Texas. Mr. Perry has worked in Washington for 40 years. Gov. John B. Connally of Texas, who is recovering from wounds inflicted by the same gunman who killed President Kennedy, has been closely associated with Mr. Johnson. He is a former secretary of the navy and has been an ally of the new president in the shifting politics of their home state.

Mr. Johnson's other prominent backers in Texas include Herman Brown, of the big construction company Brown & Root. Clifton C. Carter, an Austin businessman whose specialty has been contacts with the business community, has been in charge of Mr. Johnson's Austin office. Charles K.

Boatner, a 50-year-old former city editor of *The Fort Worth Star-Telegram*, served on Mr. Johnson's vice-presidential staff for two years before becoming information director of the United States Park Service.

A longtime campaign adviser to Mr. Johnson and an important link to other Washington figures is James H. Rowe Jr., a lawyer who has been consulted by every Democratic presidential candidate since Franklin D. Roosevelt. Mr. Rowe backed Senator Hubert H. Humphrey for the nomination in 1960 until Mr. Humphrey withdrew. Then he switched to Mr. Johnson. After Mr. Kennedy's nomination for president at the 1960 Democratic National Convention, Mr. Rowe served as liaison between Mr. Kennedy and Mr. Johnson.

Mr. Johnson's personal secretaries, Mary Juanita Roberts and Marie Fehmer, have jointly carried the burden of his immense correspondence for many years. They will almost certainly assume similar posts in the White House.

A former Johnson aide who is not expected to join the White House staff is Robert G. Baker, who became secretary of the Senate's Democratic majority under Mr. Johnson when he was majority leader and remained when Mr. Johnson left. Long a protégé of Mr. Johnson, Mr. Baker played a key role in the senator's 1960 nomination campaign. Mr. Baker resigned under fire last Oct. 7 and his business affairs are being investigated.

Johnson Pledges Policy Continuity

Asks Advisers to Reassure U.S. Allies and Foes

By MAX FRANKEL

Special to The New York Times

WASHINGTON, Nov. 23—President Johnson asked the Cabinet and other advisers of President Kennedy today to show the world that there would be no change in the broad outlines of United States policy. The new president assured Secretary of State Dean Rusk and others that he genuinely supported the policies developed over the last three years and that his expressions of support while vice president were not merely ceremonial. Mr. Johnson urged that steps be taken to reassure both the nation's allies and adversaries of the continuity of its policy. He asked the men dealing with national security affairs to remain at their desks, "working tomorrow as you did yesterday—for the president." He also asked all ambassadors abroad to forgo customary offers of resignation. Mr. Rusk requested that they send in assessments of the impact of the change in leadership here.

The emphasis today was on continuity. Mr. Kennedy's advisers, some of whom had said privately that they doubted whether the new president could simply pick up where his predecessor left off, expressed a desire to remain on the job. There were immediate signs, however, that more than declarations would be needed to persuade other Governments that Washington was not entering an interregnum.

The diplomatic community here was stunned by the assassination of President Kennedy. Many foreigners feared that American diplomacy would be injured through the loss of "sophistication." Some United States officials believed that the rush of royalty, presidents and other high-ranking statesmen to Mr. Kennedy's funeral was a sign not only of affection for the late president but also of uneasiness abroad about the future. The State Department tried to persuade foreign Governments that their ambassadors here would be appropriate representatives at the funeral, but received notices that many heads of Government wished to attend.

Quick briefings on the state of the world and the implications of the assassination were Mr. Johnson's first concerns last night and this morning. Although routine security precautions were taken to guard against the possibility of an organized assassination plot, the highest men in Government described for Mr. Johnson a period of relative calm that required no urgent decisions. Their greatest fear was that the assassination and the left-wing background of the prime suspect, Lee H. Oswald, would generate anti-Communist passions and cries for vengeance. No responsible official here believed that any foreign power or movement had any connection with the assassination. The widespread feeling was that there could be no "sensible" explanation for a senseless act. But the delicacy of the issue caused grave concern. Officials tried through the night to prevent the police and prosecutors in Dallas from drawing political conclusions from the assassination.

Though the principal foreign policy advisers were among those who told Mr. Johnson that he would eventually have to fashion a "Johnson Administration" responsive to his habits and personality, Mr. Rusk was widely expected to remain with the new team. Because of Mr. Johnson's frequent trips abroad on what amounted to goodwill missions, Mr. Rusk had always kept close touch with him. What is more, associates said, while Mr. Johnson was abroad and virtually forgotten here, it was often Mr. Rusk who urged that he be informed of some new development or that his speeches be given circulation in the United States. Mr. Johnson has spoken very highly of the secretary of state. He once told an associate that Mr. Rusk was often abused in "high places" in Washington, yet kept right on doing his job. "That," Mr. Johnson concluded, "is the mark of a really great man."

The complexity of events led officials to speculate that Mr. Johnson would rely heavily in the months to come not only on Mr. Rusk and his associates at the State Department but also on McGeorge Bundy, Mr. Kennedy's special adviser, and Secretary of Defense Robert S. McNamara.

Johnson Style: Earthy and Flamboyant

By ANTHONY LEWIS

Special to The New York Times

WASHINGTON, Nov. 23—Detachment, understatement, irony, sophistication, coolness—those were the qualities that were seen in the manner of John F. Kennedy. The trademarks of Lyndon B. Johnson are emotion, flamboyance, folksiness. He can be earthy in a manner hard to imagine John Kennedy's ever being, and no one would accuse him of reticence. Picture Lyndon Johnson as majority leader of the Senate, his greatest role before yesterday's tragedy made him president. He stands at his desk in the well of the Senate, talking quietly to another member while one arm grips the other's elbow or runs up and down his back. It was as if Senator Johnson felt a need to be in physical touch with the colleague he was trying to convert.

There was the time, in the 1960 campaign, that he flew to his Texas ranch at 1:30 one morning with a group of reporters—and spent the next hour turning on lights and driving them around in an electric cart to show off the sights. It was typical of Lyndon Johnson. He can be totally over-whelmed by the idea of the moment, and overwhelming in expressing it to others.

The morning after that tour, the senator decided to "relax" by his swim-ming pool. For two hours he sat at a control panel for the ranch commu-nications system, giving detailed orders for his daughters' departure that day, arranging baggage and answering two telephones that stood by the chair. He was not still for a moment.

That was relaxation for Lyndon Johnson. And the story tells something else besides his restlessness and energy. It indicates how much, in the past, he has been accustomed to keeping control of every detail in his life and handling everything himself—when it mattered personally. When it was not of interest, he relied heavily on the judgment of his staff. Frequently he would sign committee reports that he had not read, solely on the advice of a staff assistant that there was nothing in the contents that would hurt him politically.

Another problem is the Johnson relationship with intellectuals. His as-sociations with this group have not been close from his earliest days in Texas politics. Even though he was a New Dealer, intellectuals were not attracted to him. In part this is because Mr. Johnson does not have the earmarks of the intellectual himself. His broad stories, his backslapping, his oldstyle political campaigning are not exactly Ivy League. It is too late, of course, for Mr. Johnson to take on a scholarly mien. He is of a different generation, too, from the Kennedys and their friends, although he has said privately that he admires them for being so "hip." What is to be seen is whether the men from the universities and the foundations can work easily with President Johnson, and vice versa. Of particular interest will be whether he asks McGeorge Bundy, former Harvard dean and President Kennedy's special assistant for national security affairs, to stay on beyond the transitional period.

In one sense any discussion of Lyndon Johnson in Eastern, intellectual terms is unfair. He is a different sort of man—but this does not necessarily make him less effective as a political leader. Those who watched him closely as Senate majority leader felt that Mr. Johnson accomplished things that seemed, by ordinary analysis, beyond achievement. They never fully understood how he did it. One late night in 1958 he went through an episode that tells a good deal about the man and his technique.

The Senate had before it a series of bills to limit the powers of the Supreme Court. From every indication a majority wanted to pass them. A motion to table one measure had just failed, and it was only with some difficulty that Senator Johnson managed to adjourn the Senate for the night so the Court's supporters could regroup. He took into his office Senator Hubert H. Humphrey, Democrat of Minnesota, leader of the liberal Democratic wing. Into the small hours of the morning he lectured Senator Humphrey on what would have to be done to win the fight. Just stand up there and talk, the majority leader said. But talk about the merits—don't let them accuse you of a filibuster. When they jeer at you and slap your face, turn the other cheek. At this point Senator Johnson smashed his massive palm hard against his own face, in a shocking gesture.

For hours he went on, in a monologue, on why and how these bills should be beaten. Senator Humphrey, not usually a silent man, hardly got a word in. Once, sitting at his desk during that long evening, the majority leader suddenly whipped around and pointed at a picture of Franklin D. Roosevelt on the wall. "Look at that chin," he shouted. The performance—Senate experts referred to this Johnson approach as "the treatment"—was a virtuoso affair. But, characteristically, it had little to do with the eventual outcome of the fight. The next day, without any extended debate or pyrotechnics, Lyndon Johnson somehow went out and found quiet ways to defeat the anti–Supreme Court bills. The key measure was tabled by a vote of 41 to 40.

From incidents like that, many liberals called Senator Johnson a "maneuverer." They meant the term critically, suggesting that he was concerned only with tactics and not with substance. But they missed the point. The point was that Lyndon Johnson did care about the Supreme Court bills. He thought they were bad for the country—products of momentary hysteria. He said to senators, in effect, that they would be ashamed of passing such legislation. And he did all this for no immediate personal gain. His wealthy, conservative backers in Texas were outraged by his sinking of the Supreme Court bills. He had more antagonistic mail than he had had on any issue of the period.

As majority leader he also performed the prodigious feat of getting the Civil Rights Act of 1957 through the Senate. He did it by persuading the Southerners that blocking the bill by a filibuster would lead to a real revolt against the Senate rules. In a way President Johnson's experience as a legislative tactician is a strength and an opportunity for him. "His life has been political administration, not staff leadership," one friend said today. "In some ways what he had to do called for greater skill because he had no authority. It was consensual, and that is a high art that can be useful to a president."

As a campaigner Mr. Johnson has favored what the unfriendly might call corn. In the 1960 campaign he never failed to ridicule the Republican candidate, Richard M. Nixon, in broad strokes of sarcasm. In nearly every speech he dwelt on the religious issue, saying that no one had asked John Kennedy's older brother, Joseph Jr., where he prayed before he flew on the World War II mission that cost his life.

Emotion, freely expressed, is very much a part of Lyndon Johnson. A year or two ago a friend, commenting on the vice president's relationship with President Kennedy, said: "Kennedy doesn't cry. That is probably the biggest personal chasm between them."

And Mr. Johnson can display a powerful temper. Sometimes he is completely controlled, taking real setbacks without a word. Then something trivial will happen—someone spills a cup of coffee on his desk—and he will burst out in Texas expletives. One thing that irritates him is articles in the press ribbing his highly personalized habits, his vanity. His talk of "pressing the flesh" for shaking hands, his musical cuff links, the fact that his daughters and even his dog have the initials L.B.J.—all these are targets.

Some Johnson critics must have been surprised by his complete loyalty to President Kennedy. While Mr. Johnson was vice president, no one heard him say anything critical of Mr. Kennedy, and he rigorously resisted the natural urge to project himself occasionally into the spotlight. The truth was that he had come to admire John F. Kennedy, as a person and a politician. The admiration could almost be seen emerging during the 1960 campaign.

It was the first Kennedy-Nixon television debate that seemed to make Senator Johnson aware of his running mate's political talents. The next day, campaigning in southern Illinois, Mr. Johnson mentioned the television debate and said how great he thought Senator Kennedy had been. When the crowd responded, he praised Mr. Kennedy some more. He found that talk about Jack Kennedy was a sure winner—even, to his surprise, in Texas.

A whole broad area of difference between the two presidents is their instinctive feeling about foreign affairs. John Kennedy, partly educated abroad, wrote a book on Britain while in college and was always fascinated by foreign policy. Lyndon Johnson's heart has been in domestic affairs, though he has tried recently to travel and learn.

The sharp differences in style and personality between the late president and his successor will tend to make the transition period even harder for President Johnson. He will be dealing with another man's Administration— with men he did not appoint, men whose loyalty cannot be expected as a matter of course. Because it was a young Administration, moreover, it was still highly personal. It had not yet slid, as governments do, into bureaucratic routine. It was still a government in the image of the young president.

Still, Lyndon Johnson is a man above all others who has made his mark by bridging gulfs in ideas and personality. His favorite quotation is said to be from Isaiah I, 18:

"Come now, and let us reason together."

Death Elevated 8 Vice Presidents

Tyler, in 1841, was First, Truman the Seventh

By PHILIP BENJAMIN

Before Friday, seven vice presidents of the United States had succeeded to the presidency upon the death of the incumbent. Lyndon B. Johnson has become the eighth. Of the eight, four have become presidents following the assassination of the incumbent and four following the death of the incumbent from natural causes. In addition, three men, John Adams, Thomas Jefferson and Martin Van Buren, were elected president while serving as vice president.

John Tyler, a Virginian, was the first vice president to become president because of the death of his running mate. Tyler was playing marbles in a street in Richmond, Va., when he was informed of William Henry Harrison's death on April 4, 1841, from a cold. Among Tyler's accomplishments were the annexation of Texas and the conclusion of the war with the Seminole Indians in Florida. Tyler, a Whig, was defeated for election by James K. Polk. Tyler became a member of the Congress of the Confederacy at the start of the Civil War, but he died on Jan. 18, 1862, before the Congress assembled.

Millard Fillmore of Summerhill, N.Y., a Whig, became president after Zachary Taylor died of a "stomach colic," probably appendicitis. Fillmore was sworn in on July 10, 1850. He signed the Fugitive Slave Law, which set up Federal machinery for the recovery of runaway slaves. This hurt him in the North and prevented him from being renominated in 1852. In 1856 he was nominated on the American (Know-Nothing) party ticket, and was defeated by James Buchanan. He was politically inactive thereafter and died in 1874.

Andrew Johnson of Tennessee became president upon the death of Lincoln on April 15, 1865. Lincoln had been shot the previous night. Johnson, a Democrat, had trouble with Lincoln's Republican Cabinet. His efforts to carry out Lincoln's policies of reconstruction and reconciliation led, eventually, to his impeachment by the House of Representatives. By the margin of a single vote, the Senate acquitted him. The vote was 35–19 against him, but a two-thirds vote was necessary for conviction. After the election of Ulysses S. Grant as president in 1868, Johnson tried unsuccessfully in 1869 to become a senator. He finally won election as senator from Tennessee in 1875, but he died four and a half months after his election.

Chester Alan Arthur, a Republican, became president on Sept. 20, 1881, after James A. Garfield was assassinated by Charles Guiteau, a disappointed office seeker. Arthur's accomplishments included revival of the Navy, which had been neglected for a number of years. Like Andrew Johnson, he failed of renomination. He tried to win a Senate seat, but was unsuccessful, and returned to the practice of law in New York. He died in 1886.

The next vice president to succeed to the presidency was Theodore Roosevelt. He became president at the age of 42 on Sept. 14, 1901, when William McKinley died. McKinley had been shot by Leon Czolgosz, an anarchist, on Sept. 6. Roosevelt, a Republican, fought the corruption of politics by big business, mediated the peace between Japan and Russia in 1905 and made possible the Panama Canal. He was elected in 1904 and helped William Howard Taft to win the Republican nomination in 1908. In 1912 Roosevelt ran for president again on the Progressive party, or Bull Moose, ticket after the Republicans renominated Taft. Woodrow Wilson was elected. Roosevelt was shot in the chest during his 1912 campaign but survived. He died in 1919.

Calvin Coolidge, a Vermont Republican, became president on Aug. 3, 1923, after the death of Warren G. Harding. He was re-elected in 1924, but in 1927 refused renomination with the famous words, "I do not choose to run for President in 1928." His Administration was one of economy, prosperity and conservative policies. After retiring from the presidency, he became a life insurance director and wrote syndicated articles. He died in 1933.

Harry S. Truman, Democrat of Missouri, became president after the death of Franklin D. Roosevelt on April 13, 1945. He was re-elected in 1948, defeating Thomas E. Dewey. Few had expected Mr. Truman to win. Mr. Truman authorized the use of the atomic bomb against Hiroshima and Nagasaki, Japan, in the final month of World War II. He ordered United States troops into action when the Communists attacked South Korea in 1950. Two Puerto Rican nationalists tried to storm Blair House to kill Mr. Truman in 1950, but guards stopped them. One guard and one of the nationalists were killed in a gunfight. Mr. Truman did not seek re-election in 1952. He lives in Independence, Mo. He is 79 years old.

REPERCUSSIONS OF ASSASSINATION CONTINUE TO SPREAD THROUGH BUSINESS AND FINANCE

Officials Move to Ease Impact

Leaders Hoping to Dissipate Uneasiness of Consumers—Stock Market Closed

By EDWARD COWAN

Repercussions of the assassination of President Kennedy continued to spread through business and financial circles in this country and abroad yesterday. Because it was a Saturday, the reaction was limited. There were, however, scattered indications of uneasiness that business and consumer confidence would be ruffled—but not seriously shaken—and that the decline in stock market prices set off by the death of Mr. Kennedy Friday afternoon might resume when the stock exchanges reopen. The New York, American, Midwest and Pacific Coast stock exchanges said they would be closed tomorrow, and other exchanges were expected to follow suit. The Toronto, Montreal and Canadian exchanges also will be closed.

A Federal Reserve Board spokesman in Washington said that President Johnson's proclamation of a day of national mourning Monday did not mean that the president was declaring a legal banking holiday. The spokesman said banks would be open unless closed by their respective state governors. Oren Root, the New York State superintendent of banks, said that as of last night he expected New York banks to open tomorrow unless Governor Rockefeller issued a proclamation ordering them closed. The governor said no such proclamation would be issued.

The Federal Deposit Insurance Corporation and the controller of the currency, James J. Saxon, declared last night that they had no objection to banks closing tomorrow, where state laws or practice permitted, in the absence of an official declaration by a governor of a legal holiday. Mr. Saxon said he had received many phone calls from banks that wanted to close tomorrow out of respect for Mr. Kennedy. Mr. Saxon is the supervisor of Federally chartered, or national, banks. A spokesman for the F.D.I.C., which supervises state-chartered banks, said it had sent telegrams to state banking authorities "purely as a matter of respect to the late president." The Bank of America, which operates 846 branches in California, said it would close tomorrow in memory of Mr. Kennedy.

There were no indications that the public would make heavy withdrawals when the banks reopened. It was hoped that any tendency toward panic among investors and traders in stocks and bonds and in foreign exchange would be dissipated over the weekend.

On Wall Street, brokerage houses, customers men, partners and clerical help came to work in force yesterday. The unusual Saturday activity was to catch up on unfinished business generated in heavy trading late Friday. Brokerage men also were checking to learn whether customers wanted to change buy and sell orders placed before Mr. Kennedy was killed.

There had been a sharp decline in stock prices in heavy trading Friday in the 26 minutes between first reports of the assassination and the early closing of the stock exchanges. The big drop in prices, Wall Street men said yesterday, probably would lead to a large number of margin calls next week—requests for more cash from customers who had bought stock partly on credit.

Foreign exchange markets in London and Zurich were open yesterday. Trading was light, although somewhat more brisk than is normal for a Saturday. The most noteworthy development was a jump of 3½ cents in the price of gold in London, to $35.11 an ounce. Demand, however, was narrow and London market observers said they would not be surprised if the price receded tomorrow. Offerings of dollars in Zurich were described by sources here and abroad as light but substantial enough in relation to the demand to bring the Swiss National Bank into the market to mop up the excess.

In New York foreign exchange traders went to work at the Federal Reserve Bank soon after 3 A.M. to keep abreast of developments in London and Zurich. They conferred by telephone with central banks on the Continent, coordinating readiness to defend the dollar against speculative attack. Federal Reserve officials expressed confidence that the network of cooperative arrangements forged with other central banks in the last three years would prove ample to avert any pronounced weakening in the value of the dollar in terms of other currencies.

Following President Johnson's proclamation, 11 major department and specialty stores in the New York area announced they would be closed tomorrow. Many other retail stores were also expected to wait until Tuesday to reopen.

Bache & Co., a major brokerage house, opened its 72 offices in North America yesterday. Walter E. Auch, the partner in charge of the branch system, said the object was to "try and help clarify the situation for our clients." Bache cautioned that "periods of emotionalism and crisis are usually poor times to sell securities." The firm said Friday's drop in stock prices "may be furthered by the opening of trading." The exchanges presumably will reopen Tuesday. But, Bache continued, "reasonable value relationships" may be established swiftly, "thereby setting the base for a move upward in reflection of the good prospects for business."

Stock and bond markets were closed in London and Europe yesterday. In London there was some expectation that stock prices would be marked down tomorrow morning in sympathy with Friday's declines in New York. The Federal Reserve system can call on $1.95 billion of foreign currencies which other central banks stand ready to make available if it is needed to buy up any dangerous overhang of dollars offered for sale in the foreign exchange markets.

Most commodities exchanges in this country will be closed tomorrow. The Chicago Board of Trade said yesterday there would be no trading until Tuesday. New York commodities exchanges are expected to follow the Chicago board's lead. The New Orleans Cotton Exchange, the Minneapolis Grain Exchange and the Kansas City livestock market will also be closed Monday.

Federal Reserve officials considered yesterday's trading in the London and Zurich foreign exchange markets too light to be indicative of what might develop tomorrow. They noted that there had been no significant flow of orders from the Continent to London, the most important market on that side of the Atlantic. The intervention of the Swiss National Bank in support of the dollar did not appear to have great significance. The bank, Switzerland's central bank, has been buying dollars recently in the Zurich market to keep the exchange rate from piercing the official ceiling of 23.17½ cents a Swiss franc. The Federal Reserve bought limited amounts of foreign currencies in New York Friday to keep rates stable. The Bank of England intervened twice yesterday in the London foreign exchange market, once to support the dollar and later to support the pound sterling, Reuters reported.

Capital Weighing Political Effect

Party Chiefs Expect Johnson to Push Kennedy Program and Be Nominee in '64

By WARREN WEAVER Jr.

Special to The New York Times

WASHINGTON, Nov. 23—A shaken capital began to piece together today a new picture of national politics to replace the one shattered by an assassin's bullet 24 hours before. There were no certainties. There were only degrees of speculation, as the politicians talked in the aftermath of President Kennedy's death and the accession of President Johnson. As party leaders looked forward after a day of turmoil and tragedy, they reached one major conclusion. The new president seems almost certain to be his party's standard-bearer when the Democratic convention meets in Atlantic City nine months from tomorrow.

On the legislative side, Congressional sources expected that the president would adopt and push the Kennedy program. Although Mr. Johnson was silent on politics, as he may be for some time, no one among his associates questioned that the former vice president would expect the nomination and fight for it, if necessary. One of the major advantages that President Johnson will enjoy is that his potential opposition is almost hopelessly divided. When the political harmony of Washington's present crisis mood has faded, the president can expect to face two major groups of detractors within his own party: those liberals who find him too conservative and those Southerners who feel he has deserted their cause. Both of these groups may feel next August that they might prefer one of their own as a nominee. But the possibility of their agreeing on a candidate seems dim.

Time is also on Mr. Johnson's side. The tragedy that projected him to national leadership seems certain to produce Democratic—even partisan—

unity for some time to come. The president and the people will expect it. When that feeling dissolves, there will be little time before the convention for an organized effort against Mr. Johnson.

History would seem to favor the new president. Three 20th-century vice presidents before him have moved into the White House: Theodore Roosevelt, Calvin Coolidge and Harry S. Truman. All were nominated at the next convention—and elected. Even Mr. Truman, who was very unpopular in some Democratic quarters in 1948, was not denied the nomination.

The emerging conviction that President Johnson will head the ticket immediately focused Democratic interest on his choice of a running mate. The name mentioned most frequently was that of Senator Hubert H. Humphrey of Minnesota. The feeling among party leaders is that Mr. Johnson, as a conservative, or at least moderate, Democrat, will need some strong liberal sponsorship if he is to make a good showing in the urban, industrial states. Mr. Humphrey, it is suggested, would supply that precious commodity. Another possibility is Senator Eugene J. McCarthy of Minnesota, who is not as well known as his colleague but who would put a Roman Catholic on the Democratic ticket.

The prospect of Mr. Johnson's nomination appeared likely to produce not only a liberal running mate but also a liberal Republican opponent. While necessarily ignorant of the posture the Johnson Administration will assume, observers are inclined to believe that the new president's greatest potential weakness is his lack of appeal to independent and liberal voters. To capitalize on such a weakness, the reasoning goes, the Republicans would be influenced to nominate someone like Governor Rockefeller, former Vice President Richard M. Nixon or Gov. William M. Scranton of Pennsylvania. Of these, Mr. Rockefeller probably provides the strongest liberal reputation, but his candidacy may have been fatally flawed by his divorce and remarriage. His performance in the primaries is expected to decide this. Mr. Nixon is less readily identified as a liberal, but his considerable vote-getting record in 1960 and his political acceptability in diverse wings of the party leadership continue to make him a strong contender. Some politicians believe that Governor Scranton has gained a great advantage. The question here is whether he is prepared to assume the active national role he has thus far shunned. The Pennsylvania governor is, in some ways, like the late President Kennedy. A young, handsome Ivy

League intellectual with broad personal appeal, he is the kind of a candidate who might run well against an older, somewhat conservative professional politician from the South.

While Senator Barry Goldwater of Arizona does not appear today to meet the qualifications for running against President Johnson as successfully as some other Republicans, no one is counting him out. Mr. Goldwater is simply too popular with too many Republican leaders to write off his candidacy eight months before the convention. Goldwater backers have claimed control of 500 of the 655 votes needed for nomination at the Republican convention. Other Republicans have given the Arizona conservative about 400.

Goldwater Holds to Course for '64

Indicates Tragedy Will Not Alter His Political Plans

Senator Barry Goldwater voiced shock and sorrow yesterday over the death of President Kennedy, but he indicated the tragedy would have no effect on his political plans. In Muncie, Ind., where he attended services for his mother-in-law, Mrs. Ray Johnson, the Arizona Republican was asked by newsmen whether the assassination would change any political plans he may have for the presidency in 1964. He replied: "No, not that I can see."

Mr. Goldwater has not yet announced his candidacy, but he is considered the leading contender for the Republican nomination. The senator said he thought the death of President Kennedy and the succession of President Johnson would not affect the standing of the United States in world affairs.

"I have confidence in Lyndon Johnson," he said. "And I think now is a time that will test Americans of all faiths and both parties. We must give this man our full cooperation and our prayers and work with him; and let's see the kind of president that he will be." He continued: "President Johnson certainly has the training; he has the instincts; he has the ability. I think we must now, as a nation, unite behind him and help him all we can, and go the usual course of helping a president—of being critical when it's needed and helpful when that's needed."

The senator's comments were broadcast on nationwide radio and television. Mr. Goldwater said he would return to Washington to attend President Kennedy's funeral tomorrow. He said he and his wife had been "extremely shocked" at news of the assassination, "shocked to think that the world has to lose a young leader at a time like this and in a way like that." He said he had probably had more Senate debates with President Kennedy, while he was a senator, than any other man. "He was a gentleman," Mr. Goldwater said of Mr. Kennedy. "He was the kind of an antagonist that I've always enjoyed. He would fight like a wildcat for his points and his principles, but there was never anything personal about it."

Governor Rockefeller, the only announced Republican presidential candidate, canceled a three-day political trip to New Hampshire that was to have started today. On Friday he ordered a 30-day period of mourning in New York State. He called the death "a terrible tragedy, for the nation and the world."

EVIDENCE AGAINST OSWALD DESCRIBED AS CONCLUSIVE

By GLADWIN HILL

Special to The New York Times

DALLAS, Nov. 23—Police officials said today they had amassed evidence enough to convict Lee Harvey Oswald of the assassination of President Kennedy. "We're convinced beyond any doubt that he killed the president," said Capt. Will Fritz, chief of the Dallas Police Homicide Bureau, after questioning Oswald and others. "I think the case is clinched." While the 24-year-old warehouse worker continued to deny the killing under prolonged questioning, the Dallas County district attorney, Henry Wade, said this afternoon: "I think we have enough evidence to convict him now but we anticipate a lot more evidence in the next few days."

Oswald was arrested yesterday afternoon after the president had been killed by a sniper's rifle bullet. He was charged also with the slaying of a Dallas policeman. District Attorney Wade said he planned to present the case to the grand jury next Wednesday or the following Monday. He thought the case might come to trial in mid-January.

Police Chief Jesse Curry announced tonight that the Federal Bureau of Investigation had identified as Oswald's handwriting a letter sent March 20 to a Chicago mail order house under an assumed name for a $12.78 rifle similar to the one that killed President Kennedy. The chief said the order bore a post office box return address in Dallas in the name of "A. Hidell," which had been established as a post office box rented by Oswald. The chief said photographs found at Oswald's home in suburban Irving showed him with a revolver on his hip and a rifle in his hand, and showed him displaying two apparently left-wing newspapers, one with a bold head-line: "Be Militant."

Chief Curry said tonight that the police considered the case against Oswald had shaped up about to their satisfaction. He said the defendant would be turned over tomorrow morning to the custody of County Sheriff Bill Decker for confinement in the county jail a mile away. This signified the end of more than 24 hours of intermittent interrogation of the defendant and comparison of his statements with those of witnesses.

Chief Curry announced also that a third charge was being lodged against Oswald—assault with intent to murder Gov. John B. Connally, who was felled along with President Kennedy.

The chief summed up the day's work thus: "I thought the case was in good shape this morning. It's even stronger tonight."

As a major item of evidence, the prosecutor cited at a news conference at police headquarters a statement to the police by Oswald's Russian-born wife, Marina. She was questioned last night and this morning. Mr. Wade quoted her as saying that Oswald had a rifle, similar in appearance to that used in the assassination, in their garage in suburban Irving on Thursday night. She was said to have added that it was not there after Oswald went to work yesterday morning at the book warehouse from which came the shots that felled the president and Texas' Gov. John Connally. Police Chief Curry quoted an unidentified witness as saying that when Oswald walked into the warehouse yesterday morning, he was carrying a long package wrapped in brown paper. He told somebody this was a window shade. The rifle involved in the assassination was found near a sixth-floor window of the warehouse shortly after the crime. Other employees were quoted as stating that Oswald had stayed upstairs when they went out to watch the president go by.

District Attorney Wade said he had mistakenly identified the assassi-nation rifle last night as a German Mauser. Police officers said the rifle was a 1938 model of the Italian-made Carcano, used by Italian armed forces in both World War I and World War II. Mounted on the rifle was a four-power inexpensive Japanese telescopic sight. The rifle was a recon-ditioned weapon, with a rifle bore of 6.5 mm. caliber. A small-arms expert said the crude finish and rough workmanship on the rifle made it a poor choice for a sporting firearm. Such weapons have been sold in large quantities by war surplus stores. Officers starting a canvass of such outlets observed that the odd-sized ammunition—a little smaller than ordinary .30-caliber—might provide an important clue. The assassination, they said, involved excellent marksmanship that could only have come from regular practice recently, and this in turn would have required sizable quantities of the special ammunition.

Oswald's only utterance directed to outsiders today was an exclamation, as he was led handcuffed through a police headquarters corridor: "I want to talk to Mr. * * * in New York."

The name sounded like Abt or Apt. Oswald was permitted to telephone New York to try to reach John J. Abt, a lawyer who has handled left-wing cases. The police said he was unable to reach Mr. Abt but talked to the lawyer's wife. [Mr. Abt, however, denied that Oswald had talked to his wife. He said, "Whoever Oswald talked to it was not Mrs. Abt." Mr. Abt said he had never heard of Oswald.]

Late today the president of the Dallas Bar Association, H. Louis Nichols, visited Oswald in the fourth floor jail at police headquarters to assure him of legal representation. Mr. Nichols said Oswald declined any immediate assistance, saying he preferred representation by Mr. Abt, or a lawyer for the American Civil Liberties Union "who believes in the same things I do." Texas law, Mr. Nichols said, does not require that the court appoint a lawyer for a defendant, if he cannot engage one, until after he is indicted.

A few moments after his interview with the lawyer, Oswald, being escorted through the corridor to another period of interrogation, was asked by reporters if he wanted anything. "I'd like to have the basic fundamental hygienic right of a shower," he said.

District Attorney Wade said Oswald refused to take a lie detector test. The prosecutor said he expected to seek the electric chair for the former marine. Mr. Wade has a record of 23 convictions in 24 capital cases.

Oswald, a former marine who had recently lived in the Soviet Union and married a Russian girl, was said to have acknowledged that he was "a Marxist but not a Communist." Investigators have discovered no organizational connection with the crime. In pursuing the left-wing aspect of the case, officers last night and this morning questioned José Rodriguez Molinas, a bookkeeper at the warehouse and a man who, according to police files, has had some associations with left-wing causes. The investigator's main interest was any indication of rapport between Mr. Molinas and Oswald. But Mr. Molinas said he had merely a nodding acquaintance with Oswald, who had worked at the warehouse for only a few weeks. He appeared voluntarily for questioning, underwent a lie detector test and was released.

Oswald was arraigned at police headquarters on a murder charge last midnight and held without bail for grand jury action. He spent the night in a cell on the fourth floor of the Police Headquarters building, with a special one-man guard. This morning at 10:30 o'clock, Central Standard Time, Oswald was brought down to the Homicide Bureau on the third floor for resumption of the prolonged interrogation of yesterday. His Russian-born wife, from whom he was separated, was brought to the Homicide Bureau for a second time. Deputy Police Chief M. W. Stevenson said eventual examination by a county psychiatrist would be routine in such a case.

Chief Curry said that a palm print on a cardboard carton near the window from which the fatal shots came had been identified positively as Oswald's and was considered important evidence. The officer said also that a paraffin test of Oswald's hands had proved positive, meaning that he had fired a weapon. However, the chief noted this could have been the .38-caliber revolver Oswald was carrying when arrested. He is alleged to have used it to kill a policeman in the Oak Cliff District shortly before going into the theater. Chief Curry said his department had had no record about Oswald up to yesterday, but that the local office of the Federal Bureau of Investigation had a long "subversive" record on him.

Police Relate Story of Swift Capture

Special to The New York Times

DALLAS, Nov. 23—Police Chief Jesse E. Curry reconstructed today the swift steps that led to the apprehension of Lee H. Oswald. Moments after the fatal shot was fired at President Kennedy at 12:30 P.M. yesterday, Chief Curry said, he radioed instructions that the Texas School Book Depository

Building be surrounded and searched. Oswald, who worked in the building, was later charged with the assassination of the president.

The chief was riding in a car 40 feet ahead of the limousine carrying Mr. and Mrs. Kennedy and Gov. and Mrs. John B. Connally Jr. of Texas. The motorcade was on its way to the Trade Mart where the president was to have spoken at a lunch. Chief Curry said he could tell from the sound of the three shots that they had come from the book company's building, near downtown Dallas. The deployment of 500 officers from his 1,100-man force along the route made fast action possible in the manhunt, he said.

The first officer to reach the six-story building, Chief Curry said, found Oswald among other persons in a lunchroom. He said the building manager identified Oswald as an employee of the book-distribution concern that used the building. Oswald was not questioned then. When the main force of investigating officers reached the building Oswald had left. He became a suspect after the police had found on the sixth floor the rifle they believed was the assassination weapon. An elevator operator, the chief said, recalled having taken Oswald to the top floor before the motorcade passed by.

Soon after a description had been broadcast, Patrolman J. D. Tippit saw a man who seemed to answer it. The man was on a sidewalk in suburban Oak Cliff, about two miles from the textbook depository building. When Mr. Tippit got out of the car to question the suspect he was shot and killed with a revolver, Mr. Curry said. A citizen used the squad car radio to report this at 1:18 P.M., about 50 minutes after the president was shot. Policemen then converged on the area.

Capt. Will Fritz, head of the Police Department's Homicide Bureau, said this afternoon that Oswald had traveled the two miles by bus and cab. Captain Fritz said the 24-year-old suspect had taken a city bus, apparently found it too slow, and shifted to a taxi to reach his rooming house near the scene of the slaying in Oak Cliff. Oswald's landlady, Mrs. Earlene Roberts, said that he had run in while she was listening to a television report on the assassination, grabbed a coat from his room and run back out. He moved into the house on Oct. 14.

The killer of Patrolman Tippit fled on foot, witnesses said. A police search of surrounding buildings yielded nothing. Then a call from Julie

Postal, cashier of the Texas Theatre six blocks from where the patrolman was slain, reported that an agitated man had entered the movie house. Chief Curry said six officers searched the theater and found Oswald on the main floor in the third row from the back. When Patrolman M. N. McDonald approached him, he sprang up, the police reported, and shouted: "This is it!"

He reached for a revolver in his shirt, but was disarmed after a scuffle. In the scuffle, Oswald received a black eye and a cut on his forehead. He pulled the trigger before the gun was wrested from him, but the gun did not fire. The arrest came about 90 minutes after the assassination.

At police headquarters, Oswald was questioned for five hours, then arraigned in the murder of Patrolman Tippit at 7:15. The interrogation, directed by Captain Fritz, continued until midnight. At 1:30 A.M. today Oswald was arraigned on charges of murdering the president. He denied both charges. The questioning of Oswald was resumed today.

The police sent the confiscated revolver and the Italian-made military rifle found in the book depository building to the Federal Bureau of Investigation's crime laboratory in Washington. Fingerprints and other evidence also were flown there late yesterday, Chief Curry said. In the search of the book company's building, the police found the rifle hidden among stacks of books and boxes. The police also found three shells and an unspent bullet, a soft-drink bottle, an empty cigarette package, a piece of partly eaten fried chicken, and a sack with chicken bones. Chief Curry said a palm print on a cardboard box at the window checked with prints of Oswald's palm taken later at police headquarters. The manhunt and investigation were aided from the beginning, he said, by the F.B.I. and state highway patrolmen and Dallas County sheriff's officers.

Marxism Called Oswald Religion

Suspect "Refused to Eschew Violence," Friend Says

By DONALD JANSON

Special to The New York Times

IRVING, Tex., Nov. 23—A transplanted New Yorker said today that the question of violence had come up "frequently" in long philosophical discussions he had held with Lee H. Oswald in recent months. "Oswald refused to eschew violence as a method for achieving desired ends," Michael R. Paine said. Mr. Paine, an engineer who was born in New York and attended Harvard University for two years, said that "Marxism was a religion" with Oswald. He said Oswald, who is being held on charges of assassinating President Kennedy, "believed in Communism and thought it would take over the world." The young engineer said he had finally given up efforts to have "a useful conversation" with Oswald because "he was not logical."

"He wanted to change the free-enterprise system," Mr. Paine said, "while at the same time saying he returned to the United States from Russia because he liked the freedom people had in this country."

Oswald, a former Marine, moved to the Soviet Union to live in 1959. There he married Marina Nikolaevna, a Minsk pharmacist. Their first child, June Lee, was born in Russia.

Since last September Oswald's family has lived at the Paine home in this small town ten miles from Dallas. Mrs. Paine took Mrs. Oswald in because she was pregnant and Oswald, frequently out of work, was having difficulties supporting her. Oswald found an $8-a-week room in Oak Cliff, a section of Dallas. He lived there until he was arrested yesterday.

Mrs. Paine's friendship with Marina, a slight brunette, began when she met the Oswalds at a party in Dallas last February. Since then Mrs. Oswald has stayed at the Paine home intermittently with her daughter, not yet 2, while her husband went from job to job in Fort Worth, Dallas and, recently, New Orleans, the city of his birth 24 years ago. Two months ago Mrs.

Paine drove to New Orleans and brought Mrs. Oswald and her daughter back to Irving for another extended visit.

With the Oswalds' effects, which went into the garage, Mr. Paine said, was a long, slim object wrapped in a blanket. He said he had taken it for "camping equipment" when he moved it from the workbench. He learned only today, he said, that the blanket contained a rifle—the one authorities believe was used to kill Mr. Kennedy. Mrs. Oswald told them about it.

Oswald followed his family to Texas last month and found a job in a Dallas textbook warehouse. The Oswalds' second child, Audrey Marina Rachel, was born a month ago. Oswald came to see the babies and his wife often. He always spoke in Russian to them, and sometimes stayed overnight. He stayed Thursday night. When he left for work yesterday morning he took the blanket-wrapped "camping equipment" with him.

Although Mr. Paine is not living with his wife and two daughters now, he comes from nearby Grand Prairie frequently to visit them. It was on these occasions that he engaged in philosophical discussions with Oswald. He recalled the conversations today in an interview in the living room of his wife's modest home. In them, he said, he was never able to convince Oswald of the superiority of free enterprise. He described Oswald as "quiet" and "hard to get to know."

"At that," he said, "I've talked with him perhaps more than anyone else around here because we were both interested in philosophy and political systems."

Mrs. Paine said she noticed no particular nervousness in Oswald's behavior Thursday night. She said she was sure his wife knew nothing of any plans for violence he might have had. Mr. Paine called the 22-year-old Russian woman "apolitical" and "a very fine person" who "likes America." Mrs. Paine said she was a very good mother and friend.

Oswald had not been close to his brother, Robert, of Denton, Tex., or his widowed mother, Mrs. Marguerite Oswald of Fort Worth, although they rushed to Dallas to try to aid him when they heard of his arrest. His mother, a practical nurse, wore her white uniform to police headquarters last night, this morning and again this afternoon when she went to see him. She heard the news that her son was being charged with the president's assassination and the subsequent slaying of a patrolman and asked the *Fort Worth Star-Telegram* how she could get the 30 miles to Dallas "to hear him tell me" whether he did it. *Star-Telegram* reporters drove her to the police head-quarters, and she told how her son's defection to the Soviet Union had made her life lonely. "They all turned their backs on me," she said of her neighbors and friends. "And now they will turn their backs on me again."

She said she had not seen her son and daughter-in-law for about a year and had not realized they were living so close to her. But she offered the excuse for her son that he had remained away and out of touch so that people would not "persecute" her. Last night she stayed with her grand-children and daughter-in-law at the Paine home. Oswald's brother, a fac-tory employee, spent much of the day today at police headquarters seeking to arrange for legal aid for his brother.

Oswald Wrote to Connally About "Injustice"

'62 Letter Citing Undesirable Discharge as a Marine Was Sent From Russia

By PETER KIHSS

Lee H. Oswald once warned the Navy Department that he would "employ all means to right the gross mistake or injustice" that he contended had been done to him. The Texan who has been charged by the Dallas police with being the assassin of President Kennedy—a charge he denied—had been complaining about an undesirable discharge given him by the Marine Corps. This occurred after he had gone on inactive status as a hardship case, only to turn up in Russia. His warning was in a letter from Minsk in the Soviet Union. It was apparently written in January, 1962—and mis-dated Jan. 30, 1961—and addressed to John B. Connally Jr. as secretary of the navy. Mr. Connally is now governor of Texas, and was wounded in the same car in which President Kennedy was shot dead.

The 24-year-old Oswald had asserted in a New Orleans radio interview Aug. 21 that he was a "Marxist" and different from a "Communist." But yesterday Police Chief Jesse Curry of Dallas quoted him as having told police interrogators that he was "a member of the Communist party" and that he was apparently "proud of being a Communist." The Communist party issued a statement here categorically denying that Oswald had "any association" with the party. The statement declared that the assassination "could only be the work of a mentally deranged person or the deliberate deed of an enemy of democracy, an agent of the ultra-Right advocates of violence."

Presumably Oswald must have denied that he was a Communist when he was issued a passport by the State Department office in New Orleans last June 25. Passport applications warn that it is illegal for a member of the Communist party to apply for or to use a passport. The applications also require the applicant to swear that he has not been a member of a Communist organization for 12 months or "ever sought or claimed the benefits of the nationality of any foreign state."

Oswald had sought to become a Soviet citizen in October, 1959, but later said that Soviet officials refused to grant him citizenship. Yesterday, State Department authorities in Washington said that they had no evidence indicating involvement of the Soviet Union, Cuba or any other foreign power in the assassination of President Kennedy.

Oswald's letter from Minsk addressed to Mr. Connally as secretary of the navy, written in longhand, was made public by the Defense Department in Washington yesterday. Giving Oswald's Marine Corps Reserve serial number, it read:

"I wish to call your attention to a case about which you may have personal knowledge since you are a resident of Fort Worth as I am.

"In November, 1959, an event was well publicated in the Fort Worth newspapers concerning a person who had gone to the Soviet Union to reside for a short time (much in the same way E. Hemingway resided in Paris).

"This person in answers to questions put to him by reporters in Moscow criticized certain facets of American life. The story was blown up into another 'turncoat' sensation, with the result that the Navy Department gave this person a belated dishonorable discharge, although he had received an honorable discharge after 3 years' service on Sept. 11, 1959 at El Toro Marine Corps Base in California.

"These are the basic facts of my case.

"I have and always had the full sanction of the U.S. Embassy, Moscow, U.S.S.R. and hence the U.S. Government. In as much as I am returning to the U.S.A. in this year with the aid of the U.S. Embassy, [to] bring with me my family (since I married in the U.S.S.R.) I shall employ all means to right this gross mistake or injustice to a boni-fied US. citizen and ex-serviceman. The U.S. Government has no charges or complaints against me. I ask you to look into this case and take the necessary steps to repair the damage done to me and my family. For information I would direct you to consult the American Embassy, Chickovski Street 19121, Moscow, U.S.S.R.

"Thank you."

Mr. Connally was navy secretary from Jan. 23 to Dec. 11, 1961. He replied Feb. 23, 1962, addressing Mr. Lee H. Oswald, U.S.M.C.R. 1653230, Lalinina Street 4-24, Minsk U.S.S.R. He said that he had referred the letter to the secretary's office in Washington. In Washington, the Marine Corps said yesterday that Oswald's undesirable discharge Sept. 11, 1960, had been issued after he had requested discharge the previous July 26 to accept Soviet citizenship. A spokesman said that a Navy discharge review board had been asked to review the case and had upheld the undesirable discharge.

Connally Effort to Delay Texas Trip Is Reported

AUSTIN, Tex., Nov. 23 (UPI)-Gov. John B. Connally Jr. tried to persuade President Kennedy to call off his visit to Texas, it was reported today by Allen Duckworth, political editor of *The Dallas Morning News*. Mr. Duckworth said the governor had told members of his staff here that he was going to ask the president to postpone or cancel his trip. Governor Connally then made a special trip to Washington.

According to Mr. Duckworth, the governor was opposed to the trip on two grounds: that it was unwise politically because it would further divide Texas Democrats and that there was the possibility of an incident. Mr. Duckworth said Governor Connally had told his staff he thought the people of Texas were "too emotional" for a visit at this time.

It was reported elsewhere that Mr. Kennedy himself had made the decision to ride in the slow-moving motorcade. The original plans called only for a fast ride from the airport to a lunch at the Trade Mart.

Connally Gains, Doctors Report

Turn May Have Saved Life—Full Recovery Likely

By JOHN HERBERS

Special to The New York Times

DALLAS, Nov. 23—Gov. John B. Connally Jr. was reported in good condition today with a bullet wound suffered immediately after President Kennedy was assassinated. Physicians said that the 46-year-old governor of Texas was expected to suffer no disabling after-effects. He will remain in the hospital for 10 to 14 days.

Governor and Mrs. Connally were riding in the seat ahead of President and Mrs. Kennedy yesterday when a sniper's bullet struck the president in the head. The governor had turned to see what had happened when he was struck in the back by another bullet. Dr. Tom Shires, chief of surgeons at the University of Texas Southwestern Medical School, said the governor probably would have been killed, if he had not turned. "After consulting with Mrs. Connally and others on the scene," Dr. Shires said, "the consensus is that the governor was quite fortunate that he turned to see what happened to the president. If he had not turned to his right, there is a good chance he probably would have been shot through the heart. As it was, the bullet caused a tangential wound."

Parkland Hospital reported late today that Governor Connally's condition was good. It said: "His mental condition is clear. He is in control of all his faculties. The last X-ray of his chest was good. We are pleased with his improved progress."

From his hospital bed, the governor proclaimed Monday, the day of the president's funeral, as "an official day of mourning in Texas."

Physicians said that the bullet had traveled through the governor's body and had broken his fifth rib. It then struck his right wrist, causing a compound fracture, and lodged in his left thigh. A fragment from the rib punctured his lung.

Stevenson Warned in Dallas

WASHINGTON, Nov. 23 (AP)—Adlai E. Stevenson said today he had told a White House aide that some Dallas citizens had expressed misgivings about President Kennedy's plan to visit their city. Mr. Stevenson, chief United States delegate to the United Nations, who was harassed in Dallas a month ago, said he had not made any recommendation as to whether Mr. Kennedy should reschedule his trip to the city where he was assassinated yesterday.

Mr. Stevenson was spat on and struck with a sign in Dallas Oct. 25 when he emerged from a theater after a speech celebrating United Nations Day. Mr. Stevenson told a newsman that Arthur M. Schlesinger Jr., a presidential assistant, phoned Mr. Stevenson on the following day to get a full report on what had happened. Mr. Stevenson said that he had summarized the incident and had told Mr. Schlesinger that "some business people who had been my host expressed some misgivings about whether the president should come."

U.S. Communists Condemn Killing

Call It Action of Madman or "Enemy of Democracy"

The Communist Party of the U.S.A. asserted yesterday that President Kennedy's murder could only be the action of "a mentally deranged person" or of "an enemy of democracy."

A statement issued in New York by the party said: "In view of the fact that attempts are being made to link the suspected assassin with the Communist party, we want to reiterate our complete condemnation of the dastardly assassination of President John F. Kennedy as a monstrous crime against the country.

"We again declare that the murder of the President only serves the purpose of those who seek to destroy democracy, those who seek to throw this country into terror and fascist reaction.

"This act could only be the work of a mentally deranged person or the deliberate deed of an enemy of democracy, an agent of the ultra-right advocates of violence.

"We categorically deny all insinuations or declarations by anybody that the suspect now arrested, Lee Harvey Oswald, has any association with the Communist party.

"We further declare that all the history of our party proves that such acts of violence and terror are diametrically the opposite of the policy and program of the Communist party.

"Nobody who teaches or practices acts of terror and violence is allowed to be a member of the Communist party. As a basic tenet we reject such practices. Throughout the years our party has been vigilant against such provocateurs and crackpots from coming into our party.

"Attempts to use this brutal act to whip up hysteria against the Communist party or progressive movements only compound the despicable crime against the President and the country, and fail to get the real perpetrators and cover up those who have encouraged this brutal and tragic deed."

Pravda Accuses Rightists

MOSCOW, Sunday, Nov. 24 (AP)—*Pravda* charged today that United States right-wingers were trying to use the assassination of President Kennedy to stir up anti-Soviet and anti-Cuban hysteria. The organ of the Soviet Communist party said the Dallas police "for provocative purposes" were trying to blame United States Communists for the crime. *Pravda* was skeptical about the arrest of Lee H. Oswald and said "the more details are reported, the darker and more suspicious all this story becomes." The newspaper was echoing charges made last night by the Moscow radio.

It continued to depict Mr. Kennedy as the victim of opponents of efforts to improve East-West relations. "Definite quarters," *Pravda* said, "are now striving to cover up the traces of the bloody crime and use the tragic death of the President for stirring up anti-Soviet and anti-Cuban hysteria. The murder of the United States President is a monstrous crime, which has shocked all the world, and the indignation of the Americans is perfectly understandable. But the very method of this terroristic act is not new for the United States. It is reminiscent of other much smaller acts of gangsters whose connections often lead to very high-placed extreme right-wing quarters and their patrons."

The Moscow radio said Oswald was charged with Mr. Kennedy's slaying after 10 hours of interrogation "but there was no evidence which could prove this accusation. The police are trying to involve the Communist party of the United States in the assassination of the President," it said.

Movie Amateur Filmed Attack; Sequence Is Sold to Magazine

By RICHARD J. H. JOHNSTON

An amateur movie camera enthusiast in Dallas recorded a 15-second close-up sequence showing the actual impact of the assassin's fire on President Kennedy. The 8-millimeter film clip in color was sold by the photographer, Abraham Zapruder, for about $40,000 to Time-Life, Inc. *Life* magazine will publish the pictures in its issue dated Friday, Nov. 29. The issue will be on the street next Tuesday. The editors said that time limitations did not permit reproduction in color. The pictures will be printed in black and white.

Mr. Zapruder, president of Jennifer Juniors, Inc., a dress shop in downtown Dallas, declined yesterday, in a telephone conversation, to discuss the film or the arrangement for its sale. A secretary to Mr. Zapruder, speaking from the offices of the dress shop, said that the Secret Service had sent agents to examine Mr. Zapruder's film and had permitted him to keep or sell it.

The film was developed Friday night. Time-Life editors said yesterday that it had been studied by their Dallas representatives, who were authorized to make the purchase. The film was sent by air to the Chicago laboratories of the magazine. From a description given by the *Life* representative in Dallas, the editors said, it appears that the pictures were taken with a telephoto lens. Mr. Zapruder's secretary said that Mr. Zapruder was "one of hundreds" who were taking pictures of the presidential motorcade. *Life* editors here said that they were unable last night to give precise details as to what the film showed, but that they were assured that it depicted the impact of the bullets that struck Mr. Kennedy.

The photographic department of the Associated Press in New York acknowledged late yesterday that the AP had bid for the pictures but that Mr. Zapruder had sold the film to Time-Life, Inc. A spokesman said he understood the price was in the vicinity of $40,000. Mr. Zapruder's secretary would neither confirm nor deny the figure, nor would Time-Life spokesmen discuss it. The AP spokesman, however, said the figure was "well over $25,000 and close to $40,000."

SECRET SERVICE FACES CHANGES IN ITS PROCEDURES AS A RESULT OF THE ASSASSINATION

Security Setup to Be Tightened

Slaying Is Said to Disprove Myth That Agents Can Dictate to Presidents

By FELIX BELAIR Jr.

Special to The New York Times

WASHINGTON, Nov. 23—The assassin's bullets that took the life of President Kennedy shattered the proud record of the century-old United States Secret Service and the 400 men who wear its star. It also shattered a myth about the men who protect the lives of presidents. Over the years the myth has grown that the Secret Service can dictate to the president what he may and may not do where the safety of his person and his family are involved. It is a myth that presidents have helped perpetrate by their grumblings over the protective measures exercised by the Secret Service. The Kennedy assassination seems likely to turn this myth into reality. Until yesterday, the service had prided itself in never having lost a president. It received the assignment of protecting presidents in 1901 after the assassination of President McKinley.

Every agent knew today that some changes would be made. Security procedures would be tightened. If a president decided to venture on foot beyond the White House grounds, he would be preceded, flanked and followed by agents forming a protective screen. The same system would be followed on motor trips beyond the grounds. The motorcycle escort, which President Kennedy first frowned on and then banished, was back on the job today. How far the tightening of security would go depends on the personal habits of Lyndon B. Johnson as president. But, if necessary, he would be "told" —either that or Congress would be advised that its orders to safeguard the life of the president could not be discharged.

Such was the mood of the 58 frustrated and angry young men who make up the Secret Service's White House detail as they moved quickly and quietly today about their assignments between the Executive Mansion and President Johnson's private residence in Washington's Spring Valley section six miles away. They wanted to talk about yesterday's calamity at Dallas. Their consciences were clear. They had done everything they could in setting up security arrangements that had to include the Dallas police. But they knew that the service was somehow on trial in the public mind, and the order had come from high in the White House to "clam up."

They knew that people in Government and across the nation were asking whether there was no way to protect the life of the president against the twisted mentalities of potential assassins that exist in every big city. Men grown old in the business of guarding presidents gave this answer: "A president is just as safe as he permits himself to be." Another way of saying the same thing is that nobody can protect the president by means that he will not accept.

That is why nobody in a position to do so even thought of telling John F. Kennedy yesterday that he must use the protective "bubble-top" or the bullet-proof side windows with which the rented Lincoln Continental touring car is equipped. The removable top is made of clear molded plastic. It was designed for protection against weather. The plastic is not bullet proof, but it may deflect a bullet fired from a considerable distance. President Kennedy had let it be known repeatedly and sometimes curtly that he wanted no part of the "bubble-top" on a clear day. Dwight D. Eisenhower disliked the "bubble-top" as much as President Kennedy did. On his visits to New York City the general usually dispensed with it in clear weather at the Manhattan end of the Queens-Midtown Tunnel.

Not even the chief of the whole service is immune to presidential ire. One was ousted by former President Truman for his premature assumption of protective duties with Gov. Thomas E. Dewey when he appeared a certain winner in the presidential election of 1948.

Secret Service agents knew even before he went to the White House that President Kennedy would be hard to "cover." He was vigorous and impulsive. Movement was instinctive. It was natural for him to leave the mansion with the king of Morocco and walk across Pennsylvania Avenue to Blair House at the height of the rush hour without a word to agents who came pounding down the driveway in hot pursuit.

But, according to some of those who have known him longest, there were more profound reasons for the late president's apparent disdain for ordinary security measures. As president, he was also the leader of the non-Communist world. He considered it important to appear to the world as a free man among free men. What better way to demonstrate the difference between a free and open society and a police state than to appear openly before the public without a protective screen? The same attitude led the president to reach out from his open car or to leave it altogether to shake hands with a well-wisher. It was that way in Rome in July when a man grabbed the president around the neck, kissed his cheek and toppled him over a wooden barricade. This incident occurred as the president walked along a barricade separating him from the crowd in front of Rome's city hall. He only wanted to shake hands with the Italian people.

In Cork, later, a good-natured crowd broke the police lines. One admirer continued to grip the president's hand as his car started off. Mr. Kennedy tried pushing the man away with his left hand. A Secret Service agent intervened, and the man let go. The president fell twisting into the rear seat with the agent tumbling on top of him. No one was hurt.

The president did not disregard police lines only on foreign streets. When he visited New York a week before his death he banned the usual motorcycle police escort. After his car stopped for a red light at the Avenue of the Americas and 54th Street, it was immobilized by a surrounding throng of youngsters attending a convention of the Catholic Youth Organization nearby. It took a band of uniformed patrolmen with their nightsticks raised as a precaution to free the vehicle. Ringing in the ears of more than one Secret Service man today was the remark of a ranking police official at the time: "If anything happens, the police and the Secret Service will be left holding the big fat bag."

Members of the White House detail had become increasingly jittery during the last year. Mr. Kennedy's insistence on showing himself and his disregard of readily available security techniques and equipment caused them concern. But there was nothing they could do about it. They expect it will be different with President Johnson. They believe that any man who saw yesterday's tragedy at Dallas must appreciate the need to cooperate on all security suggestions. Those who talked with him on his return to Washington late yesterday testified to his "stunned and shaken" condition.

Fortunately for the men charged directly by Congress with his protection, Mr. Johnson learned as vice president to accommodate himself to the necessary precautions. But not at first. He began by asking that the two agents assigned to his movements be withdrawn. But Congress stepped in to make the protection mandatory rather than at the vice president's discretion.

Most presidents have encouraged the myth about the power of the Secret Service to tell them what to do. General Eisenhower used to say "they" would not permit him to witness the explosion of a nuclear device. Franklin D. Roosevelt complained about the jerkiness of his outmoded private railroad car at the end of an eight-car special. He said "they" insisted on retaining the car because its heavy steel plates provided great protection. Harry S. Truman grumbled that "they" always had to tag along and slowed him on his 6 A.M. walks "in the middle of the morning."

But no one could prevent Mr. Truman from flying to Kansas City, Mo., to spend Christmas with his mother in weather so hazardous that all commercial planes had been grounded from the Atlantic Coast to the Mississippi River and 100 miles beyond. And President Roosevelt continued to take his special train up the west side of the Hudson River in wartime despite its easy identification as the presidential train.

All presidents have shown irritation at the ministrations of their protectors. It began with Theodore Roosevelt, who delighted in spontaneous departures from the mansion for Rock Creek Park to tramp through woods and streams while agents in city clothes tried to keep up. Warren G. Harding acknowledged to fellow members of the Chevy Chase Country Club his embarrassment about the several unidentified Secret Service men who preceded him on the golf course and tried unsuccessfully to make themselves part of the background foliage in their severe black suits. Since the Harding days, the job of protecting the president has increased in complexity just as the presidency itself has become more complex. The transition from travel by railroad to jet aircraft and from the revolver to the submachine gun only suggest some ways in which the task of the Secret Service has enlarged.

Until now, only one Secret Service agent has been able to tell a president what to do about his own safety. He was Deeter B. Flohr, who was President Eisenhower's chauffeur on the road and on the golf course. Only the close relationship of the two men and General Eisenhower's fondness for the big agent could result in the incident that occurred one day on Augusta National Golf Course. General Eisenhower had badly topped a tee shot and became so enraged that Mr. Flohr grew alarmed. The president's face was discolored and the veins of his neck became rigid. Mr. Flohr commanded the president to "stop that." He told the president to get into the electric cart or he would pick him up bodily and carry him back to the clubhouse. General Eisenhower obeyed.

Two Bullets Reported to Have Hit Kennedy

WASHINGTON, Nov. 23 (UPI)—President Kennedy was shot twice yesterday, White House sources said today. The first reports said the president was killed by one bullet. Staff doctors at Parkland Hospital in Dallas said yesterday only that the sniper's bullet pierced the midsection of the front part of his neck and emerged from the top of his skull. The White House sources said they understood that one bullet hit Mr. Kennedy in the neck. He bent forward, turned his head and was struck in the skull by the second bullet, the sources said.

The Kennedy Wound

Fatal Shot Struck Base of His Skull, Causing Immediate Unconsciousness

By HOWARD A. RUSK, M.D.

The world is still numb, stunned, and in a state of continuing shock as it grieves over the tragic death of President Kennedy. We who mourn can be grateful for the fact that he felt no pain, that unconsciousness was instantaneous and death was swift and certain. A high-velocity bullet that ripped through the base of the skull tore away the bone and brain tissue, striking the vital areas of the brain, the pons and medulla that control and regulate the vital functions of respiration and circulation. After such a devastating wound from a high-powered rifle, what chance is there for life and what does life hold if one is saved?

Such wounds are common in war. In World War I, even though a bullet missed the vital areas of the brain controlling the basic functions of the heart and respiration and if the great blood vessels of the brain were spared, recovery was very rare because of secondary infection producing meningitis, abscesses and even infection in the blood stream itself. In World War II, if one survived the initial assault, the chances for recovery were much greater, for neurosurgical teams operated directly behind the front lines, where immediate emergency surgery was done. The patient was then evacuated to a base hospital and then by air to specialized centers in the United States. This emergency surgery plus antibiotics to control infection, and a better knowledge of the use of plasma and blood, saved many lives.

The status and future of the survivor then were dependent upon the areas of the brain that had been damaged or destroyed. If a bullet went through the silent area of the frontal lobe and damage was minimal, sometimes there was little change in the individual. Some wounds in the frontal lobe, however, could produce the same symptoms as a therapeutic lobotomy. This is a surgical procedure, sometimes performed in cases of severe and uncontrollable psychoses, in which a portion of the frontal lobe is deliberately removed. After such a procedure, the individual usually changes from a dynamic, driving, manic type to a passive, quiet, lethargic personality. If too much of the frontal lobe is destroyed, these patients may revert to a vegetative existence. If the main damage is in the temporal lobe of the brain the patient is left paralyzed on the opposite side, possibly with loss of sensation, and aphasia.

Aphasia is that tragic condition commonly suffered by victims of a stroke. The ability to think is intact but although one recognizes an object he is unable to put the word and object together. Aphasia is one of the most frustrating disabilities. We all know the frustration when we are unable to remember an old friend's name. Multiply this frustration by infinity and that is the way the aphasic patient feels. Usually much can be accomplished by patient, long-term training. But the process is tedious, frustrating, and sometimes heartbreaking.

If the injury is in the posterior portion of the brain, the area where the bullet that killed the president made its exit, the cerebellum is damaged. Then the individual is left with ataxia, evidenced by severe intention type of tremors that occur when one tries to perform a basic act or grasp an object. Damage to the cerebellum is also usually accompanied by a loss of equilibrium. If the base of the brain is damaged, as was the case of the president, the pons and medulla are injured. Then unconsciousness is instantaneous and death occurs usually in a matter of minutes because these centers control the vital body functions of circulation and respiration.

This was substantiated in a medical report issued by Dr. Tom Shires, chief surgeon at Parkland Hospital and professor of surgery at the University of Texas Southwest Medical School. He stated:

"Medically, it was apparent the president was not alive when he was brought in. There was no spontaneous respiration. He had dilated, fixed pupils. It was obvious he had a lethal head wound.

"Technically, however, by using vigorous resuscitation, intravenous tubes and all the usual supportive measures, we were able to raise a semblance of a heartbeat.

"I am absolutely sure he never knew what hit him."

If a patient recovers from severe brain damage, he may have any one of these specific disabilities or a combination of all of them. However, there is often another devastating condition that comes after severe brain damage. These are epileptiform convulsions due not only to the damage itself but also to adhesions that are part of the healing process. These convulsive seizures can usually be more or less controlled with modern drugs. However, even if the convulsions are rare, the sword of Damocles hangs over the injured head of the individual, for he knows not when a convulsion will strike and therefore lives in a world of continuing fear and anxiety.

The most tragic patients coming to rehabilitation centers are those with severe brain damage. They are always depressed, at times confused with problems in locomotion and hand function and often unsteady in gait. In some, intelligence has been spared but the means of communication has been lost. The road back to some kind of life limited by disability is a tough, frustrating, and difficult road. Even with all of the modern facilities and opportunities in rehabilitation and with courage in depth on the part of the patient, a satisfying, productive, dignified life is often not attainable.

We must be grateful that our president suffered no pain or anguish. For us, and for his loved ones left behind, there is at least the consolation that he was spared any suffering and the future did not present the insurmountable odds that often the bravest cannot conquer.

Walker Says Assassination Shows the "Internal Threat"

SHREVEPORT, La., Nov. 23 (AP)—Former Maj. Gen. Edwin A. Walker said here today that "the death of Mr. Kennedy is not as surprising as it is tragic." In a statement he said, "The tragic events of yesterday demonstrate the internal threat that can never be underestimated." Mr. Walker resigned from the Army two years ago in a dispute over his anti-Communist indoctrination of troops. "My sympathy for the Kennedy family is no less than it is for the millions of people who have sustained equal losses in the fight for freedom," he said. "The sacrifices of our leading American family is the sacrifice of every American for peace. There is every need at this grave hour for strength and unity without recrimination that only reflects differences in beliefs regarding an acceptable price for peace."

Dallas Asks Why It Happened;
Worry Over "Image" Is Voiced

Special to The New York Times

DALLAS, Nov. 23—Was Dallas to blame? Or was this a chance tragedy that could have happened in any city that happened to entertain a president of the United States? At every level of the social and economic scale, Dallas citizens searched themselves today for the answer. The defensiveness was massive. It verged sometimes on combativeness. It came out often without prompting. Almost surely it came in the presence of an identified Easterner.

This city of 750,000 calls itself the Southwest's capital of aviation, insurance, finance and manufacturing. In recent years it has also become known as a center of sometimes extreme conservatism. Residents took little comfort in the news that the man charged in President Kennedy's assassination, Lee Harvey Oswald, had a record as a Communist sympathizer.

"People are going to be driven to the conclusion that maybe this wouldn't have happened if Dallas hadn't been so conservative," one businessman said. In one way or another, men and women asked, "What will the rest of the nation think of Dallas?" But putting this worry about Dallas's "image" first was not universal. Many thought first and spoke first of a family's grief and the blow to orderly government.

But Dallas appeared self-conscious and defensive as if a mass conscience had been aroused. There seemed to be guilt feelings that ordinary men and women were not able to handle. "What can you do?" an industrial engineer in his middle years asked helplessly. He was representative of many. Physicians, observing patients and friends, commented on this reaction. At the Trade Mart yesterday, as the word got around that the president had been shot, one man's spontaneous outburst was: "Those damn fanatics! Why do we have them in Dallas?" A taxicab driver listened to the conversation of his passengers for a few moments. He broke in and asked where they came from. "New York? Uh!" he remarked. "Are you here to take pictures of our black eye?" He was both sad and defensive, but not combative. "You can't blame the city," one of his passengers ventured. "But everybody won't say that," the driver said.

A man with shock plainly on his face said: "This is a tragic day for Dallas. Oh, this is a tragedy." A waitress felt the same way. "Dallas can't hold its head up this morning," she volunteered. At an all-night lunchstand, a young man who had witnessed the assassination said sadly: "I had to come downtown and talk to somebody about it. I just can't get it out of my mind. What are the people in New York saying about us? I am sure you'll be fair, but it's too bad we have this reputation." A man working at the lunchstand bared his feelings this way: "I think Dallas died right with him. We're the ones that are going to suffer. History will never erase it."

A statement by Mayor Earle Cabell reflected, in a degree, a widespread feeling: "There are maniacs all over the world and in every city of the world," he said. "This was a maniac. It could have happened in Podunk as well as in Dallas." Carle E. Welch, who holds the title of mayor pro tem, commented: "I challenge anybody who says this reflects on the character of the people of Dallas."

Was this kind of reaction strange to local professional people who encounter the emotional problems of patients every day? "No," said a neuropsychiatrist, "not in consideration of the dynamics, coming after the case of Stevenson." (Adlai E. Stevenson, chief United Nations delegate, was struck by a picket sign and spat upon during a recent visit to Dallas.) "We were embarrassed once previously," he continued. "It has a great deal of meaning as far as the image of the city is concerned." A Dallas psychoanalyst put it this way: "Dallas is very, very proud of Dallas. In an individual it is almost a narcissistic thing. Instead of worrying about the grief of others, he worries about the image of the city. But many were very distressed and upset and were thinking first of Mrs. Kennedy and then what was going to happen to the country and the world situation."

Dallas's reputation as a center of conservatism is not entirely without foundation. *The Dan Smoot Report,* a weekly periodical described as "uncompromising constitutional conservative" by its author, Dan H. Smoot, is published here. It goes to 50,000 subscribers. A commercially sponsored broadcast version is used by 55 television and 100 radio stations.

Dallas is also the home of several persons and organizations firmly identified with conservatism. Former Gen. Edwin A. Walker lives here, as does oilman H. L. Hunt. The local branch of the John Birch Society, which operates largely out of the public eye, is said to attract a large number of supporters.

Dallas Times Herald Asks Prayer to End Bitterness and Hate

Special to The New York Times

DALLAS, Nov. 24—*Following is an editorial published this afternoon on the front page of* The Dallas Times Herald:

Terrible history had been made in Dallas, and the magnitude of our city's sorrow can only be measured against the enormity of the deed.

John F. Kennedy, President of the United States of America, is dead. Killed in Dallas. No matter what the explanation of the act, the awful reality of it overwhelms us. He died here.

We do not know, we may never know, why it happened in Dallas. And it is no comfort to our grief that an insane chance, operating with blind destiny, brought our President's death to us.

But this we know, that as a city we must show the world the deep unity of our grief, the depths of the stunned void that is in each of us.

Let us go into the open churches, the cathedrals, the synagogues, and there let us pray to God to teach us love and forgiveness. In the quiet of our homes, let us search our hearts and, through the terrible cleansing power of our grief, remove any vestiges of bitterness and hate.

What happened here could have happened in any city. But first there had to be the seeds of hate—and we must pray that Dallas can never supply the atmosphere for tragedy to grow again.

The bullet that felled our President was molded in an unstable world. But to our great sorrow, it found its mark here.

Widow of Texas Policeman Hears From New President

WASHINGTON, Nov. 23 (AP)—President Johnson telephoned his sympathy today to Mrs. J. D. Tippit, wife of the Dallas policeman slain by a gunman shortly after the fusillade that cut down President Kennedy yesterday. District Attorney Henry Wade has charged Lee H. Oswald with the Tippit slaying as well as the assassination. His theory is that Mr. Tippit was shot after stopping Oswald for questioning on the basis of a broadcast description. Pierre Salinger, White House press secretary, told of the telephone call but did not report what was said beyond the fact that Mr. Johnson had extended his sympathy. In Fairfax, Va., residents of that Washington suburb began collecting money today for the Tippit family.

Killing of President Not a U.S. Offense; States' Laws Apply

Special to The New York Times

WASHINGTON, Nov. 23—The assassination of a president is not covered by Federal law, according to the Justice Department. Lee H. Oswald will be tried under Texas statutes for murder. According to the Texas Penal Code, Article 1257, "The punishment for murder shall be death or confinement in the penitentiary for life or for any term of years not less than two." There is no bail. If the penalty is death, it is carried out by electric chair.

President James A. Garfield's assassin, Charles Jules Guiteau, was tried in Washington on Nov. 14, 1881. He was found guilty Jan. 25, 1882, and hanged at the jail in Washington on June 30, 1882. Leon F. Czolgosz, who shot President William McKinley in Buffalo, N.Y., on Sept. 6, 1901, was tried in the Supreme Court of New York and convicted. He was electrocuted on Oct. 29, 1901, at Auburn State Prison, at Auburn, N.Y. John

Wilkes Booth, assassin of President Abraham Lincoln, was shot by cavalry soldiers in Fredericksburg, Va., on April 25, 1865.

Jack Rosenthal, a Justice Department spokesman, said that a military trial here for Oswald was out of the question. The president was not a military man, he said, and he was not shot by a military man on a military reservation. Even if a military man did the killing and it was off a military reservation, civil authorities would have jurisdiction. However, in some such cases, military and civilian authorities do confer.

TEXTS OF KENNEDY'S ADDRESS
IN FORT WORTH AND OF
HIS UNDELIVERED DALLAS SPEECH

Following are the transcript of President Kennedy's last address, which he made Friday morning at Fort Worth, and the text of the speech he was to deliver at Dallas:

FORT WORTH ADDRESS

I know now why everyone in Texas—Fort Worth—is so thin, having gotten up and down about nine times. This is what you do every morning.

Two years ago I said that—introduced myself in Paris by saying that—I was the man who had accompanied Mrs. Kennedy to Paris. I'm getting that, somewhat that same sensation as I travel around Texas. Nobody wonders what Lyndon and I wear.

I'm glad to be here in Jim Wright's city. About 35 years ago a Congressman from California who had just been elected received a letter from an irate constituent which said: "During your campaign you promised to have the Sierra Madre mountains reforested. You've been in office for one month and you haven't done so."

Well, no one in Fort Worth has been that unreasonable, but in some ways he has had the Sierra Madre mountains reforested, and here, in Fort Worth, he's contributed to its growth, he speaks for Fort Worth, he speaks for the country. And I don't know any city that's been better represented in the Congress of the United States than Fort Worth.

And if there are any Democrats here this morning, I'm sure you won't hold that against us.

Three years ago last September, I came here, and the Vice President spoke at Burk Burnett Park and I called in that speech for national security policy and a national security system which was second to none—a position which said not if, when and how, but first. That city responded to that call as it has through its history, and we have been putting that pledge into practice ever since.

And I want to say a word about that pledge here in Fort Worth, which understands national defense and its importance to the security of the United States.

During the days of the Indian War this city was a fort. During the days of World War I even before the United States got into the war, Royal Canadian Air Force pilots were training here. During the days of World War II, the great Liberator bombers, in which my brother flew with his co-pilot from this city, were produced here.

The first nonstop flight around the world took off and returned here in a plane built in factories here. The first truly intercontinental bomber—the B-36—was produced here. The B-58, which is the finest weapons system in the world today, which it demonstrated most recently in flying from Tokyo to London with an average speed of nearly 1,000 miles per hour, is a Fort Worth product.

The Iroquois helicopter from Fort Worth is a mainstay in our fight against the guerrillas in South Vietnam. The transportation of crews between our missile sites is done in planes produced here in Fort Worth.

So, wherever the confrontation may occur—and in the last three years it's occurred on at least three occasions, in Laos, Berlin and Cuba, and it will again—wherever it occurs, the products of Fort Worth and the men of Fort Worth provide us with a sense of security.

And in the not too distant future a new Fort Worth product—and I'm glad that there was a table separating Mr. Hicks and myself—a new Fort Worth product—the TFX—Tactical Fighter Experimental (nobody knows what those words mean, but that's what they mean, Tactical Fighter Experimental)—will serve the forces of freedom and will be the number one airplane in the world today.

There's been a good deal of discussion about the long and hard-fought competition to win the TFX contract, but very little discussion about what this plane will do.

It will be the first operational aircraft ever produced that can literally spread its wings through the air. It will thus give us a single plane capable of carrying out missions of speed as well as distance; able to fly very far in one form, or very fast in another.

It can take off from rugged, short airstrips, enormously increasing the Air Force's ability to participate in limited wars. The same basic plane will serve the Navy's carriers, saving the taxpayers at least one billion dollars in costs if they built separate planes for the Navy and the Air Force.

The Government of Australia, by purchasing $125 million of TFX planes before they're even off the drawing boards, has already testified to the merit of this plane and at the same time its confidence of the ability of Fort Worth to meet its schedule.

In all these ways, success of our national defense depends upon this city in the western United States, 10,000 miles from Vietnam, five or six thousand miles from Berlin, thousands of miles from trouble spots in Latin America, in Africa or the Middle East. And yet, Fort Worth, and what it does and what it produces, participates in all these great historic events.

Texas as a whole and Fort Worth bear particular responsibility for this national defense effort. The military procurement in this state totals nearly one and a quarter billion—fifth highest among all the states of the Union. There are more military personnel on active duty in this state than any in the nation, save one. And it's not Massachusetts.

I don't recite these for any partisan purpose. They're the result of American determination to be second to none.

And as a result of the effort which this country has made in the last three years, we are second to none.

In the past three years we have increased the defense budget of the United States by over 20 per cent, increased the program of acquisition of Polaris submarines from 24 to 41, increased our Minuteman missile-purchase program by more than 75 per cent, doubled the number of strategic bombers and missiles on alert, doubled the number of nuclear weapons available in the strategic alert forces, increased the tactical nuclear forces deployed in Western Europe by over 60 per cent, added five combat-ready divisions to the Armies of the United States and five tactical fighter wings to the Air Force of the United States, increased our strategic airlift capability by 75 per cent and increased our special counterinsurgency forces which are engaged now in South Vietnam, by 600 per cent.

I hope those who want a strong America and place it on some signs will also place those figures next to it.

This is not an easy effort. This requires sacrifice by the people of the United States. But this is a very dangerous and uncertain world.

As I said earlier, on three occasions in the last three years the United States has had a direct confrontation. No one can say when it will come again. No one expects that our life will be easy—certainly not in this decade and perhaps not in this century.

But we should realize what a burden and responsibility the people of the United States have borne for so many years. Here a country which lived in isolation, divided and protected by the Atlantic and the Pacific, uninterested in the struggles of the world around it, here in the 18 years after the Second World War, we put ourselves by our own will, and by necessity, into defensive alliances with countries all around the globe.

Without the United States, South Vietnam would collapse overnight. Without the United States the SEATO Alliance would collapse overnight. Without the United States, the CENTO Alliance would collapse overnight. Without the United States there would be no NATO, and gradually Europe would drift into neutralism and indifference.

Without the effort of the United States and the Alliance for Progress, the Communist advance onto the mainland of South America would long ago have taken place.

So this country, which desires only to be free, which desires to be secure, which desires to live at peace, for 18 years, under three different Administrations, has borne more than its share of the burden, has stood watch for more than its number of years.

I don't think that we are fatigued or tired. We would like to live as we once lived, but history will not permit it. The Communist balance of power is still strong—the balance of power is still on the side of freedom. We are still the keystone in the arch of freedom. And I think we'll continue to do as we have done in our past—our duty. And the people of Texas will be in the lead.

So I am glad to come to this state, which has played such a significant role in so many efforts in this century, and to say that here in Fort Worth you people will be playing a major role in the maintenance of the security of the United States for the next 10 years.

I'm confident as I look to the future that our chances for security, our chances for peace are better than they've been in the past. And the reason is because we're stronger. And with that strength is a determination to not only maintain the peace but also the vital interests of the United States. To that great cause Texas and the United States are committed.

Thank you.

TEXT PREPARED FOR DALLAS

I am honored to have this invitation to address the annual meeting of the Dallas Citizens Council, joined by the members of the Dallas Assembly—and pleased to have this opportunity to salute the Graduate Research Center of the Southwest.

It is fitting that these two symbols of Dallas progress are united in the sponsorship of this meeting. For they represent the best qualities, I am told, of leadership and learning in this city—and leadership and learning are indispensable to each other.

The advancement of learning depends on community leadership for financial and political support—and the products of that learning, in turn, are essential to the leadership's hopes for continued progress and prosperity. It is not a coincidence that those communities possessing the best in research and graduate facilities—from M.I.T. to Cal Tech—tend to attract the new and growing industries. I congratulate those of you here in Dallas who have recognized these basic facts through the creation of the unique and forward-looking graduate research center.

This link between leadership and learning is not only essential at the community level. It is even more indispensable in world affairs. Ignorance and misinformation can handicap the progress of a city or a company—but they can, if allowed to prevail in foreign policy, handicap this country's security. In a world of complex and continuing problems, in a world full of frustrations and irritations, America's leadership must be guided by the lights of learning and reason—or else those who confuse rhetoric with reality and the plausible with the possible will gain the popular ascendancy with their seemingly swift and simple solutions to every world problem.

There will always be dissident voices heard in the land, expressing opposition without alternatives, finding fault but never favor, perceiving gloom on every side and seeking influence without responsibility. Those voices are inevitable.

But today other voices are heard in the land—voices preaching doctrines wholly unrelated to reality, wholly unsuited to the sixties, doctrines which apparently assume that words will suffice without weapons, that vituperation is as good as victory and that peace is a sign of weakness.

At a time when the national debt is steadily being reduced in terms of its burden on our economy, they see that debt as the greatest single threat to our security. At a time when we are steadily reducing the number of Federal employees serving every thousand citizens, they fear those supposed hordes of civil servants far more than the actual hordes of opposing armies.

We cannot expect that everyone, to use the phrase of a decade ago, will "talk sense to the American people." But we can hope that fewer people will listen to nonsense. And the notion that this nation is headed for defeat through deficit, or that strength is but a matter of slogans, is nothing but just plain nonsense.

I want to discuss with you today the status of our strength and our security because this question clearly calls for the most responsible qualities of leadership and the most enlightened products of scholarship. For this nation's strength and security are not easily or cheaply obtained—nor are they quickly and simply explained.

There are many kinds of strength and no one kind will suffice. Overwhelming nuclear strength cannot stop a guerrilla war. Formal pacts of alliance cannot stop internal subversion. Displays of material wealth cannot stop the disillusionment of diplomats subjected to discrimination.

Above all, words alone are not enough. The United States is a peaceful nation. And where our strength and determination are clear, our words need merely to convey conviction, not belligerence. If we are strong, our strength will speak for itself. If we are weak, words will be no help.

I realize that this nation often tends to identify turning points in world affairs with the major addresses which preceded them. But it was not the Monroe Doctrine that kept all Europe away from this hemisphere—it was the strength of the British fleet and the width of the Atlantic Ocean. It was not General Marshall's speech at Harvard which kept Communism out of Western Europe—it was the strength and stability made possible by our military and economic assistance.

In this Administration also it has been necessary at times to issue specific warnings that we could not stand by and watch the Communists conquer Laos by force, or intervene in the Congo, or swallow West Berlin or maintain offensive missiles on Cuba.

But while our goals were at least temporarily obtained in those and other instances, our successful defense of freedom was due—not to the words we used—but to the strength we stood ready to use on behalf of the principles we stand ready to defend.

This strength is composed of many different elements, ranging from the most massive deterrents to the most subtle influences. And all types of strength are needed—no one kind could do the job alone. Let us take a moment, therefore, to review this nation's progress in each major area of strength.

First, as Secretary McNamara made clear in his address last Monday, the strategic nuclear power of the United States has been so greatly modernized and expanded in the last 1,000 days, by the rapid production and deployment of the most modern missile systems, that any and all potential aggressors are clearly confronted now with the impossibility of strategic victory—and the certainty of total destruction—if by reckless attack they should ever force upon us the necessity of a strategic reply.

In less than three years, we have increased by 50 per cent the number of Polaris submarines scheduled to be in force by the next fiscal year—increased by more than 70 per cent our total Polaris purchase program—increased by 50 per cent the portion of our strategic bombers on 15-minute alert—and increased by 100 per cent the total number of nuclear weapons available in our strategic alert forces.

Our security is further enhanced by the steps we have taken regarding these weapons to improve the speed and certainty of their response, their readiness at all times to respond, their ability to survive an attack and their ability to be carefully controlled and directed through secure command operations. But the lessons of the last decade have taught us that freedom cannot be defended by strategic nuclear power alone. We have, therefore, in the last three years accelerated the development and deployment of tactical nuclear weapons—and increased by 60 per cent the tactical nuclear forces deployed in Western Europe.

Nor can Europe or any other continent rely on nuclear forces alone, whether they are strategic or tactical. We have radically improved the readiness of our conventional forces—increased by 45 per cent the number of combat ready army divisions—increased by 100 per cent the procurement of modern army weapons and equipment—increased by 100 per cent our ship construction, conversion and modernization program—by 100 per cent our procurement of tactical aircraft—increased by 30 per cent the number of tactical air squadrons—and increased the strength of the Marines.

As last month's Operation Big Lift—which originated here in Texas— showed so clearly, this nation is prepared as never before to move substantial numbers of men in surprisingly little time to advanced positions anywhere in the world. We have increased by 175 per cent the procurement of airlift aircraft—and we have already achieved a 75 per cent increase in our existing strategic airlift capability. Finally, moving beyond the traditional roles of our military forces, we have achieved an increase of nearly 600 per cent in our special forces—those forces that are prepared to work with our allies and friends against the guerrillas, saboteurs, insurgents and assassins who threaten freedom in a less direct but equally dangerous manner.

But American military might should not and need not stand alone against the ambitions of international Communism. Our security and strength, in the last analysis, directly depend on the security and strength of others—and that is why our military and economic assistance plays such a key role in enabling those who live on the periphery of the Communist world to maintain their independence of choice.

Our assistance to these nations can be painful, risky and costly—as is true in Southeast Asia today. But we dare not weary of the task. For our assistance makes possible the stationing of 3.5 million allied troops along the Communist frontier at one-tenth the cost of maintaining a comparable number of American soldiers. A successful Communist breakthrough in these areas, necessitating direct United States intervention, would cost us several times as much as our entire foreign aid program—and might cost us heavily in American lives as well.

About 70 per cent of our military assistance goes to nine key countries located on or near the borders of the Communist bloc—nine countries confronted directly or indirectly with the threat of Communist aggression—Vietnam, free China, Korea, India, Pakistan, Thailand, Greece, Turkey and Iran. No one of these countries possesses on its own the resources to maintain the forces which our own chiefs of staff think needed in the common interest.

Reducing our efforts to train, equip and assist their armies can only encourage Communist penetration and require in time the increased overseas deployment of American combat forces. And reducing the economic help needed to bolster these nations that undertake to help defend freedom can have the same disastrous result. In short, the $50 billion we spend each year on our own defense could well be ineffective without the $4 billion required for military and economic assistance.

Our foreign aid program is not growing in size—it is, on the contrary, smaller now than in previous years. It has had its weaknesses—but we have undertaken to correct them and the proper way of treating weaknesses is to replace them with strength, not to increase those weaknesses by emasculating essential programs.

Dollar for dollar, in or out of Government, there is no better form of investment in our national security than our much-abused foreign aid program. We cannot afford to lose it. We can afford to maintain it. We can surely afford, for example, to do as much for our 19 needy neighbors of Latin America as the Communist bloc is sending to the island of Cuba alone.

I have spoken of strength largely in terms of the deterrence and resistance of aggression and attack. But, in today's world, freedom can be lost without a shot being fired, by ballots as well as bullets. The success of our leadership is dependent upon respect for our mission in the world as well as our missiles—on a clearer recognition of the virtues of freedom as well as the evils of tyranny.

That is why our information agency has doubled the shortwave broadcasting power of the Voice of America and increased the number of broadcasting hours by 30 per cent—increased Spanish-language broadcasting to Cuba and Latin-American readers—and taken a host of other steps to carry our message of truth and freedom to all the far corners of the earth.

And that is also why we have regained the initiative in the exploration of outer space—making an annual effort greater than the combined total of all space activities undertaken during the fifties—launching more than 130 vehicles into earth orbit—putting into actual operation valuable weather and communications satellites—and making it clear to all that the United Status of America has no intention of finishing second in space.

This effort is expensive—but it pays its own way, for freedom and for America. For there is no longer any fear in the free world that a Communist lead in the space will become a permanent assertion of supremacy and the basis of military superiority. There is no longer any doubt about the strength and skill of American science, American industry, American education and the American free enterprise system. In short, our national space effort represents a great gain in, and a great resource of, our national strength—and both Texas and Texans are contributing greatly to this strength.

Finally, it should be clear by now that a nation can be no stronger abroad than she is at home. Only America which practices what it preaches about equal rights and social justice will be respected by those whose choice affects our future. Only an America which has fully educated its citizens is fully capable of tackling the complex problems and perceiving the hidden dangers of the world in which we live. And only an America which is growing and prospering economically can sustain the worldwide defense of freedom, while demonstrating to all concerned the opportunities of our system and society.

It is clear, therefore, that we are strengthening our security as well as our economy by our recent record increases in national income and output—by surging ahead of most of Western Europe in the rate of business expansion.

And the margin of corporate profits—by maintaining a more stable level of prices than almost any of our overseas competitors—and by cutting personal and corporate income taxes by some $11 billion, as I have proposed, to assure this nation of the longest and strongest expansion in our peacetime economic history.

This nation's total output—which three years ago was at the $500 billion mark—will soon pass $600 billion, for a record rise of over $100 billion in 3 years. For the first time in history we have 70 million men and women at work. For the first time in history average factory earnings have exceeded $100 a week. For the first time in history corporation profits after taxes—which have risen 43 per cent in less than 3 years—have reached an annual level of $27.4 billion.

My friends and fellow citizens: I cite these facts and figures to make it clear that America today is stronger than ever before. Our adversaries have not abandoned their ambitions—our dangers have not diminished—our vigilance cannot be relaxed. But now we have the military, the scientific and the economic strength to do whatever must be done for the preservation and promotion of freedom.

That strength will never be used in pursuit of aggressive ambitions—it will always be used in pursuit of peace. It will never be used to promote provocations—it will always be used to promote the peaceful settlement of disputes.

We in this country, in this generation, are—by destiny rather than choice—the watchmen on the walls of world freedom. We ask, therefore, that we may be worthy of our power and responsibility—that we may exercise our strength with wisdom and restraint—and that we may achieve in our time and for all time the ancient vision of peace on earth, goodwill toward men. That must always be our goal—and the righteousness of our cause must always underlie our strength. For as was written long ago: "Except the Lord keep the city, the watchman waketh but in vain."

Kennedy and Reporters

Daily Contacts With President Formed Personal Bond Beyond a Formal One

By TOM WICKER

Special to The New York Times

DALLAS, Nov. 23—To reporters who watch a president day in and day out, year in and year out, who write minutely of his movements and actions, who constantly seek to divine his thoughts and attitudes, who know perhaps more than they can legitimately tell of his personality and character and actions, a president can never be the lofty, regal figure he seems to others. Inevitably, even those politically opposed to or dubious about him are drawn into his personal radius. They become, however tenuously, part of his entourage. They believe they know the man, if not the president. They love him, dislike him, ponder him, occasionally feel pride in or contempt for him—but they can never be indifferent about him. This was particularly so of John F. Kennedy. For if in the latter part of his life both president and press felt a generalized estrangement, a suspicion of each other, still between man and reporter there was a personal bond in the enduring interest each had in the other.

No president paid more attention not only to the press but also to reporters. Once in a drizzling rain at the airport in Columbus, Ohio, as he turned away from an adulatory crowd with whom he had been shaking hands, he made his way over to where the press stood. "That was a splendid piece you wrote the other day," he said to a reporter as the rain came steadily down on both of them. "Really excellent." He was talking about an account of a background briefing he had held a few days earlier. Again, at a first private interview he gave to one reporter, Mr. Kennedy quickly eased the atmosphere with a few blunt words about a critique of his speaking style. "You're right," he told the reporter. "I can't read a speech worth a damn."

Once after he had held two days of intensive talks with the head of a foreign Government, the president appeared in the White House rose garden and made a murky speech to a religious group. His news secretary, Pierre Salinger, was asked for an explanation of some impenetrable sentences. Mr. Salinger called back in an hour: "The president said to tell you that he doesn't know what he meant. He said that is just the way he gets after two days with——" [the visiting head of government].

But it was not only such personal incidents, the compliment on a story, the frequent complaints (it seemed as though he read every word printed in the major publications) that built the bond between Mr. Kennedy and the men who followed him. There is much to remember, on this day of sad recollection. Memories come at random, some sharp, some hazy, colored no doubt by time and hope and personal feeling. They are not of great events. Those belong to everyone. But of little things.

The night on his plane, for instance, as he returned from Trenton, after speaking for Richard J. Hughes, who was running for governor of New Jersey. "I'd really like to have that yacht Eisenhower laid up in Philadelphia," he confided. "But he said he did it for economy reasons and if I took it out of mothballs now they'd never let me hear the end of it."

Or the day in Palm Beach when he left the yacht *Honey Fitz* for a return to Washington. Already on the dock to walk to his waiting car, he had to stop and turn back to give a last hug to little Caroline, running after him.

Once, standing in Pierre Salinger's office, a door opened to the rear. There was the president of the United States, a newspaper in hand, eyeglasses cocked up on his forehead. Not too many knew that he wore glasses—a fact he did not like publicized.

Sharp and clear stands a moment from one of his last hours, when the president of the Fort Worth Chamber of Commerce had presented him with a Texas 10-gallon hat. The crowd of 2,000 or so waited expectantly for him to put it on. But one thing that John Kennedy, political man that he was, never would do, was to put on a "funny hat." "Come to Washington Monday and I'll put it on for you in the White House," he joked. One is glad that on that last day he did not yield so intensely personal a point.

A reporter might also remember the night in Miami Beach when the president regaled a Democratic audience with good-natured derision of his old friend, Senator George A. Smathers of Florida, "his most valuable adviser." Mr. Smathers's advice, as Mr. Kennedy told it, had been wrong at every point.

Or anger on Mr. Kennedy's face at a news conference when he replied hotly to a loaded question . . . The day he laughed with reporters in the White House rose garden about the time Mr. Salinger drove off the first tee at Hyannis Port and hit the clubhouse . . . The phrases and manner of one of the most felicitous speeches he made, his talk on the publication of a book of the John Adams papers . . .

The delight on his face when the bearded mayor of New Ross in County Wexford, Ireland, accused "some pressman" of having put the loudspeaker out of action . . . The exasperation and embarrassment he showed when a pompous Navy officer placed him atop a pedestal on the flight deck of a carrier off San Diego last summer . . .

The frequent occasions when, harassed by the pain in his always troublesome back, he would have to drag himself up the ramp to his plane, even up the two or three steps from the rose garden to the White House portico.

In the soaring Cathedral of Cologne, during his triumphal tour of Europe last summer, the president sat by Chancellor Adenauer—the young, handsome head by the old, skeletonal profile of the older generation from which John Kennedy hoped to assume world leadership. Just once, that young head turned upwards, wonderingly, and paused a long time and gazed at the marvelous old building that represented so much of the permanence and nobility of the civilization he was undertaking to preserve.

There was the family pride and delight in his voice that night in Harrisburg when he told 12,000 Democrats: "I should introduce myself. I am Teddy Kennedy's brother." Edward M. Kennedy had just won the Democratic senatorial primary in Massachusetts.

And there was the tart message, delivered by Mr. Salinger, to the author of an article on that primary campaign. "The president said to drop in on him sometime and he'll teach you something about Massachusetts politics." Like so many valuable lessons, that one never was learned.

He did not, of course, know so much about the reporters as they knew about him. How could he, with all the cares he had, with his life so nearly circumscribed by Hyannis Port and Palm Beach and high office? "Tell me," he once said to a reporter aboard his plane. "Do they feed you when you fly on the press plane?"

It did not matter. What did matter was the bond that all knew was there—far more personal than professional, more real sometimes than the job of writing about what he did and said. That bond was forged in small events, not great ones—not Cuba, not steel, not Oxford. And it is that bond that brings to some today's plain and intense grief.

History, no doubt, will measure him unemotionally and impartially. But those who went with him almost all the way cannot. They knew him; mostly they liked him. They believed he knew them as much as he could; they thought he liked them as much as he could.

Now Lyndon Johnson is president, and the only things certain are that soon enough, in some manner, there will be a bond with him too.

In Memoriam

The leaden skies of yesterday were like a pall. A sense of grief seemed to hang in the air. Such a feeling was inevitable, for it was as though the very wind was keening in the woodlands, the trees themselves sensitive to human emotions. Late November is the year's own time of the long sleep, the summary if not the farewell. The hills are bare to the buffeting of winter.

And yet, the hills still stand. The trees are still rooted and rugged. Rivers flow to the sea. And beyond the gray clouds the sun keeps to its course and the stars are in their appointed places. The eternities prevail. We live with those eternities, though ourselves mortal; it is the human dream, the hope and aspiration, that persists. Take away all else and those are the human eternities.

Robert Frost, in his last book, wrote lines that sum it up:

> *We vainly wrestle with the blind belief*
> *That aught we cherish*

Can ever quite pass out of utter grief
And wholly perish.

Dark days come, inevitable. And time persists, time that is both dark and light and forever changing. The time of the stars, the time of the hills, the time of man. And nothing cherished ever wholly perishes. Gray November is a passing thing, and year's end is no end at all, but another marker on the great rhythm. A tree falls, and a seedling is already rooted.

Man persists, man with the capacity to dream and hope and dream again. Man, with his capacity for shock and grief, but also with his inheritance of faith, of belief, [h]is participation in the great truth of continuity.

The Death of the President

A nation still stunned in shock and grief is today attempting with difficulty to readjust to the loss this country and the world have suffered in the death of President John Fitzgerald Kennedy.

Even now it almost seems impossible that this depraved crime could have been committed in our country, which has contributed so much to the theory and practice of orderly, democratic self-government. And yet, for the fourth time in our history, it has happened; and, as the bells toll today for John F. Kennedy, every American must feel, mixed in with his sorrow, both remorse and shame that it could have happened here.

We mourn with the late president's family, to whom this blow has been inexpressibly cruel. While no grief can touch theirs in its personal intimacy, the nature of the American presidency is such that the office belongs to every one of us—and, in a very real sense, whatever happens to the president happens in some degree to each of us. Today's national grief is more than formal; it too is personal, only intensified by that special, youthful appeal of the man who today lies in solemn state in Washington beneath the Capitol's dome.

John F. Kennedy was a man of his generation, an eloquent spokesman for that strange new world which the Second World War had ushered in. More than any president since Woodrow Wilson, he believed in the power of ideas. His quick intelligence gave him an extraordinary grasp of the vast scope of the presidential office; his deep intellect molded a philosophy of government that rare oratorical powers enabled him to articulate with grace and with distinction.

He was a man of the world, who understood the role of the United States in this world. He was a man of peace, who at first hand had experienced war. He was above all a man of political sophistication, who appreciated what the United States could do and what it could not do in its relations abroad. While a brilliant exponent of American democracy, he never fell into the trap of believing in the myth of American omnipotence.

He was a man of moderation, as he demonstrated repeatedly during his too-brief years in office; he was also a man of courage, as he showed in that moment of acute crisis over Cuba a year ago.

Magnificent in the presentation of his programs, President Kennedy had thus far proved less successful in carrying his proposals through a recalcitrant Congress. But he was not given the chance to prove his mettle in this respect.

He has been murderously cut off in the prime of life and power; the Nation has suffered another day of infamy which the American people will never forget.

The Accused

While he lived and served as president of the United States, John Fitzgerald Kennedy stood for the concept of this nation as one ruled by law and directed by the utmost concern for justice and fair play. The act which snuffed out the president's life was first and foremost a repudiation of these concepts, a retrogression to the most barbaric practices of the most primitive man.

An individual has now been charged with the horrible crime which deprived the nation of its elected head. The most fitting tribute to President Kennedy's memory can only be concern that the accused receive the most scrupulous protection of our laws with full opportunity for his defense before a properly constituted court. Whatever the verdict, no doubt about its fairness must be allowed to stain the historic record of deep devotion to "equal justice under law" which was so brilliantly written by John F. Kennedy while yet he lived.

President Johnson's Tasks

As President Johnson assumes the majesty, the power and the awesome responsibilities of the high office destiny has thrust upon him, he must also take up the enormous burden of the tasks confronting the chief executive of this nation and the leader of the free world.

There is some consolation in this hour of tragedy that he does not have to meet an immediate crisis, as did President Truman when he assumed office on the death of President Roosevelt. Except for the war in Vietnam, the world is not engulfed in hostilities and the prospects for peace look brighter than they did some time ago.

But the Western world also seems to be drifting into disarray; the cold war continues and the peace we seek still escapes us. President Johnson must assume a legacy of unfinished business that will test his statesmanship to the utmost.

Foremost among the tasks he faces are those of foreign policy. Like President Kennedy he has dedicated himself to the advancement of the cause of freedom, not by waging war but by waging peace. He, too, recognizes the sober fact that we confront an implacable Communist drive which must be met. But he, like his predecessor, also realizes, as does Premier Khrushchev, that a major war in this nuclear age spells suicide for all mankind and that there can be no military solution for existing problems.

To meet the Communist challenge, he must keep up our military power to such proportions that no aggressor dare test it. He must seek to repair and strengthen our alliances, most particularly the North Atlantic alliance. In that effort he can count on the full support of the rest of Europe, especially of Chancellor Erhard. The latter has made it plain to President de Gaulle that, while upholding the French-German treaty of reconciliation as an essential basis for European unification, he also regards it, not as a vehicle for French hegemony, but as a stepping stone toward a wider European unity and an Atlantic community. Equally serious problems confront the new president in Latin America, where the Alliance for Progress is in trouble, in dealing with South Vietnam and Cuba, in furthering disarmament and foreign aid.

In strengthening our might, we arm only for defense, to ward off aggression, not for conquest or domination. President Kennedy was the great champion of continued negotiations with Soviet Russia to ease international tensions and if possible reach a détente. That is also the policy President Johnson can be expected to pursue.

The new president must also face tremendous unsolved problems in the domestic field, of which civil rights is only the most obvious in a list of pressing issues that include unemployment, education and taxes. There is hope that, under the impact of the tragedy, President Johnson will be accorded the full support of a united country. He deserves it and must have it to meet his responsibilities and steer this nation safely through a stormy sea.

The Presidential Succession

The assassination of John F. Kennedy forces once again on the American people the necessity for correcting an important defect in the Constitution. If the late president had survived his wounds but been seriously incapacitated, a cloud might have settled over the most critical functions of government, for the Constitution leaves uncertain the procedures to be followed.

The succession is clear in the event of the president's removal, death or resignation. But if illness or injury makes it impossible for him to govern, neither the Constitution nor any law provides how succession shall be determined. Nor is there legal provision for resumption by the president of his official functions when he is restored to health.

President Wilson, gravely ill toward the end of his second term, never was superseded. His illness contributed to the defeat of United States entry into the League of Nations, a factor of importance among the causes of World War II. The consequences of uncertainty could be far more serious today when the president alone must decide on use of our vast nuclear retaliatory forces.

In 1958, President Eisenhower dealt with most aspects of this problem through a private agreement with Vice President Nixon. A similar agreement was made in 1961 by President Kennedy and Vice President Johnson.

These agreements provided that the vice president would serve if asked by the president. If the president were unable to make this decision, the vice president would decide "after such consultation as seems to him appropriate." Included under this head would be discussion with the Cabinet and legal advice from the attorney general. The president himself would decide when his inability to serve had ended.

These arrangements are unsatisfactory. They do not provide for the case when a president is unfit to serve but insists on exercising his functions. And, in any event, so critical a matter as the exercise of presidential powers should rest on law rather than private, unofficial agreement.

Many years of debate over this issue have led to a proposed constitutional amendment which has been approved by a Senate Judiciary subcommittee after extensive hearings. The amendment would delegate to the Congress authority for establishing the necessary procedures. Prompt passage of this measure is more than ever a matter of urgent national interest.

Topics

"When Lilacs Last in the Dooryard Bloom'd"

A bereaved country reached in vain for words until a great poet, Walt Whitman, wrote: "When lilacs last in the dooryard bloom'd / And the great star early droop'd in the western sky in the night, / I mourn'd, and yet shall mourn with ever-returning spring." So a singer of America wrote of President Lincoln, whose fearful trip was done that terrible day in April of 1865.

North and South

The printers of 1865 took the one-point column rules and turned them downside up into six-point shrouds of black. Historians and journalists groped in the language that he had used with such deceptive simplicity and found that simple words could not fully explain him. The preachers and the politicians, North and South, spoke mightily. And the people who didn't speak and couldn't find the proper expressions sought some meaning.

In the good columns of *The Springfield Journal,* the home-town paper that Lincoln called his "friend," they remembered that as president-elect he had told his neighbors, leaving: "To this place, and the kindness of these people, I owe everything. Here I have lived a quarter of a century, and have passed from a young to an old man. Here my children have been born, and one is buried. I now leave, not knowing when, or whether ever, I may return . . ." Four years after a second American Revolution called the Civil War, he returned to Springfield.

Hatred in Texas Newspapers

Of his life, Lincoln had once told a contemporary that it was but one thing: "the short and simple annals of the poor." But along the edges of the Confederacy that was, in *The Frankfort Commonwealth,* they spoke this way about a native son who was born near Hodgenville, Kentucky: "When Abraham Lincoln fell, the South lost its best and truest friend."

Such was the sympathetic reaction in most parts of the South.

But from Texas came a horrible statement in the pages of *The Dallas Herald* which said, "God Almighty ordered this event or it could never have taken place." And in *The Tri-Weekly Telegraph,* in Houston, ten days after the assassination, these shocking words appeared: "From now until God's judgment day, the minds of men will not cease to thrill at the killing of Abraham Lincoln. . . . We saw successively in his public documents how super-ruling became his purpose, and how callous to all the usual motives of humanity he grew. . . . Whoever would impose the fate of servitude and slavery on these Confederate States, whatever fatal Providence of God shall lay him low, we say, and say it gladly, God's will be done."

"The Gift Outright"

When President Kennedy took the oath of office on Jan. 20, 1961, another great poet sang of America in words that echoed Walt Whitman's. Robert Frost's vast television audience enabled him to be seen by more people than had ever in the history of mankind heard a poet recite. The dedication of his poem, "The Gift Outright," was: "For John F. Kennedy."

> *The land was ours before we were the land's.*
> *She was our land more than a hundred years*
> *Before we were her people. . . .*
> *Something we were withholding made us weak*
> *Until we found out that it was ourselves*
> *We were withholding from our land of living,*
> *And forthwith found salvation in surrender. . . .*
> *To the land vaguely realizing westward,*
> *But still unstoried, artless, unenhanced,*
> *Such as she was, such as she would become.*

It was, at the same time, a tribute to a still-young country personified by the new president.

Washington

The Cruel Lessons of Fortune and Caprice

By JAMES RESTON

WASHINGTON, Nov. 23—History seems determined to teach this nation that it must make more provision for fortune and caprice. All our assumptions, even about human ability and mortality, are subject to error. Franklin Roosevelt, who thought he was marked by fate to make the peace, died before the end of the war. Harry Truman, who was marked early in his

ENTHUSIASTIC ADMIRERS: The crowd in Fort Worth jamming a barrier outside the hotel to welcome President Kennedy as he arrived to address the Chamber of Commerce.

BETTMANN/CORBIS

CROWDS GREETING THE PRESIDENTIAL COUPLE: President Kennedy and his wife, Jacqueline, in the presidential limousine in Dallas on November 22, 1963, moments before he was shot. BETTMANN/CORBIS

MOMENTS BEFORE ASSASSINATION: President and Mrs. Kennedy and Governor and Mrs. John B. Connally riding through Dallas in the motorcade. Shortly after this picture was taken, rifle fire hit the president and the governor. ASSOCIATED PRESS

AT TIME OF SHOOTING: A spectator took this picture with a Polaroid camera just as the president slumped after being shot. BETTMANN/CORBIS

MOMENTS AFTER ASSASSINATION: An amateur photographer watching the motorcade took this picture soon after the president and Governor John B. Connally were shot. The left arrow points to Mr. Kennedy's foot hanging over the side of car, and the right arrow indicates Mrs. Connally. The man standing in rear is a Secret Serviceman. ASSOCIATED PRESS

SILENT MOURNER: A woman pauses on hearing the news.
NEAL BOENZI/THE NEW YORK TIMES

LEARNING THE NEWS: Attorney General Robert F. Kennedy with two of his children at his home in McLean, Va., after he was notified of the assassination. He left for Andrews Air Force Base to meet the jet carrying his brother.
BETTMANN/CORBIS

THE NEW PRESIDENT: Lyndon B. Johnson takes the oath before Judge Sarah T. Hughes in the plane at Dallas. Mrs. Kennedy and Representative Jack Brooks are at right. To the left are Mrs. Johnson and Representative Albert Thomas. BETTMANN/CORBIS

A SADDENED MEETING: Attorney General Robert F. Kennedy greets his sister-in-law. ASSOCIATED PRESS

ESCORTED BY WIDOW: Mrs. Kennedy, her stockings still stained with her husband's blood, enters vehicle for the trip to Bethesda Naval Hospital. ASSOCIATED PRESS

RETURN TO THE CAPITAL: President Johnson speaks at Andrews Air Force Base on arrival from Dallas. With him is Mrs. Johnson. The plane carried President Kennedy's body. ASSOCIATED PRESS

CHARGED WITH ASSASSINATION: Lee Harvey Oswald, in handcuffs, at police headquarters in Dallas. He was charged by police with the murder of President Kennedy. ASSOCIATED PRESS

FAMILY OF ACCUSED: Mrs. Marina Oswald, wife of Lee Harvey Oswald, carrying one of her children as she left police headquarters in Dallas where she had attempted to visit her husband. With her was her daughter, in foreground, and Mrs. Marguerite Oswald, mother of the accused. ASSOCIATED PRESS

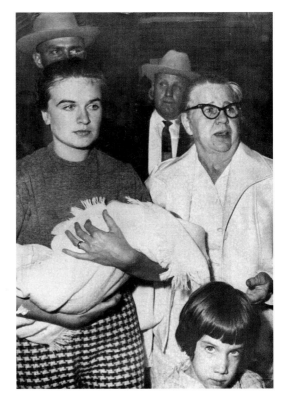

ASSASSIN'S VIEW: This photograph was taken through the window from which President Kennedy was shot. The arrow points to a car in approximately the same position as the president's limousine was at the time of the shooting.

ASSOCIATED PRESS

SCENE OF THE SLAYING: The framed window indicates where the gunman stood as he fired his rifle at the passing car. At the time the president was shot, his car was at about the same position as the white truck shown above at the right. ASSOCIATED PRESS

HERO'S FAMILY: Mrs. J. D. Tippit, whose husband was shot to death as he tried to capture President Kennedy's assassin, with her children, Brenda Kay, 10, Curtis Ray, 4, and Allen, 13. ASSOCIATED PRESS

"READY FOR SHOOTING": Mail-order catalogue describes carbine bought by Lee Harvey Oswald, which officials described as the weapon used to kill John Fitzgerald Kennedy. BETTMANN/CORBIS

THE FIRST DAY BEGINS: As rain sweeps the capital, President Johnson is driven from his Washington residence to his suite in the Executive Office Building for meetings.
BETTMANN/CORBIS

RETURN TO THE CAPITAL: The honor guard as it preceded the ambulance bearing the coffin of President Kennedy to the White House. BETTMANN/CORBIS

GUARD OF HONOR: An honor guard, composed of representatives of the Army, Navy, Air Force and Marines, stands at its post at the shrouded North Portico entrance to the White House. ASSOCIATED PRESS

IN REPOSE: The flag-draped coffin of President Kennedy in the East Room of the White House. A priest kneels in prayer at left. The guard of honor represents the armed services.
GEORGE TAMES/THE NEW YORK TIMES

career for oblivion and defeat, survived to organize the greatest coalition of nations in history. Dwight D. Eisenhower, who was stricken twice in office and counted out, lived on to be the oldest president in the long story of the nation. John F. Kennedy, the youngest elected president, who came to office proclaiming the emergence of a new generation of leaders, is dead at 46. And Lyndon Johnson, who at first opposed Kennedy and later joined and served him, has succeeded to the presidency only after reaching the reluctant conclusion that he would never get it.

Accordingly, this is no time for anything but very modest speculation about the future. Time has been more cruel to President Johnson than it was to Harry Truman. He has come into the White House near the end of the statutory four-year term rather than at the beginning, and like Sir Alec Douglas-Home, the new British prime minister (who was also thrown up by a stroke of fate), he has less than a year to go before the election. Policy under the new president, therefore, will probably remain very much as it was under Kennedy, but the execution of policy will undoubtedly be much different.

The Administration of John F. Kennedy was a very personal affair. It was organized to fit his personality and style. He had his own strong views on policy, foreign and domestic, and his own highly original concepts about his personal staff and his Cabinet. He was a reader, an analyzer and a catalyst, and was to a very large extent his own foreign secretary, with gifts of grace, wit and knowledge that enabled him to fulfill the diplomatic and ceremonial aspects of his job.

President Johnson is a totally different type of man. He has not been a deep student of foreign affairs over a long period of time. Unlike Kennedy, he is not a great reader or analyzer of documents. He is a doer, who spends more time on how to get things done than on meditating on what to do.

The prospect is, therefore, that the White House staff of brilliant intellectuals and Boston politicians will decline in power and the Cabinet will rise. Johnson drives his staff with all the energy of an impatient Army officer, which is quite different from what Kennedy's aides are accustomed to; but, ironically, Kennedy's Cabinet is likely to have more power under Johnson than it did under Kennedy. Moreover, there is no urgent need for the new president to take new policy initiatives in the field of foreign affairs. His urgent problems are to get organized, to get something through the Congress, and to get ready for the election.

The death of President Kennedy has transformed the political scene. That is fairly obvious. It has improved the Republican party's chances of victory. It has hurt Senator Goldwater, who is identified in many minds with the extreme Right. It has certainly not increased the popularity of Texas in the North, and therefore, by indirection, it has complicated President Johnson's political problem.

Everybody in the Democratic party will rally behind the new president now. He will almost certainly be unchallenged for the presidential nomination, and there is already considerable talk here that Senator Hubert Humphrey will be strongly backed for the vice presidential nomination, and may even replace Mike Mansfield as majority leader before then.

Beyond these speculations, however, it is probably imprudent to go. Each of the last three presidents has developed in office in wholly unpredictable ways, and President Johnson is not likely to be an exception to this rule.

DAY THREE

___

November 24, 1963

"All the News That's Fit to Print"

The New York Times.

LATE CITY EDITION
U. S. Weather Bureau Report (Page 80) forecast: Sunny and cool today; fair, mild tonight. Cloudy, milder tomorrow.
Temp. Range: 46—32; yesterday: 53-

VOL. CXIII..No. 38,656. © 1963 by The New York Times Company, Times Square, New York 36, N. Y. NEW YORK, MONDAY, NOVEMBER 25, 1963. TEN CENTS

PRESIDENT'S ASSASSIN SHOT TO DEATH IN JAIL CORRIDOR BY A DALLAS CITIZEN; GRIEVING THRONGS VIEW KENNEDY BIER

Associated Press Wirephoto

FAREWELL: Kneeling with her mother at John Fitzgerald Kennedy's coffin in the Capitol, Caroline touches the flag

Mrs. Kennedy Leads Public Mourning

By MARJORIE HUNTER
Special to The New York Times

WASHINGTON, Nov. 24 — Mrs. John F. Kennedy, firmly holding the hands of her two children, followed the coffin bearing the body of her husband as it left the White House today for the last time.

Her eyes swollen, she moved quietly to the edge of the steps of the North Portico and paused to watch the coffin placed in the caisson by military bearers.

Her son, John Jr., tugged at her hand and pointed to a black, riderless horse, part of the ceremonial procession. She leaned down and spoke to him.

Mrs. Kennedy wore a simple black suit and black lace mantilla. John Jr., who will be 3 years old tomorrow, and Caroline, who will be 6 on Wednesday, wore similar pale blue coats, while anklets and red shoes.

As the three stood there, framed against the black-draped doorway, there was an eerie silence. It was broken only by the occasional sound of hoofs of the restless gray horses that were to pull the caisson up Pennsylvania Avenue to the Capitol.

Mrs. Kennedy was composed, but appeared to be on the verge of tears as she and the children stepped into a black limousine for the slow ride to the Capitol. In the car, too, were President and Mrs. Johnson and Attorney General Robert F. Kennedy.

Still holding the hands of her children, Mrs. Kennedy followed the flag-draped coffin into the Capitol Rotunda. She stared straight ahead as the coffin was placed on the catafalque, a simple funeral bier draped in black broadcloth.

John Jr., wide-eyed and bewildered, was restless. Clutching a tiny flag, he was led away by a military aide.

Later, after the tributes had been spoken, Mrs. Kennedy walked slowly to the coffin, touched it with her fingertips, knelt and kissed it. Caroline was by her side. They were rejoined by John Jr. at the door.

Shortly after 9 o'clock tonight Mrs. Kennedy returned to the Capitol and again kneeled before the coffin and kissed it.

Mrs. Kennedy walked into the Rotunda on the arm of her husband's brother, Robert, who stopped at the rope holding

Continued on Page 2, Column 8

CROWD IS HUSHED

Mourners at Capitol File Past the Coffin Far Into the Night

Texts of eulogies spoken in Washington, Page 4.

By TOM WICKER
Special to The New York Times

WASHINGTON, Monday, Nov. 25—Thousands of sorrowing Americans filed past John Fitzgerald Kennedy's bier in the Great Rotunda of the United States Capitol yesterday and early today.

Mr. Kennedy's body lay in state in the center of the vast, stone-flooring chamber. Long after midnight the silent procession of mourners continued.

Some wept. All were hushed. As the two lines moved in a large circle around either side of the flag-covered coffin, almost the only sounds were the shuffle of feet and the quiet voices of policemen urging the people to "keep moving, keep moving right along."

By 2:45 A. M. today 115,000 persons had passed the bier.

Yesterday afternoon a crowd estimated at 300,000 lined Pennsylvania and Constitution Avenues to watch the passage of the caisson bearing the body of the 35th President of the United States, slain in the 47th year of his life by an assassin's bullet.

A Riderless Horse

Behind the caisson, following military tradition, came a riderless bay gelding, with a pair of military boots reversed in the silver stirrups.

The horse was Sardar, the thoroughbred that belongs to Mrs. John F. Kennedy.

Mrs. Kennedy, her two children, President and Mrs. Johnson and Mr. Kennedy's brother, Attorney General Robert F. Kennedy, rode in the first car of a 10-car procession that followed the caisson.

The procession moved at a funeral pace, to the sound of muffled drums, from the White House to Pennsylvania Avenue. It was a journey Mr. Kennedy had made formally four times.

At the Capitol, brief ceremonies of eulogy were held in the Rotunda before the admission of the waiting thousands who swarmed over the plaza and stretched in a long line up East Capitol Street.

At the conclusion of the cere-

Continued on Page 2, Column 1

World's Leaders to Attend Requiem Today in Capital

Mrs. Kennedy Will Walk Behind the Caisson to Mass at Cathedral

By JACK RAYMOND
Special to The New York Times

WASHINGTON, Nov. 24 — Mrs. John F. Kennedy, joined by world and national leaders, will walk behind the horse-drawn caisson that bears her husband's body from the White House to St. Matthew's Roman Catholic Cathedral tomorrow.

Following a requiem mass, John Fitzgerald Kennedy, the 35th President of the United States, will be escorted in a solemn state procession to Arlington National Cemetery to be buried with military honors.

The gravesite, on a beautiful grassy knoll, provides a sweeping view of the capital city and it is itself easily in view from the Memorial Bridge approach to the national burial ground.

The state funeral procession will begin at 10:30 A.M. at the Capitol, where the closed, flag-draped coffin of the President

Continued on Page 6, Column 5

Officials of Nearly 100 Lands in U.S.—They Will Meet Johnson

By MAX FRANKEL
Special to The New York Times

WASHINGTON, Nov. 24 — An emperor, a king, a queen, princes, presidents, premiers and ministers from every continent converged on Washington this evening to pay final tribute to

List of leaders expected at the funeral, Page 6.

President Kennedy and to make the acquaintance of President Johnson.

Representing nearly 100 nations, the foreign dignitaries will include the largest assembly of ruling statesmen ever gathered in the United States for any event.

Their arrival here, through the night, virtually overwhelmed an already tense and overburdened capital. Nonetheless, each visitor received the protocol deference and police protection of more normal

Continued on Page 6, Column 1

ONE BULLET FIR[ED]

Night-Club Man W[ho] Admired Kennedy [Is] Oswald's Slayer

By GLADWIN HILL
Special to The New York Times

DALLAS, Nov. 24 — [Pres]ident Kennedy's assassin, [Lee] Harvey Oswald, was [fatally] shot by a Dallas night-club [oper]ator today as the police [were about] to move him from the [city] jail to the county jail.

The shooting occurred [in the] basement of the mun[icipal] building at about 11:20 [A.M.] central standard time [(12:20] P.M. New York time).

The assailant, Jack R[uben]stein, known as Jack [Ruby,] lunged from a cluster of [news]men observing the transf[er of] Oswald from the jail [to an] armored truck.

Millions of viewers saw [the] shooting on television.

As the shot rang out, a [Dallas] detective suddenly recog[nized] Ruby and exclaimed: "Jack, [you] son of a bitch!"

A murder charge was [filed] against Ruby by Assistant [Dis]trict Attorney William F. [Alex]ander. Justice of the [Peace] Pierce McBride ordered him [held] without bail.

Detectives Flank Him

Oswald was arrested F[riday] after Mr. Kennedy was [shot] dead while riding th[rough] Dallas in an open car. He [was] charged with murdering [the] President and a policeman [who] was shot a short time [later] while trying to que[stion] Oswald.

As the 24-year-old pri[soner,] flanked by two detec[tives,] stepped onto a basement g[arage] ramp, Ruby thrust a .38 [cali]ber, snub-nose revolver [into] Oswald's left side and fi[red a] single shot.

The 52-year-old night [club] operator, an ardent admir[er of] President Kennedy and his [fami]ly, was described as ha[ving] been distraught.

[District Attorney He[nry] Wade said he understood [that] the police were looking [into] the possibility that Os[wald] had been slain to pre[vent] him from talking, The [As]sociated Press reported. Wade said that so far [no] connection between Os[wald] and Ruby had been es[tab]lished.]

Oswald slumped to the [con]crete paving, wordlessly c[lutch]ing his side and writhing [in] pain.

Oswald apparently lost

Continued on Page 18, Colu[mn]

JOHNSON AFFIRMS AIMS IN VIETNAM

Retains Kennedy's Policy of Aiding War on Reds—Lodge Briefs President

By E. W. KENWORTHY
Special to The New York Times

WASHINGTON, Nov. 24 — President Johnson reaffirmed today the policy objectives of his predecessor regarding South Vietnam. He called upon all Government agencies to support that policy with full unity of purpose.

This was disclosed by White House sources after a meeting between President Johnson and Henry Cabot Lodge, United States Ambassador to South Vietnam.

The meeting lasted nearly an hour. It was described as being devoted to a full review of the conclusions reached by participants in a strategy conference on South Vietnam held in Honolulu last Wednesday.

In another move today that emphasized the President's desire to convey at home and abroad the impression of continuity, Mr. Johnson asked all members of the White House staff to remain at their jobs.

This was announced by Pierre Salinger, White House press secretary.

Some Expected to Leave

Mr. Salinger said the President would leave up to the officials involved how long they wished to serve him.

Inevitably some of these officials—especially those from the universities and foundations—will decide to leave their posts after an interval.

But the President's request today would seem to insure that during the difficult days of adjustment and transition he would continue to have the benefit of the experience of key policy figures.

Attending the meeting between the President and Ambassador Lodge today were Secretary of State Dean Rusk, Secretary of Defense Robert S. McNamara, Under Secretary of State George W. Ball, John A. McCone, director of the Central Intelligence Agency, and McGeorge Bundy, special assistant to the President for national security affairs.

Secretaries Rusk and McNamara, Ambassador Lodge and Mr. Bundy all took part in the Honolulu conference.

As a result of the meeting, White House informants said, President Johnson laid down a

Continued on Page 5, Column 1

Millions of Viewers See Oswald Killing On 2 TV Networks

By JACK GOULD

The fatal shooting of Lee H. Oswald, who was held as the assassin of President Kennedy, was seen as it occurred yesterday by millions of television viewers.

The National Broadcasting Company telecast the dramatic happening live. Less than a minute later the Columbia Broadcasting System telecast it by means of tape, made as the shooting occurred.

C. B. S. headquarters recorded the pictures from Dallas as they were received here over a closed circuit. Officials, upon seeing the contents of the Dallas relay, put the tape out over the network instantly.

The incident marked the first time in 15 years of television around the globe that a real-life homicide had occurred in front of live cameras. The closest parallel occurred in October, 1960, when Inejiro Asanuma, Japanese political leader, was knifed on a public stage in

Continued on Page 10, Column 8

JOHNSON SPURS OSWALD INQUIRY

President Orders F. B. I. to Check Death—Handling of Case Worries Capital

By ANTHONY LEWIS
Special to The New York Times

WASHINGTON, Nov. 24—President Johnson directed the Federal Bureau of Investigation tonight to look into "every aspect" of the murder of Lee H. Oswald.

He spoke with the director of the F.B.I., J. Edgar Hoover, and ordered the redoubled investigation.

The action came as official Washington was showing increasing concern about the entire handling of the aftermath of President Kennedy's assassination.

Officials were convinced that Oswald was the assassin. But their concern was over the public impression of the criminal proceedings.

Tonight they were consider-

Continued on Page 11, Column 3

BUSINESS OF CITY WILL HALT TODAY

Mayor Says Only Essential Services Will Be Provided

Changes in events here are listed on Page 9.

By LEONARD INGALLS

Normal public business and social activity in the city will be almost completely suspended today out of respect for President Kennedy.

Mayor Wagner announced yesterday that the city would continue in full mourning throughout the day. Only essential city services will be maintained, he said.

"Those city employes not engaged in activities imperative to the health, safety and welfare of our citizens are to be released from duty and their offices closed through Monday," Mr. Wagner said at City Hall.

Proclamation of the day as a legal holiday by Governor Rockefeller in observance of Mr. Kennedy's funeral permits banks and other institutions to close.

Classes at schools and colleges will be suspended. Department stores and specialty shops will be shut. Securities exchanges and commodity markets will not operate. Most places of entertainment will be closed. There will be no deliveries of mail and post offices will be shut.

Special memorial services for the murdered President have been scheduled at churches and synagogues.

At St. Patrick's Cathedral

Continued on Page 9, Column 1

Pope Paul Warns That Hate and Evil Imperil Civil Order

Special to The New York Times

ROME, Nov. 24 — Pope Paul VI, alluding to the assassination of President Kennedy, said today that it showed how much "capacity for hatred and evil still remains in the world."

Without mentioning Mr. Kennedy by name, the Pontiff spoke of "the crime that has aroused in these days the deploration of the whole world." He said it illustrated "how great the threat to civil order and peace still is."

The Pope was addressing thousands of people gathered in St. Peter's Square for his usual Sunday-noon benediction.

"We cannot, at this moment of prayer together, take our thoughts from the crime that has aroused in these days the deploration of the whole world," he said.

"After dwelling upon the man who is no longer with us and after comforting those who still live in mourning and grief, our thoughts show us how much the capacity for hatred and evil yet remains in the world, how great the threat to civil order and peace still is, and how great is the need for the grace

Continued on Page 4, Column 1

NEWS INDEX

JOHNSON SCORED BY CHINESE REDS

Views Called 'Reactionary'—Taiwan Aid Attacked

By United Press International

TOKYO, Nov. 24—Communist China bitterly criticized President Johnson today and termed him a supporter of the late President Kennedy's "trickery policy."

"Since the emergence of the Kennedy regime," the Chinese Communist press agency Hsinhua said, "Johnson has positively supported various reactionary policies of the Kennedy Administration and participated in formulating and promoting such policies.

"Johnson has supported Kennedy's trickery policy and has called for the maintenance of such a policy in a series of his speeches."

The Chinese Communists reported the assassination of President Kennedy in a four-paragraph dispatch eight hours after it occurred. But they made no comment.

Hsinhua said Mr. Johnson "was one of the central figures in the Kennedy Government and has made frequent trips abroad."

The Chinese statement added that Mr. Johnson believed "the United States, in making two-faced antirevolutionary plots, must maintain a strong position on the basis of strong force."

"He also looks toward Cuba with animosity and has called for the elimination of the Cuban revolutionary Government," it

Continued on Page 7, Column 6

Copyright 1963—Dallas Times-Herald and Photographer Bob Jackson, from United Press International Telephoto

OSWALD IS SHOT: Lee Harvey Oswald cringes as Jack Ruby attacks him at Dallas jail. Policeman is J. R. Leavel[le]

SUNDAY, NOV. 24, brought new shocks to a nation still reeling from the death of its young leader. At 11:20 A.M. central time, in a corridor at the Dallas city jail, a small-time hustler and strip-club operator shot and killed Lee Harvey Oswald at point-blank range. And with that, the story suddenly shifted back to Dallas, to Chicago, to wherever something could be learned about a man named Jack Ruby. In Washington and elsewhere in the country, of course, the mourning continued. Kennedy's body was moved from the White House to the Capitol. President Johnson turned his attention to Vietnam and other urgent matters of foreign policy. High-ranking dignitaries by the hundreds, and ordinary Americans by the thousands, poured into Washington in anticipation of Kennedy's funeral the next day. Eulogies and tributes rang out from every pulpit in New York.

But the coverage on Day Three necessarily begins with Ruby. The opening section also includes other news from Dallas, further reporting on Oswald's tangled and tormented life—notably a detailed portrait by Peter Kihss—and a handful of fascinating bits and pieces, including one on the murder weapon that the Warren Commission would later seize upon and confirm.

The nation's capital, by contrast, presented a stately and splendidly reassuring picture of reason and order. With the funeral less than a day away, a moment of extraordinary national solidarity played out on the streets of Washington and in the Capitol Rotunda, where thousands of Americans filed by Kennedy's bier until, with great regret, the police closed the doors. Marjorie Hunter's soulful story about Jacqueline Kennedy, truly a profile in courage that day, Tom Wicker's report from the Rotunda, Nan Robertson's interviews with mourners who had driven hours for one last glimpse—these best capture the texture of the day.

As before, the editorials and other commentary close this particular chapter. James Reston's piece and the lead editorial make the same doleful observation: that American culture is riven by a fundamental ambiguity—nobility, grace and tenderness on the one hand (all very much on display on the streets of Washington and in the churches of New York), violence and anger on the other hand (all very much on display in Dallas). America has been living with this contradiction since its inception and lives with it even today.

PRESIDENT'S ASSASSIN SHOT TO DEATH IN JAIL CORRIDOR BY A DALLAS CITIZEN; GRIEVING THRONGS VIEW KENNEDY BIER

One Bullet Fired

Night-Club Man Who Admired Kennedy Is Oswald's Slayer

By GLADWIN HILL
Special to The New York Times

DALLAS, Nov. 24—President Kennedy's assassin, Lee Harvey Oswald, was fatally shot by a Dallas night-club operator today as the police started to move him from the city jail to the county jail. The shooting occurred in the basement of the municipal building at about 11:20 A.M. central standard time (12:20 P.M. New York time).The assailant, Jack Rubenstein, known as Jack Ruby, lunged from a cluster of newsmen observing the transfer of Oswald from the jail to an armored truck.

Millions of viewers saw the shooting on television. As the shot rang out, a police detective suddenly recognized Ruby and exclaimed: "Jack, you son of a bitch!" A murder charge was filed against Ruby by Assistant District Attorney William F. Alexander. Justice of the Peace Pierce McBride ordered him held without bail.

Oswald was arrested Friday after Mr. Kennedy was shot dead while riding through Dallas in an open car. He was charged with murdering the president and a policeman who was shot a short time later while trying to question Oswald. As the 24-year-old prisoner, flanked by two detectives, stepped onto a basement garage ramp, Ruby thrust a .38-caliber, snub-nose revolver into Oswald's left side and fired a single shot. The 52-year-old night-club operator, an ardent admirer of President Kennedy and his family, was described as having been distraught.

[District Attorney Henry Wade said he understood that the police were looking into the possibility that Oswald had been slain to prevent him from talking, the Associated Press reported. Mr. Wade said that so far no connection between Oswald and Ruby had been established.]

Oswald slumped to the concrete paving, wordlessly clutching his side and writhing with pain. Oswald apparently lost consciousness very quickly after the shooting. Whether he was at any point able to speak, if he wanted to, was not known. The politically eccentric warehouse clerk was taken in a police ambulance to the Parkland Hospital, where President Kennedy died Friday. He died in surgery at 1:07 P.M., less than two hours after the shooting. The exact time Oswald was shot was not definitely established. Four plainclothes men, from a detail of about 50 police officers carrying out the transfer, pounced on Ruby as he fired the shot and overpowered him.

Ruby, who came to Dallas from Chicago 15 years ago, had a police record here listing six allegations of minor offenses. The disposition of five was not noted. A charge of liquor law violation was dismissed. Two of the entries, in July, 1953, and May, 1954, involved carrying concealed weapons.

The city police, working with the Secret Service and the Federal Bureau of Investigation, said last night that they had the case against Oswald "cinched." After some 30 hours of intermittent interrogations and confrontations with scores of witnesses, Oswald was ordered transferred to the custody of the Dallas County sheriff. This was preliminary to the planned presentation of the case, next Wednesday or the following Monday, to the county grand jury by District Attorney Wade.

The transfer involved a trip of about a mile from the uptown municipal building, where the Police Department and jail are. The route went down Main Street to the county jail, overlooking the spot where President Kennedy was killed and Gov. John B. Connally was wounded by shots from the book warehouse where Oswald worked. The original plan had been for the sheriff to assume custody of Oswald at the city jail and handle the transfer. Late last night, for unspecified reasons, it was decided that the city police would move the prisoner.

Police Chief Jesse Curry declined to comment on suggestions that he had scheduled the transfer of Oswald at an unpropitious time because of pressure from news media. Chief Curry announced about 9 o'clock last night that the investigation had reached a point where Oswald's presence was no longer needed. He said that Oswald would be turned over to the county sheriff today. Asked when this would take place, the chief said: "If you fellows are here by 10 A.M., you'll be early enough." When newsmen assembled at the police administrative offices at 10 o'clock, Chief Curry commented: "We could have done this earlier if I hadn't given you fellows that 10 o'clock time."

This was generally construed as meaning that preparations for the transfer had been in readiness for some hours, rather than implying a complaint from the chief that the press had had any part in setting the time.

Chief Curry disclosed this morning that to thwart an attempt against Oswald, the trip was to be made in an armored van of the kind used to transfer money. "We're not going to take any chances," he said. "Our squad cars are not bullet-proof. If somebody's going to try to do something, they wouldn't stop him."

A ramp dips through the basement garage of the municipal building, running from Main Street to Commerce Street. Patrol wagons drive down this ramp and discharge prisoners at a basement booking office. The garage ceiling was too low for the armored car, so the van was backed up in the Commerce Street portal of the ramp.

The plan was to lead Oswald out the doorway in the center of the basement and about 75 feet up the ramp to the back of the armored car. At about 11 o'clock, Chief Curry left his third-floor office, followed by plainclothes detectives and newsmen, to go to the basement. Oswald was still in a fourth-floor jail cell. As the group with the chief walked through a short corridor past the basement booking office and out the door onto the guarded ramp, uniformed policemen checked the reporters' credentials. But they passed familiar faces, such as those of policemen and collaborating Secret Service and F.B.I. agents.

Ruby's face was familiar to many policemen who had encountered him at his two night clubs and in his frequent visits to the municipal building. Neatly dressed in a dark suit and wearing a fedora, he was inconspicuous in a group of perhaps 50 men who for the next 20 minutes waited in a 12-foot-wide vestibule and adjacent portions of the ramp.

Television cameras, facing the vestibule, were set up against a metal railing separating the 15-foot-wide ramp from the rest of the garage. Some newsmen clustered along this railing. Across Commerce Street, in front of a row of bail bondsmen's offices, a crowd of several hundred persons was held back by a police line.

Soon Oswald was taken in an elevator to the basement. He was led through the booking office to the open vestibule between two lines of detectives. Captain Fritz, chief of the police homicide division, walked just ahead of him. Oswald was handcuffed, with a detective holding each arm and another following. On Oswald's right, in a light suit, was J. R. Leavelle and on his left, in a dark suit, L. C. Graves.

As they turned right from the vestibule to start up the ramp, Ruby jumped forward from against the railing. There was a sudden loud noise that sounded like the explosion of a photographer's flashbulb. It was Ruby's revolver firing. A momentary furor set in as Ruby was seized and hustled into the building. Policemen ran up the ramp in both directions to the street, followed by others with orders to seal off the building.

About five minutes elapsed before an ambulance could be rolled down the ramp to Oswald. The ambulance, its siren sounding, was followed by police and press cars on the four-mile drive to the hospital.

The hospital's emergency department had been on the alert for possible injuries arising out of the projected transfer. Oswald was moved almost immediately into an operating room, at the other end of the building from the one where President Kennedy was treated.

The bullet had entered Oswald's body just below his heart and had torn into most of the vital organs. Dr. Tom Shires, the hospital's chief of surgery, who operated on Governor Connally Friday, took over the case. The gamut of emergency procedures—blood transfusion, fluid transfusion, breathing tube and chest drainage tube—was instituted immediately. But Dr. Shires quickly reported through a hospital official that Oswald was in "extremely critical condition" and that surgery would take several hours.

Oswald's brother, George, a factory worker from Denton, Tex., got to the hospital before the assassin died. The police took Oswald's mother, wife and two infant daughters into protective custody. They were escorted to the hospital to view the body, then were taken to an undisclosed lodging place in Dallas.

Governor Connally is still a patient at the Parkland Hospital. The excitement of the Oswald case swirled around the temporary office the governor had set up there.

Back at the jail, Ruby was taken to the same fourth-floor cellblock where his victim had been the focus of attention the last two days. Reports that filtered out about his preliminary remarks said that he had been impelled to kill President Kennedy's assassin by sympathy for Mrs. Kennedy. It was reported he did not want her to go through the ordeal of returning to Dallas for the trial of Oswald. District Attorney Wade said yesterday he was sure the prosecution of Oswald could be carried out without the personal involvement of any members of the Kennedy family.

A half-dozen lawyers who have worked for Ruby converged on police headquarters in the next hour or two. They said they had been directed there by relatives and friends of Ruby and had not been called by Ruby himself. One lawyer said that he had arranged for a hearing before a justice of the peace tomorrow morning to ask for Ruby's release on bail. "He's a respectable citizen who's been here for years and certainly is entitled to bail," the lawyer said. "We'll make any amount of bail. He is a great admirer of President Kennedy and police officers." The last remark was an allusion to the fact that Oswald was accused of fatally shooting the Dallas patrolman after the president's assassination. Ruby, the lawyer said, "is a very emotional man."

Chief Curry called the second formal news conference of the last three days in the police headquarters basement assembly room at 1:30 P.M. His face drawn, he said in a husky voice: "My statement will be very brief. Oswald expired at 1:07 P.M. We have arrested the man. He will be charged with murder. The suspect is Jack Rubenstein. He also goes by the name of Jack Ruby. That's all I have to say."

Sheriff Bill Decker commented that the police "did everything humanly possible" to protect Oswald, as he said they had in the case of President Kennedy. "I don't think it would have made a bit of difference if Oswald had been transferred at night," he said. "If someone is determined to commit murder, it's almost impossible to stop him."

Ironically, it appeared that Ruby might have had a number of far easier opportunities for killing Oswald than the method he finally used. He was reported to have circulated repeatedly the last two days among the throng of people that was constantly in the third-floor corridor near the homicide bureau. Oswald was led along this corridor a number of times as he was taken down from the fourth-floor jail for interrogation.

Millions of Viewers See Oswald Killing on 2 TV Networks

By JACK GOULD

The fatal shooting of Lee H. Oswald, who was held as the assassin of President Kennedy, was seen as it occurred yesterday by millions of television viewers. The National Broadcasting Company telecast the dramatic happening live. Less than a minute later the Columbia Broadcasting System telecast it by means of tape, made as the shooting occurred. C.B.S. headquarters recorded the pictures from Dallas as they were received here over a closed circuit. Officials, upon seeing the contents of the Dallas relay, put the tape out over the network instantly.

The incident marked the first time in 15 years of television around the globe that a real-life homicide had occurred in front of live cameras. The closest parallel occurred in October, 1960, when Inejiro Asanuma, Japanese political leader, was knifed on a public stage in Tokyo. Tape recordings of this were played back on Japanese TV stations ten minutes later.

The Dallas shooting, easily the most extraordinary moments of TV that a set-owner ever watched, came with such breath-taking suddenness as to beggar description. It had been a quiet and subdued morning on TV, with emphasis on religious services and plans for the funeral of President Kennedy today. N.B.C. had just done a "remote" from Hyannis Port, Mass., on the condition of the late president's father, Joseph P. Kennedy. C.B.S. was giving a news report from its studio after having carried a sermon in which violence was decried.

Under stand-by arrangements for instant switching to Dallas, the two networks took their audiences to the now familiar overcrowded corridor in the Dallas Police Department. And once again there appeared in view the figure of Oswald with a plainclothes man at each side.

On the home screen all three appeared to be looking toward the left side of the screen. Out of the lower right corner came the back of a man. A shot rang out, and Oswald could be heard gasping as he started to fall. Tom Pettit, N.B.C. correspondent, said quickly: "He's been shot! He's been shot! Lee Oswald has been shot. There is absolute panic. Pandemonium has broken out."

Robert Huffaker, staff newsman for television station KRLD, the Dallas affiliate of the Columbia network, happened to be at the C.B.S. microphone. "He's been shot!" Mr. Huffaker exclaimed. "Oswald's been shot!"

On the faces of the police officers there was shock, and then a viewer could see the officers swarming over the back of the assailant, Jack Ruby, a night-club operator.

The television coverage showed Ruby being whisked away and Oswald being sped in an ambulance to Parkland Hospital. The TV sequence was over almost as soon as it started, and the viewer could not help but respect the composure of the commentators and the cameramen. The ability of television to cope with the Oswald murder reflected the extent of network preparations since the president's assassination. Hundreds of persons in the networks' news staffs have been on duty almost around the clock, organizing and presenting programs throughout the day and night.

All networks concurred yesterday in a decision not to resume regular commercial programming until tomorrow morning. One official estimated that the expenses for the special four-day news coverage would run from $2 million to $3 million for each network. But a larger economic consideration pertains to advertising revenue that will not be realized. If both the networks and the hundreds of individual stations are considered, it was said, the total industry loss could amount to $100 million. The three networks together realize a total of about $14 million a night from the sale of prime time. To this must be added the loss of individual station income from the sale of spot announcements.

In today's coverage of the funeral and burial services for President Kennedy, beginning at 7 A.M. and continuing until late afternoon, the networks will pool their picture resources while carrying the commentary of their own reporters. The same arrangement was followed for the inauguration of President Kennedy.

Johnson Spurs Oswald Inquiry

President Orders F.B.I. to Check Death—Handling of Case Worries Capital

By ANTHONY LEWIS

Special to The New York Times

WASHINGTON, Nov. 24—President Johnson directed the Federal Bureau of Investigation tonight to look into "every aspect" of the murder of Lee H. Oswald. He spoke with the director of the F.B.I., J. Edgar Hoover, and ordered the redoubled investigation.

The action came as official Washington was showing increasing concern about the entire handling of the aftermath of President Kennedy's assassination. Officials were convinced that Oswald was the assassin. But their concern was over the public impression of the criminal proceedings.

Tonight they were considering ways to bring out for the public the evidence pointing to Oswald. The feeling was that it would be tragic and divisive if there were any doubts in the country and the world about the events. Today's shooting of Oswald, on top of past events, might create such doubt, it was believed. At the Justice Department, officials said there was "strong evidence" of Oswald's guilt. Agents of the Federal Bureau of Investigation actively assisted the Dallas police in their investigation of the crime.

Despite a Dallas police statement this afternoon that the case was closed, the F.B.I. continued its inquiries. An official made clear that the decision to go on rested not on any doubts but on the importance, in this of all cases, of leaving no remote possibilities untouched. "The case will not be closed until all the facts are in and every lead followed up," a Justice Department official said. The F.B.I. is also helping in the inquiry into Oswald's murder. Asked whether any bureau agents were in the corridor when Oswald was shot, an F.B.I. spokesman declined comment.

Even before today's sudden dénouement, there were elements in the Oswald case disturbing to persons concerned about civil liberties. Among the elements were the lengthy questioning of him without access to a lawyer and the police statements to the press declaring him, in effect, guilty. The feeling in Washington generally was that, for the sake of the American conscience and the world's opinion, it was vital that Oswald be treated and tried fairly. Today's event was thus the more disturbing.

The Justice Department showed its concern by sending the head of its criminal division, Assistant Attorney General Herbert J. Miller Jr., to Dallas this afternoon. The decision was made by the deputy attorney general, Nicholas deB. Katzenbach. Mr. Miller will talk with F.B.I. men working on the case and with the United States attorney in Dallas, Barefoot Sanders. He is also expected to confer with state and local prosecutors and police officials.

What is generally not understood abroad—perhaps not altogether appreciated in this country—is that the Justice Department has no control over local police or prosecutors. It can advise and confer, but that is all. The department, through Mr. Sanders, was in close touch with the Dallas officials for the last two days. The visit by Mr. Miller is designed to re-emphasize the Federal interest and willingness to cooperate.

Evidence Offered

By FRED POWLEDGE

Special to The New York Times

DALLAS, Nov. 24—The police offered today a mass of evidence they contend proves beyond reasonable doubt that Lee H. Oswald assassinated President Kennedy. The evidence, made available by the local police, the Federal Bureau of Investigation and the Secret Service, included finger and palm prints showing that Oswald was near the window where the assassin's bullets were fired; ballistic evidence that Oswald's rifle had fired the bullets, and a letter Oswald wrote ordering the weapon from a mail-order store.

Local authorities said they had an airtight case against the young malcontent, who was shot to death this afternoon, by a Dallas cabaret operator, 48 hours after the president's death. Federal authorities were more cautious in their statements about the case. But everyone concerned privately expressed the belief that Oswald, now beyond the reach of justice, was the murderer of the president. Capt. Will Fritz, homicide specialist for the Dallas Police Department, said after Oswald's death today that, in his estimation, "the case is closed." Chief of Police Jesse Curry said he felt certain now that Oswald was the president's murderer.

Henry Wade, Dallas County district attorney, who was to have prosecuted Oswald, said, "I think we have sufficient evidence to prove Oswald was the man who killed the president." Tonight the district attorney added that he felt that it was "beyond reasonable doubt and as a moral certainty" that Oswald was the assassin. He said he had "no concrete evidence or suspicions" that other persons were involved in the killing.

Oswald also was charged with the murder of Patrolman J. D. Tippit shortly after the president's assassination Friday. Mr. Wade had announced that he would ask a jury to send Oswald to the electric chair. "I have no doubts in this case," he said. Capt. O. A. Jones, of the police department's criminal investigation division, said today that unless new evidence turned up, the case would be closed. "In our opinion we had a conclusive case against Oswald," he said.

The police had formally charged Oswald with murder in the deaths of the president and the patrolman and with assault with intent to murder Texas Gov. John B. Connally Jr. The governor was wounded during the shooting. Oswald maintained his innocence during two days of police questioning. Captain Fritz said after his death that the young man "said absolutely nothing before or after he was shot."

A Dallas homicide detective, J. R. Leavelle, explained that authorities would continue to compile evidence in the Oswald case. When the evidence is collated, he said, a decision almost certainly will be made to close the case. The decision will be made by Chief Curry and a municipal justice court. Detective Leavelle said he thought the procedure would take about two days.

Already the authorities have collected evidence of all sorts. Gordon Shanklin, F.B.I. agent in charge at Dallas, said today that the rifle that killed the president had been traced to Oswald. Numerous witnesses have declared that Oswald was inside the Texas School Book Depository building when the shooting took place. The president and Governor Connally were shot as their limousine passed in front of the building. Other witnesses have said that they saw a rifle being withdrawn from a window of the building.

The F.B.I. agent noted these other pieces of evidence, which have been assembled by the Dallas police, the F.B.I. and the Secret Service:

A bullet that Secret Service men removed from a stretcher at Parkland Hospital after the shooting, and two bullet fragments removed from the presidential automobile matched bullets fired by the rifle agents found inside the warehouse. The bullets were fired by a 6.5mm. Italian made Mannlicher-Carcano rifle, the agent said.

The rifle was traced to Oswald. The F.B.I. agent said the young man ordered a 6.5mm. rifle with telescopic sight from a Chicago store last spring. The rifle was sent to an "A. Hidell," at Oswald's post office box here. It arrived by parcel post on March 20.

Samples of Oswald's handwriting were sent yesterday to the F.B.I. laboratory in Washington, where they were found to match the handwriting in the letter ordering the rifle.

F.B.I. identification experts developed a latent finger print and a palm print from a brown paper bag found near the window of the school book warehouse. The bag was apparently part of a chicken lunch the assassin ate in the building. The finger print matched Oswald's left index finger. "The palm print was identical with the right palm print of Oswald," said Mr. Shanklin.

Dallas policemen obtained a statement from Oswald's Russian-born wife, Marina, that he had had a rifle in the garage of her living quarters on the night before the assassination. The young woman also said the rifle was not there on the next day. Authorities said the wife's testimony would not have been admissible in Texas courts, however.

A search of Mrs. Oswald's living quarters produced photographs showing her husband holding a rifle and a pistol.

A paraffin test, used to determine whether a person has fired a weapon recently, was administered to Oswald shortly after he was apprehended

Friday, one hour after the assassination. It showed that particles of gunpowder from a weapon, probably a rifle, remained on Oswald's cheek and hands.

One of Oswald's fellow workers at the school book warehouse said the young man carried a long package to work with him on Friday morning. Police have said that Oswald told the worker the package contained window shades.

Oswald's behavior, when he was arrested in a Dallas motion picture theater, betrayed his knowledge that he was being sought by the police. Witnesses quoted him as saying, "This is it!" when the police apprehended him. He drew a revolver and attempted to fire it at a patrolman, but it failed to discharge. In a television interview tonight, Mr. Wade said that "cards" were found on Oswald "identifying him with the assumed person" who ordered the rifle from the Chicago firm. He did not elaborate. The district attorney also said that Oswald, in fleeing the scene of the assassination, rode a city bus for a short time. He "told the driver that the president had been shot, and laughed," said Mr. Wade.

Map Reported Found

DALLAS, Monday, Nov. 25 (AP)—Lee H. Oswald was reported today to have left behind a map with the path of the president's death bullet clearly marked. *The Dallas Morning News* in a copyrighted story said officers found the map during a search of Oswald's room. The newspaper quoted what it called a reliable source as saying:

"This was a map of the city of Dallas. Oswald had placed marks at major intersections along the motorcade route—three or four as I recall. There was also a line from the Texas School Book Depository building to Elm Street. This was the trajectory of the bullets which struck the President and Governor Connally."

The map may have been the "major evidence" Dallas policemen said they held against Oswald, but declined to reveal.

OSWALD, A MAN OF MANY TROUBLES, TOOK MARXISM AS HIS GOSPEL WHILE A TEEN-AGER

Onetime Marine Hated the Corps

Assassin, Always Poor, Once Tried Life in Soviet Union—Backed Castro's Rule

By PETER KIHSS

A teen-ager who discovered Karl Marx's socialism as a new gospel. . . . A Marine who believed the occupation of Japan was imperialistic and who developed a grievance against the Corps. . . . An American who went to the Soviet Union and then decided factory life under Communism there was not for him. . . . A propagandist for Castro Cuba who tried to penetrate anti-Castro operations as, in effect, a fifth columnist. . . . A man who has been said by one of his most recent associates to have "refused to eschew violence. . . ."

This was Lee Harvey Oswald.

His troubled life came to an end yesterday at the age of 24 years, one month, six days. The end came with a bullet wound in the abdomen. The shot was fired point blank by a night club operator in the Dallas police headquarters where Oswald had been charged with the assassination of President Kennedy two days earlier. Oswald denied killing the president.

For three days the life and mind of Lee Oswald have been the center of national inquiries, ransacking the memories of schoolmates, fellow servicemen, neighbors. The story is far from final, far from firm.

He was born Oct. 18, 1939, in New Orleans. His father had died before he was born. His widowed mother, Mrs. Marguerite Oswald, raised him with two other sons. Most of his early life, he said, was spent in Fort Worth, but his family moved around considerably. He remembered his mother as working in shops. She remembered him as going to work at odd jobs at an early age, always bringing home what he earned and never spending it on himself, she said. "He was a boy who helped his mother," she said.

One school he went to was Ridglea Elementary School in Fort Worth, where he was taught in sixth grade in 1951 by Mrs. Howard L. Green. Mrs. Green said yesterday he was "not under-privileged" and "had plenty to eat," not needing an occasional nickel or dime loan from his teacher as some did. He and another child may have had "a little bit of troublemaker" in them, Mrs. Green said, but "there was nothing in his background that would turn him away from a free society toward Communism."

Mrs. N. M. Merrett was principal when the school was first opened in the suburban community of Ridglea West in September, 1949. Oswald was a transfer student, entering in the fourth grade. He was "kind of smily, a boy with curly hair, hair that was tousled, the way curly hair gets," Mrs. Merrett remembered yesterday. "He was a very lively boy, a wiggly boy, always on the move."

On citizenship, he made an A in the fourth grade, B's in the fifth and sixth grades. His grades were low in spelling, English, arithmetic. He had a grade of 4 in a standardized achievement test in the fourth grade, against a normal 4.5; 4 in the fifth grade, against a normal 5.5; but 7.4 in the sixth grade, as against a normal 6.5.

"Back in 1959, when the news came about his trip to Russia," Mrs. Merrett said, "I remembered what I could about Lee. At that time I said to myself that I could not have foreseen that he would be a person who would go bad."

When he was 13 and 14 years old, Oswald lived in the Bronx, from September, 1952, until January, 1954. It was a rootless period. He attended Trinity Lutheran School, 2125 Watson Avenue, for three weeks. Then he transferred to Junior High School 117, 1865 Morris Avenue, as a seventh grader. When his family moved to a new school zone, he transferred in March, 1953, to Junior High School 44, 1825 Prospect Avenue, remaining there until January, 1954. Oswald's grades were barely passable, according to school records dug out by Nicholas Cicchetti, the present principal of Junior High School 44. His teachers rated him satisfactory in courtesy and effort, unsatisfactory in dependability, cooperation and self-control.

It was 1954 when he entered Beauregard Junior High School in New Orleans. One classmate, Edward Collier, said: "We called him Yank because he had a Yankee accent."

He had a lot of fights. One friend he had was Edward Voebel. In a Columbia Broadcasting System telecast yesterday Mr. Voebel said that he met Oswald when another boy punched Oswald in the mouth. Mr. Voebel said some other youngsters had put the puncher up to it, although he might not have known Oswald. Mr. Voebel and two other boys picked Oswald up off the ground, and brought him back to the school to put cold compresses on his mouth. Like others had done, Mr. Voebel said Oswald was a "loner," not interested in extracurricular activities. He doubted Oswald's own story of having been interested in Marxist ideas at 15.

Although reported a below-average student at Beauregard, Oswald scored well on his achievement tests when he entered Warren Easton High School in New Orleans. With 55 per cent considered average, he made 88 per cent in reading, 85 per cent in vocabulary. On his high school questionnaire, he listed as his favorite subjects: civics, mathematics and science. Vocational choices: biology and mechanical drawing. Favorite pastimes: reading and outdoor sports, such as football. Close personal friends: none.

He entered Warren Easton on Sept. 8, 1955. Shortly he was uprooted again. On Oct. 5, 1955, his mother wrote the school saying the family was leaving for San Diego, Calif. Six months later, school officials received a letter from Arlington Heights High School in Fort Worth requesting his transcript.

In Tulsa, Okla., Mrs. James Giles told C.B.S. yesterday she had taken a world history class with Oswald. She said: "If the teacher asked a question in world history class, Lee would give the answer. But he did it in such a way as to come back with a question in kind of a sarcastic way. He was lonely, and he didn't seem to be living like the rest of the students. He didn't seem happy in any way. He didn't seem to be able to converse with anyone, as a friend would converse with anyone."

In Salt Lake City, Kathleen Willett, another former Fort Worth student, said she had sat next to Oswald in biology class. He did not study, she said, he got poor grades; he "never seemed to have any friends—maybe that was part of his trouble."

This was the time, according to a reporter, that Oswald remembered becoming interested in Marxism. The reporter, Aline Mosby, a United Press International correspondent, interviewed him in Moscow in 1959, three years after those schooldays. "I played baseball and football in high school," Oswald told her. "I had a certain amount of friends, but I don't have many attachments now in the United States. In my childhood I enjoyed a few benefits of American society. I was a bookworm. I'm a Marxist. I became interested about the age of 15. An old lady handed me a pamphlet about saving the Rosenbergs. [Julius and Ethel Rosenberg were convicted on March 29, 1951, of conspiracy to commit espionage for the Soviet Union; they were executed on June 19, 1953.]

"I still remember that pamphlet about the Rosenbergs. I don't know why. Then we moved to North Dakota and I discovered one book in the library, *Das Kapital*. It was what I'd been looking for. It was like a very religious man opening the Bible for the first time. I started to study Marxist economic theories. I could see the impoverishment of the masses before my own eyes in my own mother. I thought the worker's life could be better. I found some Marxist books on dusty shelves in the New Orleans library and continued to indoctrinate myself for five years."

This meant it would have continued through his Marine Corps career. He was seven days past 17 when he enlisted in the Marines at Dallas on Oct. 24, 1956. From then to January, 1957, he underwent recruit training in San Diego; then through February, advanced training at Camp Pendleton, Calif. From March to May, 1957, he was trained in aviation electronics operations at Jacksonville, Fla. Then he went overseas—Marine Air Group 11, First Marine Air Wing, at Atsugi Air Base in Japan, from July, 1957, to October, 1958.

He had already had problems, seemingly. In Los Angeles, for instance, Donald Goodwin, a former Marine sergeant, said he had been Oswald's section chief at Camp Pendleton. "He was good with a rifle," Mr. Goodwin said, "but he was such a hothead I was glad when he was finally shipped out for radar training. He was always having beefs with the guys in the barracks. Never could figure out what it was about, really. Just to get into a fight and vent his emotions, I suppose. If he had any Commie leanings at that time, I didn't know about them, We weren't exactly close acquaintances. But I did know about his temper and the habit he had of lipping off at the wrong time."

In Japan, Oswald received two summary courts-martial. On April 11, 1958, he was convicted of having an unregistered pistol. For this he was demoted from private first class—the highest rating he had achieved—to private. On June 18, 1958, he was convicted of using profanity to a non-commissioned officer; he could not be demoted any further, and got a note on his record instead.

Peter Connor, an apprentice ironworker in West Haven, Conn., said he had served with Oswald in Japan. Mr. Connor called him "a real aggravator," whose almost constant smile was a steady annoyance to barracks mates. Oswald had a reputation for competence as a technician.

He had a hair-trigger temper, but he always got the worst of it in fist fights, Mr. Connor went on. "One thing about him, he never fought his way into the shower," Mr. Connor said. "He was one of the sloppiest guys I ever met in my life. He was a pretty insistent kid," Mr. Connor reported. "If he said something, he really meant it, but he was not much for conversation. When his fellow Marines were heading for a night on the town, Oswald would remain behind or leave before they did or after they did. No one ever knew what he did in town."

What Oswald thought, he said later in Moscow, was that serving with the occupation forces in Japan was "imperialistic." He told Miss Mosby he had watched American technicians show Chinese how to use guns in Taiwan, and that kind of experience for three years gave him the impression "things aren't quite right."

He got back to California in December, 1958, to the Third Air Wing at El Toro. There he applied for a discharge for hardship reasons to support his mother. On Sept. 11, 1959, he was put on inactive reserve status. Government records indicate he was issued a passport in Los Angeles one day earlier. He told his sister-in-law, Mrs. Robert L. Oswald, on a visit to Fort Worth, that he "wanted to travel a lot," and he talked "about going to Cuba." Mack Osborn, a real estate dealer in Lubbock, Tex., said yesterday, however, that Oswald, who had shared a double bunk with him for about six months at El Toro, had "spent most of his spare time studying Russian."

By Oct. 13, he turned up in Moscow. His occupation was listed as shipping export agent. On Oct. 31, he appeared at the United States Embassy. He said he had applied for Soviet citizenship. "I have made up my mind, I'm through," he said. He told Miss Mosby: "I've been waiting to do it for two years, saving my money, just waiting until I got out of the

Marine Corps, like waiting to get out of prison. For two years I've had it in my mind not to form any attachments because I knew I was going away. My mother doesn't know. She's rather old. I couldn't expect her to understand. Capitalism has passed its peak. Capitalism will disappear as feudalism disappeared."

He said the United States was a place of hatred. He was against racial segregation. "I've seen poor niggers, being a Southern boy," Miss Mosby quoted him as having said, "and that was a lesson. People hate because they're told to hate, like school kids. It's the fashion to hate people in the United States."

His mother said she had tried to call him in Moscow. The telephone clicked, she said; he hung up on her. On Nov. 2, he wrote out an affidavit in Moscow: "I affirm that my allegiance is to the Soviet Socialist Republic."

But on Nov. 14, he said that Soviet officials had refused to grant him Soviet citizenship. They told him he could remain as an alien resident. He wound up in Minsk as a factory worker. Later he said he had tried for a Soviet exit visa as early as July 20, 1960. The United States Embassy got word of his desire to return home in February, 1961. By May, 1961, he was reporting that he had married a Russian woman, Marina Nikolaevna, a pharmacist in Minsk, and that she would need a visa to accompany him home.

By January, 1962, Oswald had the idea of appealing to Senator John G. Tower, a Texas Republican, who was a stranger to him. His handwritten letter said: "I beseech you, Senator Tower, to raise the question of holding by the Soviet Union of a citizen of the United States, against his will and expressed desires." The senator referred the letter to the State Department. The department reported that Oswald had a mother living in Vernon, Tex., and a pregnant Soviet wife, and was unable to pay for his return here.

On May, 24, 1962, the United States Embassy in Moscow, on instructions from the State Department, renewed Oswald's old passport, and amended it to include a daughter, June Lee, born Feb. 15, 1962. This was based on a decision that he had not expatriated himself. The passport was made valid only for return to the United States. At the same time, his wife was granted a visa. The family needed Soviet exit permits.

The embassy lent the family $435.71 for travel expenses, presumably based on a claim of destitution. On June 13, 1962, Oswald, his wife and child arrived in New York. Between October and last January, the travel loan was repaid.

In Washington, the Marine Corps indicated it had received a request from Oswald while he was in the Soviet Union July 26, 1960, to be discharged so that he could accept Soviet citizenship. A board of officers was convened at the Naval Air Station, Glenview, Ill., and recommended that he be separated as undesirable. He was given an undesirable discharge as of Sept. 13, 1960.

In January of last year, this came to Oswald's notice, and he wrote a bitter letter from Minsk to John B. Connally Jr., then secretary of the navy and now governor of Texas. He contended he had been in the Soviet Union with "the full sanction of the United States Embassy, Moscow," and asked that the Navy Department "take the necessary steps to repair the damage done to me and my family." He wrote that he was returning home, and "I shall employ all means to right this gross mistake or injustice to a bonified [sic] US. citizen and ex-serviceman."

Last May 9 the Oswald family—his wife expecting a second child—moved into a one-bedroom home at 4907 Magazine Street in New Orleans. Mrs. Lena Garner, the landlady, said: "He wouldn't speak to anyone. When he passed me or my husband in the yard he wouldn't say anything. He just kept walking with his head down." Twice, she said, he plastered the porch with propaganda in favor of Premier Fidel Castro's regime in Cuba. She told him to remove the signs. He told her he was a Russian, she said.

"We always had to go and ask him for the rent," Mrs. Garner said. "When he left, he owed me for about 15 days." She said Oswald had told her he was sending his wife back to Texas to have her baby. He sneaked out, she said, and left the apartment dirty.

Her husband, Jesse James Garner, a taxi driver, found it hard to believe Oswald could have shot President Kennedy. "He was too quiet, too reserved," Mr. Garner said. "He certainly had the intelligence, and he looked like he could be efficient at doing almost anything."

A. P. Eames 3d, a field clerk with the United States Engineers, was a next-door neighbor at 4903 Magazine Street. He said Oswald was frequently bringing home armfuls of books from the public library. He called Oswald "a very arrogant person in that he would not greet you or make any attempt to be congenial or neighborly."

Mr. Eames's wife, Doris, said: "His little Russian wife was just the opposite. She couldn't speak English, but she seemed very friendly, except when he was around. He didn't seem to want her to mix with anyone. She always smiled. She learned to say hello, although she never spoke English. She would try to answer back when someone greeted her. I don't believe he ever took her anywhere. The only place we ever saw them go together was the corner grocery store. Whenever they spoke, he and his wife always spoke in a foreign language."

One man said Oswald used to price cosmetics for his wife in a drugstore, and then send her with money to buy them after the deal had been arranged. There were some complaints that he used to dump trash in everyone's garbage can along Magazine Street.

Last June 24, Oswald applied for a new passport. He said he was a photographer, and he wanted to take a trip abroad for three months to a year, and would leave between October and December of this year. He listed as his proposed itinerary England, France, Germany, the Soviet Union, Finland, Italy and Poland. The passport was issued on June 25, which indicated he must have replied negatively to questions as to whether he had for 12 months been a member of a Communist organization or ever sought foreign nationality.

In July, he introduced himself to Carlos Bringuier, New Orleans delegate of the anti-Castro Cuban Student Directorate, as a man who wanted to fight Communism and who could help train exiles for an invasion effort. Mr. Bringuier was suspicious, and put Oswald off. Some days later, Mr. Bringuier found Oswald distributing literature with pro-Castro pickets on Canal Street. The Cuban upbraided him and proposed to punch him; Oswald spread his arms as a ready example of nonviolent protest. They all wound up in court; Oswald paid a $10 fine for disturbing the peace.

On Aug. 21, during an interview on radio station WSDU, he said he was secretary of the New Orleans chapter of the Fair Play for Cuba Committee, and a Marxist but not Communist. Vincent Theodore Lee, the Fair Play group's national director, said that the organization——sympathetic to the Castro regime—had never had a chapter in Louisiana or Texas, and had never had Oswald as an official or representative. Oswald might have obtained Fair Play literature, Mr. Lee said.

The Oswald family slipped away from the home they had rented from Mrs. Garner just about that time.

Last Sept. 23, he sent his wife and child from New Orleans to Irving, Tex., to live with Mrs. Michael R. Paine, a Quaker friend they had met in Dallas in February. A month ago, their second child, Audrey Marina Rachel, was born there.

A neighbor of Mrs. Paine's, Mrs. William Randall, was having coffee one day with Mrs. Paine and Mrs. Oswald, and reported there was a job open in the Texas School Book Depository Building in Dallas. Mrs. Paine said yesterday that Oswald had followed up the tip, seemed very happy to get the job, and spoke hopefully of being able to rent an apartment next year with his $50-a-week earnings. Meanwhile, he stayed at a rooming house in Dallas and visited his family weekends.

He got into long discussions with Mr. Paine, a Bell Helicopter engineer, when Mr. Paine also came to visit. Mr. Paine said "Marxism was a religion" with Oswald. "He wanted to change the free-enterprise system, while at the same time saying he returned to the United States from Russia because he liked the freedom people had in this country," Mr. Paine said. "Oswald refused to eschew violence as a method for achieving desired ends."

Last Friday, a rifle bullet from the schoolbook warehouse building killed President Kennedy. Another wounded former Governor Connally, who was riding in a car with the president.

Friend Offers to Take Oswald's Family Into Her Home Again

By DONALD JANSON

Special to The New York Times

IRVING, Tex., Nov. 24—"I would be very pleased to have her again if she wants to live with me."

Mrs. Michael R. Paine was speaking today of Mrs. Lee Oswald. She had just heard the news of the shooting of her friend's husband. Mrs. Oswald and her two baby daughters had lived with Mrs. Paine in this small town near Dallas while Oswald sought to earn enough money to get an apartment.

After President Kennedy was assassinated the police told Mrs. Paine they were bringing Mrs. Oswald and the children back to her two-bedroom home in this quiet residential neighborhood. Subsequently, policemen were stationed in the home to insure the protection of the Oswald family.

Then Mrs. Oswald called from Dallas, where she and her children and mother-in-law had spent the night at the Executive Inn in rooms rented by *Life* magazine. She said the police had decided to keep them in protective custody elsewhere in Dallas. Speaking in Russian, Mrs. Oswald, who has learned little English during her year and a half in the United States, asked Mrs. Paine to send her things she needed. Responding in Russian, Mrs. Paine agreed. She also sent toys. She said Mrs. Oswald did not seem distraught. Her husband died shortly afterward.

Mrs. Paine said Oswald had called her three times yesterday. He asked to speak to his wife and requested Mrs. Paine to try to get John Abt of New York, an attorney, to defend him against charges of assassinating Mr. Kennedy. Mrs. Paine was not able to reach Mr. Abt, but had planned to try again today.

Mrs. Paine, a tall young brunette, was born in New York. She became Marina Oswald's best friend through her interest in the Russian language. A Quaker, she worked with the Young Friends Committee of North America in Philadelphia before moving here with her husband four years ago. She said the object of her work was to improve international relations, and that knowledge of the Russian language would be useful. Last summer she taught Russian at St. Mark's, an Episcopal school in Dallas.

Mrs. Paine, who wants to do more teaching, said she had met the Oswalds at a small party in the home of a friend in Dallas last February. At the party, she said, Oswald told of his three-year stay in the Soviet Union and of his preference for Marxism over capitalism. He said he had met Marina, a pharmacist, in Minsk and married her a month and a half later. Their first child, now 22 months old, was born there. The other child is one month old.

Mrs. Paine said she had never engaged in political or philosophical discussions with Oswald because she did not enjoy argument. "He had very fixed ideas," she said.

Mrs. Paine's husband, an engineer at Bell Helicopter Company, sometimes debated with him, but also found him inflexibly pro-Marxist. Mr. Paine, although not living with his family, visits often. Neither Mr. nor Mrs. Paine realized until Friday that the luggage they had helped Oswald to put in their garage had included a rifle.

The police say the rifle had been used to assassinate President Kennedy. "As a Quaker and a pacifist I would not have allowed them to keep it here," Mrs. Paine said today.

Mrs. Oswald has stayed with Mrs. Paine twice, for two weeks last May and from Sept. 24 until yesterday. Each time it was because Oswald had lost a job and could not support his family. His last job was as a $50-a-week stock clerk at the Texas School Book Depository Building in Dallas, where the assassination was carried out.

The first time she had felt any sympathy for Oswald was when he had looked "very bleak" in bidding good-by to his family in New Orleans Sept. 23. Mrs. Paine had gone there to bring Mrs. Oswald and the baby back here after Oswald had lost a job. Oswald came to the Dallas area a short time later, but never lived full-time with his family again.

While visiting his wife, Mrs. Paine said, Oswald seemed to be a loving father and husband. He liked to play with his babies and Mrs. Paine's children, who are a little older. Oswald was handy around the house, Mrs. Paine said. He had planed doors to make them fit better and had moved furniture and done other chores. He liked to watch football and late shows on television. But he never made any friends, she said. Even the party he and his wife had been invited to last February had included them because the group was interested in Russia, and Marina was Russian. He was never close to his mother, of Fort Worth, or his older brother, of Denton, Tex. He was a loner.

His 22-year-old wife is different, Mrs. Paine said. She says the slight young woman is likeable and "quite intelligent." Mrs. Oswald is learning English so she can work as a pharmacist. Mrs. Paine said Mrs. Oswald liked the United States "very much." Of her husband's death, Mrs. Paine said that it was probably better for Mrs. Oswald because "it will mean less total strain."

Dallas Policeman's Widow Also Weeps for Husband

DALLAS, Nov. 24 (AP)—Mrs. John F. Kennedy is the focus of sympathy today, but another woman also weeps for the man she has lost. She is Mrs. Marie Tippit, whose 39-year-old husband, Patrolman J. D. Tippit, was slain by Lee H. Oswald shortly after President Kennedy's assassination last Friday. The police say that Oswald might have escaped capture if Patrolman Tippit had not intercepted him.

"I just don't know what we are going to do," Mrs. Tippit said in her neat, three-bedroom brick home. She is the mother of three children, a girl 10 and boys 4 and 13. "I depended on my husband so much. He spent all his extra time with us, and the family just got used to him making all the necessary decisions. The problem of raising three children suddenly seems too great. Older children need a father's guidance."

Despite the tragedy that struck the White House, those most deeply involved have found time to let Mrs. Tippit know that she is not forgotten in her sorrow. Attorney General Robert F. Kennedy telephoned to express the sympathy that the president's widow feels for Mrs. Tippit. In return, Mrs. Tippit told him "to express my concern to Mrs. Kennedy and tell her I certainly know how she feels." Another call came from President Johnson. He took time in the midst of a historic governmental transition to remember the policeman's widow.

OSWALD'S KILLER DESCRIBED AS EMOTIONAL MAN WHO "HATES ANYTHING DONE" TO U.S.

Ruby Is Regarded as "Small-Timer"

Club Operator Known for Temper and Loyalties—Comes From Chicago

By JOSEPH A. LOFTUS

Special to The New York Times

DALLAS, Nov. 24—Strong emotions and loyalties were long the marks of the man who slew President Kennedy's assassin today.

Jack Rubenstein, who long ago adopted the name of Jack Ruby, was a small-time operator in the night club and gambling world. In petty ways he had broken the law in Chicago and Dallas many times, but was not on record as having committed a felony. Ruby, 52 years old, about 5 feet 10 inches tall and heavy set, talked gruffly and might personally "bounce" an offending patron from his night spot. He learned violence in Chicago's ghetto.

He also had a reputation for kindness and generosity toward anyone who did him a favor. He knew many policemen because of his club operations. Ruby yearned to rise above his background of limited education and poverty. Though not connected with politics, he identified himself emotionally with the New Deal in the nineteen-thirties and with President Kennedy's New Frontier. As a young man in Chicago he would strike anybody who disparaged President Franklin D. Roosevelt.

Ruby and his sister, Mrs. Eva L. Grant, were so devoted to President Kennedy they felt devastated by his death. "Jack must have gone out of his head," Mrs. Grant said today. "He hates anything done to this country." Weakened by radical surgery two weeks ago, her grief compounded by her brother's deed, she said the thought occurred to her that she had unwittingly driven him to it.

"I'm lying there on the couch," she recalled in her small apartment in a northwestern section. "I said somebody will shoot him [Oswald]. You know what I meant? I meant the Communists would shoot him so he wouldn't talk."

That was Friday, the day the president died. Her brother, who lived elsewhere, came to her apartment three times that afternoon and evening, she recalled. "He hasn't slept and he hasn't eaten," she said.

Mrs. Grant, a reddish-blond woman of 54, repeatedly referred to her fancied guilt. She sat slumped in her weakness. Her face was ashen. "I said the Communists will never let him [Oswald] get the chair. I don't know if I embedded that in his mind. I feel so guilty, I don't know what to think. We talked. He came here three times. He made his mind up. 'We can't open a night club.' "

Ruby went to a newspaper and inserted an advertisement saying his two clubs would be closed temporarily in respect for the president. "He was the only one to put an ad in," she said. "He loved every president; that's the whole problem. We were more affected by the president getting shot than when my father died."

Mrs. Grant said she and her brother were among a family of four girls and four boys. A brother, Earl, operates the Cobalt Cleaners in Detroit. She preferred not to identify the others. "We were a big, Orthodox Jewish family," she said. "He's such a good Jew. This [the shooting of Oswald] is something we don't believe in. I don't know what possessed him to do it."

Mrs. Grant was divorced 18 years ago. "He is such a guy," she said affectionately. "If he had money, I had money. You know why we haven't any money? If he had $300 and met somebody who was in trouble and needed money, he would give him half of it."

Mrs. Grant said her brother had not married. He came here in 1948. He owns the rock 'n' roll Vegas Club in the Oaklawn section, which she manages for him. He operates the Carousel, but does not own it, she said. The Carousel, a strip-tease spot, occupies the second floor of a building across from the Adolphus Hotel on Commerce Street. The city directory lists Ruby's address as the apartment house where his sister lives. But she said he had his own apartment in Oak Cliff, some miles away. Their telephone numbers are not listed.

A taxicab driver said Ruby was a generous tipper who spoke with kindness. If a patron of the Carousel telephoned for a cab, the driver said, Ruby would require the patron to deposit 50 cents to protect the driver in case the patron changed his mind.

Ervin Mazzei, former regional director for the American Guild of Variety Artists, recalled having met Ruby at a party. He described him as "neurotic and excitable at all times." He added that Ruby was in good standing with the unions. A Carousel girl once told him Ruby had beaten her, Mr. Mazzei said, and later Ruby told him he had the case quashed for $100.

Police records showed a series of petty charges against Ruby, beginning in 1949. One, in 1953, was marked "investigation of concealed weapon." The others were disturbing the peace, violating dance hall ordinance, and violating the liquor laws. The last was the only charge that carried a notation of disposition. It was marked "dismissed."

Tony Zoppi, entertainment reporter for *The Dallas Morning News,* described Ruby as "a highly emotional man given to flashy dress and a desperate yearning for social acceptance."

"I have suffered long enough and skimped enough all my life," Ruby recently told a friend. "I want to live a little." With that he told of plans to move into a luxury apartment. George Senator, who worked at one of Ruby's clubs, was his roommate. He said Ruby had been in a state of shock since the assassination, mourning particularly for the Kennedy children. "He's been going around the apartment saying, 'Those poor kids,'" Mr. Senator said. "It bothered him tremendously."

Ruby's attire often included wide-brim hats and high-collar shirts. He recently went on a diet and dropped from 210 to 190 pounds. He was known as the "Chicago cowboy" when he first came to Dallas. He frequented the old Plantation Club, dressed in an immaculate Western costume. The audiences at his clubs usually were made up of convention delegates. The police dropped in every night to check his operation. That contact with detectives made him known around City Hall. Nobody who saw him shoot Oswald today took his appearance seriously until it was too late.

Chicagoans Recall Jack Ruby as Ticket Scalper and Chiseler

By AUSTIN C. WEHRWEIN

Special to The New York Times

CHICAGO, Nov. 24—Jack Ruby, who murdered the president's assassin, was recalled by acquaintances in his native Chicago today as Jack Rubenstein, a fancy dresser, ticket scalper and cautious chiseler.

Ruby, nicknamed "Sparky," peddled cigars, janitor supplies, novelties, and automobile accessories. He also scalped tickets to sporting events and theaters, acquaintances recalled. He was described as a steady, but small-time, gambler. One Chicagoan remembered him as a "hustler who always had a buck in his pocket and dressed like he owned a mint." There were also reports that he was a street brawler and had a hot temper.

Ruby was identified as the son of a contractor named Joseph, said to be dead now, and was born and grew up in the West Side Jewish "Ghetto." Although he apparently had times when he was financially well off, he was often short of money. A preliminary check showed no one meeting his description with a Chicago police record.

The conflicting reports about Ruby's intemperate fighting fitted a picture of many unanswered questions about him. He left Chicago about 15 years ago to help his sister, Mrs. Eva L. Grant, run her bar in Dallas. But apparently he returned to Chicago about six years ago to promote a "talent discovery," a 12-year-old Negro boy who sang, danced and played the piano. However, Ruby was unable to get bookings from New York agents. Friends recall that when they joked that the boy was really a midget, Ruby's temper rose.

He also frequented sporting events, either scalping tickets or trying to crash the gate. Sometimes he hawked programs. He was said to have been beaten once when he tried to crash a prize fight and injured so badly he needed a metal plate in his skull.

Sometimes he scalped Notre Dame football tickets in South Bend, Ind., bars. Not long before he went to Dallas he became connected with a manufacturer of salt and pepper shakers and peddled them and other items.

He was said to have three brothers and four sisters. The family was described as being Orthodox Jewish. Carl Anis, who said he knew Ruby about 1941, described him as a "nice guy, the last guy to do anything like this [the murder]." However, he was described as a toe-to-toe slugger, who boasted that he was a clean fighter because "I got principles."

David Bryon, interviewed on a television show, recalled Ruby as a "loner," not impulsive but with a temper that flared. He also said Ruby always seemed to have money. Mr. Bryon said he had visited Ruby in Dallas and been told he didn't want it known that he had changed his name from Rubenstein. Mr. Bryon was reportedly questioned by the Federal Bureau of Investigation about Ruby.

Ruby was also identified as a former organizer for the Waste Material Handlers Union. In 1959, Senate investigators described the union as a link between the underworld and James R. Hoffa, president of the International Brotherhood of Teamsters.

Ruby was last seen in Chicago at a basketball game in the Chicago Stadium three years ago. He said then that he was operating his sister's nightclub in Dallas and that Ruby was his "stage name."

'62 Ruling Upset Dallas Gun Curb

U.S. and Texas Codes Say Citizens May Bear Arms

By OSCAR GODBOUT

A Dallas ordinance making it "unlawful to have in one's possession within the city or upon any property owned by the city any firearms, rifle, revolver, pistol or any other weapon" was declared unconstitutional 14 months before President Kennedy was killed.

Ruling on a case in which a man was accused of having a revolver in his possession, Judge Newton Fitzhugh of the County Criminal Court of

Appeals of Dallas County said, in September, 1962: "The ordinance here involved [is] null and void, an unconstitutional and unauthorized invasion of a natural right the citizens of this state have never relinquished to their rulers."

Thus both the Texas Constitution, cited by Judge Fitzhugh, and the United States Constitution, in the Second Amendment, guaranteed Lee H. Oswald's right to have a firearm—the rifle he used to assassinate President Kennedy on Friday. And yesterday Oswald met his end at the hands of a man with a firearm—a man who had also abused the same constitutional guarantees.

The rifle said to have killed President Kennedy was one of the least suited for long-distance, accurate sniping. The firearm, the Italian service arm in 6.5 millimeter, Model 1938, differed little from the original first made in 1891. Although the 1938 Model is somewhat improved over earlier versions, a marksman seeking an accurate rifle would normally prefer any one of a number of other kinds of rifles. It is not considered particularly accurate in standard form, but it could be adapted for better marksmanship at long distance. The addition of a telescopic sight would greatly improve its potential. One major dealer currently offers, for $12.78, the same kind of rifle that killed Mr. Kennedy. For $19.95, it can be equipped with a telescopic sight of four-power magnification. Military ammunition for the gun costs $7.50 for 108 cartridges.

A group of the nation's most knowledgeable gun experts, meeting in Maryland at the time of the shooting, agreed that, considering the gun, the distance, the angle and the movement of the president's car, the assassin was either an exceptional marksman or fantastically lucky in placing his shots.

When the nations of the North Atlantic Treaty Organization switched to a common-sized cartridge for small arms, several years ago, their old rifle and pistols became obsolete. These were sold to American gun dealers and imported in huge quantities to be sold cheaply. The Italian rifle was one of hundreds of kinds. The importation of these guns caused great concern to American firearms makers. They felt the impact on sales of domestically produced sporting rifles. The imported military rifles can be used without alteration for hunting. Often they are specially adapted. A number of mail-order houses specialized in selling such rifles, often with the addition of cheap Japanese telescopic sights or surplus military-sniper telescopes, at prices far under those for commercially made guns.

There have been a number of efforts in Congress to halt the "dumping" of such surplus arms. The latest was a bill introduced in August by Senator Leverett Saltonstall, Republican of Massachusetts, on behalf of Senator Edward M. Kennedy, Democrat of Massachusetts, the president's brother, and Senators Thomas J. Dodd and Abraham A. Ribicoff, Connecticut Democrats. The bill would have limited foreign imports severely. Senator Dodd also introduced a bill recently to restrict the interstate sale of firearms by mail.

In this country, there are no prohibitions on the purchase and ownership of rifles and shotguns, except in some states that restrict it for persons convicted of felonies. In most states, concealable firearms such as pistols are regulated by the police through licensing and the issuing of permits. But rifles, not considered concealable, are free of such regulations. Federal firearm laws cover machine guns, concealable weapons such as pistols and cut-down rifles and shotguns and explosives, as well as the mailing of concealable guns. Again, ordinary rifles and shotguns are not affected.

A dispute is still under way between groups favoring licensing, registration or even prohibition of all firearms and the gun-owners of the country. It has been estimated that at least 25 million Americans own one or more firearms. The Second Amendment to the Constitution states: "A well-regulated militia being necessary to the security of a free State, the right of the people to keep and bear arms shall not be infringed." The United States itself sells surplus rifles and pistols to the public through the Department of Civilian Marksmanship and the National Rifle Association, which handles sales.

Dallas Is Groping for a Reason Why

Some Say "Crackpots" Have Touched Off Violence

By JOHN HERBERS

Special to The New York Times

DALLAS, Nov. 24—"We think it's this Western tradition," a minister's wife said. "They are used to shooting at everything they don't like."

This was one explanation for a series of impulsive acts of violence that has occurred in Dallas—the abuse of President Johnson in a hotel lobby during the campaign in 1960; the attack on Adlai E. Stevenson, chief delegate to the United Nations, a few weeks ago; the assassination of President Kennedy, and the slaying today of the president's assassin.

Dallas does have a Western tradition, but it is not predominant. The city is really neither Western nor Southern. A civic leader who has been concerned about the rise of right-wing extremism here explained it like this: "Dallas has a lot of professional people who are responsibly conservative and individualistic. It has some leaders who are interested in making money under the free and open Texas tradition. These people have attracted a lot of crackpots and the crackpots have inflamed the weak-minded and emotionally unstable."

Jack Ruby, the night-club operator who shot Lee H. Oswald, was described as a Chicagoan who was attracted by the Western tradition in Dallas. His club in the heart of Dallas is decorated in Western decor, with the picture of a steer's head on a street sign. A friend of Ruby's said he was an efficient bouncer. "He was tough all right, but you can't run a night club here and be a sissy," he said.

One block from Ruby's club is a similar night club called "The Horseshoe." It is decorated with pictures of scantily clad women, some of them wearing pistols on their hips. Both night clubs are in the shadow of a partly completed, 50-story office building. Dallas has several skyscrapers going up. A taxi driver was asked if the city needed that much office space. He replied: "I don't know about that, but you see that new building there.

It was built by a bank. Another bank is building that tall structure. They couldn't stand to let the first bank get ahead of them."

"Something has happened here," Dr. Thomas A. Fry, pastor of the First Presbyterian Church, told his congregation today in a memorial service for President Kennedy. "We are proud of our heritage and our image. But something has happened like a cancer you cannot quite put your finger on. We have allowed the apostles of religious bigotry and the purveyors of political pornography to stir up the weak-minded. These events should cause us to see to it that never again will we allow persons to brand a president a Communist unless he can back up his charges in court with facts, to call a person an adulterer with nothing more than a picture of a man in front of the house to prove it." Dr. Fry was referring to literature distributed in the city by extremists.

Oswald's slaying today added to the feeling of defensiveness, confusion and hurt that has been evidenced here since the president was killed. People on the street have felt throughout that there was some kind of conspiracy involved in the president's death. Hundreds of persons gathered under clear skies today at the spot where President Kennedy was shot. They placed scores of floral wreaths in the small park that adjoins the street. Many of them stood in small groups discussing Oswald's death.

"I said all along that there was something else behind this," a woman said. "This shooting proves it. He won't be able to talk now." A waitress said, "I just don't believe Oswald was acting on his own." These people said they found it difficult to believe that the president's assassination was the act of a single demented person. Extremists here have contended that any left-wing activity was part of a worldwide conspiracy. Oswald has been a defector to the Soviet Union and was a self-proclaimed Marxist.

There was anger against Ruby for shooting Oswald before he could be brought to trial. "This makes it worse than ever for Dallas," a businessman said. "It seems like the police would have had enough sense to keep out people like that; it will be hard to convince the nation that Dallas people aren't wild-eyed gunmen." Some residents expressed doubt that the authorities had enough evidence against Oswald to convict him. "I don't believe he did it," a woman said.

Dallas also has a strong Southern tradition, even though most residents claim Western ties first. It is a city of many churches and their members turned out in great numbers today, obviously deeply grieved and disturbed over what had happened. A minister said, "I think it is significant that the president received a warm and genuine reception by thousands of its residents before he was shot by a single emotionally disturbed man. Dallas cannot be explained in a few words. It is a lot of things."

Right-Wing Group in Dallas Debut

Assailed Kennedy With Ad on Day of His Death

Special to The New York Times

DALLAS, Nov. 24—A right-wing "organization" that took President Kennedy to task Friday in a full-page advertisement in *The Morning News* is new to the city. "The American Fact-Finding Committee," headed by Bernard Weissman, is apparently not known even to other ultra-conservative groups here.

In the ad the committee assailed the president, on the day of his assassination, for his policies on Latin America, Cuba, Vietnam, Poland and Yugoslavia, and on the sale of grain to Communist countries. It asked why Gus Hall, Communist leader, had "praised every one of your policies and announced that the [Communist] party would endorse and support your reelection in 1964. Why have you scrapped the Monroe Doctrine in favor of the spirit of Moscow?" the ad continued. It demanded replies to that and other questions "now." It declared that Dallas would "reject your philosophy and policies" more emphatically next year than it did in the 1960 election.

Mr. Weissman, a 26-year-old salesman, has not been here long. He has an apartment in East Dallas with a new, unlisted telephone number. When reached he expressed regret that the president had been assassinated, but refused to give details about his group. He said it was "a local organization which wanted to show its position on national issues." The ad, which gave only a postal box number, identified the committee as "an unaffiliated and nonpartisan group of citizens who wished truth."

Spokesmen here for the John Birch Society and the Defenders of American Liberties, extreme right-wing groups, said they had never heard of Mr. Weissman or the committee. Civil rights leaders also knew nothing about the group. A Negro lawyer said that such groups "come and go" in Dallas. Like others, he said, this one may last a few days, then disappear. "This is the way it is in Dallas," he commented.

Knight Denounces the Dallas Police

LOS ANGELES, Nov. 24 (UPI)—Former Gov. Goodwin Knight was sharply critical today of the Dallas police force in connection with the fatal shooting of Lee H. Oswald. He said President Kennedy's assassin had been entitled to a fair trial and protection.

"One of the great fundamentals of American justice which John Kennedy many times praised and worked for was violated during the last two days in Dallas," Mr. Knight said. "Apparently the evidence against Oswald was overwhelming, but under our great system of American justice he was still entitled to a fair trial and he was still entitled to protection."

Mr. Knight accused the Dallas district attorney, chief of police and other officials of "trying Oswald via television and newspapers when they should have been directing their attention toward gathering the evidence and making sure that the accused would face a trial. This is a crime of the century, yet because of the carelessness of these officials in Dallas the American people will now forever be denied the whole truth of the assassination."

Any Aid to Oswald Is Denied by Tower

WASHINGTON, Nov. 24 (UPI)—Senator John G. Tower, Republican of Texas, said today that he did not help Lee Oswald return to the United States from the Soviet Union. "The facts of the matter are just exactly opposite," Mr. Tower said in a statement. He said that his office had received a letter from Oswald in January, 1962, stating that he was a citizen of the United States being held against his wishes in the Soviet Union.

"I forwarded this letter to the State Department for their analysis. The State Department informed my office shortly thereafter, in February of 1962, that Mr. Oswald had sworn to an affidavit that he owed his allegiance to the Soviet Union and that he had renounced his American citizenship. Given that information, I closed the case. I had no intention of interceding in behalf of anyone who had renounced his American citizenship and sworn allegiance to the Soviet Union."

Texas Increases Connally Guard

At Least 20 Extra Troopers Are Assigned to Hospital

TYLER, Tex., Nov. 24 (UPI)—The chief of the Texas Highway Patrol ordered at least 20 extra men into Dallas today to guard Gov. John B. Connally Jr., who is recuperating in a hospital. "We have complete respect for the Dallas Police Department and we do not mean to imply that we do not," Col. Homer Garrison Jr., head of the Department of Public Safety, said.

Governor Connally was shot when President Kennedy was assassinated. He was reported to be up and around today at Parkland Hospital and well enough to shave himself. A temporary headquarters for his staff has been set up at the hospital. "The governor's security is always our prime concern," Colonel Garrison said. "By law, we guard the governor in the mansion. Wherever the governor is . . . that's where our prime concern is. Here [at Parkland Hospital] we will use whatever security measures we think necessary for his protection. We have complete respect for the Dallas Police Department. This just happens to be our special assignment."

Colonel Garrison stressed that there was nothing "unusual" about extra police units being brought into Dallas. He refused to specify, however, how many additional troopers were ordered into the city. But it was learned that at least 20 additional troopers were brought in from the Tyler district.

Tyler is 98 miles east of Dallas. Colonel Garrison took personal charge of the security guard for Governor Connally. He said that nobody could see the governor without clearance. "And that includes the Secret Service and the F.B.I.," he said.

Connally Leaves Bed

DALLAS, Nov. 24 (UPI)—Gov. John B. Connally Jr., wounded during the assassination of President Kennedy last Friday, was able to walk from his bed to a chair and sit up today. Governor Connally stayed in the chair a few minutes and then walked back to bed, smiling.

His wife, Nellie, was composed earlier today when she said that her husband "is now apparently out of danger." Mrs. Connally, in a news conference at the Parkland Hospital, where her husband is recuperating, also described the last minutes of President Kennedy's life. "I had such a good feeling about the way they had received him in this city," she recalled. "I had just turned to him and said, 'You can't say Dallas doesn't love you, Mr. President,' and that was it."

Pharmacist Says He Gave F.B.I. a Tip on the Rifle

DAYTON, OHIO, Nov. 24 (UPI)—Duane Creviston, local pharmacist, said today that he had recognized the rifle used to kill President Kennedy as the same type he had seen in a catalogue advertisement and that he had then notified the Federal Bureau of Investigation. The pharmacist, whose hobby is collecting rifles, said that he had spotted the advertisement in a catalogue issued by Klein's Sporting Goods Company of Chicago.

Mr. Creviston said that he immediately recognized the rifle when he caught a glimpse of it on television Friday night. He said that he understood his tip to the F.B.I. had led them to the source of the rifle. The local F.B.I. office refused to comment.

Oswald Purchase Confirmed

CHICAGO, Nov. 24 (AP)—Milton P. Klein, president of Klein's Sporting Goods here, confirmed today that his concern had sold the rifle that killed President Kennedy. Mr. Klein said a copy of the sales slip showed that the rifle had been purchased from his mail-order company and shipped to Dallas in March, 1963. The Italian-made, bolt-action 6.5-millimeter rifle, with telescopic sight, was sold for $19.95, Mr. Klein said.

Marlin W. Johnson, special agent in charge of the Chicago office of the Federal Bureau of Investigation, said his investigation had disclosed that the rifle was sent to a Dallas post office box that had been rented by Oswald.

Lone Assassin the Rule in U.S.; Plotting More Prevalent Abroad

By FOSTER HAILEY

A study of assassination attempts of the last century in the three countries where they have been most frequent—Czarist Russia, Japan and the United States—reveals no clear pattern or motivation beyond a common urge to right a wrong.

There is one clear distinction between most of the attempts to kill Government figures in other countries and those in the United States. In Russia and in Japan the assassinations generally were the culmination of detailed plans made by well-organized groups, usually involving high Government figures. The motivations were political, or nationalistic. In the United States, in all except two cases, the attempts were made by a single person, often with little advance planning and often without any real grievance against the personage attacked. That seems to have been the case with Lee H. Oswald, the killer of President Kennedy who was himself slain yesterday.

The two exceptions to this American pattern of violence have been the conspiracy headed by John Wilkes Booth against Abraham Lincoln and the attack by two Puerto Rican nationalists on Blair House in 1950 in an apparent attempt to kill President Truman. The original Booth plan was to kidnap Lincoln and hold him hostage for the release of all Southern prisoners held in Union jails. It seems doubtful that the four who, like Booth, died for the conspiracy had any real knowledge that he intended to shoot the president that night of April 14, 1865.

Oscar Collazo and Griselio Torresola, who on Nov. 1, 1950, attacked Blair House with blazing guns, were members of an extreme Puerto Rican nationalist group that demanded complete independence for their country. Collazo survived the return fire of White House guards (Torresola was killed), was captured, tried and is now serving a life sentence in the Federal prison at Atlanta. He denied that the attackers intended to kill Mr. Truman. He said their plan was to dramatize the Puerto Rican demands by "making a demonstration." Since both were well armed and opened fire on the guards, that explanation was discounted at his trial for the murder of the guard who was killed.

The history of the other American assassins, as learned after their captures, was of men who were eccentric, if not legally insane. Two were found by courts to be insane and died in custody many years after their acts. One was Richard Lawrence, who tried to kill Andrew Johnson. The other was John Schrank, who shot and wounded former President Theodore Roosevelt.

Had the trials of two others who were executed for their acts—Leon F. Czolgosz and Giuseppe Zangara—been delayed until the initial hysteria had died down, they might also have been adjudged mentally incompetent. Czolgosz was tried and was executed within 45 days of the date on which he shot President McKinley at Buffalo on Sept. 6, 1901. Zangara was electrocuted in the state prison at Raiford, Fla., only a month and five days after he had fired at President Franklin D. Roosevelt in Miami on Feb. 13, 1933, killing Mayor Anton Cermak of Chicago instead.

The only other assassin who was legally executed—he was hanged— was Charles J. Guiteau, a 38-year-old part-time lawyer, part-time itinerant evangelist, who shot and fatally wounded President Garfield in the railroad station at Washington, July 2, 1881. There was clear evidence that he was at the very least eccentric. He even wrote a song to commemorate his execution.

One physiological characteristic all nine men involved in the American assassination attempts have had in common is their size. All were small men, including Oswald. The tallest was only 5 feet 7½ inches. Most were dark-haired and of ruddy or swarthy complexion. None was sturdy and nearly all had suffered some serious illness during their relatively short lives (most were in their thirties). Zangara had what he described as "terrible stomach aches" that he thought were caused by his childhood in a poor family in Italy.

Czolgosz, it was learned after his execution, had suffered some sort of breakdown three years before he shot McKinley and had been able to work only intermittently afterward. Before that he had been known as a steady worker who always did his share or more of a job.

Most psychologists agree that American assassins have been antisocial persons who, in times of stress, give vent to the violence that lies dormant in most human beings. None of the assassins was well educated, none well to do. Only Booth had ever received any public attention. The stresses of modern society are likely to create more persons of that type.

The pattern of assassination in Russia and in Japan was entirely different. Those who led the terrorist groups in Russia in the last century were largely intellectuals—students, school teachers, other professionals. They often enlisted military persons, police and even members of the aristocracy in their plots. But the hard core remained the intellectuals.

A strange individual named Necheyev was the generally accepted intellectual father of the terrorist movements in Russia that led, after many attempts, to the assassination of Alexander II on a snowy street in St. Petersburg on March 14, 1881. Necheyev provided inspiration for a movement called the "People's Will Party" or "Will of the People Party." Two of his lieutenants were Zhelyabov and Sophia Perovsky. Some authorities credit the latter with being the real iron will of the terrorist groups. Certainly it was she who gave the signal to the bomb throwers on the day that Alexander II was killed. Previously, Madame Perovsky herself had placed the dynamite that was intended to blow up a train on which the czar was returning from a Black Sea vacation. The charge exploded prematurely under a preceding train, killing many innocent persons.

The "People's Will Party" was a splinter group. After it was crushed by the Czarist police, the Social Democratic party arose, espousing the doctrines of mass revolution expounded by Karl Marx. The Bolsheviks (the present-day Communists) were the majority faction of this party. Most of the followers of Necheyev were credited by historians as being dedicated Russian patriots who felt there was no other way than assassination to rid themselves of oppressive rulers. It was an irony that Alexander II was perhaps one of the most enlightened of the czars. On the day he was killed by a bomb he had just put his royal signature to what would have been Russia's first Constitution.

In Japan, the year 1932 is known to some as the "Year of Assassination." That island country, which did not emerge from feudalism until the middle of the last century, has a long record of violence. In 1932 the violence was organized and, on three days, Feb. 9, March 5 and May 15, it took the lives of three Japanese leaders. Many others were marked for death but, for various reasons, escaped assassination.

The organization that planned the assassinations was called Ketsumeidan, a direct successor to the Kokuryukai, or "Black Dragon Society." The latter flourished in the first quarter of the century, and others, such as the Genyosha, preceded it in the 1880's and 1890's. The aim was to promote a more aggressive expansion policy and bring an end to parliamentary government in Japan. The last goal was achieved in fact as Japan marched on to the attack on Pearl Harbor under the control of the militarists.

The three persons killed, in order, were Inouye Junnosuke, a former finance minister and with a powerful voice in Government, Baron Dan Takuma, director of the Mitsui companies, and Premier Inukai Tsuyoshi. The first two were killed by two young men named Konuma and Hisanunia, respectively. Premier Inukai was slain by a group of Army and Navy officers led by a Lieutenant Koga, who invaded his official residence. Investigation tended to implicate a member of the imperial family in the plot, but that was never brought out in court. A Shinto priest close to the imperial family also was involved.

Another plot was organized the following year, but it was discovered and stopped before anyone was killed. Most of those involved were military officers. The plot was not even revealed until 1935, and when a trial was held the conspirators were given such light sentences that the whole thing seemed a mockery to most thoughtful Japanese.

MRS. KENNEDY LEADS PUBLIC MOURNING

By MARJORIE HUNTER
Special to The New York Times

WASHINGTON, Nov. 24—Mrs. John F. Kennedy, firmly holding the hands of her two children, followed the coffin bearing the body of her husband as it left the White House today for the last time.

Her eyes swollen, she moved quietly to the edge of the steps of the North Portico and paused to watch the coffin placed in the caisson by military bearers. Her son, John Jr., tugged at her hand and pointed to a black, riderless horse, part of the ceremonial procession. She leaned down and spoke to him. Mrs. Kennedy wore a simple black suit and black lace mantilla. John Jr., who will be 3 years old tomorrow, and Caroline, who will be 6 on Wednesday, wore similar pale blue coats, white anklets and red shoes. As the three stood there, framed against the black-draped doorway, there was an eerie silence. It was broken only by the occasional sound of hoofs of the restless gray horses that were to pull the caisson up Pennsylvania Avenue to the Capitol.

Mrs. Kennedy was composed, but appeared to be on the verge of tears as she and the children stepped into a black limousine for the slow ride to the Capitol. In the car, too, were President and Mrs. Johnson and Attorney General Robert F. Kennedy.

Still holding the hands of her children, Mrs. Kennedy followed the flag-draped coffin into the Capitol Rotunda. She stared straight ahead as the coffin was placed on the catafalque, a simple funeral bier draped in black broadcloth. John Jr., wide-eyed and bewildered, was restless. Clutching a tiny flag, he was led away by a military aide. Later, after the tributes had been spoken, Mrs. Kennedy walked slowly to the coffin, touched it with her fingertips, knelt and kissed it. Caroline was by her side. They were rejoined by John Jr. at the door.

Shortly after 9 o'clock tonight Mrs. Kennedy returned to the Capitol and again kneeled before the coffin and kissed it. Mrs. Kennedy walked into the Rotunda on the arm of her husband's brother, Robert, who stopped at the rope holding back the crowd while she went on through. She walked slowly to the side of the coffin, knelt beside it and then, with her hand on the flag again, kissed the coffin. Standing, she turned, looked long at the crowd and then rejoined the attorney general. They walked slowly out of the front entrance, passing the crowd, seeming to look at its faces.

After walking down the steps beside the line filing up, Mrs. Kennedy was heard to say, "Let's walk a bit." They walked west to the bottom of Capitol Hill, stopped to chat with some nuns they met, and finally got in a limousine when a crowd began to gather. The limousine carrying Mrs. Kennedy and the children back to the White House this afternoon had to be rerouted over side streets because of crowds.

Tomorrow, Mrs. Kennedy will again follow the caisson by car from the Capitol to the White House. There, she will alight to follow the coffin by foot for five blocks to St. Matthew's Cathedral for the funeral mass. White House aides declined tonight to say if the children would attend the service or the burial, which will be held in Arlington National Cemetery.

Mrs. Kennedy will meet with foreign heads of state at the White House at 3:30 tomorrow afternoon, shortly after the burial, it was announced tonight. The State Department was flooded all day with requests of foreign dignitaries to meet her.

The solemn ceremonies of the day began in late morning for Mrs. Kennedy and her children when they attended a private mass in the East Room, where the coffin rested under a crystal chandelier. The mass was celebrated by the Rev. M. Frank Ruppert of St. Matthew's Cathedral. Present were members of the family and close friends, including Under Secretary of the Navy Paul Fay and Charles Spaulding of New York. Joining Mrs. Kennedy at the White House before the procession to the Capitol were her stepfather and mother, Mr. and Mrs. Hugh D. Auchincloss of Washington and Newport, and her stepsister and stepbrother, Miss Janet Auchincloss and Jamie Auchincloss.

Mrs. Kennedy's sister, Princess Stanislas Radziwill of London, arrived yesterday to stay with her sister until after the funeral. Attorney General and Mrs. Kennedy also are staying with her much of the time. Other members of the family at the White House during the mourning were two of President Kennedy's sisters and their husbands, Mr. and Mrs. Stephen Smith and Mr. and Mrs. Peter Lawford. Arriving from Hyannis Port, Mass., aboard the family plane, the *Caroline,* late today were Mr. Kennedy's mother, Mrs. Joseph P. Kennedy; a sister, Mrs. Sargent Shriver; and a brother, Senator Edward M. Kennedy.

President Kennedy's mother, one of her daughters, two daughters-in-law and one son-in-law visited the catafalque in the Rotunda just after 10 P.M. Kneeling and praying beside the coffin for several minutes were the senior Mrs. Kennedy, Joan Kennedy, wife of Senator Kennedy; Mrs. Robert Kennedy, and Mrs. Shriver, who is the president's sister Eunice. Standing by was Mr. Lawford, the actor, husband of the president's sister Patricia, who was not present.

Crowd Is Hushed

Mourners at Capitol File Past the Coffin Far Into the Night

By TOM WICKER

Special to The New York Times

WASHINGTON, Monday, Nov. 25—Thousands of sorrowing Americans filed past John Fitzgerald Kennedy's bier in the Great Rotunda of the United States Capitol yesterday and early today. Mr. Kennedy's body lay in state in the center of the vast, stone-floored chamber. Long after midnight the silent procession of mourners continued.

Some wept. All were hushed. As the two lines moved in a large circle around either side of the flag-covered coffin, almost the only sounds were the shuffle of feet and the quiet voices of policemen urging the people to "keep moving, keep moving right along." By 2:45 A.M. today 115,000 persons had passed the bier.

Yesterday afternoon a crowd estimated at 300,000 lined Pennsylvania and Constitution Avenues to watch the passage of the caisson bearing the body of the 35th president of the United States, slain in the 47th year of his life by an assassin's bullet. Behind the caisson, following military tradition, came a riderless bay gelding, with a pair of military boots reversed in the silver stirrups. The horse was Sardar, the thoroughbred that belongs to Mrs. John F. Kennedy.

Mrs. Kennedy, her two children, President and Mrs. Johnson and Mr. Kennedy's brother, Attorney General Robert F. Kennedy, rode in the first car of a 10-car procession that followed the caisson. The procession moved at a funeral pace, to the sound of muffled drums, from the White House to Pennsylvania Avenue. It was a journey Mr. Kennedy had made formally four times.

At the Capitol, brief ceremonies of eulogy were held in the Rotunda before the admission of the waiting thousands who swarmed over the plaza and stretched in a long line up East Capitol Street. At the conclusion of the ceremonies, Mrs. Kennedy and her daughter, Caroline, stepped a few feet forward. Each reached out and touched the flag and the coffin it covered. Mrs. Kennedy knelt, kissed the coffin, then rose and led her daughter away.

President Johnson had already come forward, following a soldier who walked backward carrying a wreath of red and white carnations. As the soldier placed the wreath at the foot of the coffin, the man who had taken Mr. Kennedy's place in office stood with his head bowed, then withdrew. The wreath was marked "From President Johnson and the Nation." Numbers of other wreaths and sprays, sent despite a White House request that flowers be omitted, were arranged in nearby rooms.

After a short interval, during which staff workers of the Senate and the House of Representatives and their guests were admitted to the Rotunda from the North and South Wings of the Capitol, the great central doors of the Capitol were thrown open to the people. Across the East Plaza, in long, silent lines, they came—patient, quiet, thousands upon thousands of them. They moved slowly up the towering marble steps, above which, on Jan. 20, 1961, a platform had been built for the Inaugural of John F. Kennedy as president of the United States. As they entered the Rotunda, they formed two lines, each moving in a great semi-circle around the Rotunda. Only

red velvet ropes and 25 feet of stone floor separated them from the catafalque upon which rested Mr. Kennedy's coffin.

Enlisted men from each of the armed services stood motionless at the
four corners of the catafalque. As the guard changed every half hour, first
an Army officer, then a Marine Corps officer, then an officer from the
Navy and the Air Force took up his position at the head of the coffin.
They rotated command of the guard through the night. Behind the commander, a sailor held the flag of the president. To the sailor's right stood
an unattended American flag.

Yesterday afternoon the dusty footprints of the military men who had
placed the coffin upon the catafalque were still visible on the catafalque's
black velvet drapings. At each side of the coffin were sprays of chrysanthemums and white lilies.

That simple scene was all the people saw as they filed past—the coffin
covered with its flag, the motionless guards, the two listless flags upon
their standards, the traditional flowers of death.

The police were nearly overwhelmed by a crowd far beyond their ex-
pectations. Within the Rotunda, however, all was order and silence. The
lines moved rapidly around the circle—about 35 persons a minute in each
line—and were directed out the west door to the wide porch that overlooks
the Mall and the Washington Monument.

Outside, virtually the whole Metropolitan police force was on duty. At
4:30 P.M., the lines of those waiting to get in the Capitol stretched across
the East Plaza back end six blocks, past the Supreme Court building on
East Capitol Street.

At 9 P.M. the waiting line stretched for 30 blocks, with four to six
persons abreast. And the line was growing, as people joined it faster than
it moved through the Rotunda. Originally, it had been planned to close the
Capitol's doors at 9 P.M., reopening the Rotunda for an hour this morning.
When the size of the crowds became apparent, it was decided to keep it
open as long as people came. Thousands were giving up late yesterday,
however, under the impression that the doors would be closed by the time
they reached the Rotunda. Families from as far away as Baltimore and
Richmond left without having gotten near the Capitol. However, millions
throughout the county were watching on television. The brilliant lights

needed for the cameras played steadily on the Rotunda and broadcasters spoke constantly in low monotones into their microphones.

Across the wide lawns and the paved drives of the Capitol Plaza, the people coming and going swarmed like ants. Most were good-natured. There was little pushing and shoving, and no fighting was observed. But confusion was constant as people tried to find out where to get into line, how long it was and how to get out of the jammed plaza. Even Mrs. Kennedy was inconvenienced by the crowds in the plaza. When she left the Capitol, in a limousine with her children and Attorney General Kennedy, her planned route along Independence Avenue was impassable. She was rerouted over other streets, led by a motorcycle escort.

Throughout yesterday among the throngs that watched the procession and those that jammed around the Capitol, there were few evidences of open emotionalism. Not many people wept or cried out. The mood was rather one of sorrow and respect. Even among teen-agers, of whom thousands and thousands seemed to be present, there was quiet. People passing through the Rotunda were told that no photographs were to be taken; only a few, looking somewhat furtive, broke the restriction.

The police said some persons began lining up at midnight Saturday. Yesterday morning, hours before the procession began, crowds began to form along the streets and in Lafayette Square across Pennsylvania Avenue from the White House.

A half-hour before the procession began, the news reached the White House that Lee H. Oswald, charged with the murder of Mr. Kennedy in Dallas on Friday, had been shot down in that city. Among the crowds many had transistor radios, and the news from Dallas swept rapidly. It was a constant subject of conversation in the crowd, and one gray-haired woman, seated on a bench in Lafayette Square, told her husband: "I told you last night, Henry, I had a feeling something like this would happen. That man held so many secrets, someone had to kill him." Another woman exclaimed: "My God, how long will this go on?"

On the lawn before the north portico of the White House, a small crowd of White House employees and workers in the Executive Office Building was permitted to assemble. The circular drive in front of the mansion was lined, shortly after noon, with black limousines. Near the northeast gate, an honor guard and the bearers of flags of all the states were lined up.

At 12:40 P.M., President and Mrs. Johnson arrived at the north portico and entered the black-draped doors of the building that will now be their home. Shortly thereafter, the empty caisson, draped in black and drawn by six gray horses, came up the drive and stopped under the portico. It was the same caisson upon which the body of Franklin D. Roosevelt was carried from the White House to the Capitol in 1945.

Behind it was Sardar. The horse was given to Mrs. Kennedy in March, 1963, by President Ayub Khan of Pakistan when she visited that country. The White House said Mrs. Kennedy had requested that the horse be used as the traditional symbol of a fallen warrior. A black-handled sword hung in a silver scabbard from the saddle. Mrs. Kennedy has ridden the horse in the hunt country around nearby Atoka, Va., where the late president built a new home. The other horses were Army stock from Fort Myer in Virginia.

Then Mr. Kennedy's military aides, Maj. Gen. Chester V. Clifton of the Army, Brig. Gen. Godfrey McHugh of the Air Force and Capt. Tazewell T. Shepard Jr. of the Navy, lined up at attention behind the caisson. Eight enlisted men of the various armed services carried the coffin out onto the north portico, down the few steps and placed it on the caisson. The military aides moved to the front. The caisson pulled slowly away, followed by the black horse. And a limousine slid into place at the foot of the steps.

Mrs. Kennedy, in black and wearing a black mantilla, came out, holding Caroline and John Jr. by the hand. The children were dressed in identical shades of blue. The three entered the car and 2-year-old John Jr., apparently unaware of the nature of the occasion, bounced up on the seat and peered out the rear window. Attorney General Kennedy followed them into the car. President and Mrs. Johnson took the jump seats, and the limousine pulled away.

In rapid order, other limousines drove up to the steps and were filled. In the second car were Mr. Kennedy's sisters Patricia and Jean, and their husbands, Peter Lawford and Stephen E. Smith. In the third were Mrs. Kennedy's stepfather and mother, Mr. and Mrs. Hugh D. Auchincloss, and others of the Auchincloss family. Mrs. Robert Kennedy, several of her children, and Sargent Shriver, the husband of the former Eunice Kennedy, were in the next car. Mrs. Shriver, her mother, Mrs. Rose Kennedy, and Senator Edward M. Kennedy, the youngest brother, were flying to Washington from Hyannis Port, Mass., and were not in the procession. A number of employees of the Kennedy family and the White House rode in another car.

Other cars with officials, security agents and policemen joined the line. As the procession moved slowly onto Pennsylvania Avenue, turned briefly on 15th Street, and then rounded on to the long straight stretch of Pennsylvania that reaches from the Treasury Building to the Capitol, the line was about two city blocks long.

In advance of the caisson, on foot, were policemen, the escort commander—Maj. Gen. Philip C. Wehle of the Military District of Washington—five military drummers, a drum major and a company of Navy enlisted men. They walked at funeral pace, 100 paces a minute. Behind them was a special honor guard, composed of the Joint Chiefs of Staff led by their chairman, Gen. Maxwell D. Taylor, and followed by Mr. Kennedy's military aides.

The national colors immediately preceded the caisson. Between it and the car carrying Mrs. Kennedy and President Johnson, there were personal flags, the marching body bearers, and the riderless Sardar. Three clergymen also marched in the procession. They were the Very Rev. Francis Bowes Sayre Jr., dean of the Cathedral of Saints Peter and Paul (Washington Cathedral), Protestant Episcopal; the Right Rev. John S. Spencer of Sacred Heart Shrine (Roman Catholic), and the Very Rev. K. V. Kazanjian, rector of St. Mary's Armenian Apostolic Church. Dean Sayre was born in the White House on Jan. 17, 1915. His mother was the daughter of President Woodrow Wilson, the late Mrs. Jessie Woodrow Wilson Sayre.

Crowds lined the entire route at least 10 deep, and twice that thick at some places. Others stretched up the side streets, hung from windows of buildings along the street, lined open-tiered parking buildings and mounted the pedestals of the street's numerous statues. At 25-foot intervals, soldiers with fixed bayonets lined the street on each side, standing at parade rest.

The Secret Service and the police, nervous after the Dallas motorcade that ended in death for Mr. Kennedy, took unusually stringent security precautions for Mr. Johnson. As the president's car passed 14th Street, for instance, a police official was designating an officer to watch each building on the street. It was from a building beside a Dallas street that Mr. Kennedy was shot through the head by a sniper with a high-powered rifle.

For the first few blocks, the crowds stood silently, almost unmoving, as each element of the procession passed. As at the Capitol later, there were few evidences of emotionalism—very little, for instance, of the weeping, screaming and kneeling in the street that was observed at the last such occasion, the funeral procession for President Franklin Roosevelt 18 years ago.

A sizable group of reporters and photographers was allowed to walk in the street at the rear of the procession. Many of them had followed Mr. Kennedy in happier times when he drove to the Capitol along the same route for his inauguration, for two addresses to Congress in 1961, and for his State of the Union Messages in 1962 and 1963. But their presence at the rear of the procession had been apparently mistaken by the crowd as an invitation for others to join. By the time the rear of the procession passed 11th Street, hundreds were seeping out from the curbs to walk behind Mr. Kennedy's coffin. Many were teen-agers, and some surged past the reporters as if to walk beside the cars ahead.

At Ninth Street, apparently on orders from a Secret Service car that pulled out of the procession, the police formed a cordon across the avenue and stopped the crowd, which was massed from curb to curb and extended back for more than a block. The reporters were let through the line at that point and continued along the avenue. Again, however, the crowds began coming from the curbside to join in. Finally, at John Marshall Place, a few blocks from the point where the procession slanted off onto Constitution Avenue, a line of marines with fixed bayonets halted everyone, including the reporters. As the procession moved slowly up Capitol Hill on Constitution Avenue, and turned into the East Plaza, the restrictions were relaxed.

As seen from below, the sloping hillsides around the building were almost solidly covered with moving figures—many with children in their arms, some running, some leaping stone walls, all swarming up the hillside and the steps toward the West Front of the Capitol. The police estimated that on the other side of the building, 35,000 persons were in the East Plaza to see the procession arrive.

The caisson and the cars following reached the east steps of the Capitol at 1:50 P.M., 45 minutes after the coffin had been borne from the White House. A 21-gun salute boomed across the crowd and echoed across the vast plaza stretching north to Union Station. A military band played "Hail to the Chief." As the eight bearers removed the coffin from the caisson and bore it slowly up the marble steps, the band softly played—perhaps in honor of the service during which Mr. Kennedy nearly gave his life in World War II—the Navy hymn, "Eternal Father, Strong to Save."

The various parties from the limousines followed the coffin in the order they had arrived. Inside the Rotunda, members of the Senate, House and Cabinet and other dignitaries stood in a semicircle. Mrs. Kennedy, President and Mrs. Johnson and others who had come in the procession stood in the northeast quadrant of the hushed chamber, near a temporary lectern. The members of the Kennedy family gathered near them. Caroline and John Jr. stood holding their mother's hands, Caroline sedately, John occasionally capering about. Among those in the Rotunda was former President Harry S. Truman. He was accompanied by his daughter, Mrs. E. C. Daniel of New York.

Senator Mike Mansfield of Montana, the Democratic leader of the Senate, was the first eulogist. As television lights washed the Rotunda in a harsh, artificial glare, Senator Mansfield spoke in tones that grew ever more ringing. Four times, in praising the man who was dead, and the life he had lived for his country and with his wife, Senator Mansfield repeated:

"In a moment, it was no more. And so she took a ring from her finger and placed it in his hands."

A fifth time he said it and added—"and kissed him, and closed the lid of a coffin." The senator referred to Mrs. Kennedy's having put her ring on a finger of the president and having kissed him as the body was about to be taken to the plane for its return to Washington. At that moment, the senator said, "a piece of each of us died."

Mr. Kennedy, he said, "gave us of his love that we, too, in turn, might give. He gave that we might give of ourselves, that we might give to one another until there would be no room, no room at all, for the bigotry, the hatred, the prejudice and the arrogance which converged in that moment of horror to strike him down."

Chief Justice Earl Warren struck much the same note in the eulogy that followed. "What moved some misguided wretch to do this horrible deed may never be known to us," he said, "but we do know that such acts are commonly stimulated by forces of hatred and malevolence, such as today are eating their way into the bloodstream of American life. What a price we pay for this fanaticism! If we really love this country, if we truly love justice and mercy, if we fervently want to make this nation better for those who are to follow us, we can at least abjure the hatred that consumes people, the false accusations that divide us and the bitterness that begets violence. Is it too much to hope that the martyrdom of our beloved president might even soften the hearts of those who would themselves recoil from assassination, but who do not shrink from spreading the venom which kindles thoughts of it in others?"

Speaker of the House John W. McCormack was more personal. "As we gather here today, bowed in grief," he said, "the heartfelt sympathy of the members of the Congress and of our people are extended to Mrs. Jacqueline Kennedy and to Ambassador and Mrs. Joseph P. Kennedy and their loved ones. Their deep grief is also self-shared by countless millions of persons throughout the world; considered a personal tragedy, as if one had lost a loved member of his own immediate family."

Most of these remarks were inaudible to many in the chamber, which was not designed for speeches. Even strong voices are lost in the vast open space that rises above the stone floor to the top of the Capitol Dome.

During the eulogies, Mrs. Kennedy stood with regal bearing, seeming to listen intently. Tears rolled down the face of Robert F. Kennedy. At the moment that Mrs. Kennedy walked forward and knelt by her husband's coffin, all who saw her were profoundly moved.

Then it was over. Mrs. Kennedy and her children walked slowly down the steps of the Capitol. President and Mrs. Johnson followed. At the foot of the steps, in the softer light of the afternoon, they talked for a few moments. Mrs. Johnson held Mrs. Kennedy's hands as they spoke; once she leaned forward and placed her head near Mrs. Kennedy's. Then the president took Mrs. Kennedy's hand in one of his, patted it with the other. Mrs. Kennedy, her children and Robert Kennedy entered a car and sped away.

Mr. Johnson, headed for one of the important meetings that will constantly occupy him in coming days, entered another car with Secret Service men and a military aide. After him, alone with her driver and a security guard, rode the new first lady.

Behind them, in the stillness of the Rotunda, they left the body of John Fitzgerald Kennedy upon the same catafalque on which had rested—98 years ago—the body of Abraham Lincoln, the first American president to be murdered. Gazing on the scene with silent stone eyes from beside the north entrance was a statue of James A. Garfield, the second president to fall before an assassin.

It was time, then, for the doors to be opened to those waiting outside.

World's Leaders to Attend Requiem Today in Capital

Mrs. Kennedy Will Walk Behind the Caisson to Mass at Cathedral

By JACK RAYMOND

Special to The New York Times

WASHINGTON, Nov. 24—Mrs. John F. Kennedy, joined by world and national leaders, will walk behind the horse-drawn caisson that bears her husband's body from the White House to St. Matthew's Roman Catholic Cathedral tomorrow. Following a requiem mass, John Fitzgerald Kennedy, the 35th president of the United States, will be escorted in a solemn state procession to Arlington National Cemetery to be buried with military honors.

The gravesite, on a beautiful grassy knoll, provides a sweeping view of the capital city and it is itself easily in view from the Memorial Bridge approach to the national burial ground.

The state funeral procession will begin at 10:30 A.M. at the Capitol, where the closed, flag-draped coffin of the president lay in state today. Marching units of all services, military bands and veterans' organizations, interspersed by color guards, Government leaders and representative delegations of clergy, will take part in the funeral procession. On the journey from the Capitol Mrs. Kennedy will sit in the lead limousine, accompanied by her brother-in-law, Attorney General Robert F. Kennedy, and by President Johnson.

At the White House, where the procession will pause before proceeding to the cathedral, Mrs. Kennedy will get out of the limousine to be joined on the walk to the cathedral by the greatest assemblage of world and United

States dignitaries that this city has ever seen. The distance is a little more than half a mile.

The assemblage is comparable in a way, to that attending the funeral of King Edward VII of Britain May 20, 1910. As Barbara Tuchman pointed out in her book, *The Guns of August*, which the president read and recommended to others, the assemblage of crowned heads and others representing 70 nations on that occasion marked the end of an era.

Mr. Kennedy's funeral will be attended by representatives of nearly 100 nations. They will represent every political, ideological and geographical quarter of the globe with the exception of China. Led by Mrs. Kennedy, they will walk in slow march from the White House for five blocks to the cathedral where Richard Cardinal Cushing of Boston will celebrate a pontifical requiem mass. This is different from the ordinary requiem low mass in that a bishop says it. A low mass is one that is said not sung. A high mass is sung.

The formal lying-in-state of Mr. Kennedy in the Great Rotunda of the Capitol is scheduled to end at 9 A.M. Servicemen then will lift the coffin off the black-draped catafalque, the same that bore the body of President Lincoln nearly 100 years ago, and carry it to the caisson in the Capitol Plaza.

At 10:30 A.M. the funeral procession will form behind a police escort. With Maj. Gen. Philip C. Wehle, commanding general of the Military District, in the vanguard, marching units composed of officers from each of the five military services—the Army, Navy, Marine Corps, Air Force and Coast Guard—will lead the funeral parade. Military bands and full companies of servicemen and servicewomen, cadets and midshipmen from the military academies, units of the National Guard and other service forces also will take part.

The route of march will take the coffin west along Constitution Avenue to Pennsylvania Avenue and the White House. Aircraft of the Navy and Air Force will fly over the main funeral procession, but in keeping with tradition one plane will be noticeably missing from the usual reverse-V formation. Cordons will be posted along the route of the march. Army, Navy, Air Force and Marine Corps personnel will stand 10 feet apart on both sides of the processional route from the Capitol to Arlington.

With the exception of the justices and Congressional leaders, who will also join in the walk from the White House, the remainder of the procession will continue to St. Matthew's. At the White House the cortege will be re-formed. In slow cadence, to a drumbeat calling for 100 steps a minute, Mrs. Kennedy and the members of her family will lead the walkers behind the cortege as it leaves the White House grounds. The cortege will consist of a special honor guard representing the three services, followed by color bearers holding American flags. Clergymen will follow. A Navy seaman, in commemoration of the president's wartime Navy service, will walk alone as he carries Mr. Kennedy's personal flag, unfurled, on a staff.

Following Mrs. Kennedy will be, in this order, the president, chiefs of state, heads of government and chiefs of special delegations; the chief justice, former Presidents Dwight D. Eisenhower and Harry S. Truman, associate justices of the Supreme Court, members of the Cabinet, leaders of Congress; the members of the Joint Chiefs of Staff, personal assistants to Mr. Kennedy and close friends.

Officials of Nearly 100 Lands in U.S.— They Will Meet Johnson

By MAX FRANKEL

Special to The New York Times

WASHINGTON, Nov. 24—An emperor, a king, a queen, princes, presidents, premiers and ministers from every continent converged on Washington this evening to pay final tribute to President Kennedy and to make the acquaintance of President Johnson. Representing nearly 100 nations, the foreign dignitaries will include the largest assembly of ruling statesmen ever gathered in the United States for any event.

Their arrival here, through the night, virtually overwhelmed an already tense and overburdened capital. Nonetheless, each visitor received the protocol deference and police protection of more normal times. Officials who had worked hard to discourage such a gathering finally worked even harder to accommodate it. They accepted it as a demonstration of respect from friends and adversaries alike, as a symbolic measure of Mr. Kennedy's far-flung activities and of the responsibilities that await his successor.

President de Gaulle of France, the proud ally whose search for independence greatly troubled Mr. Kennedy in the last year, was among the first to arrive here this evening. Among the last tomorrow morning will be Anastas I. Mikoyan, a first deputy premier of the Soviet Union, whose last mission here was to close out the Cuban missile crisis and to set the stage for a year-long effort to reach a Soviet-American accommodation.

Also coming back to Washington were Emperor Haile Selassie of Ethiopia, King Baudouin I of Belgium, Queen Frederika of Greece and nineteen other chiefs of state or government. With Prince Philip from Britain came Sir Alec Douglas-Home, the prime minister. With President Heinrich Lübke of West Germany came Ludwig Erhard, the chancellor. Like the United States, these two major allies have new governments and must prepare for difficult elections and possibly further changes in the next two years.

Leaders who by themselves could have stirred this capital to pomp and excitement in ordinary days poured in at half-hour intervals at different airports around the capital. For the most part, they remarked on the sadness of the occasion and declined any statement. They chatted only briefly with the official greeters—Secretary of State Dean Rusk or his deputies, Under Secretaries George W. Ball and W. Averell Harriman, the assistant secretaries of state and protocol officers. Nearly all wished to pay their respects to Mrs. John F. Kennedy. It was finally decided tonight that she would receive the foreign dignitaries at the White House after the funeral tomorrow afternoon.

President Johnson will meet with the visitors from abroad at the State Department between 5:30 and 7 P.M. tomorrow. The new president may meet separately with some of the chiefs of government on Tuesday, but the confused schedules of all made it impossible to arrange fixed appointments. Mr. Johnson may wish to issue vague invitations to some of the visitors, like President de Gaulle, to return to Washington in the near future, but no major policy discussions are expected.

By this evening, 84 nations had assigned special delegations to the funeral; 30 others had still to indicate how they would be represented. Only a few heeded the early appeals of the State Department that representation by the ambassadors to Washington would be perfectly appropriate. Among the announced visitors will be at least 12 of royal title, 18 republican chiefs of state or government, at least 34 foreign ministers, six vice premiers or vice presidents, and two former presidents of other nations.

In magnitude, the assemblage will surpass even the gathering of 21 chiefs of state or government at the United Nations in 1960, though it will not include the colorful figures of Premier Khrushchev, Premier Fidel Castro and Prime Minister Jawaharlal Nehru. It will certainly be the greatest assembly of mourners since the funeral of King Edward VII in London 50 years ago.

For both the State Department and police authorities, the gathering poses the greatest security and protocol problems ever encountered in this capital. And it comes at a moment of enormous strain, when officials are already overburdened with the demands of a new leadership and with nervousness about the safety of the new president. Most of the high-ranking visitors will live at their embassies here. They do not have the status of official guests and thus are responsible for their own lodging and arrangements. But each will have the security guard of a regular visit—plainclothesmen at his side and residence and motorcycle escorts on trips through the capital.

From the planning standpoint, the State Department had an even more difficult time with protocol arrangements. It worked through the night from its operations center, normally employed for foreign crises, charting the movements of dignitaries and making provisions for them. It was especially difficult to work out an official order of precedence in which the foreign mourners will march from the White House to St. Matthew's Roman Catholic Cathedral and the order in which they will sit for the services.

The rivalries of international politics were clearly subdued by the world community for the gathering here. There was no representation, of course, from nations with which the United States has no diplomatic relations— Communist China, Cuba, East Germany, North Korea, North Vietnam and Albania. The governments of South Africa, Haiti, Portugal and some others with which Mr. Kennedy's Administration had strained relations, did not send their highest ranking representatives. But there was no discernible distinction in the delegations of many Communist and non-Communist nations, or in those from Israel and from Arab nations. The representatives of Morocco and Algeria, whose border war Mr. Kennedy tried so hard to end, arrived aboard the same plane.

The countries without special delegations will be represented by their ambassadors to Washington or to the United Nations, so that 110 sovereignties in all will participate in the rites for Mr. Kennedy. In addition, special representatives will be present from the Vatican; the European Economic Community or Common Market; from Euratom, the Western European Atomic Energy Association; the European Coal and Steel Community and the United Nations and its subsidiary agencies.

Airport Shields Arrivals

By MARTIN GANSBERG

Extra security measures were taken to guard European and Middle Eastern leaders who arrived yesterday at Idlewild Airport on their way to Washington for President Kennedy's funeral.

With 16 flights bringing in dignitaries on regularly scheduled planes, the police decided at 2 P.M. to close down both outdoor observation decks at the International Arrivals Building. It was the first time in the history of the airport that both decks had been closed at the same time. Albert J. Vavrick, supervisor of the Port of New York Authority force that polices the building, ordered additional men on duty from 4 P.M. to midnight, the period when most of the planes arrived. Besides the normal police complement at the airport, additional forces from the city Police Department were assigned to this shift.

The speed with which arriving dignitaries were moved to private quarters until they could get on planes for Washington reduced the danger. State Department and United Nations representatives greeted them aboard the commercial planes, whisked them through customs to airline lounges and kept them occupied until their planes to Washington were ready.

There were few interruptions in the forward movement of the arrivals. Customs regulations were waived and aides filled out necessary forms. Baggage was left to be placed on the relay plane. The first to arrive, at 1:40 P.M., was Prince George of Denmark, who came on a plane from

London. Prince Stanislas Radziwill, brother-in-law of Mrs. Kennedy, arrived on a plane from London at 2:20 P.M. Both waited in airline lounges, hidden from the press and public, until their flights to Washington were ready.

As he boarded the plane to the capital, Prince Radziwill was told about the slaying of Lee H. Oswald, President Kennedy's assassin. "It's terrible," he said. "It's terrible!" After Crown Princess Beatrix of the Netherlands arrived with her party of five, including Foreign Minister Joseph M. A. H. Luns, officials at Idlewild placed a flag at half-staff in the center of the main reception hall. The flag was mounted on a small platform that was covered with black crepe paper. The area was roped off.

Among other notables arriving later at the airport on their way to Washington were President de Gaulle, President Eamon de Valera of Ireland and Mayor Willy Brandt of Berlin. With President de Valera were his two sons Major Vivian and Dr. Brian de Valera and an honor guard of 24 cadets from the Irish Military College. The cadets were flown over at the request of Mrs. Kennedy.

Idlewild officials said that the crowds were "somewhat lighter than usual" for Sunday. Yet the open area on the first floor of the building was crowded with onlookers as each dignitary came thorough the reception hall to go to private quarters while awaiting his transfer plane. Persons barred from the observation decks asked a guard there for an explanation. "It's too windy to be out there," he said. "It's just too windy."

Business of City Will Halt Today

Mayor Says Only Essential Services Will Be Provided

By LEONARD INGALLS

Normal public, business and social activity in the city will be almost completely suspended today out of respect for President Kennedy. Mayor Wagner announced yesterday that the city would continue in full mourning throughout the day. Only essential city services will be maintained. "Those city employees not engaged in activities imperative to the health, safety and welfare of our citizens are to be released from duty and their offices closed through Monday," Mr. Wagner said at City Hall.

Proclamation of the day as a legal holiday by Governor Rockefeller in observance of Mr. Kennedy's funeral permits banks and other institutions to close. Classes at schools and colleges will be suspended. Department stores and specialty shops will be shut. Securities exchanges and commodity markets will not operate. Most places of entertainment will be closed. There will be no deliveries of mail and post offices will be shut.

Special memorial services for the murdered president have been scheduled at churches and synagogues. At St. Patrick's Cathedral pontifical requiem masses will be celebrated at noon and 5:30 P.M. The first will be offered on behalf of delegates to the United Nations whose Secretariat will be closed for the day. Throughout the day the Middle Collegiate Church's "liberty bell" will toll as it has for the death of every president since George Washington. The church is at Second Avenue and Seventh Street.

Temple Emanu-El, like many synagogues, will hold a memorial service at noon. Among churches that have scheduled noontime services are the Cathedral Church of St. John the Divine; St. James's Protestant Episcopal Church, Madison Avenue and 71st Street; St. Thomas Protestant Episcopal Church, Fifth Avenue and 53d Street; the Fifth Avenue Presbyterian Church at 55th Street, and St. Luke's Lutheran Church, 308 West 46th Street. There also will be a memorial service at noon today in St. Paul's Chapel at Columbia University.

Naval guns will fire simultaneous 21-gun salutes at one-minute intervals starting at noon. The salutes will be fired from the aircraft carrier *Franklin D. Roosevelt,* berthed at the Naval Shipyard Annex in Bayonne, N.J., and by a Marine battery at the Brooklyn Navy Yard parade ground.

Railroads serving the city announced that trains would be halted at noon from one to five minutes as a mark of respect for Mr. Kennedy. Subways and buses operated by the New York City Transit Authority will stop for two minutes at noon.

The New York Telephone Company said it expected all employees to report for work at their normal times today. "Essential telephone service must be maintained," a company spokesman said. Normal weekday parking regulations will be in effect today, the Police Department announced.

There will be no change in alternate-side-of-street regulations. Mayor Wagner said departments and agencies that would provide a full range of services were Police, Fire, Health, Hospitals, Corrections, Sanitation, Transit, Housing Authority and Water Supply, Gas and Electricity. Other departments and agencies will maintain emergency and operational services ordinarily provided on a continuous basis.

Among the city's businesses and industries, most nonessential enterprises will close for the entire day or for a period of time during the funeral service for President Kennedy, which starts at noon. Some that are not closing have arranged to give their employees time off during the day if they desire to attend memorial services for Mr. Kennedy. Others have asked half their working force to come in during the morning and the other half to work during the afternoon.

Among concerns that said they would close for the day were W. R. Grace & Co., Lever Brothers Company, Metro-Goldwyn-Mayer, Inc., Webb & Knapp, Inc., American Cyanamid Company, Standard Oil Company of New Jersey, General Foods Corporation and Mutual of New York Insurance Company. The Associated Hospital Service of New York and the United Medical Service, Inc., operators of the Blue Cross and Blue Shield plans, will be closed. Some advertising and public relations agencies reported that they would open. They work closely with newspapers and radio and television networks, but a large volume of the advertising normally carried by these media has been canceled.

Governor Orders Holiday

ALBANY, Nov. 24 (AP)—Governor Rockefeller has proclaimed tomorrow a legal holiday in New York State. His office said today that the proclamation allowed all local governments, banks and private concerns to close. Essential services, such as police, fire and public health protection, will continue at the discretion of the local governments.

The governor ordered a 30-day period of mourning and closed all state offices last Friday after the assassination of the president in Dallas. In the proclamation, Governor Rockefeller said: "The people of the State of New

York together with other Americans and peoples throughout the world mourn the untimely death of John Fitzgerald Kennedy, 35th President of the United States." The proclamation declared tomorrow, "the day of the funeral service of President John F. Kennedy, to be a day of general prayer and general religious observances, enabling the people of the State of New York on that day to assemble in their respective places of divine worship in reverence and mourning for President Kennedy."

Most schools throughout the state have been ordered closed by local school boards. Governor Rockefeller has also ordered a 21-gun salute to be fired here at noon tomorrow with a 50-gun salute at sundown. A memorial service will also be held. The governor and Mrs. Rockefeller plan to attend Mr. Kennedy's funeral.

Thousands Pass Bier at Night
Despite the Cold and Long Wait

WASHINGTON, Monday, Nov. 25 (AP)—People by the thousands who had endured the cold and hours of patient waiting passed in homage last night and early this morning past the bier of President Kennedy in the Capitol. At least 115,000 had moved up the Capitol steps, and passed the coffin by 2:45 A.M. The line of those waiting to pay a final tribute extended for miles in a chill wind. Representative William J. Randall, Democrat of Missouri, drove the length of the line of waiting people at 11 P.M. He said the line was nine miles long. Original plans had called for the viewing of the flag-draped coffin to continue until 10 A.M. but military authorities announced at a late hour that all viewing would cease by 9 A.M.

The people were filing swiftly through the Rotunda and moving on into the night with their memories. They came alone, they came with children. Some were the mighty, most were the meek. Among them was the grieving widow, back for a second brief visit to the bier of her husband. An hour later the late president's mother, Mrs. Joseph P. Kennedy, moved through the line and knelt in silent prayer alongside the coffin of her son. Another mourner was Eamon de Valera, aging president of Ireland, from which Mr. Kennedy's forefathers had come.

But mostly they were just people, shuffling in awed silence, two abreast, in two semi-circles around the bier guarded by military men. As midnight approached, and the temperature dropped to 39 degrees, newsmen estimated that some 75,000 persons had passed through the Rotunda. Many on the line said they had been waiting nine hours to view the bier. Almost unanimously they said they would do it again. Earlier the police had doubled the pace by ordering viewers to go two-abreast instead of single file, increasing the rate to about 14,400 an hour. But they feared that even the all-night vigil would not accommodate the waiting thousands.

Kennedy's Mother Visits Altar Dedicated to Son Killed in War

HYANNIS PORT, Mass., Nov. 24 (UPI)—The mother of President Kennedy worshiped today before an altar dedicated to another son—Joseph P. Kennedy Jr., who was killed in World War II.

Mrs. Joseph P. Kennedy, 72 years old, attended two masses in the white clapboard Roman Catholic Church at this Cape Cod community. One son, Senator Edward M. Kennedy, Democrat of Massachusetts, and a daughter, Mrs. Sargent Shriver, also attended the church a few hours before all three flew to Washington for the president's funeral tomorrow.

Today, in church, one seat was empty. At the 11 A.M. mass, the priest, Msgr. Leonard J. Daley, noted that the empty seat in a side chapel of St. Francis Xavier Church was the one occupied by President Kennedy when he attended church while home from Washington.

"It is empty," Msgr. Daley said. "We like to think of him in the days before he became president when he worshiped at this altar." Sobs were audible among the congregation that included a 150-member uniformed veterans group.

The president's mother, his brother, and married sister had attended church earlier. The mother prayed through two masses starting at 7 A.M. Mrs. Kennedy sat in the vestry. She emerged only to receive communion with the other parishioners. Senator Kennedy and Mrs. Shriver sat in a pew.

The president's 75-year-old father, left virtually speechless from a stroke in December, 1960, was reported bearing the strain bravely.

Family Is Appreciative

HYANNIS, Mass., Nov. 24—Senator Kennedy made a statement today expressing appreciation for the sympathy shown to him and his family in the death of President Kennedy. His statement, made before boarding a plane for Washington, follows:

"I would just like to say a word. I'm going down to Washington now with my mother and my sister, Eunice. I do want to say how appreciative that both my parents have been for the tremendous outpouring of thoughtfulness and prayers that have come from all Americans in all parts of the country, from every religious group. This has been a matter which has been a source of tremendous consolation to both my parents and they certainly wanted me to express their great thanks to all of the people who've been so kind in remembering them now."

Grandmother Not Told

Special to The New York Times

BOSTON, Nov. 24—Mrs. John F. Fitzgerald has not been told and probably will not be told that her grandson, John F. Kennedy, was assassinated on Friday. She is 98 years old.

Experts Favor Telling Children About Death

Some Counsel Taking Young to Funeral—Advise Early Preparation for Event

By MARTIN ARNOLD

When and what should parents tell a child about death? A sampling of professional opinion on the subject rejected last night a widely held idea that children should be shielded from the fact of death or concepts about it.

Many parents have been concerned about this matter in recent days because of the assassination of President Kennedy. Some are also concerned that closing of schools today for his funeral would prompt children to dwell deeply on the subject.

Dr. Martha Wolfenstein, a child psychologist at the Albert Einstein Medical College, said that the closing of the schools was a good idea. "It tells children that something extremely exceptional has happened," she said. "It will help prepare them for another death—perhaps one closer to home." The small child, according to Dr. Wolfenstein, will accept death mentally but not emotionally. "A 6-year-old will say 'Daddy's dead and not coming back,' but deep down the child will still day-dream about his daddy and will expect him to come home again for many years," she said.

Dr. Wolfenstein believes that a child should be told about a death in the family as soon as possible by the person closest to the child. The way to help a child see that death is real is to take the child to the funeral, she said. She said that children would, no matter how well prepared, "give only verbal belief to the fact that a parent is dead."

It is generally agreed that a child's reaction to death depends upon his preparation and how well those closest to him react. The Rev. George C. Hagmaier, associate director of the Roman Catholic Paulist Institute for Religious Research, at 411 West 59th Street, said that the "most important thing is the way the child sees" the adult react. He said that most psychologists feel that if one is to make a choice between complete shielding of the death and explaining it, it is better to involve the child in death.

The experts agreed that a child should be told simply that someone who had died would not come back. They also agreed that it was helpful to tell a child that "his father is in Heaven" or "God wanted daddy with Him"—but only if the parent's religious conviction led him to believe it.

The two main questions a child faces with death are: Do I have to die? And who will take care of me when a parent dies?

Dr. Benjamin Spock, the author and pediatrician, said: "Children generally raise the question of death themselves by the age of 3 or 3½. They ask about dead animals, birds or insects." He said in a telephone interview that there was "no ideal way to tell a child about death." There are ways, he added, to help the child "live with the experience."

According to Dr. Spock, it is not enough for a parent to explain that the child "wouldn't be left alone because I'll be here with you. The child can picture a parent's growing older while he himself remains only 3 years old. So it must be explained that while you expect to live a long time the child will be grown up and have his own children when you die."

Dr. Spock, like Father Hagmaier, believes that religion can be very helpful in easing death for a child. "Religion gives a very real, tangible and concrete set of symbols," Father Hagmaier said, referring to the idea that a loved one had gone to Heaven or was near God.

Rabbi Israel Miller, of the Kingsbridge Heights Jewish Center in the Bronx, said, "In most cases I have found that children accept death as a natural occurrence. Although they don't understand all its implications, especially the finality of death, children seem to accept it with more aplomb than adults." He too believes that "if it is at all possible the parent should consider having his children take part in the experience of the funeral." Rabbi Miller said that he usually advises a survivor "to tell the child if he is not preschool age, but the exact form of the telling is optional, depending on the parent's understanding of the child involved."

Johnsons Go to Church on Capitol Hill

Special to The New York Times

WASHINGTON, Nov. 24—President Johnson prayed today for John F. Kennedy and his family and heard a congregation pray for the success of his Administration in banishing hate from the nation. With his wife Lady Bird and 16-year-old daughter, Lucy Baines, the president attended services at 11 o'clock at St. Mark's Protestant Episcopal Church on Capitol Hill.

Secret Service men lined the back of the brick Gothic-style church. Outside, several hundred persons gathered on the sidewalk to watch the president, who entered and left the church by a side door. The president sat in a pew near the front. When he stood, his tall figure could be seen among the parishioners.

Throughout the 70-minute service there was a note of mourning for the dead president and prayers for the living—from the opening psalm beginning "The Lord hear thee in the day of troubles" to the recessional hymn of "Before the Lord Jehovah's Throne." The Rev. William M. Baxter, the rector, said in his sermon that the murder of President Kennedy should unite the nation in a new awareness of what it had inherited in its institutions. The lesson for the sermon was taken from a passage in II Corinthians reading: "If God be for us, then who can be against us."

Mr. Baxter deplored the "take-it-for-granted attitude" that he said had developed toward national institutions and the tendency, particularly on the far right and left, to grasp for easy solutions to complex problems. As a nation, he observed, we have been brought up to believe in a "sure and enduring order" in which law and justice are "automatic fruits."

With the murder of President Kennedy, he said, the "normal order has broken down" and with it should come a realization of the frailty of our national institutions and "the chaos" that lies behind them. It has taken a crisis such as the death of President Kennedy, he said, to "bring us together into a new awareness of human reality." He expressed concern that the mood of the moment would pass and that courage would "grasp at easy answers."

Looking at President Johnson, the clergyman observed that if this mood of indifference again sets in, "our leadership will suffer from loneliness."

During the service, Mr. Baxter led prayers that God would receive Mr. Kennedy "into the arms of Thy mercy" and that He would imbue the souls of members of his family with patience. There were prayers for the health and prosperity of the new president. Mr. Johnson and his family joined prayers for the unity of the nation and removal of "all our hate and prejudice."

After the service the Johnsons went to the parish hall where members of the congregation gathered for coffee. The president shook hands with the children's choir, with the rector's family and with many parishioners. He remained about 15 minutes and then went to the White House. President Johnson, a member of the Christian Church, presumably decided to attend St. Mark's today because Mrs. Johnson, an Episcopalian, has frequently worshiped there.

They Came to Bid a Friend Good-By

"I Feel As If a Member of My Family Had Died"

By NAN ROBERTSON

Special to The New York Times

WASHINGTON, Nov. 24—"I came to pay my respects to the president," they said, over and over. "It was the least I could do."

The people watched the caisson go up Capitol Hill from the White House. Then they followed their slain president in the hundreds of thousands to see him lie in state at the Capitol Rotunda. "I feel as if a member of my family had died, I really do," said a Detroit housewife.

As the sun on a cold, sparkling afternoon sank behind the Capitol today, the patient, waiting multitude stood 20 deep across the broad sidewalks, eastward for a mile and more. Many came from other cities. Two youths walked the 40 miles from Baltimore overnight.

Hundreds began gathering at Capitol Plaza at 2 o'clock this morning, bringing blankets and pillows to sleep on ground soggy from the drench-ing rains of yesterday. Just before the president's cortege began the slow march from the White House, two young women hurried across Lafay-ette Park toward the ranks of spectators. "We were going to watch it on television in our room at the Y," said one. The Y.W.C.A. is only two blocks away. "But the more we watched," she said, "the more we felt we just had to be here ourselves. It's so awful we felt we had to do something—something."

Shortly after noon, word of the shooting of Lee Harvey Oswald in Dallas circulated in incredulous whispers through the crowd packed across Penn-sylvania Avenue from the White House. Hundreds were listening to the news on small transistor radios. The instantaneous reaction was dismay and horror at the senseless violence, rather than triumph at the fate of the man supposed to be the president's assassin.

Two hours later, as thousands pressed into the plaza east of the Capitol, they heard of Oswald's death. Announcers interrupted the broadcast of Senator Mike Mansfield's eulogy over the bier inside the Rotunda. "Oh, my God," said an Army sergeant in the crowd, shaking his head with the others. "When is all this going to end?"

When the short ceremony in the Capitol was over, Mrs. Kennedy, clad in black, came down the steps to her car. Murmurs of sympathy swept over the masses outside as the 34-year-old widow appeared. On either side, clutching her hands, were her two small children, dressed in pale blue coats. John Jr. struggled manfully down the steep incline.

Many of those who waited brought their own children, some babies in arms. Albert Osbahr, a biochemist, came to the city from Rockville, Md., with his wife and three children. The oldest child is 5, the youngest 14 months. "We wanted to give them a sense of history," Mrs. Osbahr said. "We wanted them to remember when their dad brought them down to Washington."

A student at the University of Florida, who had come up with a friend from Gainesville, said: "I guess we couldn't believe it and had to come here ourselves to make sure. But it's more than that. When I have grand-children 30 or 40 years from now, I want to say to them, 'Yes, I went to Washington to say good-by to President Kennedy.' "

Mrs. Lottie Fitzgerald Lively, 72, walked up the Capitol's 37 steep steps.

"I came because, like all the rest, I wanted to glimpse the casket. I don't know why that fine man wasn't allowed to live," she said.

Some of those who had been composed outside lost control when they caught sight of the flag-draped coffin centered in the towering Rotunda. A burly man and his teen-aged daughter began to weep helplessly as they shuffled by the bier. Close behind them in single file were 36 nuns, Felician sisters from Jersey City, who had chartered a bus to come down to the capital.

Mrs. William Matthews, a housewife from Bethesda, Md., expressed the feelings of many when she said: "I came here as I would go to the funeral of any friend, to pay my respects." A Philadelphia schoolteacher took the train today with a friend, a postman. "I felt it was my duty and my obligation to be here," she said. The postman added, "I wanted to pay tribute to a great man in the only way I could. I don't think we can find anyone in his footsteps for a long while." Mrs. Peggy Ehrmann, a Washington housewife, said she had come to honor "a man that I thought had an understanding heart and was a wise president."

All afternoon and into the night the people streamed toward the Capitol. One police sergeant, on the force 21 years, said, "It's the biggest crowd I ever saw in Washington. It beats the inaugural."

"Where are they all coming from?" another sergeant asked. Mrs. Kennedy's limousine, with motorcycle escort, had to be rerouted over side streets on leaving the Capitol. The police reported that Independence Avenue, along which she had been scheduled to go, was "full of people in the street."

Early in the afternoon, a young Nigerian watching the sad procession was asked how he thought his countrymen would react to the assassination. The African, who is a student here, said, "I think there must still be disbelief in my country. We cannot believe that a people so rich and so great as the United States would do this cruel thing. I feel sorry for you American people."

Woman Brings a Tribute of Single Chrysanthemum

WASHINGTON, Nov. 24 (AP)—Elaborate floral tributes to President Kennedy poured in today, but a young woman who never knew him brought her small gift personally—a single snow-white chrysanthemum the size of an orange.

"I wanted to do something—I brought a flower," she explained as her token to the president was placed with the costly wreaths in a nearby room, to be placed on the president's grave after the funeral tomorrow.

She identified herself as Mary Anne Marczak of Washington. Hers was the first floral gift brought by members of the public filing in homage past the president's catafalque in the Capitol Rotunda.

Night of Stars Show Will Honor Kennedy

The 30th annual observance of the "Night of Stars," to be held in Madison Square Garden tonight, will be dedicated to the memory of President Kennedy. Past observances have featured an entertainment program. Tonight, the 18,000 ticket holders will hear tributes to Mr. Kennedy by leaders in the Catholic, Jewish and Protestant faiths. A special musical program will include liturgical selections to be sung by the Concord Choral Ensemble. Isaac Stern, violinist, and Eleanor Steber, soprano, will also take part in the program. The "Night of Stars" has traditionally been observed for the benefit of the United Jewish Appeal.

St. Louis Mourns Kennedy at Rally for Equal Rights

ST. LOUIS, Nov. 24 (AP)—A crowd estimated by police at 35,000, including civic and religious leaders, gathered before the old St. Louis Courthouse near the Mississippi River today to mourn President Kennedy's death. The scene was the place where the Dred Scott case was first heard in the middle of last century. The march originally had been scheduled as an interfaith procession for equal rights.

Leaders of the three major religious faiths and Mayor Raymond R. Tucker spoke. They said that the president would have wanted them to continue the meeting, and that his death only had emphasized the steps Mr. Kennedy had taken to ease racial tension and promote equality.

It was the largest demonstration in the 199-year history of St. Louis.

Street to Honor Kennedy

FOGGIA, Italy, Nov. 24 (Reuters)—The city council of Foggia, a provincial capital of 120,000 people in Southern Italy, has decided to name the main avenue of a new residential district after President Kennedy.

U.S. Forces Abroad to Join in Kennedy Tribute Today

WIESBADEN, Germany, Nov. 24 (Reuters)—United States servicemen throughout Europe, North Africa and the Middle East will join in honoring President John F. Kennedy tomorrow.

All military units will parade in the morning and their commanding officers will formally announce the death of the commander in chief. Messages will be read from Defense Secretary Robert S. McNamara, Air Force Secretary Eugene M. Buckert and Gen. Curtis E. LeMay, Air Force chief of staff.

All civilian employees will be excused from work tomorrow and service-family schools will be closed.

Pope Paul Warns That Hate and Evil Imperil Civil Order

Special to The New York Times

ROME, Nov. 24—Pope Paul VI, alluding to the assassination of President Kennedy, said today that it showed how much "capacity for hatred and evil still remains in the world." Without mentioning Mr. Kennedy by name,

the pontiff spoke of "the crime that has aroused in these days the deploration of the whole world." He said it illustrated "how great the threat to
civil order and peace still is."

The pope was addressing thousands of people gathered in St. Peter's
Square for his usual Sunday-noon benediction. "We cannot, at this moment
of prayer together, take our thoughts from the crime that has aroused in
these days the deploration of the whole world," he said. "After dwelling
upon the man who is no longer with us and after comforting those who
still live in mourning and grief, thoughts show us how much the capacity
for hatred and evil yet remains in the world, how great the threat to civil
order and peace still is, and how great is the need for the grace of God,
for His mercy and for His pardon."

The pontiff spoke from a window of his apartment in the Apostolic
Palace. Before reciting the Angelus, a prayer commemorating the Incar-
nation, and imparting his benediction, he said: "Now let us pray as Jesus
has taught us: 'Lead us not into temptation and deliver us from evil'
through the maternal and most humane intercession of the Virgin Mary."
The phrase he quoted is from the Lord's Prayer.

As the pope spoke, hundreds of people went to the United States Embassy to express their sympathy and to sign the register. By late this afternoon more than 35,000 had signed.

Memorial services for the president were held in many cities in Italy
and at military posts. In Rome, Protestant Episcopal memorial services
were conducted by the Rev. Wilbur C. Woodhams in St. Paul's American
Church. Hundreds of Americans attended the services, and the United
States was represented by the ambassador, G. Frederick Reinhardt. A memorial was also held at the Rome Synagogue, with Chief Rabbi Elio Toaff
officiating. The United States was represented by embassy officers.

Tomorrow, the day of the president's funeral, the Basilica of St. John
Lateran, the pope's church as bishop of Rome, will be the scene of official
memorial services with diplomats and Government representatives attending. Cardinal Spellman, archbishop of New York, will say the mass, at
which many American prelates and prelates from other countries will be
present. They are here for the Ecumenical Council.

CUSHING EULOGIZES KENNEDY
AS BOTH A GREAT LEADER
AND A FAMILY MAN OF WARMTH

Extols President in Memorial Mass

Cardinal Describes Him as a "Youthful Lincoln" Who Gave the World Hope

By JOHN H. FENTON

Special to The New York Times

BOSTON, Nov. 24—Richard Cardinal Cushing, who served the spiritual needs of John F. Kennedy in joy and in sorrow, celebrated a memorial mass for the slain president today. The mass was televised nationally from the archdiocesan television center here.

The Roman Catholic archbishop of Boston eulogized Mr. Kennedy as a husband and a father who made the most of the few moments he could share with his family. The cardinal continued: "What comfort can I extend to their heavy hearts today—mother, father, sisters, brothers—what beyond the knowledge that they have given history a youthful Lincoln, who in his time and in his sacrifice has made more sturdy the hopes of this nation and its people."

Like Cardinal Cushing, two priests who also had played roles in Mr. Kennedy's spiritual life noted the sacrifice that the demands of public office required of his private life. The priests were attached to churches in Boston, where the president maintained a residence in the early years of his political career.

Cardinal Cushing married Mr. Kennedy and Jacqueline Bouvier at Newport, R.I., in 1953. He baptized their two children, Caroline, 6 years old next week, and John Jr., 3 tomorrow. Three months ago, the prelate celebrated a mass for a third child, Patrick Bouvier Kennedy, who died two days after his birth. When Mr. Kennedy was inaugurated as 35th president of the United States, Jan. 20, 1961, Cardinal Cushing offered the invocation.

This afternoon, the cardinal flew to Washington, where tomorrow he will preside at noon at a pontifical funeral mass in St. Matthew's Cathedral. After the televised mass, Cardinal Cushing recalled that he had watched Mr. Kennedy "mature with ever expanding responsibility." The cardinal went on: "I have been with him in joy and sorrow, in decision and in crisis, among friends and with strangers, and I know of no one who has combined in more noble perfection the qualities of greatness that mark his cool intelligence and his brave heart."

While others may pay tribute to Mr. Kennedy's virtues as a world leader, Cardinal Cushing said, "for me, it will be proper to recall him on this day of mourning as a husband and father, surrounded by his young and beloved family. Although the demands of office carried him often on long journeys and filled even his days at home with endless labors, how often he would make time to share with his son and daughter those few minutes that could be his."

The cardinal notified all pastors in the archdiocese yesterday that, by permission of the Holy See, one Sunday mass in each parish might be a mass of requiem, offered for the repose of the soul of the president. Normally, masses of requiem are not permitted on Sundays or feast days of major rank. Such requiem masses were offered at 10 A.M. at St. Joseph's Church, in the West End, and at Holy Ghost Chapel, at the Paulist Information Center, on Park Street, overlooking the Boston Common.

The Rev. Francis X. Quinn, pastor of St. Joseph's, recalled times when Mr. Kennedy had attended services there. During Mr. Kennedy's residency at 122 Bowdoin Street, near the Massachusetts State House, St. Joseph's was his parish. In those days, Mr. Kennedy was embarking on his political career and was away much of the time.

Father Quinn said that the Paulist Fathers headquarters, just below the State House, was more convenient for Mr. Kennedy. A priest there, who asked not to be identified, recalled that Mr. Kennedy had once taken up the collection at a mass while one of the ushers was in the sacristy, protesting that "that guy is using our vestibule as a rallying place." The priest identified the protesting usher as a Republican.

The Transcript of Cushing's Eulogy

Following is the text of Richard Cardinal Cushing's eulogy of President Kennedy on a nationally televised mass from Boston as recorded by The New York Times *through the facilities of WOR Radio:*

In the name of the Father and of the Son and of the Holy Ghost, amen. My dearly beloved, friends in Christ and guests:

A shocked and stricken world stands helpless before the fact of death, that death brought to us through a tragically successful assault upon the life of the president of the United States.

Our earliest disbelief has slowly given way to unprecedented sorrow as millions all over the earth join us in lamenting a silence that can never again be broken and the absence of a smile that can never again be seen.

For those of us who knew the president as friend as well as statesman, words mock our attempts to express the anguish of our hearts.

It was my privilege to have been associated with John F. Kennedy from the earliest days of his public life, and even prior to that time, my privilege to have watched him mature with ever-expanding responsibility, to have known some of the warmth of his hearty friendship, to see tested under pain and loss the steely strength of his character.

I have been with him in joy and in sorrow, in decision and in crisis, among friends and with strangers and I know of no one who has combined in more noble perfection the qualities of greatness that marked his cool, calculating intelligence and his big, brave bountiful heart.

Now all of a sudden, he has been taken from us and I dare say we shall never see his like again.

Many there are who will appropriately pay tribute to the president as a world figure, a tribute due him for his skill in political life and his devotion to public service.

Many others will measure the wide interests of his mind, the swiftness of his resolution, the power of his persuasion, the efficiency of his action and the courage of his conviction.

For me, however, it is more fitting and proper to recall him during these days of mourning as husband and father, surrounded by his young and beloved family.

Although the demands of his exalted position carried him often on long journeys and filled even his days at home with endless labors, how often he would make time to share with his little son and sweet daughter whatever time would be his own.

What a precious treasure it is now and will be forever in the memories of two fatherless children? Who among us can forget those childish ways which from time to time enhance the elegance of the Executive mansion with the touching scenes of a happy family life?

Charming Caroline stealing the publicity, jovial John-John on all fours ascending the stairs of an airplane to greet his daddy and a loving mother like all mothers joyfully watching the two children of her flesh and blood, mindful always of three others in the nurseries [in] the Kingdom of Heaven.

At the side of the president in understanding devotion and affection behold his gracious and beautiful Jacqueline. True always to the obligations of her role as mother, she has given new dimensions to the trying demands of being America's first lady.

The pride in her husband, which he so eminently justified, was plainly reciprocated in his pride of her. The bonds of love that made them one in marriage became like hoops of steel binding them together.

From wherever men may look out from eternity to see the workings of our world, Jack Kennedy must beam with new pride in that valiant woman who shared his life, especially to the moment of its early and bitter end.

It will never be forgotten by her for her clothes are now stained with the blood of her assassinated husband.

These days of sorrow must be difficult for her—more difficult than for any others. A Divine Providence has blessed her as few such women in history by allowing her hero husband to have the dying comfort of her arms.

When men speak of this sad hour in times to come, they will ever recall how well her frail beauty matched in courage the stalwart warrior who was her husband. We who had so many reasons for holding her person in a most profound respect must now find an even wider claim for the nobility of her spirit.

One cannot think, my dearly beloved, especially one such as myself, of the late president without thinking also of the legacy of public service which was bequeathed to him by his name and his family.

For several generations in a variety of tasks, this republic on one level or another has been enriched by the blood that was so wantonly shed on Friday last. Jack Kennedy fulfilled in the highest office available to him the long dedication of his family.

It is a consolation for us all to know that his tragic death does not spell the end of this public service but commits to new responsibilities the energies and the abilities of one of the truly great families of America.

What comfort can I extend to their heavy hearts today—mother, father, sisters, brothers—what beyond the knowledge that they have given history a youthful Lincoln, who in his time and in his sacrifice, had made more sturdy the hopes of this nation and its people.

The late president was even in death, a young man—and he was proud of his youth. We can never forget the words with which he began his short term as president of the United States:

"Let the word go forth," he said, "from this time and place, to friend and foe alike, that the torch has been passed to a new generation of Americans—born in this century, tempered by war, disciplined by a hard and bitter peace, proud of our ancient heritage. . . ."

No words could describe better the man himself who spoke, one whose youth supplied an almost boundless energy, despite illness and physical handicap, whose record in war touched heroic proportions, whose service in Congress was positive and progressive.

It was against personal background that he continued by saying:

"Let every nation know . . . that we shall pay any price, bear any burden, meet any hardship, support any friend, oppose any foe to assure the survival and success of liberty. This much we pledge and more."

All that the young president promised in these words, he delivered before his assassination. He has written in unforgettable language his own epitaph.

Two days ago, he was the leader of the free world, full of youth, vigor and promise, his was a role of action, full of conflict, excitement, pressure and change, his was a fully human life, one in which he lived, felt dawn, saw sunset glow, loved and was loved.

Now in the inscrutable ways of God, he has been summoned to an eternal life beyond all striving, where everywhere is peace.

All of us who knew personally and loved Jack Kennedy—his youth, his drive, his ideals, his heart, generosity and his hopes—mourn now more for ourselves and each other than for him.

We will miss him: he only waits for us in another place. He speaks to us today from there in the words of Paul to Timothy:

"As for me, my blood has already flown in sacrifice. I have fought the good fight; I redeemed the pledge; I look forward to the prize that awaits me, the prize I have earned. The Lord whose award never goes amiss will grant it to me—to me, yes, and to all those who have learned to welcome His coming."

John F. Kennedy, 35th president of the United States of America, has fought the good fight for the God-given rights of his fellow man and for a world where peace and freedom shall prevail.

He has finished the race at home and in foreign lands alerting all men to the dangers and the hopes of the future, pledging aid in every form to those who attempted to misinterpret his works, to misunderstand his country, to become discouraged and to abandon themselves to false prophets.

He has fulfilled unto death a privilege he made on the day of his inauguration—a privilege in the form of a pledge—"I shall not shrink from my responsibilities."

Far more would he have accomplished for America and the world if it were not for his assassination here in the land that he loved and for which he dedicated and gave his life.

May his noble soul rest in peace. May his memory be perpetuated in our hearts as a symbol of love for God, country and all mankind, the foundation upon which a new world must be built if our civilization is to survive.

Eternal peace grant unto him, O Lord, and let perpetual light shine upon him.

In the name of the Father and the Son and the Holy Ghost, amen.

Eulogies Given by Leaders

Following are the texts of eulogies to President Kennedy made yesterday as recorded by The New York Times *or transmitted by The Associated Press or United Press International:*

By Speaker McCormack

As we gather here today bowed in grief, the heartfelt sympathy of members of the Congress and of our people are extended to Mrs. Jacqueline Kennedy and to Ambassador and Mrs. Joseph P. Kennedy and their loved ones. Their deep grief is also self-shared by countless millions of persons throughout the world, considered a personal tragedy, as if one had lost a loved member of his own immediate family.

Any citizen of our beloved country who looks back over its history cannot fail to see that we have been blessed with God's favor beyond most other peoples. At each great crisis in our history we have found a leader able to grasp the helm of state and guide the country through the troubles which beset it. In our earliest days, when our strength and wealth were so limited and our problems so great, Washington and Jefferson appeared to lead our people. Two generations later, when our country was torn in two by a fratricidal war, Abraham Lincoln appeared from the mass of the people as a leader able to reunite the nation.

In more recent times, in the critical days of the Depression and the great war forced upon us by Fascist aggression, Franklin Delano Roosevelt, later Harry S. Truman appeared on the scene to reorganize the country and lead its revived citizens to victory. Finally, only recently when the cold war was building up the supreme crisis of a threatened nuclear war capable of destroying everything—and everybody—that our predecessors had so carefully built, and which a liberty-loving world wanted, once again a strong and courageous man appeared ready to lead us.

No country need despair so long as God, in His infinite goodness, continues to provide the nation with leaders able to guide it through the successive crises which seem to be the inevitable fate of any great nation.

Surely no country ever faced more gigantic problems than ours in the last few years, and surely no country could have obtained a more able leader in a time of such crisis. President John Fitzgerald Kennedy possessed all the qualities of greatness. He had deep faith, complete confidence, human sympathy and broad vision which recognized the true values of freedom, equality and the brotherhood which have always been the marks of the American political dreams.

He had the bravery and a sense of personal duty which made him willing to face up to the great task of being president in these trying times. He had the warmth and the sense of humanity which made the burden of the task bearable for himself and for his associates, and which made all kinds of diverse peoples and races eager to be associated with him in his task. He had the tenacity and determination to carry each stage of his great work through to its successful conclusion.

Now that our great leader has been taken from us in a cruel death, we are bound to feel shattered and helpless in the face of our loss. This is but natural, but as the first bitter pangs of our incredulous grief begins to pass we must thank God that we were privileged, however briefly, to have had this great man for our president. For he has now taken his place among the great figures of world history.

While this is an occasion of deep sorrow it should be also one of dedication. We must have the determination to unite and carry on the spirit of John Fitzgerald Kennedy for a strengthened America and a future world of peace.

By Senator Mansfield

There was a sound of laughter; in a moment, it was no more. And so she took a ring from her finger and placed it in his hands.

There was a wit in a man neither young nor old, but a wit full of an old man's wisdom and of a child's wisdom, and then, in a moment it was no more. And so she took a ring from her finger and placed it in his hands.

There was a man marked with the scars of his love of country, a body active with the surge of a life far, far from spent and, in a moment, it was no more. And so she took a ring from her finger and placed it in his hands.

There was a father with a little boy, a little girl and a joy of each in the other. In a moment it was no more, and so she took a ring from her finger and placed it in his hands.

There was a husband who asked much and gave much, and out of the giving and the asking wove with a woman what could not be broken in life, and in a moment it was no more. And so she took a ring from her finger and placed it in his hands, and kissed him and closed the lid of a coffin.

A piece of each of us died at that moment. Yet, in death he gave of himself to us. He gave us of a good heart from which the laughter came. He gave us of a profound wit, from which a great leadership emerged. He gave us of a kindness and a strength fused into a human courage to seek peace without fear.

He gave us of his love that we, too, in turn, might give. He gave that we might give of ourselves, what we might give to one another until there would be no room, no room at all, for the bigotry, the hatred, prejudice and the arrogance which converged in that moment of horror to strike him down.

In leaving us—these gifts, John Fitzgerald Kennedy, president of the United States, leaves with us. Will we take them, Mr. President? Will we have, now, the sense and the responsibility and the courage to take them?

By Chief Justice Warren

There are few events in our national life that unite Americans and so touch the heart of all of us as the passing of a president of the United States.

There is nothing that adds shock to our sadness as the assassination of our leader, chosen as he is to embody the ideals of our people, the faith we have in our institutions and our belief in the fatherhood of God and the brotherhood of man.

Such misfortunes have befallen the nation on other occasions, but never more shockingly than two days ago.

We are saddened; we are stunned; we are perplexed.

John Fitzgerald Kennedy, a great and good president, the friend of all men of goodwill, a believer in the dignity and equality of all human beings, a fighter for justice and apostle of peace, has been snatched from our midst by the bullet of an assassin.

What moved some misguided wretch to do this horrible deed may never be known to us, but we do know that such acts are commonly stimulated by forces of hatred and malevolence, such as today are eating their way into the bloodstream of American life.

What a price we pay for this fanaticism!

It has been said that the only thing we learn from history is that we do not learn. But surely we can learn if we have the will to do so. Surely there is a lesson to be learned from this tragic event.

If we really love this country, if we truly love justice and mercy, if we fervently want to make this nation better for those who are to follow us, we can at least abjure the hatred that consumes people, the false accusations that divide us and the bitterness that begets violence.

Is it too much to hope that the martyrdom of our beloved president might even soften the hearts of those who would themselves recoil from assassination, but who do not shrink from spreading the venom which kindles thoughts of it in others?

Our nation is bereaved. The whole world is poorer because of his loss. But we can all be better Americans because John Fitzgerald Kennedy has passed our way, because he has been our chosen leader at a time in history when his character, his vision and his quiet courage have enabled him to chart for us a safe course through the shoals of treacherous seas that encompass the world.

And now that he is relieved of the almost superhuman burdens we imposed on him, may he rest in peace.

Cushing to Offer Pontifical Mass

Cardinal to Be Celebrant at Simple Requiem Service

By PAUL L. MONTGOMERY

The pontifical requiem mass to be said for President Kennedy today in Washington will differ only in particulars from the masses offered in all the Roman Catholic churches of the world on each day of the year.

The form "pontifical requiem mass" contains three concepts. "Pontifical" means that the celebrant will be a bishop—in this case Richard Cardinal Cushing, archbishop of Boston. By the doctrine of apostolic succession, which holds that bishops are the direct inheritors of the duties of the apostles of Jesus, the bishops are created by the pope. Thus a bishop is acting for the pope and is performing a "pontifical" service. "Requiem," from the Latin word for "rest," means that some parts of the mass, which are joyous in nature, are omitted because the mass is not being offered for a joyous occasion. Certain funeral elements are added in the requiem mass. "Mass" is the central act of worship of the Roman Catholic Church. It is a re-creation, in words and symbolic actions, of the crucifixion and sacrifice of Jesus.

The mass contains prayers and recitations of two kinds, the proper and the ordinary. The ordinary of the mass is invariable in wording but some sections can be omitted. In the requiem mass, for example, the psalm "Judica me" (Give judgment for me) at the beginning is not said. The texts of the proper of the mass vary with the occasion and day of the year. It is in the proper that the solemn elements of the requiem are introduced.

The mass for President Kennedy today will be a low mass—that is, it will be said, rather than sung as in a high mass. Because it will be celebrated by only one priest, it will not be a solemn mass in the Catholic sense of the term. A solemn mass is celebrated by three men—the celebrant, the deacon and the sub-deacon. The mass is offered to God. However, it can be offered for a specific person. The church and all the faithful are considered to partake of the benefits of all masses offered.

The funeral service preceding requiem mass begins with a ceremony at the church door when the coffin is brought in. The celebrant sprinkles the coffin with holy water and recites, in Latin, the 129th Psalm and other prayers.

The mass begins with the words "*In nomine Patris, et Filii et Spiritus Sancti.* Amen" (In the name of the Father, the Son and the Holy Ghost. Amen). After several prayers, both ordinary and proper, the Gradual, Tract and Sequence are said. In the requiem, the Sequence is the famed Dies Irae (Day of Wrath), a description of the Last Judgment and a prayer to Jesus for mercy.

Other prayers in the proper of a requiem mass also dwell on the immortality of the soul. They include, in Latin, the words of St. Paul—"We would not have you ignorant concerning those who are asleep, lest you should grieve even as others who have no hope"—and part of Jesus' message in the Gospel of St. John—"I am the resurrection and the life; he who believes in Me, even if he die, shall live."

The canon, or the central part of the mass, consists of the consecration—the essence of the sacrificial act—and the communion. These parts are invariable. When this part is concluded, the celebrant pronounces absolution at the bier, sprinkling the coffin with holy water and wafting incense over it. The mass will end with this prayer: "O God, Who alone art ever merciful and sparing of punishment, humbly we pray Thee in behalf of the soul of Thy servant John, whom Thou hast commanded to go forth from this world."

During the absolution and prayers the words are English. In the rest of the mass they are Latin.

List of Dignitaries Expected at Kennedy's Funeral

Special to The New York Times

WASHINGTON, Nov. 24—*Following is the latest available list of dignitaries expected to attend President Kennedy's funeral:*

International Organizations

UNITED NATIONS

U Thant, secretary general.
Dr. Ralph J. Bunche, under secretary for political affairs.
Paul G. Hoffman, managing director, United Nations Special Fund.
Maurice Pate, executive director, United Nations Children's Fund.
David B. Vaughn, director of general services.
Carlos Sosa Rodriguez, president of the General Assembly, and his wife.
Sir Patrick Dean, president of the Security Council.
Dr. Louis Alvarado, International Labor Organization.
David Blanchard, International Labor Organization.

EUROPEAN COAL AND STEEL COMMUNITY

Albert Coppe, vice president.
Jean Monnet, former president.

EUROPEAN ECONOMIC COMMUNITY

Jean Rey, member.

EURATOM

E. M. J. A. Sassen, member of the Council.

Europe

AUSTRIA

Alfons Gorbach, chancellor.

BELGIUM

Baudouin I, king of the Belgians.
Paul-Henri Spaak, foreign minister.

BULGARIA

Miliko Tarabanov, deputy foreign minister.

CZECHOSLOVAKIA

Dr. Jiri Hajek, permanent representative at the United Nations.

DENMARK

Crown Prince George.
Jens Krag, premier.

FINLAND

Vali Merikoski, foreign minister.

FRANCE

President de Gaulle.
Maurice Couve de Murville, foreign minister.
Gen. Charles Ailleret, chairman, Joint Chiefs of Staff.
Etienne Burin Des Roziers, secretary general of the presidency.

WEST GERMANY

Dr. Heinrich Lübke, president.
Dr. Ludwig Erhard, chancellor.
Dr. Gerhard Schröder, foreign minister.
Kai-Uwe von Hassel, defense minister.
Willy Brandt, mayor of West Berlin.

BRITAIN

Prince Philip, duke of Edinburgh.
Sir Alec Douglas-Home, prime minister, and Lady Home.
Harold Wilson, Labor party leader.
Jo Grimond, Liberal party leader.

GREECE

Frederika, queen of the Hellenes.
Sophocles Venizelos, deputy premier and foreign minister.

HUNGARY

Peter Mou, first deputy foreign minister.

ICELAND

Gudmundur I. Gudmundson, foreign minister, and his wife.

IRELAND

Dr. Eamon de Valera, president.
Frank Aiken, minister for external affairs.
Maj. Vivian de Valera.

ITALY

Attilio Piccioni, foreign minister.
Piero Vinci, Foreign Ministry chef de cabinet.
Guerino Roberti, assistant chief of protocol.
Gen. Emiliano Scotti, military counselor to the president.

LUXEMBOURG

Prince Jean, hereditary grand duke.
Eugene Schaus, foreign minister.

THE NETHERLANDS

Prince Bernhard, husband of the queen.
Crown Princess Beatrix.
J. M. A. II. Luns, foreign minister.

NORWAY

Crown Prince Harald.
Einar Gerhardsen, premier.

POLAND

Prof. Stanislaw Kulczynski, deputy chairman of the Council of State.
Piotr Jaroszewicz, deputy premier.

PORTUGAL

Luis Supico Pinto, president of the Corporate Chamber.

RUMANIA

M. Milita, deputy foreign minister.

SPAIN

Gen. Augustin Muñoz Grandes, vice premier.

SWEDEN

Prince Bertil.

Tage Erlander, premier.

Olaf Palme, minister without portfolio.

SWITZERLAND

Dr. Friedrich T. Wahlen, chief of the Federal Political Department.

Pierre Micheli, secretary general of the Federal Political Department.

TURKEY

Ismet Inonu, premier.

Feridun Cemal Erkin, foreign minister.

U.S.S.R.

Anastas I. Mikoyan, first deputy premier.

YUGOSLAVIA

Koca Popovic, foreign minister.

Petar Stambolic, president of the Federal Executive Council.

THE VATICAN

The Most Rev. Egidio Vagnozzi, archbishop of Myra, apostolic delegate.

Africa

ALGERIA

Abdelkadir Chanderli, representative at the United Nations.

Haj Ben Alla, president of the National Assembly.

Amai Ouzegane, minister of state.
Cherif Guellal, ambassador to the United States.
Abdelazziz Bouteflika, foreign minister.

CAMEROON

Benoit Balla-Ondoux, foreign minister.

CONGO (BRAZZAVILLE)

E. D. Dadet, ambassador to the United States.

CONGO (LEOPOLDVILLE)

Jacques Masangu, deputy premier.

ETHIOPIA

Haile Selassie I, emperor of Ethiopia.
Ras Andare Atchew Massai.
Commander Iskander Desta.
Tefara-Woro Kidane-Wold.
Lij Kassa Wolde-Mariam.

GHANA

Miguel A. Ribeiro, ambassador to the United States.
K. Armah, high commissioner in London.
Alex Quaison-Sackey, representative at the United Nations.

GUINEA

Saifonlaye Diallo, minister of state.
Leon Maka, president of the National Assembly.
Alessane Dioh, minister of communications.

IVORY COAST

Phillipe Yace, president of the National Assembly.
Camille Alliali, minister delegate for foreign affairs.

LIBERIA

William A. Tolbert, vice president.
J. Rudolph Grimes, secretary of state.

LIBYA

Dr. Wahbi Elbouri, representative at the United Nations.

MALAGASY REPUBLIC

Louis Rakotomalela, ambassador to the United States.

MOROCCO

Prince Moulay Abdullah.
Ahmed Reda Guedira, foreign minister.
Abdelkadar Benjelloun, minister of justice.
Ali Benjelloun, ambassador to the United States.
Ahmed Taibi Benhima, representative at the United Nations.
Badir Din Senoussi, attaché to the royal cabinet.
Mohammaed Ziani, attaché to the cabinet of the foreign minister.
Gen. Mohammed Ameziane, inspector general of the royal armed forces.
Col. Moulay Hafid, director general of royal protocol.

SIERRA LEONE

Dr. John Karefa-Smart, minister of external affairs.

SOMALIA

Mohammed Ali Daar, under secretary for foreign affairs.

TANGANYIKA

Chief Erasto A. M. Mangyenya, representative at the United Nations.

TUNISIA

Bahi Ladgham, secretary of state for the presidency.
Mongi Slim, foreign minister.
Taieb Slim, representative at the United Nations.
Habib Bourguiba Jr.
Hachmi Quanes.

UGANDA

Apollo K. Kironde, representative at the United Nations.

UNITED ARAB REPUBLIC

Mahmond Fawsi, foreign minister.

Asia

CAMBODIA

Prince Norodom Kantol, president of the Council of Ministers.

CHINA

Tingfu F. Tsiang, ambassador to the United States.

INDIA

Mrs. Vijaya Lakshmi Pandit, delegate to the United Nations.

INDONESIA

Gen. Abdul Haris Nasution, minister for defense and security affairs.
Dr. Subjarwo Tjondronegoro, deputy foreign minister.

IRAN

Shaphur Gholam Reza.
Abbas Aram, foreign minister

ISRAEL

Zalman Shazar, president.
Mrs. Golda Meir, foreign minister.

JAPAN

Hayato Ikeda, premier.
Masayoshi Ohira, foreign minister.

JORDAN

Antone Atallah, foreign minister.

LEBANON

Ibrahim Ahdab, ambassador to the United States.
George Hakim, representative at the United Nations.

KOREA

Chung Hee Park, president.

LAOS

Tiao Khampan, ambassador to the United States.
Sisouk Na Champassak, ambassador to India.

PAKISTAN

Zulfiqar Ali Bhutto, foreign minister.

THE PHILIPPINES

Diosdado Macapagal, president, and his wife.

SAUDI ARABIA

Rashad Pharaon, ambassador to France.
Abdullah Hababi, chargé d'affaires in Washington.

THAILAND

Thanat Khouman, foreign minister.

VIETNAM

Tran Chanh Thanh, ambassador-designate.

AUSTRALIA

Sir Alexander McMullin, president of the Senate.

Western Hemisphere

ARGENTINA

Carlos Humberto Perette, vice president.

Dr. Miguel Angel Zavala Ortiz, foreign minister.
Brig. Ignacio Avalos, secretary of war.

BAHAMAS

Sir Roland Symonette, premier-designate.

BOLIVIA

Enrique Sanchez Delozada, ambassador to the United States.

BRAZIL

Senator Auro Moura Andrade, president of the Senate.
João Augusto De Araujo Castro, foreign minister.
Roberto de Oliveira Campos, ambassador to the United States.
Senator Zitorino Freire, majority leader.
Senator Antonio Carlos Konder Reis, minority leader.

CANADA

Lester B. Pearson, prime minister.
Paul Martin, external affairs minister.

CHILE

Carlos Martinez, representative at the United Nations.

COLOMBIA

Alberto Lieras Camargo, former president.

COSTA RICA

José Figueres, former president.

ECUADOR

Dr. Neftali Ponce Miranda, foreign minister.

EL SALVADOR

Dr. Hector Escobar Serrano, foreign minister.

GUATEMALA

Alberto Herrarte Gonzalez, foreign minister.
José de Dios Aguilar, private secretary to the Government.

JAMAICA

Sir Alexander Bustamante, prime minister.
Brig. Paul Cook, chief of staff.
James Lloyd, permanent secretary, External Affairs Ministry.
Noël Croswell, commissioner of police.

MEXICO

Manuel Tello, foreign minister.

NICARAGUA

Luis Somoza de Bayle, senator and former president.
Dr. Alfonso Ortega Urbina, foreign minister.

PANAMA

Galileo Solis, foreign minister.
Arturo Morgan Morales, of Foreign Ministry.

PERU

Dr. Victor Andres Belaunde, representative at the United Nations.

URUGUAY

Juan Felipe Yriart, ambassador to the United States.

VENEZUELA

Runaldo Leandro Mora, acting foreign minister.
Gen. Antonio Briceño Linares, defense minister.

Schedule for Funeral

Special to The New York Times

WASHINGTON, Nov. 24—*Following is the unofficial schedule of the approximate timing of the events tomorrow*:

9 A.M.—Lying in state at Capitol Rotunda ends.

10:15 A.M.—Mrs. Kennedy arrives at Capitol.

10:30 A.M.—Funeral procession from Capitol to St. Matthew's Roman Catholic Cathedral begins.

11 A.M.—Procession pauses at White House, where Mrs. Kennedy and dignitaries begin following caisson on foot.

Noon—Pontifical requiem mass begins, said by Richard Cardinal Cushing of Boston.

1 P.M.—Funeral procession starts to Arlington National Cemetery.

2 P.M.—Burial service.

3:30 P.M.—Mrs. Kennedy receives heads of state in the White House.

5:30 P.M.—Reception at the State Department for all visiting dignitaries.

Dignitaries Pose Big Security Task

Presence of Foreign Leaders Adds to Guard Problems

By BEN A. FRANKLIN

Special to The New York Times

WASHINGTON, Nov. 24—The arrival of 22 chiefs of state or heads of government and other high-ranking dignitaries for President Kennedy's funeral has posed security problems for Federal and local authorities that they described today as unequaled in the nation's history. The problems were magnified, officials said, by the suddenness of the arrivals, which ruled out the usual careful planning and "casing" of the dignitaries' quarters here.

Keith O. Lynch, the 46-year-old investigator who heads the State Department's division of protective security, said that more than 250 plainclothes agents from an assortment of Federal agencies had been mobilized by this afternoon for assignment to visiting dignitaries. Most of these agents are regular State Department security officers or investigators, Mr. Lynch said. They were called in from field offices of major cities across the country, including New York, Philadelphia, Pittsburgh, Chicago, San Francisco and Los Angeles.

The security chief said that all were "qualified and armed law-enforcement officers." Some of them, he said, carried "special equipment" —a euphemism for submachine guns. The State Department also called on the Defense Department for an undisclosed number of plainclothesmen from two agencies of the Army—the Counterintelligence Corps and the Criminal Investigation Division. Defense Department vehicles and communications equipment were being used to augment the State Department's own facilities.

The District of Columbia police also reported unusual activity. Leaves and days off for the department's 2,900 men were canceled Friday, when the magnitude of the traffic and other problems of the funeral began to be appreciated. Today, Inspector John L. Sullivan, head of the Metropolitan

Police special investigation squad and the department's liaison man with Federal law-enforcement agencies, said that the presence of the foreign delegations "gives us the greatest security job we ever had in my 23 years in this business."

The city police, under the supervision of Deputy Chief Howard V. Covell, were providing uniformed motorcycle escorts for each foreign delegation. Special foot patrols and scout-car surveillance of embassies, consulates and hotels were ordered this afternoon. Plainclothesmen assigned to coordinate their work with the State Department's security force were under the command of Inspector John B. Layton, chief of detectives.

In addition, many of the visiting foreign officials have their own extensive security teams or bodyguards with them, the State Department said. "They will be absorbed as part of the security team," a spokesman said.

The problems of protocol, transportation, communications and logistics, as well as security, were being dealt with in a special command post on the seventh floor of the State Department building.

There, about 25 State Department officials, many of them in shirt sleeves, worked [amid] a clutter of telephones between an array of maps, charts and blackboards showing the routes, the time and place of arrival, and the location of visiting dignitaries.

This center was under the supervision of William B. Connett, deputy executive secretary of the State Department secretariat and director of the department's operations center. Mr. Connett was assisted by representatives of the five regional bureaus of the department, and by officials of the Visa Bureau, the Office of Protocol and the security office.

MACMILLAN WILL LEAD
THE HOUSE OF COMMONS
IN ITS TRIBUTE TO KENNEDY TODAY

Home and Others to Be at Funeral

Bonn, Berlin and Paris Join in Expressions of Grief for Slain President

By LAWRENCE FELLOWS

Special to The New York Times

LONDON, Nov. 24—When Parliament meets tomorrow to pay its last tribute to President Kennedy, Harold Macmillan is expected to be there to speak of the dead president as he knew him. It will be the first time Mr. Macmillan has been in the House of Commons since his illness and retirement last month as prime minister.

The House of Lords had been scheduled to assemble on Tuesday, but it will also meet tomorrow to pay tribute to the man whose premature death has shocked this nation. The prime minister, Sir Alec Douglas-Home, will not be there. He and the leaders of the other political parties left for Washington tonight to attend Mr. Kennedy's funeral tomorrow. Queen Elizabeth II, who is expecting her fourth child, will be represented at the funeral by her husband, the duke of Edinburgh.

Before leaving for Washington the prime minister, Harold Wilson, the Labor party leader, and Jo Grimond, Liberal party leader, joined more than 1,200 persons in Westminister Abbey to mourn Mr. Kennedy and offer prayers for his family and country.

Anglican churches over the country were holding commemoration services for Mr. Kennedy, as asked for by the archbishop of Canterbury. The tributes extended equally to the churches of all denominations. So many persons waited in front of the American Embassy to write their condolences that the embassy staff added six writing tables to the six already there. A Salvation Army band marched through Grosvenor Square, in front of the embassy, playing solemn music.

At the 13th-century parish church of St. Etheldreda's, at Hatfield in

Hertfordshire, Queen Mother Elizabeth, accompanied by the marquess and marchioness of Salisbury, heard the rector, the Rev. John Stow, say that President Kennedy represented the generation that had grown into responsibility and power since World War II. Special prayers were said in St. Paul's Cathedral. A national memorial service will be held there next Sunday.

Bonn's Faith Unshaken

Special to The New York Times

BONN, Nov. 24—Chancellor Erhard reaffirmed today West Germany's faith in United States leadership. Before leaving for Washington with President Heinrich Lübke, the chancellor presided at a special meeting of the West German Cabinet in memory of the dead president.

The chancellor said he was going to Washington to say what he had planned to say to the president on the same day. Dr. Erhard was to have made a two-day working visit to Washington this week. The plane on which he departed today was the one that had been scheduled to take him to his eagerly awaited first meeting with President Kennedy as chancellor. Dr. Erhard assured his cabinet that cooperation between Bonn and the United States would continue.

President Kennedy had regarded the unity of the West as the most important goal of his foreign policy, the chancellor said. "We shall proceed in his spirit if we stand firm on this policy now, in cooperation with President Johnson."

Throughout West Germany this was a day of deep mourning. Pastors delivered eulogies of President Kennedy in hundreds of churches. Flowers were laid at places associated with the president—at the Schoeneberger City Hall in West Berlin, where he spoke last June, at United States consulates and America Houses throughout the country.

Brandt Pays Tribute

Special to The New York Times

BERLIN, Nov. 24—Mayor Willy Brandt of West Berlin pledged today the full support of the German people to the new American president.

"I am convinced the hands of the entire German people in both parts of our country are reaching out toward the new president," the mayor said in a radio address. Berliners knew Mr. Johnson, he added, and "have confidence in him." The former vice president flew to the city with American assurances of support on Aug. 19, 1961, at the height of the crisis less than a week after the Communists had built their wall to cut Berlin in two. Most of the mayor's speech was a tribute to President Kennedy, whose death, he said, "has struck us as that of a brother."

The Communist press in East Berlin continued to devote a large amount of space to the news of Mr. Kennedy's assassination. *Neues Deutschland,* the Communist party organ, charged that reactionary forces in the United States were attempting to lay the blame for the crime on Communism.

All through the day thousands of Berliners stood patiently in long lines in front of the City Hall and United States headquarters to add their signatures to condolence lists laid out at both places.

Memorial Rites in Paris

Special to The New York Times

PARIS, Nov. 24—Americans in Paris joined Frenchmen across the nation today to pay homage to the memory of President Kennedy. More than 1,500 people crowded into the gothic American Cathedral of Paris for a simple memorial service conducted by the dean, the Very Rev. Sturgis Lee Riddle.

Charles E. Bohlen, United States ambassador to France, read the lesson from the Scripture. The ambassador to the North Atlantic Treaty Organization, Thomas K. Finletter, and Gen. Lyman L. Lemnitzer, supreme allied commander in Europe, attended the Protestant Episcopal service. After the memorial service Mr. Bohlen went to Orly Airport to see General de Gaulle off for the United States to attend the funeral service in Washington tomorrow.

Across France, from Calais to Nice, town councils and community organizations paid their respects in varied ways. United States military bases organized ceremonies for troops based in France. A 21-gun salute will be fired at Orléans tomorrow, followed by a salvo of 50 cannon, one for each state of the Union.

Sorrow All Over World

Thoughout the world—from a simple chapel at the United States Navy Antarctic Base at McMurdo Sound to the magnificence of St. Peter's Square in Rome—people in every station of life mourned the death of President Kennedy yesterday.

In Portugal people wore black ties and placed mourning bands on their arms. In Kenya 5,000 tribesmen sent condolences to Washington after being informed by Tom Mboya, minister of justice and constitutional affairs, of the president's assassination. Memorial services were held in many countries, East and West—in Buddhist pagodas, Roman Catholic and Protestant churches and cathedrals, Greek Orthodox churches and Jewish synagogues.

In Italy, thousands of Sunday afternoon soccer fans stood in silence for a minute. Nearly 6,000 Spaniards expressed their mourning in Madrid by signing a register at the United States Embassy. In Belgrade a student wrote in a book of condolences at the Embassy: "I am one of 19 million Yugoslavs who sincerely admired his dynamism and efforts for the preservation of peace. With his death we lose a great friend."

In Israel, a three-day period of mourning has been proclaimed and a special meeting of the Knesset (Parliament) will be held today in tribute to Mr. Kennedy. Elsewhere in the Middle East statesmen and ordinary people mourned. In Beirut, Dr. Charles Malik, former president of the

United Nations General Assembly, delivered a eulogy at a high mass held at the American University. In Amman, King Hussein of Jordan announced he would attend a Roman Catholic memorial service today.

On the Indian subcontinent Urdu-language newspapers throughout Pakistan marked Mr. Kennedy's death with blade-bordered eulogies. In New Delhi, V. K. Krishna Menon, probably India's severest critic of the United States, called the assassination a "great tragedy for the world." The Indian Government announced that Prime Minister Jawaharlal Nehru would attend a memorial service today at the United States Embassy and would then go to Parliament to make a statement on President Kennedy's death. The Government's offices will be closed today.

Farther east, flags on public buildings flew at half-staff throughout Indonesia, where three days of mourning have been announced. In Africa, expressions of mourning were reported from many points. In Togo, President Nicholas Grunitzky delivered a eulogy in a broadcast. In Addis Ababa, Ethiopia, Crown Prince Asfa Wassen signed a book of condolences at the American Embassy. Liberia, a West African state with close ties to the United States, began 30 days of national mourning. A week of official mourning was begun in Algeria.

Praise for President Kennedy was expressed in newspapers in Japan, in the Philippines and in Burma. In Trinidad, hotels and clubs canceled all dancing and other entertainment. In Lima, the Peruvian House of Representatives voted unanimously to nominate Mr. Kennedy for a Nobel Peace Prize.

Mikoyan Flies to Washington as Russians Praise Kennedy

Moscow Television Broadcasts Special Program on Years in White House and Newscasts of Ceremonies

By HENRY TANNER

Special to The New York Times

MOSCOW, Nov. 24—The Soviet press, radio and television continued tonight to praise and mourn President Kennedy as Anastas I. Mikoyan was on his way to Washington to attend the United States leader's funeral. Mr. Mikoyan, one of two Soviet first deputy premiers, was regarded as the logical choice to represent Premier Khrushchev at the funeral. He has frequently carried out important missions abroad in the name of the premier.

A Moscow television station, for the second day, interrupted its schedule tonight to broadcast a special program, *In Memory of President John F. Kennedy*. The program showed some of the highlights of Mr. Kennedy's years in the White House. In one of the scenes, a little more than a year ago, the president defined in a speech the United States Government's position on civil rights more clearly than it had ever been heard by a Soviet audience.

The program also included newscasts by Eurovision, the West European television network, and Intervision, the Soviet-bloc network, of events in Washington today. There were scenes of the Arlington National Cemetery and the White House and some of President Johnson with Secretary of State Dean Rusk and other visitors. No such newscast had been shown here before.

At one point, the voice of the Soviet narrator, a woman, broke with emotion. One observer commented that President Kennedy, in death, had brought the United States closer and more clearly before Soviet eyes than ever.

At the same time, it became increasingly clear that Soviet official circles have been badly stung by reports that the president's assassin had Communist connections. Western observers felt that a dangerous and potentially catastrophic situation might build up if a trans-Atlantic dispute over the political motives behind the murder were permitted to develop. Soviet newspapers, as well as radio and television commentators, charged that the Dallas police and a part of the American press were trying to whip up an anti-Soviet and anti-Cuban campaign.

All Soviet commentators have been consistently saying that rightists, "not a leftist," were responsible for the president's death. Tonight a television announcer seized upon the shooting of Lee Harvey Oswald, President Kennedy's accused assassin, to assert that the attack on the president had been engineered by a vast organization, not a single fanatic, and that every effort was being made by the Texas authorities to cover up for the real culprit.

He compared Oswald to Marinus van der Lubbe, the Dutchman who was convicted by the Nazis of having set fire to the Reichstag, the German Parliament building, in 1933. The Soviet press agency Tass, in a dispatch from its New York correspondent, said the killing of Oswald meant that "the murderers of President Kennedy are trying to cover up their tracks." A speaker said earlier on the Moscow radio that Senator Barry Goldwater, Republican of Arizona, and other "extremists" of the right could not escape moral responsibility for the president's death.

Tass quoted tonight the Rev. Martin Luther King, the Negro integrationist leader, as having said that the president's assassination had to be viewed against the background of growing violence engendered by the racial issue in the South. It also quoted Ralph McGill as having written in *The Atlanta Constitution* that Southern editors were receiving anonymous phone calls from people who gloated over the president's death.

Mr. Mikoyan was seen off at the airport by the United States ambassador, Foy D. Kohler, high Soviet Government officials and senior officers of the embassy. Before boarding the plane he said he was going to Washington at the request of "the Soviet Government and Nikita Khrushchev personally" to pay a last tribute to President Kennedy.

The choice of Mr. Mikoyan had been announced to Mr. Kohler by Mr. Khrushchev yesterday morning. It was not known whether later, as a result of the decision by President de Gaulle and other Western heads of state to go to Washington, Mr. Khrushchev had considered making the trip himself.

Western diplomats all along had virtually ruled out the possibility that Mr. Khrushchev would fly to Washington.

U.S. Servicemen in Japan Mourn Death at All Bases

TOKYO, Monday, Nov. 25 (AP)—Guns roared out final salutes at United States bases in Japan today as American servicemen mourned the death of President Kennedy. In Yokosuka harbor, the rain-drenched cruiser *Providence* fired a single gun every half hour in a salute to the president.

Every United States base in Japan went into mourning and thousands of the 46,000 American servicemen in this country attended nondenominational prayer services. All men not holding essential jobs were excused from duty.

"I've never felt so far away from home," said a United States sailor on leave in Tokyo. "I wanted to go home when I heard the news."

A Crowd Gathers at Johnson Home

Arrival of President's Wife Is Virtually Unnoticed

WASHINGTON, Nov. 24 (AP)—For the first time since Lyndon B. Johnson became president on Friday, a crowd gathered outside his home in northwest Washington today. Mrs. Johnson arrived almost unnoticed at 2:40 P.M. after having said good-by to Mrs. John F. Kennedy at the Capitol, where the body of President Kennedy had been taken.

Mr. Johnson rode in the limousine with Mrs. Kennedy and the two young Kennedy children in the procession from the White House to the Capitol.

Waiting at home for Mrs. Johnson was a myriad of matters to be handled. Among other things, she will have to begin moving to the White House, but there has been no announcement of when the move will be made. Mrs. Johnson has been coming and going quietly in the traffic jams of Washington. She rides in a black limousine with a chauffeur and Secret Service man in the front but does not have a police escort.

Lucy, dark-haired 16-year-old younger daughter of the Johnsons, went to church with her parents this morning and returned home around 1:30 P.M. Lynda, 19, the older daughter, a sophomore at the University of Texas, is not coming here at this time.

More than 100 persons stood in the sunshine on a cool Sunday afternoon just looking at the Johnson home, which once belonged to Mrs. Perle Mesta, famed Washington party giver. The neighborhood, known as Spring Valley, has large homes with large lawns. The sightseers spread across the lawns near the Johnson home, which resembles a French chateau. It sits atop a small hill with extensive grounds around it.

Policemen stood guard around the Johnson home, and a Secret Service man was at the wrought-iron gate to the driveway. At one point Lucy ran her own errand, driving her own car, a white convertible with a black top. She is now in the family of the president, so a Secret Service man rode beside her. They returned a few minutes later with another girl, apparently a friend of Lucy, riding in the back seat.

The sightseers were interested in all of the television paraphernalia that had been set up across the street and watched reporters at their work. Telephones for the reporters have been placed on the ground underneath two maple trees across the street from the Johnson home.

JOHNSON AFFIRMS AIMS IN VIETNAM

Retains Kennedy's Policy of Aiding War on Reds— Lodge Briefs President

By E. W. KENWORTHY
Special to The New York Times

WASHINGTON, Nov. 24—President Johnson reaffirmed today the policy objectives of his predecessor regarding South Vietnam. He called upon all Government agencies to support that policy with full unity of purpose. This was disclosed by White House sources after a meeting between President Johnson and Henry Cabot Lodge, United States ambassador to South Vietnam. The meeting lasted nearly an hour. It was described as being devoted to a full review of the conclusions reached by participants in a strategy conference on South Vietnam held in Honolulu last Wednesday.

In another move today that emphasized the president's desire to convey at home and abroad the impression of continuity, Mr. Johnson asked all members of the White House staff to remain at their jobs. This was announced by Pierre Salinger, White House press secretary. Mr. Salinger said the president would leave up to the officials involved how long they wished to serve him.

Inevitably some of these officials—especially those from the universities and foundations—will decide to leave their posts after an interval. But the President's request today would seem to insure that during the difficult days of adjustment and transition he would continue to have the benefit of the experience of key policy figures.

Attending the meeting between the president and Ambassador Lodge today were Secretary of State Dean Rusk, Secretary of Defense Robert S.

McNamara, Under Secretary of State George W. Ball, John A. McCone, director of the Central Intelligence Agency, and McGeorge Bundy, special assistant to the president for national security affairs. Secretaries Rusk and McNamara, Ambassador Lodge and Mr. Bundy all took part in the Honolulu conference.

As a result of the meeting, White House informants said, President Johnson laid down a general policy line emphasizing the following: First, the central point of United States policy on South Vietnam remains; namely, to assist the new government there in winning the war against the Communist Vietcong insurgents. The adoption of all measures should be determined by their potential contribution to this overriding objective. Second, the White House statement of Oct. 2 on the withdrawal of American troops from South Vietnam remains in force. This statement, reflecting a decision of the National Security Council, said the program for training of Vietnamese troops should have progressed by the end of this year to the point "where 1,000 United States military personnel" can be withdrawn. The United States now has 16,500 military men in South Vietnam. Third, all United States agencies represented in Vietnam are to assist the present Government in its tasks of consolidation and the development of public support for programs directed toward winning the war.

President Johnson, according to a White House source, asked that all agencies in the field support these policies with full unity of purpose. When asked why the president should feel it necessary to ask for unity, the source said that since the visit to South Vietnam of Secretary McNamara and Gen. Maxwell D. Taylor, chairman of the Joint Chiefs of Staff, last September, the agencies in the field had been united on policies to be followed. However, he said that prior to that time there had been differences of views.

It is known that the Defense Department and the C.I.A. thought political reforms by the government of then President Ngo Dinh Diem should take second place to the task of fighting the Communists. The State Department, on the other hand, felt increasingly that public support for the war effort depended on political and economic reforms, particularly a cessation of persecution of Buddhists by the Roman Catholic–dominated regime.

Despite the emphasis President Johnson laid today on winning the war, officials said that at Honolulu there had been a concentration on "something besides winning the war." The conference participants, it was said, were fully aware that a sounder economic base for the new government must be built and that the lot of the villagers must be improved. It was agreed that unless these objectives could be achieved, the government might well collapse, even though the war against the Communists was going better.

Consequently, it was said, there was agreement that the United States must provide as much economic aid as possible. It was realized that the uncertain political situation in South Vietnam required a delicate balancing of economic measures. On the one hand, it was explained, there must be some austerity to curb inflation; on the other, the austerity must not be so great as to generate disaffection with the new government. All in all, officials said, the tone of the Honolulu meeting was hopeful despite recognition of the pitfalls. It is safe to conclude, officials said today, that all this was conveyed to President Johnson.

Officials cautioned against interpreting today's meeting as an indication of renewed crisis. Ambassador Lodge, they noted, had been scheduled to come here after the Honolulu meeting to report to President Kennedy. He was to have dined with Mr. Kennedy today. Following the assassination of President Kennedy, they said, it was decided that Ambassador Lodge should come as planned. It was decided also that his report to President Johnson should not be postponed until after the funeral of President Kennedy tomorrow. The ambassador, they said, wished to return to Saigon as soon as possible in order to convey to the government personally his assurances that the new Administration meant no change of policy.

Having dealt with South Vietnam, President Johnson, it was learned, will turn this week to the problems facing the Alliance for Progress in Latin America. He will confer with Secretary Rusk and Assistant Secretary of State Edwin M. Martin. The latter has been in Argentina in connection with the cancellation of contracts with United States oil companies.

President Johnson had a long, arduous, emotion-filled day. At 10 A.M. he received a 30-minute intelligence briefing at his home by Mr. McCone and Mr. Bundy. At 11 he attended services with his wife and 16-year-old daughter, Lucy, at St. Mark's Episcopal Church upon Capitol Hill. He then went to the White House to accompany the body of President Kennedy to the Capitol. On returning to his office after the ceremonies in the Capitol Rotunda, his face was drawn, and tears welled in his eyes.

After the meeting with Mr. Lodge, the president had courtesy visits from Gov. Otto Kerner of Illinois and Mayor Richard Daley of Chicago and from Lieut. Gov. Preston Smith and Attorney General Waggoner Carr of Texas. The press of business and visits kept the president in his office until after 7 P.M.

Officials at the White House and State Department worked today on drafts of the address the president will deliver to Congress Wednesday. The speech, which will be broadcast by radio and television, will almost certainly not deal in any detail with specific problems. It is the president's intention, officials said, to assure the nation and the world of the continuity of the essential purposes and policies of the United States. Beyond that, he will appeal—as President Truman did 18 years ago—for the support of the Congress and the nation and will assure them he will fill his office to the best of his ability.

Johnson Scored by Chinese Reds

Views Called "Reactionary"—Taiwan Aid Attacked

By UNITED PRESS INTERNATIONAL

TOKYO, Nov. 24—Communist China bitterly criticized President Johnson today and termed him a supporter of the late President Kennedy's "trickery policy."

"Since the emergence of the Kennedy regime," the Chinese Communist press agency Hsinhua said, "Johnson has positively supported various reactionary policies of the Kennedy Administration and participated in formulating and promoting such policies. Johnson has supported Kennedy's trickery policy and has called for the maintenance of such a policy in a series of his speeches."

The Chinese Communists reported the assassination of President Kennedy in a four-paragraph dispatch eight hours after it occurred. But they made no comment. Hsinhua said Mr. Johnson "was one of the central figures in the Kennedy Government and has made frequent trips abroad." The Chinese statement added that Mr. Johnson believed "the United States, in making two-faced antirevolutionary plots, must maintain a strong position on the basis of strong force. He also looks toward Cuba with animosity and has called for the elimination of the Cuban revolutionary Government. He once stated: 'We will never be satisfied until Communism is eliminated from Cuba and the Western Hemisphere.' "

Hsinhua asserted that President Johnson took "a strong position against the Chinese people" by his support of the Nationalists in Taiwan. "This was evident," the agency said, "when he visited Taiwan shortly after he became vice president, and guaranteed a nonreduction of United States assistance to [President] Chiang Kai-shek and assured him the United States would take responsibility for defending Taiwan."

Peking Children Applaud

PEKING, Nov. 24 (Reuters)—Chinese Communist newspapers published today 300-word identical inside-page reports on the assassination of President Kennedy. They also published 600-word biographical sketches of President Johnson with caricatures and photographs showing him grim and unsmiling.

Authoritative sources said schoolchildren here applauded yesterday when they were told of the death of Mr. Kennedy, who had been represented to them in Peking propaganda as the world's wickedest man. A diplomat from a neutral country reported that a Chinese member of the embassy staff commented when he heard of the assassination: "That's good news. He was a very wicked man."

The Chinese trade-union newspaper, *Kungjen Jih Pao,* printed a cartoon entitled "Kennedy Biting the Dust." It depicted the late president lying face down after he had been shot. The biographical sketch of Mr. Johnson contained a brief history of his political career and excerpts from his recent speeches. It said he was a millionaire who "represents the interests of big oilmen and ranch owners in the South and big capitalists and industrialists in the North."

Taiwan Warm to Johnson

Special to The New York Times

TAIPEI, Taiwan, Nov. 24—Nationalist China is mourning the death of President Kennedy. The Chinese Nationalists admired Mr. Kennedy for his ability and demonstration of toughness against the Communists, as in the 1962 Cuba crisis, but there was some apprehension here about his policies, particularly with regard to Taiwan's interests.

A major concern of the Chinese Nationalists was what they considered Mr. Kennedy's refusal to see the immediate need and feasibility of ousting the Chinese Communist regime through a United States–supported Nationalist invasion of the mainland. There is a certain amount of guarded optimism now that issues affecting Taiwan's interests may improve under President Johnson's Administration. Mr. Johnson left a lasting impression as "true friend" as a result of his visit here in May, 1961.

North Vietnamese Critical

TOKYO, Nov. 24 (AP)—*Nhan Dan,* official newspaper of the Communist party of North Vietnam, said in an editorial today that "the reactionaries now ruling in the United States will follow the aggressive path" of the late President Kennedy. The newspaper's editorial was broadcast by the Hanoi radio. The organ of the North Vietnamese Communists, who have backed Peking in its ideological quarrel with Moscow, added in an apparent allusion to Premier Khrushchev and President Tito of Yugoslavia: "The revisionists are stupefied and have expressed sorrow at the loss of a bellicose ringleader of imperialism who, they said, had goodwill for peace and was neither imperialist nor bellicose."

2 Suggest Johnson Meet Khrushchev

WASHINGTON, Nov. 24 (UPI)—Two senators said today that a "get-acquainted" meeting between President Johnson and Premier Khrushchev might be useful under certain conditions. Both senators, J. W. Fulbright, Democrat of Arkansas, and Bourke B. Hickenlooper, Republican of Iowa, opposed an early summit conference or negotiating session between the two heads of state—anything more than a chance to "feel each other out."

Mr. Fulbright, chairman of the Senate Foreign Relations Committee, said he believed Mr. Johnson and Mr. Khrushchev must be profoundly curious about each other. He saw in the Soviet leader's "expression of condolence" to the United States yesterday a hopeful sign that "he would like to maintain reasonably good relations." Mr. Hickenlooper, the committee's ranking Republican, and Mr. Fulbright generally agreed that the nation's foreign policy would remain unchanged, although perhaps carried out in a new pattern under Mr. Johnson.

Britons See Hope of Leading West

Lord Avon Says Home Has Experience "to Play Part"

By SYDNEY GRUSON

Special to The New York Times

LONDON, Nov. 24—A suggestion that President Johnson's relative inexperience with foreign affairs provides a new opportunity for British leadership has begun to appear in some London assessments of the future. The idea was broached in articles in three Sunday newspapers. Two of the articles were by well-known Britons.

One outcome of the death of President Kennedy "seems inevitable—the responsibilities of this country will be increased," wrote the earl of Avon, the former Sir Anthony Eden, who was foreign secretary and later prime minister. "Fortunately," he added, "our new Prime Minister, Sir Alec Douglas-Home, is well-equipped by his years in the Foreign Office to play the part which the new circumstances and the cause of peace will now demand."

The idea of Britain's taking up some special task was also broached by Richard Crossman, a Labor party leader. His main difference with Lord Avon appeared to be in his suggestion that the task was one for a Labor Government, not for Sir Alec's Conservatives. Mr. Crossman conceded that the leadership of the West must remain with the United States. But President Kennedy's "special contribution" to world peace, he added, must either be lost forever or assumed "by another member of the Western alliance." Mr. Crossman asked: "By whom?" and said: "One has only to ask the question to see the answer. Britain is the only country which could fill the gap—under the right leadership."

An unsigned editorial-page column in *The People* suggested that Sir Alec might become a "go-between" between the United States, Britain and France and "might even for a time be its [the Western alliance's] spokesman with Russia."

British officials, as distinct from politicians, belittle the idea that Britain, with her strained economic resources and relatively meager military strength, is in a position to speak for the Western world. But the idea's arising so swiftly after President Kennedy's death seems to reflect two things about Britain. One is that being a secondary power still frustrates many Britons and leaves them dissatisfied. The other is that the longing for past greatness is never far below any surface acceptance of Britain's present place in the world.

Castro Declares U.S. May Change

Tells Cubans Kennedy Death May Alter Foreign Policy

Special to The New York Times

MIAMI, Nov. 24—Premier Fidel Castro warned Cuba last night that the assassination of President Kennedy was "grave and bad news from the political point of view." He said it could change United States foreign policy "from bad to worse." In a two-hour radio and television address, the Cuban leader gave what he called an "objective analysis of facts, consequences and repercussions" that the assassination might have. His views, he said, represented the opinion of his associates.

Dr. Castro called the news "grave and bad" in spite of the fact that, as he said, "we have been victims of constant hostility on the part of the U.S. and among the leaders of the U.S., great responsibility for these acts fell on President Kennedy." The premier said that Cubans "hate the imperialist and capitalist system," but as Marxist-Leninists "we recognize that the role of a man is small and relative" and [his death] need cause no joy.

Discussing a possible "fight for power" that might affect Washington's foreign policy, he said that within the United States there are "ultraconservative elements" and "liberal elements," the latter being those who "think in terms of diplomacy rather than force." Quoting constantly from news-agency dispatches from Dallas, he termed information about Lee H. Oswald, who was accused of the assassination, a "Machiavellian plan against Cuba."

"Oswald never had contacts with us, we never heard of him," Dr. Castro said. "But in the dispatches he is always represented as a Castro Communist. This is all part of a defamatory campaign against the U.S.S.R. and Cuba.

"What is behind this assassination no one knows," Dr. Castro went on. He called Oswald "an individual expressly fabricated to begin an anti-Communist campaign to liquidate the president because of his policy." He said that "all people, including the United States people, should demand that what is behind this assassination be clarified," and said that "those who love peace and the United States intellectuals should comprehend the gravity of this campaign."

Excerpts From Castro Talk

Special to The New York Times

MIAMI, Nov. 24—*Following, in unofficial translation, are excerpts from a speech broadcast in Spanish last night by Premier Fidel Castro of Cuba and monitored here:*

We have to make an analysis of the facts, consequences and repercussions that the assassination of President Kennedy might have.

The policies of the administrations of President Eisenhower and President Kennedy have been characterized by a spirit of aggression and hostility. We have been victims of constant hostility on the part of the United States, and among the leaders of the United States great responsibility for those acts fell on President Kennedy.

However, the assassination of the president of the United States is grave and bad news. We should comprehend it very well. This kind of act affects the sensibility of every man.

Before an act of this nature I react in this way and I believe this is the reaction of most human beings, who repudiate assassination.

There are cases where amid repression the revolutionaries are forced to defend themselves, they are forced to kill to defend themselves. Given the circumstances that surround the assassination of the president, we understand there is no justification for it.

From the political point of view, I was saying it is grave and bad news. Some people will ask why it is that for Cubans, who have been victims of so much aggression on the part of the United States, on the part of the Kennedy Administration, it should be bad news?

Cubans should react to it like revolutionaries. We don't hate men. We hate the imperialist and capitalistic system. We should not confuse the hatred for a system with the sentiments we should have for men.

As Marxist-Leninists we recognize that the role of a man is small and relative in society. We should be glad about the death of a system. The disappearance of a system would always cause us joy. But the death of a man, although this man is an enemy, does not have to cause us joy. We always bow with respect in front of death.

The death of President Kennedy can have very negative repercussions for the interests of our country, but in this case it is not the question of our interest, but of the interests of the whole world.

Unquestionably, when there is an authority within the United States, a forceful authority, the dangers from reactionary currents are much smaller.

Then suddenly a situation arises in which a president, because of the circumstances in which he takes power—that is, being a vice president—does not gain power with the same personal authority that President Kennedy had.

And therefore a question mark begins to appear about the influence of all these forces on the Administration.

Within the United States there are reactionary or racist elements contrary to civil rights and racial fights for the Negroes, Ku Klux Klan, powerful economic interests, equally ultraconservative, partisans of direct invasion of Cuba.

Also there are liberal currents—more advanced, moderate right, certain intellectual circles that are not thinking in terms of force but in terms of diplomacy.

The death of President Kennedy could be beneficial only to those ultraconservative circles among which President Kennedy could not have been situated. The death of President Kennedy can change the United States foreign policy from bad to worse.

The information about Lee H. Oswald is a Machiavellian plan against Cuba. Oswald never had contacts with us—we have never heard of him. But in the dispatches he's always presented as a Castro Communist.

This is all part of a defamatory campaign against the U.S.S.R. and Cuba. This is a sinister trick.

The first thing that appears to be a lie is that this man was a president of the Fair Play for Cuba Committee in New Orleans.

We have searched through all our files and this man is not listed as president of any committee. Nowhere is there any mention of any Fair Play for Cuba Committee in Dallas or New Orleans.

What is behind this assassination no one knows. Oswald is an individual expressly fabricated to begin an anti-Communist campaign to liquidate the president because of his policy.

This plan to call Oswald a Castro Communist is designed to pressure the new Administration.

All people, including the United States people, should demand that what is behind this assassination be clarified. Those who love peace and the United States intellectuals should comprehend the gravity of this campaign.

Mrs. Nhu Recalls Saigon Coup in a Message to Mrs. Kennedy

ROME, Nov. 24 (UPI)—Mrs. Ngo Dinh Nhu sent a message today to Mrs. John F. Kennedy saying that the president's death must be particularly unbearable "because of your habitually well-sheltered life." Mrs. Nhu termed the assassination "that ordeal which God has bestowed on you." She compared it with the slaying in a coup d'état Nov. 2 of her brother-in-law, President Ngo Dinh Diem of South Vietnam, and her husband, Ngo Dinh Nhu. She said that "even the wounds inflicted on President Kennedy were identical" to those of Mr. Diem and of her husband.

Mrs. Nhu was in the United States on a lecture tour when the Vietnamese coup took place. Her three youngest children were brought to Rome and she joined them here later. The text of Mrs. Nhu's message to Mrs. Kennedy follows:

"Though not having the pleasure to know you or hearing from you personally, I wish to tell you of my profound sympathy for you and your little ones in your time of shock and grief. Though I have said that anything happening in Vietnam will surely find equivalence in the U.S.A., truly I would not wish for anyone [to endure] what the Vietnamese and myself are now enduring while we were so near our victory against Communism.

"But though not being proven alike, I understand fully how you should feel before that ordeal which God has bestowed on you. I sympathize the more for I understand that that ordeal might seem to you even more unbearable because of your habitually well-sheltered life, notwithstanding how particularly incomprehensible it would be if, as reported, President Kennedy's assassination comes from Communist hands.

"Indeed, such a murder, where even the wounds inflicted on President Kennedy were identical to those of President Ngo Dinh Diem, and of my husband, and coming only 20 days after the Vietnamese tragedy, would only prove to the world that even power or extreme graciousness with Communism still does not protect from its traitorous blows.

"My children and I have especially prayed for President Kennedy when we learned that he did not regain consciousness to receive the last sacraments of the church. Be assured also that our most sincere thoughts and prayers are with you and your dear ones."

South, in Its Grief for Kennedy, Finds a Spirit of National Unity

Reacts Against Extremism of Both Left and Right— Hope Rises for Easing of Social and Political Strife

By CLAUDE SITTON

Special to The New York Times

ATLANTA, Nov. 24—Grief over President Kennedy's death brought a renewed spirit of national unity today among Southerners and a reaction against extremism from either the left or the right. These were the sentiments expressed in the tragedy's sober aftermath by the region's leaders, its press and its people. They indicate that the young president may accomplish in death what he had been unable to achieve in life—an easing of social and political strife.

Comments throughout the 11 former Confederate states reflected the belief that emotionalism during recent months had drawn the nation near the precipice of disaster. There seemed to be agreement on the necessity of reappraisal—if not of positions on such critical issues as racial change, at least of the manner in which these positions have been defended. This new attitude will undoubtedly affect the South's course in next year's presidential election. Even before the president's assassination, opposition had set in against the extremes to which many of his right-wing detractors had gone in attacking him, his family and his program.

Generally, however, politics was pushed aside as the South joined the nation in mourning. State, county and city heads of government requested that public facilities close tomorrow, some for the entire day and others for the period of the funeral services. Newspapers throughout the region carried black-bordered advertisements from businesses announcing that they would shut their doors in tribute. Most Southern churches and synagogues held special worship services and some remained open at night for prayer.

Residents of middle Tennessee participated in a memorial service this afternoon presided over by Gov. Frank G. Clement at the War Memorial Auditorium in Nashville. In Birmingham, Ala., copies of President Johnson's proclamation of mourning and floral wreaths were placed on the main doors of the City Hall. In Augusta, Ga., officials of the Knights of Columbus, a Roman Catholic layman's order, formally organized a new council, named for the late president. And at Cape Canaveral, Fla., scientists postponed the launching of two satellites from Tuesday to Wednesday so that workers might observe the day of mourning. A number of Southern radio and television stations canceled all commercials and entertainment programs out of respect to Mr. Kennedy.

But there was more than the shock and grief demonstrated and apparently sincerely felt by all but the relative handful of Southerners who expressed satisfaction. A thread of guilt and national shame ran through the comments. In a statement prepared for delivery tomorrow at a Baptist Sunday School Board service in Nashville, Dr. James L. Sullivan, its executive secretary-treasurer, said: "We tend to forget that respect for those in governmental authority is both patriotic and Christian. We show neither loyalty to our country nor to the Christian spirit when we allow tirades against the president to become the favorite indoor sport in America."

C. B. Deane of Rockingham, N.C., a friend of the president during and after their service together in Congress, asserted: "History will surely record, in my opinion, that the assassin's bullet represents the hatred, bitterness, the feeling of superiority, the racial and ideological conflicts, the religious animosities, the extremist views of the right and left that are the mark of our day. Because of this friction and division, the president has given his life. Few of us can escape some of the responsibility for what has resulted from this tragedy."

W. C. Hamilton, executive secretary to Birmingham's Mayor Albert Boutwell, recalled that Mr. Kennedy had been friendly and sympathetic to that city during its racial crises. He added: "The violence of his death can only point up, to us here in Birmingham, the vicious danger of equating political differences with personal hatred. His assassination and the enormity of the consequences serve to damn all the ministers of hate and the preachers of violence, whatever their political stripe, their color or religion. The one comfortless blessing that may come out of this American tragedy is that sobered, as America has never been sobered before, we may be able to regain our perspective as intelligent and moral people and put an end to the mongering of hate, fear and suspicion, wherever they may rise."

William A. Ott, editor of *The Macon* (Ga.) *Telegraph,* wrote that the president's death could bring "a moral reawakening to America if it causes us to see the best in him and the worst in ourselves." He continued: "Let us speak out against racial injustice, against oppression of the weak and helpless anywhere at any time."

Negroes Ponder Next Rights Step

"What's Going to Happen to Us?" One Woman Asks

By LAYHMOND ROBINSON

An assassin's bullet has forced America's Negroes into a sudden reevaluation of the pace and direction of the civil rights movement. A Negro mother expressed the problem yesterday as she emerged from a memorial for the president at Harlem's Abyssinian Baptist Church: "We needed him to lead us to freedom. What are we going to do? What is going to happen to us?"

Mr. Kennedy had, beyond dispute, won a place in the hearts of Negroes alongside that of Abraham Lincoln and Franklin D. Roosevelt. In the emotional reaction to his death some Negroes have called him "America's greatest civil rights president." All over the nation, Negro leaders, shaken by the assassination, have either called off civil rights demonstrations or have converted them into memorial services. "Everything's in a state of suspension for the moment," a grim-faced Roy Wilkins said yesterday. "No one can say what our future timetable will be."

"The bullet that killed Kennedy paralyzed the civil rights drive," another Negro leader said. But Mr. Wilkins, executive secretary of the National Association for the Advancement of Colored People, the nation's oldest and largest rights group, disagreed. In a voice edged with determination he said: "I don't think there'll be any change in the steady pressure toward enactment of civil rights legislation."

Whitney M. Young Jr., executive director of the National Urban League, disclosed that the "big six" of the Negro civil rights movement would meet in New York Tuesday to chart their course. In addition to Mr. Young and Mr. Wilkins, the meeting will include the Rev. Dr. Martin King Jr., head of the Southern Christian Leadership Conference; A. Philip Randolph of the American Negro Labor Council; James Farmer, national director of the Congress of Racial Equality, and James Forman or John Lewis of the Student Nonviolent Coordinating Committee.

Louis E. Lomax, Negro author and prominent figure in the civil rights field, has called upon the nation's 19,000,000 Negroes to suspend all demonstrations at least through the holiday season in tribute to the president. Mr. Lomax said that in the emotional atmosphere surrounding the president's death civil rights demonstrations could be "dangerous" as well as irreverent. This is one of the matters that the rights leaders will take up at their strategy session this week.

Another problem to be discussed is the leaders' relationship to President Johnson. Mr. Johnson, a Southerner, is in the minds of some a basic conservative. Some Negro leaders, however, hailed Mr. Johnson yesterday as a man who might do even more than Mr. Kennedy in the civil rights field, particularly in pushing legislation through a reluctant Congress. These leaders included Mr. Wilkins and Mr. Young. Both have known Mr. Johnson intimately in his capacity as head of the president's Equal Opportunity Committee, established to open employment doors to Negroes.

Two factors, they argued, could make Mr. Johnson an effective civil rights president. One is his knowledge of, and skill in, legislative affairs, gained from his years as a Senate leader. The other factor is that, as a Southerner, Mr. Johnson might be even extremely sensitive to charges that he would be opposed to rapid progress in the civil rights field and work all the harder to speed legislation or executive action. The N.A.A.C.P. and Urban League leaders also contended, with several other prominent Negroes, that national revulsion over President Kennedy's assassination might shame Congress into acting on his civil rights program.

This optimism does not appear to be shared, however, by the Negro in the street. In interviews in New York, a significant number of Negroes said that they either did not know Mr. Johnson's civil rights view or did not trust him on the issue. From the political standpoints some observers believe that unless the 55-year-old President Johnson can erase this apprehension in the minds of some Negroes, he will fare less well at the polls next year than his predecessor would have. Recent polls have shown that Mr. Kennedy would have won a minimum of 85 per cent of the Negro vote. This would have been the highest percentage of Negro votes ever recorded for a president. President Roosevelt never topped more than 75 per cent of the Negro vote. Before most Negroes were converted into Democrats largely because of Mr. Roosevelt's economic program, virtually all Negroes were Republicans.

A PORTION OF GUILT FOR ALL

New Violence Underlines Need to Fix Public as Well as Private Responsibility

By JAMES RESTON

Special to The New York Times

WASHINGTON, Nov. 24—A tale of two cities. And two murders. In Dallas: Violence and anarchy. In Washington: Sorrow and humiliation and anxiety. Running through the private and public comments here today was a single theme: that this decent country has been made to look uncivilized; that there is a kind of rebellion in the land against law and good faith, and that private anger and sorrow are not enough to redeem the events of the last few days.

The doctrine of an-eye-for-an-eye has prevailed in Dallas, and the civil authorities in neither of these two cities have promised the nation a full objective inquiry into the deaths of President Kennedy and Lee Harvey Oswald. But thoughtful men here are not satisfied. They are determined to explore the question of public as well as private guilt in these two cases.

The chief justice of the United States raised the question of public responsibility for the present atmosphere of lawlessness in his eulogy to the murdered president at the Capitol today. We do know, he said, that such acts of assassination and murder "are commonly stimulated by forces of hatred and violence such as today are eating their way into the bloodstream of American life."

The grandson of President Woodrow Wilson, Dean Francis Sayre of the Washington Cathedral, put the point more directly in his sermon this morning: "We have been present at a new crucifixion," he said—this one following on the murder of Medgar Evers in Mississippi and the bomb-murders of four Negro children in Birmingham.

"All of us," he added, "have had a part in the slaying of our president. It was the good people who crucified our Lord, and not merely those who acted as executioners. By our silence; by our inaction; by our willingness that heavy burdens be borne by one man alone; by our readiness to allow evil to be called good and good evil; by our continued toleration of ancient injustices . . . we have all had a part in the assassination."

The American people saw two scenes on the television today that illustrate the dualism of American life, the nobility and tenderness on the one hand, and the brutality on the other.

Jacqueline Kennedy arrived in Washington years ago merely as a beauty and is leaving it, as she demonstrated at the Capitol today, as a beautiful spirit. Out of the crowd she stepped under the vaulted ceiling of the vast Rotunda, a trim and hale figure in funeral black with the golden [Caroline holding onto] her hand, and kneeled ever so slowly before her husband's flag-draped coffin, and stretched out her hand and touched the flag and kissed the coffin; and then rose as gracefully as a young girl and walked away. At least that was the way the people in Washington saw it through their tears.

In Dallas, another scene: murder at point blank range of the hand-cuffed human being suspected but not convicted of assassinating President Kennedy. This was being shown all over the world tonight, and people here were so sick of it that the tendency was to punish the culprit and be done with it. But these two murders raise fundamental questions in the minds of reflective men and women here and cannot be forgotten so easily.

Is the evidence on Lee Harvey Oswald to be left with the Dallas police and the F.B.I.? Is the public not entitled to know what was said to and by Oswald in the Dallas jail? Cannot a presidential or some other objective commission carry on a private investigation, interrogate Oswald's wife and brother, and finally present its findings to the nation?

The Dallas side of the tale cannot be left where it is without adding to the moral confusion Chief Justice Warren and Dean Sayre talked about today. More than the policemen and the politicians, the jurists and the philosophers here are insisting that the "inalienable rights" of the individual in this country, as the founding fathers insisted, came not from the state but from their Creator, and that nobody has a right to take them away.

The point at issue here was defined very clearly by Walter Lippmann. "The decay of decency in the modern age . . . ," he wrote many years ago, "the treatment of human beings as things, as the mere instruments of power and ambition, is without doubt the consequence of the decay of the belief in man as something more than an animal animated by highly conditioned reflexes and chemical reactions.

"For, unless man is something more than that, he has no rights that anyone is bound to respect, and there are no limitations upon his conduct which he is bound to obey. This is the forgotten foundation of democracy in the only sense in which democracy is truly valid and of liberty in the only sense in which it can hope to endure. The liberties we talk about defending today were established by men who took their conception of man from the great central religious tradition of Western civilization, and the liberties we inherit can almost certainly not survive the abandonment of that tradition."

Both Dallas and Washington have forgotten this foundation, and this is the point the preachers and the jurists were trying to make today. The president of the United States, said Chief Justice Warren, is "chosen to embody the ideals of our people, the faith we have in our institutions, and our belief in the fatherhood of God and the brotherhood of man."

This is probably the single hope in the tragedy. For it may be that only the shock of this ordeal can help the nation recover a clearer vision of how a free and civilized people must live.

EDITORIALS

Spiral of Hate

The shame all America must bear for the spirit of madness and hate that struck down President John F. Kennedy is multiplied by the monstrous murder of his accused assassin while being transferred from one jail in Dallas to another.

The primary guilt for this ugly new stain on the integrity of our system of order and respect for individual rights is that of the Dallas police force and the rest of its law-enforcement machinery. But none of us can escape a share of the fault for the spiral of unreason and violence that has now found expression in the death by gunfire of our martyred president and the man being held for trial as his killer.

The Dallas authorities, abetted and encouraged by the newspaper, TV and radio press, trampled on every principle of justice in their handling of Lee H. Oswald. It is their sworn duty to protect every prisoner, as well as the community, and to afford each accused person full opportunity for his defense before a properly constituted court. The heinousness of the crime Oswald was alleged to have committed made it doubly important that there be no cloud over the establishment of his guilt.

Yet—before any indictment had been returned or any evidence presented and in the face of continued denials by the prisoner—the chief of police and the district attorney pronounced Oswald guilty. "Basically, the case is closed," the chief declared. The prosecutor informed reporters that he would demand the death penalty and was confident "I'll get it."

After two days of such pre-findings of guilt, in the electrically emotional atmosphere of a city angered by the president's assassination and not too many decades removed from the vigilante tradition of the old frontier, the jail transfer was made at high noon and with the widest possible advance announcement. Television and newsreel cameras were set in place and many onlookers assembled to witness every step of the transfer—and its tragic miscarriage.

It was an outrageous breach of police responsibility—no matter what the demands of reporters and cameramen may have been—to move Oswald in public under circumstances in which he could so easily have been the victim of attack. The police had even warned hospital officials to stand by against the possibility of an attempt on Oswald's life.

Now there can never be a trial that will determine Oswald's guilt or innocence by the standards of impartial justice that are one of the proudest adornments of our democracy. Whatever judgment is made will fall short of the tests John F. Kennedy himself would have demanded. "Our nation," he declared at the time he dispatched Federal troops to the University of Mississippi to guard the legal rights of one Negro student a year ago, "is founded on the principle that observance of the law is the eternal safeguard of liberty and defiance of the law is the surest road to tyranny."

The best monument all Americans can build to his memory is the enshrinement of that principle in our day-to-day conduct. Hate and violence are the enemies of law, and never more so than when any of us decides to become his own dispenser of retribution in defiance of law.

The President's Security

Can the president of the United States be made safe against assassination? That is a question that millions of Americans are sadly pondering, in the wake of the fourth murder of a president in the past 100 years.

President Kennedy's tragic death is the first since the Secret Service was given the responsibility for guarding the chief executive. That was in 1901, after the assassination of President McKinley. He, like Lincoln and Garfield, had been haphazardly guarded, if at all. Those who have seen the dedication with which the men of the Secret Service carry out their duties will doubt whether any better protection could be devised.

If the president were to forgo all public appearances and spend his term of office a prisoner behind locked doors and armed guards, the risk might be lessened but it could never be completely eliminated. Such a course would be unthinkable. Other heads of government—even Khrushchev and Castro—expose themselves freely to their countrymen. No American president could do less.

President Johnson will undoubtedly accept the danger as a hazard inseparable from his office. However, he must take that hazard seriously and fully cooperate with the Secret Service and the local police authorities, wherever he may be.

The World Mourns

This past weekend it has been evident that President Kennedy's death sent a shock wave of sorrow around all the world. We are still far from the day when all men will consider themselves brothers; humanity is still driven by many differences. But when the news of this tragedy arrived on every continent, it brought sadness to hearts of rich men and poor, capitalists and Communists, men of every creed and every color. The great and near great from many lands who will attend President Kennedy's funeral in Washington today symbolize in their persons this vast outpouring of human sympathy.

How shall we explain this worldwide reaction which united emotionally people so different as Bolivian Indians, black men in South Africa, and "the man in the street" of Warsaw? It cannot have been merely the tragedy of a man cut down senselessly at the height of his powers; disease and violence inflict such losses on humanity every day in many lands. Nor the fact alone that he was president of the United States; the magnitude of the office would not of itself have evoked quite such response.

The cause of this nearly universal sorrow, we suspect, lies elsewhere. It came from President Kennedy's projection to all the world of his and his country's deep concern for humanity, for freedom and for peace. He summed up the goal of his life work when he declared at American University last June: "And if we cannot end now our differences, at least we can help make the world safe for diversity. For, in the final analysis, our most basic common link is that we all inhabit this small planet. We all breathe the same air. We all cherish our children's future. And we are all mortal." The fact that so much of the world mourns him today is proof conclusive that his message was heard and understood.

Farewell to a President

In Arlington Cemetery this afternoon the nation will pay its final tribute to a martyred son as he is laid to rest forever surrounded—and appropriately so—by thousands of other Americans who in humble and in lofty station had also served their country well. With the coming of dusk, the last of the national ceremonies attending the death of John Fitzgerald Kennedy will have been concluded, and a mourning people, still shaken by grief and horror, will have said good-by to a young president who had captured their love and their imagination.

His family will at last be left alone in the intimacy of their sorrow; but the people, too—even as we now turn our eyes toward the future—will not lose the memory of this brilliant man of intellect and of action, whose still-incomprehensible murder has made last weekend one of the blackest in our history.

No one who saw the solemn procession yesterday from White House to Capitol will ever forget it, particularly that moving moment when the flag-covered coffin was being lifted from its caisson to be borne into the Rotunda to the stirring, evocative strains of the presidential march. The power and the glory of the great presidential office—and the frailty and the mortality of even the most vibrant of men—were there summarized in striking contrast.

But though this president who filled that office so gracefully, if so briefly, is gone, his ideas will live after him to inspire the generation—his generation—that is inheriting the earth. He was an intensely practical man, but he was also a prophet and a philosopher. In the last paragraph of the last speech he ever wrote, he expressed some of this philosophy for himself, for his country and for the world:

"We in this country, in this generation, are—by destiny rather than choice—the watchmen on the walls of world freedom. We ask, therefore, that we may be worthy of our power and responsibility—that we may exercise our strength with wisdom and restraint—and that we may achieve for our time and for all time the ancient vision of peace on earth, goodwill toward men. That must always be our goal—and the righteousness of our cause must always underlie our strength. . . ."

What better epitaph could there be for John Fitzgerald Kennedy, 35th president of the United States, as we say good-by to him today?

The Shadow of 1964

The sudden, totally unexpected death of President Kennedy has shattered both political parties' assessments of the outlook for the 1964 presidential election.

The Democrats lost the leader whose return to office for a second term they had considered almost certain. President Johnson now has nine months before the nominating convention to prove that he deserves designation in his own right. He starts with the enormous advantage of being in the White House, endowed with fateful responsibilities and powers and having at his disposal unparalleled avenues of communication with the public. The seeming inevitability of Mr. Kennedy's renomination has kept any other ranking Democrat from seeking the kind of national attention a prospective candidate needs. The measure of President Johnson's performance will be whether anyone else tries seriously in the months ahead.

For the Republicans, what had seemed a despairing race has become a real one. Competition for the nomination will accordingly increase. Also there will be a reduced disposition within the party leadership to indulge its ultra-conservative and even extreme right wing. The party will now surely want a candidate with the broadest possible appeal to all Americans, and a program that will reinforce that appeal.

As both parties begin focusing on the great campaign of 1964, they may forget the basic truth that what the voters will think of either Democratic or Republican nominee will be influenced in important measure by the record of each party in a Congress that thus far has fallen far short of responding to the country's urgent needs. The process of adjustment to a new president, so different from his predecessor in personal style and attributes, ought not become an excuse for further paralysis of the legislative process.

There are honestly held differences of view on Capitol Hill on how best to advance the national interest, and it would be an abuse of democracy to ask that these be jettisoned. But the country has a right to expect that the differences be resolved constructively and without rancorous displays of partisanship, especially in respect to such key problems as civil rights, foreign aid, tax reduction and unemployment.

FOREIGN AFFAIRS

Instant Grief and Instant Terror

By C. L. SULZBERGER

PARIS—Instant grief like instant terror is a revolutionary phenomenon of our time. When President Roosevelt died 18 years ago I happened to be in Moscow and was struck by the speed with which this dreadful news percolated that war-weary city and the sadness that muted an emotional people who were then our allies.

But the brutal shock of President Kennedy's murder was smashed into the world's consciousness by this era's entirely new methods of communication. These transmitted all the horror of that shock and all the horror of its implications in one brief blinding moment. The full play of television and transistors brought the entire human race into the tragedy, almost as a single family, and the human race was frightened.

Like Roosevelt, Kennedy was far from wholly loved at home, but he was deeply respected abroad for the stand he took on those very issues that cost him national popularity. Roosevelt had almost finished his job but Kennedy was less than halfway along. Yet the late president had come to represent an image of youthful vigor, of a postwar generation of leadership just starting to burgeon, of the future itself.

To have this image erased with one brutal stroke and to have the actual erasure so swiftly and totally advertised has produced a strange kind of fear as well as sorrow. Not only the Americans huddled rather helplessly around their distant embassies and black-draped flags were embraced by this very personal consternation, bound by a kind of bewildered panic to their lost leader. The whole world was scared.

The world was scared because it seemed to realize not only how easily its stability could be threatened but also how complex has become the life of everyone still alive today, appalled by instant grief and acutely aware of its partner, instant terror. People seemed subconsciously to realize that for one hour and a half there was no one legally at the helm of the greatest nation charged with protecting peace, no one legally competent to push the button of nuclear war and thereby capable of deterring such a war.

During the tragically brief Kennedy Administration there has been a good deal of international bickering. All too many persons had come to forget the bleak fact that the United States, in the last analysis, is almost the total champion of freedom and that the president of the United States must in the end bear this intolerable burden alone.

It took insane tragedy to remind everyone of this and also to remind everyone that just as a young leader can be annihilated by one mad act, the world itself could be destroyed with almost equal speed by other mad acts. So the stunned mourners around the globe seemed to be mourning not only a man who had not yet had a chance to fulfill his goals and those of aspiring generations, but also to be mourning for themselves. They knew with alarming suddenness the truth of John Donne's warning that the bells beginning to toll could be tolling for them.

All over again and for unexpected reasons the world is afraid. This is the most important factor that President Johnson must deal with as he assumes the load. All over again the world is afraid of traits within its own soul which it seeks to camouflage or forget. And the instantaneous change brought by one man's death has reminded the world how closely it leans in upon itself, how inescapably happenings in one obscure corner can be transmitted like a temblor encompassing all.

The world is abruptly aware how much a single man can become the token of both peace and leadership. This is the inner sense of the gathering of the great today to bury President Kennedy, men brought together in tribute but also brought together in awareness of the inextricable web that binds them.

President Roosevelt, who like President Kennedy had a glowing gift for phrases that identified the very heart of meaning, told his countrymen under different circumstances that they had nothing to fear but fear itself. Fear, if murkily perceived, was a strong emotion everywhere this weekend. It will be a hard, hard thing for President Johnson to lay the ghost of its uncertainty.

Topics

Arlington National Cemetery

By order of Secretary of War Stanton on June 15, 1864, the Custis-Lee mansion and its original 200 surrounding acres were acquired as a site for a Union cemetery. The Government early in the Civil War had made an important decision—to transform burial sites near major battle areas into national cemeteries. Thus one was established near Sharpsburg, Md., as a memorial to the dead who fell in the Battle of Antietam. The Battle of Gettysburg was memorialized in the famous dedication of the cemetery there just a hundred years ago last week. And on the site which Secretary Stanton simply called "Lee's farm" stands Arlington National Cemetery, where John F. Kennedy will be buried today.

Here on the banks of the Potomac River, directly opposite Washington, D.C., the cemetery occupies one of the most historic sites in the nation. The 420 acres of rolling Virginia terrain has 20,000 trees and 10 miles of winding roads. It is a fitting location for the heroic and humble and some-times unknown Americans, and now becomes a still greater place of dedication.

The mansion at Arlington was built in 1802 on the estate of George Washington Parke Custis, adopted son of George Washington. The land-mark with its eight white columns was said to have been modeled after the Temple of Theseus in Athens. Here Mary Anna Randolph Custis married Robert E. Lee in 1831. He was then a lieutenant in the U.S. Army. Three decades later Lee rode down Arlington hill, across Long Bridge, along the canal, and into the heart of the city of Washington. There took place a conversation in which Lee concluded, "I look upon secession as anarchy. If I owned four millions of slaves in the South, I would sacrifice them all to the Union; but how can I draw my sword upon Virginia, my native state?" Then Lee returned to the mansion at Arlington and wrote a letter of resignation to Secretary of War Cameron.

Shortly thereafter the mansion and grounds were occupied by Union troops. Later a hospital was set up there. The first soldier buried there was

a Confederate who had died in the hospital. The title to the property remained in dispute for many years. In 1883, after a Supreme Court decision
favoring George Washington Custis Lee, the Federal Government paid him
$150,000 and obtained clear title.

Major wars still were ahead for the United States and for Arlington's
patient land. One president—William Howard Taft—is buried at Arlington
and many individuals famed in military annals—Gen. George C. Marshall,
Gen. John J. Pershing, Gen. Jonathan M. Wainwright, Adm. Robert E.
Peary, Adm. Richard E. Byrd, many, many more. Mr. Taft, the 27th president and 10th chief justice of the United States, died in Washington in
1930.

The best-known memorial in the cemetery is the Tomb of the Unknowns. Formerly known as the Tomb of the Unknown Soldier of World
War I, it was renamed on Memorial Day, 1958, when servicemen from
the Second World War and the Korean War were interred here. The inscription to these unknowns reads: "Here Rests in Honored Glory an American Soldier Known but to God." A continuous guard is maintained here
by soldiers of the "Old Guard" infantry regiment from Fort Myer, Va.
Nearby is the Memorial Amphitheater, a roofless white marble structure,
erected by the efforts of the Grand Army of the Republic in memory of
its departed heroes.

In distant places around the world for which they fought and helped to
safeguard, many American servicemen are buried in dignity and honor.
The dead and unknown are in the Ardennes; near Carthage in Tunisia; near
Manila in the Philippines; overlooking the Normandy beaches at St. Lau-
rent; in the two newest states of Alaska and Hawaii. These Second World
War cemeteries were added to those already in England, France and Belgium maintained by the American Battle Monuments Commission for the
servicemen who died in the First World War. The Latin Crosses and Stars
of David are set in precise rows, marks of honor in marble, and the headstones of the unknown bear the inscription: "Here Rests in Honored Glory
a Comrade in Arms Known but to God."

Now these hundreds of thousands of casualties are joined in a great
military cemetery at Arlington by one of their own—a once-obscure Navy
PT-boat commander who later served as the nation's commander in chief,
a comrade in arms in the long and unending struggle for peace.

Ship at Sea

Night closes round the lighted ship
The paw of God in dusky glove seizes his moving jewel.
Strike on, my portholes, amber brave,
His clutching is not willful cruel.
He grasps you in a threat of love
to make you blaze against his grip
and lift against his wave.

RUTH WHITMAN

Masefield Poem Honors Kennedy

Special to The New York Times

LONDON, Monday, Nov. 25—*The Times* of London printed today the following tribute by John Masefield, the poet laureate:

John Fitzgerald Kennedy

All generous hearts lament the leader killed,
The young chief with the smile, the radiant face,
The winning way that turned a wondrous race
    Into sublimer pathways, leading on.
Grant to us life that though the man be gone
    The promise of his spirit be fulfilled.

DAY FOUR

November 25, 1963

"All the News That's Fit to Print"

The New York Times.

LATE CITY EDITION
U. S. Weather Bureau Report (Page 9) forecast:
Fair then cloudy today; cloudy tonight. Fair tomorrow.
Temp. Range: 56—37; yesterday: 46—35.

VOL. CXIII...No. 38,657.   NEW YORK, TUESDAY, NOVEMBER 26, 1963.   TEN CENTS

KENNEDY LAID TO REST IN ARLINGTON; HUSHED NATION WATCHES AND GRIEVES; WORLD LEADERS PAY TRIBUTE AT GRAVE

LAST JOURNEY BEGINS: The body of John Fitzgerald Kennedy is borne on a caisson drawn by six horses as his funeral procession leaves the Capitol. Members of the armed services form lines on the Capitol steps down which the flag-draped coffin was carried.

GRAVESIDE: Those facing camera include Mrs. Joseph Kennedy, Mrs. Stephen Smith, behind her: Mrs. Peter Lawford, Mr. Smith, Robert Kennedy, mostly hidden; Mrs. John F. Kennedy, Edward M. Kennedy.

PRESIDENT SPEAKS

Tells Governors He'll Press Civil Rights and Tax Bills

Excerpts from the Johnson remarks are on Page 18.

By E. W. KENWORTHY
Special to The New York Times

WASHINGTON, Nov. 25 — President Johnson told a group of Governors tonight that he would press for enactment of the tax cut and civil rights legislation proposed by President Kennedy.

Furthermore, he indicated to the Governors that his plan for Congressional action on these two bills would figure prominently in the speech he will make Wednesday to a joint session of Congress.

Although several Governors agreed after the meeting that President Johnson had stated very plainly his intentions to urge passage of these bills, his remarks on these issues were omitted in excerpts from the speech issued by the White House.

Action Causes Surprise

The President met with about 30 Governors, Democratic and Republican, who had attended the funeral for President Kennedy today. The meeting, which was so hastily set up that some Governors were called back from airports to attend, took place in the former Vice President's suite in the Executive Office Building.

It could have been no surprise to the Governors that President Johnson would put his weight behind the tax cut and civil rights bills. On civil rights, he has been making speeches all over the country, and the issue deeply engaged his sympathies.

However, it did cause some surprise here that he intended to bear down on these issues in his initial speech to Congress. Officials here have been saying that the President would speak very briefly and concentrate on asserting his determination to continue the foreign and defense policies of his predecessor.

From what he was reported

Continued on Page 18, Column 1

New York Like a Vast Church

By R. W. APPLE Jr.

New York wore a veil of silence yesterday in mourning for the fallen President.

It was as if all the city's millions were in the cathedral tolling the President's body being said for John Fitzgerald Kennedy. It was as in the city itself had become a church.

In their homes, in offices and even in bars, people watched the television broadcast of the funeral rites with religious intensity. Those few in the streets spoke softly, if at all.

More than 4,000 people stood silently in Grand Central Terminal watching a huge television set erected as the President was laid to rest. Some of them grew tearful. Others made the sign of the cross.

Large and small churches, as well as synagogues, held memorial services. Among them were St. Patrick's Roman Cath-olic Cathedral, the Protestant Episcopal Cathedral Church of St. John the Divine and Temple Emanu-El.

Between noon and 12:21, the deck guns of the aircraft carrier Franklin D. Roosevelt, docked at Bayonne, fired 21 times in salute.

At noon, as the coffin companies.

Then, from the top of the marquee of the Astor Hotel, taps reverberated across the square. The buglers were Andrew Prinn of 258 West 91st Street and Stewart Koenles of 251 West 92d Street, 16-year-old Eagle Scouts.

At the same moment, planes on the taxiways at Idlewild Airport stopped. So did trains at Pennsylvania, Long Island and New York Central terminals, roads as well as buses at the Port Authority terminal.

For the next five minutes

At Charlie Yee's band laundry on National Road in Brooklyn, a small portable TV set was nestled among the shirts. Six Chinese stood there ironing and watching the funeral.

The Riverdale Country Day School in the Bronx, where Mr. Kennedy had attended the fourth, fifth and sixth grades, was almost deserted. It was closed, like all other schools and colleges in the metropolitan area.

People everywhere seemed completely preoccupied with

Continued on Page 5, Column 1

Johnson Meets With Visitors

By MAX FRANKEL
Special to The New York Times

WASHINGTON, Nov. 25 — The world's men of title and power went side by side to John F. Kennedy's grave today in a demonstration of tribute and unity that the living President never re eyed.

Then they turned, kings and Communists, dark men and light in rank and turban and uniform and morning frock coat, to pay their respects to Mrs. Kennedy and to wait for their first words with President Johnson.

Towering above them all in 220 foreign visitors. The tale provision of the famous was and in the attentions of Americans was the uniformed figure of Charles de Gaulle, the President of France.

General de Gaulle, among the celebrities first dignitaries to arrive yesterday, was among the first to leave Washington tonight. He brief conversations between Mr.

was the first chief of state to confer privately, if briefly, with President Johnson. The new President was besieged by requests for more formal audiences from a world community formerly in search of a clue to his personality and political style.

President de Gaulle reached the President's bedeie dinner at the John Quincy Adams Room at the State Department after 5 o'clock. They met privately an hour later for about 15 minutes in the other President Johnson also spent 15 minutes there with Prime Minister Hayato Ikeda of Japan and Prime Minister Lester B. Pearson of Canada.

The French President said today only an emotional journey as the representative of the French people and to discuss the great issues that have

Continued on Page 6, Column 1

A HERO'S BURIAL

Million in Capital See Cortege Roll On to Church and Grave

By TOM WICKER
Special to The New York Times

WASHINGTON, Nov. 25 — The body of John Fitzgerald Kennedy was returned today to the American earth.

The final resting place of the 35th President of the United States was on an open slope among the dead of the nation's wars in Arlington National Cemetery, within sight of the Lincoln Memorial.

Mr. Kennedy's body was carried from the Capitol to St. Matthew's Roman Catholic Cathedral for a requiem mass. From there, in a cortege, it was taken to the cemetery.

During the day, a million people stood in the streets to watch Mr. Kennedy's casket.

Across the land, millions more—almost the entire population of the country at one time or another—saw the solemn ceremonies on television.

Cushing Says Mass

At the pontifical low mass said by Richard Cardinal Cushing of Boston, and following the caisson bearing Mr. Kennedy's body to his grave, were notable figures — among them President Johnson, President de Gaulle of France, Emperor Haile Selassie of Ethiopia, King Baudouin of the Belgians, Queen Frederika of the Hellenes, and Prince Philip, husband of Queen Elizabeth II of Britain.

As the caisson reached the graveside below the Custis-Lee Mansion that dominates the Arlington National Cemetery, a flight of 50 jet planes thundered overhead — one representing each state of the Union that Mr. Kennedy often called "the Great Republic." The jets were followed by Air Force 1, the President's personal plane.

Cardinal Cushing spoke the ancient words of the Roman Catholic graveside service, interpolating the phrase "this wonderful man, Jack Kennedy." Cannon boomed a 21-gun salute across the open spaces and rows of white stones. A bugler sounded taps.

The eight body bearers who had placed Mr. Kennedy's coffin above his open grave folded the flag that had covered it for three days. It was presented to Mrs. Kennedy, who then stood erect, as her head covered by a long black veil.

Then the eight and Mr. Kennedy's brothers, Attorney General Robert F. Kennedy and Senator Ed-

Continued on Page 3, Column 1

DIGNITARIES IN FUNERAL PROCESSION: World leaders march behind the Kennedy coffin from White House to St. Matthew's Roman Catholic Cathedral. In front row, from left: President Heinrich Lübke of West Germany, President de Gaulle of France, Queen Frederika of Greece, King Baudouin of Belgium, Emperor Haile Selassie of Ethiopia, President Diosdado Macapagal of the Philippines and Gen. Chung Hee Park, President-elect of Korea. Behind Queen Frederika is Chancellor Ludwig Erhard of West Germany;

"THE BODY OF John Fitzgerald Kennedy was returned today to the American earth." As Tom Wicker's lead sentence made clear, there was really only one story on Monday—the funeral of the 35th president of the United States. In Dallas, inquiries continued. At the White House, President Johnson revealed a bit more about his legislative agenda, including plans to complete two important pieces of unfinished business inherited from his slain predecessor—a tax bill and sweeping new laws expanding the rights of America's black citizens.

But the nation's thoughts that Monday were focused less on the future than on the pageantry at hand. One million Americans lined the streets of Washington to watch silently as the cortege passed by; millions more watched on television. It was a day of images, not words—images captured sequentially but fleetingly on television as the caisson, the family, the dignitaries proceeded from Capitol to church to cemetery—images preserved forever in photographs that appeared in the newspaper the next day.

The Times devoted the first nine pages of Tuesday's paper to the funeral, and much of that space was devoted to pictures, some of them as sharply etched in the mind now as they were that day: the caisson itself, followed by the riderless horse; the widow at graveside, stunned beneath the veil; LBJ staring fiercely out from beneath his hat brim and, most memorably of all, three-year-old John F. Kennedy Jr. saluting his father's coffin.

Tuesday's paper was full of lovely writing. Russell Baker's musings on how the Kennedys had transformed the capital with wit and style bears careful reading; so, for that matter, does Arthur Krock's typically labyrinthine meditation on good and evil. For the first time, letters to the editor commenting on the assassination began to appear on the editorial page—four days after the event. Why the delay? One easily forgets that those were days of "snail mail"—no e-mail, no fax machines, for that matter no overnight express mail. It took that long to receive a suitable batch of letters and prepare them for publication.

But just as the letters columns began to catch up with the past, so the editorial columns began to look ahead, to matters involving the economy, the environment and foreign policy. The editors also urged a fair and complete investigation into the assassination, suggesting the creation of "an objective Federal commission . . . with members of Congress included." And in due course that is what happened.

KENNEDY LAID TO REST IN ARLINGTON; HUSHED NATION WATCHES AND GRIEVES; WORLD LEADERS PAY TRIBUTE AT GRAVE

A Hero's Burial

Million in Capital See Cortege Roll On to Church and Grave

By TOM WICKER
Special to The New York Times

WASHINGTON, Nov. 25—The body of John Fitzgerald Kennedy was returned today to the American earth.

The final resting place of the 35th president of the United States was on an open slope among the dead of the nation's wars in Arlington National Cemetery, within sight of the Lincoln Memorial. Mr. Kennedy's body was carried from the Capitol to St. Matthew's Roman Catholic Cathedral for a requiem mass. From there, in a cortege, it was taken to the cemetery. During the day, a million people stood in the streets to watch Mr. Kennedy's last passage. Across the land, millions more—almost the entire population of the country at one time or another—saw the solemn ceremonies on television.

At the pontifical low mass said by Richard Cardinal Cushing of Boston, and following the caisson bearing Mr. Kennedy's body to his grave, were notable figures—among them President Johnson, President de Gaulle of France, Emperor Haile Selassie of Ethiopia, King Baudouin of the Belgians, Queen Frederika of the Hellenes, and Prince Philip, husband of Queen Elizabeth II of Britain.

As the caisson reached the graveside below the Custis-Lee mansion that dominates the Arlington National Cemetery, a flight of 50 jet planes thundered overhead—one representing each state of the Union that Mr. Kennedy often called "the Great Republic." The jets were followed by Air Force 1, the president's personal plane. Cardinal Cushing repeated the ancient words of the Roman Catholic graveside service, interpolating the phrase "this wonderful man, Jack Kennedy." Cannon boomed a 21-gun salute across the rows upon rows of white stones. A bugler sounded taps.

The eight body bearers who had placed Mr. Kennedy's coffin above his open grave folded the flag that had covered it for three days. It was presented to Mrs. Kennedy, who stood erect and still, her head covered by a long black veil. Then she and Mr. Kennedy's brothers, Attorney General Robert F. Kennedy and Senator Edward M. Kennedy of Massachusetts, each touched a flaming wand to an "eternal flame" placed at the head of the grave.

That was all. For John F. Kennedy, 46 years of age, three years leader of this nation and the Western world, herald of a new generation of American purpose, the tumult and the shouting died. The captains and the kings departed.

This was a cold clear day in Washington—a day of hushed streets, empty buildings, silent throngs standing in their massed thousands to watch the cortege pass, a day of brilliant sunshine falling like hope upon a people that mourned a fallen leader but had to set their faces to the future.

Officially, the day began at 10:41 A.M. when Mrs. John F. Kennedy, with Robert and Edward Kennedy, entered the great, still Rotunda of the United States Capitol, where John Kennedy's body had lain in state since yesterday afternoon. Hundreds of thousands of Americans had filed silently past the catafalque—the same upon which the murdered Lincoln lay 98 years ago—in a procession that continued through the night and until after 9 A.M. today.

Mrs. Kennedy, Robert and Edward Kennedy knelt by the coffin for a minute, then arose, backed away several steps, turned and went down the central steps of the Capitol to the East Plaza. Between sentinels of all the armed services, posted in two long lines down the steps, the eight body bearers carried the flag-draped coffin and placed it upon the waiting caisson. Six matched gray horses pulled it away, carrying John Kennedy on this last journey to the White House.

The Kennedy family and others followed in a solemn line of cars along Pennsylvania Avenue. At the White House, the Kennedys left their car and went inside for a few minutes. Across the street, in Lafayette Square, thousands stood to watch the procession to the church forming in the White House drive.

At 11:25, the foreign dignitaries who had come to pay their respects began lining up—President de Gaulle in the uniform and cap of the French Army, the diminutive Haile Selassie in gorgeous braid, Prince Philip in the blue of the British Navy, others in top hats, sashes, medals, or simple civilian clothes like those worn by Queen Frederika. Altogether, State Department officials said, 220 persons representing 92 nations, five international agencies and the papacy came to Washington. Among them were eight heads of state, ten prime ministers, and most of the world's royalty.

In the distance, as they waited, tolled the bells of St. John's Protestant Episcopal church on the other side of Lafayette Square. The flags of the 50 states, displayed along the White House drive, were dipped in the presence of the caisson.

At 11:35, Mrs. Kennedy came down the steps of the north portico, as a choir of midshipmen sang softly. She took her place behind the caisson, flanked by Robert Kennedy on the right, Edward Kennedy on the left. Only once, as she waited, did she break her stillness to glance around at the world's great standing silently behind her. Then, to a distant skirl of bagpipes from the Black Watch, flown to Washington to march in the funeral procession, the caisson and its followers moved down the drive, into Pennsylvania Avenue, past Blair House and onto 17th Street.

Five yards behind Mrs. Kennedy walked President Johnson and his wife, discreetly accompanied by numerous security agents. Next, in a limousine, came Caroline and John Kennedy Jr., the dead president's children. On foot behind them, in what soon became a straggling, confused mass, came the visiting delegations—a contrast to the precision of the military units and bands that marched ahead of the caisson.

Along 17th Street and Connecticut Avenue, on the eight-block route to St. Matthew's Cathedral, crowds had been gathering since early morning. They massed on the sidewalks and spilled over the curbs, clustered in the buildings that line one of Washington's smartest office and shopping areas, and backed up into the side streets.

Seldom had such personages gathered at once; certainly never had such a gathering been seen walking on foot along one of the busiest streets of the nation. De Valera, Mikoyan, Erhard, Douglas-Home, Ikeda, Thant—the parade of famous figures seemed endless. Behind them came the Supreme Court justices and the Cabinet; and, after them, in a group of their own, some of Mr. Kennedy's closest associates. Another group of personal friends followed.

At the cathedral, those who were not marching in the procession had been gathering since before 11 A.M. Admission was by invitation only, and the capacity of the green-domed building limited those invited to somewhat more than 1,100. The guests were varied: Harold Wilson, leader of the British Labor party; Mrs. Nelson Rockefeller and her husband, the governor of New York; White House staff members; members of the Senate, among them Barry Goldwater of Arizona, and members of the House.

There was Gov. George Romney of Michigan and his wife; Gov. Bert Combs of Kentucky; David J. McDonald, president of the United Steelworkers of America; Mayor Richard J. Daley of Chicago and former Gov. Ernest Hollings of South Carolina; Gov. George C. Wallace of Alabama; Richard M. Nixon and Mrs. Nixon; Gov. and Mrs. William W. Scranton of Pennsylvania and Gov. Edmund G. Brown of California. Seated near the front of the church were former President Harry S. Truman and his daughter, Mrs. E. C. Daniel of New York. Former President Dwight D. Eisenhower, with his wife on his arm, was seated near Mr. Truman.

The diplomatic corps arrived in a body. Military ushers and several friends of Mr. Kennedy—among them two reporters, Hugh Sidey of *Time* magazine and Benjamin Bradlee of *Newsweek*—showed the great and the small to their seats. The church was silent. Six massive candles, in tall gold holders, stood upon the white marble altar. From the ornate, domed ceiling—designed by Grant LaFarge—paintings, carvings, inscriptions looked down upon the rapidly filling cathedral.

Then came the sound of drums. The Black Watch bagpipes could be heard, faintly at first, rising as they passed the open doors, falling into silence. Shouted military commands sounded clearly through the door. The choir in the loft above and to the left of the altar began to sing. Cardinal Cushing and a long line of prelates followed a crucifix held aloft by an acolyte as they marched slowly along the aisle to the open porch in front of the cathedral.

The caisson halted before the cathedral at 11:57 A.M. Mrs. Kennedy, walking with a sure and rapid stride, was just behind it with her husband's brothers. Cardinal Cushing in his lofty white mitre came down the steps. Mrs. Kennedy's children, clad in identical blue and wearing red shoes, were brought to her and she took them by the hand. She bent to kiss the cardinal's ring, then walked with Caroline and John Jr. into the cathedral. Members of the Kennedy family and of Mrs. Kennedy's family followed. President and Mrs. Johnson came just behind them and were seated across the aisle.

As the mass of dignitaries and foreign visitors filed in, the coffin waited outside on its caisson. At 12:08, the body bearers lifted it, carried it across the street and to the cathedral porch. Cardinal Cushing sprinkled it with holy water, then bent to kiss it. At 12:15, the acolyte carrying the crucifix moved slowly back up the aisle, flanked by two others carrying candles. The cardinal, chanting in Latin, and the prelates followed. Behind them, at funeral pace, stiffly erect as automatons, came the eight body bearers, wheeling the flag-draped-coffin—three at each side, one at its head, another trailing.

The coffin was placed in the front and center of the church, a few feet from where the family sat. The bearers marched stiffly away. The doors of the church closed on the still, waiting crowds outside. As Cardinal Cushing, in the familiar droning voice that had sounded the invocation at Mr. Kennedy's inauguration on Jan. 20, 1961, said the requiem mass Luigi Vena sang from the choir loft Gounod's "Ave Maria." Mrs. Kennedy had requested that Mr. Vena do so. He had sung the same music at her marriage to John F. Kennedy in Newport, R.I., on Sept. 12, 1953—a ceremony at which Cardinal Cushing had also officiated.

The cardinal—a tall and imposing figure in the massive church—said the mass entirely in the traditional Latin *("Dominus vobiscum. Et cum spiritu tuo.")* He moved steadily and without hesitation, sometimes in a sing-song voice that sounded more like a steady drone of sound than enunciated words—through the Introit, the Kyrie ("*Kyrie eleison*—Lord, have mercy. *Christe eleison*—Christ, have mercy"), the consecration, through all the other forms of the mass familiar to millions of Roman Catholics the world over, to the communion.

Mrs. Kennedy and Robert Kennedy were the first to receive communion. Edward Kennedy followed. Hundreds of others in the church also received communion and were given the peace of the Lord *("Pax Domini sit semper vobiscum")*. When the celebration of the mass ended ("O God, who alone art ever merciful and sparing of punishment, humbly we pray Thee in behalf of the soul of Thy servant, John Fitzgerald Kennedy, whom Thou hast commanded to go forth today from this World . . ."), the Most Rev. Philip Hannan, auxiliary bishop of Washington, ascended to the pulpit and spoke for 11 minutes in English.

In a clear, almost uninflected voice, Bishop Hannan spoke of Biblical passages in Mr. Kennedy's speeches, including one from one of the last addresses he ever made, in Houston last Thursday night: "Your old men shall dream dreams, your young men shall see visions, and where there is no vision the people shall perish." He concluded with a reading of Mr. Kennedy's Inaugural Address with its famous passage, "Ask not what your country can do for you—ask what you can do for your country."

And once again, in the bishop's unimpassioned voice—so different from that of the young president who spoke that snowy day in 1961—there rang out a challenge that had stirred a nation:

"Now the trumpet summons us again—not as a call to bear arms, though arms we need, not as a call to battle, though embattled we are—but a call to bear the burden of a long twilight struggle, year in and year out, 'rejoicing in hope, patient in tribulation'—a struggle against the common enemies of man: tyranny, poverty, disease and war itself."

The words did not seem less relevant—in the aftermath of Mr. Kennedy's murder they seemed if anything more challenging—than the day, on that crest of hope and belief, when he said them.

At 1:15 P.M., the church doors were opened, the cathedral service concluded. Once again, the procession of prelates followed the crucifix slowly up the aisle. The body bearers moved Mr. Kennedy's coffin behind them. From the street came the stirring sounds of "Hail to the Chief," to which Mr. Kennedy had stepped so often in his brisk stride.

Mrs. Kennedy, holding Caroline's hand—John had been taken from the church at the beginning of the mass—followed it. For a long moment, as the coffin was being taken down the steps and mounted for the third time upon the caisson, she had to stand in the aisle waiting. She was weeping behind her veil. But as she stood unmoving and erect, she took control of herself with an obvious effort, and moved on out of the church. Robert Kennedy followed her with his mother, Mrs. Joseph P. Kennedy, on his arm. Then came the rest of the family mourners.

President Johnson and his family followed. In the jam of persons leaving the church, the foreign dignitaries stood for long moments in the aisle. President de Gaulle whispered something to King Baudouin.

Outside the church, Caroline and John Kennedy entered a limousine with their nurse, Mrs. Maude Shaw, and were driven to the White House. Cardinal Cushing wiped tears from his eyes with a handkerchief as an Army band played a dirge. Attorney General Kennedy helped Mrs. Kennedy into a limousine. Both General Eisenhower and Mr. Truman leaned into her car and spoke to her briefly. They had been chatting on the cathedral porch as they waited for cars. Later, the two former presidents, none too friendly since the 1952 election, rode together in the procession to Arlington National Cemetery.

That procession formed up slowly in front of the cathedral in a jam of waiting limousines, and the dignitaries began to crowd to the curb. Angier Biddle Duke, the State Department chief of protocol, gave up the effort to escort each of them to a car, but all eventually found their places in the long, solemn parade. Eight Secret Service men flanked the car in which President and Mrs. Johnson rode. Another large group of agents guarded the car of President de Gaulle. So large was the Kennedy family group that President and Mrs. Johnson, whose car was immediately behind the group, were 10th in the long cortege.

Once again, on its final journey, the caisson rolled down Connecticut Avenue and Seventeenth Street, then turned right on Constitution Avenue. Behind it, Blackjack, the riderless gelding with the traditional reversed boots in the silver stirrups, pranced and pawed nervously at the pavement.

Untold thousands stood at the curbside—along the same route taken by masses of Negroes and whites last Aug. 28 in the March on Washington that Mr. Kennedy had encouraged. Past the noble white marble of the Lincoln Memorial, over the long stone reach of the Memorial Bridge, across the serene Potomac toward the green slopes of Arlington and the pillared mansion where Robert E. Lee made his tragic choice to leave the Union with his state—onward to the grave rolled the cortege of the great-grandson of an Irish immigrant.

Behind him, the leaders of the world—royalty and commoners, generals and revolutionaries—came on endlessly in their mourning-colored cars. The crowds watched silently, sorrowfully, respectfully. In the cold and warming sunshine, they stood patiently, seeming almost not to move.

More than an hour after it had left the church, the caisson arrived at the graveside. On a nearby slope, masses of flowers were arranged. The metal coffin railings gleamed with polish. Beyond the river, the Lincoln and Jefferson Memorials, the soaring stone of the Washington Monument could be plainly seen.

Mrs. Kennedy, Robert and Edward Kennedy, the Kennedy sisters Patricia, Eunice and Jean, and their mother, were seated in a single row at the front of the family group. As the limousines arrived one by one, the dignitaries took their places—President de Gaulle and Haile Selassie at the head of the grave.

For the graveside services, Cardinal Cushing spoke mostly in English. The words were familiar ("I am the Resurrection and the Life . . .") Occasionally, he seemed to be hurrying, as if to end more quickly the anguish of Mrs. Kennedy and her family. But his harsh voice rang plainly across the hillside and the watching crowds and the thousands of graves as he intoned:

"O Lord, we implore Thee to grant this mercy to Thy dead servant, that he who held fast to Thy will by his intentions, may not receive punishment in return for his deeds; so that, as the true faith united him with the throng of the faithful on earth, Thy mercy may unite him with the company of the holy angels in Heaven."

Three cannon, firing by turns, boomed 21 times in the stillness. President de Gaulle and the other military men came to the salute. Then three riflemen fired three sharp volleys into the arching sky. Sgt. Keith Clark, an Army bugler, sounded the clear, melancholy lament of taps across the cemetery. The flag was removed from the coffin, folded with whiplike precision by the body bearers, passed to Mrs. Kennedy. She and her husband's brother lit the eternal flame. Cardinal Cushing cast holy water upon

THE PEOPLE MOURN: Men, women and children wait quietly outside the Capitol for their turns to pass John F. Kennedy's coffin in the Rotunda. ASSOCIATED PRESS

FUNERAL: The solemn cortege proceeds along Pennsylvania Avenue toward the Capitol. The crowds massed on Pennsylvania and Constitution Avenues were estimated at 300,000.

FUNERAL: The coffin is placed in the Rotunda of the Capitol for the brief ceremony of eulogy.

FAREWELL: Kneeling with her mother at John Fitzgerald Kennedy's coffin in the Capitol, Caroline Kennedy touches the flag.
ASSOCIATED PRESS

AFTER EULOGY: Mrs. John Fitzgerald Kennedy and her children, Caroline and John Jr., leave the Capitol, followed by other members of the Kennedy family and, at top, President and Mrs. Johnson. Behind Mrs. Kennedy are, from left, Robert F. Kennedy and his sisters, Mrs. Peter Lawford and Mrs. Stephen Smith, with her husband.
BETTMANN/CORBIS

THE SUDDEN ATTACK: Jack Ruby closes in on Lee Harvey Oswald, in custody at the jail in Dallas. Ruby put the muzzle of the pistol against the assassin, and then fired.
DALLAS MORNING NEWS

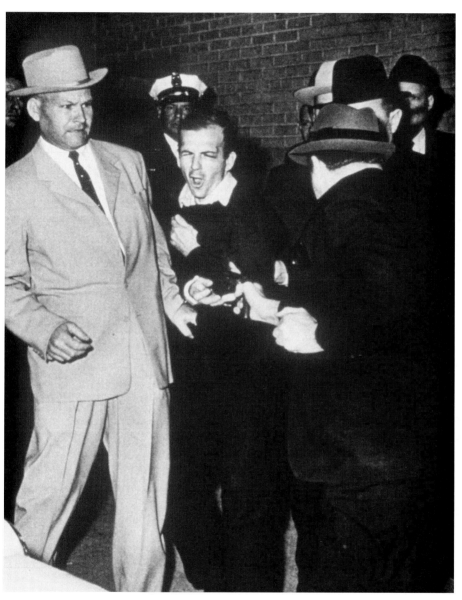

OSWALD IS SHOT: Lee Harvey Oswald cringes as Jack Ruby attacks him at the Dallas jail. The policeman is J. R. Leavelle. BOB JACKSON

FATALLY WOUNDED: Lee Harvey Oswald is taken from the jail. He died in the hospital.
ASSOCIATED PRESS

OSWALD'S WIFE: Lee Harvey Oswald's Russian-born wife, Marina, arriving at the hospital in Dallas where her husband died.
ASSOCIATED PRESS

DIGNITARIES IN FUNERAL PROCESSION: World leaders march behind the Kennedy coffin from the White House to St. Matthew's Roman Catholic Cathedral. In front row, from left: President Heinrich Lübke of West Germany, President de Gaulle of France, Queen Frederika of Greece, King Baudouin of Belgium, Emperor Haile Selassie of Ethiopia, President Diosdado Macapagal of the Philippines and Gen. Chung Hee Park, President-elect of South Korea. Behind Queen Frederika is Chancellor Ludwig Erhard of West Germany. BETTMANN/CORBIS

IN PROCESSION TO CHURCH: Mrs. John F. Kennedy, Attorney General Robert F. Kennedy, left, and Senator Edward M. Kennedy walk behind the caisson bearing the coffin in the procession from the White House to St. Matthew's Cathedral.
BETTMANN/CORBIS

BOSTON PRELATE OFFICIATES: Richard Cardinal Cushing celebrating the pontifical requiem mass for John Fitzgerald Kennedy at St. Matthew's Cathedral. ASSOCIATED PRESS

THE CHILDREN: John and his sister, Caroline, leave after hearing mass.

THE SON: John Kennedy Jr. salutes as the coffin of President Kennedy is carried from the cathedral. BETTMANN/CORBIS

BURIAL: The horse-drawn caisson bearing the body of President Kennedy turns into Memorial Bridge, November 25, 1963, on the way to Arlington National Cemetery. Crowds in foreground stand near the Lincoln Memorial. ASSOCIATED PRESS

BURIAL: Having crossed the Potomac River, the cortege proceeds down Memorial Avenue toward Arlington National Cemetery. BETTMANN/CORBIS

CROSSING MEMORIAL BRIDGE: The cortege approaching Arlington Memorial Cemetery after passing the Lincoln Memorial, in the background. ASSOCIATED PRESS

BURIAL: At the grave the widow, erect and still, receives the flag that had covered the president's coffin for three days. ASSOCIATED PRESS

PRESIDENTIAL RECEPTION: Mrs. Lyndon Johnson with visitors in the John Quincy Adams room. From left are Queen Frederika of Greece, John A. McCone, head of the C.I.A., Mrs. Johnson and Princess Beatrix of the Netherlands. ASSOCIATED PRESS

MEETING OF PRESIDENTS: President de Gaulle of France confers with President Johnson in the office of Secretary of State Dean Rusk. The two leaders talked for about 15 minutes during the reception for dignitaries. ASSOCIATED PRESS

DALLAS TRANSFER: Jack Ruby, killer of Lee Harvey Oswald, moves from the city to the county jail. BETTMANN/CORBIS

the exposed coffin. Robert Kennedy led Mrs. Kennedy away. After a few steps, she stumbled on broken turf, quickly recovered her stride and went steadily on.

The procession had been so long that many dignitaries, far back in the line of cars, were only arriving at the graveside. But if it had taken a long time for the men who followed John Kennedy to arrive at his last resting place, it seemed to take hardly any for the throng of uniforms and morning frock coats and veils and simple dark clothes to disperse and leave the dead for the living.

At 3:34 P.M., the coffin was lowered into the earth. The short life, the long day, was done forever. And none of the pomp and pageantry, none of the ceremony and music, none of the words and grief, none of the faces at the curb, none of the still figures in the limousines, had seemed to say more than the brief prayer printed on the back of a photograph of the dead president that had been distributed at the cathedral:

"Dear God—please take care of your servant—John Fitzgerald Kennedy."

Timetable of the Kennedy Funeral and Procession

Special to The New York Times

8:25 A.M.—The police cut off the line of persons waiting to view the coffin in Rotunda of Capitol.

9 A.M.—Bronze doors of Capitol closed, ending lying in state.

9:05 A.M.—Last visitors pass by coffin.

10:25 A.M.—Mrs. John F. Kennedy, accompanied by Attorney General Robert Kennedy and Senator Edward M. Kennedy, leave White House by limousine.

10:39 A.M.—Mrs. Kennedy and brothers-in-law enter Capitol Rotunda. They kneel at coffin and kiss flag draping it.

10:43 A.M.—Military bearers lift coffin from catafalque and carry it to horse-drawn caisson of funeral cortege.

10:48 A.M.—Coffin is placed on caisson.

10:50 A.M.—Cortege escorting caisson begins departure from Capitol Plaza.

10:58 A.M.—Cortege clears plaza.

11 A.M.—Cortege joins military units at Constitution Avenue as funeral procession begins.

11:35 A.M.—Cortege arrives at White House. The first section of procession proceeds to St. Matthew's Cathedral, as cortege turns into White House grounds.

11:40 A.M.—Mrs. Kennedy is joined by world and national leaders in walk behind caisson to cathedral.

12:13 P.M.—Bronze doors of cathedral close for beginning of requiem mass.

1:15 P.M.—Mass ends. Bronze doors of cathedral open for resumption of funeral procession.

1:30 P.M.—Caisson resumes funeral procession to Arlington National Cemetery. Mrs. Kennedy and dignitaries follow in limousines.

2:43 P.M.—Caisson arrives at Arlington National Cemetery.

3:08 P.M.—Army bugler, Sgt. Keith Clark of Grand Rapids, Mich., sounds taps.

3:15 P.M.—Mrs. Kennedy lights the eternal flame that will burn at the head of the grave and receives the United States flag that had draped the casket. She is escorted to her waiting limousine by President Johnson.

3:34 P.M.—Coffin is lowered into the grave.

The ceremonies were over.

Mrs. Kennedy Puts Flowers on Grave in Nighttime Visit

WASHINGTON, Nov. 25 (AP)—Mrs. John F. Kennedy made an unannounced visit tonight to Arlington National Cemetery and placed a sprig of flowers on the grave of her husband. She was accompanied to the cemetery, where Mr. Kennedy was buried this afternoon, by her brother-in-law, Robert F. Kennedy, the attorney general.

They arrived at the main entrance to the cemetery at 11:53 P.M. and left by the same gate 15 minutes later. Their White House car was followed by a second vehicle containing two Secret Service men. Mrs. Kennedy returned to the White House.

There were few people in the area when Mrs. Kennedy arrived. Earlier, however, roads leading to the cemetery were crowded with cars, which were turned away by a sign reading: "Cemetery gates close at 4:45 P.M." Military policemen and park policemen advised motorists that the cemetery would open at 8 A.M. tomorrow. Military police cruisers patrolled inside the cemetery during the night to guard against intruders. One young couple climbed a shoulder-high stone wall to get a closer after-dark glimpse of the president's grave. They were ejected by the military police.

The Texts of Eulogy at the Funeral Service and Prayer by the Side of Grave

Following are the texts of the eulogy given by the Most Rev. Philip M. Hannan, auxiliary bishop of Washington, at President Kennedy's funeral yesterday, and the prayer, part of which was inaudible, by Richard Cardinal Cushing, archbishop of Boston, at Mr. Kennedy's grave as recorded by The New York Times:

Funeral Eulogy

Mrs. Kennedy and children, beloved mother and members of the family, the president of the United States, your majesties and distinguished heads of government, representatives of the distinguished heads of state, your eminence Cardinal Cushing, your excellency, the most rev. representative of the holy father, your excellency the archbishop and bishops, Monsignor Cartwright, your excellencies, the ambassadors, the speaker of the House, distinguished members of the judiciary, the Congress, the Government, and distinguished friends of President John Fitzgerald Kennedy:

It was thought that the most appropriate commemoration of this heartbreaking event would be the expression of President John Fitzgerald Kennedy's ideals and sources of inspiration in his own words.

President John Kennedy was fond of quoting the Bible. At the last dinner of his life in Houston, Tex., last Thursday night, he applied to a friend as it should be applied to him this combination of passages from the Proverbs and the prophecy of Joel:

"Your old men shall dream dreams, your young men shall see visions, and where there is no vision the people perish."

And to those who shared his vision in this land and abroad he had said two months ago to the United Nations:

"Let us complete what we have started, for as the Scriptures tell us, no man who puts his hand to the plow and looks back is fit for the kingdom of God."

At this time of sorrow and burden, he would have us remember the passages from Joshua and Isaiah he had used in accepting the presidential nomination:

"Be strong and of good courage. Be not afraid, neither be thou dismayed. They that wait upon the Lord shall renew their strength. They shall mount up with wings as eagles. They shall run and not be weary."

Finally, in his last hours, President Kennedy had prepared these words for Dallas and for the nation:

"The righteousness of our cause must always underlie our strength, for as was written long ago, except the Lord guard the city, the guard watches in vain."

The following is one of his favorite passages from Scripture, from the book of Ecclesiastes, the third chapter:

"There is an appointed time for everything, and a time for every affair under the heavens.

"A time to be born, and a time to die. A time to plant, and a time to uproot the plant.

"A time to kill, and a time to heal. A time to tear down, and a time to build.

"A time to weep, and a time to laugh. A time to mourn, and a time to dance.

"A time to scatter stones, and a time to gather them. A time to embrace, and a time to be far from embraces.

"A time to seek, and a time to lose. A time to keep, and a time to cast away.

"A time to rend, and a time to sew. A time to be silent, and a time to speak.

"A time to love, and a time to hate. A time of war, and a time of peace."

And now is the final expression of his ideals and aspirations—[excerpts from] his inaugural address:

"We observe today not a victory of party but a celebration of freedom—symbolizing an end as well as a beginning—signifying renewal as well as change.

"Let the word go forth from this time and place, to friends and foe alike, that the torch has been passed to a new generation of Americans—born in this century, tempered by war, disciplined by a hard and bitter peace, proud of their ancient heritage—and unwilling to witness or permit the slow undoing of those human rights to which this nation has always been committed, and to which we are committed today at home and around the world.

"Let every nation know, whether it wishes us well or ill, that we shall pay any price, bear any burden, meet any hardship, support any friend, oppose any foe to assure the survival and the success of liberty.

"Let both sides unite to heed in all corners of the earth the command of Isaiah—'to undo the heavy burdens . . . and let the oppressed go free.'

"All this will not be finished in the first 100 days, nor will it be finished in the first 1,000 days, nor in the life of this Administration, nor even perhaps in our lifetime on this planet.

"But let us begin.

"In your hands, my fellow citizens, more than mine, will rest the final success or failure of our course.

"Since this country was founded, each generation of Americans has been summoned to give testimony to its national loyalty.

"The graves of young Americans who answered the call to service surround the globe. Now the trumpet summons us again—not as a call to bear arms, though arms we need, not as a call to battle, though embattled we are—but a call to bear the burden of a long twilight struggle year in and year out, 'rejoicing in hope, patient in tribulation'—a struggle against the common enemies of man: tyranny, poverty, disease and war itself.

"In the long history of the world, only a few generations have been granted the role of defending freedom in its hour of maximum danger.

"I do not shrink from this responsibility—I welcome it. I do not believe that any of us would exchange places with any other people or any other generation.

"The energy, the faith, the devotion which we bring to this endeavor will light our country and all who serve it—and the glow from that fire can truly light the world.

"And so, my fellow Americans, ask not what your country can do for you, ask what you can do for your country.

"With a good conscience our only sure reward, with history the final judge of our deeds, let us go forth to lead the land we love, asking His blessing and His help but knowing that here on earth God's work must truly be our own."

Prayer at Grave

In the name of the Father and of the Son and of the Holy Ghost. Amen.

Let us pray.

O God, through whose mercy the souls of the faithful find rest, be pleased to bless this grave and Thy holy angels to keep it . . . the body we bury herein, that of our beloved Jack Kennedy, the 35th president of the United States, that his soul may rejoice in Thee with all the saints, through Christ our Lord. Amen.

I am the resurrection and the life. Blessed be the Lord God of Israel because He hath visited and wrought redemption to His people and had raised up a horn of salvation to us in the House of David, His servant, as He [spoke through] His holy prophets of old from the beginning. Salvation from our enemies and from the hand of all who hate us. Show mercy to our fathers and to remember His holy covenants.

The oath which He swore to Abraham our father that He would grant unto us, that being delivered from the hand of our enemies we may serve Him without fear. Holiness and justice also before Him all our days. Thy child shall be called the prophet of the Most High for thou shalt go before the face of the Lord to prepare His way.

To give knowledge of salvation to his people unto the remission of their sins. Because of the mercy of God in which the ... from on high has visited us.

To enlighten them that sit in darkness and in the shadow of death to direct our feet into the way of peace.

Eternal rest grant unto him, O Lord, and let perpetual light shine upon him.

I am the resurrection and the life. He who believeth in Me, although he be dead, shall live, and everyone who liveth and believeth in Me, shall not die forever.

Lord have mercy on us. Christ have mercy on us. God have mercy on us.

Our Father, Who art in heaven, hallowed be Thy name. Thy kingdom come, Thy will be done on earth, as it is in heaven.

Give us this day our daily bread, and forgive us our trespasses as we forgive those who trespass against us. And lead us not into temptation, but deliver us from evil. Amen.

From the gates of hell, deliver his soul, O Lord, that he may rest in peace. Amen.

O Lord, hear my prayer and let my cry come unto Thee.

The Lord be with you and with thy spirit. Let us pray:

Grant, O Lord, this mercy to Thy servant departed, that he who in his desires did Thy will may not receive the punishment of any misdeeds, and that as through faith that joined him to the company of the faithful here below, Thy mercy may make him the companion of the holy angels in heaven, through Christ our Lord. Amen.

Hymn in Procession Work of Cardinal

WASHINGTON, Nov. 25 (AP)—One of the hymns played in today's funeral procession was one that President Kennedy himself may have sung as a boy in Boston, "The Cross and the Flag." The words and music of the hymn were written by the late William Cardinal O'Connell of Boston, predecessor to Richard Cardinal Cushing, who celebrated the requiem mass for the president today. The O'Connell hymn is still widely known and sung by Roman Catholic children in Massachusetts, and it is familiar to many of their parents and grandparents.

It was as the caisson neared 11th Street on Pennsylvania Avenue that a band, some distance ahead, began playing the hymn, which has a martial air. The words include these lines:

> *All o'er the land, the hearts of men are crying,*
> *Chilled by the storms of grief and strife.*
> *All o'er the land, rebellion's flag is flying,*
> *Threatening our altars—and the nation's life . . .*
> *Lift high the cross, unfurl the flag,*
> *May they forever stand—*
> *United in our hearts and hopes,*
> *God and our native land!*

Requiem Mass Communion Called No Longer Unusual

Special to The New York Times

WASHINGTON, Nov. 25—Some persons at the requiem mass for President Kennedy today were surprised when Mrs. Kennedy and other members of the president's family received communion at the service.

Catholic sources said this was not unusual in recent years since the church had made less strict its rules about the length of fasting required before receiving communion. The relaxing of fasting rules allows communion three hours after eating and one hour after drinking some beverages. Water may be taken at any time before communion.

Before the relaxation, fasting began at midnight and, as requiem masses were usually not held until after 9 A.M. at the earliest, it became a custom not to receive communion at a requiem mass because of the long fast required.

Transcript of Commentary at Requiem Mass for Kennedy in Washington

Following is the transcript of the running commentary carried on all networks on the requiem mass at St. Matthew's Cathedral by the Rev. Leonard Hurley, director of radio-television communications for the Archdiocese of New York, as recorded by The New York Times:

Commentator: The first reading from the sacred Scripture is taken from the Letter of the Apostle Paul to the Thessalonians:

"Make no haste, brethren, about those who have gone to their rest. You are not to lament over them as the rest of the world does, with no hope to live by. We believe, after all, that Jesus underwent death and rose again. Just so, when Jesus comes back, God will bring back those who have rested through Him."

The solemn reading of the Bible is followed by a lesson which serves as an additional food for thought. The first of these, for example, certainly reminds us of President Kennedy. The just man shall always be remembered. He shall fear no evil reports.

The celebrant is reading a 13th-century hymn, the Dies Irae. This hymn is a Christian meditation on the day of death. A non-Catholic has described this magnificent hymn as solitary in its excellence. The secret of its irresistible power lies in the awful grandeur of the theme. Intense earnestness and pathos of a poet, the simple majesty and the solemn music of its language, the stately meter, the triple rhythm, all combine to produce an overwhelming effect, as if we heard the final crash of the universe, the commotion of the openings of graves, the trumpet of the archangels summoning the living and the dead. And so the King of tremendous majesty, seated on the throne of justice and mercy, and ready to dispense everlasting life or everlasting woe.

Now comes the most important reading of the mass, the proclamation of the Holy Gospel. The cardinal prays that he may be worthy to perform this sacred task. All stand to demonstrate this respect for the word of God.

"At that time, Martha said to Jesus, if Thou has been here, my brother would not have died, and I know well that even now God will grant you whatever Thou asks of Him. Thy brother, Jesus said to her, will rise again. Martha said to Him, I know well enough that he will rise again at the resurrection when the last day comes. Jesus said to her, I am the resurrection in life. He who believes in Me, although he be dead, will live on, and whosoever has life and has faith in Me through all eternity cannot die. Dost thou believe this? Yes, Lord, she told Him, I believe that Thou art Christ, Thou art the Son of the living God."

The first part of the mass having been completed, we now begin the Offertory—preparation of the gifts. The celebrant has presented the bread, which is to be consecrated in just a few moments. Here the wine is presented on behalf of all who have gathered themselves in this work of worship.

As we offer our praise to God, we pray to God for John Fitzgerald Kennedy, servant of God, that he may be given everlasting rest.

In a moment the cardinal will invite all to join with the angels in unceasing prayer before throne of God.

Thus be as the Canon, the central prayer of Thanksgiving, through which Christ renews his work of redemption in our midst.

In the first part of the Canon, the priest again asks God the Father to accept the sacrifice. Then he prays for the whole church. Next he prays for the faithful on earth, mentioning by name those for whom the mass is being offered, including in a special way those who are actually present.

Spreading his hands over the offering, he prays:

"We therefore beg you to accept, O Lord, this offering of our worship, that of the whole household."

Taking the bread into his hands, he recites the solemn words which Christ used at the Last Supper:

"This is my body."

Now blessing the chalice, he recites the words of himself as he consecrates the wine:

"This is the chalice of my blood of the new and eternal covenant, the mystery of faith which shall be shed for you and for many unto the forgiveness of sins."

The prayers after the consecration call to mind the passion, resurrection and ascension of Our Lord. Now the cardinal prays for the faithful departed that they may have comfort in peace, naming in particular in this mass our late beloved president, John Fitzgerald Kennedy.

"Through Christ, and with Him, in Him is given to you God the Father Almighty in the Unity of the Holy Spirit, all honoring Glory for ever and ever."

With this element we pray:

"Our Father Who art in Heaven, hallowed be thy Name, thy Kingdom come, thy will be done on earth as it is in heaven. Give us this day our daily bread and forgive us our trespasses as we forgive those who trespass against us, and lead us not into temptation, but deliver us from evil. Amen."

Agnus Dei qui tollis peccata mundi, dona eis requiem.
Agnus Dei qui tollis peccata mundi, dona eis requiem.
Agnus Dei qui tollis peccata mundi, dona eis requiem.
[Lamb of God, who takest away the sins of the world, grant them rest eternal.
[Lamb of God, who takest away the sins of the world, grant them rest eternal.
[Lamb of God, who takest away the sins of the world, grant them rest eternal.]

The celebrant now receives the communion. The Holy Eucharist is a living symbol of union, union of all the faithful of Christ living in death. The Holy Eucharist is the daily bread that Christians everywhere devoutly pray for. To the Catholic, the sacramental body of Christ received in the Eucharist is the Christ whom those who die in the Lord will meet in heaven. It is this mystery, together with things, that enables the Christian to utter the prayer contained in the preface of this requiem mass: "To those who are faithful to you, Lord, life is not taken away—it is transformed."

When this earthly abode is no more, an everlasting dwelling place awaits them in heaven.

To wholly take part in the Holy Sacrifice and to do what Our Lord wants, the congregation receives the sacramental body of Christ from the hands of the priest.

Cardinal Cushing, having reverenced the altar, now moves to the bier. A wonderful prayer in its simplicity and confidence.

"But he was sealed with the seal of the Holy Trinity in baptism. He believed in the triune God. And therefore the church confidently hopes for mercy from the same all-loving God.

"To live in Thee, O Lord, from everlasting death on that dread day of terror, when the heavens and the earth will be shaken, as Thou dost come to judge the world by fire. I am in fear and trembling at Thy judgment, the wrath that is to come. The heavens and the earth shall be shaken. That day will be a day of wrath and of misery and of ruin, a day of grandeur and of horror, as Thou dost come to judge the world by fire. Eternal rest grant unto him, O Lord, and let Thy perpetual light shine upon him."

Pausing now, the cardinal places incense over hot coals in a censer. This action is filled with Biblical symbolism, the smoke rising to heaven indicative of our prayers of supplication.

[At this point the Lord's Prayer is recited in English, in unison.]

While the cardinal recites the "Our Father" with the people, he goes around the bier and sprinkles the corpse with holy water thrice on each side, then in the same way he incenses it. Holy water and incense becoming efficacious sacramentals for the prayer and the blessings of the Church. They're employed here because the soul of the departed benefits by their application and because the body of the departed was a temple of the most Holy Spirit.

The cardinal now says: "From the gates of hell, rescue his soul, O Lord. May he rest in peace. O Lord, hear my prayer and let my cry come unto Thee. Lord be with you and with your spirit. Let us pray.

"O God, who alone art ever merciful in sparing of punishment, humbly we pray Thee on behalf of the soul of Thy servant, John Fitzgerald Kennedy, whom Thou has commanded to go forth today from this world. Do not hand him over to the power of the enemy, nor forget him forever, but command that his soul be taken up by Thy holy angels and brought home to Paradise. May his soul and all the souls of the faithful departed, with the mercy of God, rest in peace. Amen."

[At this point, Cardinal Cushing, speaking in English, says:]

"May the angels, Dear Jack, lead you into Paradise. May the martyrs receive you at your coming. May the spirit of God embrace you, and mayest thou, with all those who made the supreme sacrifice of dying for others, receive eternal rest and peace. Amen."

MRS. KENNEDY MAINTAINS A STOIC DIGNITY THROUGHOUT FINAL HOURS OF PUBLIC GRIEF

Walks 8 Blocks to the Cathedral

She Sheds Tears Only Twice—Returns to White House to Greet World Leaders

By ANTHONY LEWIS

Special to The New York Times

WASHINGTON, Nov. 25—Mrs. John F. Kennedy went bravely through her final hours of public grief today. She walked the eight long blocks from the White House to St. Matthew's Roman Catholic Cathedral behind the caisson carrying the body of her husband to the funeral. It was a gesture that few who watched would ever forget.

She stood erect at his graveside, watching the powers of church and state bid him farewell. She carried out a final duty as the president's wife, greeting at the White House the leaders of the nations who had come to pay tribute to Mr. Kennedy. Through the long day of ceremony, she maintained the stoic dignity that she had displayed since an assassin's bullet killed her husband three days ago. Only twice during the day did her tears appear. Once was in the cathedral, the second time after the burial service.

As the ceremony at the Arlington National Cemetery ended, she turned suddenly to Gen. Maxwell D. Taylor, chairman of the Joint Chiefs of Staff, who was a step or two away. She embraced him and pressed her veiled cheek against his. Her dark eyes filled, and for an instant her face looked like that of a 34-year-old girl burdened with sorrow, instead of a president's wife. Then Mrs. Kennedy turned away. She reached out and took the hand of her brother-in-law, Attorney General Robert F. Kennedy—a hand she held often during the day—and went back to the White House for the diplomatic reception.

Today happened to be the third birthday of her son, John, Jr., called "John-John" by his father. John and his sister, Caroline, who will be 6 the day after tomorrow, were at the cathedral for the funeral service but were spared the ceremony at the cemetery. As the children left the cathedral after the service John saw the honor guard of nine servicemen carry the flag-covered coffin of his father to the caisson that would bear it to Arlington. He looked up at his mother. She whispered to him. Then he handed her a prayer book he was carrying, and his small right hand suddenly shot up a salute.

The official business of the day began for Mrs. Kennedy at 10:25 o'clock this morning. She left the White House to travel by limousine to the Capitol, where thousands of persons had filed past the bier of the president. Members of the White House staff lined the driveway. Across Pennsylvania Avenue, in Lafayette Park, the crowd was 20 to 30 persons deep. All was still.

The limousine soon reached the Capitol. Mrs. Kennedy walked up the steps with Robert Kennedy on her right and his brother, Edward M. Kennedy, on her left. They walked together into the Rotunda and knelt for about half a minute at the foot of the coffin. Then they turned and went back out into the bright sun, with the body bearers carrying the coffin behind them.

When the procession reached the White House, Mrs. Kennedy got out of the car. She stood for a few moments behind the caisson in the driveway, her head high, her slight figure still. Once she glanced around at the dignitaries gathering behind her. Then to the strange sound of the bagpipes, she began the trip to the cathedral. Past the silent crowds she walked, her two brothers-in-law on either side. Behind them came President Johnson and all the dignitaries. But the eyes of the people were on Mrs. Kennedy. She was all in black. Her face and her brown hair could be seen only dimly from the distance, behind the black veil that flew against her face.

As the extraordinary walk began, she took Robert Kennedy's hand and held it. But then, resolutely, she dropped it and walked alone. At the cathedral she waited for the children, who were driven over from the White

House. She took them, one on each hand, and led them up the steps to meet Richard Cardinal Cushing. She dipped down in a genuflection and kissed his ring.

John seemed to be crying as they went into the cathedral, but his mother said a few words to him and he stopped. She could not so easily console Caroline, who wept after the service as they followed the coffin out of the church.

The procession formed again for the ride to Arlington. The horse-drawn caisson and the limousines crossed the Potomac. Probably few noticed the few fishermen with lines in the icy water. The grave was at the base of the hill below the Custis-Lee mansion, in an open space among the tall, bare elms. A single gnarled cedar still showed green. The site, one of the most impressive in the 420-acre cemetery, had been selected by Robert Kennedy and Secretary of Defense Robert S. McNamara.

On the bank of the hill were wreaths of flowers, sent before Mrs. Kennedy could make known her wishes that flowers be withheld. At 2:35 P.M., just before the procession arrived, two large bunches of white chrysanthemums and lilies were placed above the head of the grave. They were the gift of Mrs. Kennedy.

Units from each of the armed services filed in to stand beside the 100-foot-square of green carpet covering the earth. It was noticeable that there were Negroes in each unit—a symbol of Mr. Kennedy's commitment against racial discrimination. One remembered the incident at his inauguration, when he remarked on the absence of Negro faces in a Coast Guard troop, an omission quickly remedied.

The caisson drew up at 2:43 P.M. At that moment leaves suddenly began floating down from what those waiting had thought was an empty sky. The Marine Band played the national anthem. Then, slowly and eerily, Air Force bagpipers marched forward, three drums beating hollowly. The coffin was carried up to the gravesite through two lines of Special Forces troops. Behind it, for the last time, went Mrs. Kennedy. As they reached the gravesite, the bagpipes stopped. A moment later, 50 jet fighters flew overhead in formation with a reverberating roar. Then, alone and much lower, came Air Force 1—the president's personal jet.

Robert Kennedy guided his sister-in-law to a chair. She sat at the left end of the row. To her right, in order, were Robert, Mrs. Rose Kennedy, and the three Kennedy sisters—Mrs. Sargent Shiver, Mrs. Stephen E. Smith and Mrs. Peter Lawford. Standing behind them were other members of the Kennedy family. Seven of the attorney general's eight children were there, all but Christopher George, born last summer. Little blonde Mary Kerry, 4 years old, stood out on the side. As the coffin was placed on the straps over the grave, Mrs. Kennedy and those beside her rose. The servicemen removed the flag that had covered it for three days and held it stretched tightly over the grave.

At Mrs. Kennedy's request, a troupe of Irish guards was on hand—26 cadets in shiny brown boots—from Ireland's West Point, the Army Cadet School. To commands shouted in Gaelic, they performed a brief drill, spinning their rifles slowly around.

Mrs. Kennedy held Robert's hand, then dropped it. Once or twice, as she stood to hear Cardinal Cushing's service, she leaned against Robert, as if for support. When the wind came up, she put her hand to her hat. Her veil, falling almost to her waist behind her, moved in the breeze.

At 3:03 a gun on the hill began a 21-gun salute to the dead president. In the crowd, held behind ropes 100 yards away, a baby cried. Mrs. Kennedy seemed to look at President de Gaulle of France, tall in the first row of spectators. Her friends thought his decision to come for the funeral meant something special to her as a lover of France and its civilization. At 3:06 Robert Kennedy whispered to her, then led her forward to stand next to him at the head of the grave. Three rifle volleys were fired. A bugler sounded taps.

When the prayers were done, Mrs. Kennedy took a long-handled lighter and lit a flame at the head of the grave. The gas device had been installed there during the night, at her request, to burn as an eternal flame. She handed the lighter to Robert Kennedy, who touched the flame again. Then Edward Kennedy, standing behind them with Cardinal Cushing, stepped forward and made the same gesture.

The eight men holding the flag folded it up and presented it, with a military salute, to the superintendent of the cemetery, John C. Metzler. He gave it to Mrs. Kennedy. She and Robert shook the hands of Cardinal Cushing and the prelates with him. Suddenly, she embraced General Taylor. Then, after that moment of emotion, she resolutely took Robert Kennedy's hand and filed out through the line of soldiers.

The coffin, closed at the Bethesda Naval Hospital early last Saturday morning with Mrs. Kennedy's wedding ring in her husband's hand, was still above ground. It was lowered into the earth at 3:34.

At the White House, after her return, Mrs. Kennedy met privately in the family quarters with three visiting heads of state—General de Gaulle, Emperor Haile Selassie of Ethiopia and President Eamon de Valera of Ireland. Mrs. Kennedy saw the emperor because of the circumstances of his visit to the United States last September. Mrs. Kennedy, then in mourning because of the death of her son Patrick Bouvier Kennedy the month before, interrupted her mourning and delayed a trip abroad for a day to meet the emperor. He made it known this week that he was coming here for the funeral in respect for her as well as the president.

Then she went downstairs to meet the other foreign dignitaries in a formal receiving line. She shook hands with each as they filed into the Red Room of the White House from the State Dining Room. With her in the receiving line were Robert Kennedy and his wife, Ethel; Edward Kennedy and his wife, Joan, and Mrs. Shriver and Mrs. Lawford.

There was no word tonight about Mrs. Kennedy's immediate plans— when she will leave the White House, where she and the children will spend Thanksgiving, where they will live. An announcement is scheduled for tomorrow. The general belief is that Mrs. Kennedy will want to move out as soon as physically possible. And there is some feeling that she will stay in Washington.

Perhaps her choice of residence had something to do with the decision to bury Mr. Kennedy in the Arlington Cemetery rather than the family plot in Brookline, Mass. But Cardinal Cushing said that Arlington had been chosen to avoid prolonging the funeral period into tomorrow.

For Mrs. Kennedy, as for those who only watched, these three days of public anguish were as much as could be borne.

"Majesty of Mrs. Kennedy"

LONDON, Nov. 25 (AP)—"Jacqueline Kennedy has given the American people from this day on one thing they have always lacked—majesty."

This was the introduction of a dispatch from Washington in *The London*

Evening Standard today under the headline: "Magic Majesty of Mrs. Kennedy."

Accompanying this was a three-column portrait of Mrs. Kennedy, depicted as she looked upon her husband's coffin in the Capitol Rotunda.

2 Kennedy Children Got Johnson's First Letters

WASHINGTON, Nov. 25 (AP)—The first two letters Lyndon B. Johnson signed as president were to the two children whose father was buried today.

The letters to Caroline Kennedy, 6 years old this Wednesday, and John F. Kennedy Jr., 3 years old today, told them at the beginning that they perhaps were too young to understand it all now.

Mr. Johnson wrote to them last Friday just after his return from Texas, only a few hours after he had been sworn in to succeed their father.

John Jr., on 3d Birthday, Salutes His Father's Passing Coffin

He Attends Funeral Rites With Mother and Caroline

WASHINGTON, Nov. 25 (UPI)—A little boy at his grieving mother's side saluted the passing coffin. And in that moment, he seemed the brave soldier his father would have wanted him to be on this day.

Today, John F. Kennedy Jr. was 3 years old. His world was strangely different, in little ways a child notices but does not understand. Where was his father? The tall man with the laughing blue eyes who had a big desk and saw lots of important people and stooped to spank him good-naturedly and took him on helicopter rides and called him John-John.

This was supposed to be the day of The Party—the cake with three candles to blow out, the friends singing boisterous "Happy birthdays," the gifts. He did get a letter, as did his sister, Caroline, from President Johnson. No one outside the White House knew what the letters said. But home, the White House, was quiet. Some of the furniture was gone.

And the soldiers outside, whose salutes he delighted in trying to return with one of his own, looked different. Today they did not glance down at him and sneak a wink or a smile. Their commands barked, their rifles clattered harshly.

His mother, Mrs. John F. Kennedy, left in the morning to go to the Capitol and ride back behind the soldiers and the horses and the wagon with the flag-covered box. He and his sister, meanwhile, dressed and put on their blue coats. It was cold outside. Caroline will be 6 on Wednesday. There was supposed to be a big birthday celebration at Hyannis Port on Friday, the day after Thanksgiving. John was born on a Thanksgiving Day. His father had just been elected president.

Secret Service agents came and led John and his sister out to the north portico. Mrs. Kennedy, dressed in black, met them at the door and took them to a limousine. Then she walked back up in line with their uncles, Attorney General Robert F. Kennedy and Senator Edward M. Kennedy, Democrat of Massachusetts, and the slow, sad march to the church began.

President and Mrs. Johnson and a host of aides and security agents followed Mrs. Kennedy on foot. John and Caroline rode in the car behind them. A half-mile later, in front of St. Matthew's Cathedral, the parade stopped. John and Caroline were brought around to join their mother. The little boy looked around, bewildered, and started crying. His mother spoke to him softly and he stopped.

They walked up the steps of the cathedral, and there waiting was Richard Cardinal Cushing of Boston. John seemed awed by the tall, craggy-faced man towering above him, wearing a white, two-pointed miter and black vestments. The cardinal had married the Kennedys in 1953 and had baptized both children. He is an old friend of the family. Now he was about to say the president's funeral mass. He put his arm around Mrs. Kennedy's shoulder, and she genuflected before him. He leaned down and kissed Caroline and patted John on the head.

Mrs. Kennedy, holding each of her children by the hand, walked in and down the aisle to their seats. John, who only recently started attending public worship services, grew restless during the mass. Someone picked a small book—*The Church Today—Growth or Decline*—from the literature rack at the rear of the cathedral and gave it to the boy to occupy him. He still clasped it in his hand when he left the church with his mother and sister.

They stood waiting at the bottom of the steps. Pallbearers appeared at the door with the flag-draped coffin, and as it came slowly down toward them, Mrs. Kennedy leaned down and whispered to her son. He stood apart, straightened stiffly, and raised his hand in salute as the coffin passed. He smiled softly and proudly.

Joseph Kennedy Controls Grief; Sees Part of Proceedings on TV

Special to The New York Times

HYANNIS PORT, Mass., Nov. 25—Joseph P. Kennedy, who saw the realization of a lifetime dream shattered by the assassination of his son, demonstrated his own fortitude today. As the rest of the family was exposed to the view of thousands at the final rites for the president in Washington, and of millions on television, the ailing father controlled his grief by keeping occupied. This morning, accompanied by his niece and constant companion, Miss Ann Gargan, and two nurses, he was taken on a 40-minute drive in the family car by the chauffeur, Frank Saunders.

Later the former ambassador to Britain, who is 75 years old, took a dip in the family pool. Mr. Kennedy has been confined to a wheelchair since suffering a stroke nearly two years ago, but he was able to use a mechanical walker to reach the water. In the afternoon he watched part of the funeral mass and processions in the nation's capital on television. Although his doctors reported him physically able to make the trip to Washington, Mr. Kennedy elected to remain out of the spotlight as the world paid final tribute to the son who achieved the goal that had originally been set for Joseph P. Kennedy Jr., the first of three children to die. Joseph Jr., a Navy flier, was killed when his plane exploded during a mission in Europe in World War II. His sister Kathleen died in a post-war plane crash.

The father had the company today of the Rev. John Cavanaugh, president emeritus of the University of Notre Dame, who celebrated mass for Mr. Kennedy in the Kennedy residence this morning. During the night, persistent reports that Mr. Kennedy had died led the family to authorize Miss Gargan to dispel the rumors.

During the morning drive, which took him as far as Yarmouth, the next town south, Mr. Kennedy had the car slowed down so that he could look at store windows in downtown Hyannis. Many of them displayed pictures of the president, appropriately creped or wreathed. The car had little difficulty keeping a slow pace. There were few other cars on the road, and they, too, moved slowly. The sidewalks were strangely deserted for a Monday.

Riderless Horse an Ancient Tradition

By JACK RAYMOND

Special to The New York Times

WASHINGTON, Nov. 25—The black, riderless horse that symbolized the lost leader in the funeral procession of President Kennedy today seemed spirited and difficult to handle. "He was proud," was the authoritative explanation of the military unit at Fort Myer, Va., which supplied him for the solemn occasion.

He was never out of control, firmly held close to the double bit of his bridle by a 19-year-old soldier from Robertsdale, Ala. The soldier, Pfc. Arthur A. Carlson, was assigned to Fort Myer a year ago and has been in the Army since June 15, 1962, when he joined for a regular three-year enlistment. The horse was Blackjack, a 16-year-old gelding with 10 years of service in similar duties as the caparisoned horse for official funerals at Arlington National Cemetery.

The military marching units in today's funeral procession, reinforced by a colorful Irish honor guard that flew here for the occasion, were experienced participants in the capital's frequent ceremonies.

The procession was marked by military symbols ancient and new. Guns saluted, taps were sounded beside the grave, rifle volleys were sent echoing across the Potomac Valley, and 50 airplanes escorted the president's plane across the burial grounds. The airplanes—30 from the Air Force and 20 from the Navy—flew in a formation that left the tail plane of the reverse-V missing, symbolic of a missing comrade.

But perhaps the most poignant touch of all was the sight of the huge steed, not quite black, more of a dark chestnut, spiritedly trailing the horse-drawn artillery caisson and its coffin of the deceased president. For a while this afternoon there was a report, confirmed at the White House, that the horse was Sardar, a bay gelding that Mrs. John F. Kennedy received as a gift from President Ayub Khan of Pakistan during a visit to that country last year.

The report turned out to be incorrect and was subsequently attributed to the confusion during the last few days, particularly since Mrs. Kennedy had personally ordered several changes in official plans.

In any event that big, prancing horse has been the No. 1 animal at Fort Myer stables ever since he was delivered in 1953 after breaking-in and training at Fort Reno, Okla. He has maintained that standing for a decade among 14 grays and 15 blacks that are normally kept at Fort Myer for ceremonial occasions. His role as the caparisoned, or "covered," horse in today's funeral procession stemmed from a tradition extending to the ancient days of mounted warriors.

In the ancient custom, the lost warrior's charger was led, sheathed in an armored cloth, and sacrificed at the burial of his master. In the days of the Mongols of Genghis Khan and Tamerlane, the people believed that the spirit of the sacrificed horse went through "the gate of the sky" to serve his master in the afterworld. Today, in the survival of the ancient tradition, Blackjack, a magnificent charger, was led behind the horse-drawn caisson bearing the body of the deceased president.

The sword used to dress the saddle today did not pierce it, as in the old symbolic rite, but was strapped in its scabbard to the side, while the stirrups and the boots in them were reversed as a sign that a commander had fallen and would ride no more.

Private Carlson, interviewed about today's experience, confessed to having "some trouble," but emphasized that he never feared he would lose the horse during the procession. He attributed the friskiness of Blackjack to the cold and the unusual crowd. The soldier, stepson of a retired Marine Corps sergeant, said he was assigned to Blackjack last January. He and Pfc. James P. Stimson, who rode one of the caisson horses today, take turns leading the caparisoned horse in military funerals that are routine at the Arlington Cemetery.

Last Monday the youth who served in the funeral of Mr. Kennedy served in a similar capacity at the more modest rites marking the funeral of a 90-year-old retired Army officer, Maj. Gen. Charles Evans Kilbourne, who had been the oldest living holder of the Medal of Honor.

Private Carlson said that the assignment today was part of his job and did not result from any special selection. It was his turn, he said. He was picked originally for the caisson unit mainly because of his height, he said. He is 6 feet 2 inches tall.

The funeral parade began with military precision at 11 A.M. at the head of Constitution Avenue, just as the cortege escorting the caisson reached the marching units from the Capitol Plaza. The precision, which marked the marching and timing all the way, was no accident. The marchers were drawn from specially trained ceremonial units in the Washington area. These regularly rehearse and frequently participate in the variety of formal observances—inaugurations as well as funerals—requiring traditional ceremony.

The escort commander was Maj. Gen. Philip C. Wehle, commander of the Military District of Washington. The commander of troops was Lieut. Col. Richard E. Cross, commander of the First Battle Group (Reinforced) of the Third Infantry, known as the "Old Guard."

In contrast with the small procession yesterday, when the president's body was borne to the Capitol to lie in state, the corps of muffled drums was expanded today to include military bands of the services. These played funeral dirges and patriotic airs.

The surprise participants in the funeral procession were an honor guard of 30 cadets of the Military College of Ireland in Curragh, County Killarney. This is the "West Point" of Ireland. The cadets were flown over from the ancestral home of the Kennedy family in the same plane that brought

President Eamon de Valera for the funeral. The Irish cadets executed complicated arms-handling traditional to Irish military funerals. The music for them was supplied by a United States Navy band. One tune was identified as "Garry Owen," a dirge.

Sgt. Thomas M. Satterberg of St. Paul, Minn., rode a 17-year-old gray horse, Big Boy, as section chief in front of the three pairs of matched grays that pulled the caisson bearing the president's coffin.

Riders were mounted on the near left horse in each span. On the lead horse, Skyline, was Specialist 4th Class Charles B. Wade of Franklin, Ky. The off (right) lead horse was Count Chris. The second, or "swing team," included Blue Dare and Blue with Pfc. James P. Stimpson of Willington, Tenn., mounted on Blue. The final "wheel team" was Cap and Cloudburst, with Pfc. Richard A. Pace of Marion, Ind. They were all chosen for the honor from the caisson section of the Army's First Battle Group (Reinforced) of the Third "Old Guard" Infantry.

The pallbearers, representing all the services in the various transfers at the Capitol, at the cathedral and at the burial site, were First Lieut. Samuel R. Bird, Army, of Wichita, Kan.; YN2 George A. Barnum, Coast Guard, of Lake City, Minn.; SA Hubert Clark, Navy, of Queens, L.I.; Lance Corp. Timothy F. Cheek, Marine Corps, of Ocala, Fla.; Specialist 4 Douglas Mayfield, Army, San Diego, Calif.; Sgt. James Felder, Army, of Sumter, S.C.; S-Sgt. Richard E. Gaudreau, Air Force, of Ashby, Mass.; Pfc. Jerry J. Diamond, Marine Corps, of Stow, Ohio; and SA Larry B. Smith, Navy, of Ransom, Ky. Most of these men, specially selected for the honor from regular honor guard units stationed in the Washington vicinity, have been serving as honor guard for the coffin since the president's body was brought back from Dallas.

In the final rite, an Army bugler, Sgt. Keith Clark of Grand Rapids, Mich., blew taps, the familiar mournful sound that calls for curfew and peaceful repose. The melody was created during the Civil War by General Daniel Butterworth of the Army of the Potomac, an upstate New Yorker, with the help of the brigade bugler. The general, who did not know a note of music, had been dissatisfied with the curfew call then usually sounded, the French "L'Extinction des Feux" (Lights Out).

He and the bugler created taps one night in July, 1862, while in camp at Harrison's Landing, Va., and the call was soon adopted by other corps and later made official throughout the Army. The name taps was used in an earlier "Lights Out" call and derives from the Dutch call, *taptoo,* which in American bugle calls became tattoo.

Preceding taps was a 21-gun salute, traditional throughout the world for chiefs of state, fired from three 76-mm. guns positioned on the slope just above the gravesite. The three guns were fired in turn at five second intervals. In another ancient custom, three servicemen fired three rifle volleys each with such timing that they sounded like single shots. The firing of rifle volleys over the grave of a deceased veteran derives from the old Roman custom of casting earth over a coffin, calling the name of the dead man three times and then saying *"vale"* three times. The word *vale* is Latin for farewell.

Bagpipers Who Pleased Kennedy Return for Funeral Procession

By MARJORIE HUNTER

Special to The New York Times

WASHINGTON, Nov. 25—Twelve days ago, the bagpipers of the Black Watch Scottish Highland Regiment played on the White House lawn for President Kennedy. Today, they played for his funeral march.

Mr. Kennedy had interrupted a busy schedule of appointments that afternoon to join his wife and children on the south portico to listen to the bagpipers. He was given a Black Watch dirk, engraved with the regiment's motto: "Nobody wounds us with impunity."

"I think that is a very good motto for some of the rest of us," Mr. Kennedy observed.

A second group of bagpipers that Mr. Kennedy had often heard played at the gravesite today. Soon after the crowd assembled at the cemetery, the United States Air Force bagpipe band played "The Mist Covered Mountain."

*

The last big ceremonial burial at Arlington National Cemetery before today was that of Secretary of State John Foster Dulles on May 27, 1959. He, too, was given a hero's farewell—a procession through the streets of Washington, a 19-gun salute and the playing of taps. Among those who came from afar that day were German Chancellor Konrad Adenauer, Soviet Foreign Minister Andrei A. Gromyko and Madame Chiang Kai-shek.

*

Another large crowd gathered at Arlington last June 19 for rites for Medgar W. Evers, the slain integrationist leader from Mississippi. He was laid to rest as the crowd softly intoned a freedom song, "We Shall Overcome."

*

In today's funeral procession, riding in a car and unnoticed by the watching crowd, was Lieut. Col. John H. Glenn Jr. Twenty-two months ago, after he had orbited the earth three times, hundreds of thousands of persons stood in the rain to cheer as he rode from the White House to the Capitol.

*

Gov. George Romney of Michigan and Gov. William W. Scranton of Pennsylvania rode in the same car in today's funeral procession. Both have been mentioned as possible contenders for the Republican presidential nomination. Riding in a relatively old Pontiac was the only announced candidate for the Republican presidential nomination, Governor Rockefeller of New York. With him was his wife.

Also riding together were two former presidents and sometimes foes, Harry S. Truman and Dwight D. Eisenhower. Later the two former presidents conversed at Blair House for 30 minutes after the funeral. An official present called it "a very sentimental visit."

*

The thousands that turned out to watch the funeral procession were bundled heavily with wraps and blankets and carried binoculars, cameras, and vacuum bottles and lunches. The mood of the crowds along the city's tree-lined streets was solemn. They stood cold and silent in the near-freezing weather, listening to the echo of transistor radios, and strangely still when the procession passed by.

"I never saw anything like this," said one taxi driver. "It's so solemn. Thousands of people, but you could hear a pin drop."

*

Those watching the hour-long procession were impressed not only by its length, but also by the obvious security measures taken to protect some dignitaries. In addition to several Secret Service men clustered about President Johnson's car, other high-ranking officials got similar attention. President de Gaulle of France, who appeared to be a particular attraction to the crowd, had 10 agents, Dr. Ludwig Erhard, West Germany's chancellor, had three, Anastas I. Mikoyan, a first deputy premier of the Soviet Union, had two motorcycle escorts beside his unmarked car.

*

St. Matthew's Roman Catholic Cathedral, where the funeral mass was said, was built 70 years ago. Its green copper dome, designed by Grant LaFarge, is a Washington landmark. The first funds for the church building came from Father William Matthews, the first native Maryland priest to be ordained. He sold some property and donated the money to help build the church.

*

This was to have been the night of the state dinner at the White House for Dr. Erhard. Dr. Erhard went to the White House today, with other foreign dignitaries, to pay his respects to Mrs. Kennedy.

*

Deputy Chief Howard V. Covell of the metropolitan police reported crime in Washington "well below normal for the last 48 hours."

*

The Women's Bureau said that in the last 36 hours it had processed 121 lost children—all but one safely reunited with their families by 4 P.M. today.

Funeral Traffic Delays Leaders

Dignitaries Wait at Church Half an Hour for Cars

WASHINGTON, Nov. 25 (UPI)—Some of the world's leaders were caught in a traffic jam today after the funeral service for President Kennedy at St. Matthew's Cathedral. There were so many world leaders, Cabinet members and close friends of Mr. Kennedy's at the funeral some had to wait more than 30 minutes for their limousines. The street in front of the cathedral was almost filled with the long, black cars reserved for dignitaries riding in the motorcade to Arlington National Cemetery behind the flag-draped coffin.

President de Gaulle of France, in a khaki military uniform, towered over other foreign visitors from Asia, Africa, Europe, and the Near East. So did Prince Philip, duke of Edinburgh, who was dressed in his naval uniform. The duke and British Prime Minister Sir Alec Douglas-Home and Lady Home looked over the jam and finally decided to walk a short distance to their car rather than wait for it to come to them.

Mrs. Kennedy and members of the family, President Johnson and former Presidents Dwight D. Eisenhower and Harry S. Truman moved away in their cars with little delay. One policeman said, however, that more than 200 vehicles were lined up on nearby streets for other guests and that it took time to move that many cars. All the high-ranking guests caught up with the funeral procession before it reached the cemetery, however, and apparently no one missed the graveside ceremony because of the traffic congestion.

Angier Biddle Duke, State Department protocol chief, at first attempted to escort heads of state and chiefs of foreign delegations to their automobiles. But this became a somewhat hopeless task as cars pulled up two or three abreast in front of the cathedral. Members of the Cabinet stood together on the church steps for nearly 45 minutes before deciding to search out their limousines instead of waiting to be picked up. The Supreme Court justices and their wives also came to the same decision a few minutes earlier.

Delayed Telegram Keeps Envoy Friend from Rites

COPENHAGEN, Denmark, Nov. 25 (Reuters)—A delayed telegram kept United States Ambassador William McCormick Blair Jr. from attending the funeral of President Kennedy, an Embassy official said today. Mr. Blair, a friend of the president's family, was invited to Washington in a telegram sent by Attorney General Robert F. Kennedy. The message did not reach the ambassador until early this morning. Danish telegraph officials said they would investigate the delay.

Shriver Decided Funeral Details

Selected Rituals That Were Followed by the Military

Special to The New York Times

WASHINGTON, Nov. 25—The funeral procession of John Fitzgerald Kennedy, which came off with flawless precision today, was based on long-prepared routines. The Military District of Washington, the headquarters for the capital, carries out all state pageants as part of its mission. It is based at Fort Myer, Va., overlooking the city.

The detailed arrangements for the funeral parade were ordered by Sargent Shriver, brother-in-law of Mrs. Kennedy. Mr. Shriver is director of the Peace Corps. It was Mr. Shriver, in accordance with the wishes of Mrs. Kennedy and members of the family, who selected from various proposals, all of which followed established rituals for state funerals. In making his selections, Mr. Shriver drew on the advice and resources of the Pentagon, the State Department and the White House as well as the Military District. The Military District was formed as a special Army command in 1942, ostensibly for the defense of the capital after the start of World War II. Over the years, however, its primary mission has been to provide ceremonial troops and honor guards.

Once the selections were made, the ceremonial chronology and details of position and movement fell into place almost automatically, subject to minor timing revisions. Other contingency arrangements were elaborate. Protocol, which could not be strictly adhered to in such a massive demonstration, was the province of the office of the State Department's protocol chief, Angier Biddle Duke.

The security arrangements were directed by Keith O. Lynch, head of the State Department's Division of Protective Security, which mustered more than 250 plainclothes agents from all over the nation. The entire District police force was under the direction of Deputy Chief Howard V. Covell. All the nonmilitary details were worked out in a command post at the State Department, where William B. Connett, deputy executive secretary of the department's secretariat, brought together 25 department officials to coordinate transportation, communications, logistics and protocol, as well as security. The Military District troops and others in the march were under the command of Maj. Gen. Philip C. Wehle, district commander.

The show unit of the Military District is the First Battle Group, Third Infantry, known as the "Old Guard." This is the Army's oldest active infantry unit. Its present commander is Lieut. Col. Richard E. Cross. The "Old Guard" supplied the horses and caisson for today's procession. It also furnished the guns for the graveside salute. It normally stands the watch over the Tomb of the Unknowns.

Among the major ceremonial occasions of recent years have been the visit of Queen Elizabeth II of Britain in 1957, the visit of Premier Khrushchev in 1959 and the triumphal return to the capital of Lieut. Col. John H. Glenn Jr., the astronaut, in 1962. One of the most striking demonstrations of the efficiency of the "Old Guard" in coping with great public ceremonies under difficult conditions was the Inaugural parade in 1961 of the president who was buried today. The capital had been inundated by a heavy snowfall the day before. The military unit, contributing Army equipment and personnel, helped the Sanitation Department clear the streets and carried out an impressive parade on the brilliant day of sunshine that marked the swearing-in.

28 New York Policemen Stand Guard at Funeral

WASHINGTON, Nov. 25 (AP)—Twenty-eight New York City policemen who had come to Washington on their own time and at their own expense stood guard today across the street from the church where funeral services were held for President Kennedy.

"We came down here to pay our respects to the president," Patrolman Maurice Wiesenberg said. "When we got here, the Washington police asked us to give them a hand. The crowds were more than they had expected." Mr. Wiesenberg said the delegation was the idea of Sgt. Harry Tedesco. By 1 P.M. yesterday, he said, 1,000 had volunteered. The 28 who were sent represented all the associations in the Police Department. Police Commissioner Michael J. Murphy arranged for them to take a police bus, and the policemen themselves paid the gasoline and toll expenses.

NEW YORK IS AS SILENT AS A VAST CATHEDRAL AS MILLIONS MOURN THE FALLEN PRESIDENT

By R. W. APPLE Jr.

New York wore a veil of silence yesterday in mourning for the fallen president. It was as if all the city's millions were in the cathedral in Washington where mass was being said for John Fitzgerald Kennedy. It was as if the city itself had become a church.

In their homes, in offices and even in bars, people watched the television broadcast of the funeral rites with religious intensity. Those few in the streets spoke softly, if at all. More than 4,000 people stood silently in Grand Central Terminal, watching a huge television screen as the president was laid to rest. Some of them genuflected. Others made the sign of the cross.

Large and small churches, as well as synagogues, held memorial services. Among them were St. Patrick's Roman Catholic Cathedral, the Protestant Episcopal Cathedral Church of St. John the Divine and Temple Emanu-El.

At noon, as the coffin containing the president's body was being borne into St. Matthew's Cathedral, the police in Times Square halted all traffic. People on the sidewalks bowed their heads. Then, from the top of the marquee of the Astor Hotel, taps reverberated across the square. The buglers were Andrew Frirsz of 258 West 91st Street and Stewart Koesten of 251 West 92d Street, 16-year-old Eagle Scouts.

At the same moment, planes on the taxiways at Idlewild Airport stopped. So did trains of the Pennsylvania, Long Island and New York Central railroads as well as buses at the Port Authority terminal. For the next five minutes most telegraph communications between the United States and the rest of the world were broken off by the cable companies. Between noon and 12:21, the deck guns of the aircraft carrier *Franklin D. Roosevelt,* docked at Bayonne, fired 21 times in salute.

At Charlie Yee's hand laundry on Rutland Road in Brooklyn, a small portable TV set was nestled among the shirts. Six Chinese stood there ironing and watching the funeral. The Riverdale Country Day School in the Bronx, where Mr. Kennedy had attended the fourth, fifth and sixth grades, was almost deserted. It was closed, like all other schools and colleges in the metropolitan area.

People everywhere seemed completely preoccupied with what was happening in Washington. A telephone operator who garbled a message apologized. "I just can't help it," she said, and began to sob.

Except for essential services, city and state offices were closed. So were the big department stores, the public library, the post offices, most business offices, the stock market, the legitimate theaters and the liquor stores. Hand-lettered signs were posted in the windows of thousands of small shops in every neighborhood. "Closed from 11 until 2," they said, "out of respect for the president." In one block on upper Broadway, only a dry-cleaning establishment was open at noon. A bar, a liquor store, a hardware store, a super market, a restaurant, all were closed. At Foley Square, only the New York City Criminal Courts were in session, and they adjourned at noon. A sign on a corner newsstand said:

"Closed because of a death in the American family."

Three days after the fact, many people still seemed unable to believe that Mr. Kennedy was dead. The only thing that seemed real was the picture on their television sets.

The caisson clattered up Pennsylvania Avenue and the commentator was saying: "Less than four years ago John F. Kennedy followed this same route. . . ." In Ferris Booth Hall at Columbia University, 35 students sat in a semicircle around a television receiver, watching intently. A young couple walked in, talking, and the others scowled at them in disgust.

In Washington, Richard Cardinal Cushing knelt before the altar. Then he began saying the Dies Irae, in Latin.

"That man was something to everybody," said a husky Negro in Jay's Bar at 307 West 125th Street. "He was not just something to a few people. There was a man who believed in things." He took an ample drink from his double Scotch. "I was talking about it the other night," he went on quietly. "Damned if I didn't get tears in my eyes. I don't know. . . . I just don't know. . . ."

Except for the sound of the television set and a few comments from the customers, the bar was quiet. On one wall was a sign: "In due respect to the death of our president, this juke box will not be played until further notice."

The mass continued with a prayer by Cardinal Cushing, his broad Boston accent unmistakable on a radio in a taxicab. "When my father died," said the cab driver, a Negro, "I didn't shed a tear until the funeral was almost over. When Mr. Kennedy died, I cried so much I couldn't drive this cab. I had to take it into the garage. I didn't know I could love a white man that much."

The Most Rev. Philip M. Hannan, the auxiliary bishop of Washington, was eulogizing the murdered president. Finally, he began reading from Mr. Kennedy's Inaugural Address:

"Ask not what your country . . ."

In an apartment on East 36th Street, four working girls looked stunned. None of them cried, but their eyes were swollen. They could cry no more. Two of the girls were knitting, and a third was drinking coffee. After a few moments the fourth went into the kitchen, closed the door, and stayed there until the services were over.

The cortege re-formed and began the long, slow trip to Arlington National Cemetery across the Potomac.

About 100 people, some of them shivering, watched its progress on TV screens set up inside the General Telephone and Electronics Company headquarters at 45th Street and Third Avenue. On the 47th floor of the Pan Am building, eight secretaries sat gloomily in the office of the airline's general counsel watching the same procession. None said anything.

The cortege reached Arlington, the burial service began and soon the bugler was playing taps.

In Grand Central, there was absolute quiet. The few men who were still wearing hats removed them. "So sad," murmured a woman on the balcony. "So sad." The huge screen mounted above the ticket booths of the New York, New Haven & Hartford Railroad showed Cardinal Cushing making the sign of the cross. Hundreds of hands among the throng that filled the concourse performed the same act of reverence.

The weather, ironically, was magnificent—no leaden murk like that on Saturday, but a bright sun in a cloudless blue sky. It was only 46 degrees at 3 o'clock, but there was no wind and the flags hung limp halfway up their staffs. In Central Park, 15-year-old John Rodriguez sat straddling his bicycle, listlessly watching an equally listless touch football game. He had ridden from Greenwich Village. "My mother was crying, my father was crying, everybody was crying," he said. "The more I stayed around the television set, the harder it got. I had to get and do something." In some ways, the park looked normal. The dogwalkers were there, the nurses pushing their baby carriages, the old men playing chess. But whatever they did, they did without gusto.

In Hackensack, N.J., Joseph Wilson, a keeper in the city jail, stood on the steps of the deserted county courthouse. "It has such an eerie effect," he said. At Mamaroneck Avenue and Main Street in White Plains, seven cars were lined up at a traffic light, all with their radios on. When the light changed, none moved and a policeman had to walk over to tell them to go ahead. On the New Jersey Turnpike, traffic dwindled almost to nothing. The highway had been jammed over the weekend with people headed for Washington to view the flag-draped coffin in the Rotunda of the Capitol.

Today the city will return to normal. It will be all noise and bustle and matter-of-factness. On the day they buried John Fitzgerald Kennedy, it was not.

SILENCE IS EVERYWHERE AS THRONGED CAPITAL BIDS FAREWELL TO PRESIDENT KENNEDY

Crowd Is Muted, Grief All Spent

A Million Drawn to Various Viewing Areas—Drums Beat Out Day's Somber Accent

By RUSSELL BAKER

Special to The New York Times

WASHINGTON, Nov. 25—It dawned cold, clear and quiet, this day when they buried the president. There was movement in the city, as there had been throughout the night, but it was crowd movement without the noise of crowds, and the silence was pervasive.

All through the night people had waited in lines 30 blocks long for the opportunity to file past his bier in the great Rotunda at the Capitol. And when the sun rose behind the Supreme Court Building, many had been standing for eight hours. At St. Matthew's Cathedral, where the funeral mass would be said for him at noon, and at Arlington National Cemetery, where the bugler would play taps for him, the people had begun to assemble before sunrise.

On Connecticut Avenue, the city's graceful shopping boulevard where the funeral procession would pass, the sidewalks were thickly lined before breakfast time. Children sat on the curbstones, patient and solemn, and shivered in the wan November morning.

When the huge bronze doors of the Capitol swung shut at 9 A.M., nearly a quarter of a million people had shuffled past the bier. The bier was the one that had supported Abraham Lincoln's coffin there 98 years ago, and the analogy to Lincoln's death must have been poignantly apparent to most of those who passed the coffin. The people came silently with small children—some carried sleeping babies in their arms—as though fulfilling some inner sense of obligation to the future.

And yet, the cranks and haters continued to operate silently in the night. Inspector Richard J. Felber, assistant chief of detectives, said that Washington authorities had received threatening telephone calls against "virtually every dignitary here." Many, he said, had been directed against Chief Justice Earl Warren.

As the morning advanced, it lit the city in a flood of brilliant sunlight, but the day remained cruel and raw. Nevertheless, enormous crowds were waiting silently all along the lengthy funeral route by the time the coffin had been strapped to the black caisson at the Capitol for its journey down Pennsylvania Avenue. On the high housetops along Connecticut Avenue, people followed the progress of the cortege on muted transistor radios, shivered in the wind and studied the streets below. Here and there in the waiting crowd, some stifled the impulse to sob as the dirges told the coffin's progress toward the White House. A few wept briefly, but generally it was a sober reflective crowd in which grief seemed to have been exhausted. The police later estimated it at 1,000,000, an enormous multitude in this city that normally shuns the streets during state occasions in preference for the comfort of home and television.

From the rooftops the city was a study in quiet. Flags at half staff rippled in the wind. The Washington Monument, with the sun behind it, loomed in somber silhouette over the White House. On the roof of the Army-Navy Club, looking down on the White House as the procession arrived, three white-jacketed waiters were outlined motionless against the sky.

At 11:25 A.M. the first military units that would lead the march from the White House to St. Matthew's swung out of Pennsylvania Avenue and stepped into 17th Street. And then the street, which flows into Connecticut Avenue, became a river of slowly moving uniforms. First came the Marine Corps band in red tunics, blue and red-striped trousers and white hats, their muffled drums draped in black, their brass instruments gleaming in the sunshine. Behind them came the cadets from West Point, marching with a precision to break a drill sergeant's heart.

Then the midshipmen from Annapolis in navy blue and white. The cadets from the Air Force Academy in lighter Air Force blue. And the men
from the Coast Guard Academy. Representatives from the women's service
units, honor guards from the services—soldiers, sailors, airmen, marines,
all moving until they stretched out through seven blocks. At 11:35 A.M.,
just as the coffin arrived at the White House, the strains of "Onward Christian Soldiers" drifted up through the leafless treetops of Farragut Square,
and the Navy band swung into sight.

When the procession had formed, it halted until the dignitaries who were
to walk behind the caisson could form position. Then a staccato of military
commands snapped along the column. The drums began to beat and the
line began to move. The drumbeat fell with soft and yet relentless regu-
larity—one, two, three, and a roll on the count of four. Its muffled command echoed off the city's stone and glass walls. Its melancholy roll
became the inescapable sound of the day, and events seemed to move at
metronomic command.

At 11:45, just before the caisson turned into 17th Street, the Air Force
band came into view and the melody of "America the Beautiful" swelled
on the air. But when the last strains were played—"and crown Thy good
with brotherhood, from sea to shining sea"—the drums again prevailed.
The caisson turned into 17th Street, the sidewalk crowd surged to keep
abreast of it, and the drums beat their relentless cadence. As the caisson
moved north up Connecticut Avenue, the drums beat and the hush of the
crowd became absolute, despite the constant pressing of the people to keep
pace with the coffin. In the sunlight that bathed the street, the flag gleamed
in brilliant red, white and blue. As it passed, there was only the sound of
jingling brass, the echoing clop-clop, clop-clop of the six white horses,
and the drum's insistent one, two, three and roll on the count of four.

And then came Mr. Kennedy's family, President Johnson and the dignitaries. In contrast to the majestic precision of the military unit, most of
them walked at their own pace in an ill-defined mass that stretched from
curb to curb. At their head was the president's widow, who had decided
that she would walk the eight blocks behind her husband s body. Deeply
veiled and with unfaltering step, she strode up Connecticut Avenue with
head and shoulders erect, looking neither left nor right, marching at a

soldier's pace. She was flanked by her husband's brothers, Robert F. and Edward M. Kennedy, who marched in step with her to create a tableau of resolution in the face of bereavement.

Behind her walked an assembly of the world's and the nation's leaders such as this city has never seen.

As Richard Cardinal Cushing sprinkled the waiting coffin with holy water at the church steps, the sound of a male voice singing "Jesu Domine" within was audible in the streets. The mass proceeded, and the drums were quieted for the hour as Cardinal Cushing prayed "that John Fitzgerald Kennedy may be spared all punishment and taken into Paradise."

By 1:15 P.M. the mass was ended, and outside the drums were beating again. The procession started on its final lap. Now the dignitaries and Mr. Kennedy's family were riding in closed limousines. The sun had fallen behind the rooftops and the shadowed street was colder.

Security guards had taken up walking positions beside the limousines of the statesmen. The car of President de Gaulle of France had more than any other—ten. The security agents formed a human wall around it as it moved toward the cemetery. The agents studied building windows and rooftops and examined faces and movement in the crowds with more than customary intensity.

The drums beat the message of the caisson's passage through the town—down Constitution Avenue, up around the Lincoln Memorial, across the cold Potomac and into Arlington Cemetery. There on the hillside, the trees were almost leafless and the failing sun cast its long shadows across the headstones of the nation's other fallen military men.

The hill where the grave lies, with an eternal flame lighted at the head, looks down onto the memorial to Lincoln and behind it, shimmering in the sunlight, lie the gleaming white domes and spires of Washington. The view is downward over the Potomac and in the distance lie the monuments to Jefferson and Washington and the Capitol dome.

Above, at the crest of the hill, sits the Custis-Lee mansion, home of Robert E. Lee before the Civil War. There, between Lincoln and Lee, today they placed the coffin over the grave at 2:55 P.M. The bugler sounded taps at 3:08. There was not another sound on the hillside, and the drums were quiet.

The Anonymous Also Pay Homage

Thousands Travel to Capital for Funeral on Impulse

By NAN ROBERTSON

Special to The New York Times

WASHINGTON, Nov. 25—Yesterday noon, Mr. and Mrs. David H. Harrison were sitting in their living room in Orange, N.J. Their television set was turned on, but they were reading the Sunday papers. "David," said Mrs. Harrison, suddenly, "I think we ought to go to Washington."

The Harrisons moved at once on impulse, taking their two little girls with them and leaving the dishes to soak in the sink. They left for Washington within the hour. "We'd never done anything like that before," said Mr. Harrison, an accountant, a careful man who likes to think things over. "We plan for weeks if we're just going to the Jersey shore for a couple of days. But yesterday we had a sense of real immediacy. We regretted we hadn't started sooner. We felt we couldn't waste an hour."

David and Lynne Harrison were astonished at themselves, but their story was typical. The Harrisons and thousands of others who traveled far to view the last journey of President Kennedy were compelled by deep instinct to share in history and to give their children a day that they might not comprehend now, but that they would always remember.

They dressed Judy, 5 years old, and Debra, 3, in their best clothes. Their cameras were left at home because to take them, they felt, was "touristy and sacrilegious." On the way to Washington, they talked to their daughters about what they were to see, trying to find words the children would understand.

This morning, the Harrisons rose at 6 o'clock in their motel, just across the Potomac from the Lincoln Memorial and down the hill from Arlington National Cemetery. They were luckier than many families along the route of the cortege who were haggard from a night in their automobiles. By 8 o'clock the Harrison family stood shivering on a curb at Connecticut Avenue, two blocks from the church where the requiem mass was to be said for President Kennedy.

The Harrisons are Jewish but rarely go to synagogue. When their children are older, they plan to go with them "to give them a sense of our culture, rather than religion."

"It may sound corny, but these are probably the most historical moments that we'll ever experience. Even though the children are so little, we want them to be here," Mrs. Harrison said as they waited for the procession to appear. "What struck all of us," Mrs. Harrison continued, "is this great sense of identity. The president is not a removed figure. I lost my own father a year and a half ago, but I am more shocked and sick at this. Someone so vital and alive, someone our own age. You don't expect to be present at their death." Mr. Harrison is 42, his wife 30.

The Harrisons' sense of urgency impelled them last night to drive from their motel to the Capitol, where President Kennedy lay in state. On the way they became confused and turned in "at a driveway with a little guard house" and asked directions of a "wonderful police captain."

"Say fella," the captain asked Mr. Harrison, "do you have any idea where you are?" They had turned in at the White House gate.

When they arrived at the Capitol, they were confronted with immense throngs and by now they were carrying their weary children. A policeman cautioned them that such were the crowds that they would never get into the Rotunda.

So today the Harrisons stood for the four hours, waiting for a spectacle that would unroll before them with bewildering swiftness. It was too much even for an adult to take in—the military marchers; the black-draped caisson rattling up the avenue; Mrs. Kennedy, her head held high under a flowing widow's veil; the giant de Gaulle; little Emperor Haile Selassie, resplendent in medals and braid.

"Look, mommy, they're draggin their feet along," said Judy, her hazel eyes big as the military marched by in slow step. "Why are they going so slow?"

"See darling, that's the casket," her mother said. "President Kennedy is there. That's the last we will ever see of him. And that's the riderless horse—remember, I told you about it?"

"He'll ride it tomorrow," Judy insisted.

"I don't think they can really comprehend—I don't think Debra, especially, has any conception of death," Mr. Harrison said as the coffin went by.

When it was over, Debra, in her father's arms, clutched her pink blanket and her eyeless teddy bear. Her face puckered in fleeting disappointment. "I didn't see President Kennedy," she said.

The Harrisons started back to Orange in early afternoon while the funeral was in its last moments at Arlington. At first they had thought to take the children to the Lincoln Memorial. They decided against it. "No, not the Lincoln Memorial today," Mrs. Harrison said. "The day really has had all its meaning."

Stunned Silence in Massachusetts

Memorial Services Timed With Rites at Arlington

By JOHN H. FENTON

Special to The New York Times

BOSTON, Nov. 25—Massachusetts paid its official tribute to a native son today in ceremonies timed to those in Arlington National Cemetery, where President Kennedy was laid to rest.

With Gov. Endicott Peabody in Washington attending the national services, Lieut. Gov. Francis X. Bellotti presided at the Boston rites on a plaza in front of the Massachusetts State House. The Right Rev. Msgr. Christopher Griffin, chaplain of the Massachusetts Senate, led the throng gathered in the Roman Catholic committal service for the dead.

Two battle groups of the 26th Yankee Division and a squadron from the 102d Fighter Wing of the Air National Guard stood at attention facing the Capitol. An artillery battalion from the Yankee Division fired a 21-gun salute on the adjacent Boston Common. At 5 P.M., the battalion fired a 50-gun salute, one for each state of the Union.

In suburban Brookline, where the late president was born, a delegation of high school students placed a wreath at the birthplace, at 83 Beals Street, in a municipal ceremony. Since Friday, the day that Mr. Kennedy was assassinated in Dallas, many people have walked past the three-story gray clapboard house. Many of them have paused to read the plaque commemorating the late president's birth.

Throughout the metropolitan area, as throughout the Commonwealth, Massachusetts observed the day of national mourning in stunned silence. Food purveyors and a few other places dealing in necessities were closed from 11 A.M. to 2 P.M. But all other businesses, except banks, were closed for the day. Banks were required by law to be open but they operated with only small staffs. Houses of worship of all denominations held memorial services and kept their buildings open through the day for meditation and prayer. The roar and thump of bulldozers and wrecking cranes, which have filled the air throughout the center of Boston for several months, were silent. The few pedestrians on the streets picked their way through rubble and mounds of earth and piping marking the process of a toll road extension in the area.

Tributes Offered at "Night of Stars"

Eleven thousand persons paid a hushed tribute last night to President Kennedy at the United Jewish Appeal's annual "Night of Stars" at Madison Square Garden, which is usually a festive occasion. President Johnson, in a special message, called on the audience to "complete the work he [President Kennedy] began so brilliantly. Let us build a world in which his children and ours will be proud to live."

Mayor Wagner and Senator Jacob K. Javits joined Mr. Johnson in urging a rededication to the late president's ideals. Senator Javits said that the nation "must go forward in unity" in the problems of civil rights, unemployment and world unity. Mayor Wagner said that the president had been killed "by hate in a season of hate," and that this was "a challenge we must all join to meet if his death is to be justified."

Kennedy Is Honored in Mississippi Mass

Special to The New York Times

JACKSON, Miss., Nov. 25—Civil and religious leaders in Mississippi took part here today in a solemn requiem mass celebrated by Bishop Richard O. Gerow in memory of President Kennedy. Numbers of Negro mourners knelt with white worshipers in St. Peter's Pro-Cathedral here.

The 79-year-old Mississippi Roman Catholic leader said he was "very gratified" that leaders of all religious groups and members of both races were present. He deplored what he said was "the hate that has been in the hearts of many men" and called for a rededication by Americans in praying for the nation and its leaders.

Among the civil officials who attended the mass were Mayor Allen C. Thompson of Jackson, former Gov. J. P. Coleman, former Gov. Hugh White, Attorney General Joe T. Patterson, Secretary of State Heber Ladner, State Treasurer-elect William Winter and State Superintendent of Education J. M. Tubb. Gov. Ross R. Barnett attended a service at the First Baptist Church here.

Crewmate Eulogizes Kennedy

LONG BEACH, Calif., Nov. 25 (UPI)—President Kennedy was eulogized today by a former fellow member of his PT-109 crew as the "best man—more man than I have ever known, or ever hope to know." Ray Starkey, who wept silently, made his remarks today during a memorial service aboard the cruiser U.S.S. *Oklahoma,* while Mr. Kennedy's funeral was in progress in Washington.

Taps Sounded on Train

PHILADELPHIA, Nov. 25 (AP)—A Pennsylvania Railroad local was stopped at noon in Narberth for one minute in respect to President Kennedy. The train conductor, Harry R. McAlister of Malvern, sounded taps on a bugle while 200 passengers stood with heads bowed.

GRIEVING PEOPLE FLOCK TO
KENNEDY MEMORIAL SERVICES
HERE AND ACROSS THE NATION

Speakers Warn Against Discord

"Insane Hatred" Is Blamed for Slaying of a "Brilliant and Brave" President

By McCANDLISH PHILLIPS

A solemn people, bereft of their elected president, answered the call for a day of national mourning yesterday by crowding churches and temples in New York and elsewhere in the nation. Whether in vast cathedrals or in cramped storefront churches, memorial services for John Fitzgerald Kennedy drew extraordinary attendance, including unusual numbers of people of high school and college age. Many services were timed to coincide with the requiem mass for Mr. Kennedy in St. Matthew's Cathedral in Washington.

The president was eulogized with great and sorrowing affection. Hymns that tell of timeless hope were sung. Ancient words of the Scriptures were read. But there was also a note of warning, almost of anger. Speakers said that discord and violence must not be allowed to infect the political and civil life of the republic any further.

More than 5,200 mourners took every available seat at Temple Emanu-El on Fifth Avenue at 65th Street, and about 1,000 people were turned away at the temple's entrance. It was the largest gathering in the 118-year history of the Reform congregation, exceeding the attendance at a similar service for the late Franklin Delano Roosevelt in 1945. The 2,500-seat auditorium was filled 45 minutes before the brief service began at noon. About 5,000 worshipers overflowed into the adjoining chapel. Another 1,500 took seats downstairs in Isaac Mayer Wise Hall and 750 in the assembly hall in the community house. The service was broadcast to them.

All the mourners were bareheaded, in contrast to the requirements for covered heads at Conservative and Orthodox services. Black was the predominant color of dress, though some women wore subdued browns, navy blues and dark reds. The 35-minute service began with a recitation of President Johnson's day of mourning proclamation, the singing of the National Anthem and the reading of the 91st Psalm ("I will say of the Lord, He is my strength and my fortress: my God; in Him will I trust"). Dr. Nathan Perilman, temple rabbi, said: "There are times when we feel the utter futility of words. This is such a time, when the heart of all mankind is stunned. Let this day not pass without firm resolve to drive out bigotry and hatred wherever they may be." In his sermon, Dr. Julius Mark, the senior rabbi, said that the death of Mr. Kennedy was a direct result of the "insane hatred which poisoned the hearts of otherwise decent and respectable citizens of our country.

"These hatreds, "he declared, "so vicious and depraved, were transferred to the twisted mind of the maniac who in murdering the youthful, brilliant and brave president of the United States destroyed the loftiest symbol of the American way of life." Noting that it was "not customary to recite the mourner's Kaddish for one not of our faith" but that Mr. Kennedy was "indeed a dear one many of us regarded as a member of our family," Dr. Mark led the congregation in the mourner's Kaddish: *"Yitgadal ve schmei rabbah* . . . (Magnified and sanctified be the name of God . . .)."

The Rev. Frank J. Currie said that the 1,000 persons who attended the hour-long service at Calvary Baptist Church, at 123 West 57th Street, included several hundred nonmembers who "walked in off the sidewalk." They heard the Rev. Stephen F. Olford, pastor, read the scriptural injunction that prayers be made for "kings and for all that are in authority; that we may lead a quiet and peaceable life." (I Timothy 2:2.)

The Right Rev. Dr. Horace W. B. Donegan, Episcopal bishop of New York, presided at a requiem celebration of Holy Communion at the Cathedral Church of St. John the Divine in Morningside Heights at Amsterdam Avenue and 112th Street. Three-thousand mourners attended, and more than half of them took the communion. The cathedral clergy were somberly garbed in black and white. There was no music. Women filled the choir stalls. The words were those of the Bible and the Book of Common Prayer.

An elderly woman, who had come expecting ceremony and colors, the drums of a cathedral memorial service, did not grasp the spirit of the starkly simple communion service, which as one of the clergy said afterward is "the same for president and pauper." "I expected a better service than this for a president," the woman said with evident disappointment.

Bishop Donegan read lines of special poignancy from the prayer book. "Save us from violence, discord and confusion, from pride and arrogancy, and from every evil way. Defend our liberties, and fashion into one united people the multitudes brought hither out of many kindreds and tongues."

At the Fifth Avenue Presbyterian Church, the Rev. Dr. Bryant M. Kirkland told 1,800 worshipers that "all share the blame for the violence that has gripped the land." He said Americans were blind to the "moral decay that has seeped into the land." Dr. Kirkland said that Mr. Kennedy's death marked a break in progress toward social justice, and he declared that justice was now on trial in the United States. In prayer, the Rev. Kenneth Jones, assistant pastor, implored the help of the One who can "calm both the raging seas and the madness of men."

The 1,000 persons who crowded St. Paul's Chapel on the campus of Columbia University was said to be the largest congregation ever to attend a service in the red-brick Romanesque chapel, built at the turn of the century. Here it was especially clear that Mr. Kennedy had exerted a strong appeal on young people. Dr. Grayson Kirk, president of Columbia, urged "more energy against the extremists and their poison" and "more self-discipline, which has never been congenial to our people, but upon which the future of our country depends." Dr. Kirk said that the president had possessed a special quality of courage—"the courage that goes beyond that of many intelligent men who, faced with a grave and unpleasant problem, lapse into the agony of indecision—or the error of impulsive judgment."

At Temple Rodeph Sholom, 7 West 83d Street, Rabbi Louis I. Newman said: "President Kennedy's martyrdom is an outgrowth of the violence and hatred which flourish today. The American people must take stock of itself, and realize that their beloved captain has been a sacrifice to the gospel of force and quick-trigger tactics which are shown on the cinema. . . ." Rabbi

Newman said that "the greatness of John F. Kennedy lay principally in his role as spokesman for the new generation of our times. Youthful, bouyant, vivacious and charming, he symbolized the most appealing features of the American character and personality."

About 1,400 mourners filled the main floor of the Riverside Church. Many were teen-agers and young mothers with small children. Some stayed after the service to pray or just to sit and gaze meditatively. The Rev. Eugene E. Laubach, minister of Christian education, described Mr. Kennedy as one who had become "the symbol of the American ideal, the image of the successful 20th Century man.

"When a person old and full of years slips to a quiet death, it is not hard to take comfort in the mercy of God who has called a loved one to rest," he said, "but when tragedy cuts down one young and full of promise we are stunned by the waste, the irrationality of it all." In the Call to Worship, these words of Scripture were read: "Jesus said, I am the resurrection and the life. He that believeth on me, though he were dead, yet shall he live, and he that liveth and believeth on me shall never die."

Nine Buddhists led by a monk from Taiwan stood in facing lines with a special altar between them as the monk prayed that President Kennedy be allowed to enter the "pure land."

On the altar in the Eastern State Buddhist Temple of America, 64 Mott Street, in Chinatown, were steaming hot plates of rice and stringbeans and bamboo shoots, offered to President Kennedy "because the soul is still alive."

The 35-piece New York Staff Band of the Salvation Army played the Navy hymn "Eternal Father Strong to Save" in an afternoon service attended by 1,200 army members and friends from several Eastern states, held in the Centennial Memorial Temple at 120 West 14th Street. Commissioner Holland French, national commander, presented the eulogy.

Manhattanville College of the Sacred Heart in Westchester County, which was attended by four of the Kennedys, held a solemn high requiem. One thousand persons, including 800 students, attended. Ethel Kennedy, the wife of the attorney general, his sisters, Mrs. Jean K. Smith and Mrs. Eunice K. Shriver, and his sister-in-law, Mrs. Joan Kennedy, all went to school at Manhattanville.

In an old weathered church near the seafront in Long Branch, N.J., not far from the spot where another of the nation's presidents died of wounds from an assassin's bullet, a memorial service was held for Mr. Kennedy. The undenominational program, led by Mayor Milton F. Untermeyer Jr. and Councilman Edgar Dinkelspiel, was conducted in the Church of the Presidents, a gray wooden building where three of the nation's former presidents had worshipped. It is a few hundred yards from the site of the old Francklyn Cottage, where President James Garfield died after being shot in Washington. The church is now a museum of the Long Branch Historical Society. Ulysses S. Grant and Woodrow Wilson had summer homes nearby and sometimes worshipped in it.

Episcopal Service Uses a Part of Catholic Mass

Portions of the Protestant Episcopal and the Roman Catholic requiem services were combined yesterday in a memorial service for John F. Kennedy at the Episcopal Church of the Epiphany at York Avenue and 74th Street. Mr. Kennedy was a Roman Catholic. The Collect, the Gospel and the Creed were taken from the Episcopal prayer book. These were blended with the Pro-Anaphora (before the offering up of the elements) portion, including the Day of Wrath sequence, from a Roman Catholic burial mass missal.

The Rev. Dr. Hugh McCandless, rector, wore black and said the Roman Catholic part. The curate, the Rev. David Wayne, wore a white stole and said the Episcopal part. White is customary for a funeral in the Episcopal Church; black is used in Catholic requiems, the rector said. The $200 offering was sent to Catholic Charities as a memorial to Mr. Kennedy.

U.N. Leaders and Staff Mourn at St. Patrick's

World Group in Center Pews—Bishop Griffiths Appeals for an End of Violence

By GEORGE DUGAN

The United Nations mourned the death of President Kennedy yesterday at a special pontifical requiem mass in St. Patrick's Cathedral. Among the 3,500 silent mourners who filled the Roman Catholic cathedral to overflowing were several hundred leaders and staff personnel of the world body.

They occupied central pews near a flag-draped catafalque flanked on each side by three tall, flickering candles. A few red and white roses were scattered over the top of the catafalque, apparently dropped there by sorrowing worshipers. Throughout the simple, hour-long ceremony the only sounds outside the service were occasional muffled coughs—a discordant overtone to the somber liturgy of the dead intoned by the cathedral choir.

Among the United Nations representatives were C. V. Narasimhan, executive assistant to Secretary General U Thant; Nikolai T. Fedorenko, chief of the Soviet delegation; Francis T. Plimpton, deputy permanent representative from the United States, representing Adlai E. Stevenson; Frederick H. Boland of Ireland, and A. B. Bhadkamkar, deputy permanent delegate from India. Other nations represented included Burma, Ceylon, Nigeria, Algeria, Tunisia, Norway and Holland.

The Most Rev. James H. Griffiths, auxiliary bishop of the Roman Catholic Archdiocese of New York and permanent observer for the Vatican at the United Nations, celebrated the mass. At the conclusion of the service the bishop left the high altar and circled the catafalque, sprinkling it with holy water. He then returned to his episcopal chair facing the mourners and thanked them for participating in the mass offered for the "repose of the soul of our martyred president, John Fitzgerald Kennedy."

The prelate reminded the silent throng that in the last few years Americans have been "appalled at the upsurge of violence in other sectors of the earth.

"But today," he observed, "downcast and shamed we have witnessed the injection of this detestable and contemptible pattern and factor into our own midst and we lament it and condemn it as contrary to our whole heritage. With almost perfect unanimity the nations of the world have excoriated this barbarous act of assassination. It has called forth vehement resentment. It has enkindled primitive urges of revenge." But, Bishop Griffiths added, "I firmly believe that if John F. Kennedy could speak from his bier this morning, in his great soul he would repeat the words of his Saviour, dying derelict on the cross of immolation, 'Father, forgive them for they know not what they do.'

"His passing has left a great gap," the bishop said, "a void in the soul of the nations. But we are heartened for in tyranny when the tyrant dies the whole structure may fall apart, in democracy when the leader is struck down, as in this case, the responsibility is handed on as a torch of liberty."

When the prelate finished speaking the sound of taps echoed through the building. As the last notes died the bishop led the mourners in the singing of "The Star-Spangled Banner."

The Most Rev. Joseph F. Flannelly, administrator of the cathedral, personally greeted the United Nations representatives as they quietly filed out of the edifice. Bishop Griffiths was assisted at the altar by Msgr. Francis X. Duffy, head of St. Patrick's Information Center, the Rev. John Moore of St. Monica's Church and the Rev. Vincent Fox of the cathedral staff. Because of the unusual crowd, which many observers said exceeded some Christmas and Easter masses, communion was distributed after, instead of during, the service.

Carrier's Crew Tosses a Wreath

Silent Ritual Pays Tribute to "a Good Shipmate"

By JOHN SIBLEY

Special to The New York Times

ABOARD THE *FRANKLIN D. ROOSEVELT*, at Sea, Nov. 25—With a wreath tossed into the sparkling North Atlantic, the men of this aircraft carrier paid final respects this afternoon to "a good shipmate," John F. Kennedy. The wordless ceremony took place as the giant warship steamed eastward past Ambrose Lightship for three days of rigorous sea trials after a five-month overhaul at the New York Naval Shipyard in Brooklyn.

The skipper, Capt. Gerald E. Miller, strode briskly, between two lines of rigid Marines and sailors, from the hangar deck to the edge of the starboard aircraft elevator. For 30 seconds he stood silently, his head slightly bowed, holding in both hands the black-ribboned wreath. Then he threw the wreath into the sea, watched momentarily as it drifted astern, turned about smartly, saluted the guard and returned to the bridge.

Sailors and civilian shipyard workers who had gathered on the hangar deck returned quietly to their tasks. Conversation was hushed.

Earlier, before dock lines were cast off at the Naval Supply Base at Bayonne, N.J., the *Franklin D. Roosevelt* fired a 21-gun salute. The saluting battery fired the first round exactly at noon, then 20 more shots at one-minute intervals. The Plan of the Day, issued daily by the carrier's executive officer, Capt. John R. Kincaid, contained a brief statement noting the nation's shock at the late president's assassination. The bulletin added: "We of the U.S.S. *Franklin D. Roosevelt* have a more personal sorrow at his death, not only because he was our Commander in Chief, but also because he served courageously as well in the Navy during World War II. His concern, his interest and his actions toward the Navy show he knew what only one who has served in the Navy knows: what the words 'a good shipmate' mean."

The ship's Roman Catholic chaplain, Comdr. Thomas Wootten, said crew members had shown intensely personal feelings about President Kennedy's death. Commander Wootten described the late president as an uncommon man with a common touch. Commander Wootten said a memorial mass for President Kennedy in the hangar bay this morning. A similar service was conducted in the forecastle by the Protestant chaplain, Comdr. Charles Robinson. Both were well attended.

As the Long Island shore dropped below the horizon, off-duty officers gathered in the wardroom to watch on television the late president's casket being borne to the Arlington National Cemetery. Interference by the ship's intricate electronic equipment caused violent distortion of the televised picture. But no eyes left the screen as the horse-drawn caisson moved slowly over the Memorial Bridge across the Potomac River.

Ironically, this ship got her name because of the death of a president. She was originally to have been christened the *Coral Sea*. But when President Roosevelt died on April 12, 1945, the ship, nearing completion at the Brooklyn Navy Yard, was renamed. She is the only aircraft carrier named for a president.

250,000 MOURNERS FILE SILENTLY PAST COFFIN IN CAPITOL'S ROTUNDA DURING 18 HOURS

Long Line Moves Through Night

Outpouring Greater Than Expected by the Police—5,000 Unable to Get In

By BEN A. FRANKLIN

Special to The New York Times

WASHINGTON, Nov. 25—The strong faces of America paid silent tribute to the dead president in the Capitol Rotunda today.

A quarter of a million people, bearing their burden of grief, filed past the bronze coffin under the vaulting Capitol dome yesterday and through the near-freezing night and into this morning. They waited and walked slowly to pay a brief but, to most, immensely meaningful measure of re-spect to President Kennedy.

Some waited as long as 10 hours in a line of people that stretched 30 blocks along East Capitol Street to the Anacostia River and then doubled back toward the Capitol. In the Rotunda they were granted, at the most, a 30-second meditation before the bier as the seemingly endless throng of mourners pressed on. For 18 hours, from 3 P.M. yesterday until 9 A.M. today, the steady shuffle of feet continued. Few words were spoken. The sound of patient footfalls was heard as an oddly stirring counterpoint to the echoing organ music—which some mourners felt was an obtrusion.

Television cameras in the Rotunda transmitted the images of mourners' faces through the night. The pictures said more about the nation's grief than all the eulogies. The National Broadcasting Company carried pictures of the procession without comment until 7 this morning.

Mrs. Kennedy returned once to the Rotunda at about 9 last night, joining the mourners in a final tribute there to her husband. She had been there earlier in the day. Among the mourners also was Adlai E. Stevenson, twice a Democratic candidate for president and now United States representative to the United Nations.

The great outpouring of citizens was not expected. The Metropolitan Police had to rush extra patrolmen to the Capitol Plaza yesterday afternoon to deal with the milling mass of persons waiting to enter the Capitol. It took several hours to organize orderly lines. Late last night, military authorities in charge of the funeral arrangements altered the original plan, which called for two single lines of mourners, one on each side of the coffin. They expanded the silent lines first to two abreast, then three and four.

Not all the mourners got inside. About 5,000 persons, stretched out over five blocks in the thin sunlight of morning, finally were told they could not be admitted. At midnight policemen had toured the lines, warning those near the ends that they almost certainly would not gain admission. The warning was based in part on an overnight decision to close the Capitol doors at 9 A.M. instead of 10 as scheduled. The warning, given courteously by policemen who had been on duty nearly 16 hours, was repeated hourly after 2 A.M.

"They just wouldn't believe us," a policeman said.

The last hour was marred by the only disorder of the 18-hour vigil. At 8:30 A.M., Deputy Chief Loraine T. Johnson of the District of Columbia Police, in charge of the Capitol Plaza detail, "cut" the line near the east front steps, leaving only a hundred or so persons between him and the Rotunda. He acted after a large group of persons had tried to crash the line. Unable to sort out the crashers from those waiting in line, many for five hours, Chief Johnson regretfully ordered the line to disperse.

Among those disappointed were two Cleveland high school girls, Martha Cremo and Nancy Perry. "It took us two days to persuade our parents to let us come here, and now look what has happened," Miss Cremo said. They had been in line since 3 A.M.

Former Vice President Richard M. Nixon and his wife were among the last to be admitted before the Rotunda was closed. Then hundreds of members of Congress and other Government officials entered from interior corridors, as the Nixons had, to conclude the period of the president's lying in state.

Families came in great numbers. Sleepy-eyed children, many of them awed but uncomprehending, moved slowly past the bier with their parents. A Negro father, his gaze fixed steadily on the flag-draped coffin, carried a sleeping child in his arms. Men, women and children made the sign of the cross as they reached the bier. Many dabbed their eyes with handkerchiefs. All fell silent in the Rotunda. They were a different crowd when they left. They drifted away in little groups, down the grassy sweep of Capitol Hill toward the city below.

Kennedy's Rescuer in Wartime Mourns

ALTO, Mich., Nov. 25 (UPI)—The skipper of the PT boat that rescued President Kennedy from a South Pacific island in World War II spent an hour alone in St. Adalbert's Church yesterday. "I thought it would be good to go to a [Roman] Catholic church," said William Liebenow. "The president was a Catholic and—well, I'm not a regular churchgoer."

Mr. Liebenow, chief chemist of the Chesapeake & Ohio Railway, commanded the boat that took Mr. Kennedy off the island that he and part of his crew had reached when his PT-109 was cut in half by an enemy ship. He went to church yesterday morning alone, "just thinking."

Additional List of Dignitaries at President Kennedy's Funeral

Special to The New York Times

WASHINGTON, Nov. 25—*Following are additions to a list published in* The New York Times *today of Government leaders who attended President Kennedy's funeral.*

Europe

ITALY

Cesare Merzagora, president of Italian Senate.

RUMANIA

Gheorghe Gaston Marin, vice president of the Council of Ministers.
Victor Ionescu, minister of foreign trade.
Vasile Pungan, director of North American affairs.

U.S.S.R.

Anatoly F. Dobrynin, ambassador to the United States.
Mikhail Smirnovsky, chief, American section, Ministry of Foreign Affairs.

Asia

CAMBODIA

Chan Youran, director of political affairs, Ministry of Foreign Affairs.

KOREA

Yong Shik Kim, foreign minister.
Chung Hoy Kim, ambassador to the United States.

NEPAL

M. P. Koirala, ambassador to the United States.

NEW ZEALAND

George R. Laking, ambassador to the United States.

PHILIPPINES

Amelito Mutuc, ambassador to the United States.
Senator Raul Manglapus.

THAILAND

Sukit Nimanheim, ambassador designate.

Western Hemisphere

COLOMBIA

German Zea, ambassador to the United States.

HAITI

Carlet Auguste, ambassador to the United Nations.
Fern Baguidy, ambassador to the Organization of American States.

PARAGUAY

Dr. Jan Plate, ambassador to the United States.

TRINIDAD and TOBAGO

Sir Ellis E. I. Clarke, ambassador to the United States.

ORGANIZATION OF AMERICAN STATES

Dr. José A. Mora, secretary general.
Dr. William Sanders, assistant secretary general.
Rodolfo A. Weidmann, representative of Argentina.
Ilmar Penna Marinho, representative of Brazil.
Don Manuel Trucco, representative of Chile.
Alfredo Jasquez Carrizosa, representative of Colombia.
José Bonilla Atiles, representative of the Dominican Republic.
Dr. Galo Leoro, alternate representative of Ecuador.
Hernan Corrales Padella, representative of Honduras.
Vicente Sanchez Gavito, representative of Mexico.
Andres Fenochio, alternate representative of Mexico.
Dr. Juan Bautista de Lavalle, representative of Peru.
Ward P. Allen, alternate representative of the United States.
Dr. Emilio N. Oribe, interim representative of Uruguay.

Africa

ALGERIA

Laiashi Vaker, director of economic affairs, Ministry of Foreign Affairs.

BURUNDI

Leon Ndenzako, ambassador to the United States.

IVORY COAST

Konan Bedie, ambassador to the United States.

MALI

Oumar Sow, ambassador to the United States.
Sory Coulibaly, ambassador to the United Nations.
Boubacar Casse, deputy secretary general, Ministry of Foreign Affairs.

SENEGAL

Dr. Ousmane Soce Diop, ambassador to the United States.

SOUTH AFRICA

Dr. Willem C. Naude, ambassador to the United States.

UGANDA

John K. Babiiha, minister of animal industries, game and fisheries.

Mideast

CYPRUS

Zenon Rossides, ambassador to the United States.

IRAQ

Ali Haidar Sulaiman, ambassador to the United States.

SYRIA

Salah Al-Din Tarazi, ambassador to the United Nations.
Walid Majid, chargé d'affaires of the Syrian Embassy in Washington.
Jawdat el Mufti, minister to the United Nations.

UNITED ARAB REPUBLIC

Mustafa Kamel, ambassador to the United States.
Mahmud Riad, ambassador to the United Nations.

YEMEN

Muhsin al-Ayni, ambassador to the United States.

Irish Cousin Flies In Just in Time

WASHINGTON, Nov. 25 (AP)—A nurse from New Ross, Ireland, a distant cousin of President Kennedy, arrived just in time today to attend his funeral services at St. Matthew's Cathedral. Completing a trans-Atlantic dash, Mary Ann Ryan was met at National Airport by a limousine and driven at high speed, with a motorcycle escort, to the cathedral.

Miss Ryan's trip began at Dunganstown, County Wexford, where she received, through the United States Embassy at Dublin, a request from the Kennedy family to attend the funeral. She met Mr. Kennedy last summer when he visited his ancestral home at Dunganstown, Ireland.

Police squad cars sped her on Sunday from Dunganstown, where she had been spending the weekend at home, to Shannon. There a Pan-American Airways plane made a special stop to pick her up. She was sped through customs at New York and put aboard a twin-engined plane that Pan-American had rented because there was no quick connection with regular airline flights.

Last summer at Dunganstown, Mr. Kennedy put his arm around Miss Ryan and said: "You know, you look like a Kennedy. You have the Irish smile.

"Eternal Flame" at Arlington
Will Be Only Temporary Setup

Special to The New York Times

WASHINGTON, Nov. 25—The "eternal flame" that Mrs. John F. Kennedy lighted at her husband's grave in Arlington National Cemetery today is a temporary installation. It is a cylinder of propane gas that feeds the flame at the burning jet at a pressure high enough to resist being blown out by the heaviest wind. The device was installed late last night or early this morning at the request of Mrs. Kennedy. It is the only such eternal flame in Arlington Cemetery.

No final decision has been made on the nature of a more permanent arrangement. A possibility is piping natural gas from regular mains near the Custis-Lee mansion a few feet away, with a pump in the line to maintain proper pressure.

PRESIDENT SPEAKS

Tells Governors He'll Press Civil Rights and Tax Bills

By E. W. KENWORTHY

Special to The New York Times

WASHINGTON, Nov. 25—President Johnson told a group of governors tonight that he would press for enactment of the tax cut and civil rights legislation proposed by President Kennedy. Furthermore, he indicated to the governors that his plea for Congressional action on these two bills would figure prominently in the speech he will make Wednesday to a joint session of Congress.

Although several governors agreed after the meeting that President Johnson had stated very plainly his intentions to urge passage of these bills, his remarks on these issues were omitted in excerpts from the speech issued by the White House. The president met with about 30 governors, Democratic and Republican, who had attended the funeral for President Kennedy today. The meeting, which was so hastily set up that some governors were called back from airports to attend, took place in the former vice president's suite in the Executive Office Building.

It could have been no surprise to the governors that President Johnson would put his weight behind the tax cut and civil rights bills. On civil rights, he has been making speeches all over the country, and the issue deeply engages his sympathies. However, it did cause some surprise here that he intended to bear down on these issues in his initial speech to Congress. Officials here have been saying that the president would speak very briefly and concentrate on asserting his determination to continue the foreign and defense policies of his predecessor.

From what he was reported to have told the governors tonight, he means also to assure Congress that his pledge of continuity extends to the late President Kennedy's domestic programs as well. "I think continuity without confusion has got to be our password and has got to be the key to our system," he said. "I intend to tell Congress that we intend to honor the commitments we have made at home and abroad, and I am going to tell them that I understand my own limitations, but I am going to do the best I can with your help and God's."

Despite the forthright position President Johnson took on the two controversial bills, his sincerity and modesty in the face of the staggering burden he has assumed quite evidently impressed the governors. At the end of his 30-minute speech, they gave him a standing ovation.

His speech was variously described by the governors as "impressive," "moving" and "inspirational." Republican Gov. William W. Scranton of Pennsylvania told reporters that the president "felt very strongly" that if it were not possible to get Congressional approval of tax and civil rights legislation then "we are not working together when we should be." Governor Rockefeller of New York, who is a candidate for his party's presidential nomination next year, said that Mr. Johnson had also discussed in general terms the need for Federal legislation in the field of education. Gov. Edmund G. Brown, Democrat of California, said that Mr. Johnson had astounded the governors by his familiarity with the problems of their states.

The governors did not indicate that President Johnson had any hope of getting Congress to act on taxes and civil rights before the end of this session. But they did indicate that he intended to press for action early in the next session. Despite all the pledges of support that he is now receiving, he is certain to meet Southern opposition on civil rights as adamant as that which confronted President Kennedy. In 1946, President Harry S. Truman discovered that affection and respect in which he was held as a former member of the Senate did not result in any change of heart or principles by Southern conservatives when he submitted his Fair Deal program. It is accepted as a political fact of life here that President Johnson's honeymoon, despite all his former skill as Senate majority leader, will be as short-lived next year.

In the area of foreign affairs, President Johnson has assured Premier

Khrushchev that he intends to carry on the efforts of his predecessor to improve relations between the United States and the Soviet Union. This assurance was conveyed in a telegram yesterday, thanking the Soviet premier for his message of sympathy Saturday on the death of President Kennedy. President Johnson's reply to Mr. Khrushchev was released today by the Soviet Government. It was disseminated by Tass, the official Soviet press agency, and broadcast by the Moscow radio. State Department officials confirmed the accuracy of the text. It read:

"On behalf of the American people I should like to thank you for the condolences you have expressed on the tragic death of President Kennedy. All President Kennedy's efforts were devoted to the cause of peace and the peaceful settlement of international problems and to improving relations between all countries including the Soviet Union and the United States. I intend to continue to strive toward the achievement of these aims."

Today President Johnson sent a message to all members of the armed services, calling on them to "rededicate ourselves to the continuing tasks before us, remembering always that the price of our liberty is eternal vigilance."

During a reception in the State Department this evening for the heads of Government, chiefs of state and other foreign dignitaries who came to President Kennedy's funeral, Mr. Johnson had brief private talks with President de Gaulle of France, Premier Hayato Ikeda of Japan and Prime Minister Lester B. Pearson of Canada. Then, at 8 o'clock, he met with 35 governors, thanking them for coming to the funeral and asking for their support in the coming months. Finally, at 8:45, he conferred in the Executive Office Building with Secretary of the Treasury Douglas Dillon, Walter W. Heller, chairman of the Council of Economic Advisers, and Kermit Gordon, budget director, on the economic situation and the budget he must send to Congress in January.

At 4 P.M., after the burial service in Arlington National Cemetery this afternoon, President Johnson talked with Adlai E. Stevenson on United Nations affairs. They particularly discussed cooperation in space, which is under discussion in New York. Pierre Salinger, White House press secretary, said the president ordered a continuation of the policy of seeking cooperation in space.

Tomorrow Mr. Johnson will move into the Oval Room in the White

House, from which all Mr. Kennedy's personal mementos and furnishings have been removed.

President Johnson is sending personal replies to all official messages of condolence sent him by chiefs of state and heads of government. The telegram to Premier Khrushchev, which was delivered through the United States Embassy in Moscow, was one of about 50 replies dispatched so far. Replies to messages from heads of government who did not come to Washington for the funeral are being sent by cable for delivery by United States ambassadors. Those heads of government who are here will receive letters delivered to their embassies. Mr. Salinger said that approximately 60 messages had been sent to heads of government. All of them, he said, express appreciation of the message of condolence and reaffirm United States policies, with particular reference to each country.

The reply to Premier Khrushchev, officials made plain, was intended to make response to the somewhat unusual content and tone of the Russian's message. Mr. Khrushchev's message to President Johnson was long for an expression of condolence. He spoke of President Kennedy's death as a blow "to all people who cherish the cause of peace and Soviet-American cooperation." He was particularly grieved that it occurred when "there appeared signs of relaxation of international tension and a prospect has opened for improving relations between the U.S.S.R. and the United States." In the same vein, Mr. Khrushchev said that Mr. Kennedy was a person who "tried to find ways for negotiated settlements" on problems dividing the world, and he hoped that the search for such settlements would continue.

This message was viewed as obviously indicating two concerns following President Kennedy's assassination. First, it was believed here that Premier Khrushchev was genuinely concerned with keeping alive the glow of détente that has existed since the signing of the limited nuclear test ban treaty. Second, it was felt he was also fearful of a wave of anti-Soviet feeling in the United States because of the left-wing record of the suspected assassin, Lee H. Oswald. Articles in the Soviet press emphasizing that Oswald was not granted Soviet citizenship when he applied for it and asserting that he was a "Trotskyite" testify to the fear in Moscow that the American people would think the Soviet Government was implicated in the assassination.

As a matter of fact, officials here shared these fears. Because they did not believe that any Communist Government or movement directed the assassination, they warned the Dallas police and the Texas state prosecutors from assigning any political motivations for the crime.

President Johnson's reply was calculated to assure Premier Khrushchev that the United States would continue to work for accommodations where they could be made consistently with the security of the Western coalition.

It is believed here that Moscow will draw reassurance also from President Johnson's request for all of President Kennedy's Cabinet and the White House staff to remain at their posts. The State Department, on the president's orders, has also directed ambassadors not to submit their resignations in the customary practice on a change of presidents. This means that the officials who played the principal roles in reaching an accord on the test ban treaty—Secretary of State Dean Rusk, Under Secretary of State W. Averell Harriman and McGeorge Bundy, White House assistant on national security affairs—will continue to advise the president, at least for the time being.

All the Cabinet members and high presidential appointees have submitted undated resignations to President Johnson, even though they have consented to stay on. But the submission of such undated resignations is normal procedure, which is intended to give the president complete freedom to make any changes in his official family that he desires. The expectation here is that some of the Kennedy entourage whose duties were primarily political or legislative may leave early in the next session of Congress to give Mr. Johnson the opportunity to fill the jobs of Congressional liaison with men close to him. On the other hand, it is believed that the so-called "Bundy Operation"—the small staff working with Mr. Bundy on foreign problems in cooperation with the State Department—will remain substantially intact for some time.

President Johnson's day was largely devoted to attendance at the requiem mass for President Kennedy, the burial in Arlington National Cemetery and the reception this evening at the State Department for foreign dignitaries.

Text of Statement

Following is the text of President Johnson's message to the armed forces:

We have suffered a great national loss and sorrow in the death of the commander in chief, President John Fitzgerald Kennedy. A man who knew war and hated it, he loved peace all the more and sought to make it secure in the world for your children and his. He will be remembered and honored for his valor and courage in serving that cause of peace which you serve in your fateful vigil for freedom.

Our Constitution provides for the orderly continuity of the civil offices of our Government. In the transition brought upon us by tragedy, there is no interruption in the continuity of that commitment to strength, stead-fastness and selfless sacrifice which has kept us free and the world at peace.

As you stand your guard of freedom and peace, you may know that the policies and purposes of your country are unchanged and unchangeable in seeking honorable peace, the friendship and alliance of free nations and the building of a responsible world free of the causes of hatred, division, oppression and human despair. Praying to be worthy of God's guidance, let us rededicate ourselves to the continuing tasks before us, remembering always that the price of our liberty is eternal vigilance.

Johnson Meets With Visitors

By MAX FRANKEL

Special to The New York Times

WASHINGTON, Nov. 25—The world's men of title and power went side by side to John F. Kennedy's grave today in a demonstration of tribute and unity that the living president never enjoyed. Then they turned, kings and Communists, dark men and light men, in sash and tur-ban and uniform and morning frock coat, to pay their respects to Mrs. Kennedy and to wait for their first words with President Johnson.

Towering above them all in the procession of the famous and in the attentions of Americans was the uniformed figure of Charles de Gaulle, the president of France. General de Gaulle, among the first dignitaries to arrive yesterday, was among the first to leave Washington tonight. He was the first chief of state to confer privately, if briefly, with President Johnson. The president announced later that General de Gaulle would visit the United States again early next year.

The two men met 30 months ago in Paris, and General de Gaulle showed scant deference to the then vice president. "What have you come to learn?" he asked Mr. Johnson coldly that day. They had a prompt reunion this evening, however, after a large presidential reception for 220 foreign visitors. The talk was probably the most effective demonstration of the suddenly changed stature of Lyndon B. Johnson and its recognition by the most independent of foreign celebrities.

Not much business was discussed in any of the dozens of brief conversations between Mr. Johnson and other heads of government. The new president was besieged by requests for more formal audiences from a world community obviously in search of a clue to his personality and political style.

President de Gaulle reached the president's buffet dinner in the John Quincy Adams Room at the State Department shortly after 6 o'clock. They met privately an hour later for about 15 minutes in the office of Secretary of State Dean Rusk. President Johnson also spent 15 minutes there with Prime Minister Hayato Ikeda of Japan and Prime Minister Lester B. Pearson of Canada.

The French president told Mr. Johnson he had come here today only on an emotional journey as the representative of the French people and not to discuss the great issues that have set him apart within the Western alliance, particularly from United States policies. Both men agreed that they now had to do what they could to find a mutual accommodation. Before the assassination, there had been talk of General de Gaulle's repaying a visit to Mr. Kennedy early next year.

President Johnson disclosed the general's forthcoming visit in opening his talks before some 30 governors assembled in the temporary presidential office next to the White House. The president apologized to the governors for being a half-hour late to the meeting. He explained that he had been talking with General de Gaulle at the State Department and had talked a little longer than he had expected. As a result of the conference, he said, it was decided that General de Gaulle "will come back and talk more early next year."

Tomorrow the president will receive Sir Alec Douglas-Home, prime minister of Britain, and Chancellor Ludwig Erhard of West Germany, among others. Also waiting here was Anastas I. Mikoyan, a first deputy premier of the Soviet Union, who was Premier Khrushchev's personal representative at this and other important functions. Mr. Mikoyan had no plans yet to leave Washington and was obviously waiting here for an opportunity to size up the new American leader.

For the Russians, as for the other diplomats here, the expressions of peaceful intent and continuity that Mr. Johnson conveyed to Moscow and other capitals today were plainly an insufficient guide to future American policy. The diplomats were asking about and seeking evidence of the new president's grasp of world affairs, his temperament in diplomacy and his personal influence over the new Washington. The diplomatic corps pursued this information in all quarters, fully aware that the moving spectacle of unity behind Mr. Kennedy's coffin would be short-lived and that Mr. Johnson would soon face the same rivalries and grim contests of will that tormented his predecessor.

There was virtually no conversation among the world's leaders as they walked in a loose crowd up Connecticut Avenue to St. Matthew's Roman Catholic Cathedral and later rode together to the Arlington National Cemetery. The funeral spirit still held them in silence at the White House, where they called on Mrs. John F. Kennedy. But by evening, at the State Department reception, they were again the representatives of a world suddenly looking ahead. Some of the foreign visitors broke into small groups for the first time to assess the American scene and their new problems. Among several dinners was one at the British Embassy that brought together Sir Alec and Prime Minister Pearson of Canada.

For one brief day, however, they had been the grandest assembly of world statesmen ever gathered in this capital. Their presence added color and splendor to the funeral, but it also strained the nerves of overtaxed security and protocol officials. An already anxious Washington police force was confronted early in the day with many telephone threats against the lives of a number of visitors. The calls went to the State Department, the embassies, the Federal Bureau of Investigation and "anyone else who'd listen," the police said.

"We've got a lot of nuts around, you know," a spokesman said.

He said that each report had to be checked. For example, the Royal Canadian Mounted Police relayed from Montreal a report that a French Canadian man was headed for Washington with a rifle to shoot President de Gaulle for an unknown grievance. Usually, such reports turn out to be false, but each one had to be checked and guarded against.

The final count of visitors from abroad was 220, representing 92 countries, plus five international agencies and the Vatican. Four delegations, from Cambodia, Cameroon, Guinea and the Ivory Coast, reached Washington at 5 P.M., too late for the funeral and barely in time for the start of President Johnson's reception.

The president stood before a fireplace in the candlelit reception room of the State Department, overlooking the Capitol, the Potomac and Arlington Cemetery. He revealed for the first time since Friday the demonstrative warmth he likes to display.

The manner of his handshake was virtually an index to the special feelings he had for some of the visitors. The average dignitary received a firm handclasp that was held for minutes, if necessary, until condolences and wishes had been expressed. Older acquaintances received not only the prolonged handshake but also the covering clasp of the left hand; they were held there through longer remarks and, usually, broad smiles. Among them were Emperor Haile Selassie, Sir Alec and Prince Philip, Mayor Willy Brandt of West Berlin, Secretary General U Thant of the United Nations, Jean Monnet of France, Paul-Henri Spaak of Belgium, and all the women.

Beside President Johnson stood Secretary of State Rusk, ready with a quick word of advice or background about the dignitary. He revealed an easy relationship with the president that observers here expected to become ever closer.

Mr. Mikoyan received a 35-second, one-hand shake while he posed for pictures with the new president. They chatted for a minute and a half through an interpreter, without smiles. President Johnson mingled with his guests after leaving the receiving line and then retired to a side room for brief conversations with the delegations of several countries.

Excerpts From President's Remarks to Governors

Special to The New York Times

WASHINGTON, Nov. 25—*Following are excerpts from the remarks of President Johnson this evening to a group of governors present in Washington to attend the funeral of President Kennedy:*

Gentlemen, I want to tell you how deeply I feel in your debt for not only your coming to Washington on this tragic occasion but for your being so understanding of me and being willing to come here and visit with me this evening.

I am sorry I am late. General de Gaulle had to return to Paris. He has had a long day of it and he is flying back tonight. He talked a little longer than I anticipated. Even then we did not finish, so we have another meeting set up for early in the year when he comes back to this country.

Canada is such a close neighbor and such a good neighbor that we always have plenty of problems there. They are kind of like problems in the hometown.

So, I am later than I expected to be, and I apologize for delaying you.

Circumstances over which I had no control brought me into this position that I occupy tonight. The difficulties and the tribulations are great, and this is the time when our whole system is on trial, not just the Republican party and the Democratic party but the American system of government.

From the standpoint of population, we have less people than the Soviet Union. From the standpoint of resources, in many respects she has greater resources than we have. She has 8,600,000 tillable acres of land while we have 3,000,000. She has 208,000,000 people while we have 180,000,000 people. She has greater water resources and greater potential oil and power. But the thing that is really to determine whether we win or lose in this struggle of philosophies is how well our system works. We think we have the best system.

We think that where a capitalist can put up a dollar, we can get a return on it. A manager can get up early to work and with money and men he can build a better mousetrap. A laborer who is worthy of his hire stands a chance of getting attention and maybe a little profit-sharing system, and the highest minimum wages of any nation in the world.

Those three together combine to give us the end product that we call free enterprise.

I think continuity without confusion has got to be our password and has to be the key to our system. For that reason I am going to address the Congress on Wednesday. That is the earliest day that they could receive me and I could meet those 70 to 80 heads of state who have come here from all over the world.

I am going to tell that Congress that we intend to honor the commitments we have made at home and abroad, and I am going to tell them I understand my own limitations but I am going to do the best I can with your help and God's.

We live under a system of checks and balances. We do so because our founding fathers figured properly that the only sure method of preventing tyranny was a political system in which no one person or no one group of persons could have power without limitations.

The Congress, the Executive and the courts all have powers to check each other. This is taken for granted so completely that every schoolboy knows about our "tripartite system of government." But what is not realized as commonly is that there is another check—the division of our Government into Federal, state and local systems. Each level of government has proper responsibilities and proper prerogatives. And our democracy is more richer and more enduring because of this division.

However, there is one point that must always be borne in mind. It is that a government by checks and balances will work only when people are willing to cooperate and work together for the common good. If they insist on glaring at each other, refusing to work together, and standing firmly on prerogatives and forgetting responsibilities, the nation will quickly be paralyzed.

For these reasons, I consider it vitally important to ask for your help. I want you to cooperate. I need your heart and your hand. Our country has suffered a grievous shock. The transition while a term is still going on is always a difficult test for democracy. It is doubly difficult in these days of quick decisions on matters that involve the fate of humanity.

I hope to keep in constant touch with you. My permanent purpose is to maintain the fabric of your nation intact and in the days that lie ahead I hope to work with you to this end.

Johnson Tells Israelis Close Ties Will Remain

Special to The New York Times

JERUSALEM (Israeli Sector), Nov. 25—President Johnson assured Premier Levi Eshkol today of his intention to maintain close ties between the United States and Israel. In reply to condolences sent by the Israeli leader, Mr. Johnson said President Kennedy's "friendship for Israel was in the tradition of the close bonds which link our two countries. I intend to carry on that tradition to the best of my ability," Mr. Johnson said.

Ambassador Walworth Barbour, other members of the diplomatic corps and Premier Eshkol and other leading Israelis attended memorial ceremonies this evening in the Knesset (parliament) and Yeshurun Synagogue. In the Knesset, a eulogy delivered by Speaker Kadish Luz was followed by a minute's silence in homage to Mr. Kennedy.

Soviet Promises U.S. Cooperation

Izvestia Calls on Johnson to Continue Peace Effort

By HENRY TANNER

Special to The New York Times

MOSCOW, Nov. 25—The Soviet Union pledged today to cooperate with President Johnson in the continuation of the late President Kennedy's policy of easing world tensions. The pledge was contained in an editorial in *Izvestia,* the official Government newspaper. *Izvestia* editorials are regarded as expressions of Government policy. The editorial declared that world opinion hoped President Kennedy's death would inspire his successor to follow "his best traditions in the interest of peace, for the benefit of all mankind."

The new United States president "solemnly pledged" to carry on the cause of his predecessor, the paper noted and added: "There will always be a positive echo from the Soviet people and its Government toward anything that will serve the relaxation of international tension." A joint Soviet-American effort toward "this goal would be the finest memorial" to the murdered president, *Izvestia* continued.

The Soviet press, television and radio have consistently expressed views that Oswald probably did not commit the crime, that he had no genuine connection either with Communism or the Soviet Union and Cuba and that he was being used, both in life and in death, to cover the tracks of the real culprits.

The *Izvestia* editorial repeated this contention. *Pravda,* organ of the Soviet Communist party, suggested today that if Oswald had had any Communist connections they were of the variety espoused by Leon Trotsky, a left-wing revolutionary expelled from the Soviet Union in 1929 and murdered by a Stalin agent in Mexico in 1940.

Millions of Soviet television viewers were able to watch part of President Kennedy's funeral by relay from the Telstar communications satellite. They saw the procession as it moved slowly to St. Matthew's Cathedral. "The grief of the Soviet people mingles with the grief of the American people," the Soviet commentator said. Television officials said the program had been shown in 60 Soviet cities west of the Urals. During the program the announcer read President Johnson's message thanking Premier Khrushchev for his condolences and expressing the intention to strive for the same peaceful aims as had President Kennedy.

Today's editorial in the Government newspaper pulled together some of the strands of Soviet feelings and emotions, including fears that were created here by the assassination of President Kennedy. The Soviet leaders seem to feel genuine sorrow and bewilderment over the death of a man for whom they had come to have a deep respect and with whom they felt they could negotiate in a businesslike, even hard-boiled way. "The policy of President Kennedy, though not always consistently, was based on his realization" that new steps toward the improvement of Soviet-American relations should be made, the *Izvestia* editorial said.

Soviet officials obviously assumed that there would be "no basic changes" in United States foreign policy. This belief was strengthened by President Johnson's first proclamation by his decision not to accept the resignation of American ambassadors and by other news reports from Washington pointing to continuity in foreign affairs.

Soviet official circles are far less certain that there will be continuity in American domestic affairs.There seems to be widespread apprehension here that there may be a sharp swing to the right in American politics and that this in turn will change United States–Soviet relations in the long run. Senator Barry Goldwater, Republican of Arizona, has been the target of frequent violent attacks as a "wild man" who opposed the treaty for a limited test ban and as an exponent of racism and "aggressive imperialism." During the last days many comments have dwelt on the themes that the chances of a Republican election victory next year have been greatly improved and that Senator Goldwater is a candidate for the Republican nomination.

Soviet officials have felt concern and even anger over news reports linking Lee H. Oswald, the accused assassin of President Kennedy, to leftist causes and stressing the fact that he had lived in the Soviet Union and had married a Russian girl. Foreign Minister Andrei A. Gromyko was asked about this at the airport last night when First Deputy Premier Anastas I. Mikoyan took off for Washington. His answer was emphatic and almost vehement: "We don't know this man!"

Mrs. Nina P. Khrushchev, the premier's wife, went today to the residence of the United States ambassador, Foy D. Kohler, to sign the book of condolences there. She spent about 15 minutes with the ambassador and Mrs. Kohler. On leaving the residence Mrs. Khrushchev said in halting English: "I am very, very disturbed by this news. My family is very sad."

Text of *Izvestia* Editorial

Following, as distributed by Tass, the Soviet press agency, is the translation of the text of an editorial from Izvestia, *the Soviet Government newspaper, under the heading "America's Hour of Sorrow":*

Nov. 25 is a day of national mourning in the United States of America, American people are paying last homage to President John Fitzgerald Kennedy. Tribute to the memory of the outstanding American statesman whose life ended so tragically is also paid by the people and governments of many countries of the world who sent their highly placed representatives to Washington. First Vice Chairman of U.S.S.R., A. I. Mikoyan, will represent our country at John Kennedy's funeral.

"J. F. Kennedy's death is a grievous blow to all people for whom the cause of peace and Soviet-American cooperation is dear." These words from the message of the head of the Soviet Government, Nikita Khrushchev, to the new United States president, Lyndon B. Johnson, express the opinion of all Soviet people. The broad outlook of the late president, who realistically assessed the situation and tried to find negotiated solutions for international problems, was highly appreciated in the Soviet Union.

The Soviet Government, whose general line of foreign policy is the Leninist principle of peaceful coexistence between states with differing socio-economic systems, is steadily striving for a relaxation of international tension and consolidation of peace. Of late, progress has been made on this difficult and intricate road. Its embodiment was the Moscow treaty banning weapon tests.

There were also prospects of some further steps toward better Soviet-American relations. President Kennedy's policy, though not always consistently, stemmed from an understanding of the necessity of such steps. He more than once emphasized that a course toward a military solution of differences, toward unleashing thermonuclear war, would be insane.

This sober approach to the situation in the contemporary world and the first mild attempts to blunt the acuteness of the most complicated problem of the United States—the racial problem—made the rabid American reactionaries hate President Kennedy. The lunatics prepared to hazard the fate of the American people; the "madmen," the pro-fascist racists, rose up in arms against Kennedy. Is it not possible that they made the bullet to be fired at the president's head? Is it not possible that they are now covering up the traces of the revolting crime?

President Kennedy's death has undoubtedly aggravated the situation in the United States. The struggle between the sober-minded Americans and the forces of rabid reactionaries, who will not miss the chance of using the situation for their own ends, will be very tense. It will determine the course of the election campaign, too.

As regards the peace-loving public beyond the boundaries of the United States, it would like to believe that President Kennedy's departure from life in the prime of his power will impel his political heirs to follow his finest traditions for the sake of peace, for the sake of all mankind.

The new president of the United States solemnly pledged himself to continue carrying out the cause of his predecessor. The Soviet people and their Government will always positively respond to anything that helps to ease international tension.

Common efforts for the benefit of this cause would be the finest monument to President John Fitzgerald Kennedy, who died in tragic circumstances.

Soviet Bloc Shows Uncertainty on Johnson's Political Policy

Special to The New York Times

VIENNA, Nov. 25—Radio Free Europe said today that its monitoring of radio broadcasts showed that the Communists in Eastern Europe generally considered President Johnson as standing farther to the right than President Kennedy.

The Budapest radio said that little was known about Mr. Johnson, but that many believed him to be inexperienced in foreign policy. "As for domestic policy," the Hungarian broadcast continued, "he is regarded with mistrust by New York people because he comes from the South." In another broadcast, the Hungarians said Mr. Johnson had refrained from taking sides in the debate "between Kennedy and the Southerners on Negro reforms."

The Prague radio said the succession of Mr. Johnson meant "a certain retreat to the right" in both domestic and foreign policy. However, the official Czechoslovak press agency Ceteka carried a dispatch from New

York that said "it can be expected that he will continue the Kennedy line until the end of the Presidential term next year."

The dispatch said that while Mr. Johnson once had been a supporter of Southern right-wing racial elements he changed his position "substantially" during the 1960 election campaign. The Prague radio doubted that Mr. Johnson would retain President Kennedy's advisers. It added: "In many respects, Johnson is much more a politician than was Kennedy. Many members of Congress considered Kennedy too much of an intellectual, too educated and too much of a realist. On the other hand, Johnson is closer to them by virtue of his jovial nature and Southern drawl. They feel that he will be inclined to achieve immediate aims even at the cost of a compromise if he can make political capital from such an attitude, and that he will neglect a wider concept of policy and long-term aims."

The Sofia radio asserted that "reactionary circles" were exerting pressure on President Johnson to abandon the policy of peaceful coexistence. In Poland, the Warsaw newspaper, *Zycie Warszawy*, said that Mr. Johnson is "a different type of politician and man" than Mr. Kennedy was. "It has been said of him that he is by instinct a liberal and by his Southern origin a conservative," the paper added.

The Communist propaganda line that President Kennedy was killed in a rightist plot designed to whip up an anti-Communist campaign appeared to be hardening in Eastern Europe. The English-language service of the Soviet press agency Tass, in a report from New York, said that "all circumstances of President Kennedy's tragic death allow one to assume that this murder was planned and carried out by ultraright-wing fascist and racist circles, by those who cannot stomach any step aimed at the easing of international tensions and the improvement of Soviet-American relations."

The East German press agency A.D.N. said extremist quarters had sought to use every means to pin the murder on Communists and to brand the accused assassin, Lee Harvey Oswald, as a Communist. "To make it more difficult to establish any proof that would unmask those really behind the president's assassination," A.D.N. said, "they decided to eliminate Oswald in the usual fascist manner."

A broadcast yesterday by the Prague radio, before Oswald was killed, said: "It is possible, or it may be shown in time, that Oswald—if indeed he was the murderer—was a member of the Communist party. That is possible. People are mad. They suffer from various manias. They are suicidal. Or they have a sick longing for publicity. But to link this murder [of President Kennedy] with the name or policy of the Communist party is completely lacking in logic."

Poles Mourn for Kennedy

WARSAW, Nov. 25 (Reuters)—Thousands of Poles jammed the narrow streets of the Old City of Warsaw tonight as a memorial service was being held for President Kennedy at the Roman Catholic Church of St. John's.

Yugoslavs Attend Service

ZAGREB, Yugoslavia, Nov. 25 (Reuters)—More than 6,000 persons crowded the cathedral here tonight for a high requiem mass for President Kennedy.

OSWALD TOLD UNTRUE STORY OF HIS SOVIET STAY, SAYS MAN WHO AIDED HIM ON RETURN

Helper Found Him Evasive at First

Account of Russian Trip Was Tailored for Use at Home, Informant Believes

By PETER KIHSS

The story of Lee Harvey Oswald's arrival in New York from the Soviet Union came to light yesterday. It was a story of a man first apparently hiding from help and then falsifying his Russian experience to make it look better here. "It was like pulling teeth to get information out of him," Spas Raikin, then a port counselor and social worker for the Travelers Aid Society of New York, recalled about the man charged with having killed President Kennedy.

What Oswald told Mr. Raikin was this: He had been a member of the Marine Corps on duty with the United States Embassy in Moscow; he had become acquainted with a Russian girl, married her and renounced his citizenship; he worked as a specialist electro technician in Minsk, but found things were not as rosy as Soviet propaganda promised; it took him more than two and a half years to get exit visas for himself, his wife and child.

What the facts were, as developed elsewhere, were these: Oswald had gotten out of the Marine Corps on a hardship claim to support his mother; he had immediately headed for the Soviet Union and sought Soviet citizenship; only then had he wound up in Minsk, where he married a Minsk girl; he got a $435.71 United States Government loan to pay for his family's trip here.

Also brought out yesterday were his mother's worries about Oswald when he was 13 and 14 years old. Mrs. Gussie Keller lived next door in the Bronx to Mrs. Marguerite Oswald and her son when the Oswalds had an apartment in the four-story brick building at 825 East 179th Street, at Marmion Avenue, in 1953 and early 1954. "She used to talk to me all the time and cry," Mrs. Keller said. The mother was concerned over the boy's staying and playing by himself. His father was dead, and the mother "used to tell me that if he had a father, maybe he wouldn't act that way," Mrs. Keller said.

Mrs. Oswald and Lee, the youngest of her three sons, had come to the Bronx from Fort Worth, Tex., in September, 1952. Board of Education records said the youngster had trouble with his hearing that first year, apparently as a sequel to a mastoid operation in Texas. Oswald's persistent hearing problem might not have been unusual after such an operation, but a specialist said it would not be likely to affect his subsequent mentality or behavior. His hearing cleared up in his second year here.

The Oswalds first lived at 1455 Sheridan Avenue, the Bronx, one block east of the Grand Concourse, according to the school records. This is a seven-story tan brick and stucco building opposite William Howard Taft High School. The boy went to Junior High School 117, 1865 Morris Avenue, for the seventh grade. In March, 1953, he transferred to Junior High School 44, 1825 Prospect Avenue, after having moved to East 179th Street. A neighbor of that time said yesterday that Oswald's mother was then a sales clerk in a mid-Manhattan stocking store.

Like Mrs. Keller, this neighbor recalled Oswald's playing by himself and agreed that "we all thought that he was kind of queer." This neighbor, who preferred not to have her name published, said: "He liked Western comics. All you could hear was 'bang, bang, bang.' He would play by himself with his toy guns."

Mrs. Oswald, Mrs. Keller said, "felt his teachers didn't understand him." Her dominating interest, Mrs. Keller said, was to get back to New Orleans where the boy was born. Eventually, she and the youngster did return.

When Oswald came here from the Soviet Union, it was with his wife, Marina, and 4-month-old daughter, June, on the Holland-America liner *Maasdam* from Rotterdam June 13, 1962. The Travelers Aid Society, a philanthropically supported service and casework agency, was then handing repatriation cases under a program for the United States Department of Health, Education and Welfare. The Oswalds were three of 42,891 persons helped by the New York agency last year.

The incoming Oswalds were referred by the Federal agency to Travelers Aid. Mr. Raikin, a native of Bulgaria, who is now an assistant professor of Western civilization at Rio Grande College in Rio Grande, Ohio, was assigned to help them. Owald, then 22 years old, had been cleared early by United States immigration officials as an American citizen. Mr. Raikin boarded the ship when it docked in Hoboken.

"I was under obligation to contact this man," Mr. Raikin said yesterday in Rio Grande. "I had been paging him three or four times for one hour on the ship, because the people were not allowed to disembark. For one hour apparently this man was hiding. He did not respond to the paging. Finally when the people were let down on the pier, I waited by his luggage, so I caught him there. One thing that impressed me was that he was trying to avoid contact with anybody."

Oswald was a man 5 feet 6 inches tall, slim. He wore a gray suit and a light blue tie. He and his wife, who was 20, and child had six suitcases and one bag. Oswald reported his nearest relative was his mother, then living at 316 East Donnell Street, Crowell, Tex.

Mr. Raikin found Oswald "extremely reserved in revealing any kind of information," but elicited Oswald's considerably inventive version of his life in the Soviet Union. He tried talking to Mrs. Oswald in Russian, and they "exchanged a few words, but she didn't talk very much at all," he recalled.

Oswald told Mr. Raikin he had paid for his family's transportation to New York, but had only $63 left on arrival. His brother, Robert Oswald, of 7313 Davenport Street, Fort Worth, he said, had offered him a home until he could get a job. But Lee said he thought Robert would be unable to pay for his trip to Texas. Mr. Raikin put the Oswalds on a Holland-America Lines bus to the Port Authority bus terminal in Manhattan. There, another Travelers Aid worker met them and took them to the Special Services Welfare Center of the city Welfare Department at 42 Franklin Street. Welfare Commissioner James Dumpson reviewed the center's file on the

Oswalds yesterday morning and turned it over to the Federal Bureau of Investigation for possible study.

The city agency had got in touch with Oswald's brother, and the brother promised to telegraph $200 to finance the family's trip to Fort Worth, Mr. Dumpson said. Lee Oswald, his wife and baby were put up for the night at the Times Square Hotel, and the next morning they left by plane for Texas, Mr. Dumpson said. It was a routine case of help by Travelers Aid and the Welfare Department.

Fund Begun for Mrs. Oswald

BELFAST, Northern Ireland, Nov. 25 (AP)—An Irish housewife today began a fund to help the widow of Lee H. Oswald. The housewife, Jane Addy, said she wanted to "put into practice what President Kennedy himself always preached, brotherhood and tolerance," by helping "the woman nobody wants."

Dallas Is Willing to Bare Evidence

But Oswald Case Is Delayed at Suggestion of U.S.

By FRED POWLEDGE

Special to The New York Times

DALLAS, Nov. 25—Dallas authorities were willing today to make public all their physical evidence connecting Lee H. Oswald with the murder of President Kennedy, but the revelation was postponed at the suggestion of Federal officials here and in Washington. Two local authorities involved in the case, Chief of Police Jesse Curry and the Dallas County district attorney, Henry Wade, said they would like to place the evidence before the public. Both men added, however, that they would not do so if authorities in Washington wished otherwise.

Justice Department sources in Washington said that when they discuss a subject of such grave importance as the Oswald case they must be absolutely correct. They said no pressure had been brought on officials here. They expressed confidence that all the evidence would eventually be made public. The report of the Federal Bureau of Investigation on the slaying will go first to President Johnson, who requested it.

The Dallas police and Mr. Wade contend they have conclusive evidence that Oswald killed Mr. Kennedy and wounded Gov. John B. Connally Jr. last Friday, and that he murdered a Dallas policeman, J. D. Tippit, shortly afterward. Chief Curry said today in a formal statement: "When the investigation in the case of Lee Harvey Oswald is completed insofar as the Dallas police department is concerned, we intend to make the entire file public unless Federal authorities specifically request that some part be withheld and turned over to them. Unless we are specifically instructed otherwise from Washington, we believe it can and should become public information. At this time, we cannot designate when the release will be made."

Mr. Wade said, in an interview: "I felt that all the agencies [investigating the assassination] should release all their information on Oswald. I'm very agreeable to this evidence being released if no one in the Justice Department has any objection and if it's agreeable with them. I do not want to interfere in any way with any investigation that they might have going on."

The police have already released descriptions of a number of pieces of evidence. Today Mr. Wade announced that authorities had also found a marked map, showing the course of the president's motorcade, in Oswald's rented room. "It was a map tracing the location of the parade route," the district attorney said, "and this place [the Texas School Book Depository, a warehouse from which the fatal bullets were fired] was marked with a straight line." Mr. Wade said Oswald had marked the map at two other places, "apparently places which he considered as a possibility" for an assassination. He said he had not personally seen the map, and could not describe it further.

The district attorney said the police had traced the serial number of the murder weapon, an Italian rifle with a telescopic sight, to the Chicago mail-order house that had sold Oswald a rifle last spring. Mr. Wade said that the Dallas police had obtained a palm print from the rifle that matched Oswald's hand.

Previously Mr. Wade and Gordon Shanklin, F.B.I. agent in charge here, had revealed other evidence against Oswald. This evidence included other palm and fingerprints, ballistics tests on the assassin's bullets and descriptions by several witnesses of Oswald's actions and whereabouts on the day of the murders.

The district attorney said today that he had no knowledge of any connection between Oswald and his assassin, Jack Ruby of Dallas. He referred to rumors circulating here to the effect that the two men had known each other before the president's death. Sources in the Justice Department in Washington said that they had found no evidence of a conspiracy in the Dallas slayings.

One of Dallas's newspapers, *The Times Herald,* reported today that the F.B.I. had been warned in an anonymous telephone call early Sunday that Oswald would be killed during the jail transfer. Another topic of rumor and speculation here was Chief Curry. One report was that Oswald's death yesterday, 48 hours after the president's assassination on a downtown street, had caused the city government to lose faith in its police chief.

City Manager Elgin E. Crull, the chief's superior, said today he would not accept Mr. Curry's resignation even if it were offered. Other city officials expressed their faith in the chief. The police department was criticized after the shooting of the president, Governor Connally and Patrolman Tippit on Friday. Yesterday the criticism increased.

Dallas Prosecutor's News Conference

Following is the transcript of a conference held Sunday by District Attorney Henry Wade of Dallas County on the evidence against Lee. H. Oswald, the accused assassin of President Kennedy, as recorded by WBC-TV:

MR. WADE: The purpose of this news conference is to detail some of the evidence against Oswald for the assassination of the president. This evidence was gathered by—largely by—the Dallas police who did an excellent job on this, with the help of some of the Federal agents.

And I am going through the evidence piece by piece for you. No. 1. (Some of this you already know; some of it you won't; I don't think that all of you do know.) First, there was a number of witnesses that saw the person with the gun on the sixth floor of the bookstore building, the window—detailing the window—where he was looking out.

Inside this window the police found a row of books, cases, boxes, hiding someone sitting in the window from people of the same floor looking in, on the window were some boxes where, in the little circle around the window, by the bookcases, apparently the person was sitting, because he was seen from that particular window.

On this box that the defendant was sitting on, his palm print was found and was identified as his. The three ejected shells were found right by the box. The shells were of an odd caliber of the type later determined [to have been fired from] the gun that was found on the floor.

The gun was hidden on this same floor behind some boxes and bookcases. It, as I think you know, has been identified as having been purchased last March by Oswald, from a mail-order house, through an assumed name named Hidell, mailed to a post office box here in Dallas. On his person was a pocketbook. In his pocketbook was an identification card with the same name as the post office box on it.

Pictures were found of the defendant with this gun and a pistol on his—in his—holster.

Immediately that morning—it was unusual, but that morning—a neighbor brought Oswald from Irving, Tex. He usually brought him on Monday morning, I think, but this day he went home one day earlier on Thursday night, and came back to—with this fellow—and when he came back he had a package under his arm that he said was window curtains, I believe, or window shades. The wife had said he had the gun the night before, and it was missing that morning after he left. He got out around 8 o'clock and went to the building behind some cars and went to work.

A police officer, immediately after the assassination, ran in the building and saw this man in a corner and tried to arrest him but the manager of the building said he was an employee and it was all right. Every other employee was located but this defendant of the company. A description and name of him went out by police to look for him.

The next we hear of him is on a bus where he got on a bus at Lamar

Street, told the bus driver the president had been shot, the president. [He] told the lady—all this was verified by statements—told the lady on the bus that the president had been shot. [S]he said, "How did he know." He said a man back there told him. The defendant said, "Yes, he's been shot," and laughed very loud.—

REPORTER: This was to a lady?

MR. WADE: A lady. He then—the bus, he asked the bus driver to stop, got off at a stop, caught a taxicab driver, Darryl Click—I don't have his exact place—and went to his home in Oak Cliff, changed his clothes hurriedly, and left.

As he left, three witnesses saw a police officer—officer [J. D.] Tippit motion to him or say something to him. He walked up to the car. Officer Tippit stepped out of the car and started around it. He shot him three times and killed him.

Q. Was this in front of the boarding house?

A. No, it's not in front of the boarding house.

Q. Where was it?

A. I don't have it exact. It's more than a block. It's a block or two.

Q. Was he on foot when Tippit saw him?

A. Yes, he was on foot. And apparently headed for the Texas Theatre. He then walked across a vacant lot. Witnesses saw him eject the shells from a revolver and place—reload—the gun. Someone saw him go in the Texas Theatre. A search was made of that later by a number of police officers. At the time an officer of the Dallas police spotted him and asked him to come out. He struck at the officer, put the gun against his head and snapped it, but did not—the bullet did not—go off. We have the snapped bullet there. Officers—officers apprehended him at that time.

Q. Was that an attempted suicide, sir?

A. Against the officer's head.

Q. Do you know why the gun . . .

Q. Which officer?

A. MacDonald was his name.

Q. Why didn't it go off?

A. It snapped. It was a misfire. Then officers subdued him—some six officers—subdued him there in the theater, and he was brought to the police station here.

Q. Mr. Wade, why didn't the gun fire?

A. It misfired, being on the—the shell didn't explode. We have where it hit it, but it didn't explode. It didn't fire the shell.

Q. There was one officer who said that he pulled the trigger, but he managed to put his thumb in the part before the firing pin. It didn't . . .

A. Well . . .

Q. . . . strike the—the bullet didn't explode. Is that . . . ?

A. I don't know whether it's that or not. I know he didn't snap the gun is all I know about it.

Q. You would say it was a misfire?

A. It didn't fire.

Q. Let's get the story again.

Q. What other evidence is there?

A. Let's see . . . His fingerprints were found on the gun, have I said that?

Q. Which gun?

A. On the rifle.

Q. You didn't say that.

Q. What about the paraffin tests?

A. Yes, I've got paraffin tests that showed he had recently fired a gun—it was on both hands.

Q. On both hands?

A. Both hands.

Q. Recently fired a rifle.

Q. A gun.

A. A gun.

Q. The rifle fingerprints were his, were Oswald's?

A. Yes.

Q. Were there any fingerprints . . . ?

A. Palm prints rather than fingerprints.

Q. Were there any fingerprints at the window?

Q. Palm prints on the what?

A. Yes, on . . .

Q. On the rifle?

A. Yes sir.

Q. Where are they on the rifle?

A. Under—on part of the metal—under the gun.

Q. Did he still . . . ever say anything about it, admit anything at all?

A. He never did admit any of the killings. I didn't—you ask me this—I didn't do any of the interrogation.

Q. You have not listed it then as part of the evidence?

A. No, it's not listed.

Q. Did he display any animosity towards the president, in any conversation with any officers?

A. He was bitter toward all of the officers that examined him is what I've been told.

Q. Do you think he deserved . . . ?

Q. Let's finish the . . .

A. We have—that's about all.

Q. How about ballistics tests?

Q. Ballistics test was made.

A. Well I said this was the gun that . . .

Q. Killed the president?

A. Yes.

Q. You talked with the F.B.I. [Federal Bureau of Investigation] this morning. Did you leave the rest with the F.B.I.?

A. I won't go—I'm not at liberty—to go into the F.B.I. report.

Q. Did you say the gun was mailed to a post office box in Dallas in March?

A. March of this year.

Q: Was he living in Dallas then?

A. Yes. I presume he was. He got it there.

Q. I see.

Q. Previously he lived in New Orleans.

Q. He said he'd only been here two months.

Q. Mr. Wade . . .

A. He came to Fort Worth sometime in the fall of 62. And then moved here a while, and apparently went to New Orleans for a while and came back. And when the period to that is, I'm not sure.

Q. Mr. Wade, what was the evidence that we were told was startling evidence that could not be told to the press . . . ?

Q. Saturday morning.

Q. Saturday morning. They said it came in Saturday morning, and it could not be revealed. It was . . .

A. I don't know. That wasn't me that said that, I don't think.

Q: Have you given us everything?

A. I've given you everything that I . . .

Q. Do you know that he has been recognized as a patron of Ruby's nightclub here?

A. I don't know that.

Q. Do you know of any connection between Mr. Ruby and the . . . the assassin?

A. I know of none.

Q. Are you investigating reports that he may have been slain because Ruby might have feared he would have been implicated in something?

A. The police are making investigation of that murder. I don't know anything about that. The investigation and charges have been filed. It will be presented to the grand jury on Ruby, immediately within the next week; and it'll probably be tried around the middle of January.

Q. Did the district attorney's office follow the police investigation of the assassination of the president, before sending again to Washington?

A. Before.

Q. Do you think it was unusual for Jack Ruby to be in that crowd?

A. I won't pass on that—unusual to be in that crowd?

Q. There are reports that he had planned to.

A. I haven't been here since last night, so I don't know anything about it.

Q. Mr. Wade, how do you feel about not being able to try Oswald as the killer of the president?

A. Well, we will try Ruby and ask the death penalty on him, about the same time.

Q. Well, how about Oswald?

A. I don't want to go into the whys or wherefores on anything.

Q. Has your office closed the investigation into the death of President Kennedy?

A. No sir. The investigation will continue on that, with the basis, of course, that we have no concrete evidence that anyone assisted him in this. The investigation, I'm sure, will go on with reference to any possible accomplice or person that assisted him in it.

Q. Do you have any suspicions now that there were?

A. I have no concrete evidence or suspicions at present.

Q. Thank you.

Q. Would you be willing to say, in view of all this evidence, that it is now beyond a reasonable doubt at all that Oswald was the killer of President Kennedy?

A. I would say that without any doubt he is the killer—the law says beyond a reasonable doubt, to a moral certainty, which I have—there is no question that he was the killer of President Kennedy.

Q. That case is closed in your mind?

A. As far as Oswald's concerned.

Oswald Visited Mexico Seeking Visas

By PAUL P. KENNEDY

Special to The New York Times

MEXICO CITY, Nov. 25—A Mexican Government source said today that Lee H. Oswald, the slain suspect in the assassination of President Kennedy, was in Mexico from Sept. 26 until Oct. 3 attempting without success to get visas to Cuba and the Soviet Union. There were reports here also that his movements were followed in Mexico by an unidentified United States agency.

The United States Embassy here declined to confirm or deny any knowledge of the visit. A Mexican official said it was evident that Oswald wanted to leave the continent immediately. A spokesman of the Ministry of the Interior confirmed this morning a report that appeared in the morning paper *Excelsior*. It said Oswald crossed the Mexican border Sept. 26 and traveled by highway to Mexico City the next day.

On that day he appeared at the Cuban Consulate here and applied to the then consul general, Eusabio Azcue, for a visa to Havana. According to the Government official, Mr. Azcue was suspicious of the applicant and told him he would have to apply to Havana for the visa. He said an answer might require 10 to 12 days. Mr. Azcue has since been transferred from the consulate here, but it was reported at the office that the applicant became incensed at the delay and left the consulate, slamming the door behind him.

The following day the applicant appeared at the Soviet Consulate. Both the Cuban and the Soviet Consulates are in the compounds of their respective embassies. Oswald applied to an unidentified employee at the Soviet Consulate. He was told there that his application would have to be submitted to Moscow and a reply might require up to three months.

Soviet Embassy officials today would neither confirm nor deny that the application had been made. But it was confirmed by the Ministry of the Interior official who asked that his name not be used.

Oswald demonstrated anger at the delay, according to the report, and explained that he had lived in the Soviet Union, that his wife was Russian, and their child had been born there. He offered to pay the expenses of a telephone call to his wife in New Orleans to verify the story, the report said, but the offer was declined.

"The Russian people thought there was something suspicious about the applicant, he acted so wild," the Mexican official explained. Apparently Mexican secret police had observed the American from time to time but the Government official said it had not been determined where he lived during his stay in Mexico City. It has been established, he said, that he did not meet with any of the known established leftist groups while here. Oswald entered Mexico through the port of Nuevo Laredo, presenting a tourist visa.

No Record of Travel

Special to The New York Times

LAREDO, Tex., Nov. 25—When Oswald crossed the border here on Sept. 26, he gave his destination as Mexico City. The record of his travel was maintained by the Mexican Government, not the United States Government.

Text of the Tass Dispatch on Dallas

Following, as distributed in English by Tass, the Soviet press agency, is a dispatch from New York on the situation in Dallas:

An atmosphere of uncertainty and hysteria continues to reign in Dallas, the town where President Kennedy was so monstrously killed. After Oswald, who was accused of assassinating the President, was shot there yesterday in the police station, the Mayor of Dallas appealed to the people of the town "to come to their senses and fight the hysteria."

Correspondents of the C.B.S. radio-television company report from Dallas that suspicious telephone calls were made today to the home of the Mayor, the homes of many prominent Dallas citizens. Unknown persons threatened them. In particular, he [the mayor] was threatened that the plane that he planned to take to Washington to attend the President's funeral would be blown up by a bomb. After this threat the Mayor took another plane.

The commentators draw attention to the "negligence" of the Dallas police, who could not prevent the assassination of the accused Oswald in the police station. It is recalled that only policemen and newsmen with special passes were allowed into the police station. The latter were even searched for firearms.

The foul crime in Dallas is used by certain quarters to fan anti-Soviet and anti-Communist hysteria. All the details of the crime were flashed for the past two days on the screens of TV sets. The Americans were insistently told that Oswald was a "Communist," a "Marxist," "Castroist," etc. Some papers even tried to implicate the Communist party in Kennedy's death. *The New York Journal American* was the loudest in this unseemly business.

At the same time one gets the impression that the circle of suspects in the President's assassination has concentrated only on one man. The possibility that the assassination was the doing of someone else has been thrown aside. The murderer of Oswald, Jack Ruby, a man with a criminal past, is now being pictured as a man motivated by patriotism, an "admirer" of the late President. Investigation of Kennedy's assassination was stopped with Oswald's death.

All the circumstances of President Kennedy's tragic death allow one to assume that this murder was planned and carried out by the ultra-right-wing, fascist and racist circles, by those who cannot stomach any step aimed at the easing of international tensions, and the improvement of Soviet-American relations.

Doctors Question Oswald's Sanity

Leaving Clues for Pursuit a Psychopathic Trait

By WALTER SULLIVAN

A number of leading psychiatrists suspect that Lee Harvey Oswald, charged with the assassination of President Kennedy and subsequently murdered, was paranoid or suffered from some other mental ailment. In a series of telephone interviews yesterday, however, they said the chances of a reliable assessment probably died when Oswald was shot down in the basement of the Dallas Municipal Building on Sunday.

Dr. Lewis Robbins, medical director of Hillside Hospital, Queens, pointed out that psychiatrists now have only "fragments of facts" to go on. He cited certain suggestive evidence. It is typical of the psychopathic criminal, he said, to leave a trail that makes his capture easy. In a subconscious way he wants to be caught. Oswald carried a card that linked him to the pseudonym under which the alleged assassination weapon was purchased. In a number of other respects he behaved in a manner that facilitated his identification and arrest. Many criminals evade capture, Dr. Robbins said, but few of those are psychopathic. He noted that photographs of Oswald after his capture showed him smiling.

Other psychiatrists cited what is known of Oswald's history: his father-less childhood, his lifelong aloofness. In manhood, as one of them put it, "he walked around with a load of hate." He apparently resented authority in the Marine Corps, and then in the Federal Government as a whole. Because the "grass in the other pasture looked greener," said one specialist, "he tried life in the Soviet Union, but that didn't suit him either, so he came back."

The Russians themselves received him cautiously, refusing to grant him citizenship. In Moscow he told an American interviewer that he had been interested in Marxism since he was 15. His associates in school have expressed doubt as to the truth of this statement. Back in the United States he said he was an official of the Fair Play for Cuba Committee, a pro-Castro group, but that organization denies any knowledge of him. He seems to have been inordinately fond of weapons. He was court-martialed for possessing a private pistol while attached to a Marine Corps unit that, presumably, was amply armed.

Even if a psychiatrist had known all of this in advance, would he have predicted that Oswald would commit murder? Dr. Robbins said no, and his view was echoed by a number of other psychiatrists, most of whom asked that they not be identified.

One nationally-known psychiatrist said he believed that all assassins of presidents had been mentally ill. However, he recalled, only one of them escaped death on that ground. That was Richard Lawrence who, in 1835, tried to kill Andrew Jackson in the rotunda of the Capitol. Both Lawrence's pistols misfired. He was committed to an institution for the insane for life.

John Wilkes Booth was shot before he could be captured after he killed Abraham Lincoln. Thus, like Oswald, he died before he could name his fellow conspirators, if he had any. Four accused accomplices of Booth were tried, and three of them were hanged. This psychiatrist described the Puerto Ricans who tried to kill Harry S. Truman as fanatics rather than lunatics.

Not all of those consulted felt that any psychiatric label could be put on Oswald. His violent behavior, said one, was not of itself a mark of mental illness. Paranoids, he added, "are more apt to sue than to shoot." If one considers all those who resort to violence to be mad, he added, "you would have to bag an awful lot of those people on the turnpikes."

The paranoid has been defined as one who attributes his failures to the enmity of others. As described in the *Merck Manual of Diagnosis and*

Therapy, "He displays sullen quietness, behind which lurks haughty disdain." As one man put it yesterday, the paranoiac "twists actual situations," whereas the schizophrenic "makes them up out of whole cloth."

A specialist who rebels against the use of labels pointed out that such symptoms appear in all graduations. Everyone, he said, is a little bit mad.

Slain Policeman Is Honored by Dallas

By JOHN HERBERS

Special to The New York Times

DALLAS, Nov. 25—Dallas shut off its bustling commerce today to join the nation in mourning President Kennedy and to honor a policeman who died while trying to arrest the president's accused assassin.

"Big D," as Dallas residents call the city, looked like a ghost town as residents stayed home, watching the funeral services on television, or visited churches for prayer or memorial services. There were rumors of further violence—that Jack Ruby, accused of killing Lee H. Oswald in the police station yesterday, had taken his own life with poison; that the district attorney had been assassinated—but both proved false. They showed the city was on edge.

"Dallas is a city undergoing the dark night of the soul," *The Times Herald* said in an editorial. "We are a city trying to find ourselves."

It was a cool, clear day and the city's buildings glistened in the sun. The streets were quiet, even when crowds gathered at the spot where Mr. Kennedy was shot and at a suburban Baptist church where funeral services were held for the slain policeman, J. D. Tippit. About 2,000 persons crowded around the Beckley Hills Baptist Church for the service, which was shown on television here following the president's funeral. The Rev. C. D. Tipps Jr. said the 39-year-old police officer was killed by "a poor, confused, misguided assassin, as was the president."

Mr. Tippit was shot three times when he tried to arrest Oswald, the president's accused assassin. Mr. Tippit leaves a widow and three small children. President Johnson and Attorney General Robert F. Kennedy telephoned Mrs. Tippit to express their sorrow before the funeral. The police officer was buried in a memorial court of honor in Laurel Land Memorial Park. The court was set aside a year ago for those who had given their lives in community service.

While Dallas citizens were preoccupied with the two funerals Oswald was buried in nearby Fort Worth, where he had grown up. Most Dallas residents knew nothing of Oswald's funeral until it was over.

Crowds gathered all day on the grassy plots adjacent to the place where the president was assassinated. They came not only from Dallas and adjoining communities but from distant states. They placed four wreaths on the grass, stared up at the sixth floor window of the yellow-brick building.

Meanwhile, leaders in the city continued to search for answers as to why the assassination and yesterday's shooting of Oswald had occurred. "Even if we are staggered by one violent discharge of hate following an-other," *The Times Herald* said, "the citizens of Dallas are surely engaging in the greatest spiritual self-examination any American community has undergone in this century." The Rev. Michael V. McLane said, "It may be trite, but nevertheless true, that pride goeth before a fall." He referred to the city's pride in bigness and commerce.

At the same time *The Dallas News* told citizens they needed to "banish any feelings of rancor and guilt" and to settle down to "normal living." *The News* said in an editorial: "Our foundations are sound, our leadership solid, our aspirations high. The good God who watches over us tempers our ease with difficulty. A city, like a tree, must weather the winds of adversity to reach the heights of stature."

Many of the city's ministers and other leaders insisted that there were problems peculiar to Dallas that should be corrected. "There has been brought forth in our town in the last few weeks a force of hatred that has erupted like a flame in two different instances," Dr. Walter A. Bennett, pastor of Westminister Presbyterian Church, declared. Another minister, the Rev. William H. Dickinson Jr., a Methodist, said the hate was not confined to the irresponsible. He said: "At a nice, respectable dinner party only two nights before the president's visit to our city, a bright young couple with a fine education, with a promising professional future, said to their friends that they hated the president of the United States—and that they would not care one bit if somebody did take a potshot at him."

$300 Donated for Tippits

PROVIDENCE, R.I., Nov. 25 (AP)—More than $300 was donated to Mr. Tippit's family today by the congregation attending an interdenominational memorial service for President Kennedy. The worshippers left coins and bills as they filed out of the First Baptist Meeting House after the service.

RUBY IS TRANSPORTED SECRETLY FROM CITY TO COUNTY JAIL AT MID-DAY WITHOUT INCIDENT

Death Sentence to Be Demanded

Defense Indicates a Plea of Temporary Insanity—No Link With Oswald Found

By GLADWIN HILL

Special to The New York Times

DALLAS, Nov. 25—Jack Ruby, who shot President Kennedy's alleged assassin, was transported secretly to the county jail today. The mile trip from the city jail, through the main streets, took place about noon without incident. Yesterday Ruby shot down Lee Harvey Oswald in the police headquarters basement garage as the latter was being taken on the same trip.

Ruby's transfer came as Henry Wade, Dallas County district attorney, planned to demand the death sentence for the 52-year-old night-club operator. Meanwhile Ruby's lawyers worked on a probable defense of temporary insanity. Oswald's death, Mr. Wade said, "was an assassination just like the other one," aggravated in public importance in that the victim "was under arrest and in handcuffs."

Local and Federal law enforcement officers, absorbed scarcely 24 hours ago in proving Oswald's guilt, were now preoccupied with the aspects of his death. Prominent among these was the possibility that Ruby's motive went beyond the surface indication of fanatical indignation over the killing of the president. Ruby, with a shadowy past and a local police record, mingled with newsmen and detectives in watching Oswald's departure from the city jail yesterday, and shot him. A Police Department spokesman said today no evidence had been found that Ruby had had previous contact with the 24-year-old warehouse clerk.

Ruby's chief lawyer, Tom Howard, said: "I am absolutely certain in my own mind that there never had been any contact between the two." Mr. Howard said that Ruby "has always been an emotional, high-strung man. When I saw him after the shooting, he was very very nervous, very upset, almost on the verge of collapse." He would not commit himself on a line of defense. When asked about a possible insanity plea, he said: "I think he was probably out of his mind at the time of the shooting." Nonetheless, speculation persisted about a link between the two men.

Mr. Howard said he would apply for an "examining trial," tantamount to a bail hearing, to be held immediately after Thanksgiving. Mr. Wade said he would oppose the defendant's release on bail. He has been formally charged with murder. The district attorney said he would follow, in Ruby's case, the approximate prosecution schedule he had mapped for Oswald. That calls for presenting the case to the grand jury within a week, with a trial in mid-January.

The impending courtroom clash pitted two men exceptionally experienced in the prosecution and defense of capital cases. Mr. Wade has asked the death penalty in 24 cases, and won verdicts in 23, although two death sentences were commuted. Mr. Howard said he had acted as counsel in at least 35 capital cases, "and I've never had a client executed."

Ruby's transfer was carried out with only a few police officers and newsmen aware of it. Ruby, like Oswald yesterday, was taken from the fourth-floor jail down a back elevator to the basement, which was nearly empty of observers today. Most were on the third-floor corridor.

The 5-foot 10-inch, heavy-set prisoner, handcuffed and escorted by four detectives, bent his head almost to his knees as he walked, as if to conceal his identity. At the doorway to the basement garage ramp, where he had shot Oswald, he was thrust into the back seat of an unmarked white police sedan. He lay down on the seat, with one plainclothes officer sitting by his head, and another on the edge of a seat, almost concealing Ruby's body. A guard sat with the driver.

With a motorcycle escort in the lead, and another sedan loaded with heavily armed officers following, the car swung around the block and down Main Street, through the heart of the shopping district. It was just before noon, but only a few persons were about. Most business places were closed as the city mourned President Kennedy and J. D. Tippit, the policeman Oswald was accused of killing an hour after his alleged shooting of the president and Gov. John Connally.

The county jail is at the foot of Main Street, at the corner of Houston Street. It overlooks the site of the president's death, being diagonally across the street from the book warehouse where the shots were fired. The jail has a loading platform just off the street, with a steel gate that can be closed after a vehicle has entered. The nine-story building has cells on the six upper floors.

Ruby Linked to Chicago Gangs; Boasted of Knowing Hoodlums

Police Say He Was Friendly With Several Who Were Slain, but Never Made "Big Time"—Had Union Ties

By AUSTIN C. WEHRWEIN

Special to The New York Times

CHICAGO, Nov. 25—Jack Ruby was an admitted associate of gangsters but never made the "big time," acquaintances said today. When the background of the man who had shot President Kennedy's accused assassin was pieced together, it was apparent that he been linked to several Chicagoans who were murdered. He was said to have boasted of knowing such hoodlums.

Ruby, whose real name was Leon Rubenstein, was born in Chicago 52 years ago. He was friendly with Paul Labriola, who was slain in 1954, and Paul R. Jones, now in Federal prison on a narcotics conviction, according to a police official. Ruby moved to Dallas about 15 years ago. Jones and Labriola went there in 1946, where they frequented Ruby's night club while trying unsuccessfully to bribe the sheriff, a Dallas source said.

Ruby's background ranged to San Francisco, where he lived before the war. There, on the basis of information obtained today, he was probably only on the fringe of the underworld. Tom Cahill, San Francisco police chief, said a check showed no evidence that Ruby was a "known gangster" there.

Federal investigators here focused on Ruby's connection with the Waste Material Handlers Union. In 1957 the union was expelled from the American Federation of Labor and Congress of Industrial Organizations on charges of corruption. Ruby and Leon R. Cooke, a lawyer, organized the union in 1937. Two years later Cooke was shot to death. Ruby, who bore the nickname "Sparky," left his union job—he once had the title of secretary—in 1940. That was soon after the union had been taken over by Paul Dorfman, a close friend of James R. Hoffa, head of the International Brotherhood of Teamsters.

In Palm Springs, Calif., Mr. Dorfman said Ruby was a "real nice guy" with "liberal" views. He denied he had dismissed him from the union. Ruby lost his job as an organizer on orders of the regional A.F.L. office when it temporarily took control of the union after Cooke was killed, Mr. Dorfman said. In 1959 Senate rackets investigators termed the union leadership a link between Mr. Hoffa and the underworld. Its leaders have been involved in charges of graft, beatings and killings in the years after Ruby left the union.

Earl Ruby, a brother, said in Detroit that reports about Jack Ruby's criminal connections were incorrect. But Ruby, information from many quarters made clear, knew gamblers and other "police characters" through his scalping of tickets at sporting events. He made small bets on fights and baseball games, sources said. He was said to have known Nathan Gumbin, a wealthy businessman who was killed in gangland style in 1948. The two had business dealings when Ruby was with the union, resources said, and Ruby frequented a gambling place where Gumbin went.

Theodore H. Shulman, head of the Sanatex Corporation and executive director of the Waste Trade Industries, said Ruby had been forced out of the union because of his temperament. Ruby, he said, would excitedly threaten a strike before a grievance could be discussed.

Luis Kutner, a lawyer, said that when the Senate committee was at work in 1949, Ruby apparently wanted to become the crime syndicate's "pipeline" into the committee. Mr. Kutner said Ruby became an "adviser" to the committee. But he added that he thought Ruby had been trying to impress "the boys" with his connections. "He was a nervous, ambitious, frustrated guy who never made the big time," Mr. Kutner said.

He insisted, however, that he would not say Ruby had had ties with the underworld, but that he had "tossed off names" of hoodlums. Ruby always acted "tough," he recalled, wearing "sharp" suits and the pearl-gray fedora with the broad brim turned down in front, which Al Capone had made a hoodlum fad.

Another person who remembered Ruby was Police Capt. Louis Capparelli. He was long commanding officer of the Maxwell district where Ruby was born. His father was from Russia and his mother from Poland. "He wasn't a tough guy, as they say, but he was a very aggressive salesman when he was selling something," the captain said. "He liked to be seen or heard, and I guess you could call him a frustrated policeman because he liked to be seen with a policeman."

Traced to Coast

By JOSEPH A. LOFTUS

Special to The New York Times

DALLAS, Nov. 25—Acquaintances of Jack Ruby gave further insights into his character today. But nothing indicated an association with Lee H. Oswald, whom he shot yesterday apparently to avenge the assassination of President Kennedy.

Ruby was said to have been friendly with a small-time Chicago gang, but not directly tied to it. A police source remembered him as the operator of a punchboard racket in San Francisco until a death threat forced him back to Chicago, then to Dallas.

"Hothead" best described the trait commonly known to his acquaintances and former employees. Janet Conforto, an entertainer, recalled Ruby as "completely uncontrollable when he's angry. I'm sure when he shot Oswald he thought this would make him a hero to the people in Dallas, that he was righting the wrong that Dallas had done to President Kennedy," she told *The Dallas Times Herald.* "He gets something in his mind and it just builds up and builds up."

Miss Conforto was a recent headliner at the Carousel Club, which Ruby operated. She was on the way to New Orleans when she heard the word of Oswald's slaying. She called the newspaper to verify it and told her story. "He threatened to beat me up and burn my wardrobe once when we had an argument over a night's pay he owed me," she related. "I had $10,000 worth of gowns in that dressing room. I went to a judge to get a peace bond put on him. Jack finally paid me. He got so mad at me one time he cut off the lights right in the middle of my act. He shouted at me right in front of the customers. You should hear what he shouted at me.

"He's used to fighting for everything. He carried everything to extremes. He thrived on it. He's really two people. On the other side, he can be very, very nice, very helpful. I remember him as very much for a cause, or against it. He beat up several people of the club and threw them down the stairs. He told me once he got his finger bitten off in a fight.

"I would like to say something good about him. He likes dogs. He used to keep 11 of them in the club kitchen. He gave a lot of them away."

The owner of a Dallas club said: "Ruby was a hard guy to understand, a big talker, a street brawler. But if Jack liked you, he'd do anything in the world for you. He needed love. He had some dogs up at his place and would not allow anybody to mistreat them. He was a vain person and sort of an egomaniac. He thought he was a lady-killer."

A companion and employee, George Senator, said he had known that Ruby had a pistol. "He bought it some time ago for self-protection," Mr. Senator said.

Called a Police "Buff"

NEW ORLEANS, Nov. 25 (UPI)—A former business associate of Jack Ruby said last night he believed Ruby had shot Lee H. Oswald to avenge the slaying of a Dallas policeman rather than of President Kennedy. "Patriotic he wasn't, a police buff he was," said Herbert C. D. Kelly, once part owner of the Carousel Club in Dallas. "Ruby wasn't very interested in politics, I doubt that he even voted."

Johnson Pledges Facts in Killings

Orders Full Investigation—Texas Plans Inquiry

BY CABELL PHILLIPS

Special to The New York Times

WASHINGTON, Nov. 25—The Government moved tonight to give the public all the facts on President Kennedy's assassination and the slaying of the man accused as the assassin. The White House announced a broad inquiry into the events of the last few days. The announcement said: "The people of the nation may be sure that all of the facts will be made public."

President Johnson, the statement said, ordered the Justice Department "to conduct a prompt and thorough investigation of all the circumstances surrounding the brutal assassination of President Kennedy and the murder of his alleged assassin." The Federal Bureau of Investigation, which is the Justice Department's investigating arm, will do the field work. The statement said the president had "directed all Federal agencies to cooperate."

The move was clearly designed to end any doubts in this country or abroad about the identity of the assassin and to try to make amends for the tragic mishandling of the suspect, Lee Harvey Oswald. There was also some feeling that President Johnson preferred to have the inquiry and public presentation of the facts handled by Federal authorities rather than state and local officials in Texas.

Earlier today the Texas attorney general, Waggoner Carr, announced that the state would convene a special court of inquiry to investigate the two killings and make the results public. The Justice Department reacted to that by saying it would cooperate with "any responsible inquiry." But a spokesman made clear at the time that the Texas inquiry could not supersede the department's own effort to get to the bottom of the tragedy. Representative Hale Boggs of Louisiana, assistant Democratic leader in the House, suggested today that a Congressional commission make a formal inquiry into the assassination. He said this was necessary because the facts could not be brought out in the trial of Oswald's accused slayer, Jack Ruby.

The preliminary opinion in the Government is that no presidential commission or other special body is needed. But there is a determination to bring the facts out by some device whose impartiality cannot be challenged. One problem in an inquiry's bringing out the facts is that Ruby presumably faces a trial for murder. It would be in violation of legal ethics and the minimum standards of fair procedure for any official to make public an asserted account of his activities before he is tried.

The Texas attorney general called a press conference here this afternoon to announce the court of inquiry. In a statement read to reporters at the Statler-Hilton Hotel, he said: "All Texans join with all other Americans in mourning the loss of our president. Because the shocking assassination of President Kennedy, the attempted assassination of Governor Connally and the subsequent murder of the suspected assassin occurred in Texas, it is my feeling that all facts surrounding these matters should be made public for the knowledge of all people everywhere.

"I will, therefore, upon my return to Texas, call for a court of inquiry, which is authorized under existing Texas law. Those conducting the inquiry will be the top staff of my office, including the attorney general, in cooperation with one or more outstanding jurists and lawyers. Also, top-level local and state authorities will be invited to participate actively, and Federal authorities will be asked to cooperate. A full and complete report of the findings of this hearing will be sent to the United States Department of Justice, and I want to emphasize that this will be a thorough, complete and impartial investigation, and that the full results will be made public."

It was explained later that a court of inquiry has all the powers of a court of law to obtain evidence and command testimony, but that it has no punitive power. Its principal value is in bringing the facts in a situation to public attention. Public authorities can then bring such legal action as the disclosures warrant. Texas last employed this device in exploring the financial manipulations of Billie Sol Estes. The court of inquiry also has the effect of moving the president's assassination and Oswald's slaying out of the exclusive jurisdiction of Dallas authorities. Attorney General Carr said he had spoken briefly with President Johnson today but that he had not discussed the court of inquiry with him.

Guevara Says Cuba Must Remain Alert

HAVANA, Nov. 25 (AP)—Ernesto Guevara says that with a new Administration in Washington, Cuba would have to be "alert as always and perhaps more so" to repel any attack. Mr. Guevara, the Cuban minister of industries, said at an electric power forum in Havana last night that the killing in Dallas of Lee H. Oswald "seems to have been taken from a gangster movie.

"Everything makes us think that very dark and shadowy forces are moving behind this," Mr. Guevara said. "Everything makes us think that in the months or years, the world's peace will be endangered by the greatest monopolist and warring oligarchy, with more power of death than the history of humanity has ever known. We will have to build socialism, and we will build it despite everything, even in these circumstances 90 miles from the United States, a center of imperial arrogance which unleashes insults and war actions against our country."

He said he would make no predictions, "But we have to be alert, as alert as always and perhaps more so to repel any attack with confidence in final victory, whatever the methods used to attack the Cuban revolution."

COMMENTARY

The President's Funeral

The pomp and panoply of a day of sad splendor have ended. Taps has sounded and the saluting cannon and rifles have been stilled. His Washington neighbors and fellow citizens, who devoted yesterday to his memory, are resuming their normal lives again. The presidents, princes and prime ministers who came in unprecedented numbers from lands near and far are returning to their homes. John Fitzgerald Kennedy has found eternal rest.

In time of sudden shock—such as that of this tragic weekend—we fall back naturally on traditional symbols and accustomed ceremonials. President Kennedy's funeral may well have been in many respects the most elaborate and impressive farewell a modern ruler has ever received, yet its key elements—the union of religious solemnity and military display—have been familiar for centuries. But something new was added this time: the reading of a part of his Inaugural Address, the document which above all made clear his desire—which he realized—to be a president of peace, and not a president of war.

In that address, President Kennedy expressed his deepest ambition for humanity in these words: "Together let us explore the stars, conquer the deserts, eradicate disease, tap the ocean depths and encourage the arts and commerce." He called for "a new world of law, where the strong are just and the weak secure and the peace preserved." There can be no more fitting memorial for this great spirit than the national resolve that we who live after him dedicate ourselves to realizing these, his profoundest and proudest dreams.

The Whole Truth

The full story of the assassination and its stunning sequel must be placed before the American people and the world in a responsible way by a responsible source of the United States Government.

This is a national matter, not one merely for the police of Dallas. We must be told, after a thorough investigation, all the evidence about Lee Harvey Oswald, the accused assassin. We must be told about his motives, about his past activities and travels, about his organizational affiliations, about what branches of government his life touched, about whatever knowledge the local police and the F.B.I. had of Oswald—before and after the shooting by and of the accused.

We must be told all the facts about Jack Ruby's killing of Oswald. President Johnson has rightly directed the F.B.I. to look into "every aspect" of this disgraceful shooting right in the Dallas jail. And we must be told how and why rifles and revolvers can be bought and concealed so easily in this country.

The killing of the accused assassin does not close the books on the case. In fact, it raises questions which must be answered if we are ever to fathom the depths of the president's terrible death and its aftermath. An objective Federal commission, if necessary, with members of Congress included, must be apprised of all and tell us all. Much as we would like to obliterate from memory the most disgraceful weekend in our history, a clear explanation must be forthcoming. Not in a spirit of vengeance, not to cover up, but for the sake of information and justice and to restore respect for law.

The Merrywood Example

The Federal Government's action to stop high-rise apartment construction on the Merrywood Estate, overlooking the Potomac River northwest of Washington, is a step to preserve the beautiful natural setting of the nation's capital for all Americans. The method employed could be fruitfully employed in many states and localities to guard against despoliation of scenic treasures.

The Merrywood project was an important test for the future of the capital area because the proposed tower apartments would have inevitably been followed by others. The Potomac Palisades would have fallen victim to the same kind of commercialization now encroaching on the Hudson's Palisades.

The legal device used by the Government was application of a scenic easement at Merrywood. This leaves the property in the hands of the owners but forbids them to erect high-rise buildings or to destroy trees and other adornments to the landscape. The owners will receive compensation in an amount fixed by the courts.

Under the circumstances it required courage and initiative for the Interior Department to use the scenic easement as an emergency weapon against the Merrywood project. The bulldozers were literally starting their destruction when the suit was filed. The department's action shows how creative thought can develop ways of preserving scenery without going to the great expense of actually acquiring the land.

Labor and Defense

Two years ago strikes in the construction of missile bases were causing so much delay in the defense program that Congress considered adoption of a no-strike law. Since that time a voluntary peace machinery set up by construction unions and their employers under the auspices of President Kennedy's Missile Sites Labor Commission has cut strike losses almost to the vanishing point. Strikes, which cost one day out of every 96 of working time in the five years before the program began, cost only one day out of every 1,288 last year.

In recognition of this and other contributions organized labor has made to America's military preparedness, Secretary McNamara has conferred the Defense Department's Meritorious Award on the A.F.L.-C.I.O. It was the first such award the department has made to any organization. It provides new evidence of the effectiveness of voluntary methods for preserving industrial peace where both labor and management exhibit adequate recognition of the primacy of the national interest.

Opportunity for Eisenhower

The nervousness reported in Europe over the change of presidents in the United States will not be easily dispelled. Though a vigorous restatement of American goals is essential, policy declarations can do no more than indicate general directions. Only as the new president begins to make and to carry out the difficult decisions that lie ahead will it be possible to see what the words really mean.

Furthermore, the outcome of the 1964 presidential election is now in far greater doubt than ever before. As a result, no one can predict what American policy will be a year from now. If the impending presidential campaign were to produce another "great debate" about American involvement in Europe, the coming interregnum could be a costly one. Such a debate would further the current policies of President de Gaulle, whose most persuasive argument for a Europe that would go its own way is that American withdrawal is inevitable in any event. The free world at this juncture cannot afford such a debate nor a year of confusion over American foreign policy—a year that a Republican victory would stretch to 18 months—while a new Administration sought its footing.

The central core of American foreign policy, which should be taken out of domestic politics, has two chief elements. The first is strengthening of the free world by encouraging unity both inside Europe and across the Atlantic. The second is continuation of attempts by a strong West to seek, through negotiation with the East, "to lower world tension without lowering our guard," as President Johnson recently put it. Despite opposition from the Goldwater faction here and the Gaullist faction in France, there is a great consensus on these issues both in Europe and in the United States—as there has been through three Administrations since 1947.

But neither America's friends nor opponents among Europe's leaders can be expected to pay much heed to a nation apparently divided against itself. They will be moved by a program that they believe no election is likely to change. Such a program demands a return to bipartisanship in American foreign policy.

The broad spectrum of views in the Republican party may make such a policy difficult to achieve. But there is one man who has the power to achieve it. He is Dwight D. Eisenhower. He himself has wavered recently on the American commitment to Europe and has talked of withdrawing American troops, as have some elements of the Administration. A viable program for the Atlantic world cannot be built on that basis. But if the former president were to rededicate himself to Atlantic purposes and lend his great prestige to a bipartisan policy, President Johnson could not reject it, nor could any Republican who hoped to obtain his party's nomination.

There have been indications that Mr. Eisenhower would welcome a greater public role. Here is one that is worthy of his mettle. And it is particularly fitting that he should perform it at this moment. For just as Senator Vandenberg at an earlier date brought bipartisan support to President Truman, it was Lyndon Johnson as Senate majority leader who helped to weld together a bipartisan majority on foreign policy issues for President Eisenhower during critical years of his own Administration.

The State of the Economy

The extreme fluctuations of stock prices on Wall Street do not provide an accurate reflection of the state of the economy as President Johnson assumes the burden of office.

Business conditions are good, with practically every significant indicator—industrial production, employment, corporate profits, personal income, retail sales and construction—at record peaks. It would not be any exaggeration for Mr. Johnson to describe the economy as fundamentally sound, although this hackneyed term has been so abused that it could be misinterpreted as connoting weakness. The fact is that the economy is not only healthy but should exhibit increased strength in the months to come.

Wall Street's movements cannot be ignored, of course; but it should be remembered that investors are often prone to hypochondriacal behavior, to excesses in buying as well as selling, that bear hardly any relation to general business conditions. This was the case in the spring of 1962, when the plunge in stock prices was aggravated by previous speculation involving abuses in the use of credit. The economy, however, managed to weather that storm on Wall Street, the deepest and most violent in the entire postwar period.

New internal excesses may be plaguing the securities markets, but they have no bearing on the basic economy of the country. The nation is in an even better position to cope with a decline than it was 18 months ago, when business was not moving forward as strongly as now.

Mr. Johnson faces many unresolved economic problems, particularly the persistence of far too high a level of domestic unemployment, the existence of some severely depressed areas, and the continuing threat to the international status of the dollar. But with the economy enjoying the most robust advance in our history, he at least does not have to worry about getting the country moving. This is a pledge that has been fulfilled.

Observer

WASHINGTON, Nov. 25—The great change that will transform this lovely city very quickly and forever within the next few weeks has already begun. By the time the daffodils bloom again in Rock Creek Park it will be another place and, though to the casual eye it will look very much the same, everything that gives it character will be different.

It is always so when one president passes and another takes his place. In this, Washington is unique. Its character, its social structure, its mood, its manner, the tone of its intellectual life, the quality of its leisure, everything that gives personality and distinction to great cities, right down to its real-estate values—all are a reflection of the family that lives in the White House.

For this reason, Washingtonians have additional cause to grieve the passing of President Kennedy, for he graced it with a heady and exciting cosmopolitan air that made it a stimulating place to live. The contagion of the youthful and effervescent spirit of the Kennedy family seemed to carbonate the atmosphere.

In General Eisenhower's time the town had been very much the gracious old lady, well-behaved, well-bred, gliding about discreetly in limousines, stooping now and then to a bit of gossip or backbiting, but, on the whole, very proper and rather dull. The Kennedys let in the excitement of youth. On the society pages, the pictures of aging, tight-laced hostesses were swept away by those of young stunners in Paris gowns. The town got into sports cars and invited professors in to dinner and went swimming again, frequently in full dress.

Thanks to Mrs. Kennedy, it discovered that there were other forms of art besides Greco-Roman temples filled with paper shufflers. It rediscovered exercise, studied foreign tongues, flexed its flaccid wit and decided that there would be nothing disgraceful in building a cultural center.

Now, the Kennedy Washington is beginning to recede. It will fade very quickly like an old tintype print, as the new Washington begins to pick up the reflection of President Johnson. Cruel though it is, and this is the cruelest of cities, the speculation about who is to rise on the social ladder and who is to fall is already the whispered gossip over the water coolers. Human relationships here often reach a level that might have shocked even the Borgias. This is why it is not surprising that people who rode the social crest because of friendships with the Kennedy family and who will now fade from the spotlight under Mr. Johnson are more likely to be scorned than pitied.

No one can yet foresee what the city is to become under the new president. What, for example, will happen to Georgetown, which was the social center of Washington under President Kennedy?

If this city still does not know what it is to become next, it can see clearly what it is losing. It has rarely enjoyed life quite so wholeheartedly as it has these past three years. Perhaps the Theodore Roosevelt era and the opening phase of Franklin Roosevelt's Administration were just as exciting, but as Washington counts time those lie back in ancient history.

What is going is an era when the town could go daffy over the Mona

Lisa and take to pool-jumping with collegiate glee. After years in which it naturally assumed that all professors were crackpots, it could see one in the round and even inquire what made him tick.

The Kennedys' zest for life became the city's. It will probably be a long time before Washington feels quite so excited again just to be alive.

RUSSELL BAKER.

In the Nation

The Modern Miracle and the Ancient Curse

By ARTHUR KROCK

WASHINGTON, Nov. 25—For the first time since leaders of the nations assembled at the bier of another, to pay final tribute to him and to his people, all have been able to make the pilgrimage within two settings of the sun. Only three days had elapsed from the death of President Kennedy in Texas to the hour when his requiem was intoned in Washington. Yet so complete has been man's conquest of time and distance that the requiem mass and the following interment were attended by the heads or plenary representatives of more than 100 states in the six continents of the world.

Probably it is true, as archivists are saying, that not since the funeral of King Edward VII has there been a comparable gathering of the incarnations of power. On May 20, 1910, the British sovereign was buried at Windsor after a long procession through the streets of London led by his son and successor, George V, seven European kings, the heirs-apparent or prince consorts of many others and a group of special ambassadors that included former President Theodore Roosevelt. But Edward's life had ended two weeks before his state funeral could be held because air transport was only in its crude, elemental stage. And, the electronic age being far in the future, no radio and television existed to make the whole world a spectator.

If grief had not been uppermost among those who watched the magnificent funeral ceremonies, these manifestations of ever-expanding human genius might have been accented, as in Hamlet's meditation: "What a piece of work is a man! How noble in reason! How infinite in faculties, in form and moving! How express and admirable in action! How like an angel in apprehension! How like a god! The beauty of the world! The paragon of animals!" But submerging the incidence of the scientific miracle was the thought of the ancient and abiding curse of violence which these potentates and princes from afar had come to mourn.

The young president lay dead in his coffin under his country's flag because not even the enlightened system of freedom and self-government of which he was the shining symbol has exorcised this curse from the human heart. "At his best," said Aristotle, "man is the noblest of all animals; separated from law and justice he is the worst." At Dallas both law and justice had been trampled upon by the president's assassin, by their civic guardians, and by the maddened avenger who took law and justice into his own hands.

This is the shame which all the elegists—at the Capitol, in the press, and throughout the world—lamented. And the theme common to all the elegies may eventually be sustained by factual evidence. This theme is that the violence of political differences that is current in the United States stimulated the fanaticism that expressed itself in the murder of the president. But the American people have always been violent and often venomous in political debate; fanaticism bred in personal or doctrinal grievances has taken the lives of three earlier presidents and unsuccessfully attempted the assassination of four who were, were to be, or had been presidents. Hence, there is no merit in the implication of some of the orators that Mr. Kennedy's murder should be related to the area where it occurred because of the intensity there of the controversy over his policies.

This implication especially lacks merit by reason of the only facts known about the only suspect, Oswald. He was a Marxist; at least a sympathizer with the religion of Communism; emigrated to and married in the Soviet Union; and was trying to return. This is certainly not the dossier of the "Right Wing extremists," a stigmatic label of Dallas which some members of the Administration are too prone to affix.

That inclination was revealed by the Voice of America broadcast at 1:59 P.M. last Friday of the ghastly tragedy in the city. "Dallas," the V.O.A. explained to the world, "is the center of the extreme Right Wing." This gratuitous, and as it proved false, suggestion that such was the affiliation of the assassin was deleted from the broadcast at 2:10 P.M. but it was grist to Moscow's mill, which has been grinding it ever since.

Mourning for a President

That His Work May Continue

TO THE EDITOR OF THE NEW YORK TIMES:

In this terrible hour the danger is that the tragedy of the president's death will be compounded by the destruction of his work.

Forces opposing the Administration's legislative program must not be allowed to seize this opportunity to frustrate the goals of the American people, which have been so dramatically expressed, for example, in the march on Washington for jobs and freedom.

Americans would do well to write President Johnson supporting his efforts to continue the late president's work in both foreign and domestic policy.

Unless the people give voice to their will with unmistakable firmness, untold damage may be done in areas that were of major concern to President Kennedy, such as full employment, education, medical care, civil rights, conservation, and the preservation of peace.

ERIC LOEB.
New York, Nov. 23, 1963.

Inflaming the Ignorant

TO THE EDITOR OF THE NEW YORK TIMES:

One thing this nation should learn from President Kennedy's death: politicians at every level have an awesome power over the mass of the people, a power that should always be tempered with responsibility.

If men in public life did not condone resistance to laws, churches would not be torn by bombs, college and high school students would not riot together, towns would not live under martial law, distinguished men would not be publicly disgraced, and President Kennedy would be alive today.

Assassins may be caught and punished, but are they more guilty than irresponsible men who inflame the ignorant for their own selfish reasons?

IRA D. GRUBER.
Williamsburg, Va., Nov. 22, 1963.

Memorial Proposed

TO THE EDITOR OF THE NEW YORK TIMES:

In order that the people of the United States be given some positive outlet for their sense of frustration and outrage, it seems to me that it would be an excellent idea to establish a John F. Kennedy Memorial Foundation.

I believe that such a plan would meet with a tremendous response and that the funds collected could be used to further some of the many projects to which the late president had given so much of his time and energy.

It is too easy at this time to think first of revenge. But, if the flood of emotion which has poured across the United States (and the world) can in some way be channeled to the good, perhaps we can once again feel that there is in humanity some part that is civilized. Today we have been given good reason to doubt it.

BRUCE A. DAVIS.
New York, Nov. 22, 1963.

A View From Britain

TO THE EDITOR OF THE NEW YORK TIMES:

President Kennedy's death diminishes us all. Your shock, your confoundment and your sorrow are also ours.

To me President Kennedy seemed a good and a great and a dedicated man. There are so few men of his quality in the world to stand for us. That someone should want only to destroy such a man makes a mockery of all we strive for. But John F. Kennedy is immortal now.

I am one of the "mere uncounted folk" but please accept my brotherly greeting. God bless the great American democracy.

F. W. HOUGHTON.
Bingley, Yorks, Eng., Nov. 23, 1963.

Moratorium on TV Violence

TO THE EDITOR OF THE NEW YORK TIMES:

In his moving account of American reaction to President Kennedy's assassination, your correspondent James Reston referred [Nov. 23] to the "streak of violence" in American life to which our president fell victim. The same violence now has claimed the man implicated in his death before his case could be brought to justice.

While no one knows what impelled the men who did these acts, many of us must realize with a pang that the television screen in our homes gives our children a steady, daily diet of cellophane violence.

In program after program the villain or the hero takes the law into his own hands and shoots it out. If the viewer becomes jaded there are the science-fiction cartoons where he sees newer and more deadly weapons of destruction. In some serials, the child audiences are left to wait until the next installment to know whether the mad scientific genius has indeed been successful in poisoning the water supply.

I most earnestly propose, in this sad period while we contemplate the consequences of what has happened, that the television and film industries, in the memory of John F. Kennedy, observe a one-year moratorium on all shows which portray violence for its own sake. This would not, of course, affect legitimate historical or literary dramas.

Perhaps in the course of this year, new entertainment themes could be devised which we might find that we all liked better.

Such a move would be as much a memorial to John F. Kennedy as the statues that will be erected, and would perhaps bring us closer to his goal of a nation "guided by the lights of learning and reason."

MARY B. SULLIVAN.
Riverside, Conn., Nov. 24, 1963.

Violence in Our Civilization

TO THE EDITOR OF THE NEW YORK TIMES:

Our splendid president gone from us! His youthful zeal and enthusiasm gone. Gone his unusual ability to handle men and ideas; his increasing competence in the affairs of nations, his resolute search for peace and disarmament. How useless and pointless.

Can we not, individuals and nations alike, recognize what this outburst of brutal hatred means? There is far too much selfishness and violence in our civilization. Differences of color and ideology make too many men think of killing. We badly need understanding and give-and-take negotiation before it is too late.

Let us do a better job for President Johnson than we did for President Kennedy. We owe that to both.

SAMUEL L. TUCKER Jr.
Westfield, N.J., Nov. 23, 1963.

A Friend Lost

TO THE EDITOR OF THE NEW YORK TIMES:

I write to you with the news of President Kennedy's death still fresh in my mind. I spent two of the most exciting years of my life in America. My friends were his supporters; I thought the way they did. I looked upon Mr. Kennedy as a leader, a man in whom I reposed my confidence, a man whom I grew to like, respect and finally to love as a friend. Perhaps it is the quality of all great men that their greatness transcends the barriers that surround others, so that those who know of them feel they also knew them.

I feel a deep sense of personal loss. I grieve that his political wisdom may now be absent, but I grieve too that I have lost a friend.

C. P. MATHEWS.
Oxford, England, Nov. 22, 1963.

Guarding Freedom

TO THE EDITOR OF THE NEW YORK TIMES:

I had never seen President Kennedy in person, but serving in the U.S. Navy for four years I have had the chance to respect and admire him not only as a president, but as a truly great man.

Freedom is truly a costly thing, and also very hard to come by. President Kennedy has paid for it with his life. We must never forget this deed that was done today, for if it is taken easily we have lost our main purpose for living—for a free and better life.

We must carry on to the best of our ability to keep the United States a free nation without such things as Communism endangering our freedom, not only for us, but also for our children, and other children to follow.

THOMAS I. BURKETT.

East Orange, N.J., Nov. 22, 1963.

For a Better Future

TO THE EDITOR OF THE NEW YORK TIMES:

No words can express the horror and the tragedy of our president's senseless assassination. He will not have died in vain if his untimely death serves to awaken millions of Americans and the people of goodwill of all nations to the realization that this is now "A Time for Greatness," that they cannot sit back and ignore the great issues that face us. It requires of them some participation on local, state and national levels in doing what they can to help make this a better world in which to live, not so much for ourselves, for the immediate present, but for our children and our children's children.

ARTHUR BLUMIN.

Staten Island, N.Y., Nov. 22, 1963.

To Pass Major Legislation

TO THE EDITOR OF THE NEW YORK TIMES:

For the sake of our nation's soul—in case it still has one—let Congress honor the memory of President Kennedy by promptly passing at least one of the major pieces of legislation which he believed needful to strengthen the common good.

LAWRENCE W. BEALS,
Professor of Philosophy, Williams College.
Williamstown, Mass., Nov. 22, 1963.

APPENDIX

A Day of Chasing After Grim Reports That Turned Out to Be True

Tom Wicker was White House correspondent for The Times *during the Kennedy Administration. Here he tells how he covered the assassination of President Kennedy in Dallas on Nov. 22, 1963. This excerpted account appeared in* Times Talk, *the in-house newsletter, shortly afterward.*

I think I was in the first press bus. But I can't be sure. Pete Lisagor of *The Chicago Daily News* says he *knows* he was in the first press bus and he describes things that went on board it that didn't happen on the bus I was in. But I still *think* I was in the first press bus.

I cite that minor confusion as an example of the way it was in Dallas in the early afternoon of Nov. 22. At first no one knew what happened, or how, or where, much less why. Gradually bits and pieces began to fall together and within two hours a reasonably coherent version of the story began to be possible. Even now, however, I know no reporter who was there who has a clear and orderly picture of that surrealistic afternoon; it is still a matter of bits and pieces thrown hastily into something like a whole.

It began, for most reporters, when the central fact of it was over. As our press bus eased at motorcade speed down an incline toward an underpass, there was a little confusion in the sparse crowds that at that point had been standing at the curb to see the president of the United States pass. As we came out of the underpass, I saw a motorcycle policeman drive over the curb, across an open area, a few feet up a railroad bank, dismount and start scrambling up the bank. Jim Mathis of The Advance (Newhouse) Syndicate went to the front of our bus and looked ahead to where the president's car was supposed to be, perhaps 10 cars ahead of us. He hurried back to his seat. "The president's car just sped off," he said. "Really gunned away." (How could Mathis have seen that if there had been another bus in front of us?) But that could have happened if someone had thrown a tomato at the president. The press bus in its stately pace rolled on to the Trade Mart, where the president was to speak. Fortunately, it was only a few minutes away.

At the Trade Mart, rumor was sweeping the hundreds of Texans already eating their lunch. It was the only rumor that I had ever *seen;* it was moving across the crowd like a wind over a wheat field. A man eating a grapefruit seized my arm as I passed. "Has the president been shot?" he asked. "I don't think so," I said. "But something happened."

With the other reporters—I suppose 35 of them—I went on through the huge hall to the upstairs press room. We were hardly there when Marianne Means of Hearst Headline Service hung up a telephone, ran to a group of us and said, "The president's been shot. He's at Parkland Hospital."

One thing I learned that day; I suppose I already knew it, but that day made it plain. A reporter must trust his instinct. When Miss Means said those eight words—I never learned who told her—I knew absolutely they were true. Everyone did. We ran for the press buses. Again, a man seized my arm—an official-looking man. "No running in here," he said sternly. I pulled free and ran on. Doug Kiker of *The Herald Tribune* barreled head-on into a waiter carrying a plate of potatoes. Waiter and potatoes flew about the room. Kiker ran on. He was in his first week with *The Trib,* and his first presidential trip. I barely got aboard a moving press bus. Bob Pierrepoint of CBS was aboard and he said he now recalled having heard something that could have been shots—or firecrackers, or motorcycle backfire. We talked anxiously, unbelieving, afraid.

Fortunately again, it was only a few minutes to Parkland Hospital. There at its emergency entrance, stood the president's car, the top up, a bucket of bloody water beside it. Automatically, I took down its license number—GG300 District of Columbia. The first eyewitness description came from Senator Ralph Yarborough, who had been riding in the third car of the motorcade with Vice President and Mrs. Johnson. Senator Yarborough is an East Texan, which is to say a Southerner, a man of quick emotion, old-fashioned rhetoric. "Gentlemen," he said, pale, shaken, near tears. "It is a deed of horror." The details he gave us were good and mostly—as it later proved—accurate. But he would not describe to us the appearance of the president as he was wheeled into the hospital, except to say that he was "gravely wounded." We could not doubt, then, that it was serious.

I had chosen that day to be without a notebook. I took notes on the back of my mimeographed schedule of the two-day tour of Texas we had been so near to concluding. Today, I cannot read many of the notes; on Nov. 22, they were as clear as 60-point type. A local television reporter, Mel Crouch, told us he had seen a rifle being withdrawn from the corner fifth or sixth floor window of the Texas School Book Depository. Instinct again—Crouch sounded right, positive, though none of us knew him. We believed it and it was right. Mac Kilduff, an assistant White House press secretary in charge of the press on that trip, and who was to acquit himself well that day, came out of the hospital. We gathered round and he told us the president was alive. It wasn't true, we later learned; but Mac thought it was true at that time, and he didn't mislead us about a possible recovery. His whole demeanor made plain what was likely to happen. He also told us—as Senator Yarborough had—that Gov. John Connally of Texas was shot, too.

Kilduff promised more details in five minutes and went back into the hospital. We were barred. Word came to us second hand—I don't remember exactly how—from Bob Clark of ABC, one of the men who had been riding in the press "pool" car near the president, that he had been lying face down in Mrs. Kennedy's lap when the car arrived at Parkland. No signs of life. That is what I mean by instinct. That day, a reporter had none of the ordinary means or time to check and double-check matters given as fact. He had to go on what he knew of people he talked to, what he knew of human reaction, what two isolated "facts" added to in sum—above all what he felt in his bones. I knew Clark and respected him. I took his report at face value, even at second hand. It turned out to be true. In a crisis, if a reporter can't trust his instinct for truth, he can't trust anything . . .

As I was passing the open convertible in which Vice President and Mrs. Johnson and Senator Yarborough had been riding in the motorcade, a voice boomed from its radio: "The president of the United States is dead. I repeat—it has just been announced that the president of the United States is dead." There was no authority, no word of who had announced it. But— instinct again—I believed it instantly. It sounded true. I knew it was true. I stood still a moment, then began running. Ordinarily, I couldn't jump a tennis net if I'd just beaten Gonzales. That day, carrying a briefcase and a typewriter, I jumped a chain fence looping around the drive, not even breaking stride. Hugh Sidey of *Time,* a close friend of the president, was walking slowly ahead of me. "Hugh," I said. "The president's dead. Just announced on the radio. I don't know who announced but it sounded official to me." Sidey stopped, looked at me, looked at the ground. I couldn't talk about it, I couldn't think about it. I couldn't do anything but run on to the press room. Then I told others what I had heard.

Sidey, I learned a few minutes later, stood where he was a minute. Then he saw two Catholic priests. He spoke to them. Yes, they told him, the president was dead. They had administered the last rites. Sidey went on to the press room and spread that word, too. Throughout the day, every reporter on the scene seemed to me to do his best to help everyone else. Information came only in bits and pieces. Each man who picked up a bit or a piece passed it on. I know no one who held anything out. Nobody thought about an exclusive; it didn't seem important.

After perhaps 10 minutes when we milled around in the press room— my instinct was to find the new president, but no one knew where he was— Kilduff appeared red-eyed, barely in control of himself. In that hushed classroom, he made the official, the unbelievable announcement. The president was dead of a gunshot wound in the brain. Lyndon Johnson was safe, in the protective custody of the Secret Service. He would be sworn in as soon as possible. . . .

We made our way to the hearse—Secret Service agents who knew us helped us through the suspicious Dallas police lines—and the driver said his instructions were to take the body to the airport. That confirmed our hunch, but gave me, at least, another wrong one. Mr. Johnson, I declared, would fly to Washington with the body and be sworn in there.

We posted ourselves inconspicuously near the emergency entrance. Within minutes, they brought the body out in a bronze coffin. A number of White House staff people—stunned, silent, stumbling along as if dazed—walked with it. Mrs. Kennedy walked by the coffin, her hand on it, her head down, her hat gone, her dress and stockings spattered. She got into the hearse with the coffin. The staff men crowded into cars and followed. That was just about the only eyewitness matter that I got with my own eyes that entire afternoon.

Roberts [Chuck Roberts of *Newsweek*] commandeered a seat in a police car and followed, promising to "fill" Sidey and me as necessary. We made the same promise to him and went back to the press room. There, we received an account from Julian Read, a staff assistant, of Mrs. John Connally's recollection of the shooting. Most of his recital was helpful and it established the important fact of who was sitting in which seat in the president's car at the time of the shooting. The doctors who had treated the president came in after Mr. Read. They gave us copious details, particularly as to the efforts they had made to resuscitate the president. They were less explicit about the wounds, explaining that the body had been in their hands only a short time and they had little time to examine it closely. They conceded they were unsure as to the time of death and had arbitrarily put it at 1 P.M., C.S.T.

Much of their information, as it developed later, was erroneous. Subsequent reports made it pretty clear that Mr. Kennedy probably was killed instantly. His body, as a physical mechanism, however, continued to flicker an occasional pulse and heartbeat. No doubt this justified the doctors' first account. There also was the question of national security and Mr. Johnson's swearing-in. Perhaps, too, there was a question about the Roman Catholic rites. In any case until a later doctor's statement about 9 P.M. that night, the account we got at the hospital was official.

The doctors hardly had left before Hawks [Wayne Hawks of the White House staff] came in and told us Mr. Johnson would be sworn in immediately at the airport. We dashed for the press buses, still parked outside. Many a campaign had taught me something about press buses and I ran a little harder, got there first, and went to the wide rear seat. That is the best place on a bus to open up a typewriter and get some work done.

On the short trip to the airport, I got about 500 words on paper—leaving a blank space for the hour of Mr. Johnson's swearing-in and putting down the mistaken assumption that the scene would be somewhere in the terminal. As we arrived at a back gate along the air strip, we could see Air Force One, the presidential jet, screaming down the runway and into the air.

In His Own Words:
President Kennedy's Creed and His Basic Policies

The following appeared in The Week in Review *section of* The New York Times *on Nov. 24, 1963.*

HIS CREED

ON FREEDOM AND PEACE "Peace and freedom do not come cheap, and we are destined . . . to live out most, if not all, of our lives in uncertainty and challenge and peril."

"However close we sometimes seem to that dark and final abyss, let no man of peace and freedom despair. . . . If we can all persevere, if we can in every land . . . look beyond our own shores and ambitions, then surely the age will dawn in which the strong are just and the weak secure and the peace preserved."

ON THE ROLE OF THE U.S. "Our strength as well as our convictions have imposed upon this nation the role of leader in freedom's cause. No role in history could be more difficult or more important. . . . This nation was born of revolution and raised in freedom. And we do not intend to leave an open road to despotism."

"I do not believe that any of us would exchange place with any other people or any other generation. The energy, the faith, the devotion which we bring to this endeavor will light our country and all who serve it—and the glow from that fire can truly light the world."

ON THE PRESIDENCY "I want to be a president who responds to a problem not by hoping his subordinates will act, but by directing them to act."

"When things are very quiet and beautifully organized, I think it's time to be concerned."

HIS FOREIGN POLICY

ON THE WESTERN ALLIANCE "Those who would separate Europe from America or split one ally from another—would only give aid and comfort to the men who make themselves our adversaries and welcome any Western disarray."

"The United States cannot withdraw from Europe, unless and until Europe should wish us gone. We cannot distinguish its defenses from our own. We cannot diminish our contributions to Western security or abdicate the responsibility of power."

ON DISARMAMENT "Together we shall save our planet or together we shall perish in its flames."

"It is . . . our intention to challenge the Soviet Union, not to an arms race, but to a peace race; to advance step by step, stage by stage, until general and complete disarmament has actually been achieved."

ON NEGOTIATING "Our patience at the bargaining table is nearly inexhaustible . . . our hopes for peace are unfailing."

"If they [the Soviets] have proposals, not demands, we shall hear them. If they seek genuine understanding, not concessions of our rights, we shall meet with them. . . . We shall . . . be ready to search for peace—in quiet exploratory talks, in formal or informal meetings."

ON COMMUNIST CHINA "We're not wedded to a policy of hostility to Red China. It seems to me that Red China's policies are what create tension between not only the United States and Red China, but between Red China and India, between Red China and her immediate neighbors to the south and even between Red China and other Communist countries."

ON THE BERLIN ISSUE "All free men, wherever they may live, are citizens of Berlin. And therefore, as a free man, I take pride in the words, '*Ich bin ein Berliner* (I am a Berliner).'"

"The source of world tension and trouble is Moscow, not Berlin."

ON VIETNAM "The systematic aggression now bleeding [South Vietnam] is not a 'war of liberation,' for Vietnam is already free. It is a war of attempted subjugation, and it will be resisted."

"Our object [is] to permit the South Vietnamese to maintain themselves as a free and independent country and permit democratic forces within the country to operate."

ON LATIN AMERICA "They [the Latin American nations] and they alone can mobilize their resources—enlist the energies of their people—and modify their social patterns so that all, and not just a privileged few, share in the fruits of growth."

"We are determined to reinforce the Inter-American principle of absolute respect for the sovereignty and independence of every nation. That principle was at the heart of the Good Neighbor policy—and we remain good neighbors today. That principle is the foundation of our Alliance [for Progress] and we shall always be allies for progress."

HIS NATIONAL PROGRAM

ON CIVIL RIGHTS "A rising tide of discontent . . . threatens the public safety. . . . The events in Birmingham and elsewhere have so increased the cries for equality that no city or state or legislative body can prudently choose to ignore them."

"[The] result of continued Federal legislative inaction will continue, if not increase, racial strife—causing the leadership of both sides to pass from the hands of reasonable and responsible men to the purveyors of hate and violence."

"We face . . . a moral crisis as a country and a people. . . . It is time to act in the Congress, in your state and local legislative body, and above all, in all our daily lives."

ON DEFENSE "Others in earlier times have made the . . . dangerous mistake of assuming that the West was too selfish and too soft and too divided to resist invasions of freedom in other lands. . . . The new preparations that we shall make to defend the peace are based on our needs to meet a worldwide threat. . . . Our primary purpose is neither propaganda nor provocations—but preparation."

ON FOREIGN AID "The fundamental task of our foreign aid program . . . is to help make an historical demonstration that . . . economic growth and political democracy can develop hand in hand."

ON THE ECONOMY "We seek . . . an economic climate in which an expanding concept of business and labor responsibility . . . increasing awareness of world commerce and the free forces of domestic competition will keep the price level stable."

"Anyone who is honestly seeking a job and can't find it deserves the attention of the United States Government and the people. . . ."

ON SPACE "It is . . . time for this nation to take a clearly leading role in space achievement, which in many ways may hold the key to our future on earth."

"With a good conscience our only sure reward, with
history the final judge of our deeds, let us go
forth to lead the land we love . . ."

John F. Kennedy—Inaugural Address

INDEX